FOUR CHANCELLORS AND A FUNERAL

Also by Russell Jones

The Decade in Tory

FOUR CHANCELLORS AND A FUNERAL

How to Lose a Country in Ten Days

RUSSELL JONES

unbound

First published in 2024

Unbound
c/o TC Group, 6th Floor King's House, 9–10 Haymarket, London SW1Y 4BP
www.unbound.com
All rights reserved

© Russell Jones, 2024

The right of Russell Jones to be identified as the author of this work has been asserted in accordance with Section 77 of the Copyright, Designs and Patents Act, 1988. No part of this publication may be copied, reproduced, stored in a retrieval system, or transmitted, in any form or by any means without the prior permission of the publisher, nor be otherwise circulated in any form of binding or cover other than that in which it is published and without a similar condition being imposed on the subsequent purchaser.

While every effort has been made to trace the owners of copyright material reproduced herein, the publisher would like to apologise for any omissions and will be pleased to incorporate missing acknowledgements in any further editions.

Unbound does not have any control over, or responsibility for, any third-party websites referred to in this book. All internet addresses given in this book were correct at the time of going to press. The author and publisher regret any inconvenience caused if addresses have changed or sites have ceased to exist, but can accept no responsibility for any such changes.

Typeset by Jouve (UK), Milton Keynes

A CIP record for this book is available from the British Library

ISBN 978-1-80018-308-7 (hardback)
ISBN 978-1-80018-309-4 (ebook)

Printed in Great Britain by Clays Ltd, Elcograf S.p.A

1 3 5 7 9 10 8 6 4 2

'How did you go bankrupt?' Bill asked.
'Two ways,' Mike said. *'Gradually, then suddenly.'*

Ernest Hemingway, *The Sun Also Rises*

Contents

Part 1: 500 Days of Flummer
2021: 'Unethical, Foolish and Possibly Illegal' — 3
2022: 'It's Bollocks, Utter Bollocks' — 84

Part 2: How to Lose a Country in Ten Days
2022: 'It Would Almost Be Endearing if it Wasn't So Completely and Utterly Fucking Mad' — 185

Part 3: Crazy Rich Asian
2022: 'Screams from a Madhouse' — 241
2023: 'A Whiny, Unpleasant, Bitchy Row' — 300

Part 4: P.S. They Hate You
Putting the Gini Back in the Bottle — 323

Notes — 339
A Note on the Author — 423
Index — 425
Supporters — 435

Part I
500 Days of Flummer

2021
'Unethical, Foolish and Possibly Illegal'

The Decade in Tory

The story so far.

The Conservatives had been in office for a decade. For the first five years, they were the biggest party in a coalition that was advertised as a way to reduce our national debt, make us richer, and avoid chaos. They did this by increasing the national debt by 50 per cent,[1] making the economy £100 billion smaller,[2] and creating ever-increasing homelessness, blossoming foodbanks, plunging investment, soaring inequality, crumbling productivity, rampant xenophobia, a series of desperate NHS crises, a few omnishambolic budgets, and (to the best of my knowledge) a solitary accusation of prime-ministerial pig-fucking.[3]

Most of these problems arose out of a magical plan to fix our finances that the Tories had dreamed up. They called it 'austerity', and it meant cuts to pretty much everything important – health, education, housing, food production, energy generation, staff training, climate change, transport infrastructure, and business investment – but not to things that are of no importance whatsoever, such as billionaires. To understand austerity's ruthless, immutable logic, just imagine a wealthy football manager chopping bits off his players' feet until the team feels well enough to run around and score goals.

The policy was so successful that the UK's growth forecast was cut almost constantly from 2010 to 2016,[4] and Britain's workers were paid less after a decade than they had been when the enrichment plan began.[5] That's assuming those workers had made it through the decade at all: austerity led to over 330,000 excess deaths.[6]

The Tories said they'd avoided chaos, but to an objective eye this did look a *bit* chaotic, and by 2016 the public were pissed off, and the Conservatives had run out of people to blame. Something needed to change, but what? Not the demented politics or destructive economics, obviously; and *definitely* not the government. Heaven forfend!

So instead, the Tories simply co-opted the preoccupations of a group of minor-league dingbats called UKIP and began explaining to everybody that things had gone to shit because of the existence of Belgium. It didn't really matter that this made no sense: the Conservatives had had enough of experts, and seemingly of exports too, and figured that the £100 billion they'd already cost us wasn't nearly enough. From now on, they'd cost us 4 per cent of GDP – that's £88 billion – every single year.[7]

Just £1 billion would form a tower of £10 notes 6.2 miles high. I don't want to overstate things, but that's quite a big pile of money. And the Tories planned to cost us 88 times that much, not just once, but annually. That's like misplacing a stack of £10 notes towering 545 miles high, and then losing another stack the same size every subsequent year.

To facilitate this grand ambition, the Conservatives held a referendum on who had the best fantasy, with the promise that the winning pipedream would become a new – and very, very angry – national religion. It was the most divisive and pointless political rupture in living memory, and lightly glazed polyp David Cameron celebrated by running away and playing make-believe-rustic in a shepherd's hut that cost close to the average Briton's annual salary.[8]

He was replaced as PM by a depressed avian cyborg called Theresa May, whose inimitable leadership style consisted of slowly sagging while she repeatedly listed the colours in our national flag. When we could bear no more of this, she subjected the nation to an utterly pointless general election so she could prove she was strong and stable. It proved she was powerless and rickety, and she barely scraped a majority.

This meant she now had no chance of governing, but it was also somehow impossible for her to resign. For a surprisingly long time, not a lot happened. She seemed to just totter around in baffled sorrow, enduring the loss of 60 ministers in two years,[9] record-breaking parliamentary defeats,[10] and the stage collapsing around her while she delivered a chorus of death-croaks to slack-jawed journalists and her slack-brained fan club. And then as an encore, she treated us all to an unforeseen outbreak of dangerously original dancing, before finally quitting.

She had been ousted by a man who promised to boost our democracy by becoming prime minister without being elected: Boris Johnson. There were some who thought Johnson was the worst politician in history, but I disagree. He was, in fact, the worst *thing* in history. He was what would happen if you made the movie *Confessions of a Window Cleaner* prime minister for a laugh. He was both a shaggy-dog story, and a dodgy-shag story, and he only seemed to be coherent for a few minutes per day, largely by accident.

He immediately repeated all of Theresa May's Brexit fuck-ups, unlawfully suspended parliament,[11] lied about it to the Queen,[12] and then followed up with yet another general election, which in any sane nation would have concluded with his immediate consignment to the bin. But this was Britain in 2019, so he won. Massively.

If this seems unlikely, remember that the mayor in *Jaws* corruptly swept evidence under the carpet, railroaded medical authorities into lying, was more enraged by the defacement of public art than by the spiralling death toll on his island, urged his population to dive into shark-infested waters cos he was prioritising the economy, and was last seen dressed as a deckchair and teetering on the edge of a nervous breakdown while chain smoking in a hospital.

He was still the mayor in *Jaws 2*.

Boris Johnson was still the prime minister in 2020 and celebrated by taking a poleaxe to our ability to trade with our largest market, while trashing our global reputation for being a stable, mature democracy. Covid raged on, but he mostly ignored it for months so he could focus on an urgently needed Shakespeare biography that still hasn't emerged four years later. And then he finally engaged with the real world long enough to hand billions to his mates so they could ineptly fight the pandemic, while he stayed in his gruesomely ornamented love nest, dividing his time between shagging, bullshitting, and acting as a super-spreader.

His devotion to the rules of lockdown were such that when he tested positive for Covid, his own team had to install a 'puppy gate' on his apartment to prevent him from wandering the halls of Downing Street dispensing infectious spume onto his staff, who had to be trained in techniques to cope with his frequent childish temper tantrums.[13]

And that's where the last book left us.*

If this was a *Star Wars* movie, the yellow conveyor belt of exposition would now fade into infinity, the music would dip into a minor key, and an ominous vessel of evil would glide into view. But before we get to Priti Patel, there was some actual good news. No, really! There was, believe it or not, A New Hope . . .

A Vaccine Arrives

That hope took the form of a vaccine for Covid-19.[14]

The pandemic had begun a year earlier, in Wuhan, China. From there it had swiftly spread across the world, ravaged a dozen nations, closed most of Europe, Asia and the Americas, and eventually made Britain's government reluctantly publish a poster telling people to put their tissues in the bin.[15]

---

* *The Decade in Tory*, Russell Jones, published by Unbound, 2022.

Nobody could have foreseen it, but these extreme measures didn't save us, and eventually – way too late – the government realised it had to get off its arse and act, otherwise all the workers it was relying on to generate the wealth hoarded by Tory donors would become dead, which would be most inconvenient. Even so, their delay in acting had dire consequences. By August 2020 the UK had the highest Covid deaths-per-capita in Europe,[16] the third highest death toll in the world,[17] and the largest drop in GDP in the G7.[18] It was a grim time, but by the last month of 2020 there seemed to be an end in sight.

The government was determined to make the most of it, and so up stepped health minister Matt Hancock, the dad from a gravy advert, to claim that our approval of the vaccine was a definitive, incontrovertible benefit of Brexit.

'It is absolutely clear,' he said, 'that because we've left the EU, I was able to change the law so that the UK alone could make this authorisation decision. So because we've left the EU, we've been able to move faster.'[19]

Within minutes Hancock's words were echoed by Jacob Rees-Mogg, a super-villain made of string-cheese,[20] and by Nadine Dorries, a Boris Johnson superfan who was equal parts stupid and wrong.[21] The 'Brexit made the vaccine possible' claim became an important statement, not least because it formed the basis of the government's primary defence against every subsequent accusation of farcical corruption, ineptitude, lies, sloth, idiocy, and greed.

And true to form, it was complete bollocks.

When the vaccine was approved on 2 December 2020, the UK was still in the transition period of our departure from the EU, and European regulations were still in effect. A UK government press release says as much, stating that during the transition period 'EU legislation which we have implemented . . . allows the MHRA to temporarily authorise the supply of a medicine or vaccine.'[22]

The MHRA – the UK's Medicines and Healthcare products Regulatory Agency – was working in tandem with the European

Medicines Agency, applying the same science, the same judgements, the same regulations. Asked whether Brexit had sped up the process, the head of the MHRA said the agency had 'been able to authorise the supply of the vaccine using provisions under European law'.[23]

Thousands reported Dorries and Rees-Mogg for spreading misinformation on Twitter, and both *Channel 4 News's FactCheck* and the independent Full Fact service said Hancock's claim was wrong.[24] But it was too late: the gaslighting had been farted out into the national atmosphere, and government ministers seemed insouciant in the extreme about the country being deluded. I almost can't blame them.

Well, I can. And I do.

But it is still easy to understand why they acted as they did. Tory MPs took their lead from the prime minister, and the bullshit was an inevitable side-effect of the stream of hooey pouring from Boris Johnson. The constant, light shower of hogwash we experienced was splashback from the nation's top Armitage Shanker.

Johnson seized on the potential of a vaccine, combined it with a temporary downward fluctuation in the numbers of daily Covid deaths, and stirred in his pathological need for approval and attention. In early December 2020, he promised a five-day Christmas relaxation of the lockdown rules, despite warnings from health experts. For the first time in their 100-year history, the *British Medical Journal* and *Health Service Journal* issued a joint editorial, pleading for Downing Street to 'reverse its rash decision to allow household mixing ... because we believe the government is about to blunder into another major error that will cost many lives'.[25]

The blundering went ahead regardless, with some concessions: a week before Christmas, Johnson had to scrap his 'let's play chicken with death' plans for the worst-affected parts of the country, but for the rest of us it felt like all bets were off.[26] Sure, go and cough on Auntie Janet! Drool onto Granny! Rub your sweaty face all over asthmatic cousin Frank!

The mere suggestion of relief from lockdown sent to millions the implicit message that social mixing was now if not exactly *safe*, then certainly safe enough.[27] Masks became less common in public, households mixed, festive parties were thrown, and the deadly consequences of the prime minister's yodel of vacant boosterism took root.

Barely a week into 2021, the dire predictions of health experts were shown to be true. A death toll of 1,325 in a single day was the highest the UK had yet seen, and we went straight into lockdown again. But if the stable door was going to be slammed too late, it was politically expedient that it at least be slammed as noisily as possible.[28]

Thus, the mephitic fumes parted and in wafted Priti Patel, shrouds flapping, with a hostage to fortune.

Police had discovered and broken up an illegal party, at which 300 people had been handed down fines of £15,000 for 'blatant Covid breaches', and Patel was out in force, decrying the 'insult to those hospitalised with Covid, our NHS staff and everyone staying at home to protect them'.[29] It was stirring stuff, and you'll feel even more stirred when you find out this was barely a week after an illegal party was held in Downing Street.[30]

Imports and Exports

But the public was still a year from discovering that. And in the interim, there was plenty of news, not least the *real* end to the Brexit transition period that Matt Hancock would have us believe had already concluded, just before the vaccine turned up. In truth the only effect Brexit had on vaccines was – and this will become a recurring theme – a higher risk of delays at the border when importing new doses.[31] That's because on 1 January 2021 the implementation period of our exit from the EU drew to a close, and from now on it was official policy for absolutely everything to be a right palaver.

Brexit was done. Boris Johnson had told us as much, so you can take that to the bank. All our problems had been wished away, and the sunlit uplands were just around the bend, over the next hill, only a hair's breadth beyond the reach of our outstretched fingers. Yet somehow, things didn't seem to be entirely as advertised.

Despite a much-boasted 'tariff-free' trade deal the government had signed and trumpeted on Christmas Eve, by the second week of January it was admitted that many items – insignificant fripperies such as food and clothing – didn't qualify as tariff-free at all. Not that it mattered immediately, because tariffs only applied if you were importing or exporting, and suddenly that wasn't happening very much. The road haulage giant DPD suspended all deliveries from the UK to the EU, explaining that new red tape was making their service untenable. One-fifth of its parcels since the end of transition had to be returned to sender because the bewildering piles of new paperwork were incomplete or wrong.[32]

As you worked your way down the logistics food-chain, things got no better. First, the type of store the Tories noticed – Fortnum & Mason – announced they were 'unable to send any products to European countries at this current time, due to Brexit restrictions'.[33] Marks & Spencer warned of the 'significant' impact of 'very complex administrative processes', and their chief executive told ITV, 'Tariff-free does not feel like tariff-free when you read the fine print.'[34] John Lewis and Debenhams, who like many retailers were already struggling massively due to Covid, were now forced to close their websites serving shoppers in the EU.[35]

And these are, of course, only the retailers large enough to make headlines. Countless smaller businesses suddenly found 'tariff-free trade' and 'taking back control' meant large tariffs, additional taxes, mountains of paperwork, transport delays, rising costs, and fleeing customers.

At ground level, individual buyers and sellers were lumbered with large, unexpected bills. A bathroom shelf ordered from France for €47 now attracted import fees of an additional €30. A bicycle made in Britain and sold to the EU now attracted charges of another €100. Up-market trainers ordered from the UK cost £270, but by the time duties and tariffs were applied, the customer in France faced a bill of £378.[36] Each of these sounds like a minor, inconvenient expense, but collectively they had an impact. Newly competitive, global Britain was suddenly costing customers 50 per cent more than the supposedly sclerotic, uncompetitive Europe.

On top of costs, there were the delays. Longer port inspections, stacks of paperwork, and sheer governmental ineptitude meant fresh food would rot while waiting to be imported or exported, with one industry hit particularly hard: fishing.

Only two weeks after Brexit finally happened, protests began. Lorryloads of seafood descended on Westminster, the trailers bestrewn with slogans decrying 'Brexit carnage' and the 'Incompetent government destroying shellfish industry'.[37] Fishermen had threatened to unload their rotting cargo on the steps of Downing Street, but in the end didn't. Perhaps the stench already emerging from the centre of government rendered it pointless.

The fate of fisheries had, of course, been talismanic throughout the Brexit campaign, with grey-skinned, wheezing toad-man Nigel Farage opportunistically co-opting the entire industry for his adventures in grifting xenophobia.[38] Off the campaign trail and away from the cameras it was a different story. He had turned up to just *one* of 42 meetings to support fishing when he was a member of the EU fisheries committee, and as soon as the Brexit campaign was won, the industry was back on his ignore list.[39]

Yet despite the damage done, the government seemed to think it had got away pretty lightly, primarily because it's hard to turn footage of somebody wearily filling in a pile of export documents or *not* ordering some fish into a compelling TV news clip. There had been predictions of highly televisual chaos at Dover and Folkestone in the immediate aftermath of Brexit. But it didn't happen, not least because you don't get a queue at a port if hauliers have stopped exporting and Covid is keeping everybody else at home.

So, the (very temporary) absence of footage from a gridlocked

Felixstowe meant the government felt it was off the hook. Dominic Raab, the Etch-a-Sketch nonentity who was pretending to be foreign secretary, went so far as to shrug off the protests, insisting that the fact the value of exported British fish had plummeted to just 2p per kilo while the government failed to secure promised fishing rights around our coast was 'a great deal for the fishing industry'.[40]

Lockdown Rebels

The month-long spike that had followed Boris Johnson's insatiable compulsion to have a fun Christmas was the sharpest rise in Covid deaths the UK ever experienced. The death toll climbed by a further 33,000, reaching over 111,000 lives lost.[41]

So it was clearly time to abandon all precautions.

Johnson's early announcement of a path out of lockdown was driven by multiple pressures: the financial cost of the Covid support package, the social cost of keeping people from their loved ones, Johnson's inherent need to be worshipped, and dark rumblings from one of the noisiest internal pressure groups that infested the party. The Covid Recovery Group (CRG) was a loose band of around 70 Tory backbenchers led by Steve Baker, a man I wouldn't wish on my worst enemy, because I don't need to: he and Jacob Rees-Mogg had already met when they worked together in the equally inaccurately named European Research Group (ERG).

As Brexit turned into an unholy and execrable mess, the ERG briefly withdrew from sight, tinkered around with their badges and letterheads, and re-emerged as the CRG. It was all-change, except for their attitude to science, evidence, and shits given about their fellow man, which they had already demonstrated in writing when they'd addressed the PM at the end of 2020.

They had warned Johnson that they'd only support life-saving lockdowns if the government published 'a full cost-benefit analysis'[42] of whether it was sufficiently profitable to take action to prevent hundreds of thousands of deaths in the fifth most deadly pandemic in history.[43] Perhaps they'd been emboldened by the PM's views on the relative values of lockdowns and your nana: 'No more fucking lockdowns – let the bodies pile high in their thousands', he was reported to have said.[44]

The CRG exploited the fact that Johnson loved to be loved, which meant he'd say or do anything to make people pleased to have met him, even if it directly contradicted something else he'd said five minutes earlier. Recognising the PM as fundamentally weak and malleable, the CRG began to make explicit threats. Steve Baker told Johnson that he believed the existence of lockdowns 'hammers freedom' – for example, the freedom to stay alive – and that 'inevitably the prime minister's leadership will be on the table' if Baker and Rees-Mogg weren't granted their wish to be released from all responsibility to other humans.[45]

Johnson hadn't yet finished his second year as PM, and the very people who put him there were already plotting his demise.

And yet, at least by comparison with the thicket of chaos that defined 2020, the first month of 2021 brought some rare competence. Enjoy it while it lasts.

The government had created the new role of minister for vaccine deployment, and handed responsibility to Nadhim Zahawi,[46] who is what happens when you ask a toddler to draw an *Apprentice* candidate on the side of an excised bull's testicle. The elderly and clinically vulnerable were given the vaccine as a priority, along with frontline health workers. In just the first three months of the programme, over 20 million doses were delivered. By the end of 2021, more than 100 million doses had been delivered.[47] The nation began to think we might actually come out of this alive.

Don't count your chickens: before January was out, the usual suspects from the CRG began to up their demands to include an end to the wearing of masks too. It didn't seem to matter that the vaccination rollout was still in its infancy, that the death toll was still climbing towards 125,000,[48] or that over 40 million Britons still hadn't even received a first dose.[49] Masks off, and let's cede victory to Covid!

The charge – actually, the retreat – was led by two people. One was Jonathan Gullis, a discarded early draft of Chewbacca that someone dragged out of the bin and taught rudimentary table manners. It was common to hear accusations of politicians 'dumbing-down', but Gullis had moved beyond this, and could be dumb in any direction you care to name. This was something the kindly people of Stoke had been prepared to overlook, and they elected him to be their MP. Gullis went viral – ironically – in January by refusing the pleas of the Speaker to wear a mask in the House.[50]

The other leader of the anti-mask movement was embarrassment's Desmond Swayne, the reanimated corpse of Alvin Stardust, whose dominant feature was to be the most mindless imaginable person in any given situation. He went around telling the kind of people who believed the vaccination was an affront to their right to fatally infect granny – or that Bill Gates had planted microchips in the vaccine – that they should 'persist' in their protests, and that the scale of the pandemic was being exaggerated with 'manipulated' figures.[51]

Over the coming months increasing numbers of Tory MPs, including senior frontbenchers, would rebel against the wearing of masks. They were almost always from the libertarian wing of the party, endlessly stretching the definition of individual responsibility to mean zero responsibility.

Some observers on social media suggested this was simply a cretinous act of performative public health vandalism, stripped of any rationality beyond generating headlines for a few noisy backbenchers who longed to stake their claim on the most gormless side of a vacuous culture war. But other people insisted Tory opposition to masks was a perfectly legitimate defence of individual rights, and that they shouldn't have to cover parts of themselves up for the wellbeing of innocent bystanders.

If you're struggling to decide which argument holds water, imagine those same people demanding the right to not cover their genitalia in a primary school. Case closed.

Institutional Racism

Off we pop, then, to see how racism has been getting along.

Black Lives Matter had first erupted as a grassroots movement in the aftermath of the acquittal of George Zimmerman for the murder of Trayvon Martin in 2013, and over the coming years had spread across the world, and into the collective consciousness. It gained yet more international headlines following the 2020 murder of George Floyd by a police officer acting with shocking impunity. There were months-long rolling demonstrations in 260 cities across the globe, and Britain saw its largest anti-racism protests since the abolition of slavery.[52]

In Bristol a long-controversial statue to one of that trade's biggest beneficiaries, the slaver Edward Colston, was torn down and thrown into the harbour to cheers from thousands on the spot, and millions watching from home. Left unimpressed, however, was a Lego version of Al Murray's Pub Landlord character going by the name of Ben Bradley MP, who appeared to defend Colston on the grounds that slavers 'didn't know any better'.[53]

Colston had been the most senior non-royal at the Royal African Company – second only to the king[54] – during a period when the business enslaved over 84,000 African people, of whom 19,000 died during forced transportation to the Caribbean.[55] I'd hazard a guess that even in the 1700s people 'knew better' than doing that. But Bradley, ethical scholar that he is, thought differently, and was swiftly joined by Bristol's Tory councillor Richard Eddy, who proclaimed Colston a 'hero'.[56]

Even Boris Johnson could see that if the Tories continued to publicly defend mass-murdering slavers, they might end up on the wrong side of history, and the PM swiftly kicked the ball into the longest grass he could find by setting up the Commission on Race and Ethnic Disparities. He acknowledged what he called the 'incontrovertible, undeniable feeling of injustice' behind the Black Lives Matter movement, and told the protesters, 'I hear you.'[57]

And then he swiftly shoved his fingers in his ears again. He asked his political advisor Munira Mirza to select members of the Commission, despite her history of describing the anti-racist movement as a 'bogus moral crusade',[58] labelling institutional racism 'a myth' and calling for government policies to improve diversity to be 'dismantled'.[59] True to form she appointed as the head of the Commission arch-Brexiteer Tony Sewell, who had said, 'I find the mantra "institutional racism" a hurdle because we are putting in the wrong interventions.'[60]

When the Sewell Report eventually emerged in April 2021, it found the 'claim the country is still institutionally racist is not borne out by the evidence', and my flabber had never been so gasted. The guy who didn't believe in institutional racism appointed somebody who didn't believe in institutional racism to find out if there was any institutional racism. And amazingly, they concluded that there was no such thing as institutional racism.

Who'd a thunk it?

Still, it takes some cojones to maintain there's no evidence of institutional racism when 16- to 24-year-old Black Britons were 11 times more likely to be victims of homicide than their white counterparts.[61] And when Black and ethnic-minority Britons – even those in work – were twice as likely as white people to be in 'deep poverty',[62] with the figures barely changing for 40 years.[63] And when Britons of Black African heritage were 3.7 times more likely to die in the pandemic than white Britons.[64] And when even David Cameron cited the research that shows, 'People with white-sounding names are nearly twice as likely to get call backs for jobs than people with ethnic-sounding names.'[65]

But who cares about all that? Apparently not right-wing Tory favourite Kemi Badenoch, who welcomed the report's conclusion that none of this was happening – or that if it was, it didn't matter – with the boast that Britain was 'one of the fairest countries in the world'.[66]

Number 10's most senior Black special advisor resigned from his post. His mentor, Tory peer Lord Woolley, explained that the resignation was due to the 'grubby, divisive' findings of the report. 'Black people around the country are incandescent with rage that their lived experience of persistent race inequality is being denied and belittled.'[67]

That's putting it mildly. The report's foreword explained how slavery had 'not only been about profit and suffering' but had – and here's a positive spin for the ages – allowed African people to culturally 'transform themselves into a re-modelled African/Britain'.[68]

How nice for them.

You might wonder how the 12 smart, ethnically diverse people appointed to the Commission could write such a shoddy piece of evidence-denying, insulting, monumental horseshit. Simple, really: the commissioners hadn't written the report at all. They'd contributed to parts of it, certainly, but those sections had been subsequently edited to such an extent that the original meaning had all but vanished. Commission member Kunle Olulode ridiculed the cherry-picked data that the bowdlerised final report relied on, saying, 'We did not deny institutional racism or play that down as the final document did. The idea that this report was all our own work is full of holes.'[69]

What's more, the final manuscript hadn't even been made available to the commissioners for reading, let alone been signed off by any of them. It was alleged that significant portions had been rewritten by somebody inside Number 10.

Huge swathes of the media and public openly mocked the findings, including the Runnymede Trust, instantly placing them on a constantly updated Tory hit-list of woke naysayers. MPs John Hayes, Tom Hunt and Darren Henry each made formal complaints to the Charity Commission that Runnymede – a racial-equality charity – was saying things about racial equality, which was clearly a breach of their remit. The Charity Commission found in favour of Runnymede.[70]

Only two years after the Sewell report, the UN had to write to the British government, expressing its 'very deep concern' at failures to address our 'structural, institutional and systemic racism',[71] and the Metropolitan Police was found to be institutionally racist in a landmark report.[72]

Tony Sewell, who had been blind to all of this, was given a life peerage by Boris Johnson.[73] And compared with the general population, Black and ethnic-minority Britons were still twice as likely to be in deep poverty in 2022.[74]

The Poshest Shop in Britain

Also in poverty: Boris Johnson. Please don't weep onto the book, the ink might run.

The lumbering haystack of hooey was reported to be struggling with the financial pressures of having to take care of himself, which might explain why he looked as though he didn't. The explanation for his poverty was simple: he's a craven, selfish, sexually incontinent moral vacuum.

They say you should never speak ill of the dead. But Boris Johnson is still alive, so I'll make the most of the opportunity.

Not only was Johnson funding yet another divorce, caused once again by his positively barnyard breeding habits, but as one MP reminded us, 'Boris has at least six children', and needed donations to keep them in private school. Unfortunately, top moralist Jeremy Hunt was too busy to offer the advice he had delivered to the rest of us: 'If you haven't got the money, you shouldn't have children.'[75]

In the year before he entered Downing Street, Johnson had earned £160,000 in a single month from just two speeches, and a further £275,000 for his regular newspaper column in the *Telegraph*[76] (earnings he had pooh-poohed as 'chicken feed'[77]). And he now topped this up with his novelty job of running the country into the ground for a measly £150,000 per year.

Yet suddenly our poor, benighted PM complained of his poverty. It is a tale of woe. On top of his estimated net worth of at least £1.6 million,[78] exclusive use of a free central London flat and a country estate, a private plane, and a bottomless expenses account, our prime minister – and here you should brace yourself for some powerfully touching stuff – our prime minister had to *pay tax*, buy his *own food*, and support nearly *two-thirds* of the children generated by his incomprehensibly fruitful loins.[79] Those are just the ones he acknowledges, of course, not the rumoured total of 12 children, and rising.[80] And naturally it doesn't include the unwanted one for which he'd (reportedly) been able to scrape together enough money to pay for another furtive mistress to abort.[81]

As a genre, poverty-porn has the kind of heart-rending tales you usually need to really gear up for. Such was the case here. Distressing news stories told us that Johnson's destitution was so extreme that he'd become the recipient of urgent food parcels. Put out of your mind the 30p meals upon which Lee Anderson says the rest of us can survive,[82] or the foodbank basics on which over 2.5 million Britons relied in 2021.[83] The Johnsons' food parcels came from Daylesford, a store owned by billionaire Tory donors Lord and Lady Bamford, which was described by *Forbes* magazine as 'the Poshest Shop in Britain'.[84]

Johnson and his then-fiancée (and soon-to-be third wife) Carrie Symonds had been gifted 30 giant boxes of 'luxury organic food' and at least 100 gourmet takeaway meals in a single year. Each was lovingly prepared by the personal chef Daylesford provided for the task, and then smuggled into Downing Street via a back door by the Bamfords' butler, who arrived in disguise, exactly like you would if you were doing nothing clandestine.[85]

Retail cost of the donated food was estimated at £27,000,[86] and Johnson didn't declare the gift.[87] A Number 10 spokesman said, 'The cost of food for personal consumption is entirely met personally by the prime minister',[88] but this telling of the story didn't seem to align perfectly with the food being delivered with a label 'charged to LB's account' (LB being either Lord or Lady Bamford).[89]

Anyway, praise the Lord – or Lady – food was now aplenty, but Mr Johnson had a new almighty challenge to overcome: slightly beige decor. You may mock, but this is a recognised problem for the exceedingly spoiled. Won't somebody think of the millionaires!

Thankfully somebody *did* think of the millionaires, and that somebody was you. Congratulations! As a taxpayer, you provided the PM with an annual grant of £30,000 to spend on decorating the official Downing Street residence, presumably on the basis that the last thing we needed was Boris Johnson becoming bored by his lampshades and barrelling off to find something new to fuck up, like a horny Hulk who'd been sleeping in a bush.[90]

Yet £30k a year wasn't enough for Johnson and Symonds, who recoiled in horror at what they termed the 'John Lewis furniture nightmare' of the tastefully, expensively decorated free flat they'd been given to live in.[91] The couple seemingly longed for their home to be turned into a horrific eruption of lurid ornamentation, delivered by their friend, the designer Lulu Lytle. Pop onto the internet for a preview of Lytle's style, which seems to be an attempt to fuse a grand mal seizure with a vestibular migraine, and then make Johnson pay through the nose for it.

Or rather, make you, me and a cadre of Tory donors pay.

For Johnson's financial woes were deeper than had yet been revealed. Enter Richard Sharp, investment banker, Tory donor, and former City colleague and friend of Rishi Sunak.[92] He was also the man who had given (via his personal charity) at least £40,000 to the right-wing Institute for Policy Research (IPR). IPR funds the TaxPayers' Alliance and NewsWatch, a right-wing group which almost exclusively targets the BBC and argues for the corporation to be privatised or abolished.[93]

As Johnson desperately tried to find ways to fund the lifestyle of a Roman emperor, Richard Sharp offered to step in and help, arranging an £800,000 personal credit facility for the sleazy Caesar from an old friend, Canadian businessman Sam Blyth.

When news of this broke, months after Johnson had stopped

being PM, Boris pleaded ignorance. Richard Sharp, he insisted, 'knows absolutely nothing about my personal finances – I can tell you that for one hundred per cent ding dang sure'.[94] Absolute ding-dang dingleberries. Sharp gave evidence to parliament confirming he'd known since September 2020 about Sam Blyth's intention of helping Johnson financially. He'd even warned Blyth how to proceed.

'Things need to be done by the book,' Sharp had warned. 'There are rules in this country'.[95]

More warnings emerged, this time official ones from the Cabinet Office, who had written to Johnson when he was still PM, formally telling him to stop seeking financial advice from Sharp, on the grounds that Sharp had applied to be the next chairman of the BBC.[96] Yeah, the right-wing, abolish-the-BBC thinktank donor. That's the guy we need!

Duly warned, and duly not giving a twirly purple shit, a few days after getting the warning letter from his officials, Johnson approved Sharp for the top job at the Beeb anyway.

Sunlight is the best disinfectant. Sharp and Johnson preferred to keep things in the dark. Sharp hadn't bothered to disclose any of this to the independent panel tasked with rooting out conflicts of interest for the guy heading up the national broadcaster. Well, I say 'independent': there were four members, appointed by government ministers. One panel member was a Tory donor, another the wife of the former owner of the *Spectator*, who had appointed Boris Johnson to be that publication's editor. The former commissioner for public appointments revealed that it could have been even worse: he'd had to 'push back' against government moves to pack the entire panel with allies, which he described as 'tilting the process'.[97]

Like Sharp, Johnson didn't bother to declare any of this. In case you care – and there's no reason you should, since the prime minister clearly didn't – the ministerial code says, 'Ministers must ensure that no conflict arises, or could reasonably be perceived to arise, between their public duties and their private interests, financial or otherwise'.[98] And the job application for the BBC chair reads, 'You cannot be considered for a public appointment if . . . you fail to declare any conflict of interest.'

'There are rules in this country,' Sharp had said, but when a damning Commons report applied those rules, it concluded his failure to fess up constituted 'a breach of the standards expected' of the chairman of the BBC, and that he 'should consider the impact his omissions will have on trust in him [and] the BBC'.[99] But for months, he didn't. Sharp clung on to his position at the Beeb, sullied like everything else that strayed too close to Boris Johnson, that ethical black hole who was barrelling across the political universe in dogged pursuit of acquisitive havoc.

Yet in the end, Sharp was consumed. A BBC investigation found he had breached its code of practice,[100] although it made no difference: by that time he'd already resigned from his post, explaining that the scandal meant he 'may well be a distraction from the corporation's good work'.[101]

But in the meantime, we were stuck with a PM secretly in hock to a foreign national to the tune of £800,000, an arrangement that the chairman of the BBC – whose 'position bears responsibility for the corporation and is required to uphold its impartiality and political neutrality' – had covertly helped to arrange.[102]

—

Sadly, all that new money still wasn't helping the PM. His fiancée, Carrie Antoinette, was deep into a decorative splurge so excessive that even Johnson despaired, telling aides, 'The cost is totally out of control – she's buying gold wallpaper!' and that the price was 'tens and tens of thousands – I can't afford it'. Symonds and Johnson had overshot the £30,000 allowance by a country mile, and Johnson suddenly discovered it was up to him to fund the rest.

The Cabinet Office refused to sign off any extra spending, so Symonds's first instinct was to call for the sacking of the Cabinet Office's Director General of Propriety and Ethics, Helen MacNamara.[103]

Meanwhile Johnson's first instinct was not to touch his secret £800,000 credit facility, but instead to touch Lord Bamford for a further £58,000 to cover the extra costs. Perhaps Bamford felt running a personal luxury foodbank for a profligate, shag-happy millionaire was generous enough, and he declined to help out.

So the PM attempted to set up a blind trust to pay for his lampshades and whatnot, into which donors could pour money, and Johnson could conveniently deny all knowledge. Just like he had about Richard Sharp. The official purpose of such a trust would be to 'preserve Downing Street for posterity', saving for the nation a gaudy outrage of a sofa, brassy gold wallpaper that looked like an estate agent's soul, and a £3,675 knockoff of a drinks cabinet owned by Rudolf Nureyev.[104]

To fill the coffers of the Downing Street Trust, Johnson put in his usual amount of effort: he opened his phone book, looked one entry below Lord Bamford, found Lord Brownlow, and dipped into *his* pocket instead. The cash was described as a donation to the Tory Party, allowing a Downing Street spokesman to say 'all reportable donations to the Conservative Party are correctly declared to the Electoral Commission', and that they had been 'declared in government transparency returns'.[105]

Downing Street spokesmen can say what they like, but Dominic Cummings revealed the prime minister had arranged for donors to 'secretly pay' for his love-nest to be grotesquely vajazzled, a move Cummings described as 'mad and totally unethical . . . foolish, possibly illegal', and which the rest of us described as: a normal Tuesday in Johnsonville.[106]

So an investigation was begun, although not by the BBC. The prime minister told parliament, 'I paid for Downing Street's refurbishment personally,' and promised that Lord Geidt, his ethics advisor – which is a bit like being in charge of shovels at the Augean Stables – would get to the bottom of things.[107] To assist Geidt in this task, Johnson declared that he had 'no idea how the revamp was being funded'.

Just like he had no idea about Richard Sharp.

Geidt felt reassured by what Johnson had claimed. 'At no point in the eight months until late February 2021,' Geidt said, 'was the prime minister made aware of either the fact or the method of the costs of refurbishing the apartment having been paid.'[108]

But what is the point of being Boris Johnson's ethics advisor if you're simply going to believe Boris Johnson's assurances? The man had been sacked for lying from practically every job he'd ever had. As early as November 2020 – four months earlier than the evidence he'd given to Geidt – Johnson was exchanging messages with Lord Brownlow on the downlow, asking for more funding for the renovation works, because despite spending £3,550 on two candleholders, his gaff was 'still a bit of a tip'.[109]

That's two candleholders *plus candles*. So let's not suggest any untoward extravagance.

Downing Street shuffled words around in an attempt to find an arrangement that allowed them to still deny everything. Of *course* the PM hadn't taken Tory Party funds for his refurbishment, they explained. However, Lord Brownlow was seemingly happy to record a different tale in writing, and sent an email discussing his contribution which read, 'I am making a donation to the Party. It includes the £15,000 you and I have agreed – plus £58,000 to cover the payments the Party has already made on behalf of the soon-to-be formed "Downing Street Trust".'[110] He also made direct payments of a further £60,000 to Soane Britain, vendors of Lulu Lytle's graceless experiments with the acceptable boundaries of interior decor.[111]

Having parted with almost £120,000 to assist Johnson and/or his Trust, Brownlow was granted a private meeting with ministers to pitch a £120 million Great Exhibition 2.0.[112] The poor Downing Street spokesman was trundled out once again, issuing further denials. This time it was to explain that the Great Exhibition 2.0 hadn't gone ahead. Instead, the 'Unboxed festival' had been commissioned. When asked by journalists, Number 10 was unable to describe any difference between the two events.[113]

Unboxed was unofficially called the Festival of Brexit. Government audits later called it an 'irresponsible use of public money', a 'recipe for failure' and 'vague and shape shifting', making it a perfect representation of what it celebrated.[114] It had a stated goal of attracting 66 million visitors. It attracted just 0.36 per cent of that target.[115]

But back to the refurb, and eventually the Electoral Commission fined the Tory Party £17,800 for its participation in the iffy financing.[116] Johnson shrugged it off – somebody else's problem – but the rumblings from his backbenchers had, for once, less to do with the kidney pudding in the Commons Tea Rooms, and more with disgust at the PM. As the months progressed, this uneasiness with his character became an increasingly difficult problem for Johnson, as his party's 'oh it's just Boris' nonchalance about his behaviour tipped into 'fuck me, not Boris again'. Meanwhile further details of his decorating expenditure leaked, until a final bill for turning the Downing Street flat into a 3D rendition of neuralgia was reported at £200,000.[117]

Thankfully future prime ministers still get £30,000 a year to paint over it.

Lessons to Be Learned

But before we get to future prime ministers, let's pay a visit to a previous one from a cleaner, less self-serving age. Or so it says here.

Pause for a moment, and contemplate the words of David Cameron, who in 2010 delivered a speech entitled 'Rebuilding Trust in Politics'. 'I believe that secret corporate lobbying goes to the heart of why people are so fed up with politics,' he said. 'It arouses people's worst fears and suspicions about how our political system works.'[118]

It had been five long, event-filled years since Cameron had waved goodbye to the nation, hummed a little tune, and left us to clean up his mess so he could pootle off and spend – presumably – a lot less time watching TV. An ally of Cameron's said of his term in office, 'If there was an Olympic gold medal for "chillaxing", he would win it.'[119]

The former PM, a languid, limpid, lackadaisical polyp in a Savile Row suit, had committed himself to his high office in the following documented ways: countless hours playing *Angry Birds*; knocking back a whisky or a G&T, and then half a bottle of wine over lunch; afternoons spent singing to himself on his personal karaoke machine; lavish dedication to cheap TV; and playing tennis all alone against a machine he had named in honour of his Lib Dem deputy. He called it 'The Clegger', presumably on the basis that all it did was spout balls all day.[120] In short, it was an orgy of self-serving, idle frippery while George Osborne beat the shit out of our futures, and the nation began to slowly fall apart.

So, few of us were prepared for the sudden burst of energy displayed by the nonchalant Etonian butterbean when a crisis hit the thing that was dearest to his heart: the vast pile of money due to him from Greensill Capital.

Throughout much of Cameron's premiership, his friend, the financier Lex Greensill, had, without being appointed to any official role,[121] used a business card bearing the royal coat of arms which described him as 'Senior Advisor, Prime Minister's Office'.[122] He had somehow ended up with a security pass to the prime minister's rooms, and a desk nearby, despite having no contract for any sort of governmental job.[123] It was reported this arrangement had granted Greensill unrestrained and privileged access to 11 government departments and agencies,[124] a situation that prompted the Cabinet secretary to comment, 'We cannot explain how these decisions were taken or why . . . it does not look appropriate.'[125]

Pause for a moment, and contemplate the words of David Cameron, who in 2011 had said, 'We'll extend to ten years the period during which ex-ministers must seek advice from the Advisory Committee on Business Appointments.'[126] Yet only one year after the PM resigned in the wake of the Brexit vote, Lex Greensill had stopped advising Cameron, and Cameron began advising Lex Greensill instead.

I can imagine a look of puzzlement on your face.

It makes no sense.

What could Dave tell Lex that Lex hadn't already told Dave a few months before?

But perhaps you're overlooking the direct-to-the-heart-of-government connections a former prime minister could offer, which were pretty valuable to the right kind of person, and also to the wrong kind of person with the right kind of wallet. Cameron was paid more than $1 million a year to do 25 days' work for Greensill Capital, and it was claimed he told friends he expected to end up squeezing $60 million out of the company.[127]

Pause for a moment, and contemplate the words of David Cameron, who in March 2010 had said, 'There is a deepening suspicion that politicians are out to serve themselves and not the country. A couple of months ago I said that [lobbying] was the next big scandal waiting to happen.'[128]

Anyhoo: a few months after Lex Greensill had stopped being not remotely employed as an advisor to the prime minister's office, his business won two giant public contracts. What are the chances? One deal was for an app to help NHS workers and pharmacists. When lobbying for the contract on behalf of Greensill, Cameron reassured the government that the company would 'never sell an employee's data'. Cameron later emailed – again on behalf of Greensill – to ask that the contract include a stipulation granting the company access to electronic data of all 1.4 million NHS staff.[129]

Lex Greensill became a billionaire, and Cameron got his $1 million a year, and everything was going swimmingly for people who weren't taxpayers, pharmacists or the NHS, right until the moment the pandemic turned up and Greensill Capital teetered on the brink of collapse. Cameron's prospective $60 million was about to go down in flames, so he greased himself up, slid gracelessly out of his preposterous squillionaire's woodshed, and set about working for the good of the nation, or at least all the bits of the nation he could see from his TV chair in Chipping Norton.

His thumbs, highly trained from his hours playing *Angry Birds*, now pounded out multiple text messages to YTS scheme Chancellor Rishi Sunak, begging him to bail out Cameron's billionaire financier friend as part of the fund set up to help ordinary businesses through Covid.[130] Cameron arranged secret drinks between Greensill and quasi-sentient spork Matt Hancock.[131] He also secretly lobbied his Old Etonian buddy Jesse Norman, a Treasury minister, for access to emergency taxpayer loans.[132]

Cameron had predicted a lobbying scandal. He wasn't wrong. The government's chief commercial officer, Bill Crothers, was found to be 'closely involved in bringing Lex Greensill into the heart of government', at the same time – and this is frankly astonishing – as Crothers was working as an advisor to Greensill Capital.[133] He argued this was fine because his advisory role was unpaid so he had no interest; but he had an $8 million stake in Greensill Capital, which seems to be *a bit* of an interest. He had also failed to disclose to the government appointments watchdog that he'd taken the post.[134]

The deal for the emergency bailout of Greensill Capital didn't go ahead, the company collapsed, 440 people lost their jobs, and thousands more were at risk.[135] Cameron walked away with $10 million.[136]

What of Greensill's app for the NHS? The Public Accounts Committee later found the contract delivered 'no material benefits to the NHS' and resulted in 'money and promised savings vanishing into thin air'.[137]

When all of this finally became public, we were supposed to believe in Boris Johnson's outrage. He ordered an inquiry, which miraculously cleared Cameron of wrongdoing, on the basis that our lobbying laws were ludicrously lax.[138]

And so a second inquiry was held, this time by the Cabinet Office. It found Lex Greensill had 'extraordinarily privileged' access to government, but that Cameron 'did not breach the current lobbying rules'.[139] The word *current* was not an accident. The Cabinet Office suggested the rules needed updating, mainly because they were based (as so many of our rules are) on the laughable theory that decent chaps in government couldn't possibly act like scoundrels.

In essence, this was the finding of yet another inquiry, the third, this time by the Treasury Committee. It said the rules had 'insufficient strength', and that Cameron had shown 'a significant lack of judgement'.[140] This will come as a shock to everybody who remembered him idly smashing up the country with a Brexit referendum that he seemingly only ran so he could get half a dozen backbench zealots off his back, freeing him up to continue watching *Midsomer Murders* and hurling digital pigeons around on his phone.

Pause for a moment, one last time, to contemplate the words of David Cameron, who in the aftermath of the Greensill inquiries said, 'There are important lessons to be learnt. As a former prime minister, I accept that communications with government need to be done through only the most formal of channels, so there can be no room for misinterpretation.'[141]

Three successive inquiries *and the culprit* said the regulations weren't up to snuff, so in the absence of any meaningful action by the government, Labour put forward a parliamentary motion to establish a committee to recommend stricter lobbying rules.

Every single party voted in favour of a new committee, except for the Conservatives. Every single Tory MP in the chamber voted against. The motion failed by 95 votes, and lobbying rules remained the same.[142]

Voter Suppression

Margaret Thatcher's government was notorious for its heartlessness, and she was followed by a Major administration that quickly became mired in scandal. The Cameron ministry had seemed too rich and privileged to have any clue about the effects of its policies on the 99 per cent who didn't live in bucolic, Home Counties luxury; and Theresa May's regime merely drifted from crisis to crisis while everybody waited for it to fall over and die.

Somehow, Boris Johnson managed to combine every one of those traits. His government was cruel, sleazy, spoiled and chaotic, and Britain was only prepared to put up with – at most – three of those things from the Tories at any given time. The polls were terrible for the party. The public consistently placed Labour 10 to 15 per cent ahead and had done so for months; and it was clear that the Conservatives would lose badly if Johnson's administration collapsed under the weight of its own ridiculousness.[143]

The Tories now faced a terrible choice.

On the one hand, they could start doing things competently. They could develop policies which helped the millions of struggling Britons. They could invest in the fabric of our shared society, our schools, our hospitals, our roads, and our power grid. They could re-join the Single Market to soften the Brexit that was shattering our economy and bringing imports, exports, fishing and farming to a standstill. And they could ditch all the culture war gibberish, stop telling quite so many palpable lies, ease off on the corruption, and kick out Boris Johnson, that saggy, idle bit of fluffy fantasy, wrapped around a moral emptiness, like Darth Bagpuss.

Or, on the other hand, they could keep doing all their usual shit, but add some additional cheating.

After literally seconds of thinking about it, the Tories opted for a new law to finally wipe out the scourge of voter ID fraud that blighted our nation. The only problem with this approach was that there was no such blight. In 2019, only one case of voter impersonation reached court, out of an electorate of 47 million voters across 650 constituencies.[144]

Data for 2022, which covered local elections in England, Scotland and Wales, elections to the Northern Ireland Assembly, multiple mayoral elections and six Westminster by-elections, found not a single provable case of voter impersonation. It found over 120 cases of electoral campaign fraud by political parties, but not one case of impersonation by a voter.[145]

Just during the timeframe of this book, the number of Tory MPs convicted of sexual offences exceeds the total number of voter ID fraud convictions since 2010.[146]

So on the face of it, it did seem a bit excessive to introduce primary legislation and spend £180 million to prevent a fraud that didn't exist.[147] You'd only bother with such a costly, pointless exercise if there was some other, less well advertised benefit to your party.

Fortunately, there was.

The new law required voters to show photo ID at polling stations: it could be a driving licence or passport, or one of a range of other acceptable forms of ID. But the government's research showed 4 per cent of people didn't have such ID. That's around 2.1 million voters about to be excluded from democracy.[148]

Those 2.1 million were predominantly poorer, from minority communities, or aged under 30, all groups which tended to have lower than average levels of disposable income, therefore be less likely to take foreign holidays or own cars. Among Black Britons, 47 per cent of voters didn't have a driving licence, which may explain why the civil rights group Liberty said the new law 'feels like an opportunistic attack on the rights of some of the most marginalised people in society'.[149]

And of course those poorer, younger, marginalised – and now disenfranchised – groups were not famed for backing the Conservative Party. The first elections under these new rules happened in May 2023, and less than a week later Jacob Rees-Mogg – who had sat in Cabinet when the Voter ID laws were passed – admitted in public that it was simply a 'clever scheme' to 'gerrymander' future elections in favour of the Conservative Party.[150]

To ensure votes were denied efficiently, the government had produced a list of acceptable identity documents. During the pilot scheme for the legislation, railcards for 16–25-year-olds were permitted. By the time the law was enacted, those railcards had been excluded, whereas older person's railcards were still allowed. Similarly, an Oyster Card for people aged over 60 was an acceptable form of ID, but an Oyster Card for students aged 18+ wasn't.[151] The range of permissible identification leaned heavily towards older, more Conservative voters, and away from the young.

It wasn't all bad news; just mostly. If you didn't have any ID, you could still apply for one via a government website, and it would be provided by your local council. But by January 2023, only 10,000 of those 2.1 million excluded voters – that's 0.5 per cent – had applied for the identification required to vote in that spring's elections.[152]

In those halcyon days before The Moggster admitted what was *really* going on, it remained important for the government to provide a rationale for their assault on democracy, and to gain our trust they sent out somebody who looked like an attempt to fuse Lieutenant Gruber from *'Allo 'Allo!* with the concept of parental abandonment. Of course the Tories weren't cheating, said Matt Hancock: they were providing fair-minded justice and boosting confidence in our voting system. 'I think people across this country want to know for sure that elections are fair.'[153]

He wasn't able to identify any previous unfair elections, but that didn't matter. The great thing about the new law was that anybody questioning it could easily be made to sound like they were in favour of electoral fraud. In truth, the critics were opposed to the government disenfranchising 2 million voters. A member of the New York City Council couldn't believe this blatant, legalised voter suppression, calling it far worse than that practised in any US state.[154]

And despite Hancock's protestations, Britons already knew our elections were fair. We had a shit voting system, granted: our first-past-the-post arrangement is 'one of the least democratic systems by global standards' according to the Centre for Welfare Reform.[155] But within that grossly unrepresentative system, Britain still managed to score 93 per cent in a ranking of fair elections, putting us 14th out of 210 nations and territories.[156] And this was reflected in public opinion:

at least 90 per cent of Britons thought voting in person at a polling station was a safe, trustworthy way to have their voice heard, according to the Electoral Commission.[157]

So naturally, the Tories' next move was to suggest abolishing the Electoral Commission.

They claimed the Commission was 'unaccountable' and must be either completely abolished, or changed so fundamentally that it could no longer publish data undermining the pretence behind Tory gerrymandering. Instead of having an independent Electoral Commission, in future we would have one which received its guidance directly from the Conservative Party.

This meant, according to the Fair Vote UK campaign group, that in future ministers 'can effectively rig election rules in their favour'.[158] Bob Posner, the chief executive of the Electoral Commission for 15 years, called the changes, 'Entirely inappropriate. It is unprecedented in democracies for something like that to be imposed. Very, very undesirable.'[159]

It was merely a happy coincidence that destroying the Electoral Commission would also halt that body's investigations into the funding for Boris Johnson's flat refurbishments, or the influence of the multiple Russian oligarchs who had donated to the Conservative Party.[160]

I can understand people reading this becoming a little worried. It didn't seem justifiable for the government to propose abolishing the body responsible for ensuring fair elections. But if you happened to be one of those worried people, relax: you could do something about it. You lived in a free society and had the right to go out and protest.

So naturally, the Tories' next move was to curtail the right to protest.

The new Police, Crime, Sentencing and Courts Bill made 'noisy protest' illegal, and granted the police the power to prevent any rally that didn't meet certain conditions, the most ludicrous of which was that protests should no longer be seriously annoying.[161] I'm not sure why it should be necessary to explain this to our democratic leaders, but seemingly it is: the entire point of protests is to be noisy and seriously annoying. That's what protest is for. When was the last time a protest achieved its goals by being consenting and silent?

What do we want?

Exactly what we've got now.

When do we want it?

Shhhhh.

Fortunately, this sort of despotic assault on both voting and the fundamental right to protest against your government was balanced by our free press, who were known for holding power to account and enlightening the public. At least until November, when Priti Patel introduced a new law – the National Security Bill – which allowed journalists, charities and NGOs to be treated as though they were foreign spies. The National Union of Journalists described it as a 'disaster for the free press and a huge danger for journalists', and the campaign group Index on Censorship said, 'This bill represents a severe threat to media freedom, free expression and the public's right to know.'[162]

So in effect, the government had limited the right to vote, then advocated dismantling the body that oversaw fair elections. If you protested this unprecedented assault on democratic rights, you could face ten years in prison. And if a journalist reported your case using any source the government wasn't happy with, they could be jailed. Amnesty International called the moves 'deeply authoritarian, [a] dark day for civil liberties in the UK, [and] part of a hugely worrying and widespread attack on human rights from across government'.[163]

So naturally, the Tories' next move was to campaign to end human rights in the UK.

David Cameron, Theresa May and Boris Johnson had all talked up an imminent withdrawal from the European Convention on Human Rights (ECHR), as did Liz Truss and Rishi Sunak when it was their turn in Downing Street.[164] In every case, it was nonsense. The ECHR has nothing to do with the EU and we never voted to leave it, no matter what you think might have appeared on the Brexit Referendum voting slip. The ECHR was created by the Council of Europe, which is an entirely separate body to the EU. The British helped to draft its human rights legislation in 1951, and it was first suggested by Winston Churchill in 1943.[165] You don't get more flag-shaggy than that.

Tory demands that we unpick human rights regulations were – just like demands for Brexit, and just like their howls of anti-woke outrage – based on nothing definable. The moment you attempted to move their objections to human rights out of the box marked Fuzzy Irritation into the one labelled Unambiguous Policy they fell apart, as box-faced clatterbrain Dominic Raab found out for himself when he appeared before a select committee in November. He was there to answer questions about exactly which rights must go, but despite him spending literally years agitating for an end to the ECHR he couldn't name one case that required a repeal of the act.[166]

There was no need to rescind human rights. There was no need to demand voter ID either. There was no need to treat journalists as spies, or to ban protest. Each of these policies was symptomatic of a dangerous lurch towards anti-democratic authoritarianism.

Superforecasting

We had reached May, and *Superforecasting*'s number one fan, Dominic Cummings, returned to parliament for the first time since his sacking in November 2020.[167]

Cummings, a real-life version of Lucius Malfoy who's been involved in a flash fire, had come a long way since his days of attempting to impress his right-wing peers at Oxford with a trip to Alton Towers, culminating in him being attacked by a squirrel that leaped at him from a bin.[168] Amazingly, he didn't superforecast that event.

I have no idea if the squirrel passed something on while it was biting at him, but it might explain the subsequent contagion of the Conservative Party with Cummings's nut-based ideas. He was made special advisor to Michael Gove way back when Gove was both education minister and a vocal opponent of what he called 'anti-knowledge culture'.[169] This was, you understand, in the heady days before Gove had 'had enough of experts'.

Gove, advised by Cummings, was determined to modernise education and prepare our kids for the technology revolution, and proved it with their scheme to get pupils to learn more Latin and Classical Greek.[170] He then set about improving our schools by scrapping the programme dedicated to fixing them,[171] before finishing his blitz on anti-knowledge culture by launching £7 billion of funding cuts to education.[172]

There was no gainsaying Gove because, according to the National Association of Head Teachers, he had created a 'culture of bullying and fear'.[173] But in truth Gove had manoeuvred himself into a position where he could justifiably deny any such thing: all the blood was on the hands of his sidekick Dominic Cummings, to whom, like a true Tory, Gove had outsourced kicking duties.

Cummings had a knack for that kind of work. Only two years into it, in 2012, he was named in a bullying case that resulted in a female senior civil servant being awarded £25,000.[174] The diplomatic affairs journalist Patrick Wintour said Gove 'would often feign ignorance of his adviser's methods, but knew full well the dark arts that Cummings deployed to get his master's way'.[175]

Champion loafer David Cameron, the glazed protuberance who was PM at the time, called Dominic Cummings a 'career psychopath',[176] and that career went into overdrive after Gove lost the education brief, a rare event that Cummings hadn't superforecasted. In search of a new outlet for his psychopathy, Cummings became campaign director at Vote Leave, where he was personally responsible for most of the irresponsible things that organisation did.

He dreamed up the slogan Take Back Control, which kickstarted years of rampant political pandemonium. He originated the claim that Brexit would allow another £350 million a week to be spent on the NHS,[177] which culminated with Brexit costing the country £800 million a week and the NHS in permanent crisis.[178] And he ended up admitting Brexit might have been a mistake, and one which – for once – he hadn't managed to superforecast.[179]

Having won the Brexit campaign, Cummings followed Boris Johnson into Downing Street, officially as the prime minister's chief aide, but unofficially as the de facto prime minister. Cummings told Boris Johnson to 'get on with dog walking' and leave the running of the country to him.[180] It didn't seem to faze Cummings that he was making decisions he admitted were 'well outside my "circle of competence"',[181] or that his strategy for running the country boiled down to advertising for a small army of 'weirdos and misfits' to mishandle operations inside Number 10,[182] while he ponced off to Barnard Castle to engage in extremely unlikely eye tests.[183]

It was all going swimmingly for a while, just as Dom's superforecasting suggested it would. Nobody was held responsible for anything; governance was being systemically smashed up in alignment with his wishes; and Johnson was losing a bit of weight as he coped with Dilyn the dog and his 'uncontrollable romantic urges'.[184]

That's Dilyn's urges, not Johnson's, which for legal reasons I'm compelled to stress are entirely controllable.

Sure, fine, the bodies were piling high, but that was well within the stated parameters of the PM's Covid strategy.[185] Things outside were record-breakingly shit, but inside Number 10 everything was lovely for Dom, until suddenly one morning it wasn't. Another bad day for superforecasts. Cummings had pissed off Carrie Symonds, complaining about what he called her 'completely unethical and clearly illegal [attempts to] appoint her friends to jobs'.[186] Doesn't sound like the kind of thing that would raise an eyebrow in the modern Tory Party, but Cummings's objections put him on the wrong side of Johnson, and bingo! he was gone, like a fart in the wind. Just him, his box of belongings, and a professional photographer to capture Cummings, standing forlornly and only slightly artfully as he waited for a bus home in the rain.[187]

This meant Johnson now had responsibility for both running the country *and* walking the dog, which may account for why only one of those things was done well.

Dilyn looked the picture of health, though.

Anyway, after months away from public view – which he seems to have spent perfecting the glassy-eyed stare of an unqualified accountant doorstepped by *Watchdog* – Cummings returned to our lives in May 2021 to give evidence to a parliamentary inquiry into the government's handling of the pandemic.

He told the inquiry that Matt Hancock was 'completely incapable of doing the job' of health secretary, and 'should have been fired for at least 15 to 20 things' on the grounds that Hancock had displayed 'criminal, disgraceful behaviour'. According to Cummings, this included both holding back Covid testing, and meddling in efforts to build a testing system, merely to satisfy a 'stupid promise' Hancock had made to deliver a ludicrously unachievable number of tests per day.[188]

The only reason Hancock wasn't sacked, according to Cummings – and let's face it, according to almost everybody else too – was that Johnson was also 'unfit for the job' as prime minister. The PM had blithely dismissed Covid as 'just a scare story' and tried to give up prime ministering mid-pandemic so he could make a few quid writing a book about Shakespeare.[189] As a result, Hancock had remained in post, and 'tens of thousands of people died, who didn't need to die'.[190]

It's genuinely amazing that Johnson wasn't among the dead, given that he'd offered to be injected 'live on TV with the virus so everyone realises it's nothing to be frightened of'. Johnson, ever attuned to what was going on outside his own monumental ego, made this suggestion on 26 May 2020, one week after UK Covid deaths had reached 50,000.[191]

A Guide to Not Recognising Anything

Matt Hancock responded to Cummings's accusations by claiming he hadn't watched the evidence to the inquiry, which was his own personal take on a suddenly fashionable bit of political bullshit: the use of the phrase 'I don't recognise those figures'.

Maybe it's my age, but I grew up in a time when leading political figures – Margaret Thatcher, for example, or Denis Healey – had supreme intellectual confidence. It didn't matter if you agreed with them or not: they knew their minds and what they stood for, and they'd happily face even the most painful journalistic scrutiny, secure in their beliefs and their ability to face criticism head on. Political interviews lasted an hour, live on television, with nowhere to hide. Even lesser politicians had to face the music. Traditionally, when presented with a true (but politically damaging) bit of evidence, a minister would be expected to wriggle out of trouble with verbal dexterity, find a convenient scapegoat, or resign.

But the first option required brains; the second required sackable underlings who wouldn't blab the truth to the press; and the third required personal sacrifice. Clearly, none of these options were available to the thicket of turds running our country since 2010, and few of them could withstand so much as a minute of uninterrupted questioning. So a new method of evading responsibility was needed, and it came in the form of 'I don't recognise those figures'.

It's a group of words that doesn't quite deny the evidence, and certainly doesn't go to the trouble of responding to it, but instead tiptoes a narrow path that allows the politician to pretend – without admitting as much – that reality isn't reality at all. And helpfully, it rolls off the tongue too quickly for a casual observer to have time to contemplate what it implies, which is: fuck the truth, I've got a career to think about.

Once this rich seam of linguistic irresponsibility had been discovered, it was ruthlessly mined for variations. 'I don't recognise those (embarrassing) figures' was quickly joined by 'I haven't seen that (humiliating) report', 'I haven't heard that (damning) quote', and Hancock's personal favourite: 'I didn't tune in when an eyewitness was telling a public inquiry that I killed shitloads of people'.

Shmonflict of Interest

And so the story was: Hancock didn't see Cummings at the inquiry. Of course he didn't. Hancock had, he claimed, been too busy dealing with 'the vaccination rollout'.[192] Yet the Dim Reaper had still found time to get busy rolling with Gina Coladangelo, and you, you lucky thing, got to watch. CCTV footage of their fumbling was leaked to the press, taken while the social distancing rules forbade 'intimate contact with people outside your own household'.[193]

I can't work out which was worse for his wife: the time after she discovered Matt Hancock was cheating on her, or the time before, when she still had to live with the fact that he'd singled her out.

Hancock had fancied Coladangelo since they'd met at university, after which she went off to become a director of a lobbying company specialising in influencing healthcare policy, and he went off to practise the look of somebody who'd started a support group for divorced men, to which nobody had turned up.

Because this is the way things worked in our fabulous democracy, the healthcare lobbyist Coladangelo was then, in the words of the *Telegraph*, 'quietly appointed' by her old pal and admirer Hancock to be a non-executive director at the Department of Health, for the miserly sum of £1,000 per day. There was no public record of her appointment, and her parliamentary pass was discreetly sponsored by Lord Bethell, a Conservative hereditary peer who worked as a junior health minister and was also a former lobbyist.[194]

Coladangelo's appointment was yet another unsettling demonstration of the chumocracy, but it didn't break the rules about who a departmental head could hire, because there *were* no rules about who a departmental head could hire.[195] Anything goes, even when it transpires that the lobbyist/pal/lover in question has a brother who was a director of a healthcare company that received a series of lucrative NHS contracts.[196]

Conflict of interest, shmonflict of interest.

'I'm quite sure that whatever the rules were at the time were followed,' said Grant Shapps, warming up for Partygate, and continuing his unbroken record of being wrong at every conceivable opportunity.[197] The rules about departmental appointments might not have existed, but rules about social contact definitely did, and they were broken. Tongues had been slipped, buttocks had been fondled, and heads had to roll.

However, a person's actions having consequences was an alien and terrifying concept for Boris Johnson; and so, despite having every justification, he still didn't sack Hancock. He tried to claim credit for Hancock going, though, telling journalists, 'When I saw the story on Friday we had a new secretary of state for health in on Saturday.' Of course, he'd personally done nothing to bring that about.[198] Instead, loverboy resigned with a letter that might as well have had *Fathers 4 Justice* emblazoned across the top. 'I want to reiterate my apology,' he said. 'I also need to be with my children at this time.'[199]

The Rarity of Common Sense

We had reached June, and time to visit Brendan Clarke-Smith, a member of the Common Sense Group of Conservative MPs.[200]

There will now be a brief pause while you chuckle ironically.

Clarke-Smith had already demonstrated what he probably sincerely felt constituted Common Sense, with his claim that it was 'simply not true [that] people can't afford to buy food on a regular basis',[201] at a time when over 2 million people relied on foodbanks, a 5,000 per cent increase since the Tories had won power in 2010.[202] What we needed, he declared, was 'less celebrity virtue signalling [and] more action to tackle the real causes of child poverty'.[203]

To tackle the real causes of child poverty, Clarke-Smith immediately rushed to vote against providing free school meals to children too poor to eat. The notion of feeding hungry kids, he declared, was 'nationalising children', and he wanted no part of such socialism. 'We need to get back to the idea of taking responsibility,' he said, and I'll be sure to pass that message on to the next hungry six-year-old I meet.[204] Get up that chimney and take some personal responsibility, you idle bastard!

Later the same year, Clarke-Smith was signatory to a letter from the Common Sense Group, accusing the National Trust of being part of a 'woke agenda'.[205] The Trust, which includes among its official duties a requirement to educate visitors, had introduced content at some locations explaining the exhibit's relationship to Britain's historical slave trade.[206] And this meant, according to what I'm still referring to as Brendan Clarke-Smith's Common Sense, that the organisation was 'coloured by Cultural Marxist dogma'.[207]

Cultural Marxism is a term that academic experts in Austria – let's face it, a nation with some history in this area – described as a 'far right antisemitic conspiracy theory'.[208]

Brendan doesn't like the far right, and indeed seemed highly attuned to their presence. So attuned, in fact, that in June 2021 he compared the England football team's gesture in support of anti-racism to the performance of a Nazi salute.

Ah yes, the famously anti-racist Nazis.

Footballers backing basic human rights also tried the patience of Clarke-Smith's fellow MP Lee Anderthal – forgive my typo, I meant Lee Anderson – who went one further, boycotting the England team's matches entirely because the players had taken the knee to support Black Lives Matter.[209] Unlike Clarke-Smith, Anderson didn't claim taking the knee was Nazism. He knows the works of the far right when he sees them, as is proven by the time he'd posed for photographs with a group of men adorned with white supremacist tattoos, one of whom has been described as a 'veteran far-right stalwart'.[210] Anderson chose to call them 'real salt of the Earth people'.[211] So you can trust his word on this far-right stuff.

And at least Lee Anderson seemed to know his mind, or might be able to recognise it if it showed up. Brendan Clarke-Smith, however, was all over the place, moving swiftly from saying taking the knee was Nazi symbolism, to expressing his belief that the Black Lives Matter movement were communists. This claim arose from the Common Sense dictum that if a solitary member of a global protest movement admits to being a 'trained Marxist' – as was the case with a solitary member of BLM – then the entirety of a global organisation supported by at least 63 per cent of people was also Marxist and must therefore be vigorously opposed.[212]

When the PM's spokesman was asked if Boris Johnson agreed – and forgive me if I'm struggling to link up the pieces of Clarke-Smith's wildly scattered attempts at logic – that Black Lives Matter was simultaneously Marxist *and* Nazi, he said, 'I don't see the connection.'

But Clarke-Smith could see connections all over the place. Anti-racism had 'sinister motives', he wrote, including destroying the nuclear family.[213] I'm pretty sure the police shooting Black people destroys nuclear families too, but perhaps Mr Clarke-Smith – one of the brightest stars in the political fundament – was off school the day that bit of Common Sense was being taught.

Betting on Benton

Clarke-Smith wasn't the only Common Senser having a hell of a 2021.

Somehow Scott Benton – who had also signed the letter condemning the National Trust – managed to hold down a full-time job as the member for Blackpool South, while also holding down a full-time position as a town councillor 70 miles away in Calderdale. He'd promised to step down as a councillor if he was elected to parliament in 2019, but by 2021 he still hadn't got around to it.[214]

Hadn't got around to a lot of things, actually; not least registering his financial interests, which he'd failed to do six times, and which led to a parliamentary inquiry.

'I have no doubt that the complaints [. . .] made about me to Calderdale Council and the parliamentary authorities will be found to be without substance,' he said.[215] Well, maybe you should retain a *few* doubts, Scott, because the complaints were found to be entirely substantial, and in January 2021 he was found to have breached the rules.[216]

In July, more scandal: Benton was revealed to be one of seven Tory MPs who had taken free tickets to major sporting events, handed to them by the gambling industry. Benton accepted over £8,000 of tickets to England football games, Royal Ascot and Wimbledon.[217]

The tickets had arrived in the lead-up to a government review of gambling legislation, and what do you know: by August – the following month – Benton was directly and vigorously lobbying gambling minister John Whittington over the 'extreme worry and anxiety of the whole gambling industry' about rumoured candidates to head up the Gambling Commission.

The government ended up appointing to the commission the only candidate Benton hadn't objected to.[218]

Unsurprisingly, it didn't seem difficult for Benton to become embroiled in a sting operation: he was later caught on camera by *The Times*, who set up a fake gambling investment company which offered to pay Benton thousands of pounds per month. In return, he offered on camera to break parliamentary rules, leak confidential documents, and lobby on behalf of the gambling industry.[219] He even admitted that he'd already asked two parliamentary questions on behalf of the betting companies who paid for his services.[220]

When the news broke in early 2023, Scott Benton was suspended as a Tory MP.[221]

Gove in the Jungle

But back to 2021, which until now had been notable for repeated claims of ineptitude, corruption, hypocrisy, Nazism, racism, graft, grift, sleaze and scandal. In August it was time to introduce some just-plain-weirdness.

And so, off to Scotland where we find Michael Gove, a man permanently startled to discover he's a bestial melding of a turbot and Jar Jar Binks, having it large in an Aberdeen nightclub. You may think, hang on a minute, that sounds very out of character. Yeah? Just wait.

Gove was warned on arrival that the club was 'playing jungle and going hard'. He responded, 'I love dancing,' and set to it. In an elegant two-piece suit. All on his own. For a solid hour.

And witnesses said he had expected to get in for free.[222]

See: in character.

Gove reportedly told door staff that he was exempt from the £5 entrance fee because he was the chancellor of the Duchy of Lancaster, which is a fucking bold move in front of an Aberdonian bouncer. Clearly, he was bursting with sudden confidence, and witnesses described his behaviour as 'merry'. I have no idea what led him to act this way. Perhaps he was celebrating his divorce, which is not to be sniffed at. Perhaps he was trying to find chemistry with the youth vote, in a frankly welcome attempt at youthanising the party. Perhaps he genuinely does love jungle.

Regardless, in the interests of accuracy I've checked the government website for an official description of the chancellor of the Duchy of Lancaster, and I can assure you the words 'this dude gets to bust moves for free' don't appear.

When asked whether Gove had tried to avoid paying, a friend, who had clearly memorised the latest ministerial catchphrase, responded that he 'did not recognise' the claims.

The Jet Set

Life was becoming more and more complicated for Boris Johnson. Everywhere he turned, a crisis loomed at him, and it didn't seem to matter that he was the direct cause of most of them. As far as he was concerned, it all seemed terribly unfair, and in June it was revealed that he wanted to resign soon so he could 'make money and have fun'.[223]

As a leader, he'd turned out to be the direct antithesis of King Midas: every single thing he'd touched since coming to power in July 2019 had turned to shit. His handling of his party and parliament was calamitous. His response to Covid had left us with one of the worst mortality rates in the world. His oven-ready Brexit had skipped the middleman and gone right into the toilet. The economy was feeble, the Cabinet was irrepressibly loopy or busy throwing shapes in Aberdeen, and the entire party was wading ever deeper into a swamp of sleaze. Even to Johnson's most avid supporters it was becoming increasingly clear that domestic politics wasn't his natural forte.

So now it was time to prove international politics wasn't either.

He'd fought the 2019 general election on a manifesto pledge to 'lead the global fight against climate change', but Covid had understandably paused all serious attempts to deliver on this.[224] Only now, as the vaccine rollout allowed a return to some kind of normality, was it possible to show leadership on carbon emissions, and Johnson chose the biggest stage of all: the G7 summit in Cornwall, where global leaders gathered under a banner promising 'to create a greener, more prosperous future'.

Inspired, the prime minister tweeted that he also looked forward to asking fellow leaders to join him in 'building back better, fairer and greener', and then travelled the 250 miles from London to the venue by private plane.[225]

There was a perfectly good rail service, but no.

He had a ministerial car, but no.

He could even have made positive headlines by doing the journey on a single charge of an electric vehicle – but no.

Personally, I was shocked to learn Johnson didn't travel everywhere in a hot air balloon inflated entirely by his own ego. But apparently not: he needed a private jet, and he needed one now. Even when he was merely foreign secretary, he had complained openly to journalists that he wanted his own plane, partly because the RAF jet sometimes loaned to the ministers wasn't always available, and partly because he didn't like the colour. 'Why does it have to be grey?' he'd whined.[226]

So, a year into his time in Downing Street, Johnson had paused from his day job of not doing enough about the pandemic, and ordered his plane painted dazzling white, thus rendering it useless for its primary function as a combat-ready RAF carrier.[227] And then he splashed out another £900,000 to daub a massive Union Flag on the tail.

It was painted upside-down.[228]

Anyway: less than a month after his environmentally destructive flight to tackle climate problems at the G7, he was back in Cornwall, this time for a private family weekend away. He took the taxpayer-funded RAF plane home again. He then popped to Blackpool for the day, again by private jet.

In just one month, October 2021, he personally pumped out 21 tonnes of CO_2 by gadding around in *another* £47 million private plane, this time loaned to him by the ever-helpful Lord Bamford.[229] Over the course of a year he generated 52 tonnes of CO_2, all on his own.[230] And to cap it all, in November he took a completely different private jet – not his white, Union-Jacked one, which presumably he was bored with by now – back from the COP26 climate summit in Glasgow, just so he could attend a dinner at a men-only private members' club in London.[231]

Out of His Tree

During one of the rare occasions when Boris Johnson was on the surface of planet earth, he woke up one morning with a brand-new brain, into which flooded a yen for a treehouse to entertain his young son Wilf. It was to be installed at the prime-ministerial residence, Chequers, and there is nothing wrong with that, especially as the kits for even a quite substantial treehouse sell for around £1,500.

But Johnson, as we have seen from his forays in decorating and takeaways, did not possess the tastes or restraint of a normal man. Plans were drawn up for the prime minister's dream treehouse, and by the time the design was finished its estimated cost had spiralled to £150,000. Shameless beyond description, Johnson reportedly chose to approach Lord Brownlow to fund this madness. Luckily for Brownlow, the treehouse plan was shelved after Johnson's security team politely explained to the genius running the country that if you don't want the prime minister's son to get shot at, it might be wise to avoid placing him on a high, brightly lit, unguarded platform in the front garden.[232]

Cabotage

We'd been climbing towards the sunlit uplands of Brexit for over a year, yet by the autumn of 2021 exports of goods to the EU had slumped by £20 billion,[233] and 40 per cent of UK goods had vanished from EU shelves.[234] Deciding to unilaterally impose sanctions on ourselves hadn't turned out to be anywhere near as much fun as 52 per cent of us had once imagined.

Boris Johnson had told us Brexit meant, 'We will be an independent coastal state with full control of our waters, with the UK share of fish in our waters rising substantially from roughly half today to closer to two-thirds.'[235] I'm not sure if he believed that, or if he was simply regurgitating whatever half-formulated jumble of preening idiocy had made its way into that morning's *Daily Mail*. Whatever the reason, one year, one election, and one ocean of palpable regret later, fish and shellfish exports had plummeted by 83 per cent.[236] Johnson referred to this as 'teething problems', as if the whole thing could be magicked away by slightly better admin.[237] Absolute balls: the collapse of the industry was a direct result of the trading isolation he'd cynically fought for, and was a result he'd been warned would come to pass.

Almost all food and drink exports suffered. Only a year earlier, Liz Truss had crossed the interdisciplinary divide between responsible governance and unloading a rifle into her own foot, when she delayed signing a vital multi-billion-pound trade deal with Japan because she wanted to make a hoo-ha about the status of British cheese. Japan bought just £102,000 of the UK's Stilton, and without wishing to put words in Truss's mouth, she quite clearly felt that was enough of a disgrace to pause billions in trade.[238]

£102,000 of Stilton was £0.000816 of cheese per Japanese citizen. It was less than a single Japanese sushi restaurant had recently spent buying a single tuna.[239]

But for Truss, cheese sales meant everything, right until the moment they didn't.

In its first year, Brexit caused an 84 per cent drop in UK cheese exports to Europe – down from £45 million to just £7 million – and Truss was suddenly uncharacteristically reticent. I can't find a single Instagram photo of her weeping over piles of unsold cheddar. Whisky exports were also down, from £105 million to £40 million. Beef exports down 92 per cent. Salmon exports stopped almost entirely, down a staggering 98 per cent.[240]

Imports were little better. Despite many Tories agitating to leave the EU since the 1990s, celebrating wildly in 2016, and then engaging in five long, agonising years of highly fissile wrangling over its implementation, they treated the materialisation of Brexit as a bolt from the blue. What do you mean we were meant to prepare for it? What do you mean it has consequences?

Import checks at border posts had to be pushed back six more months because the government had failed to build the border posts in time, meaning prolonged delays to imports,[241] which was not great news for a nation that had to buy almost half of its food from overseas.[242] And our exit from the EU also brought another long foreseen yet completely ignored outcome: a crisis in cabotage.

Cabotage sounds like an Uxbridge English Dictionary definition for 'vandalising Andrew Bridgen' but is in fact a technical term for the transport of goods between two locations inside the same country.

Because the EU has seamless internal borders, its definition of cabotage allows movement of goods between member states too. For decades, a driver from Spain could conveniently bring imports into the UK, and then return to Spain with his truck full of British exports. The arrangement made the European haulage industry financially viable: almost no lorries were making expensive return journeys with empty trailers. It filled gaps in logistics networks, prevented driver and vehicle shortages, and had green benefits that would baffle Boris Johnson, since its efficiency reduced the total number of journeys made.[243]

But when the UK left the EU, we exited the cabotage scheme too, and all those benefits stopped. Sunlit uplands klaxon!

Within a couple of months, 26 per cent of HGVs returning from the UK to the EU were empty.[244] Drivers suddenly found they could make far more money being paid to drive full wagons around the EU than they could by coming to Brexit Britain, spending a fortune on fuel, and driving home empty. Not to mention the huge delays and inconvenience at the ill-prepared ports, which, if anything, grew worse over the coming year.

In increasing numbers, drivers simply stopped making the journey to Britain. It became harder and harder to get things delivered – food, medicines, clothing, fuel, raw materials, and parts. Supply chains broke down across almost every industry.

The crisis had been growing slowly for months, but in the autumn of 2021 it all came tumbling down. The first domino to fall was fuel, and BP reported almost a third of their UK filling stations were out of supplies.[245] In London and the south-east of England, 40 per cent of all filling stations were out of either petrol or diesel, and a further 22 per cent had no fuel whatsoever.[246]

First there was a lack of HGV drivers, then a lack of fuel, and then inevitably the impact spread across the nation, damaging more deliveries, more supply chains, more industries. Retail suffered, not just from lack of supplies, but from lack of customers. Shops had prayed for a rush as Covid eased and much-needed business returned. But punters stayed home, partly due to the risk of running out of petrol during a trip to the Arndale Centre, partly because they couldn't afford the fuel in the first place. Shortages and panic buying across the country had pushed forecourt prices to a (then) record of £1.47 per litre.[247]

Seven per cent of UK firms reported problems obtaining vital raw materials, which might not sound much, but it naturally affected their ability to supply to yet more companies, and inevitably hit almost everybody. In construction, a lack of raw materials directly impacted one in every six businesses.[248]

Then a *real* crisis hit the nation. Still reeling from the pandemic, we were suddenly faced with – God, I can hardly bring myself to type it – McDonald's running out of milkshakes.[249]

Yawning gaps appeared on supermarket shelves, and not just in non-essentials or luxury goods. Throughout the autumn, 16 per cent of essential food items were unavailable, and over a quarter of other food items.[250] Life in post-Brexit Britain felt like your granny's stories of the war, with oranges, grapes and even carrots becoming rare and exotic treats, towards which customers would race, only to find Tesco had resorted to stocking their shelves with cardboard cut-outs of the missing products, just to make the place look less depressing.[251] Empty promises for empty bellies, as prices rose and rose. The Food and Drink Federation described it as 'terrifying' that food inflation in the hospitality sector was at 18 per cent in October 2021, months before the Ukraine War – later widely presented as the sole reason for the cost-of-living crisis – was even a twinkle in Putin's deranged eye.[252] The price of basics – the staples that form the core of every diet, and the bulk of food bought by the poorest households – soared by up to 80 per cent during 2022/23.[253]

Tory backbenchers were quick to apportion blame anywhere but on Brexit or the government. As one in four Londoners were unable to buy essential foods,[254] Conservative vice-chairman Andrew Bowie assured us Britons were suddenly fighting over carrots because of 'the huge success with Eastern European economies drawing people back into those countries'.[255] He seemed to have overlooked that his explanation implied Brexit Britain was experiencing less than stellar success.

Still, he probably felt confident that he'd really done a number on rational thought, only to find himself swiftly outdone by his colleague Chris Loder. Loder claimed the crisis was a good thing for Britain – huzzah! – and the complete breakdown in our ability to supply even basic foodstuffs was to be celebrated. 'It is in our mid- and long-term interest that these logistics chains do break,' he said. 'It will mean the farmer down the street will be able to sell their milk in the village shop like they did decades ago.'[256]

This might have held water if we all lived in villages from the 1950s. Or, for that matter, if it wasn't for the British Poultry Council warning that one in six of their agricultural jobs were unfilled, and that Brexit had resulted in Britain, a nation of turkeys who had voted for Christmas, now most likely running out of festive birds by December. Yes, even in the village shop.[257]

Farmers launched a protest outside that autumn's Tory conference under banners reading 'Don't let Brexit obliterate us, Boris', and for a good reason.[258] But also, for a bad reason. In fact, for a fucking awful reason. During the year, 35,000 healthy pigs had to be slaughtered and simply thrown away because Brexit had left us without enough trained agricultural workers to safely prepare them for the table.

That's 35,000 animals needlessly shot and chucked in a pit, and all of it entirely avoidable: we had 500,000 agricultural vacancies, but the government had granted just 115 migrant labour licences to do the work.[259] Thousands of tonnes of crops had also been left to rot in fields, and all this while more than 2.5 million Britons were reliant on foodbanks.[260]

This was catastrophic enough on its own, but it was made still worse by the broken promises about replacing EU subsidies. Before the Brexit referendum, the government had pledged to match EU funding for farmers if we left the EU.[261] Boris Johnson had said it would be 'mad' not to continue to support farmers.[262] But now our obsession with migration had led to crops rotting and tens of thousands of pigs being shot and thrown into a pit.

The Environment, Food and Rural Affairs Committee called on the government for a 'radical rethink' of the post-Brexit limits on seasonal agricultural labour. Having caused this problem, a rethink was the least the Tories could do, until suddenly they realised they could do even less, so they did. By the end of 2022, only 2,481 seasonal workers were granted visas, which is half of one per cent of what was required.[263] And the post-Brexit subsidies for Britain's farmers fell by between 22 per cent and 36 per cent.[264]

Meanwhile the HGV crisis lumbered on. The industry groups Logistics UK and the British Retail Consortium called on the business secretary to act: the chronic shortage of drivers was 'increasingly putting unsustainable pressure on retailers and their supply chains'. Again, there was a quick, simple solution: grant European HGV drivers cabotage rights in the UK again. It should have been easy. But we'd reckoned without Business Secretary Kwasi Kwarteng, a dead-eye functionary from the Death Star, warming up for his brilliant future performance at the Treasury.

'I am sure you would agree,' he told desperate logistics groups, 'on the importance of utilising the strength of our domestic workforce.' It was supremely unimportant to him that there *wasn't* any strength in our domestic workforce. There wasn't even a workforce. Brexit had driven hundreds of thousands of workers away from Britain, and as a result hundreds of thousands of vacancies were unfillable.

Even if Britons had been available to take up the slack, you can't *force* people to work as HGV drivers. In the unlikely event we miraculously found spare workers who were willing and capable of driving a goods vehicle, they'd still need months of training to get licences, but – yep – that part of the country wasn't working either. The DVLA, responsible for issuing licences, had record backlogs of 3.3 million people experiencing a delayed application process.[265]

So, to summarise: Kwarteng's solution to the HGV crisis was to train Britons who didn't exist to take jobs they didn't want, using licences we couldn't issue, so they could drive lorries which we didn't have.[266] What could possibly go wrong?

A government source said reintroducing cabotage rights 'seems like the obvious solution', but there had been 'a lot of pushback from the Home Office', which lived in fear of being seen to betray whatever they imagined Brexit to be. That was the unofficial line. Officially, a government spokesman said, 'We have a highly resilient food supply chain,'[267] just as Britain went Mott the Hoople because Nando's ran out of chicken.[268]

Mask Rebels

In possibly the first ever use of these words in connection with Desmond Swayne or Jonathan Gullis, they suddenly found themselves at the cutting edge.

The efficacy of masks as a protection against Covid had been scientifically proven, and a study in *Science Focus* found their mandatory use could have kept the UK's pandemic death toll at 52,000, rather than the figure at the time of writing, which is over 217,000.[269] So naturally, Gullis and Swayne launched a battle to oppose the use of masks.

Since they'd started their corpse-friendly campaign in the first months of 2021, increasing numbers of Tory MPs had joined in, and between them they'd invented a spectacular array of increasingly bizarre reasons why face masks – which had already prevented over half a million cases in the USA – were somehow not working in Britain.[270] The British Medical Association denounced this approach as 'wilful negligence', but I'm reasonably sure the members of the BMA had been to university, which meant they were now part of the New Elite, and could be ignored.[271]

Quick to join Gullis's gang of vandals was the contrarian's contrarian Jacob Rees-Mogg, an apparition of a pitiless Victorian dentist that appears to you just before you die. Mogg seemed to suggest the Covid virus agreed with him on the necessity of drudgery for the lower orders, and the importance to people like him of being in the right club. Tory MPs didn't need to wear masks, Mogg told parliament, because they all knew one another, and existed in a 'convivial, fraternal spirit'.[272] Whereas, he argued, opposition members needed face masks because they were not working hard enough.[273] Hard work had turned him from the mere child of a Conservative millionaire who sat in the House of Lords into a Conservative millionaire who sat in the House of Commons. And if he could do it, so could you.[274]

Rees-Mogg's latest fruitless lunge towards logic was built around his belief that Covid was able to recognise (and agree with) his Conservative views, and who am I to argue? After all, a virus is a technically dead agent of destruction that has no brain, so maybe Jacob had a point.

By now – autumn of 2021 – the vaccine was certainly making life safer for those who'd been given it, but that wasn't everybody by a long way. Fewer than half of the UK population had yet received the vital second dose.[275] We were still seeing thousands of deaths every month, and tens of thousands hospitalised or unable to work due to illness.[276] Yet care minister Gillian Keegan felt this was the perfect moment to tell Sky News masks were not only 'less relevant', but that we must be wary of them becoming a 'sign of virtue'.[277]

For God's sake, let us avoid virtue!

Government guidelines still recommended masks in 'crowded and enclosed spaces', but by the time MPs crowded into the House of Commons for the first time since March 2020, all but two government ministers refused to wear one in parliament. Every MP on the opposition benches still wore a mask. Almost the entire Tory Party didn't.[278] The libertarian wing had won, and whether you were prepared to accept mild inconvenience for the sake of others was no longer a matter for science or common decency. It was an issue of tribal politics, adopted and flaunted by a government supposedly tasked with keeping us safe during a pandemic.

Missing in Action

Parliament had been reconvened because events in Afghanistan had – somehow – taken the Tories by surprise. Let's start with a little background.

The wars in Iraq and Afghanistan had begun two decades years earlier, and for absolutely criminal reasons. The politics behind the wars were a disgrace. The wars themselves, an outrage. The results, catastrophic.

In the UK, the decision to go to war was based on lies emanating from the very top, and opinion polls showed it was never backed by more than a wafer-thin majority of Britons, peaking briefly at just 52 per cent.[279] It had been driven through parliament despite most MPs knowing it would be a disaster, yet being unwilling to face down a jingoistic tabloid press. Beyond winning the initial campaign there was no viable plan to make it work. The strategy, such as it was, boiled down to smashing everything up, calling naysayers unpatriotic, and hoping success would magically emerge from the mayhem we'd caused. The costs were huge, the benefits negligible, innocent millions suffered, and the entire project destroyed Britain's international standing. Five years later barely a quarter of voters still thought it was a good idea.

Phew, good job we wouldn't make that kind of mistake again!

The west was exhausted by it all, probably a bit bored, certainly ashamed, and politicians decided they'd had enough. In February 2020, Donald Trump negotiated and announced a withdrawal of American forces from Afghanistan. In August 2021 the new – and yet also very old – US President Joe Biden implemented the plans. The world had had at least 18 months' advance notice of these events.[280]

Britain, with troops on the ground, had little say in matters. We were too militarily weak to remain in the country alone, and too politically weak to persuade the Americans to change their minds. I know *The West Wing* was a liberal fantasy of beautiful people, eloquently doing ethical things for noble reasons, but it contained a kernel of truth: historically, US administrations really did liaise with the Brits over international affairs.

Did: past tense. Those days were gone. Burning our bridges to Europe had also devalued us in the eyes of the USA.

Alone, we seemed clueless. In July Boris Johnson had reassured the House of Commons that there was 'no military path to victory' for the Taliban.[281] One month later the Taliban marched up that military path to Kabul, and took both the city and the country in just ten days.

We'd frittered away our 18 months of notice. We'd been outmanoeuvred by the Taliban, contemptuously ignored by our partners in the 'special relationship' and had intentionally denuded ourselves of either soft or hard power. Britain had no choice: we immediately began pulling our presence from the country, and to give you a sense of how brilliantly the government handled events, the official parliamentary report on the fiasco is entitled 'Missing in action: UK leadership and the withdrawal from Afghanistan'. It described 'a disaster in terms of planning, execution, and consequences for the UK's wider interests'. The former National Security Advisor called Britain's actions 'a bad policy, badly implemented. It is an act of strategic self-harm'.[282]

In charge of this specific piece of national self-harm was a man with an unbroken track record of raddled idiocy. A man gifted with bottomless clodhoppery. A man you could depend upon, at all times, to capture the shitegeist. His life had been cursed by tragedy, but it was always somebody else's tragedy, so he never gave a shit. Both his brain and his body appeared to be operating in low resolution: boxy, rigid, and prone to glitches. He looked like an escapee from *Minecraft*, or perhaps an irritating piece from *Tetris* that you could wearily depend upon to drop from the sky at the worst possible moment and snuff out all hope of success. And his name was Dominic Raab.

Raab, who as foreign secretary was responsible for this crisis, immediately announced he wasn't responsible for this crisis. The job, he said, belonged with military intelligence, and in his opinion it was 'not the Foreign Office's lead responsibility' to deal with all that pesky foreign stuff. That much was obvious: it had been eight months since Raab's last call to any government even neighbouring Afghanistan, and in the militarily frenzied month between Johnson confidently claiming the loss of Kabul would never happen and it, y'know, *happening*, Raab had undertaken only one international engagement on the subject.[283]

On 21 July – 25 days before Kabul fell – an official report warned the UK government that its embassy may need to be mothballed in a hurry due to the speed of the Taliban advances. The government response was so lackadaisical that by the time we acted on this advice, we had only nine hours left to close the embassy, hadn't practised how to do it, and in the rush, we failed to remove sensitive documents. The files identified Afghans who had been working with the UK, almost certainly condemning them to death. The appalled former head of the British Army said the government had been 'asleep on watch'.[284]

We'd had plenty of warning. Donald Trump – even Donald

Trump – had managed to be more competent than we were, and had laid out the withdrawal policy over a year earlier. A handover plan had been signed with the Taliban months earlier in May.[285] But Raab had still decided to go on holiday during the Taliban advance, and during the subsequent evacuation he refused to even speak with Foreign Office staff because he considered them to be 'time-wasters', which ironically led to even more delays.[286] Parliament described him as displaying 'a fundamental lack of seriousness, grip or leadership at a time of national emergency'.[287]

Raab had been advised to urgently dismount from his sun-lounger and call Afghanistan's foreign minister to co-ordinate action, but didn't do so because he'd told staff he was 'unavailable'. Perhaps he'd reached an exciting bit of his Dan Brown novel, or was doing a donkey ride. He definitely wasn't paddle-boarding, despite persistent rumours, because as he explained at the time, 'the sea was closed'.[288]

That's one in the eye for people who reckoned he was fundamentally unserious.

As 15,000 Afghans desperately tried to arrange an escape from the country, Raab's department helped – and believe me, that's stretching the word – with another example of his brilliant leadership. The government set up three separate evacuation channels, managed by three separate departments, who often didn't talk to one another. Rather than implementing a phone system, there were at least six different email inboxes to which Afghans were supposed to address urgent appeals for help.

You know how when your house is on fire, and you urgently email the fire service? Like that.

And once a terrified email was received, it was common practice to simply forward it from one email recipient to another, in the hope it might eventually land on the desk of somebody who knew what the Jabba the Heck they were supposed to be doing.

There was no system to track which emails had been responded to, and during a shift-change the very existence of one email account was forgotten about completely. They just . . . forgot. All those messages from desperate people who had risked their lives to aid Britain were left unanswered. A senior official said she had 'never in my career seen anything [. . .] so badly managed'.[289]

One more fatal fuck-up, and it would technically qualify as a spree. But months later Raab was still pooh-poohing criticism about his calamitous leadership. He laughed in a way he clearly hoped would help him blend in with the humans, and said any condemnation of him was 'silly season stuff'.[290] Parliament didn't see it as silly. They described the government's response as 'arbitrary and chaotic', and nothing illustrated that more clearly than the mind-boggling farce swirling around Nowzad, a charity based in Kabul that looked after stray dogs.

Nowzad had been founded by former Royal Marine Commando Pen Farthing, and was mainly staffed by Afghan locals. Farthing appealed for evacuation, and in the middle of the night – literally 1.30 a.m. – Ben Wallace, a novelty pencil eraser who had been made defence minister, tweeted that 'if [Pen Farthing] arrives with his animals we will seek a slot for his plane'.[291]

Evacuating stray dogs rather than humans seemed on the face of it to be quite, quite mad, so staff in London sought urgent clarification of what was described as 'policy by Twitter'. A call was made to Number 10, and shortly after it was confirmed that Nowzad's animals would indeed be given priority.

And so it was that scarce governmental resources in a desperate crisis were dedicated to organising a 230-seat plane to fly out of Kabul, carrying a solitary human and 173 dogs.

Senior Foreign Office officials believed Boris Johnson had personally mandated this prioritisation of dogs. Johnson denied it, saying any claims he was involved were 'total rhubarb',[292] but the parliamentary report found there to be 'no plausible alternative explanation', and noted that when asked about it, the PM's representative had evaded the question about Johnson's alleged intervention six times.[293]

Apropos of nothing, the writer Jon Ronson asserts psychopaths have a particular fondness for dogs 'since they are obedient and easy to manipulate'.[294]

When Raab returned from his holiday, looking tanned and rested, Downing Street told the press the prime minister had 'full confidence' in him, and probably patted him on his head too, and told him he was a good boy.[295]

Open dissent on the backbenches hadn't broken out in a major way yet, but discontent was growing fast. To respectful silence, the Afghan veteran Tom Tugendhat, now a Tory MP, delivered a scalding speech to the house, berating the government for its failure of duty to the Afghan people. He accepted it was too late to reverse the withdrawal, and so 'now we need to turn our attention to those who are in desperate need [. . .] supporting the United Nations High Commissioner for Refugees, the World Food Programme.

'I support refugees,' he said. 'We just need to get people out.'[296]

The entire house roared its agreement. Boris Johnson leaped into action, gaining glowing headlines when he announced Operation Warm Welcome, his plan to urgently home a further 20,000 Afghan refugees in Britain.[297]

By December 2022, over one year later, we had accepted just four.[298]

Transcendentalism

Dominic Raab was a poster-boy for a certain strain of modern Conservative. Those, like the PM, who retained their confidence in Raab came from various factions of the party. Some were merely selfish and acquisitive libertarian Dementors, divorced from any responsibility to the world. Some were brazen sociopaths, addicted to disruption for its own sake. More than a few hadn't given it much thought, they simply responded with rage and confusion to anything that stank of progress.

But all of them, regardless of other motives, shared one characteristic. They were obsessed with blaming society's ills on the supposed permissiveness and anti-establishment culture of the 1960s, when taxation funded a cohesive society. They didn't see social problems as being an inevitable consequence of the rabid individualism of the Thatcherite 1980s, when a pathological hatred of contributing tax to something cohesive and unifying became so normalised that the very existence of society was ultimately denied.

By 2021 this blame game was all they had left. We could all see from our windows that the fabric of Britain was falling apart; and we could all see from our wages that the promised riches hadn't emerged. There was little still underpinning the politics or economics of today's Tories, so they turned instead to blaming everybody not in government.

Without a hint of irony, the shamelessly greedy ended up claiming that the morally concerned had undermined the shared bonds of society by paying tax, respecting others, and working in our vital services. Bloody hippies.

The Tories had embraced a form of transcendentalism every bit as vivid and detached as that of a drug-addled dropout. To modern Conservatives – as to acid-tripping bohemians – both individual conscience and the tangible world had lost all relevance. All that mattered was the dream state in which they sought solace. Evidence of demonstrable reality or predictable consequences were secondary to the boundless mysticism of Brexitania. The only difference between today's right-wing zealots and the LSD pioneers was that acid's advertised effect was to dismantle the mind until, all barriers gone, the tripper experienced oneness with the infinite. Whereas the Brexit headbangers chose to block out reality by demanding ever-higher barriers, higher, higher, higher.

Sadly, just like those seeking to get higher by surrendering their minds to dangerous substances, the Tories had sustained a wide number of acid casualties. Dead-eyed, fried-brained, soulless zombies still convinced that their dangerous experiments with self-gratification had revealed to them a unique wisdom, and now stumbling around the place, pitiable figures barking nonsense at their demons.

So let's see what Gavin Williamson had been getting up to.

The Idiot-to-Scoundrel Ratio

Williamson, a substandard pottery manager who had bewilderingly ended up as education secretary, was a lifetime collection of blunders lent physical form, fitted with the teeth of a starved horse, and sent skittering around Westminster with instructions to break everything. It often felt like the only thing standing in the way of him causing even greater harm was that he was in charge of schools at a time when schools were mostly shut. His face was an ever-changing mask, flitting between wildly misplaced confidence, angry defiance, and the haunted suspicion that he might be out of his depth. He was. He'd be out of his depth in a raindrop.

The evidence for this arrived with astonishing frequency, often multiple times a day. During 2020, he'd informed parents of the 'vital importance' of primary-school kids going back to class in the middle of the pandemic. And then, *the same afternoon*, he informed them of the 'vital importance' of kids staying at home instead.[299]

But this was merely a warm-up for the pan-directional, ignominious spatter of anarchy that surrounded his attempts at organising exams,[300] during which Williamson whizzed through seven impossible and contradictory policies in just 48 hours.* He was U-turning so fast I'm surprised he didn't drill himself into the ground, and it was a miracle he survived the humiliation and mockery that followed. *ConservativeHome* listed him as the least popular minister among party members, and it looked like the only thing saving him from the sack was that without his presence in Cabinet, an embarrassed Boris Johnson would be at the bottom of the chart.[301]

Williamson must have known this couldn't last, and by 2021 he seemed to be experiencing some kind of breakdown. In March he volunteered himself for a breathtakingly despondent online interview, in

---

* Detailed in *The Decade in Tory*, pages 450–3 (Unbound, 2022).

which he reeled madly from pathos ('Not every day has been brilliant') to bathos (offering to an unforgiving world the news that the only thing keeping him sane was conversations with his dog).[302]

Amazingly, not even turning into Dr. Doolittle (and do it badly) could get him sacked. But the reshuffle in response to Raab's mishandling of Afghanistan took out Williamson too. He was gone from the Cabinet.

Even more amazingly, Raab himself wasn't sacked, merely demoted to justice secretary. After what was described as a 'lengthy and difficult conversation with the prime minister', he was also given the consolation prize of pretending to be deputy PM.[303]

With Williamson gone and Raab bumped down a few steps, it was important to maintain the ratio of idiots-to-scoundrels that Boris Johnson preferred around his Cabinet table. So the new foreign secretary was Liz Truss, a food-obsessed Gilead commander's wife famed for posing serenely in orchards,[304] bizarre and impassioned speeches about the disgrace of cheese,[305] and fuming about the existence of 'new-fangled products such as Angel Delight',[306] a dessert that had been around for six years before Liz Truss was even born.[307]

Pricktionary Corner

Truss wasn't the only baffling new appointment. To a satirist, Nadine Dorries becoming minister for culture was a bit like Imelda Marcos walking into your shoe shop, and my God she didn't disappoint. She immediately went on the attack against anything she didn't fully understand, which was ambitious to say the least. The list of Things Nadine Doesn't Fully Understand is not renowned for its brevity. First up: her battle against 'woke'.

Wokeness doesn't merely fill the role once taken by 'political correctness gone mad' in those halcyon days when the right-wing press could still print those words without being laughed at. There is a real definition. It means 'alert to racial prejudice and discrimination', originating in African-American vernacular, and then extended to incorporate not just racism, but sexism, homophobia and prejudices against other minorities too.

But that was not what the new anti-woke right meant by it. What they meant by it was . . .

. . . hold on, I'm thinking.

. . . nope, I've got nothing.

You can't define what they meant by 'woke', but that's the entire point. Their use of the pejorative 'woke' described, essentially, anything they didn't like. It was a folk-devil, a bunch of scary noises in the dark, designed to frighten the unthinking. Wokeness was Grendel's mother come to gobble you up, a shape-shifting terror, ever lurking, constantly threatening, yet with a description lost to the ages. Nadine Dorries, Jacob Rees-Mogg, Lee Anderson and the gang regurgitated the word constantly, but could offer only the vaguest hint about what they meant by it.

So rather than wait for a definition from the guys in Pricktionary Corner, here's what I think they *really* meant: an entirely normal bit of evolution.

There is a – probably apocryphal – story about Sir David Attenborough and a cameraman, out on the Serengeti filming a pride of lions. The lions suddenly begin to take an interest in the two delicious-looking humans watching them from a ridge. They prowl with purpose towards the defenceless men.

The cameraman puts down his equipment and reaches into his bag. He pulls out a pair of trainers and begins to rapidly change out of his heavy hiking boots.

'I don't know what you're doing that for,' says Attenborough, 'you'll never outrun a lion.'

'I don't need to outrun a lion,' says the cameraman, 'I only need to outrun *you*.'

Whether true or not, the story tells us something very real about the driving force behind evolution and competition. Attenborough's instinct was that the thing deciding whether he lived or died was a lion. In fact, it was a cameraman. This is the essential nature of both Darwinian evolution and classical market forces: it's all in the little differences.

Most businesses beat their rivals by that little difference. A one per cent advantage here, an infinitesimal outperformance there, an imperceptible reputational polish everywhere. If that one per cent appears to always shift behaviour in the direction of socially progressive viewpoints, it's because there is (to be coldly clinical about it) no profit in embracing hatred or estranging marginalised groups. Whereas a spirit of inclusion and acceptance makes the corporations look like good guys while they put their hands in your pockets.

The evolution of ideas is driven – as with Attenborough's lion story – by tiny changes of perspective that make us all reappraise how we view the world. Nobody steers this stuff; it just emerges naturally out of group dynamics and a race to gain an advantage. It is market forces in action, something the Tories have always told us are vital to our survival.

A sensible government would adopt 'wokeness' entirely. It would encourage unity and understanding, if not out of morality, then at least out of self-preservation. It wouldn't even need to believe in the 'wokeness', it would simply recognise an opportunity to exploit our kindness, just like a corporate PR department.

The government since 2010, however, had chosen to treat this as a wedge issue, and encouraged its fans to tune into GB News to find somebody – anybody – who would echo back to them their evidence-free instinct that all this modernity was a liberal conspiracy; and one somehow funded and directed by a mash-up of George Soros, an army of furious, statue-smashing transexuals, *Guardian*-readers, and top crisp salesman, Gary Lineker.

And now the Tories had appointed their own champion of the anti-woke as culture minister. She didn't always get the greatest reviews from colleagues, however. 'She often speaks without thinking,' said an admiring colleague about Nadine Dorries.[308]

Dorries seems to have taken this less as an expression of concern than as a guiding principle, and got stuck straight in with an appearance on the *Telegraph* podcast, during which she railed against her natural enemies: joined-up thinking and the BBC. The Beeb, she averred, was merely a broiling nest of nepotism, populated by 'people whose mum and dad worked there', and that was something Dorries hated.[309]

She'd seemingly forgotten about employing both of her daughters in her parliamentary office for a wage bill of £80,000 a year.[310]

And then it was off to her first appearance before the Culture Select Committee, where Dorries was pressed about a tweet in which she described the journalist James O'Brien as a 'public school posh boy fuckwit'. Her abusive message was perfectly acceptable, she explained, because it justified her proposal to ban people from sending abusive messages.[311] Take that, so-called logic!

It's unclear whether the time she threatened to nail a journalist's testicles to the floor using the reporter's own front teeth was merely a signifier of her relentless backing for free speech.[312] But rather than waste too much time attempting to pick bits of sense out of Nadine's raving tangles of verbiage, let's just note that she sent her own daughter to the very same public school James O'Brien went to, and move on to her plans for Channel 4.[313]

She told the select committee she didn't think the broadcaster had 'a sustainable and viable model', and that it was therefore appropriate that she should privatise Channel 4, 'because it's in receipt of public money'. And this would have been an excellent argument if Channel 4 had been in receipt of public money. It wasn't. The broadcaster's status as a private company was an inconsequential detail that hadn't intruded on Nadine's years spent obsessing about the company's future.

When a fellow Tory MP on the committee patiently explained these absolute basics to Dorries, her reply demonstrated all the mental agility demanded by her high office, and the linguistic grace we expect from a best-selling novelist.

'And . . . so . . . though it's . . . yeah and that . . .'[314]

An anagram of Nadine Dorries is 'Inane Disorder'.

Jog On

Sometimes it's the little things. After delivering his keynote speech at the Tory Conference in Manchester, Boris Johnson decided to let the press see him complete his daily jog.

And so his chauffeur-driven Land Rover arrived outside the luxurious Midland Hotel, and out stepped the PM in his performatively slovenly running regalia, to trudge through the arduous 10 metres to his hotel door in the shattered style of somebody completing a gruelling marathon.

The press caught the images of our hard-working prime minister pounding the pavement, and that's what made the papers.[315]

Ten metres.

Oh Shit!

In the early years of Boris Johnson's premiership there was a sudden fad for Britain to beat the world at everything, and before you knew it, the phrase was everywhere. We were offered world-beating Covid apps which didn't work; world-leading test and trace which failed miserably; world-conquering border technology which was a shambles. You couldn't rely on much from the Johnson government, but you could pretty much guarantee any promise of 'leading the world' would quickly turn into an absolute torrent of shit.

Although nobody expected things to be quite so on-the-nose as November's Environment Act.

'World-leading Environment Act becomes law' read the official government press release, but the legislation mostly became known for allowing the dumping of raw sewage directly into our nation's rivers and seas.[316] The House of Lords had rejected the original bill, returning it to the Commons with an amendment to place legal duties on water companies to refrain from pouring billions of gallons of untreated excrement into our waterways. Hundreds of Tory MPs voted to overturn the Lords' amendment.

Let's put what happened next into context.

In 2010, after a decade of work, the Labour government had left behind the cleanest rivers and beaches since before the industrial revolution.[317] In 2020, after a decade of Conservative rule, raw sewage was dumped into our rivers over 400,000 times.[318] By the end of that year, not a single river, lake or stream in England met the basic 'good health' standard. Not one.[319] And now the Tories had voted against future protections, only days before Boris Johnson was due to host the COP26 climate conference in Glasgow.

Water had been privatised under Thatcher in 1989, promising a shiny new era of investment, efficiency, and low, low bills. Between 1991 and the COP26 shindig in 2021, not a single reservoir had been completed in the UK.[320] Britain's privatised water companies replaced just 0.05 per cent of pipes every year, which was a tenth of the European average.[321] The maths of this implies that our pipes – which already leaked over 1 trillion litres every year – were expected to last a further 2,000 years.[322] In just two years following the sewage vote, water companies in England undertook 775,000 separate dumps of sewage, equivalent to a relentless stream of shit and piss lasting over 5 million hours.

The public were appalled at the decision, so the Conservatives defended it on the grounds that *not* pouring millions of gallons of infectious human waste all over the fucking country would be expensive. Fortunately, I might have identified a way to resolve the funding issues. Britain's privatised water companies declared profits of £2.9 billion in 2021 alone. Their chief executives earned up to £2.9 million, and the companies have paid out dividends of £16 billion since the Tories came to power in 2010.[323]

Is it churlish of me to suggest that if the profits are all theirs, so are the responsibilities?

Anyway, having listened to your outrage, in January 2023, while you probably weren't looking, 292 Tories voted for new regulations delaying any reduction of phosphates in our rivers – related to human excrement – for a further 15 years.[324] And those low, low water bills? They rose by the highest amount for 20 years.[325]

Privatisation

I don't want to seem sniffy about privatisation as a concept. Some things certainly should be private: there's no reason whatsoever why the state should run your corner shop, pub or supermarket.

But there are many vitally important pieces of national infrastructure that we used to own as a collective society, and which were privatised to make them better. After all this time it is perfectly reasonable to ask: did they improve?

Look at water. No new reservoirs for 30 years. Infrastructure expected to last two millennia. Unimaginably vast leaks. The land swimming in sewage. Huge shareholder dividends. And still, every summer, water shortages on one of the dampest islands on the planet.

Look at trains. Public subsidies have doubled since the service was privatised.[326] Despite this, the average price of a journey has increased by a quarter.[327] Our trains are, by some margin, the most expensive in Europe, costing up to five times as much of a person's salary compared to France or Italy.[328] Research by *Which?* magazine found that 20 years after privatisation, less than half of passengers are satisfied, and only one in five passengers thinks things are improving.[329] £3.2 billion in dividends to shareholders.[330]

Look at energy. We have the highest electricity bills in the world.[331] A profound lack of energy security. Decade-long delays in building new capacity.[332] And in 2022, shareholder dividends for a single company, Centrica, of £3.3 billion, more than triple the year before.[333]

Look at Royal Mail. Sold off for at least a billion less than it was worth.[334] Over 11,000 jobs lost. Over a million customer complaints per year.[335] A fifth of services closed, yet dividends to those lucky shareholders who bought it at half its proper value – £220 million a year.[336]

Sure, it's worked out great for those shareholders. But surely there must be a time when we ask if privatisation has worked for the nation?

If that time isn't now, when is it?

Deeply at Odds

The reek in the air wasn't all emanating from our rivers. All around us, everywhere we looked, the nation appeared to be sinking into a swamp. After a decade of austerity, the state was so enfeebled that it was incapable of withstanding the slightest shock, and a combination of Brexit and Covid had cruelly exposed our fragility. For millions, even the notion of home ownership was a bleak, existential joke. Fuel supplies barely existed. Food costs were rising at 18 per cent per year. Farming was teetering. Fisheries ruined. Passport offices, the benefits system, dentistry, even road surfaces – they all seemed to be crumbling. The NHS was in crisis. Schools were falling apart. Trains didn't work. Border posts didn't work. Trade *definitely* didn't work.

And parliament didn't work. When we needed them most, the governing party was – like Raab – missing in action, obsessed with overcoming tofu, privatising already private companies, ensuring footballers didn't kneel down, and spearheading popular uprisings to defend statues of long-dead slavers. The only time Tory backbenchers took time away from these urgent national problems, it was to seemingly focus on their own personal enrichment.

Almost a quarter of the governing party held second jobs that earned them over £15 million between the fall of Theresa May and the fall of Liz Truss.[337] Just like the privatised utilities, they seemed to be strong on extracting wealth for themselves, but lousy at delivering services we expected them to. The public felt far too many of these MPs had second jobs that reeked of something fundamentally wrong, even if we couldn't always put our fingers on exactly what. MPs gave the impression they were benefiting from their time holding government roles in ways that many felt entirely uncomfortable about.

For instance, the mere mention of former transport minister Chris Grayling was shorthand for graceless buffoonery after his repeated ministerial failings, yet now he had a side-hustle as an advisor to Hutchison Ports Europe, which earned him £100,000 a year. It wasn't only Opposition MPs asking questions when Hutchison was awarded £35 million of government money.[338]

Andrew Mitchell, former international development minister and nemesis of plebs, got £182,600 for 35 days' work offering advice to various investment groups.[339] Geoffrey Cox, the former attorney general, earned over £1 million in a year as a barrister, while still trying to persuade us he was working full-time as somebody's MP.[340]

These former ministers were all backbenchers now, of course. Serving ministers were officially banned from holding second jobs, but many, including the Tory Party's Bez, Jacob Rees-Mogg, got around this by taking them in an unpaid capacity. The unholy relic kept his positions in multiple investment companies on the grounds that he earned no money from them.[341] But because of that bit in the Bible that relates to situations like this, the staunchly Christian Rees-Mogg had led the government's attempts to relax standards on making vast piles of money from second jobs. And then in November 2021, there were accusations he'd flouted those rules by accepting – and not declaring – a £6 million loan from one of those companies he was officially not being paid by.

He was able to show that the loans had been fully repaid, and that they'd only been needed – all £6 million of them – to refurbish his second home in Westminster. Jesus would have been so proud. But Jacob Rees-Mogg had not broken any rules, which is a shame, because it would have been lovely to refer to him as Felonious Monk.[342]

To be fair, some Conservative MPs disapproved of the practice. 'We are paid handsomely for the job we do,' said Lee Anderson, 'and if you need an extra £100,000 a year on top then you should really be looking for another job.'

In 2023 Lee Anderson, while still a serving MP and working as deputy chair of the Conservative Party, took a £100,000 second job as a presenter on GB News.[343]

The public were a little more consistent than Anderson on the subject. Polls found 68 per cent felt MPs holding second jobs was wrong, and politicians' most common justification for iffy moonlighting – that it gave them insight into ordinary working lives – might have rung more truly if any of them took a second job as a hospital porter or did a shift on a building site.[344] But they all seemed to be getting fifty grand for a morning's work advising massive companies, and then those massive companies all seemed to land some kind of gigantic government contract. Whether that scenario was accurate or not, it was certainly the perception.

Which brings us to Owen Paterson, former environment minister, passionate Brexiteer, and unsuccessful scourge of badgers. Paterson had grown up on a Shropshire farm, and gained qualifications at the National Leathersellers' College[345] – which actually exists – before going on to manage his family tannery for two decades.[346] I can't find any scientific or medical training in his background, and indeed he had refused to even accept briefings from scientists when in his environment role.[347] So it's not immediately obvious what advice he could offer to a medical testing laboratory. Regardless, one such lab, Randox, had been paying him £100,000 a year to do 16 hours of advisory work every month.[348] He also accepted £12,000 for 24 hours of work advising a sausage distributor in Northern Ireland.[349]

The Venn diagram of people with expertise in medical diagnostics *and* in putting sausages into post boxes is two circles, positioned at some distance from one another.

At the height of Covid, Randox had landed a £133 million deal to supply testing kits. No other company was given the chance to bid for the contract.[350] And that was just one of the £600 million of Covid deals the company landed, about which the government later admitted they were 'unable to locate' vital papers showing how the firm came to be appointed.[351]

The rules over lobbying were pretty feeble, and the Tories had intentionally left them that way in the aftermath of the Greensill scandal, but one thing was clear: MPs must not lobby for companies they were being paid by. Regardless, Paterson represented his employer Randox in a call to health minister Lord Bethell just before the Covid contract was awarded. Nobody in government was able to produce minutes of the call, despite it being a requirement that any meeting between a business and a minister is recorded.[352]

The contract was later extended by a further £347 million, having been approved by Matt Hancock. Paterson had directly approached Hancock for aid in landing the agreement.[353] And again, no other company was able to bid for the contract.[354]

It's probably unrelated, but Randox had donated £160,000 to the Tories since they came to office.[355] What is certain is that a year after landing the contracts, Randox declared profits which were 'more than 100 times greater' than the previous year.[356]

Parliament's spending watchdog later found ministers had 'played fast and loose' with the rules when dealing with Randox and Paterson. Hancock had only recently been given a free stay at the country estate owned by the head of Randox, and had failed to declare it in the register of hospitality, which ministers are required to keep. When this was discovered, his spokesman said Hancock didn't need to declare it, because he was not there in a ministerial capacity.[357]

Just so we're clear, he was *not* a minister when he was accepting free, secret hospitality from a company's owner; but he returned to being a minister when it was time to sign off a contract to that company. It was almost as if he could flicker between states, like Schrödinger's Twat.

The Parliamentary Committee on Standards began looking into Paterson's activities and found that 'no previous case of paid advocacy has seen so many breaches or such a clear pattern of behaviour in failing to separate private and public interests'. The committee recommended Paterson be suspended from the Commons for 30 days due to his 'egregious' behaviour.

Paterson was being paid £81,932 as an MP. His punishment was to keep being paid that, but spend a month in his lovely Shropshire farmhouse, lolling around in his pants, watching *Loose Women* until it all blew over. But he was having none of it, mostly because if he was suspended, his constituents would have had the right to petition for a by-election, and neither he nor the party wanted to face voters. They knew there was a strong chance they'd lose.

'The process I have been subjected to does not comply with natural justice,' Paterson declared. 'A fair process would exonerate me.'[358]

And so, operating on the rationale that any process capable of finding them guilty must be unfair, a group of leading Tories set about designing a – very much in air-quotes – *fair* process that would always find them innocent. Andrea Leadsom, a former Cabinet minister and current melted waxwork of Margaret Thatcher, put forward an amendment to pause Paterson's suspension long enough to set up a new, Tory-majority committee that would make it all go away. Johnson backed the idea, and the government issued a three-line whip, meaning every Tory had to back it, whether they liked it or not.

Many didn't like it one bit. It went to a vote, and as a mark of how uncomfortable his own party now found Johnson, 97 of his own MPs risked retaliation by abstaining or absenting themselves, including Angela Richardson, parliamentary private secretary to Michael Gove. She was sacked for her troubles. Another 13 Tory MPs went further than mere abstention, and actively voted against the measure. But Johnson had a massive majority, and plenty of his backbenchers didn't seem to give a lukewarm speckled fuck about decency; so despite the rebellion, the amendment passed, and Paterson's suspension was paused.[359]

Public response was cacophonous. Across all branches of the media, left, right and centre, commentators deplored the move. The chairman of the Committee on Standards called it 'deeply at odds with the best traditions of British democracy'. Tory MP and former Chief Whip Mark Harper – not a man to rebel – said the affair was 'one of the most unedifying episodes' of his 16 years in parliament.[360] Aaron Bell said it 'looks like we're moving the goalposts, and for that reason I can't support it'.[361]

In a panic, the government U-turned. Angela Richardson was un-sacked, cos that's totally normal, and the Tories tried to pretend nothing had happened. Less than 24 hours after his suspension had been suspended, Paterson was suspended again.[362] But as a keen advocate for personal responsibility, he decided he wasn't gonna stick around to face his punishment, and quit parliament with immediate effect.

The subsequent by-election should have been a shoo-in. Paterson's seat of North Shropshire was one of the safest in the country, and he held a majority of over 23,000. Other than a brief interlude in 1904, when the constituency changed its name, it had been in Conservative hands for two centuries, and should have been unassailable.

The Liberal Democrats handsomely won the by-election in a gleeful orgy of public fury and tactical voting by opposition parties.

Senior Tory backbencher Roger Gale said the result 'has to be seen as a referendum on the prime minister's performance', and that for Boris Johnson, 'one more strike and he's out'.[363] In normal circumstances you'd have to agree, but Johnson was not normal. He should have gone already, following his illegal prorogation of parliament in 2019, or been sacked after he'd been found to have lied to the Queen. He should have been ousted in the national interests during his disgraceful, deadly mishandling of Covid in 2020. A properly functioning party would have dumped him after DominicCummingsgate, and after Wallpapergate, and after Afghanistangate, and after Patersongate.

Yet still he clung on. He had more gates than Wembley Stadium, and more endings than *The Lord of the Rings*.

He survived because there was no longer anything unusual about what was happening. It had become normalised. You can see that much in his party's response to the Randox scandal. In any other political era, Paterson's actions would have been extraordinary, but by 2021 he was surrounded by amoral enablers, who shrugged off corruption and stupefying greed. Hundreds of his fellow Tories had voted against tightening lobbying rules in the wake of David Cameron's Greensill scandal, barely six months earlier. And they voted to overturn parliamentary standards for Paterson too. A quarter of them were constantly grubbing around for money on the side, and they still backed – albeit with rising concern – the most degenerate, destructive and asinine figure to have entered Downing Street since Mr Blobby paid a visit. They voted for this. They planned it. It arose out of their every choice.

Owen Paterson was not an aberration, but a culmination.

Party On!

We didn't know it at the time, but we'd just witnessed the first crucial blow that led to Johnson's demise. Until Paterson, the PM's tactic was to be agile, jabbing at critics, dashing from oncoming assaults, bewildering his detractors with a barrage of waffle and obfuscation, and always supremely confident that the press wouldn't bother checking if any of his bullshit promises had accidentally ended up being fulfilled.

Paterson was a haymaker, though: an ear-ringing, percussive wallop that left the PM staggering. He just didn't know it yet. He was still swiping wildly at the air, still confidently booming to his cornermen, still on his feet. But his legs had turned to jelly, and from this moment onwards the swipes became desperate.

Everybody was now counting down until the moment a killer punch landed. This was especially evident among his own MPs, many of whom were increasingly revolted by the prime minister. Traditionally, Tories seemed to be born with three things: a silver spoon, a knack for self-preservation, and a carefully concealed knife for sticking into their leader's back. Johnson's years spent plotting his route to power added a new element to the mix: he'd trained every one of his MPs in the art of constant rebellion. As Johnson's approval rating fell, so did any sense of loyalty to him. They were quick to find a microphone.

'It was so unethical,' said one Tory MP. 'I thought, do I really want to be associated with these people?'[364]

'The stench of sleaze and the mind-blowing incompetence could be massively damaging to us,' said another.

'This has gone straight into my top 10 fuck-up chart,' said one poor soul who had been keeping a tally. I feel for him, I truly do.

Even the *Daily Mail* turned, although it aimed at the wrong target. They called the attempt to save Paterson by suborning parliamentary process a 'dark day for democracy' under a headline reading 'Shameless MPs sink back into sleaze'.[365] But this wasn't caused by shameless MPs, but by a shameless prime minister, who had whipped his backbenchers into helping him dismantle the offices of state.

A high-ranking Tory advisor put his finger on the crux of the problem: 'Boris has few friends.'[366] There was nobody close who could tell Johnson he was fucking up because, as with all narcissists, he didn't like other people. And he definitely didn't trust them. Narcissists always prefer the company of other narcissists, and now Dominic Cummings was gone, so Johnson was alone.[367] The only MPs he'd been able to rely upon for constant and unthinking support were the constantly unthinking Brexiteer sect that had powered him to Downing Street, a loose grouping around Jacob Rees-Mogg, Nadine Dorries, Iain Duncan Smith and – until recently – Owen Paterson. And having just witnessed one of their own being driven from a safe seat, their loyalty and confidence were somewhat tested.

Like a staggering boxer near the end of a round, the PM's best hope was to duck for cover, pray for the bell, and hope the short break at Christmas would give him time to recover.

Let's see how that went.

—

Not well.

On 30 November the *Mirror* ran the first of a series of explosive reports alleging Johnson and dozens of his team had packed 'cheek by jowl' into small Downing Street rooms for a series of parties the year before.[368] The nation was shocked, but the press weren't. Most of what emerged had been circulating unofficially since January, but it had taken over ten months for disgruntled whistle-blowers to go on the record.

The revelations perfectly reflected the nation's now settled view of Johnson as a clumsy, self-seeking vandal who didn't give a damn about the rules, and there was an immediate sense in the air that this was terminal. Number 10's first move was flat denial. 'This is total nonsense,' said a spokesman, but it quite clearly wasn't. Within hours three things had become obvious: there was a lot more to this story; the public *really* cared; and consequently there might be an opening for PM in the very near future.

Manoeuvres began. Senior MPs hoping to succeed Johnson practised combinations of words that blithely reassured the public no parties had taken place, but also made it plain that parties had *definitely* taken place, but they had personally remained squeaky clean throughout.

'I didn't attend,' said Sajid Javid. 'I don't know who attended these parties, but I don't even think there were parties that I'm aware of.'[369]

Javid made being villainously slippery look easy.

Let's see how George Freeman made it look.

The science minister, a doomed attempt to find a socially useful purpose for a pigeon's knuckle, pootled off to commit hara-kiri on the *Today* programme in defence of Boris Johnson's honour, which is right up there with setting yourself on fire on *Gardeners' Question Time* for the glory of Discworld.

Freeman said he knew nothing, because he hadn't been at the rule-breaking parties, but 'I've asked the people who were, and they have all said the rules were followed.' It was a bracing retort to reason, and you could hear the wooden thunk of forehead on desk all the way from Westminster.[370]

The poor man had barely made it back to his ministerial car for a bit of a cry before the Number 10 spokesman was shoved out to try a new approach. The government was no longer denying parties had happened. Sure, they said, fine: there were parties, but they must have been *legal* parties because the PM was there. And we could all trust Johnson – a man who had just caused national outrage by bending the rules to save Paterson – not to bend the rules to save himself.

It didn't work. Public anger was palpable. Worse still, the crisis had already been named Partygate, and when you add a gate to a scandal, you're in real trouble. In desperation, one more attempt from Downing Street.

'Mr Johnson has followed coronavirus rules at all times, and it is categorically untrue to suggest otherwise.'[371]

This statement was categorically untrue, so a couple of days later the language had been massaged again to the familiar language of indistinct non-denial. 'We don't recognise these accounts.'[372]

Johnson did what we all expected him to do: set out a specific plan to make other people pay for his mistakes. It was named, with characteristic humility, Operation Save Big Dog, and was a roadmap of exactly which innocent underlings should be sacked instead of Boris Johnson. His chief of staff and his private secretary were named, an act of crashing disloyalty that instantly made it far more likely that they'd do nothing to save the PM.[373]

By now somebody – in the name of suffering Christ, *somebody* in Downing Street must have worked out that all this illegality might end up involving the police. So the strategy shifted again: forget about denials, forget about sacking the tea-boy, and instead lay the groundwork for avoiding fines. This was a job for Dominic Raab, a CGI construct from a videogame about an inept spy who can't find his way out of his hotel room.

'The police don't normally look back and investigate things that have taken place a year ago,' said Raab, which must have come as a shock to the police, who – and this is the real takeaway from the whole affair – do have a tendency to focus on crimes that happened in the past. Doctor Who has got the future covered. The past is kinda the police's thing. Even so, the fact-checking service Full Fact genuinely had to clarify, for the benefit of the *justice minister* Dominic Raab, that 'police often investigate alleged offences which took place years before'.[374]

And then photos began to emerge: a dozen people drinking wine in the Downing Street garden, including Boris Johnson, Carrie Johnson (they had married by now), and Dominic Cummings. After a quick rummage in the excuses box, Number 10 decided to claim this was a 'work meeting', and that Carrie Johnson was only present because it was 'her garden'.

This didn't explain why they were all getting pissed at a 'work meeting'. Or answer the obvious question: if Carrie Johnson attended work meetings, what was her security clearance?

'We won't get into that,' said the spokesman, and vanished inside to see if any whitewash was left over from their previous attempts to paint over the truth.[375] The whole escapade became bizarrely fascinating. Every lie was only there to cover up multiple previous lies, and there seemed to be no end to it.

They'd invented Mandelbrot bullshit.

―

Perhaps Downing Street felt things couldn't get much worse, but if so, they were feeling in the wrong place, because things did. The next day, the press moved from photographic evidence to video footage, and you'd need to have a heart of stone not to laugh your head off at the thought of Johnson suddenly realising it might not have been the best idea in the world to hire a cameraman to capture all the times something illegal happened in his house.

Back in March, Boris Johnson had proudly launched his new press briefing room. The announcement was accompanied by a carefully stage-managed photo of the room, a discordant assemblage of shonky materials seemingly hurled together in anger and spite. The walls had been painted the precise shade used for blue-screen superimposition, as if Lulu Lytle was worried the nation's satirists were about to run out of material. As one Tory aide commented, 'I can't believe something with blue walls got past whatever committee approved it! The internet is going to thank them for years to come.'[376]

To break up the blue, they'd installed a couple of panels of offensively orange wood, a TV, a bland plinth, Henry the Hoover squatting in the corner, and four Union Flags. Three Union Flags wouldn't have been enough. With three Union Flags you might have mistaken it for the briefing room of Estonia or Paraguay. It had to be four.

This ghastly chamber had cost us £2.6 million, and no, I can't even begin to explain why. But five months later no press briefing had yet taken place, and instead Johnson used it to watch Bond movies in the evenings.[377]

Yet the official purpose of this room was to house Johnson's newly appointed £100,000 press secretary Allegra Stratton. Stratton never got to give a press conference, but her practice session was good enough. It had been filmed a year earlier, but her team still had the foresight to ask her opinion on illegal parties that Downing Street later spent weeks denying happened. A giggling Stratton was filmed saying, 'This fictional party was a business meeting . . . and it was not socially distanced.'[378]

It was impossible to watch the footage and not reach the conclusion: not only did Stratton and all those present know parties had happened, but they also knew it was wrong, and suspected that one day they'd have to answer questions. Yet somehow, Downing Street still managed to be wrong-footed by the whole affair.

Stratton resigned in floods of tears, which seemed very real.

Johnson said he was 'shocked' by the video, which did not seem real at all. He marched straight to parliament to tell them he was 'furious to see that clip', and to prove how angry he was he thumped random bits of nearby air for a few seconds, like a cross baby who's been at the sherry.

'I can understand how infuriating it would be to think that the people who have been setting the rules have not been following the rules,' Johnson told MPs. 'I repeat that I have been repeatedly assured since these allegations emerged that there was no party, and that no Covid rules were broken.'[379]

It was absolute crap, and everybody knew it. Johnson was a manipulative liar, a lawbreaker, and the ultimate unreliable narrator, weaving bullshit out of whatever he saw around him.

He was Britain's very own Keyser Dozy.

2022
'It's Bollocks, Utter Bollocks'

Born to Run

2022 began as almost every year since the Conservatives came to power had begun, and you can't say they aren't sticklers for tradition.

Britain had been frogmarched into an escalating series of surreal calamities. Brexit was a disaster, the NHS was in crisis, the government was bathed head-to-toe in impropriety, and senior Tories were still acting as though the public purse was their personal feed-trough. The air crackled with anger about Partygate, and the government desperately needed something that would distract the public.

Enter Liz Truss with the first scandal of what turned out to be quite a busy year, scandal-wise. She had insisted on having lunch at an 'incredibly expensive' private dining club, overruling official guidance. Truss had 'refused to consider anywhere else' despite lunch being quoted at £3,000. The five bottles of wine she ordered cost £719.[1]

Undeterred by the fuss over this, Truss took to hosting regular 'fizz with Liz' dinners at the same venue, in an effort to woo MPs and prospective donors who might back her to be leader. While Russia was manoeuvring tanks and troops at the Ukrainian border, our foreign secretary's top priority seemed to be establishing herself as a frontrunner to replace the wounded Boris Johnson. The lessons of Dominic Raab's disaster in Afghanistan had clearly not been learned.

As part of her bid for power, she kickstarted her habit of accompanying every official announcement with a portrait of herself that aligned with what she clearly considered the very quintessence of Britishness. She released a photo of herself in a tank, posing like Thatcher.[2] She released a Christmas photograph of herself, posing like the Queen.[3]

You half expected her to lunge for a family pet so she could treat us to her depiction of Cat Bin Lady.

Her Instagram swelled to hundreds of photos that to an untrained eye seem like the desperate wail of an unhinged mind. Here I am, milking cows. Now I'm dressed as Satan. Now as a fighter pilot. Now as Dracula. Yesterday I was on a zip-wire, but today I've gone surfing . . . wait for it . . . on dry land.[4] On and on and on it goes. It's hardly a surprise that one Tory MP described her as a 'very odd person . . . not good or bad – just very weird'.[5]

Weird Liz was even given permission to hire an 'Instagram guru', who would accentuate the prime-ministerial bits of her fantasy life and de-emphasise the bits where she spent her afternoons clutching a newborn calf and gawping blankly, as though she'd just struck her head on a low beam. Little Rishi Sunak, safe from such hazards, had also hired a specialist to 'overhaul the Chancellor's digital profile' and establish his brand.

They came up with 'Dishy Rishi'.[6]

The internet preferred Eunuch Sunak, but the internet doesn't always get what it wants.

Johnson's Christmas Gift

So: plenty of cash to persuade us Rishi was dishy and Truss was competent, but not much money for the NHS. The service was under incredible pressure. Austerity and ideology had landed hospitals and care services with a decade of mismanagement and underinvestment, after which yet more ideology – this time against Brussels – exacerbated the problem.

Since Labour's last full year in office, wages for an average frontline NHS nurse had fallen by more than £10,000 in real terms.[7] More than 22,000 EU-born health workers had left the NHS since the Brexit referendum.[8] George Osborne's decision to slash bursaries for training new nurses had led to a 40 per cent drop in domestic student applications,[9] and the number of nursing staff joining the NHS from the EU's 27 nations had fallen by 87 per cent.[10]

The staffing crisis in the NHS was an entirely avoidable catastrophe, caused exclusively by Conservative policy.

And then came Covid, which not only swamped understaffed hospitals already battling with record-shattering waiting lists of 4 million patients awaiting elective treatment,[11] but killed over 1,500 NHS staff, and left tens of thousands more either too sick to work, or in self-isolation.[12]

In January 2022, in regions across the country, hospitals declared critical incidents, not due to a train crash or natural disaster, but due to chronic staff shortages. In Lincolnshire, four of the largest hospitals announced 'critical incidents', leaving the county with barely any medical capacity. A major incident was declared across all London hospitals to prevent them being overwhelmed.[13] The crisis was national, deep, and desperate.

Boris Johnson emerged from hiding to inform us that we must 'make sure that we look after our NHS any way that we can', which sounded lovely, but was in stark contrast with his actions. Right through the winter, he giddily repeated all the mistakes that he'd made the previous year.[14]

The Omicron variant of Covid had first been identified in South Africa in November 2021 and spread rapidly across the globe.[15] There was justifiable concern, and the World Health Organization (WHO) warned against any assumptions that the new variant would be mild. It wasn't. It was far more transmissible, and therefore more deadly.

'Last week, the highest number of COVID-19 cases were reported so far in the pandemic,' said a WHO spokesman, as infections had risen by 65 per cent across Europe.[16] The Netherlands rushed into lockdown. Portugal curbed flights, as did much of Europe and North America. Severe travel restrictions were implemented in more than 50 nations across the world, from Japan to the USA.[17]

In the UK, we had no international travel restrictions. In fact, we never introduced any, at any point during the pandemic: flights in and out of the country went ahead as if we simply didn't care about protecting our borders when the people crossing them were rich enough to afford business class. Officially, our response to the fifth worst pandemic in history seeping across our borders amounted to nudging people towards a voluntary, self-administered Covid test two days before flying.[18] Unsurprisingly, Omicron quickly became the dominant strain in the UK, and began gleefully kicking seven shades out of the NHS.

Boris Johnson said he would 'look after our NHS any way that we can', but his interpretation of those words was the opposite of yours and mine. He had cut the self-isolation period from ten days to seven, making the spread of infection more likely,[19] and then confidently announced all this fresh death did not 'justify any tougher measures before Christmas'.[20]

He hadn't been able to justify tough measures the previous Christmas either, and 33,000 people had died in the surge of cases that followed.[21] A year on from that, Christmas went ahead as normal, Omicron had a great time, and by 8 January 2022 the UK had over 200,000 current cases,[22] and had passed the horrific figure of 150,000 dead.[23]

Less Good and Very, Very Bad

Across every branch of government things were going badly. Inflation rose to the highest level for almost 30 years.[24] Energy costs spiralled, with costs-per-household already predicted to reach £2,255 by

October 2022.[25] And remember, this was still two months before Russia invaded Ukraine, the event that became the Conservatives' go-to excuse for the cost-of-living crisis.

In reality, the reasons were complex. A breakdown in global supply chains. Increased demand from growing economies. Delays to essential maintenance during the pandemic, which now interrupted supply.[26] Much of the world was affected by these issues, to which Britain could add one additional, unique problem, which had been accurately predicted four years earlier by experts at the US Embassy in London. Discussing Brexit in 2018, the diplomats predicted it would cause 'the worst kind of inflation' and that 'the economy is going to tank'.

'The British government is not interested in telling people, "You know this thing that 52 per cent of you said that you wanted, here are the range of options: there's less good and then there's very, very bad"', said one official, with the 'very, very bad' option being leaving the single market.

Which is what we did, for no reason.

'They haven't actually done a lot of macroeconomic modelling of this,' the Embassy staff went on, 'almost deliberately, like, "We don't want to know!"'[27]

Brexit-related lorry queues at ports grew to prodigious lengths. There was 30 km of standing traffic at Channel ports, and the tailbacks of HGVs at Dover became so enormous that they showed up on satellite images, making them the third artificially created thing that could be seen from space (the others being the Great Wall of China and Boris Johnson's ego).[28]

There was no hiding how terrible things were becoming, and attempts to blame it on a war that hadn't yet happened only decreased trust in our leadership, as was reflected in opinion polls. An in-depth study revealed 73 per cent of the British public didn't trust the government to make decisions that would improve their lives, which surely can't be unconnected with Brexit – the most consequential policy decision of the last decade – being an unmitigated, broiling, Biblical curse that we could neither escape from, nor fix, nor – still in large numbers – even accept was happening. Far from the EU being a danger to our democracy, the study found lack of faith in Westminster politics was the biggest threat.[29]

And the biggest single cause of that lack of trust was Boris Johnson, who had both spearheaded Brexit and was still prime minister.

Culture Wars

But if you can't win the important battles, focus attention on incredibly trivial ones that you *can* win. Or better still: on battles that are destined to go on for years, so there's never any reason for you to put forward a viable solution. And thus, we get culture wars, reducing politics to a series of banal slogans designed to bisect the population into friends and enemies, us and them, the deserving and the undeserving.

Culture wars represent a withdrawal from the system that has lent stability to governance since Magna Carta; namely that politics is the realm of reasoned debate, from which rational, functional, stable policy can arise. Now, all of that was suddenly dispensable. Facts, logic and calm consideration mattered less than being on the right or wrong side of some artificially created cultural divide.

Of course, once you take that route, what inevitably follows is an ingrained tribalism where your 'team' can do no wrong; therefore, the rules don't apply to anybody you agree with. It's an abandonment of the fundamental principle that laws have precedence over the current ruler, so the nation doesn't become a mere plaything, subject to whatever whim the occupant of Downing Street wakes up with that morning.

But if the Tories had accepted that laws were still paramount, they would have had to dump Boris Johnson, and by now his political survival had become the animating force of the entire government. To many of them, he was the great and infallible leader, Kim John-Sun. His followers and apologists eschewed all evidence, damned all reason.

It was us vs them, and 'them' almost always turned out to be the most vulnerable, who had been magically inflated to positions of deadly power and influence.

People taking the knee for racial equality were actually performing Nazi salutes. You, the privileged white people, were the real victims.

Desperate immigrants fleeing war and depravation were actually invading our shores in a quasi-military takeover. You – the Britons who had invaded their homelands for half a millennium and were now selling arms to their dictators – you were the real victims.

Trans people dominated your lives, despite trans people being just 0.2 per cent of the population,[30] and four times more likely to be victims of assault than any other group.[31] You – the straight person who has about a one-in-a-thousand chance of ever even *meeting* a trans person – you were the real victims.

And if there was still such a thing as paramount law, it now had to be forced through the Culture War Reality Filter, forcing everybody into two groups. Laws would protect *our* team, yet would leave us free of all restrictions. The very same laws would restrict *their* team, but would offer them no protection whatsoever. It didn't matter that this was legally impossible and morally indefensible: it was the cornerstone of all culture-war thinking. It was simplistic and hit voters in their selfish, frightened hindbrain, and therefore it tended to dominate debate to the exclusion of more important things.

But for once, in January 2022, it wasn't working. Something else had cut through the noise. Partygate simply would not go away, and throughout the month more and more evidence seeped into the public sphere.

Plonko Paralytiko

The story had changed again. It had to. You can't continue to deny Christmas parties had happened when photos emerge of two dozen people crammed into the office, toasting one another with glasses of wine and posing in Christmas-cracker hats next to a trestle table full of catered food. Granted, that specific party didn't exactly look like a hedonist's apocalypse, but it was still illegal at the time, and one of the attendees, Conservative London mayoral candidate Shaun Bailey, resigned in disgrace.[32]

Reports of other parties became more and more damaging.

Oliver Dowden, an adenoidal, Tango-coloured Morph cosplayer who had somehow landed the role of Tory Party chairman, had told a Covid briefing, 'You can meet one person outside of your household in an outdoor, public place provided that you stay two metres apart.' As he was speaking an email invited around 100 Downing Street staff to a drunken shindig.[33] Almost every working week ended with 'wine-time Friday', at which so much was consumed that people were sent to the off-licence with a wheely suitcase, which they filled and returned to Number 10. And of course, you can't risk your Plonko Paralytiko being served at the wrong temperature, so a dedicated 34-bottle drinks fridge was purchased.[34]

Boris Johnson had personally turned up at several of these events, giving a speech at one in which he'd called it 'the most unsocially distanced party in the UK'.[35] Publicly, he still claimed these were work-related events. Nothing to see here, just important and serious prime-ministerial meetings.

However, a quick skim-read of my history books failed to identify previous PMs who had held official meetings to which their wife was invited and everyone got pissed; or vital political business being conducted while people knocked back suitcases full of wine, ran a DJ set, and got so hammered that they broke the swing in the Downing Street garden.[36] Johnson attempted to convince the public that when he'd turned up to one of these 'meetings' and witnessed these events, he had managed to work out it was actually a wild party in a mere 25 minutes, which was quick thinking by his usual standards. He hadn't attempted to stop these parties, of course. He'd simply left everybody to get on with it and . . . what? Went to a different meeting, without telling a soul?

Chinny reckon.

When Prince Philip died in April 2021, the Queen had attended a socially distanced funeral, sat in spartan seclusion in Westminster Abbey, grieving the man to whom she'd been married for over 70 years. The night before, two parties had been held in Downing Street, at which things got so out of hand that staff vanished into secluded offices to fuck one another, in a rare break from their usual habit of fucking everybody else.[37] While the PM and his acolytes were still publicly denying any of this had even happened, some poor bugger on Johnson's team was tasked with phoning the Queen to apologise for it.[38]

Shelley Williams-Walker, Johnson's one-time head of operations at Number 10, had been given the nickname 'DJ SWW' by other members of the Downing Street staff after she'd taken charge of the playlist at the lockdown-breaking party on the eve of Prince Philip's funeral. Boris Johnson awarded her a damehood in 2023.

Martin Reynolds, Johnson's principal private secretary, was found to have invited more than 100 people to a rule-breaking party, and told them to 'bring your own booze'. He later wrote – not entirely accurately – 'We seem to have got away with it.' Boris Johnson awarded him the Order of the Bath in his resignation honours list in 2023.[39]

Shaun Bailey had been the unsuccessful candidate for London mayor. He resigned after he was pictured alongside his equally calamitous campaign manager, Ben Mallett, at an illegal Christmas party inside Downing Street. Mallett, the poor lamb, was merely given an OBE by Johnson, whereas Bailey was given a peerage and a seat in the House of Lords for life.

―

But that was still a year away, and in the meantime every day brought new cracks in the wall of bullshit Johnson was attempting to build. Reports stated the PM had not merely attended multiple parties, but had instigated several of them too, pouring wine in previously dry offices.[40] The usual suspects trundled out to try and patch things up: Michael Fabricant, an Oompa-Loompa who'd been loaded into a cannon and launched head-first into Dougal from *The Magic Roundabout*, took the 'hey, at least nobody lost an eye' route.

'The way it's been characterised, you would think there were sort of, pole dancers,' he said.[41] OK, I'll give you that: there weren't pole dancers. No hookers got murdered. It wasn't the final act of *Scarface*. Johnson didn't start a new Great Fire of London. Whoop-de-doo. There was merely constant illegal partying, shagging, fighting, vomiting, an award for 'sexist of the year', and red wine spilled over (hopefully) Lulu Lytle's startling contribution to design standards.[42]

Worse still: karaoke.[43]

At the ABBA-themed party that Johnson attended in his own apartment above 11 Downing Street, classified intelligence documents had been left lying around for anybody to see.[44] Mamma Mia! Carousing could be heard all over Downing Street, and some reports say it could even be heard by reporters on the opposite side of the road, who must surely have said 'Thank You for the Music'. A pissed-up reveller leaned against a panic button – S.O.S. – and security staff – please let it have been a Super Trooper – charged up the stairs to rescue the PM, only to find Johnson didn't want rescuing: he was having a whale of a time at a party in full swing. Yet Downing Street still denied that such a party ever happened, despite the police having a record of the incident, including a note that they'd decided not to issue a fixed penalty notice on the spot.[45]

One Of Us Is Lying.

—

'Nobody told me that what we were doing was against the rules,' said Boris Johnson, the man who had defined the rules and then gone on TV to read the rules out to us on camera. Unsurprisingly not many people bought his story.[46] And this wasn't helped by the record of conversations within Downing Street.

Jack Doyle, Johnson's director of communications, sent desperate messages to Number 10 officials, frantically trying to come up with a justification for any of this. 'I'm struggling to come up with a way this [party] is in the rules,' he said, admitting that the latest excuse 'blows another great gaping hole in the PM's account'.[47]

So Johnson decided to prove to a sceptical public there hadn't been any parties, and announced an inquiry to be led by Cabinet secretary Simon Case. Case immediately recused himself from investigating whether parties had happened on the grounds that he'd been at one of the parties he was meant to be investigating.[48] And so the gig went to Sue Gray instead, a senior civil servant who briefly became the most famous totally unrecognisable person in the country.

And the moment the inquiry was announced, Downing Street staff said they felt 'the implication' from on high that they should begin shredding files and destroying evidence. Which is exactly what they did.[49]

Some idiot said Jacob Rees-Mogg's name three times, and he turned up to defend all of this. As always, it was utterly macabre. He looked like he had dressed as a dildo for Halloween, and then the wind changed direction and he got stuck. His response to Partygate, yelled over the sound of shredders, was that it was 'fundamentally trivial', and we should focus on more important things than national security, destroying evidence and a dipsomaniac liar smashing our democratic norms to pieces.[50]

But many of his colleagues had had enough, and not just the few remaining moderates. Letters of no-confidence started turning up at the door of Graham Brady, the chair of the backbench 1922 Committee.[51] Even the Brexit ultras turned on their man in open, public condemnation. Steve Baker said Partygate was 'appalling' and that it 'looks like checkmate' for Johnson.[52] Dominic Raab reassured a packed Commons that the backbenchers were 'behind the prime minister', and then behind the prime minister backbencher David Davis stood up and told Johnson, 'In the name of God, go.'[53]

Christian Wakeford must have misunderstood, cos the PM stayed but *he* went. He defected to Labour, which probably helped

Johnson – nothing pulls the Tories together like a common enemy, and Wakeford was now both Labour and from Burnley, which ticks both boxes. As he defected, Wakeford accused government whips of blackmail, claiming they'd warned him to back Johnson or else schools in his constituency would lose funding; that the *actual government* threatened to starve kids of education funding unless its MPs turned a blind eye to illegal activity inside Downing Street.

Johnson said he would act if there was proof of such blackmail, but he had 'seen no evidence'.[54] William Wragg, another of his own backbenchers, said the same blackmail threats had happened to him,[55] and his story was repeated by 12 more Tory MPs.[56]

No, not that kind of evidence, said Team Johnson, and then attempted to change the subject.

Operation Red Meat

Pop on the galoshes of despair, and let's wade into the absolute abattoir that was Operation Red Meat, an in-no-way-desperate attempt to steer the news cycle away from Boris Johnson's troubles, and instead make people angry about immigration. Again.

Operation Red Meat, a series of half-baked policy wheezes that would enrage, engage and engorge readers of the *Telegraph*, began with some officially sanctioned hatred of foreigners. The government tweeted that it was in discussions with Ghana about a bold scheme to force people claiming asylum in the UK to go there for processing.

People with long, short or indeed *any* memory might recall Operation Warm Welcome, Boris Johnson's scheme to roll out the red carpet for asylum seekers, which was barely two months old. Well, ignore all that: now we'd moved on to Operation Red Meat, and we were telling asylum seekers to fuck off again.

The Ghana announcement would have worked beautifully as a distraction tactic, if it hadn't been for the pesky government of Ghana, which tweeted that they could 'state categorically that Ghana has not engaged with the UK on any such plan and does not intend to consider any such operation in the future'. They said Johnson's Operation Red Meat should be renamed 'Operation Dead Meat', a rebuff so brutal you could almost hear the entire UN wincing.[57]

The Tories deleted their tweet about Ghana and tried to pretend none of this had just happened. But Operation Dead Meat urgently needed a success, so the next announcement was that we would deploy the military to stop small boats in the English Channel, an operationally impossible and financially unaffordable tactic which never got off the crayon-bestrewn drawing board, and which even Tory MPs labelled 'Operation Dog's Dinner'.[58]

Perhaps spurred on by all this renaming business, along came Conservative Chief Whip Mark Spencer, famous for his habit of inventing clever new insults for Tories.* The most Wildean examples of Spencer's wit were:

Anthony Mangnall (Anthony Wanknall)

Tom Tugendhat (Tom Tugentwat).[59]

It was widely suggested that – what with all the blackmail claims, inability to hold the party together, and the droll sophistication of a seven-year-old – Spencer might not be very good at Chief Whipping. It's hard not to be weirdly impressed by this, but he had managed to degrade a role previously held by Gavin Williamson, a man who wandered blindly from fuck-up to fuck-up like he was attempting to complete a Duke of Edinburgh Award for profound failure.

Anyway, back to the chief whip: Spencer got into a terrible tizz over his fellow MP Nusrat Ghani, who claimed she had been sacked as a minister after being told her 'Muslimness [was] making colleagues uncomfortable'.[60] Spencer tweeted that he had never used the words attributed to him, which is fine, except nobody had attributed the words to him. His name had never been mentioned.

---

* What kind of person would do that?

It was now, obviously.

So he quickly – but not quickly enough – did the same thing his party had done over the Ghana fiasco: deleted the tweet. He then appears to have undertaken a very short and intense nervous breakdown, after which he wrote essentially the same tweet again, except this time he denied any of the events from his first draft of the tweet had even occurred.[61]

Fine, but Number 10 said they and Nusrat Ghani had discussed the events more than six months earlier.[62]

So now, in the middle of his attempt to distract from questions of ethics, Boris Johnson had to set up an ethics inquiry into exactly how Islamophobic the Tory Party was.[63] The mission wasn't helped by the arrival of Michael Fabricant, a man so galactically absurd that it's sometimes hard to remember he isn't fictional. He said Nusrat Ghani was 'hardly someone who is obviously a Muslim'.[64]

So the claims of Islamophobia didn't hold water because she didn't look Muslim enough to abuse? Is that it?

Having royally buggered up three attempts at Operation Dead Dog For Dinner, we moved onto the grand finale: Levelling Up, a slogan in search of a policy. In the absence of any specific action, the government promised – once again – to level up the country at some unspecified point in the future, just as a report showed the wealthiest areas of the nation would get ten times more funding than poor areas,[65] and cash for 'levelling up' public transport was cut by 50 per cent.[66]

Objectively, every part of Your Dog Died During The Operation had gone very, very badly, so Liz Truss decided to help out. That in itself should be a red flag. Her tactic was to promise she would fix Brexit in a month, which not only undermined Johnson's key electoral claim to have Got Brexit Done, but also seemed queasily familiar.[67] It was essentially the same promise we'd heard once a year since 2016, from – in order – David Davis, Theresa May, Liam Fox, Jacob Rees-Mogg, Boris Johnson, and Lord David Frost.

Foie Gras and Fur Coats

We hadn't finished with Jacob Rees-Mogg. At the start of the year, the unholy result of the Child Catcher angrily impregnating a bassoon was released from his crypt and given a new job: minister for Brexit opportunities. It was 11,116 days since UKIP had begun campaigning for Brexit, so the time was ripe to work out what the hell it was all for.

Back in 2018 Rees-Mogg had been able to look half a century into the future, and predicted it could take 50 years to see any advantages from Brexit.[68] But by the time he began his new job in 2022, Mystic Mogg's powers of prognostication had failed him, and he was reduced to having to beg readers of the *Sun* to flag up any possible benefits to leaving the EU, and tell him what the rippling fuck to do next.[69] After a couple of months scratching around, he was asked to summarise his findings.

'If you go through the Dartford Tunnel, there have to be signs saying how you get out of it every 25 metres,' he explained. 'But in this country we use yards for road signs, so the signs say 121 yards in one direction and 1152 yards in the other.'[70]

And that was it: the number-one opportunity arising out of Brexit. Rounding up numbers on signs inside the Dartford Tunnel.

The Public Accounts Committee took a different view. In their February report into Brexit they said, 'the only detectable impact so far is increased costs, paperwork and border delays'.[71] Five weeks into 2022, and once-every-blue-moon emergency measures to force lorries to park on major roads so they wouldn't clog up Dover had been implemented more than 20 times already. Even so, vast queues of HGVs at ports were common. Dover's Tory MP, Brexiteer Natalie Elphicke, complained bitterly about the 'miles of traffic jams' which haunted her constituency, and which she'd literally campaigned to make happen. But she insisted they were 'not because of Brexit, but because of Brussels bureaucracy and red tape'.[72]

Like most of her fellow Leavers, she seemed outraged to discover that Britain not being part of the EU would mean Britain was treated as if it wasn't part of the EU.

Brexit meant we no longer had to accept rules drawn up by people in other countries, and to celebrate, Jacob Rees-Mogg, only days into his new job, supported a plan to unilaterally adopt other countries' regulations for anything we import, which is quite a turnaround from all that 'regaining our independence' stuff.[73] He said there was 'no point' in testing things we bought from overseas – I guess we'd find out if that imported pork was deadly when people started dying. Downing Street was forced to deny they were scrapping tests on imports,[74] and a Whitehall insider was quoted as saying, 'It'll just be Rees-Mogg not knowing what he's talking about.'[75]

Mogg's next move was a plan to cut 65,000 civil-service jobs, once again failing to understand that the expanded civil service was *his fault*.[76] UK civil-servant staff numbers had been forced to increase by 23 per cent since the referendum, simply to cope with the extra paperwork involved.[77] The number working solely on Brexit had trebled in the two years to 2021.[78]

But there were – finally – some glad tidings for working-class Red Wall voters who had turned to the Tories in a desperate bid to improve their lives. The government proposed lifting a ban on importing foie gras and fur coats.[79] Welcome news for the fine people of Stoke-on-Trent.

Fraud

While Mogg was busy turning his signature policy into an object of ridicule, Liz Truss was busy trying to turn herself into Brexit's latest saviour. Unpicking her reasoning wasn't difficult: a desperate attempt to gain the attention and approval of the party membership ahead of what already looked like yet another leadership election.

It mattered not a jot that 'I will fix Brexit' was palpable nonsense, because her target audience was entirely divorced from the real world anyway. All they wanted was more promises that we could be a country with no taxes but exceptional public services; a land of high-paid jobs where nobody had the right to ask for a pay rise; a utopia where smiling workers who couldn't afford to heat their homes delivered luxury imported food to millionaire pensioners who had voted to block imports; a wealthy trading nation which never had to negotiate with foreigners.

To win over this gleefully crazy demographic, practically the entire Conservative frontbench started jostling for position, every one of them engaged in freeform impressionistic stabs at creating a new reality via the medium of arrant bollocks.

Rishi Sunak, Thunderbird 0.5, had become popular during the deepest trough of the pandemic, when he'd handed out billions in furlough money. It is, of course, hard *not* to be popular when handing out vast piles of cash, and this gave Sunak a false understanding of how deep the admiration for him went. He was about to find out, because now it was time to get that money back.

Unfortunately, after a dozen years of Conservative short-termism and financial mismanagement, Sunak was out of options. If he raised taxes, it would destroy his precarious popularity with the party members who would choose Johnson's replacement. If he made members happy by keeping taxes low, the financial markets would have a shit-fit, and the economy would tank even further. And unless he was prepared to equitably tax the wealthy, he'd have to impose yet more austerity on a population that was already facing a historically huge cost-of-living crisis. Inevitably, this would burn through the Tory's dwindling support in the new seats they'd won in 2019 and condemn the party to certain electoral defeat.

Sunak's long-standing preference was the traditional one that dates back to Nigel Lawson, the chancellor who powered Thatcherism: slash taxes, cut the state to the bone, cross your fingers, and say 'tadaah' if the economy accidentally grows. This was the approach of George Osborne in 2010, and later of Liz Truss, sped up and backed by

Benny Hill music: the idea that endlessly shrinking the social realm would allow a cowed market to rush in and prosper.

But it's a fantasy. Markets don't float outside of society; they exist within it. Shrink the state, and you shrink the arena within which markets can operate. Since 2010, with the – I nearly said 'honourable' – exception of invited guests to the Covid VIP lanes, Britain's private sector has not been famous for booming as the state shrinks. Instead, it has stagnated, tax receipts have fallen way below what's required to manage our public finances, and consequently the infrastructure that makes a country into a country has crumbled before our very eyes.

Small-state libertarianism is a busted flush, and the sane approach would be to fix that flush, keep flushing, and rid us of this shitty idea for good. Even some senior Tory MPs privately accepted this. 'Modern politics is not in the same place [as under Nigel Lawson], it doesn't matter whether Rishi thinks it should be or even if I think it should be,' said one Tory minister, saying of Sunak's approach: 'It's bollocks, utter bollocks.'[80]

That minister wasn't alone in his assessment of Sunak's grip on finances. Lord Agnew, the minister for countering fraud, resigned because there was simply too much fraud for him to counter it anymore. He didn't go quietly either, standing at the House of Lords dispatch box, raging over what he called Sunak's 'lamentable' handling of fraud surrounding Covid loans.[81]

Around £4.3 billion of allegedly fraudulent loans had been casually written off by Sunak, part of what Agnew called 'total fraud loss across government estimated at £29bn a year', which the Tories were doing next to nothing to either prevent or recoup. Instead, Agnew claimed, the government 'appears to have no knowledge or little interest' in such rackets, and was frozen by a mixture of 'arrogance, indolence and ignorance'.[82]

Agnew said the lost money was 'one of the most colossal cock-ups in recent government management', and considering the competition for that title, that's quite a claim. But not as worrying as his claim that the Treasury under Sunak had warned crime agencies to 'butt out' when police and Lord Agnew had attempted to crack down on fraud.[83]

And not as great a claim as that made in a National Audit Office report a year later, which found Agnew had underestimated Sunak. And I didn't think that was possible. Sunak had overseen as much as £58 billion in losses[84] – reported as 'the single biggest financial loss by any government in history'.[85]

While £58 billion was being simply thrown away – that's enough to form a stack of £10 notes 400 miles tall – Sunak was reported to have threatened to resign if Boris Johnson raised National Insurance to fill the hole in the nation's finances,[86] and Nadine Dorries scrapped £44 million of funding for children's educational TV programming because we could no longer afford it.[87]

Ambushed by Cake

And still Partygate ground ludicrously on. Dominic Raab battled manfully to make it all go away, but he was fatally hindered by his own sterling native imbecility, and the blatant dishonesty of his PM.

Raab conceded to journalists that the Ministerial Code says ministers must resign if they are found to have lied to parliament, then produced the satisfied smile of somebody who has considered every possible response to that statement. Except for this one: the journalists asked if Johnson should resign if he was found to have lied. No, said a flummoxed Raab, of course not.[88]

Next up to the plate: Conor Burns, whitewashing Johnson by claiming he hadn't been to a noisy, drunken party at all. He had simply been 'ambushed with a cake', a form of words met with widespread ridicule. Burns became even more ridiculous when he later admitted 'there actually wasn't a cake', so Johnson had managed to be ambushed by a nothingness.[89] Steve Barclay was not available for comment.

Or maybe he was. It's never easy to tell with Steve Barclay. Of all the people appearing in this book, Barclay is the one safest from character assassination, because he was born without one.

All of this added to the sense that nobody had a grip on anything. Johnson promised the Sue Gray report would be published in full. Raab said it wouldn't.[90] Downing Street said it would. Then Johnson said he'd only publish highlighted 'findings', Number 10 repeated it would be the full report, while the Cabinet Office suggested it would be heavily redacted.[91] Leaks from inside Cabinet said they might only publish a summary, and then Boris Johnson clarified matters by telling parliament, 'I will do exactly what I said', which by this point could have meant absolutely anything.[92]

In private, Johnson's parliamentary party was getting deeply shirty about the entire thing. One MP, described as 'normally very loyal', texted the *Financial Times* to say the situation 'was awful. I'm considering my position'.[93] Another called Johnson 'a bastard [who would] probably wiggle off the hook'.[94]

Enter hook, stage left. Just as everybody was braced for the Partygate report to see daylight, the police suddenly decided to get involved, and we reached the stage where the government was grateful to be facing criminal investigations, because it gave Johnson an excuse to delay publishing Sue Gray's findings.

The Metropolitan Police – why is it always the Metropolitan Police? – said there was no reason to delay publication, but was reported to have asked Sue Gray to 'make minimal reference to Downing Street parties' so as not to prejudice further investigations.[95] This rendered the full Sue Gray report meaningless if published immediately, so instead she published an update, which listed 12 events that met the threshold for criminal investigation, including at least two Johnson had personally attended.[96]

Johnson, a man without shame, bounced into the House of Commons to perform something between an apology, a fightback, and a libel action waiting to happen. He turned his fire on the opposition leader, claiming Keir Starmer 'spent most of his time [as Director of Public Prosecutions] failing to prosecute Jimmy Savile', the disgraced paedophile disc jockey.

It was absolute bullshit, of course, but what else did you expect? The independent fact-checking service Full Fact confirmed that Starmer was 'not the reviewing lawyer for the case',[97] and BBC Reality Check 'found no evidence that Sir Keir was involved at any point in the decision not to charge Savile'.[98]

Johnson said he would not apologise for the slander.[99] The Speaker of the House condemned Johnson's lies about Savile, warning him that 'words have consequences'. They certainly did. A mob, incited by the PM's words, attacked Keir Starmer and his Labour colleague David Lammy outside parliament, accusing them of protecting paedophiles. Starmer said, 'The PM knew exactly what he was doing. It is a conspiracy theory of violent fascists,' and many agreed.[100]

Under pressure from all sides, Johnson eventually relented, didn't quite apologise – because narcissists never can – but did admit Starmer had 'nothing to do' with the case. So Johnson avoided the consequences the Speaker had threatened him with.[101]

An anagram of Alexander Boris de Pfeffel Johnson is 'Xenophobe Slanderer Fends Off Jail'.

—

Johnson's communications director Jack Doyle quit in disgust at the PM's smear campaign.[102] So did Munira Mirza, who for 14 years – dating back to Johnson's time as Witless Dickington, the mayor of London – had been his loyal policy chief and was commonly described as 'Boris's brain'. So it doesn't sound like she was much of a loss.[103]

Some of his backbenchers couched their growing concerns in diplomatic language. Conservative peer Baroness Warsi said Johnson should 'think long and hard about what is in the best interests of this country'.[104] Tobias Ellwood said Johnson should 'lead or step aside', with the clear implication that Ellwood had a preference for the latter.[105]

But some were blatant. Aaron Bell, clearly revolted by Johnson's antics, asked: 'Does the prime minister think I'm a fool?' (Yes. Nobody is asking me, but yes, Johnson thinks *everybody* is a fool.) Andrew Mitchell said the PM 'no longer enjoys my support'.[106] Angela Richardson, who was sacked for rebelling over Paterson and then un-sacked for being right to rebel over Paterson, was suddenly gone again: she resigned from her post in protest. Even Andrew Bridgen, a man so irrepressibly uncomprehending that you'd think he'd been bitten by a radioactive idiot, managed to observe: 'Boris Johnson has lost the moral authority to lead the country.'[107]

In the interests of balance, I should record that the prime minister did still have supporters, although they seemed so unquestioningly loyal that you could imagine one of the higher primates performing the same cheerleading duties in return for fruit. Stuart Anderson, who – and I'm not making this up – had decided to become a Tory MP after reading a book called *Politics for Dummies*,[108] still backed Johnson.[109] So, unsurprisingly, did Crystal Meth Barbie Nadine Dorries, and aristocratic goth earthworm Jacob Rees-Mogg, who managed to keep a straight face while saying, 'My experience is very few people lie in public life.'[110] He then told journalists Britain had a 'presidential system', which was a lie, and that therefore 'a change of leader requires a general election', which was also a lie, but one that fitted the mood of the country. Even the Tory-supporting *Spectator* called Mogg's comments 'laughable'.[111]

Dominic Cummings agreed. He said that, despite the overwhelming evidence, the public still 'underestimate the extent to which [Johnson] lies to literally everybody literally all day – including to Carrie and about Carrie. "Lies" isn't even a useful word with him – he lives inside a fog of invention and "believes" whatever he has to in the moment. E.g., he both knows he's lying about the parties AND thinks he did nothing wrong. This doesn't make "sense" unless you've watched him carefully or similar sociopaths.'[112]

Within days 15 Tory MPs had gone public with their demands for Johnson's resignation, including the leader of the Scottish Tory Party.[113] It wasn't enough yet, but the vultures were circling.

Guto Harri and Steve Barclay

As a mark of Johnson's confidence in his long-term survival, he appointed a new communications director, Guto Harri. And as a mark of his confidence in Johnson's long-term survival, Guto Harri said he'd be returning to his previous job in six months.[114]

Harri was responsible for making the PM look good, which would have been a tricky proposition at any time, but wasn't helped by the fact he'd previously described Johnson as a 'sexually incontinent [and] divisive' figure who was 'dragging the country down'.[115] In response, Boris Johnson had threatened to prosecute Guto Harri for blackmail. So clearly, this was destined to become a winning team.[116]

They came up with a two-pronged strategy: offer an immediate grovelling apology for the parties, and rebrand Johnson as a serious man.

The apology took more than two months to appear, and when it was finally forced through Johnson's gritted teeth, all we got was a claim that 'it did not occur to me' that the drinks, Christmas crackers, party hats, and DJ meant it was a party.[117]

Prong One was a ludicrous, farcical failure, so it was on to Prong Two: demonstrating that the PM was serious. Harri said he was 'proud to join a team of capable, grown-up' people,[118] and his evidence for this was his description of Johnson as 'not a total clown', as proven by the revelation that the PM had started Harri's job interview by delivering a passionate rendition of 'I Will Survive'.[119]

They'd already ruined ABBA for me, and now it was Gloria Gaynor's turn.

Guto Harri wasn't supposed to tell the country their prime minister was a fool, but c'mon: it was hardly a secret at this point. He got a bollocking from Johnson for making a 'disastrous' start, and it was agreed Number 10's new head of public communications would not communicate in public again.

Johnson also appointed a new chief of staff, Steve Barclay, a man so lacking in personality that he failed his Myers–Briggs test. He was like an explosion in a nothing factory. Some are born humdrum, some achieve humdrumosity, and some have humdrumosity thrust upon them. For Steve Barclay it was all three, and fittingly he now held three jobs: he'd already been a (non-dancing) chancellor of the Duchy of Lancaster and Cabinet Office minister, and now he was chief of staff too, in the forlorn hope he could help dig Boris Johnson out of the shit.

Even for politics nerds, it's hard for anybody to know who or what Steve Barclay is. He vanishes behind the big personas, those artificial constructs who constantly attract attention. Boris Johnson, for example, isn't Boris Johnson. That's an act. He was born and raised in New York, and used the name 'Al' for years – his family still call him that, when they're not on telly perpetuating his myth.[120] He relocated to the UK in 1977 to attend Eton, where he 'suddenly adopted the eccentric English persona which he's now widely famed for'.[121] All those mannerisms are false. All those gaffes are deliberate. He intentionally messes his hair up before going on camera.[122] His scarecrow aesthetic is a carefully planned guise, not a real person.

And Jacob Rees-Mogg is not, despite appearances, a Monopoly piece cursed into life by a passing witch. Nor is he a petty aristo lifted directly out of the Catholic snobbery of *Brideshead Revisited*, and able to trace his grandiose family back to the Norman Conquest. His grandfather was a van driver. His mother, raised by a grocer, was hired as a secretary to the City editor of the *Sunday Times*, William Rees-Mogg. According to William's colleague, Hunter Davies, she threatened to quit, but Rees-Mogg Senior was 'so absorbed by the gold standard that she might as well not have existed'.[123]

'Hey, have you heard about Gillian? She is going to leave.'

'Who?'

'Your blooming secretary, that's who! You have missed your chance there, William.'

So William married her, did his duty by the Pope, and we ended up with Jacob Rees-Mogg. Psychologists would have a field day delving into Junior's relationship with his mother, whose background he appears to have entirely expunged from his persona. Instead, this grandson of a van driver clung to his nanny, still employing her into his fifties,[124] while he carefully cultivated his public image as a kind of Earthworm Jim via Savile Row, poncing around in monocles and top hats, and oozing condescension in a ludicrous patrician drawl.

Fatuous pretences such as Johnson and Mogg draw all the attention, but if you were to look in the nooks and crannies behind the crooks and nannies, you'd find plywood abomination Steve Barclay, diligently unleashing carnage on the infrastructure of the state.

An anagram of Steven Barclay is 'Cravenly Abets'.

Few were convinced Barclay doing three jobs at once would solve Johnson's problems, not least because 'the whole of the mess', as one Downing Steet aide put it, 'is really a story about the PM not listening to advice'. And now Fat Malfoy had to stay awake and focus long enough to take counsel from a man who was like walking Rohypnol.[125]

The Institute for Government was concerned. 'Either [Barclay] is a chief of staff, and chancellor of the Duchy of Lancaster responsibilities will be neglected,' they said, 'or he's de facto deputy PM, and you're lacking a chief of staff.'[126] They also pointed out that Dominic Raab was already officially the deputy PM, which left him in limbo. And that was a particular problem for Raab, who could spend weeks trying to find Limbo on a map.

So now we had two ministers doing one job that doesn't have to exist, and one minister doing three jobs that nobody could possibly succeed at. When asked to explain to parliament how the hell this was going to work, Barclay didn't turn up to answer questions.[127]

Or maybe he did, and people just assumed he was the curtains.

A Collapsing, Disreputable Government

Despite the palpable success of Harri's and Barclay's appointments, the prime minister's troubles persisted, and rivals plotted.

Sunak seemed to have positioned himself right behind Johnson, ready to pounce, although this may have been an optical illusion: something about his height makes it difficult to be sure how far away he is. Aside from Sunak, the main frontrunner to replace the PM was Liz Truss, a betwattled, utterly solipsistic cartoon Margaret Thatcher who was so thick you could stand a spoon up in her, and who emitted the desperate energy of Alan Sugar's sixth-most impressive Apprentice. In any other era, she would have seemed catastrophically underwhelming, but by comparison with her Cabinet rivals she managed to look merely depressingly middlewhelming, and that was as much as we could hope for in these dark days.

In a grim omen of her future mastery of our nation's finances, in January it was discovered Truss had blown £500,000 on a private jet to Australia so she could sign a trade deal that would almost certainly make us poorer.[128] On the day she flew out, the most expensive scheduled commercial ticket available was £7,712. And it got there faster. But no, half a million quid on a private jet, please.

It was almost worth the money just to hear the response of the Australians. Their former prime minister called Truss 'demented' and urged her to rush 'back to her collapsing, disreputable government'.[129] So she did, deal in hand, and on second thoughts, it wasn't worth the money at all.

Former Tory minister George Eustice said the agreement Truss had signed was 'not a good deal for the UK' and accused her of 'shattering' our negotiating position because she'd been in such a desperate hurry to sign something – anything – in order to boost her profile.[130] Rishi Sunak later suggested the deal was 'one-sided' in favour of Australia, and was bad for British farmers.[131] He wasn't wrong. UK officials had warned Truss her deal would hit agriculture jobs for 15 years, making it the worst-affected sector of the UK economy in terms of employment.[132]

Truss's actions were also a crippling embarrassment to her colleague Alok Sharma, who had to host the COP26 climate conference the day after her flight. He exhorted delegates to unite in their battle against climate change because any agreement was 'just words on a page . . . unless we honour the promises made',[133] while Liz Truss generated 500 tonnes of CO_2 all on her own.[134]

The ink had barely dried on Sharma's climate deal before spindly mantis Jacob Rees-Mogg was up on his hind legs, urging the House of Commons to open new coal mines in what he called 'our own green and pleasant land', which doesn't immediately suggest an easy familiarity with the realities of coal mining. His rationale was that we needed coal to support our 'heritage railways', so remember to tell your grandkids that their slow, agonising heat-death is worth it, cos it allowed Mogg to look at antique steam trains until he got that fizz in his special place.[135]

The Mad Woman in the Attic

As January ended, it was time to celebrate Brexit's birthday.

Sadly, nobody got ambushed with a cake. We couldn't afford one. Leaving the EU to save us £350 million a week was costing us £800 million a week.[136] But we were Global Britain now, and to show how mighty we had become, we signed a whopping new trade deal with Greenland.

It was worth £12 million.[137]

Now we just needed to find another 6,600 Greenlands, and we'd break even.

But perhaps the world in which Nadine Dorries lives is awash with mythical Greenlands. The woman who once told the BBC, 'I feel like I'm in Groundhog Day, with things constantly changing around us' was back, this time to prove she was not merely struggling to understand the basic premise of that movie; she was also having a bit of trouble grasping what interviews are for.[138] She video-called *BBC Breakfast* from what appeared to be her loft, yet despite the early hour, her tone was that of somebody telling the bouncers at Wetherspoons, 'Well, don't call it "bottomless prosecco" then!'

'Why? Why are you asking me that question?' demanded the *literal* Cabinet minister when asked about the major political events of the day.[139] From there she moved on to insisting we could ignore any Tories calling for Johnson to quit, since these were the same faithless pseuds who had also called for Theresa May and David Cameron to quit.

Dorries had called for Cameron to resign in 2016,[140] and for May to resign in 2018;[141] but who needs logic and consistency when you have a hot pash for Boris Johnson?

Yet despite the giddy experience of watching live as Dorries's mouth flapped along in the wake of her meandering, rudderless mind, the most startling thing about the interview (or whatever Nadine imagined was happening to her) was the setting. The culture secretary, best-selling author and avid devourer of ostrich anus during her unsanctioned spell on *I'm a Celebrity* was seated next to a wall of 12 bookshelves containing just one book.[142]

The whole thing looked like she'd got hammered the night before, and accidentally agreed to take part in a diorama depicting the term 'mad woman in the attic'.

To her credit, it was spot on.

Avoiding Scrutiny

The central argument of Brexit had been about sovereignty, and for good reason: every other argument was embarrassingly easy to disprove.

It's pretty simple to count the number of immigrants, or to measure how much trade is done. But how can you measure something as infinitely vague as a feeling of sovereignty? Even during the referendum campaign in 2016, government ministers had been surprisingly candid about this, with one telling *Channel 4 News*: 'Boris and Michael [Johnson and Gove] don't buy the economic arguments that we'd be freer to trade outside the EU. They don't buy the immigration arguments', so instead the Leave campaign chose to focus on 'sovereignty, which literally means nothing to anybody'.[143]

The admissions went even further with the publication of the Brexit White Paper in 2017, delivered by the Brexit department under Brexiteer David Davis, which explicitly says, 'Whilst Parliament has remained sovereign throughout our membership of the EU, it has not always felt like that.'[144]

So we weren't leaving the EU in order to improve trade, or freedom, or immigration. We were leaving so we could regain our sovereignty – except the government admitted we already had sovereignty, in its own White Paper asking for it back.

It beggars belief, frankly.

Even so, this bullshit won the referendum, Brexit happened, and the sovereign powers we already enjoyed were returned to the Westminster parliament that already exercised them. Among those powers – indeed, responsibilities – is the requirement that parliament hold the government to account, which is why government is required to release documents for MPs to scrutinise and question. A lot happens in government, so typically around two sets of detailed documents are released every day.

But as March 2022 arrived, the Tories waited until Easter Recess was imminent and MPs were just about to go on holiday, and then released 120 documents in 48 hours. MPs were swamped, and scrutiny became impossible as the Johnson administration attempted a shoddy, shabby, grubby avoidance of the basic principle of accountability. Among the many reasons many couldn't wait for the demise of Johnson was so parliament could return to its proper business: ensuring Number 10 was transparent, honest and held to account.

Thank the sweet lord, then, that by March 2023 we had honest and ethical Rishi Sunak as PM. Once again, along came the Easter Recess, and once again the Tories flooded MPs with too many documents to read. In just 48 hours, 150 papers were dumped – up from 120 the year before – just as parliament was closing shop and heading for its spring break. That was more data in two days than in the previous 44 days combined, once again making it impossible for parliament to hold the government to account.[145]

Mordaunt Magic

More astonishing news from the grown-ups in charge. Mohamed Amersi, a telecoms mogul who had given over half a million quid to the Tory Party, suddenly demanded the repayment of £200,000 because he hadn't been given what he'd been promised.

No, not a peerage. No, not some sinecure or other at a national institution. No, not access to VIP lanes for government contracts. It was more serious than that.

Amersi hadn't been granted a magic show from former defence minister Penny Mordaunt. He was promised a magic show, and goddammit, he wanted a magic show.[146]

Mohamed Amersi was 61 years old.

Shockingly Weak

While the solemn and professional management team leading Britain were busy having a squabble over balloon animals, 70s disco classics and the quantum state of cake, Russia had been slowly increasing its military presence on its border with Ukraine.

Tensions had been building for months, although few thought Russia's gangster president Vladimir Putin would be crazy enough to actually start a war. Most assumed he was sabre-rattling, partly to demonstrate his ludicrous strong-man act for his domestic audience without having to take his shirt off during the Moscow winter, and partly to make a few kopecks by boosting the price of Russian oil and gas.

When the invasion began in February, Boris Johnson could scarcely believe his luck. He was so excited he had to be practically dragged away from his Union Jack Fleshlight. Now, at last, was his chance to prove to the world that he was *not* merely a fly-tipped, leaking bin-bag full of bullshit and Viagra who had only recently proven himself capable of organising a piss-up; he was, in fact, the second coming of Winston Churchill.

The Ukraine invasion also had the happy side-effect of providing Johnson with the ultimate reason for not quitting over Partygate – WAR, WAR, WAR! He didn't mention that in February – literally days before the invasion – he had mocked the very idea of a conventional conflict. 'The old concepts of fighting big tank battles on European land mass are over,' he had told a parliamentary committee, which was pressing him on why he'd broken his promise to increase our military hardware. He'd pledged 138 fighter jets for the RAF. He'd delivered just 48.[147]

As opposition leaders and multiple members of his own party demanded the PM's resignation, his most loyal backbenchers now had a new excuse to keep this abject failure in office. 'Don't they know there's a war on?' they demanded in April.[148] By Christmas they had spaffed their way through three prime ministers in as many months, war or not. Yet as the Ukraine conflict began, Douglas Ross, Andrew Bridgen and others withdrew their calls for Johnson to quit, and the immediate threat to his career eased a little.[149]

China would later come out in opposition to unilateral sanctions, but Brexit Britain had already unilaterally sanctioned itself in 2020, and we'd be damned if we were going to treat Russia any better than the people of Grimsby. So we launched what Foreign Secretary Liz Truss called the 'toughest sanctions regime against Russia', and everybody else called 'light to no sanctions'.[150]

Our initial crackdown on Putin and his allies targeted just five banks and three individuals, two of whom had already been sanctioned by the USA for years while we'd turned a blind eye.[151] Johnson, practically humping the dispatch box, invited us to admire his 'massive package of economic sanctions', but legal experts said his plans were flaccid, and his policies were shooting blanks. Our sanctions would have absolutely no effect, they said, because years of 'grotesque underfunding' of our law enforcement agencies meant the UK was effectively incapable of policing sanctions anyway.[152]

A regime for tackling the hundreds of billions in dubious Russian monies flowing through London had been in place since 2016. It had no effect, not least because the Conservatives' former justice minister, Lord Faulks, said Downing Street under Theresa May had 'leant on him' to drop anti-money-laundering proposals in 2017 and 2018.[153] As a result, in the five years leading up to the Ukraine War, the UK had handed down only six fines to sanctioned oligarchs, with a total value of just £12 million. To put that into context, over the same five-year period US authorities had issued fines equivalent to £1.1 billion, almost 100 times more.[154]

Faulks called Britain a 'laughing stock' over our failure to tackle the problem. The campaigning group Spotlight on Corruption called Britain's track record 'shockingly weak', and under Boris Johnson that certainly didn't appear to be about to change in a hurry.[155]

Following the invasion of Ukraine, the EU immediately applied sanctions to 424 Russian individuals.[156] Britain upped our sanctions list to a whopping eight,[157] although we also revealed that implementing those scant sanctions would take us 'weeks and months', so everybody targeted knew they could have a nice long lie-in, and then take a leisurely stroll to the bank to move all their assets out of the UK before they were frozen.[158]

Of course there were plenty of assets that couldn't be moved, mostly housing. The anti-corruption group Transparency International UK recorded that just since 2016, £1.5 billion of UK property had been bought by Russian oligarchs. Labour said that in the light of the Ukrainian invasion, we should give the owners 28 days to get on the right side of the law, and then impose sanctions or fines.[159] The Tories leaped into inertia, said they'd give the oligarchs six months, but then refused to say when any new legislation to make this happen would be brought forward. So in effect, an infinite amount of time to fess up.[160]

Johnson told MPs Putin had 'singled out' Britain because we were 'in the lead on global sanctions'.[161] Of the paltry 18 oligarchs we had sanctioned by March – described by Boris Johnson as having 'the blood of the Ukrainian people on their hands' – eight had previously been given so-called golden visas to live in the UK, after they coughed up £2 million each under a controversial scheme that might as well have been called 'we hate immigrants unless they're fucking minted, in which case: no questions asked'.[162]

The scheme was backed by, yep, Boris Johnson. American diplomats expressed 'dismay and frustration' at the river of dirty Russian money still pouring through London, and Johnson's own anti-corruption chief accused the government of delaying a bill to stamp it out.[163]

Six Russian donors had given the Tory Party £2 million just since Johnson became PM.[164] In the five months following February's invasion, the Conservative Party accepted an additional £62,000 in donations from Russia-linked donors.[165] An independent report by the Centre for the Study of Corruption found Johnson's administration was 'more corrupt than any UK government since the Second World War' and that there was an 'absolute failure of integrity at Number 10'.[166]

Next door at Number 11 wasn't much better. Ethical paragon Rishi Sunak called on firms to stop investing in Russia,[167] but seemingly hadn't mentioned this to his own wife, Akshata Murty, who held a £690 million stake in Infosys, her father's company, which had refused to withdraw from Moscow.[168]

'IT'S BOLLOCKS, UTTER BOLLOCKS'

'I'm an elected politician and I'm here to talk to you about what I'm responsible for. My wife is not,' said Sunak when challenged on this vast hypocrisy.[169] None of the businesses he had just asked not to invest in Russia were elected politicians either, but let's skip past that and see if things got any better over the coming months.

Not much, no.

Infosys said they'd pull out of Putin's Russia. Eight months later, in November 2022, they were still operating in Moscow, Sunak was by then PM, and his wife was still getting £11.5 million in dividends from a company that was defying his own government's express policy.[170]

And as for sanctions: eventually, with a teeth-grinding sluggishness that teetered on apathy, they were increased to cover over 1,000 individuals. But by December 2022 a cross-party group of MPs castigated the government for the UK's 'persistently low levels of enforcement'. Over 720 sanction breaches had been reported. Only eight fines were handed down. Of those only two exceeded £50,000, which is chickenfeed for a Russian billionaire.[171]

Meanwhile our Foreign Secretary Liz Truss was pictured in Moscow's Red Square, although it's a miracle she found the place. She'd only recently offered to support 'our Baltic allies across the Black Sea', and nobody had the heart to tell her these are two different locations, 700 miles apart.[172]

An anagram of Elizabeth Truss is 'Haziest Bluster'.

Regardless, after that minor mix-up somebody guided her to Russia, where she was pictured gazing at the vast horizon, the very image of steely determination, wrapped in a Russian-style fur hat and coat, and perfectly framed against a background of the Kremlin. The photo bore a startling resemblance to an iconic image of Margaret Thatcher from three decades earlier, and if the coincidence seemed too good to be true it's because it was no coincidence at all. There were countless examples of Truss dressing as Thatcher, in some cases down to the last detail.[173]

'I don't accept that. I am my own person,' she later told Radio 4, in defence of an outfit that was an exact carbon-copy of the one Thatcher wore in a famous 1979 election broadcast.[174]

By now Truss was so obsessed with polishing her image as the new Iron Lady that she was having five publicly funded Instagram portraits a day taken.[175] Almost nothing of value to Ukraine or the UK was achieved by her flight to Moscow, simply a great day out for the wannabe PM, her dressing-up box, and her official photographer.

The Covid Bloom

Despite our impressive array of governmental Flickr accounts and military-grade Instagram filters, Russian tanks still rolled across the Ukrainian border, while we were still suffering the consequences of lazily allowing a pandemic to roll across Britain.

Our death toll managed to be at once deeply shocking and hardly surprising. The government frontbench couldn't be arsed following their own mask guidelines, and that harbinger of calamity Liz Truss was back again, this time announcing she'd tested positive barely minutes after sitting in a packed House of Commons, wearing no mask, surrounded by hundreds of elderly, overweight, vulnerable colleagues and a few trillion Covid particles.[176]

Meanwhile, after Johnson's 2021 decision to prioritise Christmas (again) Covid infections had blossomed (again), and by the start of February 2022 the UK recorded its highest daily death toll for a year.[177] Christmas was saved, though, mainly because the last thing the PM wanted was to deliver more bad news to a public that was already furious over Partygate. In January he had cancelled the requirement to wear face masks in schools.[178] Just three weeks later, 415,000 school children were off sick with Covid,[179] the government had to reintroduce face masks again, and for all that death and illness, Boris Johnson was still in trouble.[180]

And so was former health minister Matt Hancock. In a just world, he would be in The Hague alongside Noel Edmonds for crimes against knitwear, but the closest we got to that was February's High Court judgement that he'd acted unlawfully in appointing Dido Harding to a top job in the Covid response team.[181]

Project Here

Dido Harding had landed that job, in large part, because we have a crazy electoral system. On the back of a small majority of parliamentary seats, we hand power to a party that rarely gets more than 37 per cent of votes, and the leadership of that party gets almost total executive authority. If they wanted to illegally employ Dido Harding, there was nothing to stop them. Courts might later find the appointment unlawful, but by that time the damage was done, and our elected dictatorship had already moved on to its next fiasco.

That such a democracy worked at all was dependent on the strange notion that anybody who became prime minister was, by definition, a decent cove. He – and it was almost always a he – would do moral things, behave with integrity, and operate within a framework that was feeble enough to permit practically any depravity the premier could think of, short of murder or talking shit about Paddington. This model just about worked, right up until it didn't.

The paradigm fell apart because we shoved into that floppy set of hazy guidelines a careless, lying, narcissistic vandal with a lifelong ambition to be the untrammelled monarch of the entire world. Boris Johnson understood the fragility of the UK's political standards, and then drove a coach and horses through them.

He could do so because he knew full well most people wouldn't notice until it was too late. Politics is a minority sport, and most of us simply don't pay enough attention. The Conservatives' client media – with comfortably twice as many national newspapers supporting Tories compared to Labour[182] – wouldn't hold Johnson to account or give voters adequate warnings about what was happening. The BBC were cowed and compliant, and the arrival of the internet had gutted the economics of traditional media, leaving them reaching for cheap commentary and click-bait, rather than expensive investigation. And even if the press did attempt to grapple with Johnson, he had a plan to nullify it all, which with typical rodomontade he had publicly announced in a TV interview back in 2006.

'I've got a brilliant new strategy,' he said, 'which is to make so many gaffes that nobody knows which one to concentrate on. They cease to be newsworthy, you completely out-general the media in that way, and they despair. You shell them, you pepper the media. You've got to pepper their positions with so many gaffes that they're confused. It's like a helicopter throwing out chaff, and then you steal in quietly, and drop your depth charges wherever you want to drop them.'[183]

In February 2022, yet another of those depth charges blew up. The First Minister of Northern Ireland resigned over Johnson's magnificent array of broken promises regarding Brexit. The PM had assured us there would be no border checks between Northern Ireland and the rest of the UK. It was a lie. It couldn't *not* be, because Brexit had at its heart a contradiction.

A Britain outside the EU needed a border somewhere, which is simple enough for England, Scotland and Wales, which are surrounded by water, but a lot more complicated for Northern Ireland, where the UK had a land border with the EU. And a pretty unruly one too. The Irish Troubles had roots centuries deep, had erupted into decades of violence, killed over 3,700 people, and injured 45,000 more. But in 1998 the 30-year nightmare ended with the signing of the Good Friday Agreement (GFA).

The GFA could only work because both Ireland and the UK were members of the EU, accepting the same standards and policies. This meant there was no reason to have a hard border between the two countries, no reason to check passports or confirm goods traded between North and South met the required standards. So the GFA could magic away the divisions. Unionists could believe they were in Britain. Republicans could believe they were in Ireland. And in every respect that mattered at the street level, they were both right. Peace broke out.

But the GFA explicitly stated that a border could not exist between Northern Ireland and the Irish Republic. Any such border would breach the treaty and risk a return of terrorism. And this became a problem when we had to find somewhere for a post-Brexit boundary for Britain's sovereignty.

If we placed the border between the UK and Northern Ireland, that would effectively leave the province subject to EU rules and break up the union. Not ideal if your country is called the United Kingdom of Great Britain and Northern Ireland.

If we placed the border between the Irish Republic and Northern Ireland, we would be in breach of the GFA, and not only risk a return to armed conflict, but also risk trade deals with the EU and USA, both of whom were guarantors of the GFA.

And if we didn't apply a border at all, the entirety of Britain would have to continue accepting EU rules over import and export standards, which pretty much nullified the point of Brexit (if there ever was one).

Johnson had solved this problem with his usual tactic: lavish helpings of thick, lustrous bullshit. He introduced a Brexit agreement that put a border between GB and NI, right down the Irish Sea, and told everybody there was no such border. There was. And no amount of pretending made it go away. So in 2022 the Unionist First Minister of Northern Ireland resigned in protest.

Under the terms of the GFA, Northern Ireland had a power-sharing executive: if one party stepped down, the other party was obliged to leave too. So when the First Minister resigned, his counterpart from Sinn Féin also had to stand down.[184] And suddenly Northern Ireland had no government, and sectarian tensions began to grow again with attacks on police stations and officers.[185] The New IRA became active, and within months the terrorism threat level was raised to 'severe'.[186]

'Project Fear', they'd called it.[187] Now it was Project Here.

Ukraine

In March, as World War Three ramped up, the Tories decided to prove to the Russians that we had a serious government for serious times. So we knighted Gavin Williamson, a prattling tower of ceaseless inadequacy with dentistry like a graveyard in the moonlight. It didn't seem to matter that he was – and it's hard for me to see how the lawyers could have a problem with this assertion – the most stupefyingly inept person to attain high office in living memory: he was Johnson's pal, and seemingly that's what mattered.

An anagram of Boris Johnson is 'Job Honors Sin'.

So Williamson got a knighthood for 'services to the nation', which included being sacked after 'compelling evidence' suggested he was behind leaks from inside the National Security Council, almost sending us to war with China over the contents of a phone mast, fucking up an entire year of exams, voting to starve kids in a pandemic, and telling a giggling Russia to 'go away and shut up'.[188]

Russia didn't. Which brings us back to the war.

—

A truly gigantic refugee crisis was emerging in Ukraine. Poland and Germany prepared to accept a million displaced people each. Throughout Europe, nations immediately suspended the need for entry visas, giving unfettered admission to anybody fleeing the war. Most of Europe granted Ukrainians automatic residence, with access to employment, benefits and housing for up to three years. No documents required, no fees charged, no questions asked.

Here in Britain, Home Secretary Priti Patel boasted that we'd set up 'the first visa scheme in the world' to aid Ukrainian refugees; and this was true, but only because every other country had suspended the need for visas altogether.[189] Millions fled Ukraine, so we proudly announced we would provide 300 visas. By March, over a month after fighting had started, we had issued just 50.[190]

More people than that had attended illegal Downing Street parties.

The Tories had airlifted 173 dogs out of Kabul.

They had granted over 700 Russian millionaires 'golden visas' to come and buy our houses from under us.[191]

Regardless: 'We are a very, very generous country,' said Boris Johnson. I hadn't reached the same conclusion, but I stand corrected. And disgusted.

Under pressure, Johnson announced that Ukrainians fleeing the war could come to the UK without a visa, if they had family here. Sounds like that's an improvement, until you hear that the government's definition of 'family' excluded adult refugees' parents or siblings.

If by some miracle a refugee did have . . . whatever escaped that absurdly narrow definition of family . . . the standard visa we were offering required an in-person interview, a fee of £95 and full medical records for a decade. Tough to provide if your house and all your belongings have just been blown up by Putin. Even if a refugee could provide those things, the UK visa granted a maximum stay of just six months.[192]

Priti Patel, looking lost without the lion and the wardrobe, told parliament she had set up a dedicated visa application centre in Lille, which would process applications.[193] There was no such centre.

So Patel said there would be one at Calais. That didn't turn out so well either.

'We have staff in Calais, we have support on the ground. It is wrong to say we're just turning people back, we're absolutely not,' said Patel. 'We're supporting those that have been coming to Calais.'[194]

But when Ukrainians reached UK official services in Calais, they were met by a poster reading: 'No visas delivered in Calais'. Some assumed they could get a visa in Dover, so tried to board a train, but train operators were slapped with £2,000-per-person fines for bringing in Ukrainians without visas.[195] And British Border Force officials turned back more than 300 people at the border.[196] All of which does sound a *bit* like turning people back.[197]

In the middle of all this, up popped Daniel Kawczynski, with things to say about the ethics of helping refugees. He knew all about ethics: only two months earlier, he had defended his claim of £22,000 in expenses to learn Polish, which he could already speak because it was his native language.[198] A month before that, a leak had shown him pitching his services to Saudi Arabia while working as a full-time MP for Shrewsbury – not a constituency famous for being in Arabia. But he'd only shill for the Saudis in return for 'good remuneration' because, poor lamb, 'I need it to pay school fees'.[199]

As the refugee crisis grew, this tower of moral certitude tweeted that 'left-wing demands' to help people in war were 'illiterate and immoral', and said civilians fleeing Russian bombardments should remain in 'frontline states' for their own good.

Having bravely volunteered Ukrainian civilians for the front line, he bravely deleted his tweet because people were mean to him; but not before it was seen by other Tories. 'What utterly risible, illiterate, immoral and offensive bile,' wrote Simon Hoare. 'You do not speak for the Tory Party. I'm not sure you speak for humanity.'[200]

Three days later Kawczynski bravely deleted his Twitter account.[201]

Meanwhile, Britain opened a visa application centre in the Ukrainian city of Lviv, but it could only be used by Ukrainians of British descent. Any other refugees had to make it to Poland or Moldova before they could apply, by which time Britain was denying them entry because they'd already made it to a third country. Just in case there was some unforeseen loophole that could be exploited by terrified families running away from barrel-bombs, the government pressed ahead with plans to make arriving 'without permission' into a criminal offence, a law which would apply to Ukrainians too. The UN's refugee agency UNHCR described our refugee framework as 'deeply concerning'.[202]

Lacking the ability to enter the non-existent visa application centre in Lille, refugees were now advised to call our 'free application hotline', which also didn't yet exist. And when it did finally open it wasn't free, and it only accepted calls made from within the UK.[203]

Exhausted, confused, shell-shocked, and bureaucratically bewildered Ukrainians in Calais were met by British officials, who told 150 of them that they had to apply in person at yet another centre, this time in either Paris or Brussels. And the cost of applications had by now somehow grown to £2,200 per person.[204]

So – deep breath – refugees had to travel from Ukraine to Calais without either flying over or setting foot in any country in between. Once they'd done this, they could apply for a visa we wouldn't give them, at a centre that didn't exist, manned by people who told them to fuck off, and who charged a fee that was unjustifiable. But if they didn't like it, they always had the option of applying to enter the UK by phoning a number that only worked if they were already in Britain.

Our home secretary had woven a wall of unbreachable gibberish.

An anagram of Priti Patel is 'Plait Tripe'.

As if things weren't bad enough, Britain then stopped all other visa applications, meaning there was no longer *any* safe route for Ukrainian refugees to reach Britain.[205] Boris Johnson said the UK was 'way out in front in our willingness to help refugees',[206] and literally the same day his government published a briefing to explain how their anti-refugee laws could be used to enable the deportation of refugees, including Ukrainians.[207]

The next day things got even more unutterably callous, as Plymouth's Tory MP Kevin Foster tweeted that refugees could still apply to come here under 'our seasonal worker scheme'.[208] So we were prepared to save you from being bombed, but only if you agreed to pick sprouts for us, and then piss off back to your war again after six months. In April 2022, Foster tweeted that it was 'a badge of honour to be on this list of people sanctioned by Putin's regime in response to our nation's support for Ukraine and its fight against tyranny'. At the time of writing, in February 2023, it was still his pinned tweet.[209]

And every evening, Downing Street was lit up in the colours of the Ukrainian flag by a governing party which decried 'virtue signalling' at every turn.[210]

—

The public were generally pretty outraged by all of this. Polls showed three-quarters of Britons supported us offering practically unlimited shelter for Ukraine's civilians,[211] and in response the government said – and I'm paraphrasing, but only very slightly – 'fuck it then, you do it', and essentially made the entire refugee process into a home-made free-for-all.

Private citizens could now volunteer to home Ukrainian refugees and families, instead of it being organised by the 'natural party of government', whom we had elected to do this stuff for us. Over 130,000 registered to take part in the scheme.[212] The only problem: anybody wanting to participate needed to know the *specific* names of the Ukrainians they would sponsor, which migration experts said meant, in practical terms, that 'only those with connections to the UK will benefit'.[213] Insiders working on the scheme described it as 'designed to fail'.

'[The government] want to keep the numbers down,' they said. 'Everything they do feels as if it is to do that. I've even had a barrister and lawyers on the phone saying they couldn't understand the system.'[214]

Keen to help, a month into this chaotic process the UK government admitted it had been giving Ukrainians the wrong guidance all along; the official information on how refugees could fly to the UK had made it literally impossible for refugees to fly to the UK.[215]

In April 2022, Boris Johnson said, 'the United Kingdom stands unwaveringly with [Ukraine] and we are in it for the long run'.[216]

By July 2022, 12 million people had fled their homes in Ukraine. Britain had offered safety to just 0.7 per cent of them.[217]

The Partygate Party

Operation Red Meat had rotted to nothing. Now it was the turn of Operation Save Big Dog, which quickly reached the 'he's dragging his arse on the rug again' stage.

In April the Metropolitan Police finally finished their investigation into Partygate and handed down 126 fixed penalty notices. This included fines for the prime minister, his wife Carrie Johnson, and that acme of ethics, Chancellor Rishi Sunak. Under Johnson, 10 Downing Street became the most fined address in the country, and even the *Telegraph* assigned its crime correspondent to covering the travails of our prime minister.[218]

So obviously, it was time to throw a party! Johnson decided to host a dinner to charm his recalcitrant MPs at a luxury hotel in Westminster, which required his guests to walk past the Covid Memorial Wall and the assembled mourners. It was a perfect opportunity for the Tories to show some contrition and humility.

'Well, we had a lot of fun,' said Michael Fabricant, a wig with an idiot hanging off it. 'It's great, we had a photo taken, it was absolutely super.'[219] His major complaint was about reports that his posh dinner had been 'washed down with fine wines'. Not at all, he tweeted. It was merely a passable house Merlot.[220]

Good effort, Fabricant, but you're veering away from relatability again.

Yet despite this strenuous effort to avoid basic empathy, and despite Johnson's pretensions at being an indispensable wartime leader, public opinion on Partygate was settled. Two-thirds of voters wanted him to resign, and close to 90 per cent of us thought he had knowingly lied about events.[221] Because he had.

So no sooner had the port and cigars been finished at Boris's 'everybody love me' shindig than the plotting resumed. Those who had called on Johnson to resign, and then called on him to remain, now called on him to resign again. They were joined by many others, some of them very senior: recent chief whips, or members of Johnson's personal band of fluffers, the ERG.

'The gig's up,' said Steve Baker.

'Do the right thing and resign,' said Craig Whittaker. William Wragg described being ordered to go out and defend the indefensible as 'utterly depressing' and said, 'I cannot reconcile myself to the prime minister's continued leadership.'[222]

'The problem isn't just Boris. The problem is the party which chose him,' said Chris Patten, the former Conservative chairman. 'They are said to want Liz Truss, which I don't think would be a frightfully good idea, to put it mildly.' He was not wrong.[223]

That was in public. Off the record, Tory MPs were brutal. The party was 'fucking deluded', said one, and the quotes kept on coming.[224]

'I have never known dysfunction like this.'

'Draw a line under the whole disaster, one way or the other.'

'It's an f'ing mess. That is all I know.'[225]

Alex Chalk, the solicitor general, had laid out his stall years before. He said in September 2019, 'If there is a scintilla of a suggestion that the British government would act unlawfully, forget it, game over. That is a really important red line for me.'[226]

126 fines, and he didn't resign.

They Aren't Going to Get Away With It

In March, P&O Ferries hit the news with their heart-warming decision to sack, with immediate effect, 800 employees and replace them with cheaper agency workers.

There was no warning and no consultation, and the bad news was delivered via a pre-recorded video message. 'Please do take some time to absorb it,' said the man on P&O's television, and then the sacked workers were instantly escorted off the premises.[227]

P&O said the company would 'not be a viable business' unless it could save £100 million, and therefore it had no alternative.[228] Their parent company, DP World, had paid out £270 million in share dividends the previous year; but sure, it had no alternative. Across the political divide, the decision was greeted with outrage and severe criticism. P&O had only just accepted £15 million in furlough money, the parent company was highly profitable, and what's more, the sackings appeared to have breached UK employment law.

This was a big test of the government, and of Brexit too. It was the first opportunity since leaving the EU to demonstrate that Britain had protected workers' rights, that employment law would be vigorously applied, and that the consequences of violations would be severe. Chests were beaten. High horses ascended. Soap boxes were mounted, and acts of extreme political bumptiousness were performed on televisions across the land.

'No one should treat employees in that way in the 21st century,' said Transport Secretary Grant Shapps, and announced that he'd instructed his legal teams to investigate what laws had been broken, and whether it was possible to withdraw government contracts from P&O.[229]

Business minister Kwasi Kwarteng said failure to give sufficient notice was 'a criminal offence and can lead to an unlimited fine', and deplored the fact that P&O 'does not appear willing to abide by the rules that we have put in place to protect British workers'.[230]

'We will take them to court, we will defend the rights of British workers,' promised Boris Johnson in the House of Commons. 'P&O plainly aren't going to get away with it.'[231]

They got away with it.

'There's no fine, there's no legal action, there's only words and hot air,' said the union representing many of the sacked workers. Grant Shapps quietly dropped his outrage, Boris Johnson had seemingly lied to parliament about taking them to court, and Kwarteng's unlimited fines were limited to zero. Instead of punishing P&O's owners, the Tories gave them £548 million from the overseas aid budget, and announced plans to give them a further £50 million in tax breaks by involving them in the establishment of freeports in London and Southampton.[232]

Ten Years of the Internet

Bearing all of this in mind, imagine the size of the balls on Nadine Dorries as she initiated a crackdown on liars. In April she launched a new Online Safety Bill, which she said would stop those who 'use the internet to exploit innocent people' with fake news and misinformation.[233]

Dorries was asked if this meant executives at social media giants could be put in prison if they didn't comply.

'Absolutely,' she said.

'The government's current proposals mean tech bosses wouldn't be personally liable,' explained the head of safety at the NSPCC.[234]

The culture secretary, trapped forever at Lambrini o'clock, decided to promote her bill by attending a meeting at Microsoft, where she 'immediately asked when they were going to get rid of algorithms'.[235] I'm gonna guess they said 'never', not least because algorithms are the basis of all computer software. But you can't expect the minister responsible for social media to know that. It was only a couple of months since she'd claimed 'we've had ten years of the internet' (it was invented in 1969),[236] and that she was 'amazed to learn' young people watched programmes on YouTube.[237]

Clearly she felt a need to connect with da yoof, so took it upon herself to rap – yes, rap – details of the Online Safety Bill on TikTok, looking for all the world like your auntie undertaking a prolonged and hearty celebration of doing well in a meat raffle in a Wetherspoons car park. She even finished with a mic-drop, and I momentarily wondered if somebody had slipped acid into my coffee.[238]

But she wasn't done with TikTok, so it's still not safe to go back there. She decided to publish an interview on the platform, in which she explained what her Ministry of Fun was really all about. She began by revealing her in-depth knowledge of broadband, which she said was there so you could 'downstream your movies'. But her job wasn't all about technological expertise: she was also responsible, she told us, for 'tennis pitches'.[239]

She blamed these gaffes on dyslexia, and that may be the case: I'm no expert. But I don't think those living with dyslexia normally blame the condition for them being simultaneously cross, obsessed, and profoundly ignorant about Channel 4.

'I have come to the conclusion that government ownership is holding Channel 4 back from competing against streaming giants like Netflix,'[240] she tweeted, and almost immediately Netflix announced it had lost 200,000 subscribers in just three months, and the service's share price fell 35 per cent.[241]

I Won't Remove My Clothes Again

Allow me to introduce David Warburton, a B-grade politician full of class-A drugs.

Back in December 2018, Warburton had delivered a moving and impassioned speech in the House of Commons. 'Children in England have been targeted by drug gangs and coerced by intimidation, violence and criminal incentives into the so-called county lines system of selling drugs across the country. What work is being done,' he demanded to know, 'to address this appalling exploitation of children and young people?'[242]

Fast forward to April 2022, and reports emerged of that same David Warburton in a flat with a young person. He encouraged her to order cocaine, snorted 'line after line after line' of it, and then – despite the young woman repeatedly saying she did not want to do anything sexual with him – Warburton allegedly stripped naked, got into bed with her, and 'ground his body against hers and groped her breasts'.

In mitigation, he texted her the next day to say 'promise I won't remove all my clothes again' if they could continue to meet up.[243] So that's OK then.

He denied any wrongdoing. 'I have enormous amounts of defence,'[244] he declared, full of the unlimited confidence for which Bolivian Marching Powder is famous. His defence might have been enormous, but it was dwarfed by the indictments, not least audio recordings of the evening and photos of the drugs in question. Warburton, who at this stage you'd be forgiven for assuming was working for the prosecution, had posed in his victim's flat, gazing into the camera next to an upturned baking tray coated with lines of cocaine.*

It wasn't the only allegation he faced. Two female former aides came forward to claim similar conduct by Warburton. In making the complaints they'd had to bypass the usual channels, which traditionally began with a report to the MP's parliamentary office. In this case, it was made a little more awkward: the person employed to handle HR in Warburton's parliamentary office was Warburton's wife.[245]

(If you've been wondering why it's a bad idea for MPs to employ family members in their office, wonder no longer.)

Warburton had also breached the parliamentary code of conduct by accepting – and failing to register – a £150,000 loan from Russian-born Roman Joukovski, who gave Warburton the money via an offshore trust in the Seychelles. Warburton, coincidentally, had lobbied on behalf of Joukovski in letters to the Financial Conduct Authority,[246] in an attempt to overturn an earlier refusal to certify the businessman as a 'fit and proper person' in 2014.[247]

The Tory Party withdrew the whip from Warburton pending investigations into the accusations of drugs and multiple sexual assaults. But they didn't suspend him immediately. Conservative whips had been warned weeks before about his behaviour but did nothing until it

---

* There was a widely spread social media story that Warburton had claimed the piles of cocaine was actually his dandruff. There's no evidence for him saying this, which is a shame, because it would have been hilarious.

became public.[248] Yet despite the findings of the FCA, and despite the findings of the Commons watchdog, Warburton received no parliamentary sanctions. The commissioner for standards said the 'matter was closed after Mr Warburton apologised for breaking the rules'.[249]

Warburton admitted himself to a psychiatric hospital to be treated for the 'shock and stress' of being caught doing that shitty thing he voluntarily did.[250] He managed to get treatment despite 60 per cent of children's mental health referrals being rejected after a decade of underfunding from the government,[251] which he had consistently voted for.[252]

Within three months of being let off because he said sorry, Warburton was feeling well enough to get himself accused of forging documents while applying for an £800,000 bank loan, and failing to declare a donation from a billionaire of £25,000.[253]

—

Warburton must have been feeling hot under the collar, and it wasn't entirely down to being presented with the consequences of his actions. 2022 was the fifth hottest year on record, and the nine previous years were the warmest on record too.[254] It was a sharp signifier of the escalating, terrifying climate and energy crises, which Boris Johnson pledged to tackle with a 'long-term plan' for low-carbon domestic energy production.[255]

The long-term plan lasted approximately two weeks.

The low-carbon bit was first to go, with Jacob Rees-Mogg urging us to extract 'every last drop' of oil from the North Sea, and then singing the praises of fracking, saying an earthquake a day under the homes of people living in the much-fracked county of Lancashire was the equivalent of 'a rock fall in a disused coalmine'.[256]

And then the wind-power bit ran into trouble, when over 100 Tory MPs threatened a mutiny over their use. The size of the impending rebellion was 'certainly way more than [Johnson's] majority', said one, menacingly, and the plan was watered down. Nine of Johnson's Cabinet were on record signing letters that called for cuts to onshore wind power, including the usual suspects: Priti Patel, Nadine Dorries and Jacob Rees-Mogg, the three things that you end up with when you piss off the wrong genie.[257] It didn't seem to matter to them that they'd been elected on a manifesto promising a 'world leading' wind-power sector and a 'moratorium on fracking'.[258] Manifesto pledges meant nothing (except for the one about Brexit, which also meant nothing but still had to be done).

And while we're on the subject of manifesto pledges:

'We will not raise the rate of income tax, VAT or National Insurance,' they promised.[259] National insurance was raised to 13.25 per cent.[260]

'We will keep the [pension] triple-lock,' they said. The pension triple-lock was suspended.[261]

'No one will have to sell their house to pay for social care,' they said.[262] People still had to sell their homes to pay for social care.[263]

'We will build Northern Powerhouse Rail between Leeds and Manchester,' they said. It was cancelled.[264]

'We will build 40 new hospitals,' they said.[265] There was only funding for six.

'We will spend 0.7 per cent of GNI on international development,' they said. It was cut to 0.5 per cent.[266]

And finally: 'We will host the UK government's first ever international LGBT conference,' they said. But that conference was cancelled in April, after hundreds of participants boycotted it in protest at the Tories' failure to outlaw conversion practices for transgender people.[267] Both Johnson and his predecessor, Theresa May, had promised to make conversion therapy – a non-scientific attempt to suppress or change a person's sexuality or gender identity – illegal in Britain. Honest Boris then reneged on this pledge, instead offering to prevent the practice via Olympically hazy 'non-legislative measures'. After an outcry, he then U-turned on his U-turn, but only partially. ITV reported the ban would now outlaw 'only gay conversion therapy, not trans'.[268]

This coincided with Tory backbencher Jamie Wallis coming out as the first openly transgender MP, and therefore a member of a party that – at least for the half hour the policy could be expected to last – was OK with him being 'cured' out of existence.[269]

I've Lost My Clothes

The real tragedy of David Warburton was that despite his vigorous efforts, he didn't even manage to be the most stupefying and idiotic scandal to plague Boris Johnson's dying days in office. The party was a well-oiled machine, but the most well-oiled part of it was the MP who called a senior colleague at 4 a.m. one morning, tired, emotional, and in need of help.

'I'm in a brothel,' he slurred. 'I don't know how I got here, and I can't find my clothes.'[270]

Yet even bewildered-and-naked-in-a-brothel guy didn't manage to be more cringeworthy than Lee Anderson, who as part of his epic battle against common decency told parliament foodbanks were unnecessary, because anybody could cook a meal for 30p.[271]

According to the foodbank charity The Trussell Trust, the main reasons people needed foodbanks were problems with the benefits system, challenging life experiences, ill-health, and lack of support. 'Foodbank need in the UK is about lack of income, not food,' said the charity's head of policy.[272]

According to 30p Lee, the main reasons we had 2 million more foodbank users than when his party took office was that we'd all forgotten how to cook in the last ten years, while ordinary people were engaging in unacceptable acts of kindness. 'Every do-gooder is starting these little projects to make themselves feel good,' Anderson complained.[273]

And he knew this because, as he told the House of Commons, he helped out in a foodbank in his own constituency. Under his eye, those in need had to take a mandatory cookery course before being fed. This didn't entirely explain why the foodbank remained open after he'd taught people how to cook, which he had already told us was the cure; but oddly enough, Lee wasn't keen on debating the issue any further.[274]

Not a Loan

Across all levels of government, from the prime minister down to the woe-begotten Warburton, there hung a fog of sleaze, indecision, gaslighting and floundering incompetence.

The fallout from their non-handling of P&O, combined with long-predicted – but still extravagantly fluffed – problems with post-Brexit border controls led to six days of 23-mile tailbacks at Dover in April. Operation Brock, the government's plan to address queues caused by Brexit, had somehow failed to consider HGV drivers needing a wee.

'We've got nowhere to go, there's absolutely nothing provided for us whatsoever,' said one driver. 'There's no water, no food, no toilet facilities, no washing facilities, absolutely nothing.'[275]

The Tories had six years to plan for this.

Meanwhile it was time for the Queen's Speech, in which the government's latest transient guess at a legislative programme would be spelled out to parliament. It was delivered by Prince Charles, the Queen herself being unable to travel to Westminster. She didn't miss much, just a priceless gold hat emblazoned with a 317-carat diamond and over 4,000 other jewels being driven in a custom-made Rolls-Royce to a £2.5 billion palace, where it was placed next to a gold chair in which sat one of the world's richest men, who explained to 2 million hungry Britons that there was no money.

Energy bills soared by 54 per cent, shattering all previous records. It was predicted that without intervention, average bills would soon reach £4,200.[276] Millions were plunged into fuel poverty, and the nation's fear and panic was soon joined by raw fury when we discovered France, hampered as it was by the Evil Empire of the EU and those dastardly nationalised energy companies, had managed to cap price rises at 4 per cent.[277]

The government leaped into apathy. The chancellor introduced a £200 'energy rebate' to massage down our bills, which was laughably inadequate, and was made yet worse when it emerged the 'rebate' had to be paid back, turning it into a mandatory loan in all but name.[278]

The diminutive Sunak was only capable of clearing low hurdles, which was fortunate, because the low hurdle he had to clear this time was 'being smarter than his colleagues'. He opted to hide from the fallout, and instead Greg Hands was given half a brief and thrown to the wolves.

'It's not a loan,' claimed Hands on BBC's *Question Time*, 'because it doesn't create an obligation on the individual to repay.'[279]

'So if we don't want to pay it back, we don't have to?' asked presenter Fiona Bruce.

We did have to, because it was a loan, and Hands floundered as the audience pelted him with laughter and abuse. His reception was a stark warning to all but the most insensate, yet somehow Northern Ireland Secretary Brandon Lewis managed to stumble into exactly the same bear trap as Greg Hands, without any assistance from Fiona Bruce. During a radio interview on the subject, Lewis even managed to get into an argument with himself.

'It is a loan, let's remember. No it isn't.'[280]

It was the perfect moment for Sunak, still angling to be the next PM, to show a common touch, and prove how much he sympathised with our plight. With this in mind he headed off to the supermarket to be filmed being ordinary, filling up his ordinary car at an ordinary location. It was an entirely believable, relatable and ordinary event, but for one small detail: Sunak, the 222nd richest person in the UK and one of the wealthiest men ever elected to parliament, wanted us to believe he drove a £12,000 Kia Rio.

When challenged, Sunak admitted the car wasn't his: he'd borrowed it from a Sainsbury's worker for the photo-op. When pressed he claimed he really drove a VW Golf, which he perhaps thought was more believable.[281] He actually owned four luxury cars, including a top-of-the-range Jaguar and *two* Land Rovers,[282] and his publicity stunt made him look like an idiot, not least because while he was cosplaying at being normal, he managed to be filmed in flapping disarray when required to use a credit card at a petrol station. And this was the man overseeing the nation's money.[283]

An anagram of Rishi Sunak is 'Runs his Kia'.

His leadership bid was falling apart before it had formally begun, and he desperately needed to look like a man of the people, sympathetic to our plight, approachable, decent, and engaging. So he donated £100,000 to foodbanks.

No, hold on, let me correct that.

He donated £100,000 to Winchester College, his alma mater, and one of the most expensive private schools in the world.[284] Then he headed off for a break at his £5.5 million seafront home in Santa Monica, leaving behind a series of baffling questions about his family's tax arrangements.[285]

—

Akshata Murty, Sunak's wife, was claiming 'non-domicile' status in the UK, allowing her to avoid paying tax on foreign earnings. These earnings included the £11.5 million a year she was pulling down from her shares in Infosys, which was still operating in Russia despite Sunak telling businesses to adhere to sanctions.

It was a bad time to be Rishi Sunak. Until now, all he'd had to do to be popular was take his jacket off on Instagram and not be Boris Johnson. Suddenly, political skill was needed, and it began to look like he had none. Was he really nothing but a rictus grin and a tiny suit? Where was his depth? The longer you looked at Sunak, the less of him there appeared to be, and rumours spread he was thinking of giving it all up and heading off to be a tech bro in California.

Somehow, despite his best efforts, he had failed to maintain his popularity with the public. But what were those efforts?

Well, in the two years he'd been a low-tax chancellor, he'd raised taxes 15 times.[286] And had only just delivered yet another package of increases, which left Britain paying the highest tax burden for 70 years.[287] His spring statement had led the Office for Budget Responsibility to declare a 'historic fall in living standards', and inflation was at a 40-year high.[288] He couldn't even be trusted to competently pay for a can of Coke during a photo-op, and now it emerged his unbelievably wealthy wife wasn't paying tax.

Sunak claimed she didn't have to pay tax in the UK because she was an Indian citizen. But non-dom status isn't automatic, and it isn't an accident. It costs around £30,000 a year, and you have to go through a complicated application process to be declared non-dom.[289] Murty had done so,[290] and her status had saved her an estimated £20 million in tax, single-handedly wiping out the entire tax contribution of over 3,300 average British workers.[291] It wasn't even as if she needed the money. If she had paid all of that £20 million in tax, she'd still have been left with over £700 million in the bank.

Things then got even worse for Sunak when it was revealed that during the first 18 months he'd been chancellor, he had not only held permanent residence (Green Card) status in the USA,[292] but he'd also been listed as a beneficiary of trust funds set up in the British Virgin Islands and Cayman Islands, both of which are, you guessed it, tax havens.[293]

And then it was reported Infosys, the firm owned by Sunak's wife's family which was currently skirting the UK sanction regime to operate in Russia, had won £50 million of public contracts in the years running up to 2021.[294]

So in a single week we'd learned Sunak was chancellor of one country, legally domiciled in another, claimed his wife didn't pay tax cos she was from a third, got paid by a tax-haven trust fund in a fourth territory, and was part of a government giving money to his wife's company, even though it was operating in defiance of sanctions in a fifth.

And this from a government that had accused Remainers of being 'citizens of nowhere'.[295]

Of Johnson's 22 ministers, only five were prepared to confirm that neither they nor their families used tax havens or non-dom status.[296]

And this from a government that had said we were 'all in it together'.[297]

Sunak, laser-focused on what was *really* pissing us off about all this, ordered an inquiry into who had leaked embarrassing shit about his family's tax affairs, and a government spokesman complained that 'divulging the tax status of a private individual is a criminal offence'.[298] Meanwhile Boris Johnson – yes, really, Boris fucking Johnson – ordered an ethics inquiry into his main rival for the premiership, which was led by Lord Geidt, the guy who had managed to clear Johnson over Wallpapergate.

Geidt cleared Sunak of breaking ministerial rules.[299]

We Used to Be Better Than This

Having been fined for Partygate, Boris Johnson now promised to 'set the record straight' by finally telling the truth about the thing he'd always denied lying about.[300]

It's wrong to suggest Boris Johnson was unprincipled. He had one principle, which was to look after Boris Johnson at all costs. And so the rough beast slouched towards Westminster, his chosen arena for this baring of the soul.

He was there to attend a meeting of the 1922 Committee, at which he would wear his very best Contrite Face and butter up his backbenchers with a charm offensive. He got the offensive bit right, at least. One MP found it so tonally crass that he left after three minutes, describing it as 'a pantomime'.[301]

Meanwhile somebody had changed the batteries in Steve Baker, and he whizzed from microphone to microphone, spurting out a constant stream of opinions about his own party's leadership. The Cabinet was 'fat, dumb and happy', he said, and the PM's appearance at the

1922 Committee had been little more than 'the usual festival of bombast and orgy of adulation'.[302]

That adulation had limits. Justice minister Lord Wolfson resigned from his position, saying Johnson was 'inconsistent with the rule of law'.[303] Mark Harper, a former chief whip and held in high regard within the party (if not without it), sent a letter to Graham Brady, the chairman of the 1922 Committee, calling for Johnson to resign because he was 'no longer worthy of office'.[304] David Davis accused the PM of 'moral delinquency' and declared, 'We are better than this – or at least we used to be.'[305]

This last statement was not about Partygate, or about Johnson (who had never been 'better than this'), but about immigration policy. Davis was appalled by the latest plan for handling asylum seekers, because in the middle of all this turmoil some idiot had let Priti Patel out of her pentagram, and she surfaced with a fresh idea about Rwanda.

In essence, it was the same idea she'd had about Ghana, which would have worked perfectly if she'd bothered to tell the Ghanaians about it. Having learned her lesson, she had made a few phone calls and found £120 million, and now was going to get asylum seekers to fuck off to Rwanda instead. Something had to be done about migration, and it certainly wasn't going to be the sensible thing, which was providing a safe route for people entering the country, where they could do jobs that we desperately needed doing, pay tax we urgently needed paying, and power economic growth we desperately longed to happen.

Migration had been a defining issue during Brexit,[306] and those behind the campaign – most of whom had sat in power for the subsequent six years – had assured us they had the solution to it.

It turned out they had loads of solutions. Pick one!

Patel, the answer to the question 'What did Bellatrix Lestrange do next?', had suggested putting immigrants on an uninhabited island in Scotland, until they realised all the ones big enough to put humans on . . . had humans on.[307] Her department suggested shipping migrants to a volcano in the middle of the Atlantic, until they realised the government isn't a Bond villain.[308] Then they had proposed covering the entire south coast of England with giant wave-generating machines that would push migrants back into the sea, so they could drown. So maybe the government *is* a Bond villain after all.[309]

They'd recommended chasing immigrants around the oceans on jet-skis until they, I dunno ... I guess got bored and sailed back to Afghanistan instead?[310] At one point, the government had endeavoured to make it illegal to steer a dinghy. Not to *own* a dinghy, you understand. Not to *launch* a dinghy. Just to *steer* a dinghy.[311]

And when that didn't work, they'd attempted to make it illegal to 'glamorise' crossing the English Channel, a phenomenon that didn't, on the face of it, seem to be a major issue. There is a reason James Bond movies are so often set in Barbados rather than Bexhill-on-Sea.

After this had failed, they suggested everybody who wanted to come to Britain should be sent to Papua New Guinea instead, perhaps hoping they wouldn't notice the difference between 70 million hectares of tropical rainforest and Eastbourne. The Tories had attempted to bluff Ghana into the same deal, been made to look ridiculous, yet seemingly enjoyed the experience enough to create something called a 'Clandestine Channel Threat Commander', possibly in the hope smuggling gangs would simply laugh themselves to death. The Royal Navy almost did: they called the policy 'completely potty', but that barely slowed down the hamster wheel of demented suggestions being spun by trundling maniac Priti Patel.[312]

Between 2010 and August 2022, the Tories had implemented 168 changes to immigration and refugee policy, which averages out at more than one per month.[313] Since 2019 there had been over 40 different policy announcements about small boats alone.[314] Not one of these measures had reduced either migration or small boat numbers.

Seemingly nobody in government had considered providing safe routes for migrants, so asylum seekers could walk through a gate to be met by Border Force staff, rather than risking their lives in glamorous, unsteerable, volcano-proof dinghies, and landing on deserted beaches in the jungles of Dorset. But instead of the sane, practical, cheap, and safe solution, Patel decided what this country needed was a burgeoning industry in people-smuggling, matched by boom-time for batshit crazy solutions. And that's how we ended up with the idea of sending migrants to Rwanda, where their application for asylum in Britain would be processed, and then, once accepted, they would never be allowed into Britain anyway.[315]

This was supposed to stamp out illegal immigration. Seemingly nobody questioned why, given the circumstances, anybody arriving in Britain would even *attempt* to legally cooperate with our immigration forces, if the guaranteed end result of following the law was to be shoved into a camp in Rwanda.

Never mind the illogicality of this scheme: the impracticality alone should have consigned it to the bin. In 2022, 60,000 people were given asylum in the UK.[316] It sounds a lot, but there were over 280 million migrants worldwide.[317] We accepted around 0.02 per cent of them.

But sending even that comparatively small number to Rwanda would require detention and application facilities in the country. Detaining 60,000 people would mean Rwanda building the equivalent of every prison in the UK, and then doing it again next year, and every subsequent year after that as numbers grew exponentially.

Britain was the sixth biggest economy in the world, and our argument against migration was that we couldn't afford to do any of this stuff.[318]

Rwanda was the 22nd poorest country in the world, so obviously it'd be *fine*.

Physical limitations on space in detention centres would ensure asylum seekers arriving in Rwanda would be released almost as soon as their feet hit the ground, just to make room for the next lot of arrivals. Once out of the detention centres, migrants would most likely find themselves homeless, jobless, unable to speak the local language, and desperate to get out of there. People like that are prime targets for smuggling gangs, who might as well set up a stall outside the detention-centre gates. And the cycle of people-smuggling would repeat itself all over again.

All Priti Patel had done was invent snakes and ladders for cunts.

When the policy had achieved its main goal of gaining approving, unquestioning headlines in the *Daily Mail*, details of the scheme began to ooze into the public realm, and it was an absolute farce. Rwanda said they could only handle 1,000 of our 60,000 migrants, and a few days later quietly downgraded that to a mere 200, at a cost of £120 million.[319] You could buy every one of those migrants a typical house in posh, desirable Wiltshire for less money.[320] The United Nations High Commissioner for Refugees called the plan a mere 'symbolic gesture' that would prove 'extremely expensive as well as illegal and discriminatory'.[321]

Regardless, the first flight of asylum seekers was loaded with passengers ready to be unwillingly dumped in a country they had no intention of living in. The first plane to leave had just seven people on board. The cost of the flight was £500,000, which in terms of luxury travel puts them in the same league as Liz Truss.

But before the plane left the ground there was a problem. It turned out the government's illegal immigration bill was an *illegal* immigration bill: both Britain's High Court and the European Court of Human Rights ruled against it on the grounds that those on board faced 'a real risk of irreversible harm' if flown to Rwanda, and the whole thing was cancelled.[322]

So naturally, Liz Truss said she was prepared to leave the European Convention on Human Rights.[323]

Human rights don't apply to *that* kind of human.

Within months, Rwanda demanded another £20 million, even though not a single migrant had yet landed in the country.[324] What happened to the original £120 million? It's a good question, especially as the *Financial Times* reported that the country's president, Paul Kagame, had seized power after his party slaughtered thousands in the genocide 30 years earlier, and although he'd won an election, it was one plagued by reports of rigging and irregularity. He was, to all intents and purposes, an autocratic dictator.[325] Rwanda's opposition leader warned that money passing through his government's hands was 'not being scrutinised'.

'We don't know really how they will use this money, because the problem we have in Rwanda is accountability,' she said in 2023.[326] But by 2023 our second unelected PM in a year was that master of accountability Rishi Sunak, a man who had shrugged away £54 billion of fraud and other unaccountable losses.[327] So what if an unelected leader in Rwanda might misplace a piddling £120 million?

Nothing Short of an International Scandal

Despite his being cleared by Lord Geidt, the Mr Magoo of ethics inquiries, most leading Tories had by now written off Sunak's hopes of being the next prime minister. 'He has shown colossal naivety,' said a former Tory Cabinet minister. 'The worry is that this is symptomatic of a party in terminal decline and that we are in a death spiral.'[328]

So it's not all bad news.

Those symptoms of decline cropped up everywhere you looked. In the week Sunak was battling to explain his family's unconventional blend of budget cars and expensive tax-minimisation schemes, the Conservatives' Wakefield MP Imran Ahmad Khan was found guilty of sexually assaulting a 15-year-old boy and got 18 months in prison.[329] Tory Crispin Blunt, chair of the all-party group on LGBTQ+ rights, wrote on social media that the conviction was 'nothing short of an international scandal'. After public outrage he deleted that message and backtracked. 'I strongly believe in the independence and integrity of the justice system,' he said, and then, just in case you thought there might be some consistency in Blunt's mind, he almost immediately leaped back to asserting Khan 'did not get a fair trial'.[330]

Half of Westminster's all-party LGBTQ+ grouping resigned in

protest at his chairmanship, and then Blunt resigned from the group too, rendering their resignations pointless.[331] So now, barely a week after the Tories had to cancel their LGBT conference because hundreds objected to Conservative policy, a Conservative led to half the gay members of parliament no longer being members of the group for gay parliamentarians.

Tractor Pull!

Wanking news! Conservative whips had been informed about one of their backbenchers watching pornography on his phone in the House of Commons, and an incensed Neil Parish took to the airwaves. This sort of thing had to be 'dealt with and dealt with seriously', he told GB News.[332]

It was dealt with barely two hours later, although Parish ensured nobody took it seriously at all. Parish – for he had been the porn aficionado in question – explained that he'd actually been trying to look at footage of tractors, and accidentally landed on 'another website with a very similar name', where 'I watched it for a bit'.

Having enjoyed CornHub, he then 'went in a second time' for another dose of tractor porn.[333]

Or maybe he was just looking at the trailers.

When not laughing about the facile idiocy of his excuse, the public were feeling rightly sickened by the level of gaslighting they were subjected to. The government had expected us to believe a top guy in Downing Street drove to Barnard Castle to test his eyesight; that the prime minister didn't know he was at a party when he raised a glass and called it 'the most unsocially distanced party in the UK right now';[334] and that an MP could mistake a naked woman for a combine harvester. It was hilarious, fascinating, and utterly grotesque, like a witnessing a car accident involving an octopus and John McCririck. But it couldn't last.

Failures of Leadership and Judgement

It was the fuck-around of times, it was the get-found-out of times.

Finally, after dominating the news cycle for months, at the end of May 2022 the Sue Gray report into Partygate was published. Dragging the facts into the daylight had been a difficult journey over ground littered with obstacles, booby-traps, and an unprincipled, rugby-tackling, one-man game of Shag, Marry, Avoid who was determined to dodge all consequences.

Along the way, Downing Street staff had admitted to shredding evidence; the Metropolitan Police had at one point decided not to investigate their own handling of Partygate; and it turned out this decision was made by the most senior officer on the case, who just happened to be Sajid Javid's brother.[335]

After that, Boris Johnson had ordered his MPs to block a further investigation into whether he had misled parliament, but they rebelled and ordered one anyway.[336] And when Downing Street was asked about believable claims that Johnson had begged Sue Gray to ditch the entire thing, the best the spokesman could come up with was 'I don't recognise that characterisation' and 'I'm not going to be getting into line by line what may or may not have been said.'[337]

Yet despite the best efforts of the government that had ordered it, the report finally turned up. It was damning. There were email trails not only showing the parties were pre-planned, but also that officials had known at the time that they weren't permitted. Johnson's private secretary had written that Number 10 'seemed to have got away with it', which is hardly something you'd write if innocent, and Sue Gray found 'failures of leadership and judgment' at the heart of government.[338] Once again Johnson was revealed, to nobody's surprise, to have personally attended multiple parties.

Well, to *almost* nobody's surprise. Boris Johnson was still so amazed at what Boris Johnson had been up to that his hair stood on end. Even as he went to parliament to tell them how 'humbled' he was by the report, he was still claiming 'I wasn't there', and telling anybody who could still be bothered to listen that he was as 'surprised and disappointed as anyone else in this House as the revelations [came to light]'.[339]

He seemed to think the country should still trust him to be prime minister, even though he couldn't be trusted to know what room he was in, or why he'd gone there. In the end, he had to create an entire new branch of government – the Office of the Prime Minister – simply to prevent him from getting pissed out of a suitcase and smashing up our constitutional norms.[340]

—

Graham Brady, the chairman of the 1922 Committee, had confirmed he'd received 30 letters of no-confidence in Johnson back in January, and over the subsequent months, as disgruntled Tories became less and less gruntled, the number had steadily climbed. As we reached the start of June, Brady announced he had now received 54 letters, enough to trigger a confidence vote.[341]

If the prime minister could retain the support of 180 of his own MPs he would win, and technically this meant he'd be safe for a year – party rules said no further vote could be triggered for 12 months. But everybody knew this meant nothing. Johnson had manoeuvred his predecessor Theresa May out of office just five months after she'd won a confidence vote.

The Tories might not have done much to govern the country in the preceding months, but glittering Jesus, they could buckle down when it came to in-fighting. A pro-Johnson whipping operation was powered up. The anti-Johnson rebels launched their bid. An orgy of intimidation, persuasion and duress broke out across Westminster, although none of it done very competently. The Tories descended into a confederacy of the strong-armed, the grease-elbowed and the ham-fisted.

Everybody knew Truss, Sunak and Jeremy Hunt were angling to replace Johnson, and the first to make his move was Hunt, choosing this moment to tweet that the Conservatives lacked 'integrity, competence and vision' and that therefore he would 'be voting for change'.[342] The public broadly agreed. Dozens of his colleagues did. A large majority of Tory voters did too. Win or lose, the mere fact it had come to a confidence vote felt terminal for Johnson. No matter what happened next, it seemed like the beginning of the end for his premiership.

And it seemed even more that way when the results of the vote came in: 148 of his own MPs had no confidence in him. That was 41 per cent of them.

He'd retained even less support than the clattering, robotic, electorally disastrous Theresa May had in 2019.[343]

—

While this was going on, tractor-enthusiast Neil Parish described how his 'hugely supportive' wife had chased him around the house with a pair of scissors, threatening to cut his Johnson off, and Britain could sympathise – we all wanted to cut our Johnson off too.[344] Despite the unexpectedly large mutiny against him, Tory rebels had failed to oust the PM, but now the public had a chance to show our anger.

Parish announced he would resign from his seat in June to spend more time with his family of furious castrators. His constituency, Tiverton and Honiton, had been held by the Tories since 1923, and Parish had enjoyed a luminously comfortable majority of 24,000.[345] It felt about as safe as any seat could possibly be.

The Tories lost it to the LibDems, breaking the record for the largest majority ever overturned. The dignified response of Helen Hurford, the Tory candidate, was to run away from the count and lock herself in a nearby dance studio.[346] Inspired by Hurford, our heroic leader Boris Johnson ran away from his own Red Wall party conference. It was 'no loss to us', said one Conservative MP.[347]

On the same day the Tories lost Tiverton because the local MP had an erotic fixation with farm machinery, they also lost the Wakefield by-election because the local MP was in jail. The Red Wall conference lost the prime minister because he was a cowardly lawbreaker, and full-fat culture-warrior Oliver Dowden cancelled himself by quitting as party chairman.

'Our supporters are distressed and disappointed by recent events,' wrote Dowden in his resignation letter, 'and I share their feelings. We cannot carry on with business as usual. Somebody must take responsibility.'[348]

That somebody should have been Johnson, of course; but he was all brass neck, leaden wits and shag-pile head, and was still being enabled by his loyal lieutenants, who awoke from whatever world they lived in and started shouting gibberish into ours.

'We've done incredibly well,' said Priti Patel about losing four by-elections in a row, two of them by record-breaking amounts.[349] She predicted there would be no further resignations,[350] but rather there would now be a 'moment of reflection'.[351]

Good try, but Johnson was so incapable of reflection that he could easily pass for a vampire. After the disastrous by-election results, he said he would 'listen to voters',[352] but polls showed two-thirds of even Conservative voters wanted him to resign,[353] so he stopped listening to voters again, and instead announced his intention to stay in office until 'the mid-2030s'.[354]

Enough was enough. Tory grandee and sinister count – that's not a typo – Michael Howard said Johnson should quit. The previously fiercely loyal leader of Welsh Conservatives, Andrew RT Davies, began to openly criticise the PM.[355] Johnson's ethics advisor, Lord Geidt, who hadn't found anything wrong with any of the previous scandals, finally admitted the PM probably *had* broken the ministerial code, and resigned with what seemed to be a pitch for a place on the British Olympic Understatement Team: Geidt said it had been an 'exceptionally busy' year.[356] He was the second of Johnson's ethics advisors to find themselves overwhelmed by the workload. His predecessor had quit when Johnson refused to act over bullying by Priti Patel.

Perhaps incapable of finding somebody willing to take on such a Herculean task, or simply deciding that morality was no longer a necessary part of his life, Johnson abolished the role of ethics advisor entirely. This was 'quite a big mistake', in the words of the government's former anti-corruption advisor (and husband of Dido Harding), Tory MP John Penrose. And given the circumstances, he knows a thing or two about mistakes and corruption, so listen up. 'You can't just pretend that it doesn't matter, and that there's no job to be done,' he said.[357]

There certainly was a job to be done, but nobody was doing it.

Not just ethics either: everything stopped.

There was still no agreed plan about soaring energy bills. There was still no workable strategy for food inflation. The Ukrainian refugee scheme was a shambolic free-for-all. Immigration centres were overflowing as applications remained unprocessed. Basic services atrophied, with people waiting up to a year for something as simple as a driving licence.[358] Businesses couldn't import raw materials. They couldn't export finished products. HGVs waited for days at our ports, with food rotting on the docks when it wasn't rotting in the fields. Farming was facing an 'existential crisis'.[359] The NHS was swamped. There was no agreed plan about Brexit, or about the cost of living, food supplies, the Irish border, or practically anything else you could name.

Westminster slowed to a crawl as the PM and his ministers blew the entire energy of government on a protracted public squabble about whether truth was important or was just a petty nuisance, plaguing the God-given right of our gelatinous tyrant to make up new realities as he went along, and then force us to live in them. When asked about the Tory's post-Brexit economic plan, Brexit chief negotiator David Davis said, 'We don't really have an agreed economic plan full stop,' which felt indicative of everything.[360]

Despite all this, Johnson was all bravado, bounding in front of cameras to front it out. 'I've got a new mandate from my party which I'm absolutely delighted with,' he said. 'It's done.'[361]

Only three weeks after Johnson had won the no-confidence vote, dozens of Conservative MPs began submitting letters to force a second vote.[362]

Chicken Kyiv

We had reached July, and it was an absolute casserole.

The government urged the nation to believe nobody was responsible for any of this shambles, least of all the PM; so nobody should resign, and everybody should keep voting for us, and *for God's sake look at the small boats*. Do not, under any circumstances, look at Downing Street. It was powerless people in small boats that were damaging your lives, so nobody should be sacked for fucking up the entire country. Business minister, flocculent walnut and master of the Freudian slip Paul Scully shrugged off any need for action on the grounds that 'politicians are held accountable at the bollock box'.[363]

The Master of Bollocks buggered off to Ukraine in a hurry, so he could pretend to be Churchill again in front of some people who hadn't yet seen through his act. Research found that every single visit Johnson had made to the country coincided perfectly with some Number 10 scandal or other – how could it not, since there seemed to be a new scandal in Downing Street twice a day, and three times on Fridays?

Shit Aslan had turned into the Cowardly Lion, running away to Ukraine whenever things became awkward in SW1. His own party dubbed him Chicken Kyiv, and credit where it's due, that might be the best thing the Conservatives achieved during a dozen years in office.[364]

—

With Johnson off playing soldiers, Dominic Raab was left in charge, and the cubic rube had barely got his chair how he liked it before the entire nation immediately ground to a complete halt. Epic tailbacks grew at our ports, affecting not just HGVs this time, but tourists too, who faced five-hour delays at customs checkpoints.[365] This coincided with the biggest rail disruption for 30 years,[366] while airports found themselves incapable of handling perfectly unexceptional passenger numbers. Vast queues sprang up and thousands of flights were cancelled.

Grant Shapps blamed the airlines for 'seriously overselling' flights and putting two passengers on every seat. I think it's a bit rich for Shapps to criticise two people occupying a single space, when the man had more simultaneous identities than Jason Bourne (somebody else people would travel halfway around the world just to punch).

But regardless, Shapps was wrong, which is such a certainty in life that you might as well tattoo it on your neck. The problem was 'completely to do with Brexit', said Ryanair boss Michael O'Leary. Over 8,000 job applications from EU citizens to be baggage-handlers, security workers or air traffic control staff had been rejected on the grounds of them being a bit too foreign, and now there was nobody to do the work, so everything simply stopped. We'd gone from 'they need us more than we need them' to 'please can somebody sort out our basic shit' in a year.

'We are hide-bound and hamstrung by a government so desperate to show Brexit has been a success,' said O'Leary, 'when it's been an abject failure.'[367]

As everything everywhere fell apart, Tory backbencher and bewitched thumb Mark Jenkinson tweeted that this was 'a vision of Labour's Britain', seemingly at a complete loss about who had been in charge for the last dozen years.[368]

The Streisand Effect

Back in 2003 a relatively unknown Malibu artist began a project to capture the entire California coastline as a montage of interconnected photographs. Among his hundreds of aerial snaps was one which accidentally included the home of Barbra Streisand, and she wasn't happy about it. She sued in an attempt to suppress pictures of her home becoming part of a public art piece.

Streisand lost the case.

Before the lawsuit, the image of her house had only been downloaded six times. In the month following the lawsuit, 420,000 people downloaded it, and the act of drawing attention to something by attempting to hide it became known as The Streisand Effect.[369]

In June 2022, *The Times* published a story claiming Boris Johnson had attempted to give the then Carrie Symonds – at that time his mistress – a £100,000 role as his chief of staff when he had been foreign secretary. It was very similar to the time he'd attempted to give his earlier mistress Jennifer Arcuri a £100,000 job when he'd been mayor of London.[370] The Carrie plan had collapsed after his advisors learned of it.

The story appeared in the first edition of *The Times* and was confirmed by Dominic Cummings and other 'political sources with knowledge of the incident'. It also appeared in the *Daily Mail*, and in a biography by Lord Ashcroft.[371] And then it vanished. After a call from Number 10, *The Times* simply spiked the story. Downing Street said it wasn't true, so all those other sources were ignored and – poof – the news blinked out of existence.

But in the interim, it had been picked up by other outlets, who also reported that the story had been spiked. The incident became Carriegate, which felt like the thousandth gate of the year.

Streisand could have warned them.

Michael Fabricant, if not the most evil Tory then at least the most embarrassing one, took time off from rubbing balloons on his hair, and attempted to dismiss the reports. He tweeted that Johnson had merely asked 'whether a highly qualified person, his wife Carrie, could be Chief of Staff of the FCDO [Foreign, Commonwealth and Development Office]'.[372]

Carrie hadn't been his wife at the time, though. His wife was still Marina Wheeler, who was waiting at home, battling cancer, and attempting to raise a small proportion of his children. That's the first point. The second: I'm not entirely convinced 32-year-old Carrie's degree in Theatre Studies and Art History made her the most highly qualified person for a top role in the nation's diplomatic service.[373]

There were false rumours of a gagging order over the incident, but that wasn't why the story was suppressed. The real reason Number 10 had leaned so heavily on *The Times* was because of fears that more embarrassing details were about to emerge: when Johnson was foreign secretary and independently assessing Carrie for a role as his chief of staff, his fellow MP Conor Burns had walked in to find Carrie performing a blowjob on BoJo on the office sofa.[374]

Was this the reason Carrie had acquired the nickname Princess Nut Nut?[375] Who knows, but you can insert your own gagging-order joke here.

Sex Scandal of the Week

Everyday office life in Johnson's government now included blowjobs, drunkenness, parties, illegality, bullying, dereliction of duty, watching porn, avoiding tax, and hoofing lines of class-A drugs. You must be wondering whether things could get any worse.

Spoiler: they could.

Put your hands together and then keep them to yourself for Chris Pincher. Back in 2017, as yet another round of sexual misconduct allegations swept across the party, Pincher was one of those who resigned – in his case, quitting as a whip after being accused of making unwanted overtures towards Olympic rower and Tory activist Alex Story. Story called Pincher a 'pound shop Harvey Weinstein', and the Tories instantly raced to find out what a pound shop is.[376]

Despite resigning, Pincher, an early adopter of being unable to acknowledge real-world experiences, said, 'I do not recognise either the events or the interpretation placed on them,'[377] only for more allegations to land. Labour's Tom Blenkinsop said he'd also been touched up by Pincher and had responded with a clear and unambiguous 'fuck off'.[378]

After the bare minimum period of fucking off, Pincher was back in government by 2019, and in 2022 Boris Johnson returned him to his former department as the deputy chief whip. There he remained until one July evening, when Pincher became 'incredibly drunk' at Tory drinking den the Carlton Club, and the groping started again.[379] He fondled two men in a part of the club called Cad's Corner, and nothing says 'we deplore this completely unexpected event' like providing it with a named and designated venue.[380]

Pincher swiftly resigned, and it's likely the Tories would have closed ranks, and the incident faded quickly from memory, were it not for the actions of Boris Johnson, both before the incident and after it. When he'd appointed Pincher in February, the PM had been warned about his behaviour by a male Tory MP who had also been the unwilling object of Pincher's handsy affections.[381]

What stage of crazy had we reached? Well, Boris Johnson, star of the previous week's best sex scandal, denied Conor Burns had walked in on him getting a blowjob in the office; and then Neil Parish, star of the week before's best sex scandal, said Chris Pincher should lose the whip, just as Parish had.[382]

Days after the crisis blew up, Johnson still hadn't given clear answers about what he knew of Pincher's history, and it all became terribly awkward. So the PM suddenly abandoned a gathering of Northern Tories, despite them being told he was already 'on the train to Doncaster'. To avoid watching Pincher being roasted alive by the party and press, Johnson sodded off to Ukraine again, opting to roam while the fiddler burned.[383]

Forgive me if this process sounds eerily familiar, but in his absence the government launched a series of short-lived denials followed by partial admissions of anything we'd already discovered. Via a spokesperson, the PM said he had not been aware of any allegations at the time he promoted Pincher. That story lasted a day, before being amended to the PM not being aware of any 'specific' allegations. The next day, four additional specific allegations appeared in the press, and the whip's office confirmed they'd been told about these incidents in February too,[384] but 'under HR law, you are not allowed to deny someone employment on the basis of rumour'.[385]

It goes without saying that under HR law, you aren't obliged to promote anybody to deputy chief whip.

Twenty-four hours later the story morphed again: Number 10 admitted Johnson had known about the allegations when he gave Pincher the job but thought they had been 'resolved'. And to prove Johnson was – as per Guto Harri's instructions – now a serious and trustworthy figure who had learned his lesson about lying to the public, he refused to deny he'd joked 'Pincher by name, Pincher by nature'.

And so, the Groper of Tamworth got his job in the whip's office, responsible for ensuring government business was carried out and that MPs were kept in line. This, despite Pincher's behaviour being so widely known that in May he'd been assigned a government minder to make sure he 'left events without drinking too much and getting into trouble'.[386]

Arch loyalists charged out to debase themselves for the honour of Boris Johnson, the guy who was bullshitting about illegal parties while the country fell apart. Despite Pincher losing his job twice for essentially the same offence, Peter Bottomley said, 'I hope Christopher Pincher is soon back in government',[387] and Michael Fabricant claimed that if the PM had a weakness, it was that he was if anything *too* loyal, which must have come as a surprise to the wife Johnson left at home so he could get blowjobs from Carrie.[388]

So, to summarise: Johnson got in trouble because of his Johnson, Pincher got in trouble for pinching, Fabricant fabricated, Bottomley reached rock bottom, and James Cleverly ... well, he remained the exception to the rule.

The Doolally Army

If Owen Paterson's corruption, Rishi Sunak's tax affairs, Gavin Williamson's knighthood, and David Cameron's lobbying had taught us anything – beyond the fact that Boris Johnson was the Citizen Kane of awfulness – it was that his government was prepared to shrug off absolutely any breach of the rules and permit absolutely any depth to be plumbed, provided it was done by an absolute plum from the government benches.

Brexiteers, they called themselves, a term that was designed to suggest the freewheeling, anything-goes swagger of romantic piracy, without ever acknowledging that pirates were a bunch of dangerous criminals who couldn't be trusted with anything of value. Each act of pillage the government committed was a collaboration between the feckless, bloviating wastrel at the tiller, and the heartless non-entities sleeping, high, drunk, or absently cheering from below decks, safe in the knowledge the damage done would never hit *their* jobs, *their* savings, *their* lives.

Until it did.

Meanwhile those we had assumed to be the last remaining conscientious people on board – the chancellor, the Treasury – were, in large part, just as responsible for delinquency and dereliction as the PM.

Chris Pincher was not an aberration, but a culmination.

—

Among those still defending the PM was grizzling Uncle Fester impersonator Thérèse Coffey, who shuffled onto our television screens to flatly assert that 'Tory men do not have a particular problem over sexual misconduct'.[389] It's a pity she hadn't managed to make it to court to see the conviction of Imran Ahmad Khan for sexual assault barely a month before.

Or the 2020 imprisonment of Charlie Elphicke for sexual assault.[390]

Or Mark Menzies, who paid a 19-year-old male escort for sex and asked him to procure some crystal meth for him.[391]

Or Mark Garnier, who referred to his secretary as 'sugar tits' and ordered her to go shopping for sex toys.[392]

Or Stephen Crabb, who texted a 19-year-old he'd just interviewed for a job and told her he wanted to meet her for sex.[393]

Or Brooks Newmark, who sent 40 sexually explicit images to a single mother,[394] and then to an undercover reporter investigating his habit of sending sexually explicit images to single mothers.[395]

Or Andrew Griffiths, who resigned after sending, in just three weeks, over 2,000 sexually explicit messages to a barmaid that he'd never even met.[396]

Or Damian Green, who resigned after accusations of being handsy with a Tory activist half his age.[397]

Or David Warburton, who promised not to discard his clothes again if the much younger woman he had groped would let him back inside for some more drugs.

Or the Tory MP who had already discarded and mislaid his clothes by the time he found himself hammered and confused in a brothel.

Or the unnamed minister who asked his secretary to 'come and feel the length of my cock'.

Or the other unnamed minister who groped a female journalist and said, 'God, I love those tits.'[398]

Or Roger Gale, who said people subjected to this tsunami of sexual assaults by sitting Conservative MPs were just pretending to be 'wilting flowers', and that the women on the receiving end of this special brand of gallantry had been 'mainly responsible' for the situation.[399]

Coffey had, in fact, been able to overlook all of the other 36 people appearing on a spreadsheet of sexually untrustworthy Tories that was passed around Conservative aides and staffers, as a kind of field-guide to the degenerate and dangerous arseholes they'd be working for.[400] She'd also overlooked Boris Johnson, who was accused of groping journalist Charlotte Edwardes and one of her colleagues during a single meal. One grope per lunch wasn't good enough for him.[401]

Anyway, as you can see, there was no problem with the Tories and sexual misconduct. So the Pincher business came as a complete surprise, despite the BBC's Nick Robinson saying his behaviour was so infamous around Westminster that 'dogs on the street' knew about it.[402]

—

Coffey, Fabricant and the rest of Boris Johnson's doolally army might have been happy to continue defending this dissolute crap, but not many others were. Across the Conservative Party, multiple MPs began refusing to go out and face the press, finally tiring of their role in a stitched-up human centipede through which the PM's bullshit had to pass before reaching the public.

On 5 July Boris Johnson – and this will shock you – suddenly discovered he needed to make an urgent call to Ukrainian president Zelenskiy rather than face the wrath of parliament.[403] It didn't help much. By the six o'clock news, he'd been forced to deliver a humiliating and not totally believable apology for making Pincher deputy chief whip, and two minutes later the resignations began.[404]

First out of the door: Health Secretary and furious gonad Sajid Javid, who said he could 'no longer continue in good conscience'.[405] This took Sunak by surprise, so he also rushed to resign on principle, quickly, before anybody else's principles got the limelight. He was clearly the one the Johnson camp felt most likely to succeed him as prime minister, so they poured abuse on him via their client media, calling him a 'traitor' and launching into 'anyone but Rishi' rhetoric that was conveniently forgotten when Sunak became our wonderful new PM three months later.[406]

Within an hour of Sunak's resignation, the party's vice-chair Bim Afolami quit live on air, with the words, 'I can't serve under the prime minister.'[407] Alex Chalk, who had promised to quit if there was 'any scintilla of a suggestion' of illegality yet had ignored 126 Partygate fines, now resigned in disgust over zero fines.[408]

But naturally, while the dismal Chalk was busy looking for his spine, there still remained the usual collection of gawping, cloth-brained twazzocks, delighted to leap to Johnson's defence.

'I believe the Conservative Party is the only party capable of giving us good government,' said Steve Baker while in the background the government degraded into its constituent atoms and blew away in the wind.[409]

'Walpole did 21 years, and I'd like to see the prime minister do better than Walpole,'[410] said Jacob Rees-Mogg, emitting the energy of Skeletor's cousin who works in accounts.

While the future of the government was being wrangled over by ministry insiders, the Minister in Cider was having her own problems. Nadine Dorries would struggle to keep up with glaciers, let alone fast-moving political events, so all this sudden activity was something of a challenge to the poor, befuddled thing. She publicly congratulated Nadhim Zahawi on being made health secretary just after he was made chancellor.[411] Meanwhile the Garden Gnome of Sauron, Priti Patel, said she would not be resigning as home secretary in case 'something awful like an attack happens', only for her to urge the PM to fuck off 24 hours later, presumably realising Johnson would be worse-than-useless in any crisis that didn't involve a photo-op in Ukraine.[412]

Six more ministers walked out, saying the government 'cannot function'.[413] Almost as if to prove the point, by the end of the day dozens more had quit. There were 43 departures from Johnson's government in 24 hours. It was the first ever example of shits deserting a sinking rat, and yet somehow, while everybody else was busy resigning, one man managed to get himself sacked.

I have a soft spot for Michael Gove. Well, I say soft spot. Technically, it's quicksand. Trying to describe Gove is like trying to find the right words at the scene of a nasty accident. He is an eerie creature, about whom I can't shake the feeling that he should be permanently accompanied by the sound of a theremin. He looks like a mudskipper that's been cursed to work in an office until he repays his debt to a gangster genie. Dozens of ministers had urged the PM to quit, but when the hapless Gove also politely told Johnson he should step down, Number 10 described Gove as 'a snake', and he was fired for his trouble.[414]

He should have been used to it by now: he'd been sacked by every single prime minister he'd worked under.

—

Reshuffles began happening hourly, although it's hard to see how any of them helped Johnson. Nadhim Zahawi was only in his new job as chancellor a day before telling the PM, 'You must do the right thing and go now.'[415] Zahawi had promised he would be 'a man who could get things done', and he was not wrong: in the 24 hours he'd been in post he had lost half his Treasury team, tried to oust his boss, faced a reshuffle, and was suddenly revealed to have been placed under investigation by the National Crime Agency two years earlier.[416]

Michelle Donelan resigned as education secretary after just 35 hours in the job.[417] Perhaps keen to save on paperwork, five more ministers resigned in a single, round-robin letter which read: 'It has become increasingly clear that the government cannot function.'[418]

No shit. Oliver Dowden had resigned as minister without portfolio weeks before, but now we had portfolios without ministers, not least the government's flagship Levelling Up department, which ironically got flattened. Only one of its five ministers remained by the end of the day.[419] The entire government looked like an extended, high-risk game of Gobshite Kerplunk.

Tradition dictated that 'men in grey suits' would visit a prime minister with the bad news that the game was up. After a couple of days of this, it felt like men in white coats would be more appropriate. Everything, absolutely *everything*, was unravelling before our very eyes. It's all very well leading a populist government, but not only was Johnson's bunch no longer popular, they weren't technically even a government anymore. Johnson insisted there was a 'wealth of talent' to replace those who had gone, but the whips were reported to be unable to find anybody willing to fill the empty spaces around the Cabinet table.[420]

As former Conservative MP Rory Stewart put it: 'In the end [Johnson] has to go because he will lose ministers faster than he can replace them and Nadine Dorries cannot do all the jobs in government.'[421] He underestimated her. She could not do *any* of the jobs in government.

Barrel-scraping reached new lows. Peter Bone, a child's drawing of their vampire grandad, was made deputy leader of the House of Commons,[422] from where, rather than backing Johnson, he publicly supported Liz Truss as the next PM. Bone had won the accolade of being 'Britain's meanest boss' when he was paying his staff just 87p per hour, and he had fought against the introduction of minimum wage which, he said, would 'condemn hundreds of thousands to the dole queue'.[423] Right as always, Bone: the minimum wage did not cause any increase in unemployment.[424]

With skills like this, you will not be shocked to learn he was so good in his new role that even Liz Truss sacked him the moment she became leader.[425]

But he was a genius compared to new Northern Ireland minister Shailesh Vara, who was so baffled by his brief that he had to ask if he needed a passport to visit Derry.[426] Fellow prodigy James Cleverly became the third education secretary of the week, and was joined in that department by a new junior, Andrea Jenkyns, who only the previous day had been photographed dressed as an irradiated lemon, giving the middle finger to voters and glaring at the public with eyes like searchlights as she raged around the streets with robotic remorselessness.[427]

From some angles, Britain's government could now be mistaken for a documentary about what happens when you provoke a troop of bonobos: a cacophonous orgy of squabbling, shagging, shrieking, and hurling shit at one another. The previous record for mass resignations had been set in 1932, when the government lost 11 ministers.[428] After two days of turmoil, Johnson finally bowed to the inevitable and announced his resignation, by which time 62 of the government's 172 ministers, private secretaries and trade envoys had quit in disgust.[429]

He'd shattered the record.

Finally, after 12 years of trying, the Tory government had achieved something #WorldBeating.

Fight!

And so, Boris Johnson became the third successive prime minister to have their career destroyed by Boris Johnson. Yet he couldn't even get that much right. After he'd delivered his humility-free resignation address from the steps of Downing Street, a senior government source told journalists, 'That speech was a fucking disgrace.'[430]

You'd think his resignation would mean he'd resigned, but no: the Tories, ever sticklers for tradition, proved incapable of Getting Exit Done, and Johnson stayed in Downing Street, barely even pretending to lead the country anymore. He didn't bother turning up to chair three separate COBRA meetings about various crises,[431] opting instead to throw a party for himself.[432] He'd learned his lesson, clearly. And then it was back to cosplaying, this time dressing up as Tom Cruise to arse around in an RAF jet, like the Honey Monster being cast in a knock-off movie called *Top Gunt*.[433]

It was at this stage of the proceedings that the government chose to stage a no-confidence vote in itself. Labour wanted a confidence vote to shift Johnson out of Downing Street as fast as possible so somebody – anybody – could start addressing the cost-of-living crisis. But Johnson didn't really care about that, he just wanted to save his skin for another few hours and decried the entire thing as a 'deep state' plot to reverse Brexit.[434] Yet the only way he could avoid judgement on his own leadership was to call a confidence vote on the entire government instead. They won, because not even they would be stupid enough to bring down their own government while they were 20 points behind in the polls.

Even so, they couldn't get through the process without a fiasco: Tobias Ellwood, the chair of the Commons Defence Committee, was stripped of the Conservative whip and made to sit as an independent

MP because he'd missed the vote. He'd been in Moldova before heading to the front line in Ukraine as part of his task of 'promoting the prime minister's efforts' there, and couldn't make it back because of the travel chaos overseen by Dominic Raab. So they effectively sacked him for being pretty much the last minister still doing their job.[435]

For the rest of the Tories, it was time to begin the first leadership election of the year. Their top priority was to urgently find a new PM who could prove to the nation that the squalid Boris Johnson was an exception to the norm. Quick and clean: that's what was needed.

This doesn't entirely explain why the party decided the leadership campaign should deprive Britain of a functioning government for an epic eight weeks – longer than practically any modern general election. And as for clean: more than one candidate immediately leaked dossiers listing the seediness of their rivals. Details included the use of hard drugs, prostitutes, tax dodges, illegal loans, and what one Tory source described as 'explicit photographs that could be used as kompromat'.[436]

None of this boded well, but then the boding got worse when a perfectly ludicrous 14 candidates threw their hats into the ring, or 11 if you only count Grant Shapps once. Under party rules, in order to stand, a candidate needed nominations from only eight MPs, but Ben Wallace – who had been favourite just days earlier[437] – couldn't even scrabble together that many, so decided to simultaneously remain our defence minister and a life model for ornamental rubber doorstops.[438]

And so the competition began.

Enter the Dunderdome!

—

The pantheon of numb-nuttery began with Liz Truss, dragged away from Instagram long enough to fill in the application form to become PM. Truss gained widespread support from the usual suspects: Jacob Rees-Mogg, Jonathan Gullis, Mark Francois, and Daniel Kawczynski, catalogue models for the extremes of the human form, and entirely unconcerned that Truss emitted the energy of Philomena Cunk battling to understand the off-side rule.[439] She was what they wanted, and don't let them forget it.

Truss's response to the massive unpopularity of Boris Johnson was to first define herself as the 'Boris Johnson continuity candidate',[440] and then to deny she was the Boris Johnson continuity candidate at all, heavily foreshadowing the stability and fortitude which became her trademark.[441] Some people boast that they are single-minded, but Truss's dedication to efficiency had got her down to a lot less than that.

By stark contrast, Jeremy Hunt's pitch was that he was caring, intelligent and competent, a claim only slightly undermined by the fact he couldn't remember the nationality of his own wife.[442] It's certainly true that he was the least fist-chewingly right-wing major candidate, predominantly by keeping his absolutely horrible political views static while the rest of the party goose-stepped off to find even horribler ones.

In normal circumstances, a candidate for PM being technically sane would be an advantage. Not so with this electorate, which consisted almost entirely of furious 80-year-olds from Guildford who earnestly believed they were living in the movie *Zulu*. This reduced the technically moderate Hunt's chances of victory to practically zero, so to increase his appeal he selected Esther McVey as his running mate, and described her as a 'star'.[443]

Perhaps the star he meant was a white dwarf, which physicists will tell you is incredibly dense, produces absolutely no material of worth, and rapidly collapses.

The other big hitter was Rishi Sunak, standing to become prime minister so he could overturn the economic legacy of Rishi Sunak. Most people's gut reaction was: this can't be our next prime minister, he looks like he's barely out of short trousers! And then the camera panned down, and we realised he was barely in them. Every ensemble ended mid-shin, as if he'd ordered a range of vastly expensive business suits that came with capri pants.

Regardless, his campaign got off to a blistering start, with a fellow MP describing him as a 'treacherous bastard',[444] and the nation reminding him that they weren't thrilled at the prospect of replacing the guy who was fined for illegally partying with the *other* guy who was fined for illegally partying.[445]

Sunak quickly flipped through the Rolodex of things a man with no beliefs can claim and plucked out the card labelled 'Honesty Candidate'. Unfortunately, this didn't entirely square with the subterfuge surrounding his family's tax affairs, so his next idea was to proclaim himself a 'serious candidate for a serious time'.[446] Fat chance. We all still remembered him as the chancellor of the exchequer who didn't know how to use a credit card at the garage where he'd taken the Kia Rio he was pretending to drive.

Days into his campaign, and with two false starts already under his tiny, tiny belt, Sunak then told his fellow MPs that his only weakness was 'striving too hard for perfection',[447] before appearing in front of a *Ready for Rishi* campaign banner on which he'd misspelled the word 'campaign'.[448]

It's almost impossible to satirise this shit.

But I'll try.

Grant Shapps stood out by refusing to get drawn into anti-trans debate, which was the first recorded instance of Shapps having clarity about an identity.[449] His unwillingness to pick on a minority wasn't the only reason Shapps gained little support from the culture warriors on the backbenches: 'The last time Grant said he'd help me win an election,' said one Tory, 'I nearly ended up in prison.'[450] I think we'll put him in the 'maybe' column.

Tom Tugendhat did well in the contest, either despite or because of his zero ministerial experience. He had been fiercely critical of the shallow, moronic approach of Johnson, with his endless repetition of three-word slogans and careless lack of understanding about the Brexit he was selling us. So Tugendhat launched a campaign using a *two*-word slogan, repeating 'Clean Start' 16 times during a single short

TV interview.[451] He then went on to prove his grasp of detail by proposing a new 'Viking Alliance' of nations which he described as 'not all in the EU', and said would consist of Ireland (which is in the EU), Sweden (which is in the EU), Iceland and Norway (both associated with the EU via the European Economic Area).[452]

Kemi Badenoch had spoken of her aspiration to be Britain's first Black prime minister, but it looked like she'd be *Britain First*'s Black prime minister after that fascist organisation gave her their backing.[453] She proudly opposed net zero climate policies on day one of her campaign, then U-turned on day two, telling a husting that she would definitely commit to net zero targets. And then she U-turned again, telling another audience she'd delay net zero.[454]

Thatcher had said, 'The lady's not for turning.' Badenoch spun round so much she'd be a more effective member of society if you painted MOT up one side of her, TEST on the other, and plonked her on the pavement outside Kwik Fit. But, keen to bolster her position as the anti-woke candidate, she held a second campaign launch at which unisex toilet cubicles were pointlessly bestrewn with makeshift 'men' and 'ladies' signs, as though the culture wars had turned her into some sort of effluent-obsessed Mary Wokehouse.

Somehow even this made her more relatable than Nadhim Zahawi, who was now in charge of the nation's money but seemingly couldn't even keep track of what was happening with his own. His leadership hopes barely lasted a week, not least because when asked about the non-dom, tax-haven status of his own vague wealth he told Sky News, 'I don't think it's right to go into numbers because I'll probably get it wrong.'

Also, can I be prime minister please?

Zahawi launched his bid for power with a tagline that looked like a leak of his Facebook password: NZ4PM. He wanted everybody to know he'd reached his high office as a result of his fierce competence and laser-like focus on the details, but if you visited NZ4PM.com it took you to the leadership page of Penny Mordaunt.[455]

That's a real person, by the way, not a minor *Addams Family* character. There were rumours that Jacob Rees-Mogg would also throw his top hat into the ring,[456] and if he teamed up with Mordaunt, we could simply cancel parliament and replace it with repeats of *The Munsters*. But Mogg didn't stand, so we were left with Mordaunt bringing to the contest all the dazzling skills we had come to expect from a Tory leader: she was a former magician's assistant who had failed to make it into the top ten in a celebrity diving show.[457]

To avoid discussing the vast gap in useful experience she could bring to the role, Mordaunt concentrated on reminding the public that she'd been a reservist in the Royal Navy and therefore, 'perhaps better than any other candidate', she understood the military.[458] This must have come as a surprise to Tom Tugendhat, a lieutenant colonel who had served in Iraq and Afghanistan.[459] It also startled those who recalled she'd been defence secretary for a mere 85 days.[460] It definitely stunned senior officers from the navy, because they reported 'she isn't [currently] a trained or paid reservist, she's never qualified or been commissioned', and complained that the martial fervour with which she represented herself was 'deeply misleading'.[461] One of her medals was a badge for drinking rum, for Christ's sake,[462] and her rank – commander – was merely honorary after her 12 gruelling weeks chairing peace-time meetings in the Ministry of Defence.[463]

Daniel Craig held the same honorary rank for playing James Bond.[464]

When she wasn't getting hammered and pretending to be Captain Pugwash, Mordaunt demonstrated her competency for the job of PM via a heart-warming campaign video featuring footage of convicted murderer Oscar Pistorius, who didn't complain, and Jonnie Peacock, who did: he's a Paralympian who hadn't given permission to appear in the video and demanded to be removed.[465] So her campaign had to be edited and relaunched two hours after it started.

She immediately gained the backing of non-league Tory backbencher Jack Brereton, who you'd assume would be a natural Sunak fan, given that he managed to spell his *own name* wrong on a leaflet in which he reassured his constituents that he would 'continue the levelling of Stoke-on-Trent'.[466]

Don't laugh; it can't be easy to only make it halfway to being an idiot savant.

Yet Brereton still somehow managed to outperform Steve Baker. Baker's opening – and, as it turned out, closing – gambit revolved around a poster with a design seemingly stolen from a gym in the 1980s. Behind an image of Baker was a random smattering of squiggles and geometric shapes, one of which intersected with his head to make it seem like he'd been struck with a meat cleaver. That was strange enough, but then we get to his tagline.

Obama went with 'Yes We Can'.

Johnson plumped for 'Get Brexit Done'.

Baker took a radically different approach and opted for: 'I will be relaunching Conservative Way Forward to redefine the territory on which the Conservative Party operates'.

Perhaps worried that this rolled off the tongue a bit *too* easily, Baker had printed it using five different font sizes. The end result looked like a riddle in the style of an eye test, performed by a smug optician with a hatchet through his brain.[467]

Unsurprisingly, his campaign ended – and I mean this very literally – before it had even begun, and he lent his backing to Suella Braverman,[468] a human-sized guinea pig that had mindlessly gnawed through very nearly half of *International Law for Dummies*. Presumably on the basis that she earnestly believed this is what the party, nay, the country was crying out for, Braverman – or should we call her Heinrich Hamster, or maybe Joseph Gerbils? – ran a leadership bid based on a promise to 'eliminate' rules protecting us from being tortured.[469]

If it's becoming hard to keep up with the sheer number of ludicrous candidates, brace yourself for the previously – and indeed subsequently – unheard-of Rehman Chishti, who had seemingly been invented merely so he could be defeated, like a nameless pre-titles bad guy in a Bond movie. YouGov didn't even include him in their list of politicians by popularity,[470] and bear in mind that list included disgraced idiot Neil Hamilton, who hadn't been an MP since 1997.[471]

It didn't help that Chishti's bid for power began with a publicity photo that aimed for 'staring at manifest destiny' but came across as 'I can't work out how to use the toilet on this train'.[472] He gained the support of literally nobody,[473] backed the losing Tugendhat before doubling-down and backing the losing Sunak, and then – poof – he was gone, like the dream that never was.

Fortunately, this lot were quickly whittled down to just eight remaining candidates.

1. Kemi Badenoch (Mary Wokehouse)
2. Liz Truss (Mary Madhouse)
3. Rishi Sunak (Mary Poorhouse)
4. Suella Braverman (Mary Workhouse)
5. Tom Tugendhat (Mary Guardhouse)
6. Penny Mordaunt (Lairy Alehouse)
7. Nadhim Zahawi (Scary Shithouse)
8. Jeremy Hunt (Dopey Titmouse)

—

It fell upon Nadine Dorries, seemingly plucked at random from a brawl outside a kebab shop, to set the tone for the campaign. She began by tweeting an image of Rishi Sunak wielding a knife at Boris Johnson, barely a year after her fellow Conservative David Amess had been stabbed to death. Her colleagues seemed less than delighted. Greg Hands described the tweet as 'appalling . . . dangerous and distasteful', Simon Hoare went for 'utterly, utterly tasteless. Crass and tasteless',[474] and Angela Richardson tweeted, 'FFS Nadine! Muted'.[475]

The format of the leadership election was kept simple, so that Nadine could join in. Tory MPs would vote for candidates in a series of knockout rounds until only two were left standing, and these would be put to the party membership for final selection. Jeremy Hunt was knocked out quickly by MPs who were – let's not be coy – people who had met him and knew what he was like. This was doubly galling for Hunt, since he'd also had a worse leadership election than Stewart Lewis, who still remained well liked by 12 per cent of voters.

It's worth noting at this stage that Stewart Lewis didn't exist: a polling company had invented him, just to see if he could outperform Jeremy Hunt and Nadhim Zahawi.[476]

He could.

Shapps and Javid had withdrawn before voting even started and then, as if to persuade members of the general public that we had any say in this lunatic process, a series of televised debates were organised. The first was won by Tom Tugendhat, with 36 per cent approving of him, compared with just 6 per cent for Liz Truss.[477] So Tugendhat was bumped out in the next round of votes by MPs. The second debate was most notable for the presenter passing out in the middle of Liz Truss explaining that her local hospital was 'being held up by stilts', at which point the entire thing was cancelled for being too dumbfounding even for the Tory Party.[478]

At no point during any of the rounds of voting did Liz Truss hold first place. She only made it into second place when all other options had been ruled out, by which time it was down to her vs Sunak.[479]

She had begun her campaign with a speech in which she outlined her new direction and unassailable leadership potential, which she demonstrated by getting lost while attempting to leave the small function room, wandering into the scrum of journalists, the dreamlike serenity of her expression unable to mask stupefied panic rising behind her eyes.[480]

None of us can say we hadn't been warned. As Truss promised billions in tax cuts, 78-year-old youngsters from the Tory membership briefly felt an erotic twinge in their dusty nether parts and cheered her to the rafters. But in making these promises she'd ignore the Institute for Fiscal Studies, which was already warning that her financial plans would be a calamity. She refused to confirm she would publish forecasts about her mad plans, which had been drawn up by the Office for Budget Responsibility. She wanted to be Conservative prime minister: what the hell did budgetary responsibility have to do with anything?

Or consistency, for that matter? Her leadership bid was built around a refusal to help with the growing, ruinous cost-of-living crisis, and she insisted there would be 'no handouts' under a Truss premiership, only to U-turn on that the moment it looked unpopular.[481]

She then did a second U-turn, this time on her plan to cut public sector pay for everybody outside London. Her team said there had been a 'wilful misrepresentation of our campaign' by people who had accurately reported her own press release, which said she would cut £8 billion by reducing wages. Tory MP Simon Hart said her plan would amount to a £3,000 pay cut for workers in Wales. Other Conservatives calculated it meant an average £1,500 pay cut for teachers, nurses and armed forces outside of South East England, and one called the policy Truss's 'dementia tax' after the disastrous tax proposal by Theresa May.

'That is no longer my policy,' said Truss barely 24 hours after it had been her policy,[482] but by that time members of her own party were already going on record about her 'worrying lack of grip on detail in what is already a woolly economic plan'.[483]

Many things about her were worrying. For one thing, she seemed as thick as a submarine door. She was a wooden, clunky performer, seemingly always caught unawares by perfectly obvious questions. In debates she appeared uninformed and poor at thinking on her feet, or off them for that matter: she was sat down when it became clear she didn't know the difference between Derbyshire and Gloucestershire.[484] She accused the civil service, without any evidence, of being plagued by a 'creeping antisemitism', and then she sent out a press release that praised 'Jewish values' such as 'setting up your own business'. The president of the Union of Jewish Students rebuked her for falling back on 'antisemitic tropes [and] an inaccurate and offensive portrayal of the Jewish community'.[485]

Yet despite her gauche demeanour and her disturbing lack of either firm policy or much common sense, she made it into the final shortlist of two candidates, and literally five minutes later announced she was 'ready to hit the ground from day one'.[486]

Fair's fair: Liz Truss ploughing straight into the ground was one of her few accurate predictions.

—

Meanwhile Rishi Sunak was at least conceding that if he became prime minister his biggest challenge would be fixing the economic crisis left behind by Chancellor Rishi Sunak. He announced we couldn't afford the massive, unfunded tax cuts Truss was selling, although he seemed much cagier about how much fresh austerity there would be in place of tax increases for very, very rich people, such as himself. He'd personally saved £300,000 thanks to cuts to capital gains tax that he had voted through parliament, which is more than half what the average Briton would earn in a lifetime of work.[487] But despite his accurate assessment that the Tories had already wrecked the economy, in most other areas his campaign was a sea of baffling ineptitude, sprinkled lightly with gaffes.

An old video emerged of man-of-the-people Sunak describing the circles he moved in. 'I have friends who are aristocrats,' he said, 'I have friends who are upper class, I have friends who are working class . . . well, not *working* class.'[488] To prove that being worth £700 million and attending Winchester College didn't mean he was out of touch, footage showed him delivering a speech about Levelling Up earlier in the summer, during which he promised to take money out of 'deprived urban areas' so he could ensure 'areas like this are getting the funding they deserve'. He was speaking to Conservative activists in Tunbridge Wells, one of the most affluent towns in one of the least deprived counties in England.[489]

'He says one thing and does another,' said former Tory chairman Jake Berry, 'from putting up taxes to trying to block funding for our armed forces and now levelling up.'[490]

So it suddenly became important for Sunak to demonstrate that he wouldn't just be the prime minister of the Home Counties (and parts of the Cayman Islands), but would appeal to every corner of the four nations that make up the UK (and parts of the Cayman Islands). His first ploy: proving how seriously he took relations with Scotland by referring to the time he had 'set up an economic campus for the government and the Treasury in Darlington', which the geographers among you will note is a town in England.[491]

On and on and on the election went, while these two gawping architects of our national decline played spin-the-bottle to find today's policy. Plans were announced, abandoned, reconstituted and re-launched practically daily, with the pair of them road-testing new material like intensely unfunny comedians given a series of prime-time shows that appeal to 0.3 per cent of the public.

That 0.3 per cent cast their ballots for our new prime minister. They chose Liz Truss. She had won with the narrowest margin of victory recorded since party members had been given the vote.[492]

—

And so, Boris Johnson returned to being a humble MP for the people of Uxbridge, although it's doubtful his constituency noticed. He immediately headed for a holiday in Slovenia, which must have been exhausting because straight after that – literally the following week – he needed a holiday in Greece to recover, and then straight from there to a *second* holiday in Greece, before finally doing some work – he attended the Queen's funeral. And then he shook off his grief with his fourth holiday in seven weeks, this time to the Dominican Republic.[493]

But in case you're worried that he'd be missed by his constituents, let me put your mind at ease: they didn't even know he existed. In the seven years he'd been their MP, Hansard shows he'd mentioned Uxbridge just four times, twice on a single day in 2015.[494]

To a man born with a normal sense of shame, the appropriate move would be to slink quietly out of the limelight and into a long, dark afternoon nap of the soul; but Johnson has no such shame and is no such man. In his statement offering bog-standard support to incoming Prime Minister Liz Truss, he took time out to compare himself to Lucius Quinctius Cincinnatus, the Roman patrician oft-cited as a selfless exemplar of civic virtue and humility.[495] Having led a conquering army, Cincinnatus voluntarily relinquished power and returned to working a plough on his modest farm,[496] which sounds exactly like Boris Johnson, who had to be pried from office in disgrace, then promptly abandoned his duties as an MP so he could go on back-to-back luxury holidays before rushing home to attempt to grab power again.[497]

Boris Johnson left office with the worst public approval rating of any post-war leader.[498]

—

But it wasn't over for him yet; or, sadly, for us.

Back in April 2022, parliament's Privileges Committee had been entrusted with investigating whether Johnson had knowingly misled the House of Commons with his various lies about Partygate. Everybody knew he had lied – it was blindingly obvious – but correct process is important, so the seven members of the committee set about their year-long task.

The phrase 'knowingly misled' was important here: it's easy to *accidentally* mislead parliament, and it happens all the time. MPs mistakenly give the wrong figure during a debate, unintentionally misquote somebody, or are inadvertently inaccurate. We should remember that MPs are, for the most part, human beings, and it's bloody tough to think on your feet, especially if your feet are made of clay and your brain is made of mud. When such a mistake is made, MPs are expected to correct the record quickly, and in almost every case they do.

But *intentionally* lying to the House of Commons is something else again. Nobody should get away with that.

The long-standing chair of the Privileges Committee, Labour's Chris Bryant, immediately recused himself from the inquiry on the grounds that he'd already said in public what everybody knew: that the prime minister was a bullshitter, and when Johnson told parliament 'the guidance was followed and the rules were followed at all times', he knew that he was lying. His top aides had warned Johnson not to use that line in the House of Commons, because they knew it wouldn't stand up to scrutiny.[499]

How could it? Guidance-breaching parties had definitely happened – there were photographs and films of them. They'd definitely been pre-planned: the invitations were not merely emailed around in an unplanned spasm; they had first been given a bit of love and attention by a graphic designer, creating a 'Jingle and Mingle' logo, and urging recipients to 'save the date' for a 'holiday party'.[500] And attendees had known what they were doing was wrong: they'd been recorded saying everything was OK 'as long as we don't stream that we're, like, bending the rules' as they danced drunkenly around the room and your nana died. Johnson had personally been at parties, and had received – and accepted – fines for it.

But Bryant, like pretty much the entire House of Commons, wanted to give Johnson no possible justification for later claiming the committee's process had been unfair. He stood aside, and instead the Tories gave the chairmanship to Labour's Harriet Harman. Her appointment was approved by the entire Commons, and four of the committee's seven members were Eurosceptic Tories.[501] This was no partisan stitch-up.

Harman was supported in her work by Sir Ernest Ryder, a former Lord Justice of Appeals and highly respected judge. And facing them, Johnson's own legal team, led by Lord Pannick, one of the country's top barristers, at a cost to the taxpayer of £245,000.[502] Cuts during the previous decade meant legal aid was unavailable to ordinary members of the public if they earned more than £12,475 a year.[503] Boris Johnson had earned more than £6 million in the year between quitting as PM and the inquiry publishing its report, yet he was given almost a quarter of a million quid to defend himself.[504] The Cabinet Office was unable to name any other former minister whose legal representation had been paid for out of the public purse.[505]

All that money, and it didn't help one bit. After a year of evidence and deliberation, the Privileges Committee found Johnson had intentionally, knowingly misled the House, and committed 'repeated contempts of parliament'.[506] They recommended a suspension from sitting in parliament of 20 days; and to ensure he could respond fairly, they sent the report to Johnson – intended for his eyes only – the day before it was due for publication.

Johnson was having none of it. Rather than face consequences, he resigned from parliament with immediate effect, and accused the committee of being a 'kangaroo court'. It was the latest in a long series of selflessly heroic acts from Johnson, and yet another reason why his admirers' constant habit of painting him as a new Churchill made no sense. Johnson's detractors could back up their criticisms with a list of all the terrible things he had done. Johnson's supporters could only list wonderful things somebody else had done, during a war 80 years earlier, in a vain attempt to sloppily paint over Degenerate Boris with a fresh coat of Noble Winston, and hope nobody noticed.

By June 2023, as the inquiry finished its work, Johnson's war on reality was reaching its climax. This was his *Downfall* moment, when he would slam the doors of the bunker, lash out at demonstrable facts, and go absolutely tonto because he felt fate catching up with him. His final acts as an MP were to leak many of the report's findings, and condemn the process his own government had initiated.

His actions were held to be yet more contempt of parliament. The Privileges Committee report said Johnson had 'impugned the committee and thereby undermin[ed] the democratic process of the House', and was 'complicit in the campaign of abuse and intimidation of the Committee'.

But by this time, Johnson had already run away from responsibility, choosing to spend more time with his lucrative speaking engagements. So the findings of the inquiry didn't affect him much; but in light of his behaviour, the recommended suspension was increased to a near-record 90 days.

Yet it was still merely a recommendation: the committee didn't have power to implement this ban. The report still had to face a debate and a parliamentary vote. There was still a chance to defend the name of the man who had just attempted to torch the standing of parliament, got himself in a terrible muddle, and instead ignited the threadbare remains of his own shoddy reputation.

Out rushed Johnson's defenders, plucked almost entirely from the group he had only just showered with unworthy gongs as part of his ludicrous resignation honours list: the newly knighted Jacob Rees-Mogg, the newly knighted Michael Fabricant, and the always benighted Brendan Clarke-Smith.

It didn't help. When it came to the vote, 352 MPs backed the committee's findings, and only 7 members supported Johnson. Neither Fabricant nor Rees-Mogg were among them.[507] Nor was Brendan Clarke-Smith, who decided to go and watch cricket instead of voting.[508] Johnson ended up with fewer allies than he has children, so who knows: perhaps he's breeding his own electorate? But until that day, his exhausted carnival had reached an end. His influence gone. His parliamentary pass revoked. He had quit parliament, his reputation was in tatters, and Boris Johnson became the first – the only – prime minister in the 750-plus-year history of our parliament to be found to have deliberately misled the House of Commons.[509]

Incessant Carnage

Partygate was never about parties. It wasn't about cake, or DJ sets, or fines. In a sense, it wasn't even about Boris Johnson. It was about the fundamental upon which all moral authority is built: honesty.

Every lie he told chipped away at the integrity of politics and the institution of parliament. Neither of those things had been held in particularly high regard even before Johnson's beshitting of public office, but his wholesale adoption of bullshit as a tool for governing risked it all. If Johnson had been allowed to avoid the consequences of his behaviour – as he had done for most of his life – the framework of Britain's democracy risked collapse. For without agreed truths, there can be no concord about anything. There can be no diplomacy if nothing anybody says can be trusted. There can be no international agreements built on lies. No summits or alliances – not even a legal system could long survive in a world where bullshit takes precedence over truth. The lying had to end, not merely as a punishment for Johnson, but as a social and political imperative.

Of course, not everybody saw it that way. Not the 7 who voted against parliament to support the Bullshitter in Chief; nor, seemingly, the 225 Tory MPs – including ethical paragon Rishi Sunak – who decided to abstain during the privileges vote.[510]

So, what can we say about the outgoing Johnson? Hopefully, not much. He's dominated our conversation for too long, and at risk of seeming hypocritical, I can't wait for a day when politics is reported without any reference to his existence. To the man himself, I would simply point out that there is much to be said for a vow of silence.

Before we take that vow, one last bit of commentary.

Alexander Boris de Pfeffel Johnson is an empty, self-centred, dipsomaniac, bloviating wastrel who presided over the abasement of parliament, one precious standard at a time. He was the worst possible leader at the worst possible time, and his actions over Brexit and Covid will damage Britain, Europe, and much of the Anglocentric world for decades to come. The man is moral degradation made flesh, a pusillanimous, avaricious scoundrel who treated our political system with the same tendresse that torch-wielding barbarians applied to the gates of Rome.

He only got away with it for so long because he was posh enough to get a free ride from our class system, and for a long time plenty of people thought he was funny. He isn't. He is a thug and a vandal, and this latter-day Lord of Misrule didn't leave much unscathed in his wake. He scathed the institutions of government; he scathed our relationship with our neighbours and allies; he scathed our economy, our political stability, trust in our democracy, his own party, and – inevitably – his reputation and political career.

Yet for all the things he destroyed, only his own career mattered a jot to him. Not even his reputation mattered much, because Johnson, perhaps the perfect distillation of narcissism in public life, never gave a tuppenny fuck what anybody else thought of him anyway – not unless their misplaced adoration could boost his endlessly hungry ego, or be turned to his political advantage. He didn't even bother to keep it secret, writing as long ago as 1988 that all an aspiring politician needed for success was to surround himself with 'a disciplined and deluded collection of stooges'.[511]

Those deluded stooges – the likes of Dorries, Rees-Mogg, and (intermittently) Michael Gove – never seemed to realise that for Johnson, all relationships are transactional, and any loyalty goes one way only. He would cast aside any supposed friend, any bilateral agreement, any misapprehending voter, any heartfelt promise, any cherished custom, vital law, or national institution if it didn't offer a direct and immediate benefit to himself. He had long since judged that what happens to Boris Johnson is infinitely more important than what happens to Britain or any of its people.

If this sounds like a bit of far-fetched, partisan exaggeration, you haven't yet understood the character of the man. He is simply incapable of seeing the world as normal people do. He is a full-blown narcissist, which means during a vital chapter in his childhood he somehow failed to fully develop the capacity to emotionally empathise. To make matters worse, his background and education didn't really require much compassion or interest in the wellbeing of others. So he never found any reason to try to learn the skill, or even learn how to ape it for longer than the minimum time required to get what he wants out of you.

His success as the guy employed to make up lies about the EU for the *Telegraph* meant for years he was – quite literally – financially and emotionally rewarded for indulging his worst instincts. It brought to him adoring members of the Tory Party, who reassured him that his aberrant behaviour was exactly what the country needed. So by the time he reached Downing Street – and probably for much of his life before that too – he had become steeped in absolute, limitless selfishness.

Yet even that isn't his most potent psychological flaw. For above and beyond all the petty self-interest and grubby indulgences is the simple fact that he'd never been punished in a way that damaged him significantly. He felt bulletproof. Indestructible. Teflon.

So he became increasingly cavalier about his actions. He was content to stand up in parliament and speak the lies that ended his career as an MP. Why wouldn't he? What consequences could there possibly be for a man who had thus far got away with everything?

To an objective observer, it may seem mad that he still believed in his innocence. Yet I truly believe he did. The reason for his shock at the outcome of the Privileges Inquiry was simple: he had become incapable of thinking anything he did could possibly be wrong. If unlawfulness benefited him, that must mean it was justified, and reality would simply have to bend to fit his worldview. And he thought we were all fools for not behaving just as he did.

This is the nature of his narcissism. This is the quintessence of Johnson.

But now, thank God, he was gone. The incessant carnage of his premiership was over, and we could finally settle into a long and stable period of sound governance.

Part 2
How to Lose a Country in Ten Days

2022
'It Would Almost Be Endearing if it Wasn't So Completely and Utterly Fucking Mad'

Tufton Street

Bearing a black door that looks remarkably similar to that of Downing Steet, 55 Tufton Street is home to most of the right-wing thinktanks that drive the Conservative Party's obsessions. The organisations inside number 55 (or next door in 57) haunt our airwaves and TV news channels, pretty much guaranteed to be the 'not a member of a political party or a comedian' booking on any topical debate programme you can name.

The residents of Tufton Street specialise in two things: turning their ideological preoccupations into government policy, and inventing incredibly bland names for themselves. If your eyes have ever glazed over when *Newsnight* or *Question Time* introduces a guest from the TaxPayers' Alliance, the Centre for Policy Studies, or the Institute of Economic Affairs, half their work is already done.

Their innocuous names disguise the unnerving reality of these groups, who often refer to themselves as 'The Nine Entities', conjuring images of black-cloaked demons chanting around a pentagram in a candle-lit basement. But the primary reason for unease must surely be the secretive nature of the groups. Most in Tufton Street disguise their sources of income – in fact the transparency campaign group Who Funds You lists them as among the most opaque it has ever investigated.[1] Yet research suggests most are funded, directly or via intermediaries, by far-right, extreme libertarian American groups, such as fossil-fuel billionaires the Koch brothers, far-right Trump supporter Robert Mercer, and by oil businesses such as Exxon.

Those are the large US donors we know about, thanks to deep digging by armies of investigative reporters. Millions more dollars have poured into Tufton Street from further anonymous US donors in the last decade.[2]

And groups within Tufton Street are also closely connected to far-right populist parties throughout Europe, including the Sweden Democrats (who trace their organisational heritage back to WW2-era Swedish Nazis)[3] and Brothers of Italy (a party with roots in neo-fascism).[4]

Although the thinktanks are each technically independent, they operate a 'revolving door' policy, with members drifting endlessly between one and another. Many – perhaps even a majority – were started with the aid of Matthew Elliott, founder of Conservative Friends of Russia.[5]

As early as 2012, Elliott was targeted by Sergey Nalobin, whom the UK's Home Office believed to be a Russian spy, 'tasked with building relations with MPs [and] a regular fixture on the Westminster drinks circuit and at political party conferences'. Nalobin became a central fixture in Conservative Friends of Russia. He was introduced to Boris Johnson. He was pals with William Hague. He was endorsed by Malcolm Rifkind, a senior Conservative Friend of Russia who was simultaneously chair of the Commons Intelligence and Security Committee.[6]

In short, Tufton Street, funded by 'dark money' from undisclosed sources, trades on political connections with the Conservative Party and weekly invitations onto BBC politics shows, and uses these avenues to launder a set of pretty extreme views into the public domain.

Among those views are: weakening Europe with a constant barrage of anti-EU rhetoric; economically isolating Britain by separating us from our biggest market; turning the UK into an ethical basket-case with a constant slew of let's-kick-out-migrants posturing; and undermining Britain's long-term energy independence via a constant opposition to green power sources, combined with flagrant climate-change denial.[7]

They don't see it like this, of course. They see it – or at least, sell it – as releasing individuals from the shackles of the state so we can operate in complete freedom (except for having to work for corporations that nobody votes for, and which we can never remove from power).

Their worldview leads to an increasingly extreme, bordering-on-demented form of economic libertarianism, a bracingly crackpot theory advanced by Jacob Rees-Mogg's late father William in his book *The Sovereign Individual*.[8]

Sovereign individualism advocates a world in which any taxation whatsoever is an affront to human rights, where the billionaire class should be free of all responsibility to nations, and where disaster capitalism and super-elitism should be cherished. For all their demands for post-Brexit national sovereignty, the acolytes of this theory believe the super-rich should (in the words of William Rees-Mogg) 'cease to think of themselves as party to a nation', and simply ignore the plight of those left behind, the 'losers' who 'do not excel in problem-solving or possess globally marketable skills'.[9]

Presumably a 'globally marketable skill' describes whatever the hell it was Jacob Rees-Mogg or Liz Truss were doing.

The Nine Entities can fairly be described as a single entity, since the groups meet regularly to 'agree on a single set of right-wing talking points', which will help them to secure 'more exposure to the public'.[10] And the monolithic power of that unified entity has a profound, unelected, and largely opaque influence over politics and news media. Tufton Street drives much of the debate within the right of the Tory Party. Its obsessions bounce straight from those agreed talking points onto GB News and the pages of the *Telegraph*.

Tufton members run the CapX news website. Tufton members

appear almost daily – without anybody mentioning that they're funded by far-right libertarian oilmen from the USA – on British talk radio and televised political debates. Boris Johnson launched one of the groups. Michael Gove is member of another. So is Dominic Raab. Owen Paterson delivered lectures for them. The groups are intimately entwined with government to an extent that it becomes hard to see where opaquely funded far-right lobbyists end, and parliamentary democracy begins.[11]

And don't expect them to be held to task by the BBC either. Richard Sharp only resigned as a director of Tufton Street's Centre for Policy Studies a month before he became chairman of the BBC.[12] The corporation's editorial guidelines state: 'we should make checks to establish the credentials of our contributors and to avoid being hoaxed', but that doesn't seem to apply to contributors pouring out of Tufton Street. In 2019 BBC guidelines were updated again, promising that the affiliations and funding of thinktanks 'should be made available to the audience, when relevant to the context', but when is that guideline actually applied?[13] Tufton Street mouthpieces are invited constantly onto mainstream talk shows, without the audience being told these 'research organisations' are fronting for political dark money.

It's not as though the thinktanks keep this stuff a secret, at least not consistently. One of them, the Institute for Economic Affairs (IEA), was explicitly set up as a front organisation. Today they present themselves as independent, objective researchers, following the socio-economic evidence wherever it leads them, without fear or favour; but they are far from it. One of the IEA's founders gave instructions that it should masquerade as a 'scholarly institute' from the beginning, and warned that it should 'give no indication in our literature that we are working to educate the public along certain lines'. Any honesty 'might enable our enemies to question the charitableness of our motives. That is why the first draft [of the Institute's aims] is written in rather cagey terms'.[14]

Legitimately independent research organisations – actual universities and genuine academic institutes – have got their number. The policy director of the London School of Economics' Grantham Institute said of the Tufton Street grouping: 'This zealous ideological clique are trying to imprint their extreme agenda on government policy. It's clear they enjoy preferential access to some parts of government [. . .] This small cabal is undermining the democratic process, which should be based on robust and open debate, rather than clandestine meetings between ideological bedfellows.'[15]

Yet this clandestine, ideologically driven, and intentionally misleading clique was about to become very important indeed. It wasn't hidden anymore, it was blatant. Above a tweet of a headline reading, 'Has Liz Truss handed power over to the extreme neoliberal think-tanks?', the policy director of the IEA simply replied: 'Yes.'[16]

The Tufton Street agenda was about to step through a rather more famous black door, directly into Downing Street.

A Funeral

On 6 September 2022 Liz Truss became both Britain's prime minister, and a tricky future trivia question. First job: set the tone with a speech as airless and insipid as all those that had gone before. The audience were observed checking their watches to see if time was still passing.

In a mark of respect for her predecessor, she informed her supporters that Boris Johnson was 'admired from Kyiv to Carlisle' before waiting for an ovation that appeared to have popped out for a piddle. She looked around, baffled, as silence reigned for five haunting seconds.[17] Eventually sheer embarrassment forced a tiny smattering of applause from the faithful, so Truss, perhaps feeling she hadn't quite gained the audience's full confidence, reassured them: 'I campaigned as a Conservative, and I will govern as a Conservative.'[18]

Fair play: she was true to her word.

Just as Johnson had before her, Truss filled her new Cabinet with people who were never going to tell her she was berserk. She preferred to let voters discover that the hard way. To facilitate this process, she placed the NHS in the tobacco-stained hands of her closest political ally, Thérèse Coffey, an ideological bedfellow who looks like an extreme close-up of a cross, overheated baby. And then – because running Europe's largest employer isn't enough to keep somebody busy – she made Coffey deputy prime minister as well.

Coffey set about the health service in her inimitable fashion, insouciantly shrugging off the fact that the NHS faced a shortfall of 40,000 nursing staff, which would rise to 90,000 if the government failed to hit its target of recruiting an unprecedented 50,000 nurses in a year. It wouldn't hit that target, obviously, because frankly the government didn't seem to care. Nursing training bursaries had been slashed by the Tories, leading to a 40 per cent drop in student applications.[19] Inflation and a decade of low-to-zero pay increases had eaten 20 per cent of nurses' wages, and the government seemed determined to do nothing to resolve that situation. Poor wages meant retaining staff was becoming more difficult, and as those who remained struggled with soaring workloads, stress levels rocketed.

A record 400 burned-out NHS staff were quitting due to stress every single week – that's over 20,000 a year. And the problem showed no signs of slowing, as the pandemic continued to quietly ratchet up the pressure while the government mostly ignored it.[20] During the weeks the Tories had spent pootling around in search of a new leader, Covid hospitalisations hit 15,000 at least once every single month.[21]

Result: the number of nurses leaving the NHS in London alone had risen by a quarter in a year,[22] and over two-thirds of NHS Trusts reported a 'significant and severe' impact from staff leaving for better-paid jobs in retail or hospitality.[23] Why wouldn't they? The typical starting salary for nursing was around £27,000.[24] The starting salary for the Aldi graduate programme was £44,000,[25] and trainee managers at Aldi have to wipe surprisingly few geriatric arses.*

---

* Figures correct in December 2022.

So we weren't retaining enough existing staff, we weren't creating a cohort of replacement staff, and we weren't importing nurses from overseas either: the colour of our passports was far more important than, y'know, breathing.

In short, the Tories had created appalling working conditions in the health service: lousy pay, gruesome hours, and shocking levels of pressure. And given the missed opportunities to resolve the situation, it's hard to believe it was unintentional, as demonstrated by the latest beef-witted ministerial decision: not only did Coffey refuse to give nursing staff a pay increase to match inflation, she also went on TV to say nurses were welcome to quit if they wanted to, and that she didn't care much anyway because she had 'an open route for people to come into this country' to replace them.[26]

I'd have paid good money to be a fly on the wall when Suella Braverman heard about this open invitation to tens of thousands of fresh immigrants. Braverman, who is what happens when a Horcrux gets into a guinea pig, had replaced Priti Patel as home secretary and took to it like a house on fire: people screaming, calling the emergency services, desperately trying to save their children, etc. The traditional role of home secretary in any Tory administration is to be as obdurate and mean-spirited as humanly possible, but Braverman took it to new extremes. She appeared determined to make Patel look like Nelson Mandela.

As for the rest of the reshuffle: presumably on the grounds that you should always give your audience what they expect – and by now people overseas expected Britain to produce something idiotic, with a misleading label – the new foreign secretary was James Cleverly.[27]

Truss was determined to draw a line under the grubby cronyism of her predecessor's era, which must be why Jacob Rees-Mogg's business partner Dominic Johnson was appointed as trade minister. But he wasn't an MP, which meant he had to be given a peerage so he could speak in Westminster. He served in the role for just 26 days before being sacked by Rishi Sunak, but he remains a Lord for life, claiming £332 per day, tax free.[28]

A single person on Universal Credit could claim £334 per month.[29]

Dominic Johnson had donated over a quarter of a million pounds to the Conservatives.[30]

And speaking of his pal Jacob Rees-Mogg: in July the sinister minister had declared, 'I have no desire to serve another prime minister', but he now served another prime minister as business secretary in Liz Truss's Cabinet.[31] Meanwhile, in charge of finance was Kwasi Kwarteng, whose previous ministerial responsibilities were for Brexit, business, growth, and energy. All of those things were going just *swimmingly*, so he was invited to continue his winning streak, this time as chancellor.[32]

Kwarteng was a big fan of small states, not listening[33] and cryptocurrency,[34] so to prevent him sending visitors into a trance with his small-talk, Truss appointed as chief secretary to the Treasury Chris Philp, who would certainly keep meetings invigorating with his queasy resemblance to a shaved mandrill that has escaped its pen.

And then the new PM was off to Balmoral for the formality of kissing hands with the monarch and the official transfer of power. Photos emerged showing the Queen looking happy to meet Truss, and even happier a moment later to be no longer meeting Truss.[35] But it was clear that after seven decades of service, her majesty was very frail indeed. Those photos turned out to be the last ever taken of Elizabeth II.

—

When she passed away, just two days later, there was an almost universal outpouring of grief. Britain contained its fair share of ardent monarchists, and a good helping of passionate republicans too. In the middle was a solid mass of those who loved the monarchy when they were asked to think about it, and those for whom the Royal Family was little more than a largely irrelevant, long-running soap opera that we didn't watch. But all negative opinions were set aside as the nation expressed a sense of collective loss; and of respect for the person, if not always for the institution of which she was the head. The Queen had been a remarkable figure of duty and constancy, in a world where those attributes seemed increasingly rare.

Britain entered ten days of national mourning, and parliament was suspended.[36] But it wasn't long before people began to demand something – anything – from our government: the energy crisis was still looming, unpayable bills still threatened, and the Tories had spent an unconscionable seven weeks in policy purdah while a few hundred octogenarians from Maidenhead fannied about choosing a new PM. And now there was another fortnight of intensively planned inactivity while we buried the Queen.

After performing multiple U-turns during her leadership bid, Truss now seemed to think this was the key to her success, and immediately applied the strategy to the new monarch. Her spokesman announced she would accompany King Charles on a tour of the UK during the mourning period.[37] Then the next day she announced that she wouldn't be doing that, and 'never intended to'. This turned out to be one of her longer-lasting policies.[38]

Our confidence boosted by the PM's clear demonstration of her lack of brain and courage, she then completed a one-woman performance of *The Wizard of Oz* by introducing us to her missing heart. Truss pootled off to the BBC studios where she haltingly attempted to convince Laura Kuenssberg that forthcoming tax cuts would be entirely fair, while in the background a massive chart showed the poorest tenth of people would gain just £7.66 a year, and the richest tenth would gain £1,800.[39]

The prime minister then zoomed off to Washington, far enough from Britain that she wouldn't have to hear our screams of frustrated outrage when she admitted a trade deal with the United States wasn't even on the cards anymore.[40] Since 2016 Brexit evangelists had held up the promise of such a deal as a nailed-on benefit of our new freedoms, and a major prize that – as with all Brexit promises – was just over the horizon, if we all just believed a bit more emphatically.[41] It was on that basis that we'd gleefully hurled away our trading relationship with the body that bought almost half of everything we sold, but now, in the blink of an eye – or in Truss's case, many, many blinks of an eye – it was gone.[42]

And then – after unbelievably managing to get the White House to vocally consider suspending the 'special relationship' with the UK[43] – she flew home to deliver what she was sure would be a triumph, as Kwasi Kwarteng delivered their joint plan to reinvigorate the economy.

Operation Rolling Thunder

As it turned out, during the mourning period for the Queen, Truss and Kwarteng hadn't been quite as idle as we'd assumed, although Christ in spandex pants, don't you wish they had?

Before delivering their plan, the new leadership team needed to prepare the nation. The inner circle consisted of Truss, Kwarteng, Jacob Rees-Mogg, Chris Philp, and a mouse-fart made flesh by the name of Simon Clarke.

For reasons of fathomless mystery, Truss felt the best person to reassure the public would be Clarke, who was given a neat brush of the hair, handed his packed lunch, and sent off to sell a fat slice of stark madness to ITV's Robert Peston. None of Clarke's handlers had thought it necessary to explain to him that admitting basic governance was beyond the government's capabilities wouldn't boost confidence, so Clarke unveiled to Peston his theory of why everything was so unutterably shit. It was, he said, because since 2010 not one of the plethora of Tory governments had been granted 'a clear run at events'.[44]

'It has been one crisis after another,' he went on, hoping against hope that nobody had spotted him personally voting for each crisis. Bad news on that score, Simon. The parliamentary record shows Clarke's votes contributed to the Brexit crisis, the supply chains crisis, the NHS crisis, the housing crisis, the welfare crisis, the crisis in the legal service, and the ongoing human rights disaster that was the management of migration.[45] He even managed to be one of Boris Johnson's staunchest and final defenders during the Partygate crisis.[46]

Few held out much hope that these dolts would do well, but not many of us expected what happened next. The Office for Budget Responsibility (OBR) had prepared an economic forecast for Kwarteng, which was waiting on his desk as he took office, and which he either totally ignored, or simply refused to publish because it showed his plans were dangerous nonsense.[47] Truss and Kwarteng sacked the permanent secretary to the Treasury, whose job it was to identify the parts of their policies that were wall-eyed madness.[48] And then they set about their grand plan, which they had ostentatiously named 'Operation Rolling Thunder'.[49] They'd borrowed the title from a US offensive in the Vietnam War, and it does make you wonder how Kwarteng gained his double-first in history from Cambridge without ever learning how that worked out for the Americans.[50]

Never a bashful man, Kwarteng bristled with confidence as on 23 September he strode into parliament to present what he called a 'fiscal event'. The speech came with a name that got the year right, but nothing else – Growth Plan 2022 – and Kwarteng delivered it with swaggering delight.[51]

He began by reassuring the public about the cost of energy. The government would borrow practically without limit to keep domestic bills under some kind of control, a move which was at the upper end of what had been predicted by currency and bond traders, but which they were just about willing to accept. What they couldn't accept was just how raddled the zero-tax, zero-responsibility libertarian wingnuts now running the country were about to become.

After a decade of Tory economic focus on keeping down public debt, our debt was already edging towards a peacetime record of 100 per cent of GDP.[52] The costs of Covid still had to be paid, the UK had an ongoing productivity problem, the damage from Brexit was profound;

and notwithstanding our local problems, most of the world was sliding into what many felt would be a decade-long recession.[53] Against this background Kwarteng, in policy lockstep with Truss, took it upon himself to set fire to what was left of the economy.

Instead of attempting to balance the books over the coming years, he cancelled the planned rise in corporation tax that was intended to service debts. This raised eyebrows in the City. Then he scrapped the 45 per cent top tax rate entirely, which raised heart rates. He reduced the Treasury's income from the basic rate of tax, which raised blood pressure. And finally, he cancelled the planned increase in National Insurance, slashed income from stamp duty, and accelerated spending on infrastructure projects, all of which raised absolutely everything except for market confidence in the UK.

As he delivered this fairy-tale there was an air of shocked silence even from some on the Tory backbenches, but then he really hit his stride. He announced 40 new 'investment zones' where taxation, building regulations and workers' rights could be largely abandoned, in the mad belief this would unleash the caged beast of competitive Britain.[54] In truth, it would do little more than unleash epidemic levels of tax-avoidance, relocate valuable investment to locations where it would generate less value for the nation, and lead to a reduction in both rights for workers and desperately needed income for the Treasury. A 2021 report sent to the Treasury by the OBR had said as much, so it was hardly a secret.[55]

And then, as a final fuck-you to common sense, Kwarteng scrapped the cap on bankers' bonuses, so that some of the richest and most irresponsible gamblers in the land could suddenly become far, far richer in the middle of a cost-of-living crisis.[56]

Even if you overlook the moral squalor of an economic model in which the rich get practically everything while the rest of us battle over crumbs from their table, trickle-down economics simply doesn't work. That's not just an opinion, it is a demonstrable fact. It's been attempted many times and failed consistently. A study by the London School of

Economics looked at 50 years of outcomes in 18 nations who implemented trickle-down policies and found giving tax cuts to the rich as a way to boost investment only benefited – you guessed it – the rich, who simply pocketed the tax cuts. Investment remained flat. Inequality increased, but not growth. The wider economy saw practically no benefits in jobs or economics.[57] Measured against its own advertised terms, trickle-down is an abject failure.

Yet this time the Tories claimed their plan was nothing like trickle-down economics. Why would anyone conclude it was? Kwarteng would simply borrow untold billions, which ordinary workers would have to repay in their taxes. And then he'd hand those billions to people who had got rich by exploiting those workers, hoarding the profits, and avoiding paying their own taxes. And then – and this is the really clever part – he'd trust those exploitative, tax-avoiding hoarders not to exploit workers, avoid tax or hoard profits this time. And then at some unspecified point in the future, money would drip from the rich down onto the rest of us, and life would be rosy again.

It was bound to work and was nothing like the much-disproven trickle-down economics; to which I say, if it walks like a duck and quacks like a duck, it's a duck. And in this case, it was a duck, and very much a dead one too.

Eton-educated Kwarteng hadn't yet realised any of this as he popped off to celebrate his success. He went straight from the traditional dispatch box whisky to a champagne reception with the hedge-fund managers who had urged him to do all of this, while they had made a fortune betting that it would crash the economy. They described Kwarteng as a 'useful idiot'.[58] Chris Philp would also have qualified as a useful idiot, if only somebody could find a use for him. Still, halfway there, Chris, so chin up.

Inside the swirling, semi-incestuous gossipsphere of finance, government and media, the traders' contempt for the Kwarteng/Truss mindset was hardly a revelation. A former Downing Street staffer, now working as an advisor in the City, went on record to say, 'The gulf between the free-marketeers and what the free market actually thinks of the free-marketeers is hilarious.' After a dinner attended by hedge-fund managers a week before the budget, it was reported, 'They were all supporters of Truss and every one of them was shorting the pound.'[59] Everybody knew what was going to happen, but they did it anyway.

One of those Truss-backing hedge-fund bosses, Crispin Odey, reportedly made returns of 145 per cent by betting the Truss/Kwarteng plan would fuck the rest of us up. Another who gambled massively against us was among the group of City financiers who donated £3.6 million to the Tory Party in the previous year.[60]

So the hedge-funders did well out of the budget, and the Tory Party did well out of the hedge-funders; but the cost to the rest of us was vast, and will probably hurt you and me for decades. Let's not forget that it's *you and me* who would have to repay Kwarteng's unfunded borrowing of £45 billion, equivalent to a pile of £10 notes towering 279 miles into the air, so they could give tax breaks to people who already had more money than they could spend. That's a stack of wasted cash so tall that the International Space Station would literally crash into it, which would go down as a pretty expensive disaster, but probably still not as expensive as the one Kwarteng unleashed.[61]

It took literally seconds for the effect of the catastrophe to show in the markets, but days for the government to realise. In the four days following the budget, the UK markets lost over $500 billion.[62] To put this into context, the Brexit argument was that we were losing £350 million a week on membership of the EU. During trading hours over that long weekend, Kwarteng's budget lost us £350 million every 21 minutes.[63]

Meanwhile in Downing Street, or perhaps Narnia: 'Great to see sterling strengthening on the back of the new UK Growth Plan,' tweeted Chris Philp, as the pound fell to its lowest ever level against the dollar,[64] lower than any time since Alexander Hamilton stopped rapping long enough to invent the US currency.[65] Sterling plummeted to within one per cent of parity with the dollar. Under the previous Labour government, the pound had bought you $2, and now it barely bought half that.[66] It seemed Kwarteng liked cryptocurrency so much, he'd turned sterling into one called Shitcoin.

'I think markets and others will see that we have a credible and responsible plan,' continued the ever-accurate Philp,[67] while outside his enclosure a cataclysmic rout on the bond markets spiralled out of control, with investors selling UK gilts at a faster rate than any time in history.[68] Government borrowing costs soared to three times higher than they'd been before the chancellor opened his mouth, just in time to punish us three times more for pointlessly borrowing billions so we could stuff the pockets of the wealthy.[69]

The International Monetary Fund intervened not once – which would have been embarrassing enough – but twice to urge the government to reconsider its demented plan.[70] The Bank of England rushed to step in, conjuring up £65 billion of imaginary money to buy security in our own bonds in a desperate attempt to prevent a £1.5 trillion – yes, trillion – collapse of pension funds, which experts predicted was just hours away.[71] The rescue worked, but the budget was still reported to have cost pensions £75 billion.[72] That's £1 per second for 2,325 years. Or if you prefer, Kwarteng cost our retirement plans £3,600 per hour, every single hour since Hannibal marched his elephants over the Alps.

Economically Reckless and Political Suicide

Back in 2012, Truss and Kwarteng had contributed to *Britannia Unchained*, a book in which they, Priti Patel, and Dominic Raab had been made to stop chewing the furniture long enough to put their delusions down in writing. Sadly, their fellow MPs from the other factional groupuscules that made up the Tory Party hadn't been paying much attention – certainly less attention than expert economists who had reviewed *Britannia Unchained* and pointed out its 'factual errors' and 'slipshod research'.[73] I'd have gone with 'demented ravings' myself, but I'm not as polite as economists are.

And sadly, their fellow Tories also hadn't paid as much attention as the Treasury officials who had cautioned Truss and Kwarteng that their plan would spark market chaos.[74] Or the OBR, which wrote an alarming assessment of the dangers, which Truss and Kwarteng subsequently withheld from publication.[75]

The thinktanks, newspaper proprietors, right-wing talking heads and functionally loopy backbenchers who powered Truss to Downing Street had been agitating for these policies for years, urging the party endlessly right, right, right. Her economic programme wasn't an accident, but a destination they'd actively sought for decades. They preened and puffed and pontificated about how amazing everything would be now that their singular wisdom had, at long last, been made manifest.

Truss was not an aberration, but a culmination.

So these policies should not have come as a great shock to the Tory Party, but seemingly they were so stupefied after being battered by years of incessant calamity that it caught them unawares. Their shock was so great that they could barely find the strength to rush to the nearest bar to get tanked up on expenses and blab to salivating journalists.

'Liz is fucked,'[76] said one backbencher, seemingly triggering an avalanche of brutal divorce chat during what should have been Truss's honeymoon period. 'Everyone who isn't mad hates it,' a Tory ex-minister told *The Times* about the budget,[77] while another called it 'economically reckless and political suicide'.[78]

Naturally, opposition parties hated the budget, but even among Tories the general opinion was that the entire plan was built not to serve the economy, but simply to scratch a wild ideological itch. 'This whole thing boils down to infectious childlike optimism in Downing Street,' said one. 'It would almost be endearing if it wasn't so completely and utterly fucking mad.'[79] Such was the collapse in confidence that one Tory MP told Sky News, 'They are already putting letters in as they think she will crash the economy.'[80]

They were not wrong.

Crayons

So to summarise: Liz Truss had been in office only three weeks, during which she'd managed to finish off the Queen, kybosh the 'special relationship', abandon our hopes of future trade, spectacularly crash the economy, and start a backbench rebellion to remove her from office.

Believe it or not, this still qualified as the calm before the storm.

Thirty years of chin-up, chest-out, arms-akimbo certainty that the Tufton Street libertarian agenda was exactly what the market was yearning for had evaporated in an hour, and suddenly the thrustingly confident Kwarteng and Truss were nowhere to be seen. For a full week, Truss was invisible,[81] and the closest we came to a hint that she still existed was a rumour that she and the chancellor had locked themselves in a room in Downing Street and engaged in a series of blazing rows.[82] While the nation waited on tenterhooks for some suggestion that Number 10 knew what was going on, the only statement Truss made was to congratulate Italian fascists on their electoral success.[83]

Things were not great for Truss, but that didn't mean they couldn't be made even un-greater. For example, the Tories had probably hoped she'd draw a line under the grotesque and lavish personal spending habits of Boris Johnson, and his wayward approach to obeying rules. But on the very day the mini-budget was being squeezed, steaming, onto the nation's doormat, Truss's past suddenly turned up, with receipts.

First, it transpired that during her final Instagram-spackled year at the Home Office, departmental credit-card spending for things related to looking electable in photos had increased 45 per cent. There had been £4,000 to a top hairdresser, £10,000 blown at Fortnum & Mason, £1,800 on what appeared to be a 'wellness app', and – in words that should soothe your mind about being led by people who don't read books, merely apply crayons – £900 to a company that provides adult colouring books.[84]

Maybe this was to prevent her from scribbling, toddler-style, all over her pristine new walls, since Truss had painted over Boris Johnson's gaudy £840-per-roll gold wallpaper.[85] Thousands had been spent at high-end restaurants, and for some reason the Home Office under Liz Truss felt it necessary to spend £1,841 at the online store of Norwich City football club. It's probably just a one-in-a-million coincidence that Truss is a Norwich City fan.

But this was nothing compared to her travel arrangements. In the first six months of 2022 she'd blown a mindboggling £1.8 million on overseas visits, something her predecessor Dominic Raab had managed to do for just £67,000. She spent half a million quid to charter a private jet to Australia, rather than take a scheduled flight on which the most expensive ticket was just over £7,700.[86] Truss's jaunt to the USA had somehow cost £229,000, when her ministerial colleague Lord Ahmed had managed to do it for £6,700.[87]

'We are committed to using public money responsibly,' said a spokesman; and we can only assume he hadn't had a chance to go outside and catch up on the economic news.[88]

So no change from the Johnson era of squander, and seemingly no change from the squalor either: it was revealed Truss's new chief of staff, Mark Fullbrook, wasn't even being paid by Downing Street, and was merely seconded to Number 10 from his actual job at his lobbying firm, Fullbrook Strategies. Not only did this finally demolish the already crumbling, paper-thin wall between (on one side) paid lobbyists acting as a shill for private concerns and (on the other) national governance that's supposed to be for the good of everybody; the move could also allow Fullbrook to avoid paying a normal level of tax on his income. This news broke just days after the government had junked reforms designed to limit so-called off-payroll working, thus making Fullbrook's dubious employment status easier.[89]

'This is not an unusual arrangement,' said a spokesman about Fullbrook's employment status.

'I've never heard of such an arrangement, and it is obviously quite wrong,' said a prominent backer of Liz Truss.[90]

The Tenth Day of Truss

In a vain effort to soothe the markets, Kwarteng issued a statement saying he'd do another fiscal plan in two months' time on 23 November. It was a heroically bold prediction about how long his career was expected to last, and within days he began telling people the plan would actually be brought forward to October. That prophecy was pretty bold too, as it turned out.[91]

While Truss and Kwarteng alternated between hiding, panicking and screaming at one another in the back rooms of Downing Street, lesser mortals were shoved in front of the cameras. The Work and Pensions departmental pixie Chloe Smith escaped from the set of *The Rings of Power* long enough to attempt to explain away a £55,000 tax cut for millionaires,[92] implemented by a government that had ended the £20-a-week uplift for people on Universal Credit.[93] It was not an easy thing to defend once you do the sums and see that £55,000 is 52 years of £20 Universal Credit uplift.

But in the interest of balance, I should record that not all opinions on the budget were negative. It's only fair to log the thoughts of its fans, just for posterity. So let's hear from the residents of Planet Zog.

Brexit-backing genius Andrew Bridgen claimed the pound hadn't crashed at all and went on to assert that the entire crisis – which he also said didn't exist – was because we didn't do enough fracking in 2020.[94]

Brexit-backing genius Greg Smith said the budget had put us on a path to 'serious economic recovery' as the economy crumbled and our life savings teetered on the brink.[95]

And Brexit-backing genius Crispin Odey said the pound had only crashed because of Remainers.[96] To be fair, that last one is technically correct: Truss campaigned for Remain. But Odey's patriotic fervour was slightly undermined by the fact that two days earlier he'd described his successful bets against UK government bonds as 'the gifts that keep on giving'.[97]

Meanwhile Brexit-backing genius Lord Frost told BBC Radio 4 listeners, 'I don't think anything's gone wrong actually,'[98] and Brexit-backing genius Dan Hannan claimed sterling only went off a cliff because Labour leader Keir Starmer did a good speech.[99]

While this lot played 'blame the lefty' in their increasingly turd-bestrewn right-wing sandpit, all hell was breaking loose. More than 40 per cent of mortgage products were withdrawn from the market,[100] which at least delivered Kwarteng's dream of wiping out stamp duty: nobody could buy a house anyway.

Our credit rating teetered. Britain had held an AAA rating since 1978 – even through the fabled economic low-point of the Winter of Discontent – until a combination of Tory austerity and Tory Brexit made us lose it;[101] and now Kwarteng's budget caused the rating agency Moody's to threaten yet another downgrade on the grounds that the budget could 'permanently weaken the UK's debt affordability'.[102] The chief economist at UBS Global Wealth Management went yet further, stating, 'Investors seem inclined to regard the UK Conservative Party as a doomsday cult.'[103]

It was the tenth working day of Liz Truss's premiership.

Oxford Commas Must Die

The entire nation's attention was taken up by this latest absurd failure, but that didn't mean the rest of government had been idle.

Meet recently appointed Home Secretary Suella Braverman, whose approach to her role involved aiming squarely for 'Priti Patel 2.0' but landing with a thud on 'Secret Squirrel gets cross at logic'. She began her brave stand against rational thought by telling the police she expected them to 'cut homicide, serious violence and neighbourhood crime by 20 per cent'. Not *solve* more crimes, you notice, simply stop a fifth of them from happening in the first place. She didn't bother to explain how this was to be achieved, and she didn't give them any additional resources.

The most obvious way to do this is to simply stop recording 20 per cent of crimes, or to misrecord them as less serious incidents. That was the conclusion of a 2015 report commissioned by the Home Office, which is exactly why such crime-stats targeting was abandoned. Braverman's sudden demand that police ignore that evidence so they could do their job of – let me check my notes – *gathering evidence* was a good indication of her headline-grabbing embrace of failure, and led one senior police officer to decry this 'throwback to the incoherent ignorance of past politicians'.[104]

She then launched into her not-medically-proven ideas for the treatment for poor mental wellbeing, which boiled down to telling stressed-out Whitehall staff to watch *Love Island* until they felt happy again.[105] *Love Island* had been such a success for mental health that two participants and one presenter had been driven to take their own lives, and a further two contestants ended up hosting *The Full Treatment*, a programme dedicated to dealing with the mental trauma arising from the show.[106]

But Braverman's therapy sessions were a positive healthcare nirvana compared to those delivered by the health minister, an adult-sized, cigar-chomping toddler named Thérèse Coffey who, faced with record-breaking waiting lists and the highest Covid hospitalisations in a year, chose to launch an urgent war against people using the Oxford comma.[107] It's not as if we lacked other things for her to focus on: she was part of a government that had inherited from Labour a guaranteed 48-hour waiting time to see a doctor,[108] but was now promising a grateful nation they would have to wait no longer than 18 weeks.[109] Twelve years of austerity and neglect, exacerbated by a Brexit which drove 22,000 NHS workers away,[110] had left the people of Britain with the worst access to healthcare in Europe.[111]

Some of the mammoth NHS backlog was certainly caused by Covid, but by no means all. The waiting list before the pandemic was already a staggering – and record – 4.3 million,[112] but now it had reached 7 million. Something needed to be blamed, and you can bet your bottom dollar – which by now was worth exactly the same as your bottom 50 cents had once been – that the government would look for something to blame other than 12 years of mismanagement and underfunding by consecutive Tory administrations.[113]

So the Tories invited a dozen private companies to bid for a £1 million contract to lead the inquiry into the UK's response to the pandemic.[114] Two thirds of those invited to bid had already been given government contracts to *deliver* the UK's response to that very same pandemic, and they were now being invited to pass independent judgement on how well they'd performed.[115]

This obviously sounds much less mad if you imagine it being barked from the back of a truck full of heavily armed Blackshirts towards a cowed and terrified public.

Coffey then began a process of 'reviewing' – with an aim of abandoning – promised measures to tackle obesity, which led to 26 former health ministers criticising the cancellation as 'unwise and dangerous'.[116] And if you need an indication of how much Cabinet-level stability the NHS has had down the years, just contemplate the fact that 26 former health ministers were available at short notice.

Coffey ignored them all, of course, and then scrapped the publication of a long-promised white paper on improving health equality, perhaps feeling that the 19-year gap in life expectancy between rich people like her and poor people like you wasn't something she needed to worry about.[117] That was certainly the view of sources close to the Department of Health: 'My understanding of why they've pulled it is [that it's] ideological – the white paper is an affront to this government's view of what makes for health.'[118]

And that's what the actual health minister did in her first two weeks in the job.

Agreeing with Jacob

Brexit news, and it was going so well that the government literally abandoned having a minister for Brexit opportunities.[119] The last person to hold that role was, coincidentally, the last person you'd want to hold *any* role: Jacob Rees-Mogg, Nosferatu attempting to pass unnoticed at a Bible study group. He'd had a splendid first few weeks as a Truss appointee, this time in charge of Business, Energy and Industrial Strategy, and in the face of inexorable climate disaster he declared his wish to 'get every cubic inch of gas out of the North Sea'.[120]

But that wasn't enough to satisfy Jacob's dark cravings, so he also proposed lifting the ban on fracking[121] and suggested in parliament that anybody unwilling to sit through an earthquake per day[122] while they waited for their kids to boil alive was only complaining because they'd been paid to whine by Vladimir Putin.[123]

So let's take a quick peek at funding. Rees-Mogg took £22,000 from the seemingly ever-present Crispin Odey, a fossil-fuel investor. In April 2022, just as other investors were scurrying away from Russia, Odey's fund bought shares in a Russian mining giant whose largest shareholder is on a US Treasury Department list of oligarchs close to Putin.[124]

But JRM never met a fact he couldn't deny, and in the same week he was pimping for greenhouse gases, his ongoing allergy to evidence was, ironically, very much in evidence.

In his previous role – leading the epic hunt for Brexit opportunities – he'd launched a public consultation to gather opinions about the return of the imperial measurements. This was presumably on the grounds that he believed Britain would boom again if only we could be made to stand for hours in the supermarket, trying to work out how many florins change we get from two-bob after buying a gill of rice. But Rees-Mogg's independent fact-finding mission hadn't been as advertised. The survey didn't include any way for people to say they *didn't* want to return to the imperial system, only ways to choose which brand of *Agreeing with Jacob* the public hated the least.[125]

Bear Traps

No matter how much they tried to ignore it, large, blunt, fast-moving nuggets of reality kept striking the new Truss administration squarely between the eyes. Kwarteng seemingly remained either oblivious or uncaring. He was reported to be 'sanguine' about the fact that he'd just sumptuously sharted inside his own spacesuit,[126] but across the gawping face of Truss it was possible to detect the first signs that she understood: she, the chancellor, the budget, and the entire government were now on exceedingly thin ice.

Urgent action was needed, so they began by addressing the most important crisis facing the nation: they cancelled the karaoke at the forthcoming Conservative Party conference.[127] This had no effect whatsoever on anything, least of all on Rishi Sunak, who stopped languishing in a hot bath of 'I Told You So' long enough to announce he wouldn't be attending the conference anyway, so he could 'give Truss all the space she needs to own the moment'.[128]

Credit where it's due: that's epic shade.

But even without Sunak's help, Truss was owning moments all over the place. She desperately wanted to persuade unconvinced voters that *her* delusions should be *their* delusions too, and apparently felt the best way to do this was via a direct appeal to a furious public. Perhaps sensing she'd be mauled if she went on Radio 4's *Today* show, she instead took a tour of what she presumably thought would be gentler questioning from half a dozen local stations. You'll be surprised to learn Liz hadn't thought it through.

For *Today* presenters, interviewing a prime minister was a workaday, unexceptional activity. But for a mid-morning presenter on Radio Norfolk or BBC Stoke, it was a once-in-a-lifetime opportunity, and they each armed themselves to the teeth, prepped to the nines, and launched into her with blistering ferocity.

'I'm prepared to take difficult decisions and do the right thing,' Truss assured listeners, to which her interviewers – every single one of them – immediately responded with demonstrable evidence that her 'right thing' had been a cataclysmic failure that made everything worse.[129] We can almost excuse Truss for placing her foot in a bear trap the first time, but she failed to learn from the experience, and began pogoing from trap to trap.

And each time an interviewer trapped her, she responded in the same way: panicky silence. Dead air as she gasped and blinked and tried to find an excuse. It sounded like the PM had slipped into Battery Saver Mode, and when she did eventually boot up again all she had for us was tin-eared nonsense. She repeated the same untruth about her fuel plans ('making sure nobody is paying fuel bills of more than £2,500') during each of the interviews, despite already having been warned about it by the fact-checking service Full Fact. They ended up writing a public letter of rebuke.[130]

Practically every commentator across the political spectrum – from the *Daily Mail* to the *Guardian* – described her radio charm offensive as light on charm, heavy on offence, and a brutal failure. What the moment required from her was contrition for the disastrous budget, empathy with those who would suffer the consequences, and a believable plan for digging us out of this shit. What Truss delivered was the sound of uncaring, uncomprehending delusion.

And then, to put a cherry on a brilliant day of radio, Chris Philp went on LBC and denied there was a financial crisis at all.[131]

A Protectionist Racket

The next morning figures showed a combination of Brexit and Kwarteng's plan for growth had left Britain as the only G7 nation with an economy smaller than it had been before the pandemic. Our GDP predictions were slashed again,[132] and in news that would further focus the Stilton-addled minds on the backbenches, pollsters put Labour a whopping 33 per cent ahead. If replicated in a general election, this would leave the Tories with just three parliamentary seats.[133]

Suddenly – brace yourself, Susan – Chris Philp was wrong: there *was* a financial crisis after all, largely involving the Honourable Member for Sodding Typical losing his expense account. Something had to be done, and backbenchers were almost trampled in their sudden rush to assassinate their own leaders in the press.

'Kwasi and Liz will have to go,' they began.

'The party has been possessed by some sort of evangelical zeal.'

'I thought Boris Johnson's Cabinet was the worst in history. That one's just beaten it.'

'We [the Conservative Party] are just a protectionist racket right now.'[134]

Rumours spread that up to ten letters of no confidence had already been sent to the 1922 Committee, and that the only thing preventing more letters was an honest belief that getting rid of Truss would either not be possible, or would do no good anyway.[135] Party rules forbade a leadership challenge in the first 12 months, and Truss had barely been at her desk for 12 days.[136] Even if this obstacle could be overcome, there was still the issue of the insane electorate, namely the membership of the Tory Party, a cohort defined almost exclusively by their calcified resentments and petty indignations, which had just selected Truss. She had been the most ideologically extreme and fact-averse of the major candidates, and had told the members exactly what they'd wanted to hear: that nobody would tax them, that humans should never be allowed to migrate (unless to a retirement villa in Spain), and that they could keep all their money after they were dead. That's how she won. Any replacement for Truss would have to appeal to the same group of superannuated, puce-faced zealots. As one Conservative MP put it, 'You can have as many leadership elections as you like. You are only going to end up with the nutter winning.'[137]

Convinced they couldn't push her out, it became economically essential to show the markets that the Tories knew how to balance the books, and politically essential to reassure the nation that the Tories knew what the hell they were doing. If you think the former was a tall order, the latter was an order so lanky it would have to duck when the moon went past. There has rarely been a more obvious demand for an unambiguous and achievable plan, and rarely a leadership team less capable of enunciating one.

Instead of lucidity, there was merely a fresh helping of mayhem. The prime minister told the House of Commons she was 'absolutely' committed to no cuts to public spending,[138] but she seemingly hadn't conferred with the permanently befuddled Chris Philp, who boldly marched off in the opposite direction to Truss, telling Whitehall to find 'efficiency savings'.[139] Whitehall's response seems pretty reasonable, given the circumstances: 'What efficiency savings are there given levels of inflation??! Amazing bullshit.'[140]

Philp's department then tweeted that the budget could save you £11,250 a year, a claim that only applied if you earned £30,000 a year, but also managed to have a mortgage that cost you £28,000 a year. It's not a stretch to assert this is a situation that has applied to absolutely nobody in history. The tweet was swiftly deleted, and the culprits went back to their day job of – bear this in mind – *adding up*.[141]

Meanwhile Kwarteng, now labouring under the sobriquet Kami-Kwasi, insisted the financial catastrophe that began the moment he opened his mouth was entirely caused by international events, only to be brusquely put right by the chief economist at the Bank of England, who insisted our crisis was 'undoubtedly UK-specific'.[142]

The Circular Firing Squad Assembles

Barely a month earlier, when she was still selling a fantasy about her being the new Iron Lady, Truss had stridently assured the nation that she was prepared to make unpopular decisions.[143] But her decisions were unpopular, so she began to cancel them.

'How many people voted for your plan?' asked the BBC's Laura Kuenssberg, to which Truss responded with a stunned silence. Maybe she was trying to remember which plan. Yesterday's, or today's? The dumbstruck moment stretched on and on. Was she thinking, or broken? What wisdom might emerge from such profound contemplation? What vision? What clarity of thought and deed? Surely, when the echoing chasm in time eventually drew to an end, Truss would conjure a maxim for the ages, words we would sew into the very fabric of our national psyche.

'What do you mean by that?' she eventually stammered, and the nation facepalmed itself into unconsciousness.[144]

Everybody knew what was meant by that, except for Truss. What it meant was that the four-day experiment with fantasy economics had cost the nation billions, and we'd feel the pain of it for years. Of course, we must not forget the real victims: Kwarteng said his fiscal meltdown had 'really ruined my sleep'. Aw. Poor lamb.[145]

Fast forward to November, and Kwarteng was attempting to rescue his reputation by telling the world he'd warned Truss she was going too fast.[146] Quite the contrast with October, when he told the media he was '100 per cent convinced that this was the right plan', and that 'if politicians were really good at reading markets, I suggest they probably would be market traders'.[147] I don't know why it should be necessary to explain to a chancellor that telling the financial industry he hadn't got a clue might be a bad strategy, but it seemingly was.

Meanwhile his allies were briefing the BBC that the problem was that Kwarteng was, if anything, 'just too clever'.[148] Sure he is, mate. He's the smartest man in the room, as long as the room only contains him, Gavin Williamson and cheese mould.

Then Simon Clarke turned up, probably. It's never easy to tell with Simon Clarke. 'If I was to describe one word for Liz at the moment, it is purposeful,' he said, just as Liz abandoned her purpose.[149] She performed a screeching U-turn on tax, the first of many.[150]

Up in Scotland, Douglas Ross, the party's top man – not a tricky position to reach, since there were only five competitors – had urged the SNP to 'match these bold plans' and copy the tax cuts, only for him to be left dangling as the 'bold plans' went in the bin.[151] Jake Berry, the party chairman, had only just finished warning Tories who threatened to rebel against tax policy that they'd lose the whip. Now he had to tell them the opposite.

After 12 years in office the Tories had left Britain with over 2.5 million foodbank users.[152] Berry, all heart, said anybody left even poorer by the Truss budget should get a 'higher salary or higher wages'.[153] Genius. 'Have you tried not being poor?' just never occurred to us before. It was tone-deaf enough on its own, without considering how directly it contradicted Simon Clarke's assertion that pay rises would just cause inflation.[154]

Meanwhile the hapless Philp had taken it upon himself to hit out at criticism of the disastrous budget, labelling it 'the politics of envy'. And you know what: he was right. We *were* envious of people living under a competent government.

As backbenchers turned on the three at the top, the three at the top turned on one another. With great power comes no responsibility. Truss refused to say she trusted her own chancellor,[155] and denied she had made the decision on top-rate tax: it was all done by Kwarteng.[156] Kwarteng's team claimed it was all Chris Philp's idea,[157] and Philp briefed that he 'wasn't the prime mover in this'.[158]

No word yet on the big boy who made them do it, and then ran away.

Uninvestable

All of this coincided with the annual celebration of Tory success at the party conference in Birmingham, and to set the tone Daniel Grainger, the chair of the Young Conservative Network, called the city 'a dump'. He was swift to apologise, explaining away any unfortunate misunderstanding with the words 'I've always enjoyed my visits to your city'.[159] I'm not sure how far back 'always' goes in this context, but during the previous year he'd tweeted, 'Birmingham is the worst city in the UK,' and, keen to avoid any confusion, repeated, 'Birmingham is firmly the worst city in the UK'. He'd also mentioned – apropos of nothing – that 'Birmingham has one of the highest Muslim population [sic] in Britain, you can draw conclusions from that'.[160]

Oh, I'm drawing conclusions, Daniel Grainger. I'm drawing them *hard*.

As a result, Grainger wasn't allowed to attend the conference, but still managed to have a better one than Liz Truss. You could spend a lifetime scrutinising events with your very best scrutin, but still never work out why she decided to deliver her speech dressed as Vivienne Rook, a fictional fascist from the dystopian sci-fi show *Years and Years*.[161] Comforting it was not. She looked like somebody in the middle of a breakdown, or perhaps trapped permanently in the denial stage of grief. She certainly didn't seem to accept what was going on around her, and nor did Jake Berry, who grinningly declared, 'What a conference it's been!' When even the true-blue fanatics in the audience sniggered at how preposterous this was, he responded, 'That wasn't meant to be the funny bit.'[162]

Oh good, they've planned a funny bit!

Was the joke at the expense of Truss's crack team of speechwriters? They'd opted to reassure the world about her competence with the revelation she had a badge for being a pretend air hostess, and then followed up with the heart-rending tale of Truss growing up in the 1980s.

'I have seen the boarded-up shops,' she told the conference, 'I have seen people left with no hope turning to drugs. I have seen families struggling to put food on the table.' Her solution to this was: we needed more Conservatism. Not one member of the Truss Brain Trust had realised the Conservatives had been running the country for the entirety of that boarded-up, hopeless, foodless 1980s.[163]

Or maybe the joke was Truss claiming she'd been the first PM to go to a comprehensive school. How we laughed: Truss wasn't even the first female Conservative leader of the previous three years to do that. Theresa May's school had been a comprehensive while she was there.

Perhaps the humour was of the ironical kind? On the morning of her speech, it was reported global finance now considered the UK to be 'uninvestable'. We had lost £300 billion during her few weeks in charge, our credit rating was lowered once again, and the pound fell immediately after her conference speech ended.[164] The punchline? She was speaking about her plans for 'growth, growth and growth'.[165]

Well, I say speaking. This, it turns out, was yet another basic skill she hadn't mastered. She was to oratory what Eric Morecambe was to André Previn: the right notes, but never in the right order. The basic rhythms of human communication had bypassed Truss, and she hurled emphasis towards random points in sentences as if she was attempting to send a secret signal that she was there under duress. Punctuation? Optional. Simply pause whenever you feel like it, or allow sentences to bleed into one another, until the entire address comes across as a deranged stream of consciousness. There might have been a full stop in the text of the speech, but it certainly sounded like she was on the side of 'the commuters who get trains into towns and cities across our country, I'm thinking of the white van drivers'.[166]

Her love of people who – let me check I've got this right – *drive vans on trains* was used as a way to distinguish herself from what she labelled the Anti-Growth Coalition. Unlike the eternally hazy wokerati, the Anti-Growth Coalition did at least have a definition: it was everybody. Every other political party, naturally. Anybody who was opposed to Brexit (for example: Liz Truss). Anybody who doesn't personally know the individual who pays their wages. People who use taxis. Anyone who doesn't work in a factory. The BBC, of course, and presumably by extension anybody who watches the BBC. Podcasters (a grouping which includes Jacob Rees-Mogg).[167] The entirety of Twitter (a grouping which includes John Redwood). And for some reason 'the talking heads'.[168] We truly were on a road to nowhere.

The overarching message was that anybody who disagreed with Truss's beliefs was classified as an enemy of growth, including Truss from 24 hours earlier, when she'd had a whole different set of beliefs. At this point you'd be forgiven for mistaking her brain for a dazzlingly high-tech stealth weapon: impossible to detect, but still capable of inflicting enormous damage.

As this became increasingly clear to the panicking Tories, it was knives out, or in Nadine Dorries's case, plastic sporks. A month earlier she'd said she would 'always show [Truss] the same loyalty and support I have to Boris Johnson',[169] but now she announced that Truss had no mandate, was cruel, and was 'lurching to the right'.[170] And then Dorries called for a general election.[171]

Was she off her meds, or finally on them?

Desperate to defend her crumbling authority, Truss again blamed all the problems on Kwarteng.[172] This caused Michael Gove to attack Truss.[173] So Suella Braverman attacked Gove.[174] And then Kemi Badenoch got in touch with the metaphysical, and attacked the very concept of attacking people,[175] after which Captain Haddock – I'm sorry, Penny Mordaunt – decided to attack Truss again.[176] The former chief whip simply tweeted, 'Arghhhhhhhhhhhhhhhhhh',[177] and the carousel of feckless recrimination spun endlessly round, just a load of old pony endlessly trying to bite the horse's ass in front of it.

Truss's approval rating was now lower than Boris Johnson's had been at the worst point of Partygate,[178] and a month into her premiership party loyalty had evaporated too. When she had been chief secretary to the Treasury in 2018 Truss had said, 'I embrace chaos',[179] but now the pandemonium was rather tightly embracing her, and it seemed less fun. 'This is the kind of chaos you only see at the end of a premiership,' said one former Tory Cabinet minister at the conference. 'It's impossible for her to recover.' Grant Shapps hinted on camera that Truss had just ten days to save her job, and for once he wasn't far out.[180]

—

Shapps showed a rare outbreak of honesty from a government that seemed committed to using smoke and mirrors, except for the ones who kept all the mirrors and smokes for their special private alone times: traces of cocaine were found in multiple toilets inside the members-only security cordon at the conference. I have no idea if them all being caned off their tits explains what follows, but if it doesn't something far more troubling was going on.[181]

Chris Philp told a fringe meeting that they would ensure 'no business under 500 employees gets subject to business regulation'.[182] It's unclear whether this meant slave labour was legal again, or merely that your local restaurants could save the expensive burden of separating their sewage from their gravy.

Then Marilyn Manson's mum, Jacob Rees-Mogg, turned up to solve the climate crisis by promising a nuclear technology that doesn't exist,[183] threatening the safety of nuclear technology that does exist,[184] and evading scrutiny of fracking projects that would only make climate change worse.[185] All of this was in pursuit of his dream Brexit, a mission that also led him to propose a series of labour-market reforms. That's code for: scrapping your rights and making you work an almost unlimited number of hours. Even Number 10, hardly a hotbed of lucidity at this point in our history, described Rees-Mogg's grand plan as 'several unworkable and half-baked ideas', and rejected the lot.[186]

If would be nice if his Venn diagram of Brexit's promise could, at some point, at least *touch* the circle containing actual Brexit.

Still, at least The Moggster had the decency to say, 'if people want to call me Tory scum, I don't mind',[187] which is a bracing dose of realism from the accursed Victorian earthworm, putting him one step ahead of Suella Braverman. She spent the conference season burnishing her reputation for being truly awful, beginning with her claim that people on benefits 'choose to top up their salaries with tax credit'.[188]

'Choose'.

Sure, it's effective applause-bait to an audience who earnestly believe the poor are unworthy. Who don't recognise that tax credits are a subsidy for the wealthy employer, not for the low-paid worker. Who think the shivering guy in cardboard shoes who delivers their Amazon order is really a stoned slacker living in sublime, publicly funded luxury (rather than a hard-working taxpayer doing an unrewarding job for little money).

That's the fantasy the Tories preferred to believe, but it's not remotely true. Every single tax-credit claimant – literally 100 per cent of them – was either in work, job-seeking, or not required to work because of a health issue.[189] You don't get to *choose* moneyed indolence. That's what the House of Lords is for.

Braverman either didn't understand her own party's tentpole benefits policy, or understood it perfectly, but was happy to perpetuate the harmful myth for political purposes. My money is on the latter, because she followed that up with a truly horrendous bit of agitprop, this time targeting anybody foolish enough to expect sanctuary in Tory Britain.

'I would love to have a front page of the *Telegraph* with a plane taking off to Rwanda,' she said. Shoving thousands of non-criminal asylum seekers into a prison camp thousands of miles away was, she said, 'my dream, it's my obsession'.[190]

Martin Luther King, eat your heart out.

Jake Berry was to later insist there was nothing unusual about sending refugees overseas. He said he was 'completely relaxed' about people sent to Rwanda. 'Many countries around Europe including Denmark, other countries in the European Union do it.' But this wasn't just a slight spin, it was an exercise in fantasy. No other European nation deported asylum seekers to Rwanda. There had been a scheme to rescue asylum seekers from the dangerous chaos of Libya and fly them to third countries, including Rwanda, but no other European country sends their own refugees there.[191]

Even so, Braverman insisted Rwanda was 'fundamentally safe and secure', and therefore an unlimited stay in a shonky internment camp thousands of miles away would be a delightful outcome for people fleeing conflict and torture. This view ran very much counter to the evidence of both the Foreign Office and the UN Refugee Agency, who determined the Rwanda policy to be 'unlawful', not least because it 'seeks to shift responsibility and lacks necessary safeguards, [and] is incompatible with the letter and spirit of the 1951 Convention'.[192]

It also ran counter to what Braverman had been told on live radio when the idea first emerged, which is that Rwandan police had opened fire on refugees who had been protesting a reduction in their food rations and had killed 12 of them.[193]

And if that's not enough evidence for Braverman, perhaps she could listen to herself from the time before she became MP, when she had written that Rwanda did not even possess a 'properly functioning legal system'.[194]

—

That wasn't the only one of Braverman's earlier claims that was at odds with reality: her CV as a lawyer listed Braverman's contribution to a seminal legal textbook in 2007, and yet once she became an MP that entry somehow vanished from her resumé. The reason emerged just as she was shitting on refugees – hold on, I might need to narrow that down – I mean the time she shat on refugees during the 2022 party conference. The textbook's *actual* author, Philip Kolvin, said Braverman 'did not make a written or editorial contribution to the book', and that her entire role in its creation boiled down to the time he 'asked her to do some photocopying'.[195]

Dishonesty, fraud, and a lack of ethics are just some of the reasons lawyers can get struck off. I'm just saying.

In another part of the conference, Andrea Jenkyns was busy

laying down a challenge to irony with her declaration that our universities 'must be bastions of freedom' and should therefore stop providing students with 'a diet of critical race theory'. I see. You can do all the free speech you like, but only if it agrees with Jenkyns's views on race. Is that the plan now?

She went on: 'The current system would rather our young people get a degree in Harry Potter Studies than in construction.' The *Times Educational Supplement* crunched the numbers and found 245,395 students studying architecture, building, planning, and engineering. This compared with zero students taking Harry Potter Studies. Absolutely none. No such course exists. Never has.[196]

It was, of course, a big stretch to expect Andrea Jenkyns to know any of this stuff. After all she was only minister for Skills, Further and Higher Education. But at least she didn't go quite as far as Miriam Cates, who carried the thesis that there was too much free-thinking liberalism in our universities to its barnstormingly illogical conclusion: her solution was to cut higher education funding so we could 'stop young people from being indoctrinated'.[197]

That sound you can hear is the Enlightenment smashing its head against a wall.

Continuing this modernising theme, let's put on our dancing shoes and visit the party organised by LGBT+ Conservatives to celebrate the party's famously relaxed and open attitudes to diversity, an event which concluded with several Tory members being ejected for hurling 'disgusting homophobic abuse'.[198] On the same evening in another part of the building, Conor Burns was accused of groping a man,[199] although he was later cleared by an internal investigation.[200] But in the interim he got himself suspended as a patron of LGBT+ Conservatives,[201] sacked as trade minister, and had the Tory whip withdrawn.[202] This meant both of Bournemouth's Conservative MPs now had to sit as independents, since each of them had contrived to be suspended in just three months.[203]

The day after his suspension for (inaccurate) accusations of serious misconduct it was revealed that Burns was set to receive a knighthood from Boris Johnson as a reward for defending Johnson against ... (accurate) accusations of serious misconduct.[204] There isn't a fiction writer on earth who'd dare to create a plot as offensively obvious as that, but while Burns was still asserting his innocence of the claims made against him, events took a sharp left-turn into the surreal with the arrival of Scary Spice.

It's hard to know what's satire anymore.

Mel B tweeted, 'Really?? You're shocked about this complaint??? Let me remind you what you said [to] me in the lift . . .'[205] I'll tell you what I want, what I really, really want. I want to find out what Conor Burns said to Melanie Brown. But she was subsequently silent on the issue, and Mr Burns said he could neither recall what the alleged serious misconduct related to, nor remember being stuck in a lift with one of the world's most famous women a few hours earlier.

'I believe I have never met Mel,' Burns said.[206] Yeah, but some people believe the world is flat, and the comparison with a sect of mad fantasists seems a suitable conclusion to the conference, an event that had been – no, honestly – designed to showcase all that's great about the Tory Party.

A Year-Long Dawdle

Everybody packed up and went home on Wednesday, probably not entirely convinced that the party conference had gone well. Somehow, despite all the catastrophic economics, flip-flopping, in-fighting, homophobia, coke-snorting, sexual misconduct, bullshitting, playing chicken with nuclear energy, and threats to stop educating our kids until they're dumb enough to vote Tory, the polls still showed a 30 per cent lead for Labour.[207]

By Friday it had become even worse, and most of the problems revolved around Suella Braverman, who combined a pantomime of over-the-top villainy with a very believable demonstration of under-the-bottom competence. The home secretary had a hell of a week, which began when she was handed an official rebuke by the Information Commissioner's Office for failure to 'ensure an appropriate level of security of personal data'. Classified documents related to policing counter-terrorism had been left at a London venue. That incident had barely hit the headlines before she was putting a much-vaunted free trade deal with the government in Delhi 'on the verge of collapse' by making disrespectful comments about Indians.[208]

From there it was just a short goose-step to reclassifying modern slavery as an 'illegal immigration issue'. She alleged the system was being 'gamed', although it's hard to know how she came to that conclusion: there hadn't been an Anti-Slavery Commissioner for the whole of 2022, because the government had neglected to replace the outgoing one. Among other duties, a Commissioner would be responsible for recommending to government ways to protect vulnerable migrants, and the Tories didn't seem in a huge rush to get that task underway, despite there being a legal duty for the home secretary to appoint somebody.

After a year-long dawdle to put somebody in place, in January 2023 the entire recruitment process was scrapped by Braverman. No reason was given by the Home Office, so I guess it's up to you to guess why Braverman delayed appointing somebody to protect the people she was busy attacking.[209] Whatever conclusion you reach, the outcome was stark: for over a year the anti-slavery watchdog had no remit to provide any information that could lead Braverman to think anything was being 'gamed', and a former police chief with expertise in modern slavery said, 'I don't know where the evidence for claiming the rise is because of abuse [of the system] has come from.'[210]

Same place all bullshit comes from, I suppose. Made up as you go along.

She Knows She's Shit

This kind of on-the-hoof, omni-directional frenzy now seemed a pattern for government. A Cabinet is supposed to know what its policy is. It's supposed to discuss it, agree it, and speak with one voice. That's the whole point. But if your leadership team consists entirely of cracked pots, you shouldn't be too surprised when things start leaking out.

For example, as Liz Truss was planning to increase immigration to boost growth and help fill our almost 1 million vacancies,[211] Suella Braverman was telling anybody who'd listen that the Tories were just about to cut immigration by hundreds of thousands.[212] While Braverman was suggesting they were about to categorise cannabis as a class-A drug, Liz Truss's spokesman was denying the government would do any such thing.[213] It was hard to believe Braverman sat to the right of Truss around the same Cabinet table, while to the right of Braverman sat . . .

Nope, there was nobody to the right of Braverman.

The whole thing felt like bedlam, and an increasingly frantic Truss attempted – yet again – to establish her authority, this time by delivering an uplifting address to the 1922 Committee. The reviews were not kind.

'I feel embarrassed to have sold [the PM] as a safe pair of hands,' said one. 'I sold them a pup.'[214]

'Funereal,' said another attendee.[215]

'It was horrific. She's not going anywhere, but she can't survive.'[216]

'She's just embarrassingly bad, and even looks like she knows she's shit.'[217]

'The mood is genuinely horrendous. Much worse than conference.'

The conference had been over for barely a week, had been an unmitigated calamity, yet was already seen as 'the good old days'. It was suggested by *The Economist* that Truss had the shelf-life of a lettuce, and then the *Daily Star* took the idea and ran with it, launching a livestream of an iceberg lettuce next to a photo of the prime minister to see which lasted longer. Over 1.7 million people tuned in.[218] Bookmakers took bets on the outcome, and Paddy Power even offered odds that the lettuce would be the next Tory leader.[219]

It couldn't have performed much worse. The Conservatives – top to bottom – were seen as an absolute liability. Private banking group TS Lombard coined a term to describe the extra cost Britain now had to pay on its borrowing, simply because the party in power was so consistently and reliably idiotic. They called it a 'moron risk premium', and the phrase spread rapidly among the world's financial centres.[220]

Here at home the government plummeted to 19 per cent in the polls, and letters of no-confidence began pouring in from previously comfortable shire Tories who realised they were about to lose their safe seats.[221] There was a realistic prospect of them having to enter the job market trailing a record like *this*, and in their port-addled minds the cost-of-living crisis was suddenly brought into sharp focus. It was publicly suggested that a new leader might fix things, to which James Cleverly responded, 'Changing the leadership would be a disastrously bad idea.'[222]

I note with interest – but not much surprise – that Cleverly didn't think it was a disastrously bad idea to be foreign secretary under that new leadership. But at least he wasn't as blunt about what came next as the anonymous Tory MP who expressed his glowing confidence in the most obvious replacement for Truss: 'We are being offered the choice of a shit sandwich, or a shit sandwich with extra shit.'[223]

While her party contemplated that delightful little palate-cleanser, Truss attempted to gain some public respect via proximity to the King. The weekly meeting between monarch and prime minister was right in the Tory wheelhouse: there is surely no better exemplar of a supposed elite right to rule combined with rigidly traditional patriotic pomp, and under normal circumstances you'd think nothing could go wrong. But what did 'normal' mean anymore? The King greeted Truss with the words 'Back again? Dear, oh dear', and if you watched the footage on a high-definition TV you could actually see the prime minister's soul leave her body.[224]

By now Truss looked like somebody who had psychically disassociated from the world and all its glories, beaten into the dust by the sheer, trudging awfulness of merely being herself all day, every day. After a month in her company the public seemed to agree with her on that, if on nothing else. We were promised an inspiring new start, and ended up watching a wet, grey flannel slowly sinking into despond. We were promised Michelin-star dining, and got a limp, white-bread, triple-decker sandwich of arrogance, delusion, and dullness. We were sold a new Iron Lady and ended up with Margarine Thatcher.

I can't believe she's not better!

Kwarteng, meanwhile, had fled to the US to attend a meeting of the International Monetary Fund in the company of Howard Davies, the chairman of NatWest, who said he had 'never felt so embarrassed'. Davies described other financial leaders seeking him out to offer consoling words. 'I'm terribly sorry to hear about your economy and your government,' they would say. 'I'm sure it's not so bad.' And he would reply, 'Well actually, it probably is. Really – it's about as bad as you think.'[225] The poor man sounded at his wits' end.

Still stuck at his wits' beginning, Kwarteng remained oblivious to what was going on around him; he had a life-long habit of listening to nobody, and consequently *oblivious* was his default setting. At least until it was forcibly changed to *oblivion*.

'I'm not going anywhere,' he reassured journalists, and then got on a plane home to be sacked, right in the middle of the IMF meeting.[226]

Christ. Poor Howard Davies.

Seemingly the Chancellor's pilot had a strong sense of the symbolic: Kwarteng's flight performed a U-turn as it came in to land, then Kwasi headed straight to Downing Street to be cordially invited to fuck off.[227] He'd been in office just 38 days, and had managed to wipe £300 billion off the value of UK assets.[228] That's the equivalent to £3,600 every single hour since the prehistoric era when Britain was still connected to Europe by land.

Yet it seemed he hadn't been sacked for any of that, but rather for the cardinal sin of doing exactly what the prime minister had told him to do. The problem was: what she had told him to do was no longer her plan. There *was* no plan. Less than 24 hours after she'd assured the media there would be no U-turn on tax, she U-turned on tax.[229]

Sacking the chancellor and cancelling another major plank of the disastrous mini-budget was supposed to turn things around. It didn't work. Sterling sank again, just as Kwarteng's replacement swept into office.[230]

Our new chancellor was Jeremy Hunt, whose face expressed the perplexed and gleeful enthusiasm of a spaniel chasing a squeaky ball into a threshing machine. He almost didn't get the job at all. It was speculated that the role had first been offered to Sajid Javid, but he had looked at the problems he'd inherit and said: no fucking chance. This rumour was denied by one of the PM's key advisors, Jason Stein, who explained that Truss 'has sat in the Cabinet with Javid for ten years and she knows who is good and who is shit'.[231] She'd barely got through suspending Stein for indulging in unauthorised honesty before another aide helpfully popped up to reveal Truss often 'pretended her relatives had died' as an excuse to hide from the public.[232]

So Truss managed to sack her preferred chancellor undermine her replacement chancellor, piss off her alternative chancellor, lose one of her most valued advisors, and slaughter a handful of imaginary relatives. All in just two days.

It was a devastating return to form.

I Am Not Hiding Under a Desk

Hunt became our fourth chancellor in four months, and the fifth in barely three years. To put that into context, think of it like this: *holy tartan shit-balls*! Or if you need more specific details, the previous five Chancellors had lasted for a combined total of 22 years.[233]

This churn of ministers wasn't restricted to Number 11 Downing

Street, or even just to the ill-starred, disordered and woeful Truss. It was endemic in a party driven more by internal squabbles over which faction has the biggest office than by service to the country. And the cost was enormous, not simply in mismanagement. Ministers leaving their post are entitled to severance of 25 per cent of their salary, meaning each time somebody was sacked or quit they got handed about £16,000. And there had been 70 ministerial resignations just since July.[234]

Between 2010 and 2022 the Tories had worked their way through 9 pensions ministers,[235] ten education secretaries,[236] 14 housing ministers,[237] and another 14 variously responsible for energy and climate.[238] Each of these departments demands long-term plans and detailed knowledge, and the decisions they make directly affect countless lives for decades to come. Yet the people in charge had barely unpacked their desktop bobble-heads and worked out the quickest route to the toilets before it was time to delete their search history and move to a new job. Was it any wonder the nation appeared to be falling apart?

Also falling apart: Liz Truss. She held a press conference to reassure the public that now Kwarteng was gone, everything was fine again. Her body language, though. Her body language.

Poker players often have a subtle 'tell': an infinitesimal physical tic which, with dedication and experience, a skilled and highly observant opponent can sometimes spot. Liz Truss's tell was gulping like a seabird battling to swallow a golf ball, blinking as if she was trying to request the Heimlich manoeuvre via some kind of face-semaphore, and throwing a flop-sweat so severe it could make a tattoo slide off. Fortunately, she only did this when she was gambling the entire country's economy on a million-to-one mad fantasy.

Nothing about her soothing media appearance calmed nerves, not even her own. She took only four questions, gave essentially the same answer to each of them – regardless of the topic – and then exited stage-left, with rumours that she'd abandoned the briefing because she was about to cry.[239]

It's hardly surprising. Her career was coming to an end, and here

I'm using the definition of *career* that means 'to move fast and without control'. Hours into the job, Hunt U-turned on practically every policy Truss believed in.[240] The only section of the parliamentary party who ever backed her – the libertarian fruitcake faction – had also started calling for Truss to quit. And now she had to face urgent questions in the House.

Truss, naturally, didn't even turn up, which left proceedings in the hands of the cross Popeye impersonator Penny Mordaunt, whose decision to volunteer the news that our great leader definitely wasn't 'hiding under a desk' was met with howls of despairing laughter.[241] Downing Street explained away Truss's absence from the seat of governance by saying she was 'fucking busy',[242] which makes a change from Boris Johnson, who seemingly couldn't be arsed turning up to run the country cos he was busy fucking.

In minutes the story changed again: now we were told Truss was holding a meeting with Graham Brady, chair of the 1922 Committee. I hope their get-together wasn't held in his office, because over 100 letters of no confidence had just arrived there, and the place must have looked like that time the Dursleys refused to let Harry go to Hogwarts.[243] And so, faced with such a scene, Truss eventually opted to traipse into the chamber of the House of Commons, where she sat in gawping stupefaction, listlessly counting her blinks while a frustrated-looking Mordaunt attempted to defend this farce.

Suella Braverman, with all the warmth of Cersei Lannister having a go at being a trauma therapist, was always itching for a fight. She defended nothing, and instead went on the attack. She blamed the nation's woes on the 'Guardian-reading, tofu-eating wokerati' who hadn't been in charge of anything for over a dozen years.[244] But it didn't matter what Braverman said. She was out of a job the day after her assault on tofu, taking only 24 hours to go from hard bean-curd to has-been turd. She'd been in office one day less than David Blaine spent dangling in a Perspex box filled with his own farts, and to just as much positive effect.

Braverman put her enforced resignation down to a minor administrative flub, a mere 'technical infringement of the rules', which she claimed to have reported to the Cabinet secretary as soon as she became aware.[245] Her take on events was that she'd forwarded a relatively meaningless document from her ministerial email account to her private Gmail, and from there had sent them to fellow right-wing Tory MP Sir John Hayes.[246] In a hurry, she had accidentally copied in somebody she thought was Hayes's wife but was actually the similarly named assistant of another Tory MP, Andrew Percy. Braverman claimed she had quickly realised her mistake and reported it to the Cabinet secretary, Simon Case. She told the chief whip that this was the first time she'd ever sent emails in this way.[247]

That was her story.

Enquiries found she'd done it at least six times, and each time it was a breach of security rules. Sources inside Number 10 said Braverman 'doesn't make any decision without consulting John Hayes', who is, to say the least, something of a character. He opposes same-sex marriage,[248] and trans rights,[249] and is resolutely pro-life in all circumstances,[250] but is, in the traditional challenge to rational thought, also a big old fan of capital punishment.[251]

As energy minister in 2013 he vowed to back coal,[252] cut subsidies for renewable energy, intentionally made onshore wind production more difficult, and scrapped a policy of zero-carbon housebuilding.[253] These ideologically driven choices added £9.5 billion to our energy bills in 2022.[254] But by 2022, Hayes had no ministerial responsibility. He had no right to see Braverman's restricted documents. He was merely an enabler for her particular brand of fundamentalist right-wing fervour.

Needless to say, Hayes's entirely unelected wife – with whom Braverman had also attempted to share internal government policy documents – also had no right to see them. And the home secretary wasn't entirely honest about reporting events to Simon Case as soon as she became aware. Instead, she had asked the accidental recipient to 'delete the message and ignore' in the hope it would all just go away, and Case only became involved when Andrew Percy reported matters to him.[255]

After a bit of light hollering between Truss and Braverman, the home secretary did the kind of resignation designed to allow ministers to preserve their dignity by pretending they haven't just been handed their arse.[256] Her resignation letter suggested any technical infringement was incidental to her resignation: she would have quit anyway due to 'concerns about the direction of this government',[257] which is a bit like complaining about the weather in Scotland. If you don't like it, wait half an hour and something different will come along.

Yet her complaint about direction didn't relate to Truss performing a twice-hourly spin of the policy randomiser wheel. Rather, Braverman was determined to push the economics of the party even further to the right, despite the academically rigorous British Election Study finding that of 275 major political parties in 61 countries, the Tories were already the most economically right-wing of all.[258]

And bear in mind Italy had just elected literal fascists.

I don't know who Braverman thought she was impressing with this gibberish, but it certainly wasn't the electorate. It wasn't even her own Conservative voters, who were by now way to the left of the policies of the party that nominally represented them. In the British Election Study's Venn diagram there is absolutely no overlap between Tory policy and the economic views of the nation. Unsurprisingly the same study described the Conservatives as 'completely unmoored from the British public', and with Braverman's resignation she had cast herself adrift from the already astray.

Regardless, any concerns about the government going in the wrong direction were immediately assuaged by the appointment of Braverman's successor, Grant Shapps, a man who can face in multiple directions at once. Shapps became Truss's second home secretary, but made up for being third-rate by there being four of him. If you think it's unfair to still bring up his false identities a decade after he'd been pretending to be Michael Green, Corinne Stockheath and Sebastian Fox,[259] consider how two-faced he was still managing to be. He famously runs a spreadsheet containing all the supporters and opponents of every likely leadership candidate, so he can figure out who is going to be the next amazingly successful Tory leader.

An anagram of Grant Shapps is 'Pants Graphs'.

On the morning Shapps was appointed, he'd been showing off his spreadsheet of Tory MPs keen to topple Liz Truss.[260] By early afternoon he was working for her and supporting her attempt to overturn her *own policies*, while Jeremy Hunt implemented the plans of Rishi Sunak.

You're not alone. This is giving me a headache too.

Maybe Thérèse Coffey can get us some paracetamol, because while Braverman was eating up bandwidth in a news cycle that was struggling to cope, Coffey, the health minister, admitted that she was fond of handing out unprescribed antibiotics to her friends and families.[261] Not only is this illegal, but it also helps to stoke antibiotic resistance and promote the emergence of untreatable super-bugs.

Coffey had no right to hand out medication. She has no medical qualifications, and it's a miracle she got any qualifications at all. She'd been 'asked to withdraw [...] on academic grounds' from her studies at Oxford, after her extreme focus on extra-curricular activities at the Conservative Association had contributed to lousy exam results.[262] Her predecessor as health minister was a medic, though. Dan Poulter was a former GP who had served under David Cameron, and found Coffey's attitude 'deeply alarming'. He described her combination of handing out unprescribed drugs like sweets, combined with a marked reluctance to take action on obesity and smoking, as the hallmarks of an 'ultra-libertarian ideological' mindset that would 'cost lives'.

Absolutely Fracking Crazy

And so, on to the clusterfuck of events that both encapsulated the premiership of Liz Truss and proved to be its final act.

Fracking in England had been subject to a moratorium since November 2019.[263] The manifesto on which the Tories had campaigned that year included a pledge that they would 'not support fracking unless the science shows categorically that it can be done safely', which to most people is a pretty unambiguous statement.[264] But in the mind of Jacob Rees-Mogg – which is the mind of a tapeworm, tragically trapped in the body of another tapeworm – fracking was a brilliant way to solve the energy crisis, make a fat pile of cash, and piss in the eye of lefty-liberals. It didn't appear to matter a jot to him that, in the words of the founder of fracking giants Cuadrilla, 'no sensible investors' would try it in the UK because the geology was unsuitable. Cuadrilla knows. Cuadrilla tried. Cuadrilla spent hundreds of millions of pounds attempting to frack in the UK, never produced a sniff of gas suitable for sale, and withdrew from the market.[265]

But it always felt like Rees-Mogg's animating force was performatively sticking it to the *Guardian*, rather than achieving anything tangible. So regardless of the certainty of failure, Frack the Ripper was determined to overturn the ban. Hi-ho, and off we go to parliament for a pointless bit of lefty-baiting.

Labour, aware that the last active fracking site in the country had caused 192 earthquakes in 182 days, were understandably sceptical that the science showed the process to be safe.[266] They put down a motion to stop Rees-Mogg's idiot plan.[267] But because they conduct politics like an us-vs-them team sport, the Tories responded by ordering their MPs to oppose Labour, even though this meant Conservatives would be voting against the Conservative manifesto.

Even the Tories didn't relish the prospect of losing a vote against themselves, so they issued a range of high-level threats. Deputy Chief

Whip Craig Whittaker sent a WhatsApp to his MPs, emphasising that 'This is not a motion on fracking. *This is a confidence motion in the government*' and issuing a 'hard 3-line whip'. Any MP failing to support the government in its current task of opposing its own agenda would be kicked out of the parliamentary party.[268]

Three MPs – including the prime minister's net-zero tsar Chris Skidmore – immediately said they'd vote against the motion regardless, and 'face the consequences'.[269] But that was just three out of an entire herd of despondent Tories who loyally traipsed off to engage in a vacuous act of environmental sabotage, only to be met by minister Graham Stuart, who informed them that 'obviously this is not a confidence vote'.[270]

Bewildered, banjaxed and directionless, they began wandering around the entrance to the voting lobbies like stunned cattle, asking one another what the hell they should do next. Downing Street chose to clarify matters by admitting they had 'mistakenly' told Graham Stuart that it *wasn't* a confidence vote, and that now it *was* again.[271]

But by the time the nation's crack leadership team had managed to work out whether it was confident in itself or not, a further 40 Tory MPs had engaged in a bit of unsanctioned decency, and had decided to vote to keep the ban anyway.[272]

All hell broke loose. A gang of libertarian Tories were seen 'shouting and bullying' their fellow MPs. Rees-Mogg joined in, which must have been like getting bollocked by a bewitched oboe. Thérèse Coffey was seen manhandling recalcitrant colleagues, physically picking up a crying MP and carrying him into the division lobby of her choice.[273] Scuffles broke out inside parliament, right in front of slack-jawed journalists and gleeful, hand-rubbing Labour members. Craig Whittaker, confronted with the spectacle of the deputy prime minister Trunchbulling MPs into lobbies to vote against her own government's manifesto, stormed away from the scene. He was heard to say, 'I am fucking furious, and I don't give a fuck any more,' before both he and his boss, the chief whip resigned.[274] And then, as if the evening wasn't anarchic enough already, they unresigned a few minutes later.[275]

Charles Walker, a distinguished Conservative backbencher, appeared on the BBC to comment on today's proceedings by Britain's so-called natural party of government.[276] He was visibly shaken. 'I think it's a shambles and a disgrace,' he said, and described his own party as 'talentless'.

'I'm livid,' said Walker, 'and I really shouldn't say this but all those people that put Liz Truss in Number 10, I hope it was worth it; it was worth it for the ministerial red box, as it was worth it to sit round the Cabinet table, because the damage they have done to our party is extraordinary.'[277]

And what was Liz Truss doing through all of this? Well, it is claimed she managed to attend the confidence motion in herself, but the record doesn't show her voting. Why? Because she 'forgot to swipe her pass'.[278]

'This,' said Jacob Rees-Mogg, 'is a government that is functioning well.'[279]

Jenga!

The next morning's polling showed people approving of the prime minister was down to 9 per cent.[280] Inflation on staple foodstuffs was up to 17 per cent, which – if you simply place the numbers side by side – appears to suggest starvation was almost twice as popular as Liz Truss.[281]

Throughout her political career she'd been known inside the Westminster village as 'a human hand-grenade', and now the whole country understood the reasons why. 'She's been dismissed and mocked by people in Westminster and the media over the years,' said her former aide in an attempt to defend her, but now the whole country understood the reasons for the dismissive mockery too.[282] Everybody, absolutely everybody, knew she was wildly incapable of the job, and it couldn't go on.

'I'm a fighter, not a quitter,' she declared, and then quit.[283]

She told her staff, 'Don't worry, I'm relieved it's over,' and they presumably all nodded vigorously. 'At least I've been prime minister,' she continued, and they presumably all made a *have you though?* face.[284] After just seven disastrous weeks in office she would now be able to claim the £115,000 per year for life awarded to former prime ministers.[285]

Her predecessor Boris Johnson's noisy and self-seeking persona had been plain for all to see, not least in his lavish furniture choices.[286] Truss, however, was deeply subfusc and woebegone, and few were prepared for her to play a strong metaphor game; but as her premiership collapsed, she announced her resignation from a lectern seemingly made from Jenga bricks. Although, true to form, she did waste £4,175 of taxpayers' money on the plinth.[287] Thanks, Liz!

The contest to make Truss prime minister had lasted 54 days. She'd been in office just 49 days and was outmanoeuvred by a lettuce.[288]

The Worst Idea for 46 Years

And so, back to their Etch-a-Sketch drawing board for another vigorous shake, and yet another PM. This would make it the third in three months, and the fifth since Brexit promised we'd finally be in control of things.

The 1922 Committee, probably stung from the credibility issues relating to a leadership campaign that lasts longer than the resulting premiership, decided not to repeat past mistakes. This time the whole thing would take less than a week. To limit the field, candidates would now need 100 nominations from MPs. A brief knockout contest would whittle potential leaders down to a shortlist of two.[289] Then the parliamentary party would recommend to Tory members the candidate most likely to bring stability, reassure the markets, and reintroduce integrity to the highest job in the land.[290]

And then polls indicated Tory members would instantly rubber-stamp Boris Johnson as PM all over again.[291]

To most of the country the return of Johnson seemed as

feasible – and as desirable – as manually sliding a turd back up your colon. Regardless, Nadine Dorries and a cluster of her fellow travellers clamoured for it. Others were not so sure. 'The serious and sensible course of action,' said one Johnson ally, 'the statesmanlike thing to do, would be to back Rishi and say the feud is over for the good of the country.'[292]

So the next day, serious and statesmanlike Boris Johnson got on a flight home from yet another holiday in the Dominican Republic to launch a bid to regain power, only two months after he'd been driven from office by a tidal wave of scandals, lies and ineptitude. William Hague said the concept of Johnson returning to government was 'the worst idea' he had heard in the 46 years he'd been a party member, and the mere prospect of more Boris caused credit rating agency Moody's to change the UK's outlook to 'negative'.[293]

We'd maintained a top rating even during the fabled Winter of Discontent in 1978. Throughout what the Tories wanted us to believe was a catastrophic Brown administration Moody's had listed us as the top-rated AAA Stable level. Since the Tories took over, with their brilliant, natural flair for managing the economy, we had experienced four downgrades and now sat at Aa3 Negative, with warnings of more to come if we welcomed back our fly-tipped anarchist of a former PM.[294]

Despite this, Johnson had the immediate backing of six Cabinet ministers: Ben Wallace, Jacob Rees-Mogg, Simon Clarke, Chris Heaton-Harris, Alok Sharma, and Anne-Marie Trevelyan.[295] If it strikes you as bananas that anybody could reach Cabinet level and sit through three years of Johnson's administration without noticing how utterly unsuited to office he is, consider this: armed forces minister James Heappey admitted 'it would be completely disingenuous to claim that on that morning, when the Cabinet was presented with [Kwarteng's] mini-budget, that there was anybody sat around the table who said that it was a bad idea'.[296]

They simply didn't know what they were doing. Any of them.

As Johnson sped home, the first candidate to officially stand was

Penny Mordaunt. Sunak's backers announced he'd reached the 100-MP threshold before he even launched an official campaign,[297] and seemingly not wishing to be left out, Johnson's team also claimed he had the support of 100 colleagues. Not many believed him. The Johnson camp was challenged to release a list of supporters but declined.[298]

Sunak was the clear front-runner, largely because he'd gained public popularity by handing out lavish piles of cash during the pandemic, and then gained fiscal popularity by accurately predicting the disaster of the Truss era (if you can call seven weeks 'an era'). Mordaunt's record was less stellar. She'd been shuffled around nine different ministerial roles in eight years. Despite being a decent dispatch-box performer, she seemed to have achieved very little beyond a reputation for salty language, and an admission that she'd only delivered a speech in parliament about the welfare of poultry so she could repeatedly say the word 'cock' as part of a forfeit for a misdemeanour in her Naval Reserve training.[299]

This now qualified her as the second-best Tory, at least until Johnson officially threw his hat into the ring and pushed her into third place.

Johnson's very own Greyfriars Bobby, Nadine Dorries, immediately showed her political nous by handing Labour their next attack line. She wrote of Sunak that 'the polls plummeted to minus 15 during the summer when there was a real possibility that he, not Liz Truss, might become prime minister',[300] and said 'only one man has a mandate at the ballot box' just as that man – Johnson – reversed out of his own fledgling leadership campaign.[301] He suddenly decided not to run.

Team Boris were furious at his betrayal and the lies that underpinned it, as though they'd never heard of the man before.[302] He'd assured his backers that he had 100-plus endorsements, but it turned out the real number was 62.[303] He'd assured them he'd learned his lesson about selfishness and would now put the country first, but sources claimed he'd really dropped out after realising a return to Downing Street would endanger the estimated £10 million he was about to make whoring himself around the after-dinner-speech and entertainment circuit.[304]

'A number of people in his team not only feel disappointed, they feel betrayed,' said Boris supporter and dying palm-tree Michael Fabricant.[305] It was even worse for Nadhim Zahawi, who published an article in the *Telegraph* backing Johnson two minutes after Johnson had released a statement saying he was pulling out of the race. Somehow Johnson's team had neglected to inform his own backers of their decision.[306]

Despite this, Johnson, still utterly in hock to his own colossal ego, continued to insist he would definitely, *definitely*, have won the race if he could be bothered to try. In his concession statement he announced that not only was he well placed to win, but he was 'uniquely placed' – yea verily, he is *The One* – 'to deliver a Conservative victory in 2024'. He boasted he could 'confirm that I have cleared the very high hurdle of 102 nominations', which he hadn't, and 'could be back in Downing Street on Friday', if he wanted to, which he didn't. And I suppose he'd only flown from the Caribbean to London to get Nadhim Zahawi to humiliate himself in the press.

Johnson wanted us to believe he hadn't failed, he'd merely been struck down with a sudden and unfamiliar attack of altruism, which led him to conclude leading the nation again 'would simply not be the right thing to do'.[307] His brief flirtation – or as he would call it, a sincere relationship – with a return to power was over. Mordaunt, with just 27 public endorsements, also dropped out so she could focus on her day job of not being in the Royal Navy. With no other candidates standing, nobody bothered asking the party membership. Rishi Sunak was declared the winner by Tory MPs, and 'the best of a bad bunch' by voters.[308]

All political careers end in failure, said Enoch Powell, but it takes a particular skill to end the same political career in failure twice in as many months. As the news spread of Johnson's withdrawal from public office, voters across the land crossed their fingers, closed their eyes, and wished, *wished*, WISHED that for just one night, they ran Nadine Dorries's nearest off-licence.

Part 3
Crazy Rich Asian

2022

'Screams from a Madhouse'

Integrity, Professionalism and Accountability

Drive-by prime minister Liz Truss was gone. From 26 October Britain was led by Rishi Sunak, an ethics chatbot wearing the hair of a Lego Elvis, who promised – and these are words you should commit to memory – 'integrity, professionalism and accountability at every level' of his government.[1]

It was immediately obvious that the most important lesson Sunak had dragged from the wreckage of Truss's premiership was this: blink less. It's the only feasible explanation for his victory speech to the nation, which had the vibe of a practice session for an Olympic Staring Competition. His eyes moved just twice as he delivered his robotic two-minute address, during which he pledged to work 'day in, day out' for Britain, except for the seven seconds after he finished speaking.[2] He'd allocated that time to standing completely still, gazing into the middle-distance in eerie silence.[3]

Sunak was a former derivatives trader and highly derivative politician. He was nothing new, simply a new face. He gave a studied impersonation of a neat, problem-solving technocrat, but was actually just as authoritarian and divisive as any of the PMs who preceded him. And he still ran a government that absolutely stank of favouritism, cronyism, corruption, and greed.

After a spell as head boy at top private school Winchester College,

Sunak had headed off to Oxford to do the so-called politician's degree: Philosophy, Politics and Economics. But once he'd graduated, he decided it would be more fun to chase money instead. He did a spell at Goldman Sachs, then joined the aggressive hedge fund that went on to help bring down RBS, a key event in the collapse of the global economy in 2007.[4] The fund's money was hidden in the Cayman Islands for tax purposes, and Sunak became a multimillionaire by his mid-20s.

Once loaded – and doubly so after he married the extremely wealthy daughter of one of India's richest men – Sunak cashed out of the hedge-fund business and cashed in on his PPE degree. He gave assured performances of his key talents – taking his jacket off while having expensively polished teeth – and charmed his way through the ranks. In no time he'd secured a candidacy in the safe seat from which former leader William Hague was about to step down. Sunak became an MP in 2015, and by 2022, at the age of just 42, ended up being in Downing Street.

It was a historic day: he was the first prime minister from a non-Christian faith since Benjamin Disraeli, and the youngest PM for 200 years, which seems appropriate for a party that had taken us back to Victorian levels of poverty.[5] Britain now had a Christian monarch, a deputy prime minister whose father was a Jewish refugee,[6] a Muslim mayor of London,[7] and a Hindu prime minister whose parents were immigrants.[8]

All this while being led by a party which regularly demanded an end to immigration and claimed multiculturalism wasn't working.

Of course, the fact that an extremely wealthy, privately educated Oxford graduate who was, for once, *not white* had made it a long way in Conservative politics shouldn't be seen as a great indication of the party's progressive nature. The Tories trumpeted loudly that they'd had three female prime ministers, while Labour had none; and now they had the first non-white PM too. But women were still 57 per cent more likely to be in prolonged poverty than men,[9] and were financially worse-off than when the Tories came to power.[10] After 12 years of Conservative policies, more than half of the UK's Black children lived in poverty.[11]

It turns out trickle-down equality isn't a thing either.

Sunak's youth, energy and novelty could – should – have been strengths, but they disguised a series of fundamental weaknesses. The first was that he had to cope with what the Tories had done to the country. To quote one recent departure from the government: 'I can't think of any PM gifted a worse inheritance by their own side', and that wasn't all down to Truss, who'd been not so much a prime minister as a punctuation mark.[12]

The party had bequeathed to Sunak the results of 12 years of austerity, which could be summarised as: a terrible economy, lousy productivity, crumbling infrastructure, a healthcare disaster, a housing crisis, transport chaos, the highest taxes for decades, and the costliest energy bills in the entire world.[13] On top of this there had been six years of political instability while this bunch of squabbling wangs had ineffectively attempted to transform their Brexit fantasy into reality. Although to be fair, by 2022 they'd mostly given up on that particular project, instead resigning themselves to delivering all the shit things that the Remain camp had warned about, while pretending they'd wanted this all along.

Unsurprisingly, the *Collins Dictionary* Word of the Year was 'permacrisis'.[14] It joined a merry bunch of previous Words of the Year during Tory rule: austerity, gaslighting, fake news, populism, post-truth, misinformation, xenophobia, and omnishambles.[15]

That was Sunak's first problem. The second was that, while he was younger than Tony Blair or David Cameron had been when they assumed office, he lacked the vital hinterland those leaders had acquired. Blair and Cameron had both held the top job in opposition for years before becoming prime minister, giving them valuable time to practise for an otherwise-unpracticable role.

And unlike those earlier leaders, Sunak had not won a popular vote – in fact he hadn't even won an unpopular one comprised of Tory members. More people voted for Matt Hancock to be covered in maggots than had voted for the new prime minister,[16] but Sunak was determined to do better than his predecessor, or at the very least outlast the contents of the Tesco salad aisle. By now, this qualified as high ambition. Yet his lack of mandate robbed him of a big stick with which to beat dissenters in his own ranks, not one of whom owed their place in parliament to a Sunak electoral victory.

Those two weaknesses were bad, but his biggest failings became increasingly clear during the first 100 days of his premiership: he was so weak he could qualify as a homeopathic remedy, and he had appalling political judgement. Aside from quite clearly thinking Boris Johnson was an oaf – which doesn't qualify as a searing insight – Sunak seemed a terrible judge of character, and incapable of acting on the rare occasion he judged a character correctly.

In mitigation, he had to select a Cabinet from his available MPs, a rivetingly terrible selection of dipsomaniac bullies, moneygrubbing fraudsters, ungovernable masturbators, and self-serving bags of howling bigotry. But even from those, he seemed to choose the worst possible candidates for every office. Before the month was out, the wheels began to come off spectacularly.

But in the meantime, the country was blessed with a prime minister worth £730 million[17] and a chancellor who once 'forgot' about seven luxury flats he owned,[18] turning up on the telly to explain to people on minimum wage that more austerity would be good for them.

—

Sunak finished U-turning on everything Truss had done, and now got started on U-turning on his own stuff. He boldly announced he wouldn't attend the COP27 climate summit, proved his humble nature by banning King Charles from attending too, and then took to Twitter to boldly throw all of that out of the window again. 'I will attend Cop27 next week,' he said, 'to deliver on Glasgow's legacy of building a secure and sustainable future.'[19]

Few held out much hope. Even his own leadership promises were now deemed unsustainable. Downing Street admitted it was undergoing a review to see whether anything he'd only just pledged was at all deliverable. 'We are looking at all the campaign pledges and we are looking at whether it is the right time to take them forward,' said his spokesman. 'We're not making commitments right now either way.'[20] He'd been PM for a week.

Under Truss, the policies the public had voted for at the 2019 election were abandoned and replaced with something to satisfy the dark urges of a tiny cohort of party members. Now that replacement was being replaced by something else, one further remove from a democratic mandate. It didn't matter much anyway: the sole purpose of the Tory government by November 2022 was to undo the policies of the Tory government of October 2022, in the hope we'd vote for another Tory government in 2024, and then do it all again.

Who needs a two-party state if one party can be both government and opposition?

The Disruptor Model

'I promise to serve you with integrity and humility,'[21] said the humble dude in the £3,500 suit,[22] and then set about appointing a Cabinet to deliver whatever the fuck he eventually decided he wanted to do.

His strategy, as so often in recent years, was to design a team that put the interests of the country second to balancing the conflicting demands of his MPs, which already threatened to tear apart this fractured, splintered government once again. Yet painting over the cracks was a necessity because, despite appearances, there was no longer any such thing as the Conservative Party.

I'm afraid this is not cause for celebration, because since the late 1980s, and turbocharged since 2016, there have been countless simultaneous versions of the Conservative Party, engaged in a furious – and to most people meaningless – 30-year battle over who gets to keep the name. A bit like Pink Floyd.

Back in the 1970s, the Tories were mostly a unified party with a clear, monolithic intellectual rationale, albeit one that wasn't always wildly popular. But suddenly, supported by the cursed ratio of only 52 per cent of her MPs, and to the surprise of many, Margaret Thatcher became leader of the party.[23] She arrived with a new approach to governance, which today we'd describe as the Disruptor Model: move fast and break things.

The thing her government most wanted to break was the post-war settlement, the broad political consensus most people over 60 had grown up with, then repeatedly voted to destroy, before finally rebelling against the consequences of their destructive choices by deciding everything was rubbish, and it was the fault of the EU.

Prior to Thatcher, for decades political consensus in the UK had been built around government intervening to support a mixed economy of manufacturing, services and finance working in mutual support, rather than betting the whole lot on the riskiest sector imaginable, and then repeatedly having to bankrupt the country to bail it out.

The post-war settlement had provided protection for workers, a nationalised infrastructure, and a welfare state funded by (among other things) high levels of taxation on the wealthy. Such tax prevented the very rich from becoming *obscenely* rich, keeping spiralling inequality under control, and inhibiting the emergence of a rentier class who might capture vital assets and then overcharge the rest of us to access them.

But with Maggie in office, those days were now over, and damn the consequences. Rentier economics were not merely allowed to let rip, but were actively encouraged, particularly in the housing sector. The theory was that rising house prices made everybody rich, assuming you already owned a home. If you didn't, well, that was your own fault for eating too many avocados and idly neglecting to be born in the 1950s.

As house prices soared, the money families would once have spent on street-level economic activity – goods and services from local traders, or perhaps starting a business – was instead sunk into piles of non-productive bricks and mortar, hampering economic growth and damaging investment in local communities.

The poll tax – and later council tax – no longer charged people more if they lived in large, costly properties, so rich people became richer, and councils lost that income. It therefore became essential to charge higher business rates, simply to fund basic council services that the rich no longer contributed fairly to. Meanwhile the rich used their new spare money to invest in more property, a rentier economic model took hold, and property prices rose and rose. This affected both domestic and commercial property, and combined with unavoidable, rising business rates, it wasn't long before running a shop in a town centre became financially ruinous.

Meanwhile older property owners suddenly discovered they were paper millionaires and loved it, securing their loyalty as Tory voters. It didn't seem to matter that they couldn't access their new, unearned millions without making themselves homeless, thus rendering those riches absolutely meaningless: they liked pretending their three-bedroom semi in Bury South placed them in the same category as Warren Buffett, and they wanted more of it!

In the years after WW2, government promises of housebuilding had been central to any election campaign. Now all of that stopped. We went from building one new home for every 14 people in the 1960s to one for every 43 people by the 2010s, despite the continued, unshakeable appetite for human beings to engage in sexual reproduction.[24]

Yet even that catastrophic failure to maintain necessary levels of housebuilding wasn't enough. Many homeowners began to agitate against the building of *any* new homes, worried that increasing the housing stock might reduce the futile, imaginary riches tied up in their own property. Meanwhile their children found themselves incapable of affording even basic housing, and instead had to fall back on a precarious, wildly expensive rental market that only served to enrich landlords yet further. Their profits allowed landlords to buy more homes to rent out, and the wheel turned.

It was a cycle of soaring house prices, impoverished mortgage-holders, insecure renters, a few vastly rich, woefully under-taxed property magnates, and appalling mass homelessness. Between 2010 and 2022, rough sleeping increased 169 per cent. On any given day in 2021, there were at least 274,000 homeless people in England – each one a real human being with real fears, real feelings, real hunger. Among the young the crisis was especially pronounced: youth homelessness increased by two-fifths in five years since 2017.[25]

As they deliberately pulled the post-war settlement apart, governments could no longer point proudly to achievements measured in improved living standards, greater wages, manufacturing success, reduced inequality, or better opportunities. So rising house prices became the key signifier of economic boom-times, even though those prices were leaving millions in unaffordable debt, while millions more were excluded entirely. The government didn't seem to care. Whenever a recession threatened, the Treasury would drum up a new wheeze to boost the cost of housing yet further, and the process repeated itself with an ever-greater frenzy.

—

A select few people made a lot of money in a hurry, by the simple expedient of not caring about what happens tomorrow. It was like a farmer boasting that he'd saved a fortune by not planting any crops. Good for you, but what do we eat next harvest-time?

And it wasn't just housing: the project to replace the post-war settlement continued on all fronts. The Thatcherites sold off infrastructure assets the nation had spent a century creating for a fraction of their value, while tax reforms hacked away at the government's own income. This in turn both necessitated and justified cutting back on investment in the things that had made the country stable and operational: education, transport, training, health.

But all of this worked fine – at least, fine for the 35 per cent of the electorate necessary to keep the Tories in power – until suddenly it didn't. There weren't any assets left to sell, and years of saving money by not investing suddenly came back to bite us on the arse. Everything began falling apart. The trains and schools and hospitals stopped working, wages began to plummet, the housing market was spellbindingly irrational, and it was increasingly clear that the Thatcherite revolution was eating its babies, as all revolutions do.

By the late 1990s, fairness and social democracy were suddenly popular again, as the nation revolted against the destruction of all the post-war social good they'd grown up with. Blair entered office with a determination to undo much of the damage (although in my opinion not enough).

Regardless, with renewed government investment the economy blossomed, repairs to our infrastructure began, and the nation appeared to love it. As the certainties of Thatcherism failed, the Tories now felt lost. In search of a new faith to invest in, they began to pull in multiple directions at once. The former monolithic creed was replaced by an eruption of minor Conservative factions, indicative of a party with ideas about society that were being proven nonsensical on all sides, and desperate to find something new to believe in.

By the 2020s there were Large State Tories, seeking to build on one of Boris Johnson's many contradictory promises: Levelling Up and investment. But there were also Small State Tories backing another of Johnson's promises: less public spending, on the rationale that we'd all race to work harder if only the government starved society of everything it needed.

There were the Christian Tories, such as Jacob Rees-Mogg, a zombie Jarvis Cocker who opposed abortion but made money from abortion medication;[26] or Steve Baker, who thought warnings about climate change classified as child abuse.[27] We had the English nationalists, essentially UKIP in a blue rosette, who were absolutely certain isolationism would make us vastly rich, just like it did for North Korea, and were endlessly obsessed with their self-created myths about migration: Priti Patel and her fellow demons.

Then there were the Neoconservative Tories, intellectually allied to the Trumpist, far-right libertarian populism funded by US oligarchs such as Peter Thiel and the Koch brothers. Michael Gove is a self-declared neoconservative,[28] and an acolyte of neocon-prime Maurice Cowling, who wrote: 'If there is a class war – and there is – it is important that it should be handled with subtlety and skill. [. . .] It is not freedom that Conservatives want; what they want is the sort of freedom that will maintain existing inequalities or restore lost ones.'[29]

I think they call that 'saying the quiet bits out loud'.

Cowling and Gove's class war wasn't the only one being waged. We also had Culture Warrior Tories, personified by Kemi Badenoch and Suella Braverman, fighting anything they thought – without definition – might be a 'woke' folk-devil, but which mostly seemed to boil down to an obsession with labels on toilets, drag artists, and a woman playing Doctor Who.[30]

There were the quixotic, who tilted at wind power; the xenophobic, who rejected the notion of humans walking to new locations; and the sclerotic, who objected on principle to any kind of modernity. And least but not last, there were the absolutely batshit, who railed against historically accurate accounts of Britain's past. Everywhere you turned there was a fresh cabal of Conservative MPs waging war on some aspect of modern life, and often seeking public funds to do research into it.[31] Not one of them talked about what would happen next year. Not one of them talked about artificial intelligence, or up-skilling our young, or preparing for climate change. Everything, absolutely everything, was a rejection of tomorrow.

This was even true of the remaining rump of old-style One-Nation Tories, who at their fringes and during their sober moments might be interchangeable with a few LibDems: traditionalist MPs for the Shires, who felt the nation's top priorities were red trousers, Barbour jackets, and the freedom to shoot whatever animals you wanted. Many of these traditionalists overlapped with another group, the Military Tories, for example Ben Wallace and Johnny Mercer.

And since 2019, we also had a new breed: Red Wall Conservatives,

Tory MPs representing formerly Labour strongholds.[32] They mostly wanted a whole load of tax-and-spend, which must be why they had joined a party that opposed to both of those things. It was entirely baffling.

Attempting to steer these flights of fancy away from the looming mountainside of reality were two other groupings. First, the Machine Politicians, whose urge to unify the party above all other considerations arose from a fundamental void: they had nothing in their lives except for the Conservatives. Here you can picture Theresa May or Rishi Sunak.

And the final group were a bunch of scatty, populist bullshitters, whose tactic was to say whatever they needed to get through the next interview, and who occasionally believed their own nonsense – Nadine Dorries – but more commonly merely hoped the public would – Boris Johnson.

The long-term success of the Conservative Party during the previous couple of centuries had been a result of them maintaining a firm, unified position within touching distance of the middle ground. By the 2020s their survival depended on them becoming shapeshifters. However you tried to define them, they could point to some groupuscule or other within the party that defied your description. And in a sense, they were all correct: there was no longer any definition of the Conservative Party that withstood scrutiny. They were now not so much a political movement as a patchwork of petty grievances and minority obsessions, thrown together by Mary Shelley's imagination.

As a result, the party no longer seemed to feel itself responsible for the actions of government, telling itself that whatever calamity was happening must be the fault of one of the other factions. Meanwhile the nominal centre of power, Downing Street, remained in continuous hock to whichever pressure group had the ascendency during any particular week.

The resulting rudderless mentality explains much of their record in government. And now it was Sunak's turn to mould a Cabinet out of this barrel of turds.

It's Not Something I Want Any Part Of

The less barmy parts of Sunak's government had already realised there was no possibility of winning a general election if they stood on their record. Unlike in 2016 or 2019, there was no scary opposition leader to use in a ready-made negative campaign. Nor could they fight an election on Getting Brexit Done, because they had spent years assuring us that they'd already finished that project, and everything was now wonderful.

So Sunak's approach was to stoke a culture war, seeking out wedge issues and distracting the country from things like food, heating, housing, and healthcare. Instead, we would focus on migrants, toilets, and transexuals.

Straight out of the blocks, Sunak reappointed as equalities minister Kemi Badenoch, who used her first parliamentary appearance since entering his Cabinet to launch an attack on the founder of *PinkNews*, an LGBTQ+ magazine. The openly gay Lib Dem MP Layla Moran called Badenoch's appointment 'disgusting', following reports the equalities minister had – among other things – questioned the validity of same-sex marriage, lent support to an anti-trans academic, urged the Financial Conduct Authority to drop plans for trans-inclusivity, and shied away from an outright ban on so-called conversion therapy for trans people.[33]

Now back in government, Badenoch falsely claimed (under the cover of parliamentary privilege) that the *PinkNews* CEO Benjamin Cohen had been sued by a Lib Dem MP, and despite calls for a correction or apology, there appears to be no record of one.[34] A member of the government's own LGBTQ+ advisory panel who had resigned during Badenoch's first stint as equalities minister described the reshuffle bringing her back as a minister as 'one of the most divisive and alarming in recent years', which Badenoch seemed to take as encouragement.[35] She appointed the anti-trans GB News commentator Mercy

Muroki – late of the much-mocked Sewell Report that found no such thing as racism – to advise on gender policy.[36]

But Badenoch was merely the warm-up act ahead of new deputy chairman Lee Anderson, who was described as 'vile and disgusting' by a fellow Tory MP after comments about the trans comedian and parliamentary candidate Eddie Izzard. 'I'm going to be honest now,' Anderson said. 'If [Izzard] does get elected and I'm still here, I shouldn't be following him into the toilets.'[37]

To be fair to Anderson, he was just executing the role he'd been entrusted with, like a performing monkey, minus the charm, intellectual dexterity, or proficiency with shoelaces. He was open about it too, stating on camera that because the Tories could no longer rely on the disputatious charms of Brexit or Jeremy Corbyn, they would need to 'think of something else' to artificially divide the electorate, and 'it'll probably be a mix of culture wars and trans debate'.

His namesake – but nothing elsesake – Iain Anderson, the Tories' former LGBT+ business chief, quit the party, saying, 'It was made pretty clear the plan is to run a culture war to distract from fundamental economic failings. It's not something I want any part of.'[38]

Sunak's first Cabinet also brought us a new education secretary, the fifth in four months. Since WW2 the average time spent as an education minister was 764 days. Michelle Donelan had lasted two. She was succeeded by James Cleverly (61 days) and then Kit Malthouse (49 days), and now we had yet another: Gillian Keegan, who had served in her previous ministerial role at the Foreign Office for less than a month. The head of the Association of School and College Leaders said the 'revolving door shows a complete disregard for the importance of what should be a key government post'.[39]

Crisis After Crisis

Politics had been an inferno for a year, so Sunak's immediate strategy was to be as boring as possible, hoping to suck the oxygen out of the news cycle. And then presumably sell it back to us at a profit.

After a dozen years in office, every dribble of talent had been squeezed from the available MPs. The Cabinet remained packed with froth-weight ninnies or returning scandalmongers. There was now barely a Tory who hadn't openly rebelled in the last 12 months, and it seemed they'd gained a taste for it. Less than a week after Sunak entered Downing Street reports emerged that 'deeply unhappy' MPs were already drafting letters of no confidence.

'My guess would be that there will be crisis after crisis and letter after letter,' said one backbencher, while another said, 'Don't rule out another leadership vote next year.'[40]

That the latest rebellion fizzled out was not due to a sudden outbreak of conscientiousness or stability, but because many Tory MPs had essentially given up. Sunak had inherited a party that knew, without doubt, that it was finished. The traditional appeal to wavering MPs – to back this or that wonky policy in the name of electability – was rendered laughable. Dozens of Sunak's colleagues were already writing their CVs, planning their post-parliamentary careers, and spending their mornings watching *Come Dine with Me* while waiting for a call back from a chum in investment banking. The PM's pleas for unity meant nothing. What was the point of all pulling in the same direction when everybody knew the direction of travel was off a cliff?

They simply no longer cared. But if they couldn't run the country, they'd make sure they would run it into the ground, and then dance in the wreckage. And so the process of dilapidation continued, with the only faction still showing any fight being the most demented one: those obsessed with an ever-downward spiral of ever-lower taxation. Despite the clear results of the recent Truss experiment, they still claimed slashing tax would solve everything; although only a lunatic would look at the previous dozen years of reduced taxation and conclude it had led to anything good. If low tax led to growth, South Sudan would be booming and Norway in dismal poverty.

What investors sought was stability. Functional infrastructure, investment in skills and education. They wanted a healthy workforce, rather than one where 7 million were awaiting treatment due to chronic, doctrinaire underinvestment in the NHS. They wanted reassurances that the government wasn't going to be struck down with paranoia about the presence of a Polish shop in Faversham, go absolutely tonto, and respond by smashing the nation's trading relations and tearing up international law. Business wants to make money, and would doubtless be keen to invest in a stable, productive country, competently led by a government still able to recognise reality.

But we didn't have one.

Instead, we were cursed with leaders who would gladly beshit the national bed in pursuit of the backing of a slack handful of obsessive halfwits from the ERG.

A Threat to National Security

Sunak kept a low profile as his maniacs raged, and pretty much the only major signal he sent to the country was that the sleazy days of Johnson were over. As a signifier of this new, transformative integrity, Robert Jenrick was back in Cabinet, just two years after he'd admitted his unlawful actions had helped a billionaire Tory donor avoid a £40 million levy that only existed because of Conservative policy.[41] And Gavin Williamson was back, vying once more to be the government's least-competent member, an accolade for which its MPs competed in a spirit of interminable, insatiable gusto. It was barely three years since he'd been sacked for an alleged national security leak.[42]

But that's nothing compared to Suella Braverman – who is what happens when you feed Priti Patel after midnight – and who was returned as home secretary a mere *six days* after she'd been sacked for a security leak.[43] I used to assume the Tories had merely become bored with defending P&O workers against fire-and-rehire; turns out they'd actively absorbed the idea as a method of filling Cabinet posts.

Former party chair Jake Berry was asked on TV to defend the reappointment of a human sieve as home secretary and once again the nature of this ungovernable government became apparent. Berry gleefully described 'multiple breaches of the ministerial code' from Braverman,[44] and went on to make public her longstanding nickname: Leaky Sue.[45]

This had been known within the party for years, but somehow had been overlooked by Sunak. Back in May she'd been investigated over claims she'd leaked sensitive details about the Northern Ireland Protocol.[46] The same year, another investigation, this time over leaking government legal plans for the BBC.[47] And then, just as Berry was blabbing about the latest fiasco, the *Daily Mail* reported she'd already been subject to a security investigation when she was the nation's most senior law officer back in January: her tendency to blab about secrets had raised 'concerns' with the security service MI5.[48]

Sunak put Braverman back in charge of MI5 again.

An anagram of Rishi Sunak is 'Hi Risk Anus'.

Braverman left the chamber of the House of Commons rather than answer urgent questions about her reappointment, because if the home secretary could ignore national security, she certainly wasn't going to make herself answerable to something as meaningless as parliamentary democracy.[49] But this didn't make everybody in the new Cabinet especially happy: sitting Tory ministers urged Labour MPs to continue their attempts to drive Braverman from office, with one telling Labour's Chris Bryant, 'She's got to go because [. . .] she's a threat to national security.'[50]

Global Factors

It turned out Braverman was a threat to health too, but in order to understand how, first we must skip back in time slightly.

Around 3.7 billion years ago, one of the earliest microbes developed the ability to move itself around at will, and immediately decided there were better opportunities in the hydrothermal vent next door. So it got on its stromatolite and looked for work.

Every single organism that has existed since has followed the same impulse, right up until 1914 when, largely to help with the admin involved in moving troops to France, the British government introduced modern border controls and mandatory passports.[51] This was the first time it had been possible to accurately track numbers crossing national borders, and since then there has been a global trend for the number of migrants – going to or from any country – to rise steadily. It has risen from around 2.6 per cent of the world's population in the 1960s to around 3.6 per cent by the 2020s, roughly 280 million people on the move to or from one country or another.[52]

The reasons for the rise in migration are complex, but include the increasing availability of modern transport, profound global inequality, the ability to transfer money back home via the international banking system, the explosion of local conflicts following the end of the Cold War, and in recent years the effects of climate change.

To these universal factors, Britain could add four more.

One: we had spent half a millennium colonising and exploiting the world, and we ended up with the largest empire that had ever existed. By the time modern passports arrived in 1914, 23 per cent of the global population lived under British rule. We ran their governments. We owned their land. We had most of the money and all of the guns, and we pointed those guns at the locals while meaningfully suggesting they learn to talk proper, like what we do. Over time, huge swathes of the global population adopted English as a first or second language, and felt an affinity with Britain.[53]

Two: our 60-year adventure in the Middle East. Dating back as far as the Anglo-American invasion of Lebanon and Jordan in 1958,[54] through to more recent and better-known actions in Iraq and Afghanistan, we had repeatedly destabilised the entire region, sending countless refugees into neighbouring countries. Inevitably, many of these refugees hoped to come to the UK – they may have had family connections here, or simply a better chance at a life because they spoke our language. In 2021, our sudden, fumbling, derisive withdrawal from Afghanistan destabilised the region again.

The third issue unique to this country arose, as with so many of our problems, directly from Brexit. Before we left the EU, Britain had been part of a 28-country returns agreement, meaning anybody travelling to the UK without right of entry could be turned back.[55] The Brexit withdrawal agreement Boris Johnson negotiated, told us was brilliant and was backed by all but six Tory MPs, didn't include such a clause. It wasn't even considered.[56]

This allowed smuggling gangs to tell migrants, perfectly accurately, that once in Britain they could not be easily returned to mainland Europe. In this respect at least, the gangs were more honest than Suella Braverman, who had introduced her latest migration-busting policy, the Nationality and Borders Act, in July 2022 with the promise that it would 'stop small boats'. It didn't, not least because once again it didn't include a returns agreement. By November of 2022, only four months after the bill was introduced, Braverman was telling parliament 'we have failed to control our borders' and began ratcheting up the rhetoric again.[57]

The fourth and final unique factor for Britain was our cosmic levels of political ineptitude. From 2010 to 2016 migration numbers had been pretty much stable: each year Britain had around 15,000 new asylum applications, and a backlog of around 30,000 applications being processed. The process often took around six months to complete, but the numbers being handled remained broadly static, and the system worked.[58]

But in 2016 there was a 35 per cent drop in the number of asylum caseworkers as the Home Office responded to yet another round of austerity, while re-allocating large numbers of remaining staff to handle the impact of Brexit. The immigration budget was reduced by £40 million.[59] Migrant numbers remained roughly the same as they had for the previous ten years – a slight increase in line with the decades-long trend, but nothing major. However, the backlog of unprocessed migrants began to grow as staff shortages made it impossible to handle applications within the six-month target period.[60]

So how did the Tories respond to not hitting their target?

They abolished the target.

The backlog instantly leaped even higher. The government, in a fluster, increased the number of caseworkers again, but (according to the Institute for Government) new workers received inadequate training and faced enormous pressure. Staff turnover increased, and experienced, specialist personnel within the Home Office began to leave for less demanding jobs. Naturally, with fewer qualified and seasoned workers and a high staff turnover, the number of cases being successfully processed fell yet further. Between 2016 and 2022 the number of caseworkers grew by 60 per cent, but their productivity fell by 80 per cent. When Labour left office, the asylum backlog was 18,954, and remained below 30,000 per annum for most of the subsequent decade.[61] But despite annual migrant numbers increasing only slightly, in just three years to 2022 the backlog exploded to over 165,000.[62]

Cue: moral panic.

Let's be clear, most of that panic was misplaced. Despite the billions living in our former empire who could speak English, we were by no means the most attractive destination for migrants. Britain didn't even make it into the top 30 worldwide.[63] We were 16th in Europe in terms of immigrants accepted,[64] and in global terms, the number of migrants reaching our shores was tiny, less than 0.05 per cent of the total. Almost 90 per cent of refugees live in developing nations, not wealthy ones like the UK, so it was hard to rationally argue that we were experiencing much of a refugee problem by comparison with almost every other nation on earth.[65]

We were just shit at the admin.

Before the government introduced – via a series of intentional political choices – turmoil, cuts and high staff turnover at the Home Office, Britain had dealt with almost every asylum application within six months. But all that changed under Priti Patel and Suella Braverman. Of those arriving by small boat in 2021, 96 per cent were still awaiting an asylum decision two years later.[66]

—

Those small boats were a new thing.

Before 2016 it had been rare for migrants or asylum seekers to cross the English Channel in a small boat: almost every migrant arrived on a plane, a scheduled ferry or – in surprisingly few but very noisily reported cases – hidden in the back of a truck. But almost all were discovered on entry, because it's quite easy to stop somebody at an airport's passport control, or to look inside a lorry at a ferry terminal.[67] Once found, they were processed quickly and either granted asylum if they had a right to it, or denied entry under the pre-Brexit returns agreement.

It worked pretty well, all things considered. Imperfect? Certainly, but very few people died attempting to enter, very few bypassed customs and border services, and we had a simple, cheap and effective process for sending people back to France.

So naturally, we stopped all of that.

It could have been sheer ineptitude, or it could have been deliberate. Of course, it's very hard to prove intent, but it's easy to guess, so I'll just do that: I think the Tories saw in migrants a useful new offshore enemy to replace the EU. You can see the reasoning: it's hard to continue blaming the nation's woes on Belgium while also boasting about how you'd just freed us from the yoke of long-lasting lightbulbs and energy-efficient vacuum cleaners. So suddenly migrants became essential to the Tories and their fellow travellers; welcomed, but only to fulfil their role as a convenient bogeyman.

In 2021, the then-Home Secretary Priti Patel had told parliament that '70 per cent of individuals on small boats are single men who are effectively economic migrants'. Her replacement, Braverman, took a break from kidnapping Dalmatians long enough to repeat the claim, saying in 2022, 'There is considerable evidence that people are coming here as economic migrants, illegally.'[68]

It wasn't until 2023 that the Home Office, under pressure from a Freedom of Information request, admitted there was absolutely no evidence for these claims. Entirely made up. Yet most of our migrant policy was built around this vapid, empty assertion. It didn't seem to bother the government that it was a lie: the 'economic migrants' story had been stabbed directly into the nation's hippocampus, and the migration crisis was reaping political dividends for the Tories.

It's Populism 101: whip up an artificial crisis involving some kind of outside threat, tell the population that you alone have the policies to fix it, and implement a crackdown on a small group lacking the power to resist.

How the polls bounced! So immediately the Tories implemented another crackdown, locking down ports at which it had once been easy to check for undocumented migrants. Now it became more difficult, so another crackdown, this time to reduce access to facilities once migrants were in the country. Then another crackdown. And another. And another.

Between 2010 and August 2022, the Tories had implemented 168 changes to immigration and refugee policy, which averages out at more than one per month.[69]

Braverman's colleagues weren't universally delighted by her posturing. Multiple MPs, peers and senior activists accused her of inflaming racial tensions, and within a few months a former member of Boris Johnson's Cabinet called her a 'real racist bigot'. Another accused Braverman of using 'racist rhetoric' to further her political ambitions. The chair of the Conservative Muslim Forum said he could no longer, in good conscience, urge minorities to join the Tory Party, and said the 'most disgusting' thing about the party was 'Braverman's anti-refugee rhetoric', and that he didn't think she could sink any lower.[70]

And the quotes kept on coming.[71]

'I think that something isn't happening properly if a minister on a weekly basis is in the news for some kind of racial insensitivity.'

'She's not stupid, she believes she has a licence to say these things because she's not white. But all her language does is exacerbate hatred.'

'The politics of this leadership plan stink,' said another, seemingly placing at least some of the blame on Sunak for giving Braverman carte blanche to lash out at immigrants. And Tory peer Sayeeda Warsi, herself a Muslim, said, 'Whether this consistent use of racist rhetoric is strategy or incompetence, however, doesn't matter. Both show [Braverman] is not fit to hold high office.'

—

And yet she did. And as it became almost impossible to enter the UK legally, market forces did their thing. Smuggling fees soared, and the number of criminal gangs exploiting the situation increased, eager to suckle on the lovely new cash-cow our government had created for them.[72] Legal safe routes vanished, and then illegal – but still safe – routes were crushed out of existence. So smugglers switched to small boats, charged extra money for the danger involved, and the business model just kept rolling along.

Destroying the business model of smuggling gangs was simple, of course. Just open safe routes into the country again, guiding asylum seekers to a secure and convenient entry point where they could be met by border staff, and processed by an efficient, well-funded Home Office. The market for criminal gangs would dry up, and the 'small boats' problem would vanish.

But where's the votes in that?

This solution required a government willing to tell its own supporters the truth: that our leaders had spent years whipping Britain into a froth of alarm about globally modest amounts of immigration, while deliberately making the entire system operate less effectively. They'd have to explain that immigrants were doing valuable work, without which many of our core services were failing. They'd have to acknowledge that 3.7 billion years of evolutionary imperative was not going to be ended by Nigel Farage stomping around the clifftops of Dover with a Go-Pro.

Explaining this to their voters was not a prospect the Tories relished. Not least because if they admitted immigration *wasn't* destroying access to healthcare, housing, school places or suppressing wages, the public might start looking for the real causes. And that would not be great for the electoral hopes of the Conservative government.

They were pretty open about it too. While the government began briefing that they'd ask the French to boost their migrant processing in Calais, a former Cabinet minister was busy telling *The Times* that they all knew this was complete balls. It wasn't about alleviating pressure on the migrant system, but about creating and then exploiting unwarranted fears, and seeding ongoing disunion among Britain's voters. 'It will open up a marvellous dividing line. If asking the French nicely to sort this out were good enough, we would have solved it years ago,' he said, but they were doing it anyway because 'this is the issue that will move the dial, the one that will cut through in Stoke'.[73]

So instead of a government honestly facing issues and uniting the nation, we had to put up with a raddled collection of irreparably asinine parliamentary zealots, on an eternal hunt for new wedge issues, and living in permanent obeisance to the next tabloid headline. The Tories had so fully embraced the idea that *any* amount of migration was too much migration that they'd become blind to the central credo of their much-worshipped Thatcher era: people getting on their bikes and looking for work.

—

By 2022 the government was onto its next false crisis: claiming the cost of hotel accommodation for migrants was £7 million per day. In truth, it was £5.6 million per day, which adds up to £2 billion per year.[74] But immigrants from outside the EU contribute 3 per cent more than they cost our economy, which adds up to £5.2 billion per year.[75] If we stopped pointlessly, cruelly storing humans in B&Bs, processed them quickly, and let them get jobs, they would easily pay for every penny of their hotel accommodation – which, of course, they would no longer even need.

Immigrants from *inside* the EU (prior to Brexit) were even better for Britain, contributing a staggering £26 billion per year to our economy.[76] That's a total contribution of £31 billion every year from immigrants, which is the same as the UK's entire primary education budget.[77] We lost all that income in pursuit of a solution to a problem that didn't exist. And then we exacerbated it with frenzied, small-state fanaticism.

Migration is a given. It will always happen. And frankly, with technological improvements and the pressures of climate change, it will most likely become more common, so we – you, me, Britain, the world – should get used to the idea.

But how we respond to migration is a political choice, and the results of the political choices made since 2010 were stark. The system for handling migrants was described by the Dean of Durham Law School, an expert in the process, as 'complex, confusing, too often wrongly applied and in a continuous state of flux, where policies are aimed at making headlines and not evidence-led'.[78] Instead of monitoring a few dedicated ports of entry, border enforcement staff now had to watch thousands of miles of coastline. Rather than a bloke with a reflective tabard and a torch in Felixstowe, we now had to send the Royal Navy out to scour the oceans. And even though we cut the budget, we ended up spending massively more money to produce worse results.

Less effective borders, spiralling costs, a blossoming criminal network, and farcical admin.

Inevitably, it led to tragedy.

Manston

In February 2022 a centre was opened in Manston, Kent, where newly arrived migrants could be held while awaiting processing.

'SCREAMS FROM A MADHOUSE'

Manston had been designed to hold a maximum of 1,600 people for just 24 hours while initial identity checks were made. But due to the vast backlog, people were soon staying for weeks rather than hours, and within months there was pressure to move residents at Manston into hotels to prevent dangerous overcrowding. More than 20 serious cases of gastroenteritis erupted at the centre in September, and in words that should concern everyone who remembers Covid – which surely means everyone – local health officials wrote to the Home Office, warning of the 'many new emerging pathogens' at Manston, and highlighting the risk of something 'potentially more serious'.[79]

'Duly noted,' replied the ludicrously named Clandestine Channel Threat Commander, and then everybody at the Home Office acted surprised when 50 cases of diphtheria cropped up weeks later, implicated in at least one death.[80]

Five separate sources reported that Suella Braverman had been given legal advice that the situation in Manston was a lawsuit waiting to happen, and that detaining people there in such numbers was illegal.[81] Five separate sources said she ignored that advice. Chinchilla the Hun was counselled to move asylum seekers into hotels, but she had 'deliberately' chosen not to sign off the plan, apparently to avoid demented *Daily Mail* headlines implying we were housing immigrants in something like a suite at Claridge's.

Braverman denies all of that, as you would expect.

The numbers living in Manston rose to over 3,000 – almost twice the capacity it was designed for. There were scant amenities for helping vulnerable families, which often included young children. They were kept for weeks in overcrowded tents in the middle of winter, sleeping on the floor among outbreaks of diphtheria, scabies, MRSA, and Covid.[82] When the independent Chief Inspector of Borders and Immigration visited Manston he was left 'speechless' at the sight. 'No prison in the country holds that many people'.[83]

As the crisis grew Braverman, keen to be seen as a woman of action, immediately raced to Manston via the only sensible mode of transport: a Chinook helicopter, at a cost of £3,500 per hour. Fortunately she wasn't in the air for long enough for it to cost more than a week's wages: she'd only travelled from Dover, about 30 minutes' drive away.[84] Looked good on telly, though. Determined. Forceful. Only slightly like a deranged hamster cosplaying General Patton.

The situation became even worse following a petrol bomb attack on another migrant centre in Dover.[85] The incident was shocking, but entirely unsurprising: government ministers and noisy backbenchers appeared to dedicate their lives to vilifying asylum seekers, and even went so far as to target specific nationalities. The Albanian prime minister's response to the political malevolence directed at his compatriots was that it 'doesn't sound very British, it sounds more like screams from a madhouse'.[86]

I don't know why this was news to him. It was well known that here in perfidious Albion we *hated* amphibious Albanians, and judging by the reaction from Tory MPs I'm only surprised they didn't set up a pitchfork-and-torches boutique outside Manston.

'Some of us [are] very sick,' read a handwritten note from a child, which was thrown in desperation over the wall of the detention centre.[87] 'There's some women that are pregnant, they don't do anything for them. We really need your help. Please help us,' to which Scott Benton replied with a tweet, 'If the conditions are so bad they are welcome to go back to France.'[88]

He was clearly struggling to understand what the words 'detention centre' meant. They'd probably have *loved* to go home, but those pesky barbed-wire fences were in the way, not to mention – and this is just a thought, Scott Benton – maybe their home had been overrun by the Taliban while Dominic Raab ordered a fresh daiquiri.

—

The firebomb attack required several hundred migrants to be relocated, including yet more people crammed into the already full-to-bursting Manston, pushing numbers up once more, from 3,000 to over 4,000.[89] The police said the attack had been driven by 'extreme right-wing terrorist ideology', and had met the threshold for a terrorist incident.[90]

You don't fuck about when it comes to terrorism, and Tory efforts to defuse the situation were headed up by Jonathan Gullis, so you could tell already it would be good. Jacob Rees-Mogg might be a stupid person's idea of what a posh person is like, but Jonathan Gullis is *everybody's* idea of what a stupid person is like. His word-cloud would just be pictures of chimps, sticky fingerprints and jam. Two days after the attack in Dover, Gullis had the banana pried from his paw, was wiped down by his keeper, and placed in front of a camera to angrily identify the precise location at which other terrified migrants were being held. In case any of his audience didn't feel sufficiently incited, he reminded them that they should find the existence of such asylum seekers 'a totally unacceptable situation'.[91]

Suella Braverman was called to the House of Commons to answer urgent questions. She failed to turn up.[92] Maybe the Chinook wasn't available? But by a bit of good luck we could rely on her backbenchers for an Olympian display of compassion and rationality.

Scott Benton, back again, said his constituents 'could only dream of' receiving the same treatment as migrants.[93] His constituency of Blackpool South isn't what it was in its heyday, but as far as I know the residents aren't subjected to scabies and diphtheria, firebombed, and forced to sleep in conditions worse than any prison in the country. Meanwhile his colleague Sir Edward Leigh, a shabbily upholstered Chesterfield crammed into a blazer he found at a regatta, decided to reveal his thoughts in public, and hoooo-boy.

'Isn't the solution,' he asked the House, 'to repeal the Human Rights Act [and] repeal the Modern Slavery Act?'

No, removing their human rights and their protection from slavery is not the solution, Sir Edward. It is not. But thanks for playing.

Nor was the solution the one Braverman subsequently came up with: that any 'illegal asylum seeker' entering the country would be banned from settling here forever. There were two issues with this plan. The first was that she had made it quite literally impossible for people to enter the country legally, as was pointed out by her Conservative colleague Tim Loughton in a cringeworthy exchange in a parliamentary committee.

'Just a bit of role play,' said Loughton, describing a theoretical but entirely realistic case. 'I'm a 16-year-old orphan from an East African country escaping a war zone and religious persecution. I have a sibling legally in the United Kingdom at the moment. What is the safe and legal route for me to come to United Kingdom?'[94]

Braverman floundered that it could be done through the 'safe and legal routes that we have' but was unable to name those routes, hampered by the minor technicality that they didn't exist. But instead of conceding this to Loughton she just handed over to a forlorn-looking civil servant, while she went back to spouting nonsense about us being 'invaded'.

The second problem with her mad solution was that there is no such thing as an 'illegal asylum seeker'. Like Braverman's safe routes, they also don't exist. The Tories might have pretended otherwise, but in early 2023 Robert Jenrick accidentally let the cat out of the bag in a written answer: 'There is no provision within our Immigration Rules for someone to be allowed to travel to the UK to claim asylum or temporary refuge or make a claim for asylum or protection from abroad,' he wrote.[95] It's right there: there was now no way to claim asylum in the UK.

But this was illegal under international treaties which Britain not only signed, but helped to design.[96] Those state that anyone, from anywhere, has a legal right to *claim* asylum in any country they come to – not simply the first on their route. That's the basis of the entire international asylum system.[97] Their stay only becomes illegal if they stick around after a claim is denied, which is how we reached the embarrassing position of the UN High Commissioner for Refugees having to explain this basic principle to Braverman,[98] who – honest to God – had somehow managed to get a master's degree in law at the Sorbonne.[99]

Giddy, springing Jesus, what has the Sorbonne become?

Seemingly oblivious to this cornucopia of inhumanity, stupidity, disease, and terrorism, Rishi Sunak rushed out to inform a doubtful nation that the UK was 'compassionate' to migrants.[100] That was certainly a unique take, and one that was quickly put into perspective by Nimco Ali, senior aide at the Home Office, who quit in the wake of Manston. She contrasted the 'vindictiveness' of Braverman with – and this will be a good indicator of how extreme things were becoming – the 'compassion' of Priti Patel, the minister who had wanted to store migrants on a frikkin' volcano in the middle of the frikkin' ocean, like Dr Evil.[101]

Ali accused Braverman of fomenting racism with her 'crazy rhetoric'. 'It's legitimising [racism]. When somebody like [Braverman] says it, you think, you're still talking about people of your own heritage to a certain extent, but you're also normalising the Nigel Farages.'[102] And the only problem I have with this sentiment is the terrifying notion that there might be more than one Nigel Farage.

So what was the outcome of the pointless, entirely avoidable crawl into the sewer of anti-immigrant bombast and bomb-blasts? Life became even worse for migrants, but migrant numbers grew. Safety for asylum seekers was diminished, but profits for people-smugglers remained strong. Braverman resisted putting people into B&Bs to avoid bad headlines, but this led directly to terrible headlines. Her money-saving scheme to endlessly pack Manston resulted in the entire population of Manston being evacuated into hotels. And the cost of such hotels soared to £5.6 million per day.[103]

And all because Braverman was obsessed with out-bigotting the bigots in her never-ending quest for a world that's right-wing enough.

Stop the Boats

If only she was any good at it. In line with Sunak's strategy of rewinding every policy he'd just announced, Braverman faced ITV News in a rivetingly terrible car-crash interview.[104]

'The prime minister has set out his priorities for the year. One of them is to "stop the boats". What does that mean?'

'"Stop the boats" means fixing our problem,' she replied.

'Will you stop the boats?'

'We want to stop the boats.'

'You *want* to stop them, but you won't *actually* stop them?'

'Come here in a year or so, and it'll be very clear we've succeeded.'

'In a year?'

'I'm not going to put a timescale on it.'

'You just did.'

I record this in full, not because it's extraordinary, but because it has become mundane in the extreme. The only rare thing about it was the opportunity to see a journalist pressing a minister in real-time, revealing not only the froth-weight stature of the home secretary but also something about the complicit nature of far too much of our broadcast media – it was genuinely rare to see a minister with their feet to the fire, or challenged on detail. Pledges such as the one Sunak made about 'stopping the boats' were reported with the bare minimum of scrutiny, and I've done the research: bare-minimum scrutiny is no scrutiny. The best we could hope for from our broadcast media would be the stunning revelation that the government says X, but the opposition says Y. It's not difficult – in fact, it should be mandatory in my opinion – for a news outlet to do basic due diligence on any governmental pronouncement before even mentioning it to the public.

And this isn't a party-political point either. The same should apply to both government and opposition MPs. If a politician announces a policy, the first things a journalist should ask are: what is the budget, what are the key performance indicators, who oversees delivery, what staff and resources do they have, and what is the schedule?

If a minister can't answer those questions, it's not a policy – it's a pipe-dream. And it should be reported as such.

—

Of course, those responsible for policy decisions such as those made by the hapless Braverman denied it was done for reasons of xenophobia. Listen, for example, to Conservative councillor Andy Weatherhead, who told TalkTV: 'There's a lot of smart language being put out there by people pushing their own political narrative [...] like "to object you must be racist, or xenophobic, or anti-this or anti-that". Why must you be?'

It was a sharp riposte to critics of the government and would have been even sharper if Andy Weatherhead hadn't been pictured in November wearing a black shirt with a fascist logo sewn on the sleeve, posing with the banners of the openly fascist New British Union. He claimed he only attended two fascist rallies 'in the spirit of education and curiosity'. He must have been an impressively quick learner, because in just two visits he made it to senior rank within the organisation, and wrote a blog attacking the 'Jewish-controlled media'.[105]

National Decline

By November, despite all the effort Andy Weatherhead was putting into education and research, the government still seemed to be making wrong decisions, as even its own ministers admitted. The development minister Andrew Mitchell was fiercely critical of the effect of our stupid migrant policy, pointing out that almost half of the international development budget was now being spent on hotels for asylum seekers.

This meant we spent less on overseas aid, taking £900 million from humanitarian support in Africa alone, which – leaving aside the morality – increased the likelihood that people struggling in Africa would migrate to find a better life. Mitchell voted against the decision to cut the overseas aid budget from 0.7 per cent of GDP to 0.5 per cent, and was on record describing his own government's Rwanda scheme as immoral, impractical, and incredibly expensive.

'When Labour left office in 2010, Britain was an acknowledged development superpower,' he said. 'Today, let's be frank, we are not a development superpower, and we need to win that back. It's impossible to deny that Britain's reputation during recent years internationally has declined.'[106]

The decline was affecting domestic politics too. New visa charges for recruiting overseas staff now cost the NHS £180 million per year, money the health service didn't have, but had to pay to the Home Office anyway. It was the equivalent of 6,800 nurse salaries, blown instead on pointless paperwork designed to be performatively horrible to foreigners and – it seemed – keep migration on the front page. The result was that it became even harder to recruit healthcare workers during a desperate NHS staffing crisis.[107]

A further £70 million a year was being spent on agency doctors to plug the gaps, which were not helped one iota by our foreign policy decisions. Analysis showed Brexit had led to 22,000 EU nationals leaving the NHS,[108] after which 4,000 fewer than anticipated European doctors decided to come and work for the service, exacerbating the acute shortage we now faced.[109]

It turns out isolationism leads to us being kinda isolated.

You could argue it was important to train our own doctors rather than bring in medics from overseas, and I would agree. But we weren't doing it. In January 2023 the Tories instructed universities to limit the number of medical school places, or risk being fined £100,000 per pupil.[110] Not content with that, the government next refused to fund a single place for British students at the University of Worcester's new medical school, which had been built specifically to train doctors.[111]

Even without the – I nearly said 'help' – of the Conservative Party, the staffing crisis was beginning to spread across every industry. Britain had 1.3 million job vacancies, more than double the amount it had run between 2001 and when Brexit was finally implemented in 2020.[112] Every job vacancy meant a business unable to perform. Every underperforming business was at risk, earning less money, ordering fewer supplies, paying lower wages, contributing less tax.

Without immigration we couldn't fill those roles, so productivity sank lower and lower. With 7 million waiting for NHS treatment by doctors we didn't train and refused to import, millions of businesses struggled even more. We quickly slumped to one of the lowest productivity levels in the G7 group of major economies, 13 per cent below the average and 23 per cent below the USA.[113]

The Confederation of British Industry (CBI) demanded an urgent rethink, saying our fixation on stopping migration meant there was no 'momentum for growth', and harming industries across the nation. Robert Jenrick's response was to encourage businesses to 'employ local people'.

Well, that would be a spiffing idea, Robert, if only such local people existed.[114]

Flying a Kite

This was the party that Sunak inherited; although as a confirmed Brexiteer who had defended Johnson as PM and then failed to be more impressive than Liz Truss – a woman who ended up defeated by a lettuce – he had nobody to blame but himself.

He couldn't just come out and admit that leaving the EU had been a terrible mistake, and he couldn't just come out and admit Brexit was causing or exacerbating almost all of our nation's deep-seated problems. He couldn't even admit he'd got what he'd campaigned for: Brexiteers can never admit they won, because admitting it would mean they were responsible for what came next. So instead, they indulged in a permanent culprit-hunt, a paranoid, omni-directional punt at blaming everybody not in charge.

Rather than accepting blame or identifying the crux of our problems, Sunak pretended it was all the fault of the wokerati, and promised to make good on the promise of Brexit, whatever that meant.[115] This was the long-awaited sequel to the exact same promise to make good on Brexit made by George Osborne in June 2016,[116] and by Theresa May during her dismal premiership, and by Boris Johnson practically daily since the referendum. Even blink-and-you-miss Liz Truss promised to make good on Brexit.

Sunak – correctly in my view – judged that his party had only one hope of political survival: to grow the economy. But having gutted manufacturing, education, science and innovation, exports, fisheries and farming, tourism, and the financial services sector, it had only one way to achieve rapid growth: re-joining the Single Market.

This offered many immediate advantages. We'd gain access to 400 million customers, while alleviating border tensions in Northern Ireland. We could begin a saner policy on migration, helping to fill the 1.3 million vacancies that were preventing companies from growing. Implementing a rational, evidence-based approach to migration could help provide the healthcare workers we urgently needed, who could then get the millions on NHS waiting lists back into the job market and boost our lousy productivity.

After a decade missing in action, any return of growth, stability and a functioning workforce might persuade investors that we were a rational country again; or at the very least one that had agreed to take its antipsychotics on a regular basis, and lay off the glue. It was all positives, assuming you didn't mind seeing brown people in your local Tesco.

As the slow march of stupidity was overtaken by reality, polls showed barely one-third of us still thought Brexit was a good idea,[117] and two-thirds supported a future referendum on re-joining.[118] Public opinion clearly wasn't averse to us aligning more closely with Europe again, so only about 100 individuals could prevent this sudden outbreak of common sense. Unfortunately, those individuals were the owners and editors of the *Telegraph* and *Daily Mail*, and the Tory Party's internal pressure group of wonkish absolutists and irrepressible refuseniks, the European Research Group (ERG).

For years the key division in Britain had been between Brexiteers (who wanted Brexit to be done) and Remainers (who didn't). Now it was between Remainers who wanted Brexit to end and Brexiteers who seemingly wanted the arguments to continue forever. At the centre of this perma-raging nexus of dissatisfaction sat the ERG, a glooping pipeline of petty grievances about wind power and foreigners; and they'd be damned if they'd let anybody solve any of the problems that they lived to shriek about. Their raison d'être centred around the blocking of *Guardian* stories on Twitter, the creation of a human shield around all depictions of Churchill, and the avid collection of appearance fees for shouting about dinghies on GB News.

Despite this, in November, only a few weeks into his premiership, Sunak decided to test the waters for a softening of Brexit. Rumours drifted out of Downing Street that the government was 'considering a Swiss-style relationship with EU', removing the majority of trade barriers and allowing something closer to free movement again, in the hope it could dig us out of the productivity trap we'd gleefully leaped into in 2016.[119] No specific policy was put forward, just a highly targeted exercise in kite-flying, to see if a handful of fantasists were finally ready for compromise.

And the answer was an uncompromising no. A senior figure from the ERG promised to go 'completely and utterly berserk' if they couldn't stick to their original plan of turning what was left of Britain into a deregulated, ultra-low-tax Singapore-on-Thames. I'm not sure I'd notice any additional berserking, to be honest. The ERG had been berserk back when nobody would execute their batshit economic theory, berserk when Liz Truss did attempt to implement it, and remained berserk after she was booted from office. And now the air hung heavy with the promise of yet more berserkness.[120]

And so, governed more by the desire to hold his fractured party together than the needs of his country, Sunak put his Switzerland plan back in its box, and once again committed himself to hard-line Euroscepticism and national decline. In a clean break from Boris Johnson, he announced he was now fully committed to Johnson's 'bare bones'

Brexit deal which would, he insisted, 'deliver enormous benefits to the country'.[121]

He couldn't tell anybody what those benefits were, or when they'd reveal themselves. But in the meantime the message was: just buy this bag of magic beans, and believe a bit harder.

I don't want to overstate the scale of the problem, but Brexit cost Britain's GDP £88 billion in 2022 – that's a pile of £10 notes 545 miles high – so everything in life could become measurably more irritating, millions of us couldn't pay our food and energy bills, and the NHS couldn't afford a survivable wage for nurses.[122]

Yet we were asked to focus on the clean-limbed, plastic managerialism of Rishi Sunak, and look on the bright side: at least the endless scandal had stopped!

Completely Underwhelming

At the height of the pandemic in 2020 there was an urgent need for personal protective equipment (PPE), and in response the Conservative government had done what Conservative governments always seemed to do: outsourced its own responsibility and created a way for corporate power to make a quick buck. They set up a 'high-priority VIP lane' to process applications for contracts coming in from government officials, ministers' offices, MPs, members of the House of Lords and other well-connected individuals.[123] The scheme was wildly successful, if your criteria for success includes wasting and writing-off almost £9 billion on PPE that was either overpriced or fell so short of standards that it was completely unusable. That's enough to pay for a dozen of the invisible hospitals the Tories had promised.[124]

Even setting aside the high court's judgement that the VIP-lane process was unlawful,[125] not much about the system looked like it had been designed to remain transparently clean. Uniserve, a logistics firm with no experience of supplying PPE, got a VIP-lane contract worth

£178 million.[126] They just happened to share an address with Cabinet minister Julia Lopez.[127] Tory donor David Meller, whose company manufactured novelty gifts for Marks & Spencer, got contracts worth £148 million.[128] Tory donor Steve Dechan was a director of a company that got a £120 million contract.[129] Globus (Shetland) Limited had given £400,000 to the Tories, and got a contract worth £93 million.[130]

And it was hardly unusual for such well-connected, deep-pocketed individuals to get a deal. In fact, it was ten times more usual than it should have been. One in ten suppliers processed in the VIP lane won a contract, compared to fewer than one in every hundred through normal, non-illegal routes.[131] And 92 per cent of VIP contracts didn't even complete the full due diligence.[132]

It's perhaps unsurprising that all of this raised concerns about the potential for sleaze and fraud. The anti-corruption group Transparency International reported that knowledge of the VIP lane was 'confined to only those within the party of government in Westminster' and therefore 'only those with connections to this party and its members would be referred through this route', and labelled it 'systemic bias'.[133] The *British Medical Journal* said that one-fifth of UK government contracts awarded in response to the pandemic raised a 'red flag' for corruption by international standards.[134] And perhaps the most scarlet of those flags was the one flapping around the Red Baroness, Michelle Mone.

It's a little bit startling to discover Michelle Mone had made it into the Lords. She'd lied about her qualifications to land her first role in marketing. After she – somewhat inevitably – lost that job, she set up an underwear firm, and marketed it by claiming her bras performed a key supporting role for Julia Roberts in the movie *Erin Brockovich*.[135] The filmmakers said this claim was a load of old bollocks.[136] But it proved the entrepreneurial Mone was prepared to do and say almost anything for self-promotion and good publicity, as long as somebody in her office was available to sweep up the mess she left behind. A director at one of her firms was found to have edited her Wikipedia page to remove various embarrassing comments about Scottish independence, and references to the time she said protesters didn't deserve human rights.[137] I'm not sure who should get them instead. Llamas?

Her looks – she was a former model – attracted TV crews, and she turned up on *The Apprentice*, something that can also be said of a wide range of unqualified, egomaniacal, lying show-offs in shiny outfits.

Growing up poor in Glasgow, Mone's ethics made her support Labour. But flashy, if occasionally untrue publicity for her knickers-and-self-tan empire had made her rich enough to pay higher tax, at which point she said paying higher tax made her 'disgusted'. So her ethics stepped in again, and made her switch her support to the Tory Party.[138] As a reward for this common touch and her recognisable face, David Cameron made her a life peer and his 'entrepreneurship tsar', overlooking the minor issue of her two businesses reporting losses of £780,000 and £135,000.[139]

Her ascendency drew glowing support from Tory bigwigs. 'Is she the best that the government could come up with?' said party donor Robert Kilgour.[140] Another leading Tory described Mone as 'a public relations creation, a personal brand rather than a serious businesswoman'.[141]

One entrepreneur said he was 'flabbergasted' that she was now enterprise tsar because he judged her to be 'a small-time businesswoman'. Another said her appointment was 'absolutely ridiculous'. And he should know because he'd met her. He described the experience as 'completely underwhelming. It's chat with no depth to it', and went on to say he hoped for more from this government – oh, naïve soul – than 'find someone who's on TV, looks good and say, "let's make her business tsar"'.[142] And it's not a person I normally turn to for in-depth commercial analysis, but Mone's friend Rod Stewart called her 'a manipulative cow' and said he hoped 'she'd choke on her profits'.[143]

Fortunately for Michelle Mone, there weren't enough profits to choke on. That is until the pandemic turned up, and a VIP lane created a wonderful new opportunity. Mone was quick to seize it; so quick in fact that she managed to recommend PPE Medpro as a supplier five days before it even existed.[144] PPE Medpro was founded by a pair of private wealth-management experts working in the tax haven of the Isle of Man. One of the founders boasted of his years of relevant experience in 'yacht management', so you can tell already they'd be good at this.[145]

Mone's lobbying on their behalf – which Matt Hancock described as 'threatening' and 'extraordinarily aggressive'[146] – ended up landing PPE Medpro with a £200 million contract to supply sterile clothing, masks and gowns for frontline healthcare workers. I say *supply*, rather than *produce*, because they'd simply bought the PPE from a Chinese manufacturer for £46 million and sold it to the UK government for three times the price,[147] but that kind of thing needs a contract from your friends in government, so Mone set about getting one. It perhaps helped that Hancock, a man so spineless he appears to be held up entirely by the starch in his turtleneck, had offloaded Mone to Michael Gove, who instantly identified her as a 'right pain in the arse' and passed her on to Whitehall staffers lacking any authority to resist her. They described her presence in the VIP lane as 'abrasive and bullying'.[148]

They didn't mention fraudulent, although that's what government lawyers seemed to imply. In legal moves against PPE Medpro, it was asserted the company had claimed it certified its PPE with test results from an accreditation provider called Intertek. Intertek denied issuing the document, which suggests it's either fake or magical.[149]

Anyway, for all her haranguing noise in pursuit of millions of quid for her yacht-managing pals, as soon as she'd got what she wanted Mone quickly clammed up again, especially when journalists began digging into who had financial interests in PPE Medpro. Mone got her lawyers to issue a statement claiming she had never taken any role 'in the process by which contracts were awarded to PPE Medpro'.[150] Matt Hancock, Michael Gove and a trail of email evidence seem to contradict that statement.

Further evidence began to suggest Michelle Mone and her husband, Douglas Barrowman, had a major and undeclared financial interest in the company. This time her legal team said, 'Baroness Mone did not declare any interest as she did not benefit financially and was not connected to PPE Medpro in any capacity.'[151]

That sounds pretty clear, but it didn't explain why documents suggested her husband had been paid at least £65 million by PPE Medpro, and the money had then been passed through various offshore accounts until £29 million of it ended up in a secret trust fund, of which Baroness Mone and her children were beneficiaries. Shortly after £29 million of PPE Medpro's money unexpectedly turned up in her trust fund, she found herself in possession of a private jet through one of her companies.[152] More questions were asked, and the traditionally noisy and aggressive Mone suddenly became a shrinking violet. Not a peep, while her lawyers seemed to suggest investigative journalism had no role in investigating *her*. They told reporters that they 'misunderstand our client's responsibilities to you. She is under no obligation to say anything to you'.[153]

That's the thing about elected officials: they're answerable. But Baroness Mone wasn't elected, so we could all fuck off. Thanks, David Cameron!

Her legal team went on to deny Barrowman was an investor in PPE Medpro, and that the gowns the company supplied 'undoubtedly helped keep our NHS workers safe' during the pandemic. Hmm. Documents indicate Barrowman invested £3 million in PPE Medpro via one of his offshore trusts. And while PPE Medpro did indeed provide 25 million surgical gowns, they failed technical inspection, and not one of them was deployed to the NHS.

This was not unique. Just 20 private companies received £7.4 billion in highly profitable PPE contracts. Masks, gowns and gloves from those contracts valued at £1 billion were judged unfit to supply to frontline NHS workers, and so were not used.[154] The Department of Health and Social Care annual report admits that of every £13 the government spent on PPE, £10 was wasted.[155]

What to do about this? You'll all have your own ideas, I'm sure, but I doubt many of you will come up with the solution the Conservatives did: hand another private contract to a company headed up by a Tory donor, paying them £4.5 million to dispose of the mountains of unusable PPE we'd just paid another bunch of Tory donors a fortune to provide.[156]

The government is – at the time of writing – still attempting to recoup £122 million from PPE Medpro, and PPE Medpro is still claiming supplying inadequate kit doesn't mean it should hand back the cash.[157] The Department of Health says the gowns were not sterile or fit 'for any purpose' within the NHS,[158] and by the end of 2022 had already spent a further £11 million (and rising) on its prolonged legal case to recoup the money.[159]

Sadly, there doesn't seem to be a fast-track lane for clawing back cash paid for faulty equipment via the kind of offshore contractual arrangements that demand a police inquiry. Because, yes, the National Crime Agency launched an investigation into Mone and Barrowman, and Isle of Man constabulary swooped into Mone's home.[160] Sadly the (then) home secretary, Priti Patel, was unavailable to pop on some police fancy dress, invite along some friendly media, and observe this particular dawn raid.

And then there emerged the by-now-traditional discovery of alleged tax avoidance too. Have a lie down, love, you look like you've had a shock. HMRC classified three schemes connected to Douglas Barrowman as tax dodges because they 'aggressively promoted tax avoidance'.[161]

Meanwhile the Baroness's previously mouthy lawyers became as quiet as a Mone. Suddenly it was no comment all round. And not much action either, at least not from Rishi Sunak, whose bold commitment to reintroducing 'integrity and accountability' into the Conservative Party led him to immediately do nothing to remove the Conservative whip from Baroness Mone.[162] Instead, she announced an immediate leave of absence from the House of Lords – while still being able to claim all its benefits and attendance allowances – so she could, in her words, 'clear her name'.[163]

And I'm sure we all wish her good luck with that mighty endeavour.

I'm a Celebrity

Matt Hancock was on a similarly fraught mission to rebuild his reputation.

Hancock – Keith Harris gone to seed after being abandoned by Orville – had thankfully overcome his fear of hidden cameras, and accepted an invitation to appear on *I'm a Celebrity . . . Get Me Out of Here*. It was a decade since Nadine Dorries was forced to apologise to the House of Commons after doing the same thing, which inevitably begs the question: how stupid do you have to be to spend ten years failing to learn a lesson from Mad Nad, drifting through events in her own sublime fog of unjudging discombobulation?[164]

Hancock's excuse was that he was doing a public service: he vowed to use the platform to raise awareness of dyslexia, something he had been tragically incapable of doing during the years he had spent being health secretary. In the event, he wasn't all that quick to raise the issue on the show either, taking more than two weeks to make a solitary mention of it.[165]

The central themes of Partygate had been: a disdain for responsibility, prioritising personal enjoyment over public duty, the utter dysfunction of our institutions, and an almost pathological childishness in the face of a crisis. Not even a year later, senior members of that administration had learned nothing. Hancock's appearance on *I'm a Celebrity* weaponised those characteristics for personal profit.

Moved by Hancock's plight, the deputy chairman of his local Conservative Association raced to express his unstinting support, telling the Press Association, 'I'm looking forward to him eating a kangaroo's penis. Quote me. You can quote me that.'[166] So I have.

Social media was awash with people equating a jungle jaunt by Hancock – who oversaw a policy of illegally discharging infected Covid patients into care homes that subsequently experienced 40,000 deaths[167] – with the sickening idea of offering a prime-time slot to serial killer Harold Shipman. This comparison seems unfair in my opinion. Harold Shipman was found guilty in crown court and died in prison. Matt Hancock was handed a small fortune to be tutted at by Boy George. No comparison at all.

His strategically iffy bid for rehabilitation took the form of trying to make us forget about all the dead grannies, and instead make himself loveable and relatable for the small, small price of £320,000. To be fair, while on the show he did make a point of saying he was raising the money for charity. His House of Commons records show he gave just 3 per cent of his fee to good causes.[168] The rest, he pocketed.

All that cash just to go on TV and ask forgiveness for his in-office fumbles. Money for old grope if you ask me, but nobody asked me. Instead, they asked Matt Hancock, who, in his chummy to-camera introduction to the show, admitted, 'There are people who'll criticise a sitting MP going into the jungle, but showing that we politicians are normal human beings is really important.'[169]

It was as though he considered himself a people person. But he wasn't a person person. Whether he's a person at all remains a question for the ages, and it's just possible he is nothing more than an excessively promoted snuffer of the elderly, held together by creepy knitwear.

He was right about one thing though: people *did* criticise him. Hancock had a nominally important job as a sitting MP, which he simply abandoned so he could make enough money to pay his divorce bill, eat kangaroo anuses, and not discuss dyslexia. A group representing bereaved Covid families hired a plane to fly a banner over the jungle camp, telling him to 'get out of here'.[170] It didn't seem like he'd be welcome home though: many of his constituents felt he should 'let someone else take over' as their parliamentarian.[171] Ofcom received over 2,000 complaints about his participation on the show,[172] and he had the whip suspended by a Conservative Party that seemed more concerned with responding to reality TV than with billions of pounds of alleged PPE fraud.[173]

The suspension of the whip had no effect on Hancock. He'd

decided to quit parliament anyway, which may or may not be related to suggestions his local constituency party had had enough of him too. His spin was that he was seeking 'new ways for me to communicate with the public', which turned out to be a stint on Channel 4's *Celebrity SAS*.[174] At the time of writing it hasn't yet been broadcast, so it's only a guess that he'll break off from charging through the waves to implore the nation to help him solve dyslexia, and we'll all call him an absolute 'king cnut.

Strike!

Meanwhile everything everywhere went on strike. Industrial action had begun in May, first with transport and rail workers, and then moving through almost every sector. Barristers went on strike. Teachers and university staff. Refuse workers, firefighters, the postal service, telecoms workers, ambulance staff, the passport office, even the Financial Conduct Authority. Almost every economic sector and area of vital infrastructure had been left dilapidated, over-stressed, under-resourced, and staffed by workers experiencing a record collapse in their standard of living.

This wasn't a one-off either. Since 1955 there have only been 12 years during which Britain's living standards have not improved. Half of those years happened since 2010. Under the Tories, each of those falls in your standard of living had equalled or broken previous records and now, in 2022, came a drop twice as large as any since records began.[175]

This coincided with the highest tax burden since 1948, and Britain facing the highest energy bills in the world.[176] And as if that wasn't bad enough, the decade before had seen the longest, deepest drop in the value of wages for over 200 years. The last time it had been this bad, Napoleon had been busy conquering Europe.[177]

Political manoeuvring and amoral, truth-averse media ensured the blame for this had been directed at immigrants rather than the government in Westminster. As a result, the squeeze on wages and living standards had been a major factor in Brexit. The Leave campaign had assured us that quitting the EU would bring about higher wages,[178] and at the general election in 2019 Boris Johnson had promised Getting Brexit Done would deliver a 'high-wage, high-skill, high-productivity economy'.[179]

Yet once the Leave campaign had won, a different story emerged. Wages had fallen by £470 per person *every year* since Brexit and would continue to do so until at least 2030.[180] And when workers asked for their wages to merely match inflation – which amounts to no pay rise at all – the government response was to treat them like traitors. Nadhim Zahawi suggested striking NHS workers were somehow giving solace to Vladimir Putin, and a nurse being able to afford food was aiding Russia's war in Ukraine.[181]

That bit of lunacy was an outlier, but across government the story remained: we cannot afford to give pay rises. Yet rail minister Huw Merriman accidentally forgot the approved party line and admitted the dispute with train workers had cost the UK £1 billion. He confessed that 'it's actually ended up costing more than would have been the case if it was just settled'.[182]

The rail strikes continued for months, and gained widespread public support from the millions of workers who had also seen their standard of living plummet. Only 42 per cent of Britons opposed the rail strikes; and even then, not with huge passion.[183]

Support for NHS strikers was even higher, reaching 59 per cent.[184] There may have been 7 million people awaiting treatment, but the added delays caused by strike days didn't appear to bother Britons very much. Three-fifths of us blamed the government for the dispute. We knew the sacrifices health workers had made during Covid, and the pressures the service was facing. During 2022, one in every four doctors between the ages of 25 and 34 left the NHS, and few blamed them.[185] They'd faced a 26 per cent cut in pay since the last full year under a

Labour government, and by 2022 many doctors were being paid a paltry £14.09 per hour, which is significantly less than they could earn working in a coffee shop.[186]

Their colleagues in nursing were, on average, £10,000 per year worse off than they had been before the Tories took office in 2010.[187] Yet in November, as strike action loomed, health minister Steve Barclay refused to attend talks. He found time to have two meetings with the nightclub giants Ministry of Sound,[188] but not to discuss the pay and conditions of NHS staff.

Stephen Dorrell, the former Conservative health minister, was scathing. 'Steve Barclay has been Secretary of State for six months. He's known for the whole of that period that there are pay issues,' Dorrell told Sky News. 'There were big issues before the pandemic . . . and now they've been made worse again.' He called the pay dispute 'both predictable and predicted, and avoidable, most importantly. It's a source of criticism for ministers that they've allowed this to drift. The responsibility, frankly, is his.'[189]

The argument from the government was that we simply couldn't afford to give NHS workers the pay rises they deserved. Presumably we couldn't afford the 31 per cent pay increase MPs had received since 2010 either, but I don't remember them voting against it.[190] And maybe NHS salaries would be more affordable if Liz Truss hadn't crashed the economy, Boris Johnson hadn't burned through hundreds of billions in pursuit of Brexit, and we hadn't given £96 billion to non-NHS healthcare providers – such as Virgin Health – during the last decade. That's a 72 per cent increase since Labour were in power.[191]

Or perhaps – and this goes back to the very beginning of their term in office – perhaps if the Tories hadn't implemented austerity, it would have made things more affordable. Research showed public spending had fallen by £540 billion.[192] If that number is too big to compute, think of it like this: £3,600 every single hour for 17,118 years. That's £1 per second, every single second since prehistoric humans first domesticated the pig.[193] As a result of this vast, almost unimaginable loss of societal investment, the report found 'the UK lives with private affluence – if only for the privileged few – amid public squalor'.

Thinking about Potatoes

Public squalor brings me neatly to Andrew Bridgen, and I'm going to surprise you here. I would argue that Bridgen's presence in parliament demonstrates representative democracy at its absolute finest: it's right and proper that incredibly stupid people can see somebody in power who is just like them.

Andrew Bridgen's brow might be low, but his standards were high. So high, indeed, that no Tory leader could possibly meet them. He'd compared being led by Cameron to being a passenger on an aeroplane who realises 'the pilot doesn't know how to land' and tried to get him to stand down via a no-confidence letter in 2013. As a mark of Bridgen's mighty influence over events, only 1,110 days later, Cameron was gone.[194]

Quite obviously marking this down as a bit of a result, Bridgen broke out a new pack of crayons and began work on his next no-confidence letter, this time to remove Theresa May, whom he accused, without a hint of irony, of being an 'insult to the intelligence' of the electorate.[195] And in 2022 he was at it again, first calling in January for the removal of Boris Johnson (whom he described as a 'moral vacuum' at the heart of government),[196] and then becoming one of the first to demand the resignation of Liz Truss.[197]

It seemed there was no Conservative leader who could persuade Andrew Bridgen to vote for them. It almost makes you wonder if he'd become bewildered at some point, and accidentally signed up for the wrong party.

Spud-u-Hate spent much of the year engaged in a long-running legal battle against the company he helped to run, his family potato business AB Produce, which is a marvellous-sounding company that in 2014 almost lost its licence due to the 'lagoons' of putrid vegetable matter it kept around the place, and the 'urine-like smell' they constantly emitted.[198]

Despite being paid £60,000 a year to deliver 'half a day to one day' of strategy work *every single month* for AB Produce,[199] Bridgen found himself unable, unwilling, or simply unconcerned about paying rent on the £1.5 million home owned by the company in which he was living. By 2022 his family had had enough of giving him £5,000 a day for his work thinking about potatoes while he refused to pay for his own housing, and it went to court.

Bridgen presumably thought his oft-deployed ethics would be enough to get him through the case. The presiding judge thought otherwise, ruling Bridgen had 'lied under oath, behaved in an abusive, arrogant and aggressive way, and was so dishonest that his claims about a multimillion-pound family dispute could not be taken at face value'.[200]

Bridgen lost the case, and seemingly his few remaining marbles. 'In actuality I won the case,' he told waiting journalists.

In actuality, he didn't.

'My brother will be compelled by the Court in due course to repay considerable sums of money,' Bridgen asserted, right before being evicted from the disputed property and ordered to pay his brother £800,000 in legal costs.[201]

Yet his difficulty in interfacing seamlessly with reality was only the beginning of his problems. He'd accepted £12,000 from Mere Plantations, and subsequently made multiple approaches to government ministers asking them to grant the company 'appropriate tax treatment' – code for 'we want to pay less tax' – without telling anybody he was petitioning on behalf of a paid client.[202]

Yet again, it looked as if an MP might be accepting cash to do secretive lobbying, and an investigation was begun by standards commissioner Kathryn Stone.[203]

Bridgen then made matters worse by attempting to pressure Stone. He told her he had heard an unsubstantiated rumour that Boris

Johnson – of whom Bridgen was highly critical – would offer Stone a peerage, but only if she found against Bridgen in the lobbying inquiry. There was no evidence for this, it was just an attempt to manipulate Stone's inquiry, and the Standards Committee described it as 'completely unacceptable behaviour'.

So Kathryn Stone could not be outmanoeuvred by Andrew Bridgen, something that also applies to all stones. She found he had breached parliamentary rules in a 'significant litany of errors'.[204] He was handed a five-day suspension from the House of Commons, but immediately called for an appeal. Having examined the evidence against him, the independent review panel not only denied his appeal and confirmed his suspension but went on to say he could reasonably have been handed a 'more severe' punishment than he had.[205]

These events seem to have broken something vital inside Andrew Bridgen. He began spouting a series of increasingly unhinged vaccine conspiracy theories, going so far as to compare our vaccination program me to the Holocaust. Enough was enough. In January 2023, Sunak finally withdrew the whip from Andrew Bridgen, casting him out of the Tory Party.[206]

I would not be surprised to learn Bridgen still thinks he won that one.

Bullying is Never Acceptable

We each have a cross to bear. For example: Gavin Williamson wakes up every day knowing full well he is Gavin Williamson.

The tubular assemblage of failures had spent his parliamentary career ricocheting from crisis to crisis while Boris Johnson pelted him with gongs, so it came as a surprise to many that Williamson was suddenly back in Cabinet. This disturbed officials. Williamson's major claim to fame – other than heroic ineptitude – was his refusal to sit at any desk that didn't have space for his pet spider.[207]

Gavin Williamson was 46 years old. That's nearly 13 in demon years.

In 2019 he'd been sacked as defence secretary by Theresa May, after she was presented with 'compelling evidence' that he'd been responsible for a leak from the National Security Council. His successor at Defence, Penny Mordaunt, then had to tackle a second leak which 'could only have come from Gavin'.

Williamson swore on his children's lives he hadn't done the first leak,[208] and said it was 'categorically untrue' that he'd done the second.

A Ministry of Defence (MoD) source said, '100 per cent it came directly from Williamson.'[209]

After a brief, but not brief enough, spell on the backbenches, the lurching, toothsome abomination had been put in charge of education by Boris Johnson, and immediately proved himself to be one of those rare people who is equally incompetent with both hands: he was effortlessly clumbidextrous. An entire year's exam results were thrown into disarray, and even the *Daily Telegraph* called his term in office 'a fiasco'.[210] He was like entropy in action: the longer you looked at him, the more disordered he seemed to be. Yet his days at Education weren't a complete waste of time: he managed to film a piece to camera as part of anti-bullying week, earnestly insisting, 'Bullying is never acceptable.'[211]

Let's see whether that comes back to bite anybody on the arse.

Given how bad he was at managing literally *anything*, it made sense that Sunak put Williamson in command of nothing at all: he was made Minister Without Portfolio, and remarkably, even though his actual job title said he had no responsibilities, he even managed to fuck that up. The former chief whip, Wendy Morton, made a formal bullying complaint about messages Williamson had sent to her, which she described as vile, threatening, and having misogynistic undertones. Once again, Williamson said he 'strongly refutes these allegations',[212] a repudiation not greatly helped by the actual transcript being published in the *Sunday Times*. He'd used WhatsApp to call Morton 'absolutely disgusting', accuse her of attempting to 'fuck us all over', and ominously told her, 'There is a price for everything.'[213]

In defence of his colleague, Oliver Dowden claimed the messages had been written 'in the heat of the moment'. It must have been bloody hot in Williamson's office, because the abuse began on 13 September and carried on until 17 October.[214]

And why did he throw this month-long mardy? Because everybody had been invited to the Queen's funeral except for him.

Downing Street said they still had 'every confidence' in Williamson, but that confidence evaporated the following day, as further details of Gavin's distinctive interpersonal skillset emerged. He had invited senior civil servants at the MoD to 'jump out of the window' or 'slit their throats', and during the few hours when he wasn't 'shouting and raging' polite invitations for his team to commit suicide, he had 'deliberately demeaned and intimidated' them instead.[215]

Anne Milton had worked under Williamson in the whip's office and wasn't shy about her opinions of the man. He 'loved salacious gossip, and would use it as leverage against MPs', she said. 'People's sexual preferences, that sort of thing. He loved all that.' And if the unspoken threat of sexual blackmail didn't work, he would coerce members over their finances. The party had aided an MP who was having minor financial difficulties, and Williamson told Milton, 'Make sure when you give him this cheque he knows that I now own him.'[216]

'I'm sure if you ask Gavin Williamson about this, he'll say it was a joke,' Milton went on. 'I don't think it was a joke. It was the seriousness with which he said it.'

Milton alleged Williamson also used MPs' mental health to intimidate them, and his attitude to officials who worked for him was defined as: 'Always tell them to fuck off [and] fuck jumped-up civil servants.'[217] None of this was a secret: a senior Tory said, 'He's a bully, no two ways about it, it's well known, it's always been well known. His only talent is bullying.'[218]

Suddenly, from having every confidence in Williamson, Sunak was telling journalists, 'I've been very clear that language is not right, it's not acceptable.'[219] Grassroots members agreed. Just ten days after being appointed, *Conservative Home* placed Williamson at the bottom of the Cabinet league table.[220] Even Jeremy Quin scored better, and let's be honest, you've never heard of Jeremy Quin. Nobody has. His own family couldn't pick him out of a line-up of one.

Join in with this if it sounds familiar: Sunak went from denying all knowledge of bullying to insisting he 'did not know about any of the *specific* concerns' over Williamson.[221] He should have: party chairman Jake Berry had warned the PM about the complaints, and Sunak had appointed Williamson to Cabinet anyway.[222]

My old dad used to say: 'You don't learn anything the second time you get kicked by a horse.' This was the third time Gavin Williamson had had to resign. He and his pet spider lasted just 14 days in office.

Bullying is Still Never Acceptable

Not every food shortage is Brexit's fault. For example, if you found it difficult to buy tomatoes during 2022, it was at least in part because Dominic Raab had thrown so many of them during meetings with his civil servants.[223] Furiously hurling salad ingredients while experiencing 'a fit of rage' was, it transpired, an important part of Raab's theory of team management.

We were still only two weeks into Rishi Sunak's attempt to be a prime minister when Raab gifted him his second bullying scandal. It had been percolating for a long time. In 2016 the campaigner Gina Miller met Raab for a debate on BBC Radio, and afterwards they were being escorted out by a young runner when Raab began being – in her words – demeaning, bullying and aggressive. Not just to her either: after he'd finished browbeating her in the corridors of the BBC, he screamed, 'Go get me a fucking car!' at the runner.[224]

Raab denied the claims.[225]

A couple of years later there were more reports about Raab's behaviour, this time in a 2018 official document to the Cabinet Office, which outlined a 'serious expression of concern', and cited 'unprofessional, even bullying conduct of the minister towards his private office'.[226]

Raab denied the claims.

The following year Raab made it to the Foreign Office. During his tenure, employee departures reached 28 per cent, compared to 12 per cent at other times.[227] His nickname became 'The Incinerator' because of the rate at which he burned through staff.[228]

Raab denied the claims.

After once again road-testing his Mr Fumblethumbs act during our withdrawal from Afghanistan, Raab was demoted to the Ministry of Justice, where he found himself having to cooperate with Priti Patel at the Home Office. Let's be clear: she was no angel. In 2020 she was found to be a bully by a Cabinet Office inquiry. Boris Johnson broke the ministerial code to let her get away with it, and the government paid £340,000 to settle the matter so details wouldn't be made public at a subsequent tribunal.[229] But even by her standards, Raab's behaviour was shocking. He behaved 'so badly and inappropriately' during high-level interdepartmental meetings that his most senior official had to phone Patel to apologise, just so it wouldn't be escalated into yet another politically embarrassing bullying complaint.[230]

Raab denied the claims.

In June there was the incident with the tomatoes, which, needless to say, Raab denied. Boris Johnson reportedly gave Raab private warnings about his conduct, although Raab denied there was a problem: 'I'm confident I have behaved professionally at all times.'[231] Shortly after this, Raab told his team at the justice department that he had 'zero tolerance for bullying'.

His staff heartily agreed, and they could speak with some authority, since they worked for Dominic Raab, who they described as being responsible for a 'culture of fear' in the department. Rather than focusing on official duties, senior officials had to spend 'all of our time managing' their minister, or insulating juniors from his rages. 'Far too many anecdotes about Raab end with him literally shaking with rage at an official,' said one.[232]

Raab denied the claims.

While Liz Truss was having her whirlwind tour of Downing Street, Raab had resigned from the justice ministry, but when that excellent judge of character Rishi Sunak became PM, he immediately handed the job back to Raab again. His re-appointment caused 15 senior civil servants to be immediately offered 'respite or a route out' of the department. Some of them were still traumatised by their first experience of Raab's behaviour, and now he was back.

But this time it was different. Officials seemed to have decided not to put up with it anymore, and within days two official complaints were made against him.[233] A dam broke, and more and more grievances were raised. It wasn't hard to find willing accusers: a survey of staff who worked in his private office found 40 per cent had reported personal experience of bullying or harassment, and 75 per cent had personally witnessed it. The head of the diplomatic service said he had warned Raab to change his behaviour. An internal departmental memo described how staff had been forced to take time off for 'extended periods' as a result of being in proximity to Raab's management style.[234]

Raab denied the claims.

Nobody, he protested, had ever raised concerns with him about his behaviour.[235] Yet an unwillingness to 'do a Johnson' and simply bullshit parliament meant awkward facts emerged: when asked in the chamber, he couldn't deny a confidentiality clause applied to the outcome of an earlier employment dispute against him.[236] Meanwhile back at the office, things had become so bad that Ministry of Justice officials established an official practice of having a civil service 'minder' present at all meetings involving Raab. And over at Number 10, the permanent secretary to the Brexit department was reported to have shared concerns about the minister's behaviour with the Cabinet Office.[237]

And Raab still denied the claims.

Rishi Sunak, who had stood on the steps of Downing Street and promised 'integrity, professionalism and accountability at every level',[238] at first refused to say whether he'd been aware of Raab's behaviour before inviting him back to government.[239] He later changed his story: he 'did not recognise' the events described, and of course you don't, Rishi: you have the visual acuity of a mole. I've done the maths, and if you were 12 per cent smaller and meeker, you'd officially qualify as 'prey for stoats'. Anyway, after not recognising things for a bit, Sunak caveated the shit out of that too: 'I'm not aware of any *formal* complaints about Dominic's behaviour,' he said.[240]

Sunak didn't want to lose two ministers – one very senior and by all accounts very, very cross and armed with fruit – within the first fortnight of his gap year at Number 10. The best solution was to kick the can down the road, so he launched an inquiry into Raab, and urged people to come forward with formal bullying complaints if they had any.

Within days, 27 people did just that.[241]

It was around this time that Rishi Sunak realised he might need an ethics advisor after all. Who'd a thunk it? Nobody had held the post for almost six months since Lord Geidt resigned, partly because of the vast workload involved in an ethics audit on the modern Conservative Party, but mainly because the government had refused to allow any appointee to launch their own investigations. Anybody accepting the role would have all the responsibilities but none of the necessary powers, and this meant 'candidates think that it could be reputationally damaging' to accept the position, according to insiders. So nobody had wanted the job.[242]

When Laurie Magnus did eventually agree to be Sunak's first ethics advisor, he did so without the authority to investigate Raab for bullying,[243] or Suella Braverman over claims she had ignored legal advice over asylum seekers and Manston.[244] This left him in office, but not in power, which a cynic might say suited the government just fine.

Raab still denied all claims.

'He just doesn't get that this behaviour is not acceptable in the modern workplace,' said one insider. 'He genuinely thinks he's just being a tough taskmaster.'[245] And to a certain extent Raab was right. 'Hit this civil servant with a tomato' does sound like something Alex Horne would say.

Eventually, after months of delay, the report into Raab's bullying emerged in April 2023. It was damning. When he ordered the inquiry, Sunak had reassured the nation that 'I won't hesitate to take swift and decisive action',[246] but when the report emerged, he hesitated, taking no action at all. Senior Tories privately condemned the PM for 'dithering',[247] while Raab's allies leaked to the media that he planned to 'fight to the death' to save his job.[248]

Instead of a death-match with fate, Raab seemingly went home and spent the evening composing a penitence-free resignation letter in which he blamed the civil service for 'setting the threshold for bullying so low' that ministers couldn't even throw food at their underlings without being held to account.[249]

It was political madness gone correct.

The Tory Government Has Failed My Generation

Sunak had already lost three of his Cabinet over well-known problems that had erupted in public almost the exact atomic instant he'd promoted them, but for some reason he seemed to feel he was growing into the job. Somebody on his team had clearly urged him to no longer deliver his speeches like a motionless, unblinking automaton. Instead, he began a curious and discombobulating habit of explaining to the public that everything was going to continue being absolutely shit while he bounced excitedly on the spot, gesticulating expansively and without reason, as if his puppeteer was having an argument in Italian.

The latest reason things would continue to be shit involved housing. Sunak, determined to pretend he was ending Johnson's habit of simply lying to the public, made his first appearance at Prime Minister's Questions, and said, 'I'm pleased we had a record number of new homes built in the last year.' The 'record number' was not just down on the previous year's total but was also far lower than records set in the 1980s, 1990s, or indeed right up to the global credit crisis in 2007.[250] Number 10 refused to publish any data supporting the 'record number of new homes' claim, and Sunak did not make a correction in parliament.

So obviously it was time for another backbench rebellion, this time forcing the government to scrap housing targets.[251] We already had the lowest level of new housing projects being granted permission since 2006, and now a key Sunak promise to deliver more housing was overturned.[252] Many MPs voted to maintain our housing crisis because they feared losing their seats if older, wealthier, home-owning constituents had to face the prospect of desperately needed new homes being built in their areas. But some defied the government on housing because they were, in the words of one rebel, simply 'a bit bored'.[253]

Ryan Shorthouse, the founder of influential Tory thinktank Bright Blue, resigned in protest. 'The Tory government has failed my generation,' he said, with a furious condemnation of '12 years of Tory rule, with punishing housing and childcare costs – combined with stagnant wages – preventing the building blocks of what Conservatives believe make the good life'. Instead of looking after the nation, he said the party had become 'bogged down in Brexit'. And despite the noisy, attention-grabbing presence of working-class Red Wall Tories such as Lee Anderson, Shorthouse now accepted the Tories were nothing more than 'the party of the rich'.

'There was kind of unashamed, almost vice-signalling about that, which really blew me away,' said Shorthouse. And while the problem pre-dated Sunak, the new PM was still 'short-sighted politically and seems to be a bad judge of character'.[254]

Sunak responded by blaming everything on Labour, a party that hadn't been in government for almost 13 years. 'It is the same old Labour ideas,' he shouted at PMQs. 'More debt, more inflation, more strikes and more migration.'[255] But it was desperate stuff, and a quick look at the facts didn't help make his case at all. Debt had risen from

£979 billion[256] during Labour's last full year in office, to a whopping £2.4 trillion.[257] Inflation was more than three times the level his party had inherited.[258] In the whole of 2009, Britain lost 456,000 days to strikes, compared with 843,000 in the *single month* of December 2022.[259] And net migration had more than doubled under the Tories.[260]

But rather than deal with any of this, they blamed Labour or focused on wedge issues designed to stoke a culture war. Their biggest tool for conducting this war was big tool Lee Anderson, who immediately launched a call to bring back the death penalty. 'Nobody has ever committed a crime after being executed', said Anderson, employing the precise logic of Judge Death.[261] Something about his forehead suggests a prodigious depth of bone. He was 48 hours into the job, and already managed to be officially rebuked by Rishi Sunak over capital punishment. 'That's not my view,' said Sunak. 'That's not the government's view.'[262]

Many complained that they didn't know what Labour leader Keir Starmer stood for, but give the guy a break: it's hard to compete with a party that boasts an omnidirectional policy agenda covering every base in the Multiverse. Spend less, said some Tories. Spend more, said others. Taxes down. Level up. Open trade. Close ports. Freeports! Free the statues! Hang the living to stop all crime! They stood for nothing and everything; and it was in that spirit that as 2023 arrived, almost one-third of Tory MPs on Twitter no longer mentioned in their bio the party they represented, possibly because they no longer knew what that party was for or against. Only one of the last four party leaders even bothered to mention they were Conservative.[263]

It was indicative of a party with no purpose and no talent. A party which didn't promote people despite their stupidity, but *because* of it. Lee Anderson and his ilk were shoved in front of cameras simply to say and do moronic, destructive, attention-grabbing things, while mundane old Simon Clarke and Steve Barclay, a pair of stock photographs made flesh, quietly got on with pulling your life apart in the background. The culture warriors were there to stick it to the libs rather than achieve anything of value; but they were too gormless to realise what was really going on.

They began to think their ascension was due to some innate brilliance, rather than the truth: they'd been selected for their consummate intrinsic stupidity and willingness to be manipulated.

So they began shooting their mouths off with wild abandon, including Anderson himself, who had likened his own government to 'the band on the *Titanic*' days before Sunak appointed him deputy chairman, yet was now conducting the band and boasting about how great the bottom of the Atlantic was gonna be.[264]

They utterly demeaned their offices, of course; but they also utterly demeaned Sunak, whose decision to place them in these positions was a stark signifier of how badly suited he was to lead.

2023
'A Whiny, Unpleasant, Bitchy Row'

Restoring Integrity . . . Again

A book has to end somewhere, and January 2023 seems as good a place as any.

The month coincided with the 50th anniversary of Britain joining the EEC[1] and the second anniversary of us leaving the EU.[2] Since then, Britain had endured perhaps the most demented 24 months of political turmoil in living memory, leading up to Rishi Sunak's stab at prime ministering – the hundredth day of which also fell at the end of January.

It was not going well. Three months into his tenure, polling found he was the least popular PM in recent history. He only outperformed Liz Truss because she hadn't survived in office for the 100 days required by the surveys.[3]

Sunak may have inherited a majority of almost 80, but everybody knew that majority had happened without his help, and everybody knew the person who had delivered it – Boris Johnson – had done so with staggering levels of bullshit. So Sunak had no real authority of his own, and couldn't really claim ownership of what Johnson had bequeathed him.

His squabbling, fractious backbenchers forced endless U-turns on him, and when they weren't doing so, Sunak himself got stuck in, and performed his U-turns unassisted. This left him seeming so weak you wouldn't be shocked to discover he was Britain's first spine donor. And he'd shown calamitous taste in ministers: Raab the bully; Williamson the other bully; Zahawi and his hazy understanding of his duty to the taxman; Braverman and her frenzied, ongoing audition to prove she's sufficiently pure-blood to join the Death Eaters.

His only offering to the country was that our descent into purgatory would, in future, be a bit less chaotic than it had been before. Not much less chaotic; just a bit. And his overarching message to the nation was hardly the stuff of our dreams. We had a multimillionaire in Downing Street who urged us to remain too poor to eat healthily, but to maintain enough fitness to work until we were 68.[4] To save money nobody paid us for a home nobody had built; and if we got sick, Sajid Javid proposed charging us to see a GP that we were already funding through our record tax – which government ministers skirted paying.[5]

But at all times we were urged to remember: the Tories were on *our* side.

—

Let's set the scene for the latest plunge into financial scandal, this time involving the party chairman.

Back in 2000, furious gonad Nadhim Zahawi had co-founded the polling company YouGov, but rather than accept the 42 per cent ownership shares to which he was entitled, he had placed them with a Gibraltar-based trust called Balshore Investments. Zahawi's father was a director of Balshore. Zahawi junior took no shares at the time.[6]

Fast forward to 2018 and Zahawi, by now a Tory MP, received a £26 million unsecured loan, with which he bought several commercial and investment properties in London, Birmingham and Brighton. The source of the loan remained secret, but the timing and the value of the loans seemed to coincide neatly with Balshore transferring £26 million to an unknown recipient.[7]

By 2021, HMRC had started investigating some of the confusing tax arrangements that seemed to congregate around Zahawi, and even though the ministerial code states ministers must declare any 'tax affairs and HMRC investigations and disputes', Zahawi didn't mention a thing.[8] He filed declaration forms for every ministerial appointment he took, but didn't make any mention of his ongoing tax investigation.

By July 2022 Zahawi had become one of the year's most enduring Chancellors, lasting almost three whole months. Yet even during the week he took office, reports began emerging in national newspapers that the National Crime Agency had begun investigating his finances under the auspices of the agency's International Corruption Unit.[9] He issued legal threats against the *Independent* when it raised questions about his tax arrangements.[10]

The legal letters didn't deter officials in the Cabinet Office though, and they raised a 'flag' about Zahawi's financial affairs. Stories made it to other national newspapers too, so unless you buy into the theory that Number 10 pays no attention to the daily news cycle, there can be little doubt details were known inside Downing Street. Even so, following Zahawi's failed attempt to become prime minister, he was appointed party chairman by Sunak. Once again, Captain Ethics seemed to have remained painfully ignorant about what was happening on the ship he was steering. Either that, or he knew but didn't understand; or perhaps he simply didn't give a lukewarm speckled shit.

'It's extraordinary that flags were raised ahead of Nadhim's appointment by the Downing Street proprietary team,' said one government source. 'These sorts of concerns would stop someone receiving an MBE or OBE. The idea he could be chancellor or even prime minister is unbelievable.'[11]

And yet here we were.

Zahawi continued to deny any relationship with Balshore. His spokesperson told the *Financial Times* that Zahawi 'has never had an interest in Balshore Investments' and that 'neither he, his wife, nor their children are beneficiaries'.[12] More than ten times – either in person or via lawyers or spokespeople – he publicly denied any connection or benefit from Balshore and swore that he had 'never had to instruct any lawyers to negotiate with HMRC on his behalf'.[13]

But more questions arose when the independent tax lawyer Dan Neidle began looking into it. Zahawi's explanation – that the offshore status of his missing millions in YouGov shares was simply because Zahawi's father, a director of Balshore, had provided start-up funding – didn't appear to hold water. Neidle's analysis of YouGov's filed accounts showed no evidence to support Zahawi's claim, so a new explanation emerged. Zahawi now said he had 'relied heavily on the support and guidance of his father, who was an experienced entrepreneur'. Yet YouGov's company secretary told a different tale. Far from Zahawi's father giving invaluable advice and guidance, she averred that 'YouGov has/had no association with Hareth Zahawi beyond his capacity as a shareholder.'[14]

Nadhim Zahawi issued legal threats against Dan Neidle too.[15]

Meanwhile Balshore had sold the YouGov shares for roughly £27 million. Had those shares been held by Zahawi in the traditional way, rather than being shoved into a Gibraltarian trust fund, £3.7 million of capital gains tax would have been due. As it was, that tax hadn't been forthcoming.

Zahawi denied any personal tax benefit had resulted from the arrangement.[16]

In fact, for months Zahawi had refused to even admit investigations were being made, his reams of legal letters notwithstanding. He'd said, 'Let me be absolutely clear. I am not aware of this. I have not been told that this is the case.' He described press reports of HMRC investigations as 'smears'.[17]

In December 2022, Zahawi agreed to pay HMRC £3.7 million in overdue taxes, pretty much exactly the amount predicted by Dan Neidle. Zahawi waffled on about the 'confusion about my finances', describing it as an innocent mistake. The presence in his bank account of £3.7 million that the taxman was due had been 'careless and not deliberate', he claimed; yet he ended up parting with almost £5 million after tax authorities also issued him with a 30 per cent penalty.[18]

As for Zahawi's claims that this was all the result of mere carelessness: 'There are no penalties for innocent errors in your tax affairs,' said the head of Revenue and Customs.[19]

So once again a government minister was, in the parlance, 'facing questions', and I can't be alone in noticing that by this stage every one of those questions began with: 'What the fuck ...?' Under pressure, Sunak set up yet another inquiry into yet another of the senior colleagues he'd appointed. The investigation looked into Zahawi's behaviour as a minister, rather than merely as a long-standing generator of massive tax errors, and found he'd committed seven breaches of the ministerial code. He'd failed to disclose matters to three consecutive prime ministers, had attempted to become PM himself, and spent months publicly stating that the news stories were 'inaccurate, unfair and are clearly smears'. It had taken him over six months to correct that false statement.[20]

The PM sacked him. Zahawi's public statement on his dismissal made absolutely no mention of his breaches and didn't include any kind of apology.[21]

Rishi Sunak then vowed to 'restore integrity' again, following the sleazy first 100 days of Rishi Sunak.[22]

They're Out of Their Mind

I know this must be disappointing for you. Perhaps you thought the lies, cover-ups, corruption, greed, and stupidity would vanish with Boris Johnson?

Sorry it didn't work out that way.

The Johnsonisation of politics had set in, and Zahawi was but the latest example of the continuing influence of the man. Johnson had set the tone for the party, just as the party had set the tone for

Johnson. Each emerged from the other, each facilitated and enabled the other. The Tories may have eventually yanked out Johnson by the roots, but the party remained the heap of manure from which he had grown in the first place.

And, never short of chutzpah, the man himself was back in the public eye in January, busily campaigning for a bit of reputational rehabilitation as we faced more hearings over Partygate. This time it was by a cross-party committee of MPs with the power to effectively push Johnson out of parliament for good. Despite their professed desire for a clean and sparkling Augean stable, the Tories had spent £220,000 of public money funding Johnson's defence, even though – and I don't think it's unreasonable to say this – he didn't really have one. So we ended up in the ludicrous situation of the National Audit Office considering an official inquiry into why the government had spent a fortune defending the indefensible during the *previous* official inquiry.[23]

While Johnson's lawyers were presumably giggling into their champagne about the river of money their client was still bringing in, the man himself faced hard-hitting questions from inquisitorial powerhouse and all-terrain idiot Nadine Dorries on her new show from Murdoch's TalkTV. The Conservative chair of the committee on ministerial appointments said she had broken government rules in taking the TV job, but it didn't seem to deter poor, baffled Nadine.[24] Perhaps she thought the rules no longer applied to her, which is one up from Johnson, who clearly believed the rules had *never* applied.

Despite the built-in controversy, mountains of promotion in the Murdoch press, and Britain's voracious appetite for car-crash television, barely 8,000 people tuned in to see Nadine's show, and only 37 per cent of them made it to the end.[25] Even the *Telegraph* could only manage a two-star review, repelled by what it called 'the blinding light of Dorries' obsequiousness'.[26]

Dorries was still technically a serving MP while presenting her soft-ball talk show; yet on the face of it she had run melancholy mad after Johnson was pushed from office, and had stopped turning up to parliament. She hadn't spoken there for a year, and there were demands she repay her £84,000 salary, since she appeared to have essentially given up politics in favour of talking bollocks to Boris Johnson for the entertainment of a handful of Tories.[27]

Which, now I think about it, isn't much of a change at all.

So now a rumpled and shapeless Johnson turned up for his interview with Dorries looking as always – and I don't know why this is true, but it is – like he was attempting to hide a large fish in each of his suit pockets. As Nadine grinned and nodded wildly, Johnson laid out his case. 'Anybody who thinks I was knowingly going to parties,' he said, 'they're out of their mind.'[28]

During one of the parties, he had said, 'This is the most unsocially distanced party in the UK right now.'

But to be fair, he really was out of his mind.[29]

Understandably, there were attempts by large sections of the party to paint Johnson out of their history. In January, Grant Shapps tweeted a peculiarly composed photo of his meeting with experts at the Cornwall Spaceport. The photo's unconventional configuration only made sense when you realised it was the same picture that had been tweeted six months earlier in June, except now the former PM had been photoshopped out, Stalin-style.[30] Johnson was becoming a non-person, which must have really annoyed Steve Barclay, because that was his speciality.

Almost Nothing Has Been Achieved

Beyond creating a bonfire of political decency, Boris Johnson's greatest gift to the nation and the government had been the insufferable curse of Brexit, and the Tories now dealt with it by the simple expedient of shouting 'La-la-la, not listening' when anybody pointed towards reality.

Reality didn't care. Reality knew that Brexit was a disaster, and that it always would be. It was crushing the life out of Britain's economy and burning its way through tens of billions of pounds every year, while the nation bemoaned our inability to fund health, education, transport, borders, energy, passport offices, the legal system, or even to feed ourselves.

By now, more time had passed since the Brexit referendum than the UK had spent fighting WW2, although it was increasingly hard to understand why we bothered. Since 2016 the UK had lost – OK, not lost so much as intentionally hurled away – four prime ministers. Two of them had to go because they realised it was impossible to make Brexit work, and the other two had to go because they told us they *could* make it work, and then found themselves smashing up the country in a doomed attempt to prove it.

Brexit had become the elephant in the room. In fact – if you've got a moment – it wasn't merely an elephant; it was an elephant that had spent the last half a decade relentlessly shitting inside the room. By 2023 everybody in the room was neck deep in steaming dung except for Nigel Farage and Jacob Rees-Mogg, who were standing comfortably on a platform built from their appearance fees, merrily shovelling peanuts and laxatives into the elephant's mouth.

Despite its public confidence, privately the government was also shitting itself. Even the Conservatives' biggest, most Eurosceptic cheerleaders, the *Telegraph*, published an editorial saying Brexit was now 'unsalvageable', and despite the Tories still making a lot of noise about their core project, 'almost nothing has been achieved'. The Torygraph predicted Britain would re-join the EU 'far sooner than anyone now imagines'.[31]

Under conditions of strict secrecy, a cross-party summit was arranged between high-ranking, pro-Brexit government figures – including Michael Gove, Michael Howard, and Norman Lamont – and their Labour, nominally pro-Remain adversaries, in a desperate attempt to 'make Brexit work'. The prepared discussion document admitted Brexit was 'acting as a drag on our growth and inhibiting the UK's potential', and now the government wanted Remainers to turn up and help them out of the terrible predicament they'd got us into.

'The main thrust of it,' said one insider, 'was that Britain is losing out, that Brexit is not delivering.'[32]

You don't say!

We ran out of food again, and not just fancy luxuries. There were national shortages of eggs, cucumbers, carrots, and cabbages. We ran out of lettuce, severely hitting Liz Truss; and tomatoes, no longer severely hitting the civil servants who worked for Dominic Raab. Asda, Morrisons and other supermarkets placed limits on the number of vegetables its customers could buy, and over 60 per cent of Britons found themselves experiencing food shortages.[33] A government built on the ineffable power of customer choice now contorted reason so much that it found itself accusing supermarkets of having 'far too many products', according to backbencher Selaine Saxby. Her more senior colleague Thérèse Coffey spent her days urging hungry Britons to 'cherish the specialisms' of our cold, wet, brown diet. Her advice boiled down to: let them eat turnips.[34]

And then the nation's biggest turnip farmer – who was in Coffey's constituency – gave up growing them. Rising costs had made it unprofitable.[35]

Unsurprisingly for a nation now reduced to living off a diet of xenophobia and unpleasant root vegetables – which we couldn't even afford to grow, let alone cook – the grand plan to turn Britain into a high-tech powerhouse was going nowhere. Battery manufacturer Britishvolt had been much vaunted by the Tories as a signifier of our technologically advanced future, yet the company collapsed in January after it failed to secure the £100 million promised to it by the government.[36]

But at least we had the lowest corporation tax in the G7, designed to attract inward investment.

It didn't work. It hadn't worked when George Osborne reduced it to 19 per cent either.[37] Business cared about bigger things than a few per cent tax on profits, and we offered almost none of those things.

Education? Underfunded by the Tories.

Training? Cancelled by the Tories.

Infrastructure? Neglected by the Tories.

Agriculture? Screwed over by the Tories.

Housing? Undelivered by the Tories.

Energy? Sold off by the Tories.

Imports? Hindered by the Tories.

Exports? Thwarted by the Tories.

A healthy workforce? Forsaken by the Tories.

Political stability? Are you fucking kidding me?

For 13 years, each time the government applied a bit of austerity, it had saved a comparatively tiny sliver of money for a year or two, yet had left Britain incapable of performing basic tasks a year or two later. If we weren't prepared to invest in our own national future, why on earth would foreigners do it? This was illustrated most clearly by the world's largest seller of electric cars, China's BYD, who declined to step in and fill the ready-made hole Britishvolt had left behind.

'As an investor we want a country to be stable,' said BYD's European president. 'Without Brexit, maybe. But after Brexit . . . we don't understand what happened.'

Britain hadn't even made it to their longlist of potential investment locations. Tesla also declined to invest here, and also explicitly cited Brexit as the key reason why.[38]

As Sunak's one-hundredth day as prime minister arrived, the IMF published figures comparing the world's largest advanced economies. The Conservative Economic Miracle™ was plain for all to see. The UK was not only the worst-performing economy out of the G7, but we had somehow even managed to perform worse than Russia, a nation strangled by international sanctions and spending tens of billions per week fighting an illegal war. Of all the advanced economies in the world, only the UK's was predicted to shrink.[39]

Prior to Brexit, the City of London had been a trading centre £1.2 trillion larger than Paris.[40] In 2023, Paris passed London as the largest financial centre in Europe. We'd lost a pool of investment so vast that it's almost impossible to comprehend, but let me try anyway.

One thousand seconds equals a little more than 16 minutes. A million seconds is 11 days. One billion seconds jumps up somewhat to 31 years.

And one trillion seconds becomes a staggeringly vast 31,000 years.

So the value of money lost from the London Stock Exchange since we voted for Brexit was the equivalent of losing £1 per second, every single second for more than 38,000 years. That's the same as losing £3,600 every single hour since the Palaeolithic era, when humans first emerged from Africa.

You probably won't be shocked to learn that polls found only a quarter of Britons were still happy that we'd left the EU.[41] Twice as many regretted Brexit, and barely a fifth of us had confidence in a Westminster government that had promoted it. By November 2022, only 2 per cent of Britons subscribed to the view that Brexit was going very well,[42] and to put that into context, 3 per cent believed the Earth was flat.[43]

Even David Davis, one of the primary movers in the referendum and later Britain's chief Brexit negotiator, seemed to have fallen out of love with the entire process, describing it as little more than a 'whiny, unpleasant, bitchy row'.[44]

—

But officially the government still insisted the problem was not Brexit *per se*. Brexit wasn't a *bad* thing. Any failings were the people's fault – we just weren't doing Brexit properly.

We didn't treat Brexit right, or perhaps we didn't love it enough. Sometimes we even angered Brexit. Maybe we didn't give Brexit everything it needed, so now we should hand over some more of our money. And some of our rights too: 'We don't need workplace rights, it'll be fine,' cried the party that brought us proven workplace bullies Priti Patel, Gavin Williamson and Dominic Raab.

No matter what, we, the ordinary voters, were to blame for what

Brexit was doing to us. Perhaps we didn't make Brexit its dinner on time, or we complained about it going out drinking with Trumpism and the guys from the Flat Earth Society. And if that meant Brexit had to sometimes – reluctantly – slap us about, well, it was for our own good in the end. The newspapers would hide the bruises. And anyway, we shouldn't listen to those former friends in the EU: they were only jealous. They didn't know how much Brexit loved us.

The whole thing had turned into a classic abusive relationship.

All the claims that it was good for us were bollocks of course, and it's essential to call out bollocks whenever you hear it. It is a truth once universally accepted, but now seemingly forgotten, that demagogues thrive in a vacuum. If you don't want a political realm awash with Farage and his ilk, you need to be truthful with the public about the lies his kind feed on. Brexit is a disaster, and vacating the debate surrounding it for fear of annoying the far right simply allows the far right all the room they need to roam around in that space, making hay.

Clocking Off

Still two years from the last possible date of a general election, and huge numbers of Tory MPs had already given up. Their polling guru explained that 'usually there are 30 or 40 retirements at an election', but there were predictions from Conservative MPs in the know that at least 80 would stand down.[45]

There was no longer any great crusade for them to be swept along by. If they could be dragged away from ranting about transexuals for a moment, and forced to explain an actual policy, all they could promise was a vague attempt to undo everything they'd done previously. They offered 20,000 new police officers,[46] which would reverse the sacking of over 20,000 police begun by David Cameron.[47] They assured us they'd repair our relationship with Europe after they'd campaigned to break it. They told us they'd fix the small-boats crisis after they'd brought that crisis into being. They told us they'd fix the social care they'd broken, the housing market they'd made insane, the inflation they'd provoked, and the health service they'd denuded. Above all, they promised to increase financial growth . . . if we gave them another decade in power. If we were prepared to do that, the Tories promised that – with luck and three consecutive decades in office – they might be able to return Britain to the economic performance levels they'd inherited from Labour, who they still insisted were a party of economic failure.[48]

Clearly not much of this was a selling point, so instead of policy they dove deeper into culture wars. Anybody who didn't wholeheartedly agree with them was an enemy, beginning, naturally, with the usual suspects. The BBC, of course, and unions. Channel 4 News. Rail workers, teachers, doctors, local councils. From there we moved onto lawyers – first merely the lefty ones, whatever that means; and after that, all lawyers who were anti-British enough to defend our human rights, and then the judges too. Ex-footballers. Current footballers. Current farmers that we were attempting to turn into ex-farmers.

Fishermen were also our enemies, as were charities, trans activists, trans *non*-activists, people who read the *Guardian*, people who wrote for the *Guardian*, God damn their eyes. The National Trust, obviously. Anybody with a podcast, or access to social media, or a library, or an education. And perhaps tiring of having to list every foe individually, there soon emerged a phrase designed to accommodate the lot: 'the metropolitan elite', a term of almost infinite vagueness that could be applied to anybody who might suggest that Britain had been fucked up by the Tory government and Brexit, rather than by Gary Lineker and the stars of *Paddington 2*.

After a couple of years of this, the only people who seemed welcome in the Conservative Party were a mythical band of highly informed yet uneducated Kentish village-dwellers who had become trapped in 1957; and the finance sector. But in a move that surprised everybody, stockbrokers, bankers and currency traders were about to join the massed ranks of the un-British.

Why is Your Chair on Fire?

The economy might have been sluggish, but Liz Truss's fantasies were still going at top speed, constantly outpacing her grip on reality. She was back, just in time to make one last appearance in this book, and if the gods are smiling on us, a final appearance in public life too.

Truss decided to print a 4,000-word apologia in the *Telegraph*, in which she reasserted her belief that nothing had gone wrong during her 49 days of being outsmarted by the ingredients of a salad. There was nothing at fault in her budget, she insisted. Jeremy Hunt – the chancellor she had chosen – was doing economics all wrong, not her: she'd been irreproachable. Don't blame Truss if the world's economic and banking system was too slow to adjust to the magical new reality that she had presented it with.

For once, the blame didn't lie with the anti-growth coalition, or with the dreaded metropolitan elite. Even the tofu-eating wokerati were off the hook, because a new villain had emerged.

'I was brought down by the left-wing economic establishment,' Truss insisted.[49]

'Can you see the "left-wing economic establishment" in the room now?' asked kindly medical experts.

The most amazing thing about this – other than the mere concept of fearsomely left-wing currency traders and hedge-funders – was that none of her friends had taken her to one side before she decided to go to print, and gently said, 'Liz, mate . . . just no.' And then an even more amazing thing happened, because literally the following day she decided her perfect budget hadn't been perfect after all. Cutting the 45p tax rate had been 'a bridge too far', she said, before heading off to confirm today's version of events in a filmed interview for the *Spectator*.[50]

True story: many years ago, my granddad, a heavy smoker, had a stroke. He was eventually sent home from hospital with severely limited movement, and instructions not to touch tobacco again. But he'd get hold of packs of cigarettes delivered by his mates from the pub, and secrete them down the side of his chair so he could sneak a quiet fag when nobody was around. A dangerous business, since he could barely hold a match.

My grandma came home from shopping one day to find him sprawled on the floor in a room filled with acrid fumes.

'Have you been smoking?' she asked.

'No.'

'Then why is your chair on fire?'

There was a long pause.

'It was on fire when I sat in it.'

Liz Truss's interview with the *Spectator*: same energy. That burning economy? Nothing to do with my matches, mate. She explained how she had spent weeks weighing up whether to sack Kwasi Kwarteng, and then months reliving the decision in her mind, and she was certain it had been the right thing to do. When it was put to her that she and Kwarteng didn't disagree on anything, she accepted they didn't.

'Yet he still had to go?'

There were then – and I've counted – 12 seconds of gasping silence while she fumbled for an answer to a simple question that she'd *literally* just told us she'd spent 100 days becoming certain about.[51] It was a soft-ball too, asked by a hand-picked, sympathetic client journalist from an in-house Tory wank-mag. And the answer she eventually stumbled into – it was because of 'market forces' – entirely contradicted her 'lefties made me do it' contention from the article she'd written just 24 hours previously.

In summary: she had campaigned on one budget. When she won, she delivered a different budget. Then she U-turned on that, sacked Kwarteng for agreeing with her, appointed Hunt (who didn't agree with her), and told the world things were finally going right. On a roll, she said she wouldn't quit, quit, and then said Hunt's completely unchanged economic plan was now all wrong again, before – keep up – she U-turned once again on her economic policies, and on her reasons for resigning.

And then, possibly just because she had too much momentum to stop now, the next day she U-turned on those things one more time.

The woman is an affront to reason.

Brexit Anniversary

It was the third anniversary of Brexit, in some ways.

You could argue Brexit had only been happening for three years, or that it had all kicked off four years before that, with the referendum in 2016. But the truth is, the nature of our relationship with Europe had been the central tension in the Conservative Party since the early 1990s. John Major's squabbles with the Eurosceptics in his party – indeed, right there in his Cabinet – had been so bad he'd taken to calling them 'the bastards' three decades before the events of this book.[52]

We'd had over 30 years of this, during which only one major party had obsessed about the EU. Labour had no noticeable fights over Europe. Nor did the Lib Dems, SNP or Plaid Cymru. The only other party obsessed with the EU was UKIP, which had existed without achievement for 20 years until it was promoted into omnipresence by the *Daily Mail*, *Express* and *Telegraph*. Riding this wave, the Conservatives had taken the decision to validate and amplify the key, evidence-free obsessions of the far right, and moved swiftly to absorb all of Nigel Farage's fixations, and most of his voters too. By 2023 Farage's party had all but vanished again, and Nigel himself was reduced to charging £63 to read birthday greetings online. You could barely blink twice before he was being pranked into supporting the IRA[53] or promoting anti-Brexit campaigners Led By Donkeys.[54]

My point is: the Tories had been consumed by Europe for far too long to call it an aberration. Feckless passions about the EU were no longer an out-of-character anomaly for the Tories. This was who they were at an ontological level.

Yet as the third anniversary of their defining, crowning achievement arrived, only 32 per cent of Britons thought we were right to leave the EU.[55] Only three of Britain's parliamentary constituencies still had a majority of voters who thought Brexit was a good thing.[56] The *Telegraph*, one of the three papers that had most driven our exit, and the one most closely associated with high-ranking Tories, now savaged Brexit.

'Almost nothing has been achieved,' read the paper's editorial. 'It can only fester, stoking tensions in Northern Ireland and strangling small firms with red tape.'[57]

The man who had negotiated Brexit, Swiss Toni impersonator David Davis, had admitted in 2018 that his government had taken away 'all the possible economic benefits of Brexit', yet couldn't even name what those benefits were ever going to be.[58] He might have attempted to sell the ongoing disaster as a result of a badly managed deal, but that didn't wash with the authors of a new joint report by top economists, who found none of this was a mistake. 'The new system is working broadly as Leave advocates promised,' they reported, which meant operating a company in Britain was now 'too onerous to compensate' for any advantages that might be found.[59]

Guy Hands, a leading figure in the City of London and a major, long-term Tory donor, called Brexit 'a complete disaster', and was clear about what this meant for the party that delivered it.

'The British population was never going to accept a state in which the NHS would be demolished, where free education would be severely limited, where regulation with regard to employment would be thrown apart. It was just complete and total absolute lies.

'The biggest issue about it, and you can take the Brexit bus as a good example, is the lies that Boris Johnson and the Conservative Party told about the NHS. In fact what they did was throw the country and the NHS under the bus.'[60]

—

So what had it cost us? Financially, it's fairly easy to find out. Between January 2022 and January 2023, it cost Britain £127 billion.[61] That's £1 per second for 4,000 years, or £3,600 per hour, every single hour since the Pyramids of Giza were begun.

If we hadn't done Brexit, we could have spent that money on new nurses to alleviate the crisis in our NHS – in fact we could have funded 3 million of them, which if anything is a bit too many. Or we could have built 460,000 two-bedroom homes, to alleviate the crisis in housing.

£127 billion could pay for the infrastructure needed to stop sewage spilling into every river in Britain seven times over. It's 4 million new teachers, or if you don't like teachers, it's the London Olympics 14 times over. It is the cost of 730 *real* new hospitals, not the 40 imaginary, unfunded ones Boris Johnson promised. It's free school meals for every child in the country for 28 years. It's almost every single farmer in the country getting £1.5 million in farming support, which surely would have helped to prevent food shortages.

It's 76 million court days, which might go some way to overturning the record backlog of 61,000 serious crime cases or reducing the record 708 days it takes to get a case to court.[62] It's 18 million wind turbines, or 2 trillion new trees planted. It's 430,000 carbon-neutral buses, which would transform our urban landscape and help tackle climate change. And those buses could move you around in more comfort, because £127 billion could fix 2 billion potholes.

It would pay for 4 million police officers, should the riots ever get so bad that we need that many. Or 3 million border-force officials, if minor-league migration is still making you more cross than what your own government was doing to you.

That's what it had cost us in *one year*, while the country was busy arguing about cake, dinghies and statues. For all their protestations about a desire for growth and a supposed record of economic competence, this is what the Conservative Party has *actually* done to the nation. Not just once either. I've quoted the cost of a single – albeit major – Tory policy over a single year. But a study by economists at Sheffield Hallam University found that at any time you care to name, the Tories are 'disproportionately likely to preside over a shrinking economy'.[63]

—

This was deliberate.

No, let me correct that: it was mostly a soup of staggering ineptitude, livened up with small, spicy chunks of pure evil. But none of it had come about as a result of some terrible, unforeseen accident. The current, calamitous condition of Britain was the result of 13 years of largely unnecessary austerity, which had progressively, year upon year, weakened the capacity of the state to respond to shocks of any kind. The Conservatives often accused Labour of failing to fix the roof while the sun was shining, but as soon as Tories gained power, they dismantled the roof and sold off the slates, as though convinced it would never rain again.

And as their hopes of further electoral victory faded, the Tories began what seemed, from an objective viewpoint, like a scorched-earth policy. The BBC must be destroyed while they had a chance. The NHS must be driven into dust. Schools must fail, councils must collapse, public transport must be ground to a halt. The civil service must be politicised, while bans on protest denuded civil society of any political views whatsoever. Any institution that conflicted with the private, minority obsessions of our failing government must be destroyed, and quickly, before they were shoved out of office for a generation.

It would be unreasonable to expect a more vivid demonstration of spiteful destruction from a vengeful, withdrawing army, slaying the cattle and salting the land in bitterness and recrimination.

It wasn't just that the Tories had left Britain incapable of coping with Covid: many nations struggled. Nor were we alone in feeling the economic consequences of the war in Ukraine, although our inflation was the worst in Europe and our energy prices were the worst in the world. And we weren't unique in battling problems with bottlenecks in international supply chains, although our decision to embrace Brexit caused it to affect us more than any advanced economy.

There was nothing especially unusual about Britain battling to overcome those rare, extreme challenges. But by 2023, we weren't even able to cope with annual winter flu, something that's been happening as regular as clockwork since time immemorial. Normal, predictable events now left us on our knees.

But we did have ten times as many billionaires as when the Tories took over.[64]

So it's not all bad news.

—

And then on 2 February 2023, a mere 48 hours after Britain had celebrated the anniversary of Brexit, Boris Johnson, the leader of the Leave movement, urged Ukraine to join the EU.[65]

Part 4
P.S. They Hate You

Putting the Gini Back in the Bottle

Classics vs Romantics

Let's finish with a bit of metaphysical philosophy. Stick with me, this isn't going to hurt.

In his 1974 masterwork *Zen and the Art of Motorcycle Maintenance*, Robert M Pirsig argues that humans can be divided into two basic behavioural types, which he calls *Classic* and *Romantic*. A Classic person doesn't care about how a thing looks, only its function. A Classic might say: yes, the house is ugly, but who cares? It's well built, and is just a box for sleeping in.

By contrast, a Romantic person is not especially interested in function, mainly in form. To a Romantic, the surface is the most important factor in assessing the essential quality of a thing. They might say: the house is pretty, so who cares if there's rot in the basement?

This leads to something commonly known as a 'platform problem': the platform you're on – in Pirsig's example, the type of personality you are – means you will tend to describe the other platform in disparaging terms. If you ask a Classic to explain Pirsig's hypothesis, they'll tell you Romantics are shallow and stupid. Ask a Romantic, and you'll be told Classics are smug and elitist. You'll recognise a lot of this terminology from both Brexit and the endlessly stoked culture wars.

I am not a Romantic in the sense Pirsig meant it. I'm certainly not remotely romantic about the past. It is, of course, easy to look back on the pre-Thatcher era with rose-tinted spectacles, and pretend everything was great, or that Britain was on its way to becoming a utopia. I entirely resist that temptation. The years from 1946 to 1979 were full of absolutely terrible things, and it's stupid to pretend otherwise. And anyway, I don't like to dwell too much on the past. I've always preferred the future – it's where I intend to spend the rest of my life.

But we can all sympathise to some extent with a perfectly natural sense of yearning nostalgia. It's obvious that many were driven to vote for Brexit by a sense of wistful, starry-eyed longing for how they thought things used to be in some mythical past. And it's hard to blame them for that: the good old days weren't all bad.

Like almost every economist, trade body, corporate leader, and (non-UKIP or Tory) politician in the entire world, I was certain Brexit would make things worse. It has. It will continue to do so. But people who voted for Brexit didn't see it that way, at least not in the few frenzied years surrounding the referendum.

I don't entirely blame them. They were lied to. They were told the truth as well, certainly, but they decided to believe the lies, because it was easier. Those lies had been drawn in primary colours: a simple story of patriotic wonder, lying just over the horizon. Brexit promised – falsely – something that looked like what the post-war period brought. And that period had a lot to offer.

From the 1940s through to the late 1970s, British governments built an average of 126,000 social homes per year, ending up with a stock of 4.4 million.[1] A decent supply of social properties helped keep down the cost of private housing too, and as a result practically every adult had an affordable home.

The state also owned and defended major industries on our behalf, and a core promise from any government – both Tory and Labour – was to deliver full employment with state-funded education, training or apprenticeships for anyone who wanted it.[2]

Fewer people needed benefits, because fairer wages than we have today meant top-ups via tax credits weren't necessary. But even so, there was a substantial welfare state which, unlike the 2020s, compared favourably with those across Europe. The popular story is that migrants come here for our generous benefits system, but by 2021, after a decade of Tory rule, Britain had the least generous benefits in northern Europe, and claimants here were worse off than their continental counterparts in 95 per cent of cases.[3]

During the post-war period Britain had a mixed economy, built from a pragmatic combination of free markets, central planning, and government intervention for the public good. There wasn't a one-size-fits-all subservience to the dictatorship of the market, which relentlessly seeks short-term profits over long-term investment.

Throughout that post-war, pre-Thatcher period, Britain's GDP growth per year fluctuated between a low of 1 per cent and a high of 6.5 per cent. Since then, if you exclude the unrepresentative (but understandable) slump-then-rebound caused by the pandemic, it has never been higher than 5.7 per cent, and has seen recessions as deep as minus 4.5 per cent.[4]

So it looked like the bold new free-market economic experiment had failed to match the mixed economy it replaced, but it did lead to a huge growth in inequality. The Gini coefficient is a globally accepted method of measuring the distribution of wealth in a society. The range is from 0 to 100: a low number means the society is more equal, a high number means it is less so.

In 1979, when the Thatcher revolution began, the UK's Gini number was 25, unremarkable by international standards.[5] By 2019 it had reached 36, which was bad enough; but if you measured accumulated wealth, rather than simply income, the UK's Gini number soared to a whopping 73.[6] During the decade from 2010 to 2020, the wealth of the richest 10 per cent of UK households had grown 574 times more than that of the poorest tenth.[7] It looked increasingly like the Thatcher revolution hadn't been about making us all richer: it was about making a few already wealthy people very rich indeed.

But let's return to the metaphysical theme of this final chapter, and quote the great diplomat and economist JK Galbraith: 'The modern conservative is engaged in one of man's oldest exercises in moral philosophy; that is, the search for a superior moral justification for selfishness.'[8]

A Plunge into Chaos

Had life been perfect before the neoliberal revolution hit us? Oh my God, no! Not in the slightest. I could write a book about the failures and scandals that rocked the nation. Sure, it would probably be a much thinner book, but nobody could deny poverty existed, governments screwed up, and there were wars and reversals and crises. Yet the general trend since WW2 had been for increased wealth, health, life expectancy, security, openness, home ownership, savings, disposable income, social cohesion, and acceptance of others.

Since the Thatcher revolution the pendulum has, to put it mildly, swung the other way. Those gains – and for the vast majority of us they had been substantial gains – seemed to have juddered to a halt, stagnated, and then begun an inexorable slide into reverse.

The action of historical inflation makes it look like we were all on poverty wages in the past. The average male manual worker got just £1,144 per year in 1968.[9] But the key factor is not how much money existed, but what it could buy. In 1968 the average income for a sole breadwinner would buy a three-bedroom semi-detached house in London.[10]

By 2020, that same ordinary semi in Romford would set you back £700,000, and the mortgage would demand an income of £175,000, which was more than *six* average salaries. Only the richest could buy property, and property ownership was the top source of income for people in the *Sunday Times* Rich List.[11] In 2023, 71 per cent of central London properties were bought for cash – something only the rich can do.[12] Poorer and middle-income Londoners, forcibly excluded from ownership, had to rent a home from wealthy owners. Rental income allowed the rich to buy yet more property to rent out, and thus the process repeated itself, locking ever more out of housing and endlessly enriching a shrinking group who had it all.

I'd call it a vicious circle, except all the viciousness was happening *outside* of the circle. Inside, it was probably lovely.

In the post-war period personal debt remained comparatively rare because – aside from mortgages – most things you needed in life could be afforded on your wage. Obviously foreign holidays were extremely rare, but that was a limitation of the nascent international airport system, not of earnings. Smartphones, PlayStations, and tropical fruit and veg weren't available, so the 1960s definition of 'most things' didn't match today's plethora. But cutting out avocado and *Tomb Raider* won't make much of a dent in the £700,000 cost of a home. Whereas in the 1960s mortgages were so cheap, you could save a deposit for that London home in under two years.[13] Today it would take a person on median income 36 years to save a deposit – just a deposit – for an averagely priced British house.[14]

So in the 60s or 70s a family would be able to clear their mortgage three decades earlier than a similar household today, and therefore have disposable income three decades earlier too. This meant they could risk starting a business, or spend money on the luxuries of the day, either of which helped to drive economic growth. Or if they preferred, they could save for a pension.

Because that's the next crisis caused by this soaring inequality: pensions. Today, 35 per cent of British adults don't have a pension,[15] and millions of us won't even start saving for one until we've got the house sorted – which won't be until we're in our 50s, even if we're very lucky. This pension time-bomb is such an enormous, terrifying financial threat just over our collective horizons that we barely dare think about it. But compare it once again to the post-war years, when state pensions certainly weren't high, but they were universal and they were secure; and you retired at 60 or 65, almost a decade earlier than people born in the year 1990 will be able to.

And yet for all this, from the late 1940s onwards, state debt was generally low and manageable; and we kept it that way while making repayments for two world wars and managing to build the NHS from scratch.

We didn't stop there. Post-war government investment and intervention – both anathema to today's right-wing – created much of today's road system, as well as publicly owned major industries, telephone services, public television, a power grid, and a science and space programme. We even managed to introduce the Clean Air Act that started to protect the environment.

Sure, the publicly owned British Leyland was terrible, but so are many things made by private industry. Twitter once launched The Peek, a mobile device that allowed you to only see the first 20 characters of tweets and absolutely no other content.[16] Pen and razor giants Bic once attempted to market disposable underwear. The Fiat Multipla really happened.

It really did. You didn't dream it.

Yet we didn't abolish all forms of capitalism because of these foolish examples, so the fact somebody made the Austin Allegro is hardly an argument for rejecting public ownership of *anything*. Public ownership allowed us to create vast national assets that benefited all, while we also gave away an empire yet remained reasonably wealthy and powerful.

We managed to do this while accepting 1.4 million non-white (and, in large numbers, non-Christian) immigrants in the 1950s alone, and yet more in the 60s.[17] Over 800 million Commonwealth citizens had the right to come here after the British Empire ended.[18] And did they? No, they did not, just as we didn't see the entire population of Romania move here in 2014, nor the whole of Albania invade Kent in

2022, despite dire warnings from irresponsible, opportunistic right-wing populists. It's a panic over nothing. Then as now, neither the potential nor the reality of mass immigration destroyed our economy, our health service, our housing market, or our capacity to earn a decent wage.

So what did?

Well, there are some clues.

In the 1970s the highest rate of income tax on the excess pay of the very richest people was 83 per cent.[19] By 2021 it was down to 45 per cent.[20] Corporation tax used to be 52 per cent.[21] By 2021 it was 19 per cent.[22] Now, I'm not suggesting an immediate return to 83 per cent taxation – a rate which, unless you're obscenely wealthy, never affected you anyway – but there are plenty of intermediate steps between next-to-nothing and far-too-much. Is it possible a return to one of those intermediate rates for the *very* wealthy might not be the worst idea in the world, if it allows us to operate a functional country?

Let me put this into context. In 2022, the wealth of Britain's 177 billionaires could – all on its own – fund the entire cost of building a million new homes, insulating every other home in the country, re-nationalising the entire water industry, repairing 90 per cent of Britain's schools, and completing the entire repairs backlog of every NHS building. All of that. The whole lot.

And after they had paid for all of that, those 177 billionaires would still have two-thirds of their money left.[23]

Not for nothing does the Nobel Prize-winning economist Joseph Stiglitz recommend a 70 per cent tax on the excess earnings of the extremely rich. He describes such a tax as a desperately needed antidote to our gaping inequality. The world, he argues, will 'plunge into chaos' if we don't take action.[24]

But we persist in our inaction. And meanwhile the tax-avoidance industry for the rich has continued to grow, happily ignored, condoned or participated in by leading members of the Tory government, including two recent Tory prime ministers (Cameron[25] and Sunak[26]), and the husband of another (May).[27] Combined with those giant tax cuts, this means the state now receives a fraction of what we used to get from the people who are sat on most of the money.

No wonder our Gini coefficient continues to climb.

The Theory of Justice

The result? Since 2010 the ten wealthiest Britons have seen their cumulative fortunes grow from £47 billion to over £182 billion, an increase of 281 per cent.[28] The UK's richest people are richer than ever.

But everybody else suffered. In 2023, average benefits were £140 per month below the minimum cost of food, energy and everyday basics.[29] Low-income households in the UK were poorer than their equivalents in Europe, and middle-income households in the UK were also poorer than middle-income households in Europe. By 2024, the average family in Britain will be worse off than its counterpart in Slovenia, which is ranked as the 84th largest economy.[30] We are fifth.[31]

As a nation we only appear wealthy because we've allowed – nay, actively encouraged – the richest few hundred individuals to hoard almost all of the loot. And one of the key reasons we struggle as a state is that we seem to elect either a Tory government in cahoots with that super-rich group, or an opposition that lives in fear of it. Neither is prepared to tax them effectively.

And here we find ourselves in the company of another philosopher, John Rawls. In his 1971 book on ethics, *A Theory of Justice*, he argues that a society is built on an intrinsically understood social contract.[32] From infancy upwards, humans instinctively comprehend fairness, and no amount of clever financial shenanigans can wipe from our minds a sense of fair play. Taxation has a utilitarian purpose, of course – combining resources to build things no single individual could create – but it also serves this underlying human need for altruism and equity.

Taxation provides education, housing, health, and opportunity for all. This isn't merely a left-wing fantasy. If you believe each person should achieve through their own labours and talents – a core tenet of capitalist thought – you must also accept that the best results emerge when every individual has a roughly equal chance to succeed. Holding back one group by starving them of resources means millions of lost opportunities. Promoting one tiny group by flooding them with resources means second-rate minds are over-promoted, and the whole of society suffers.

The Tories fundamentally refuse to engage with that idea, and the reason is simple: they don't really like you. Not even if you voted for them. In fact, they mostly hate you. They don't care about your poverty, not half as much as they care about their own nauseating wealth. They don't care about your healthcare because they go private. They don't give a toss about your schools, cos their kids don't go to those schools. They make decisions, and then opt out of the consequences of those decisions while the rest of us are trapped with them.

With reasonable taxation on stagnant wealth, they could have fixed all the problems many of us (wrongly) blamed on migration. But they just didn't like us enough to try. They were appalled at efforts to improve equality, disgusted by efforts to re-establish Rawls's theory of justice, and furious at those appealing for simple, basic decency.

A horror of taxing the obscenely wealthy infects the Conservative Party and the handful of obscenely wealthy media moguls which back it. They agitate endlessly to cut tax, which makes for a lovely headline, but doesn't address the damage caused by such cuts. They've forced us to underinvest for over a decade, and demanded from our core services endless rounds of what are euphemistically labelled 'efficiency gains', which sucked the slack out of every vital system, from education to health, from energy to the military. Britain has the lowest levels of investment in the Organisation for Economic Co-operation and Development, at just 16 per cent of GDP, compared with 30 per cent in South Korea.[33] Germany invests almost 22 per cent. In 2008/9,

German households were £591 richer than households in Britain. After a decade of austerity, that gap had grown to £4,068.[34]

Measured another way, the effects of austerity, inequality and stagnation since the Tories came to power have left the average British worker £11,000 a year worse off.[35] All of that lost income could have been taxed, and all those taxes could have cleared much of our state debts, funded the NHS, paid for stronger borders, or whatever your own personal political focus is. Instead, we chased cuts in taxation regardless of consequences, stopped investing in ourselves, and are now falling apart.

Conservative governments may wrap themselves in flags and proclaim their love of country, but by their actions they have left Britain incapable of responding to even the slightest variation from the lowest survivable performance levels, while the wealthy swim in lakes of unearned money. I'm not sure I could invent a clearer illustration of this than multimillionaire Rishi Sunak and his non-dom wife spending tens of thousands to upgrade the local electricity supply so he could power the private swimming pool in one of his multiple homes, while he led a nation where 350 public pools closed because they couldn't afford their energy bills.[36]

How is any of that good for the country?

High taxes on very high incomes are not a punishment for success. They're an absolute necessity, not merely to fund the infrastructure of the state, but to prevent a dynamic economy turning into a dead-end rentier economy – which is exactly what happened when we slashed taxes.

Unhindered by fair, equitable taxation, the rich almost immediately began capturing assets such as housing, and then charged the poor ever-increasing amounts to access those assets. Property prices rocketed. In 1979, before this wondrous revolution began, the UK's average house price was four times the average income. Now it is nine times the average income.[37] So renters and buyers became too impoverished to fund a roof over their heads, let alone power an economy;

but it didn't encourage dynamism at the top either: money that the wealthy once invested in productive entrepreneurship and innovation now sat stagnant in bricks and mortar. And occasional swimming pools.

Our government actively encouraged this trend. Most well-off people see their wages taxed at around 40 per cent,[38] but if you're rich enough to snap up a rental property, you pay only 18 per cent on the money you make from it.[39]

So money the rest of us would once have spent on the small purchases that drive the everyday economy was now sucked up by landlords, who used their unearned, under-taxed new income to buy yet more houses. Only the state can break this dismal cycle, by taxing away excess wealth and then using the tax revenues to invest in productive dynamism again. The market won't do it. The market has had half a century to do it, and it has failed utterly.

A Failed Experiment

Britain has turned out to be remarkably useful as a petri dish for everything a modern democracy should avoid. Every nation in Europe has watched, wincing from behind the sofa, as we demonstrate what happens when an advanced country goes absolutely tonto, sells off its key assets for a steal, encourages its wealthy to stop investing in the future, and then votes to unilaterally sanction itself. Across the continent support for leaving the EU in a hypothetical Brexit-like referendum has plummeted by around 30 per cent since we made our choice in 2016.[40] By 2023 the most Eurosceptic nation on the continent is the Czech Republic, where a stonking 71 per cent of the population support staying in the EU, thanks.

You can argue this is because our island status makes us feel intrinsically detached from mainland Europe, and perhaps you're right. But I think there's more to the sudden flush of pro-EU sentiment seen elsewhere since Brexit. They can see that for most of Britain, growth is no longer a reality. We are post-growth. After Covid, huge numbers of Britons chose not to return to the workplace at all.[41] It had become clear to millions that working harder wouldn't improve our lot in life, because we'd all learned the hard way that any extra work we might do simply funded those at the top of the pyramid, raising it higher, and pushing them further and further away from the source of their baroque and grotesquely gilded existence: our labours.

Over the decades of post-Thatcherism, as the wealth of the top couple of per cent sailed into the stratosphere, the rest of us saw a continuous shrinkage of our ability to even *ask* for enough money to live on: unions were intentionally castrated, and their membership crumbled.

The word 'unions' once conjured images of Arthur Scargill haranguing the nation from a picket line. But in much of the world, unions sit on the board with other directors, and help ensure a happy, productive workplace. In the UK, this is practically unheard of. To our political and business leaders, workers' representatives are not potential partners in success, but a block on their capacity to fleece the nation. A problem to be eliminated.

Anti-union legislation meant Britain's trade union membership halved between the 1980s and 2012,[42] and in the private sector only around one in ten of us joins a union.[43] It's an undeniable fact there have been some very bad unions, but it's equally true that every union in the world was, ultimately, created in response to exploitation. As union power evaporated, exploitation returned, not least by the British government.

That government used to own steel, water, car, electricity, gas, postal, and other industries. Then, because it would somehow magically 'make things better', we flogged them off to other countries. We were told these major national assets were being sold to the great British citizenry, and in a collective act of national amnesia we simply forgot that we already owned them. We were told that selling our own stuff back to us would turn our people into engaged and dynamic patriotic shareholders. But really, is any of that what really happened?

Nope.

By 2022, over 70 per cent of the UK's water industry was in foreign hands.[44] Of the big six energy companies, only one remained in British ownership.[45] Do you know any ordinary British person – literally one person – who has shares in the industries we *all* used to own a part of, but which were then sold off to a wealthy elite? If you see Sid, ask him.

Those industries used to generate money for the Treasury. Sure, sometimes they lost money too, but that's the nature of business. You don't see VW selling off the entire company because they make a loss one year; but that's effectively what Britain did.

Ultimately, what ended the post-war settlement was very simple. You voted for cuts: you got cuts. That's why by the time the Brexit referendum was urged upon the nation, you couldn't get a house or see a GP. It wasn't because of a Romanian working at your local car wash.

Every time you voted for smaller government and lower taxes, you essentially voted to reduce your own income, pension, community investment, and the availability of housing for your kids. And after 30 years of this, we got to 2016 – and your standard of living was crap.

Every time you despised those lazy scroungers on welfare, and chose meaner, crueller leaders, you kicked away a piece of the framework on which your future happiness should have been built. And by 2016, your happiness was fading, and you needed someone to blame.

Every time you turned your back on miners or shipbuilders or rail workers who fought to save their working conditions, you helped to destroy your protection from exploitative bosses. And by 2016, nobody was left to stick up for you.

Bulgarians didn't do this. Michel Barnier didn't. Refugees didn't.

It's true that Britain's economy was still pretty big by the time we turned ourselves into Brexitania, and in pure numeric terms we were the fifth-richest country on earth (although rapidly sliding down the scale).[46] But if one person has £200 trillion and everyone else has nothing, the country is still worth £200 trillion. That doesn't make the population wealthy. There is an economic trick for adjusting national wealth to reflect the real power of the population's money: the amount each person can buy with their income, once you exclude the incredibly rich hoarders who distort the data. It is called Purchasing Power Parity, and this method shows that in 2016 – around the time we were blaming the EU for how terrible the British government had made things – Britain was poorer than Equatorial Guinea, which isn't even in the top 100 of technically richest nations.[47] That wasn't the case before we all decided it was good to vote for spiteful, greedy, short-termist conmen.

Behind Brexit lay this harsh fact: we were a nation of turkeys who had repeatedly voted for Christmas. We'd had multiple chances to put our cross next to the candidate promoting enlightened self-interest, and we blew it cos we thought Ed Miliband looked funny eating a bacon sandwich.

And by the time Sunak entered Number 10, this – the privatisation, the demented house prices, the low wages for workers, the squashing of unions, the crushing of dissent . . . even the attacks on sandwiches – was all the Tories had to offer. More of the same. More failure. More decline.

—

Which brings us back to *Zen and the Art of Motorcycle Maintenance* again, and the dichotomy of Romantics and Classics.

Call me smug, but I'm a bit of a Classic, I think. Nobody examining my wardrobe or vast, distended belly could conclude I care much about surface appearances. So I can't help viewing the Brexit vote as a function, rather than simply accepting whatever label its salesmen used when they were making their hollow promises. Sovereignty, independence, freedom – all that vacuity, all that emptiness, all that shine and glitter and sparkling bullshit: it means nothing. If you look below the surface at what we were *really* rejecting, rather than at what badge was applied to it, there's a surprise in store.

I accept this doesn't apply to everyone who voted for Brexit. Maybe only to a small minority (although the vote was so close that small minority could have led to a wildly different future). But in my Classic way, I can't help concluding that we didn't vote to leave the EU at all, really. We only think we did. Given everything I've said about the yearning for what we used to be, everything we lost and want back, everything we blame on foreigners without any justification, I reach just one conclusion.

We didn't reject the dream of Europe we were all building.

We rejected the reality of a Britain we had voted to destroy.

Notes

Part 1: 500 Days of Flummer
2021: 'Unethical, Foolish and Possibly Illegal'

1. 'Public sector net debt expressed as a percentage of gross domestic product in the United Kingdom from 1920/21 to 2021/22', Statista, https://www.statista.com/statistics/282841/debt-as-gdp-uk/
2. Larry Elliot, 'UK economy £100bn smaller because of austerity – thinktank', *Guardian*, 21 Feb 2019, https://www.theguardian.com/business/2019/feb/21/uk-economy-100bn-smaller-because-of-austerity-thinktank
3. Nadia Khomami, 'David Cameron, a pig's head and a secret society at Oxford University – explained', *Guardian*, 21 Sep 2015, https://www.theguardian.com/politics/2015/sep/21/david-cameron-piers-gaveston-society-what-we-know-oxford-secret
4. Jill Treanor, 'George Osborne cuts short holiday to deal with stock market crisis', *Guardian*, 9 Aug 2011, https://www.theguardian.com/politics/2011/aug/09/george-osborne-cuts-short-holiday-for-financial-crisis
   Patrick Wintour, Nicholas Watt and Juliette Jowitt, 'Autumn statement: growth and NHS figures jolt George Osborne', *Guardian*, 4 Dec 2012, https://www.theguardian.com/uk/2012/dec/04/autumn-statement-nhs-george-osborne
   Larry Elliot, 'IMF puts pressure on George Osborne with criticism of cuts', *Guardian*, 16 Apr 2013, https://www.theguardian.com/business/2013/apr/16/imf-pressure-george-osborne-cuts
   Patrick Wintour and Larry Elliot, 'Osborne moves to cut spending to 1930s levels in dramatic autumn statement', *Guardian*, 4 Dec 2014, https://www.theguardian.com/uk-news/2014/dec/03/autumn-statement-2014-george-osborne-spending-cuts
   Chris Giles and Emily Cadman, 'Annual FT economists' survey: UK growth forecast to continue', *Financial Times*, 1 Jan 2015, https://www.ft.com/content/7964c0f8-9123-11e4-914a-00144feabdc0
5. Andrew Woodcock, 'Workers earning 45p a week less than in 2010 in real terms, new analysis finds', *Independent*, 6 Sep 2022, https://www.independent.co.uk/news/uk/politics/wages-pay-ashworth-inflation-prices-b2160967.html
6. Patrick Butler, 'Over 330,000 excess deaths in Great Britain linked to austerity, finds study', *Guardian*, 5 Oct 2022, https://www.theguardian.com/business/2022/oct/05/over-330000-excess-deaths-in-great-britain-linked-to-austerity-finds-study
7. Toby Helm, Robin McKie, James Tapper and Phillip Inman, "What have we done?': six years on, UK counts the cost of Brexit', *Guardian*, 25 Jun 2022, https://www.theguardian.com/politics/2022/jun/25/what-have-we-done-six-years-on-uk-counts-the-cost-of-brexit
8. 'Just call me two sheds Dave! Ex-PM David Cameron splashes out £25k on his SECOND luxury shepherd's hut, but this one is for his £2m holiday home', *Daily Mail*, 11 Aug 2018, https://www.dailymail.co.uk/news/article-6049377/Ex-PM-David-Cameron-splashes-25k-SECOND-luxury-shepherds-hut-2m-holiday-home.html

9. 'List of departures from the second May ministry', Wikipedia, https://en.wikipedia.org/wiki/List_of_departures_from_the_second_May_ministry
10. Heather Stewart, 'May suffers heaviest parliamentary defeat of a British PM in the democratic era', *Guardian*, 16 Jan 2019, https://www.theguardian.com/politics/2019/jan/15/theresa-may-loses-brexit-deal-vote-by-majority-of-230
11. Owen Bowcott, Ben Quinn and Severin Carrell, 'Johnson's suspension of parliament unlawful, supreme court rules', *Guardian*, 24 Sep 2019, https://www.theguardian.com/law/2019/sep/24/boris-johnsons-suspension-of-parliament-unlawful-supreme-court-rules-prorogue
12. David Allen Green, 'Scottish judges decide Boris Johnson misled the Queen', *Financial Times*, 11 Sep 2019, https://www.ft.com/content/12097e7c-d47f-11e9-8367-807ebd53ab77
13. Kirsten Robertson, '"Puppy gate" had to be made for Boris Johnson to stop him breaking social distancing rules', *Metro*, 29 Jul 2022, https://metro.co.uk/2022/07/29/puppy-gate-had-to-be-made-to-stop-boris-johnson-breaking-covid-rules-17092016/
14. 'Covid-19 vaccine: First person receives Pfizer jab in UK', BBC News, 8 Dec 2020, https://www.bbc.co.uk/news/uk-55227325
15. Tania Snuggs, 'Coronavirus: "We can all play our part" – UK public health campaign offers advice to stop spread', Sky News, 2 Feb 2020, https://news.sky.com/story/coronavirus-we-can-all-play-our-part-government-campaign-offers-advice-to-stop-the-spread-11924298
16. Michael Marmot, 'Why did England have Europe's worst Covid figures? The answer starts with austerity', *Guardian*, 10 Aug 2020, https://www.theguardian.com/commentisfree/2020/aug/10/england-worst-covid-figures-austerity-inequality
17. 'Coronavirus: Mexico death toll overtakes UK to become world's third highest', ITV News, 1 Aug 2020, https://www.itv.com/news/2020-08-01/coronavirus-mexico-death-toll-overtakes-uk-to-become-worlds-third-highest
18. Richard Partington, 'UK to plunge into deepest slump on record with worst GDP drop of G7', *Guardian*, 9 Aug 2020, https://www.theguardian.com/business/2020/aug/09/uk-to-fall-into-deepest-slump-on-record-with-worst-fall-in-gdp-among-g7
19. Georgina Lee, 'Brexit did not speed up UK vaccine authorisation', Channel 4 News Fact Check, 2 Dec 2020, https://www.channel4.com/news/factcheck/factcheck-brexit-did-not-speed-up-uk-vaccine-authorisation
20. Georgina Lee, 'Brexit did not speed up UK vaccine authorisation', Channel 4 News Fact Check, 2 Dec 2020, https://www.channel4.com/news/factcheck/factcheck-brexit-did-not-speed-up-uk-vaccine-authorisation
21. Nadine Dorries [@NadineDorries], Twitter, 2 Dec 2020, https://twitter.com/NadineDorries/status/1334122869194940419
22. Georgina Lee, 'Brexit did not speed up UK vaccine authorisation', Channel 4 News Fact Check, 2 Dec 2020, https://www.channel4.com/news/factcheck/factcheck-brexit-did-not-speed-up-uk-vaccine-authorisation
23. Georgina Lee, 'Brexit did not speed up UK vaccine authorisation', Channel 4 News Fact Check, 2 Dec 2020, https://www.channel4.com/news/factcheck/factcheck-brexit-did-not-speed-up-uk-vaccine-authorisation
24. 'Vaccine approval isn't quicker because of Brexit', Full Fact, 4 Dec 2020, https://fullfact.org/health/coronavirus-vaccine-brexit/
25. Alexander Smith, 'Boris Johnson worries experts with his Christmas Covid respite', NBC News, 18 Dec 2020, https://www.nbcnews.com/news/world/boris-johnson-worries-experts-his-christmas-covid-respite-n1251692
26. Jim Pickard, 'Coronavirus: Boris Johnson tears up five-day festive bubble plans', *Financial Times*, 19 Dec 2020, https://www.ft.com/content/3484bb65-e394-49ab-a23b-6e9001d79baa
27. Global Health Security Team, 'Boris Johnson speaks of "heavy heart" as Christmas is sacrificed to protect the vulnerable', *Telegraph*, 19 Dec 2020, https://www.telegraph.co.uk/global-health/science-and-disease/covid-coronavirus-news-vaccine-moderna-pfizer-christmas-lockdown/
28. 'Covid-19: UK sees highest daily toll of 1,325 deaths', BBC News, 8 Jan 2021, https://www.bbc.co.uk/news/uk-55594107
29. Priti Patel [@pritipatel], Twitter, 25 Jan 2021, https://twitter.com/pritipatel/status/1353709064467963904

30 'Partygate: A timeline of the lockdown gatherings', BBC News, 19 Jan 2022, https://www.bbc.co.uk/news/uk-politics-59952395
31 James Kane, 'Covid vaccine decisions have little to do with Brexit', Institute for Government, 2 Dec 2020, https://www.instituteforgovernment.org.uk/blog/covid-vaccine-decisions-brexit
32 Zoe Wood, Lisa O'Connell and Sarah Butler, 'Firms halt deliveries from UK to EU over Brexit border problems', *Guardian*, 8 Jan 2021, https://www.theguardian.com/politics/2021/jan/08/firms-including-ms-suspend-eu-exports-over-brexit-smallprint
33 Jon Henley, 'Customers in Europe hit by post-Brexit charges when buying from UK', *Guardian*, 7 Jan 2021, https://www.theguardian.com/politics/2021/jan/07/customers-europe-hit-by-post-brexit-charges-buying-from-uk
34 Oscar Williams-Grut, 'Marks & Spencer warns of "significant" impact from Brexit deal', *Yahoo! Finance*, 8 Jan 2021, https://uk.finance.yahoo.com/news/marks-spencer-brexit-deal-eu-ireland-2020-christmas-trading-084331730.html
35 Suban Abdulla, 'DPD stops delivering UK parcels to EU due to Brexit', *Yahoo! Finance*, 8 Jan 2021, https://uk.finance.yahoo.com/news/dpd-parcel-delivery-road-services-suspended-brexit-europe-ireland-110822436.html
36 Jon Henley, 'Customers in Europe hit by post-Brexit charges when buying from UK', *Guardian*, 7 Jan 2021, https://www.theguardian.com/politics/2021/jan/07/customers-europe-hit-by-post-brexit-charges-buying-from-uk
37 Lisa O'Carroll, 'Seafood lorries travel to Westminster for protest against Brexit red tape', *Guardian*, 18 Jan 2021, https://www.theguardian.com/politics/2021/jan/18/fishing-trucks-protest-at-westminster-against-brexit-red-tape
38 Fay Schopen, 'Nigel Farage is no fisherman's friend: he's been ignoring them for years', *Guardian*, 9 Apr 2018, https://www.theguardian.com/commentisfree/2018/apr/09/nigel-farage-fishermen-ignored-ukip-brexit
39 'Brexit: Nigel Farage only turned up to one of 42 EU fisheries committee meetings', *Descrier*, 16 Jun 2016, https://descrier.co.uk/politics/brexit-nigel-farage-turned-one-42-eu-fisheries-committee-meetings/
40 Polly Toynbee, 'Brexiters are waking up to the damage they've done', *Guardian*, 18 Jan 2021, https://www.theguardian.com/commentisfree/2021/jan/18/brexiters-damage-horse-racing-fishing-haulage-industry-chaos
41 'Deaths within 28 days of positive test by date of death', GOV.UK, https://coronavirus.data.gov.uk/details/deaths
42 Vickiie Oliphant, 'Boris Johnson lockdown rebellion – letter in full as 70 Tory MPs REFUSE to back Boris', *Express*, 22 Nov 2020, https://www.express.co.uk/news/uk/1363175/Boris-Johnson-lockdown-rebellion-letter-in-full-Covid-Recovery-Group-covid-rules-evg
43 'List of epidemics', Wikipedia, https://en.wikipedia.org/wiki/List_of_epidemics
44 Jessica Elgot and Robert Booth, 'Pressure mounts on Johnson over alleged "let the bodies pile high" remark', *Guardian*, 26 Apr 2021, https://www.theguardian.com/politics/2021/apr/26/pressure-mounts-on-boris-johnson-over-alleged-let-the-bodies-pile-high-remarks
45 Lucy Fisher, 'Boris Johnson told his leadership will be "on the table" without exit strategy from restrictions', *Telegraph*, 14 Jan 2021, https://www.telegraph.co.uk/news/2021/01/14/pm-warned-leadership-will-table-unless-jettisons-lockdown-restrictions/
46 'Parliamentary Under Secretary of State (Minister for COVID Vaccine Deployment)', GOV.UK, https://www.gov.uk/government/ministers/parliamentary-under-secretary-of-state-minister-for-covid-vaccine-deployment
47 'COVID-19 Data Explorer', Our World In Data, https://ourworldindata.org/covid-vaccinations
48 'Deaths within 28 days of positive test by date of death', GOV.UK, https://coronavirus.data.gov.uk/details/deaths
49 'People who have received 1st dose vaccinations, by report date', Coronavirus.Data.Gov.UK, https://coronavirus.data.gov.uk/details/vaccinations
50 Emer O'Toole, 'Jonathan Gullis: Who is the Tory MP who went viral for not wearing a mask?', *The National*, 27 Jan 2021, https://www.thenational.scot/news/19880416.jonathan-gullis-tory-mp-went-viral-not-wearing-mask/

51 Alan McGuinness, 'COVID-19: Tory MP who said NHS figures were being "manipulated" refuses to apologise', Sky News, 28 Jan 2021, https://news.sky.com/story/covid-19-michael-gove-says-tory-mp-out-of-order-to-tell-anti-vaxxers-to-persist-against-restrictions-12201020

52 Aamna Mohdin, Glenn Swann and Caroline Bannock, 'How George Floyd's death sparked a wave of UK anti-racism protests', *Guardian*, 29 Jul 2020, https://www.theguardian.com/uk-news/2020/jul/29/george-floyd-death-fuelled-anti-racism-protests-britain

53 Ben Bradley [@BBradley_Mans], Twitter, 7 Jun 2020, https://twitter.com/BBradley_Mans/status/1269677091500494857

54 Abdul Mohamud and Robin Whitburn, 'Britain's involvement with New World slavery and the transatlantic slave trade', British Library, 21 Jun 2018, https://www.bl.uk/restoration-18th-century-literature/articles/britains-involvement-with-new-world-slavery-and-the-transatlantic-slave-trade

55 Tristan Cork, 'Row breaks out as Merchant Venturer accused of "sanitising" Edward Colston's involvement in slave trade', *Bristol Post*, 23 Aug 2018, https://www.bristolpost.co.uk/news/bristol-news/row-breaks-out-merchant-venturer-1925896

56 Tristan Cork, 'Edward Colston was "a hero" for Bristol says outraged Tory councillor', *Bristol Post*, 9 Jun 2020, https://www.bristolpost.co.uk/news/bristol-news/edward-colston-a-hero-bristol-4205516

57 Heather Stewart, '"I hear you": Boris Johnson to Black Lives Matter protesters', *Guardian*, 8 Jun 2020, https://www.theguardian.com/us-news/2020/jun/08/i-hear-you-boris-johnson-to-black-lives-matter-protesters

58 Munira Mirza, 'Theresa May's phoney race war is dangerous and divisive', *Spectator*, 13 Sep 2017, https://www.spectator.co.uk/article/theresa-may-s-phoney-race-war-is-dangerous-and-divisive/

59 Jon Stone, 'Boris Johnson appoints aide who said institutional racism was a myth and railed against multiculturalism', *Independent*, 16 Jun 2020, https://www.independent.co.uk/news/uk/politics/boris-johnson-westminster-insider-institutional-racism-munira-mirza-a9568456.html

60 'School gap blamed on black culture', BBC News, 21 Aug 2000, http://news.bbc.co.uk/1/hi/education/890214.stm

61 Suen Matiluko, 'Truth, lies and racism: The story behind the "Sewell Report"', The House, https://longreads.politicshome.com/truth-lies-and-racism-the-story-behind-the-sewell-report

62 Patrick Butler, 'Black and minority ethnic people in UK twice as likely to be in "deep poverty"', *Guardian*, 6 Oct 2022, https://www.theguardian.com/society/2022/oct/06/black-and-minority-ethnic-people-in-uk-twice-as-likely-to-be-in-deep-poverty

63 'Poverty rates by ethnicity', Joseph Rowntree Foundation, 2022 Poverty Report, https://www.jrf.org.uk/data/poverty-rates-ethnicity

64 'Updating ethnic contrasts in deaths involving the coronavirus (COVID-19), England: 24 January 2020 to 31 March 2021', ONS, https://www.ons.gov.uk/peoplepopulationandcommunity/birthsdeathsandmarriages/deaths/articles/updatingethniccontrastsindeathsinvolvingthecoronaviruscovid19englandandwales/24january2020to31march2021

65 'Job applicants with ethnic minority sounding names are less likely to be called for interview', Full Fact, 26 Oct 2015, https://fullfact.org/economy/job-applicants-ethnic-minority-sounding-names-are-less-likely-be-called-for-interview/

66 Aletha Adu, 'Government says institutional racism does not exist in UK', *Mirror*, 16 Mar 2022, https://www.mirror.co.uk/news/politics/government-agrees-uk-no-longer-26487156

67 Rajeev Syal, 'No 10 race adviser Samuel Kasumu resigns', *Guardian*, 1 Apr 2021, https://www.theguardian.com/politics/2021/apr/01/no-10-race-adviser-resigns-day-after-uk-structural-racism-report-published

68 Suen Matiluko, 'Truth, lies and racism: The story behind the "Sewell Report"', The House, https://longreads.politicshome.com/truth-lies-and-racism-the-story-behind-the-sewell-report

69 Nosheen Iqbal, 'Downing Street rewrote "independent" report on race, experts claim', *Guardian*, 11 Apr 2021, https://www.theguardian.com/uk-news/2021/apr/11/downing-street-rewrote-independent-report-on-race-experts-claim

70 Nadine White, 'Runnymede Trust wins battle with Tory MPs over race report criticism', *Independent*, 1 Sep 2021, https://www.independent.co.uk/news/uk/home-news/runnymede-charity-racism-sewell-report-b1912441.html

71 Aamna Mohdin and Amelia Gentleman, 'UK failing to address systemic racism against black people, warn UN experts', *Guardian*, 27 Jan 2023, https://www.theguardian.com/world/2023/jan/27/uk-government-failing-to-address-systemic-racism-against-black-people-un-working-group-of-experts-on-people-of-african-descent

72 Jemma Crew, 'Met Police report: Rape cases ruined, Sikh officer's beard cut . . . five findings from Casey review', BBC News, 21 Mar 2023, https://www.bbc.co.uk/news/uk-65019879

73 Peter Walker, 'Boris Johnson gives peerages to string of Tory allies, but not Paul Dacre', *Guardian*, 14 Oct 2022, https://www.theguardian.com/politics/2022/oct/14/boris-johnson-gives-peerages-to-string-of-tory-allies-but-not-paul-dacre

74 Patrick Butler, 'Black and minority ethnic people in UK twice as likely to be in "deep poverty"', *Guardian*, 6 Oct 2022, https://www.theguardian.com/society/2022/oct/06/black-and-minority-ethnic-people-in-uk-twice-as-likely-to-be-in-deep-poverty

75 Katy Holland, '"If you haven't got the money, you shouldn't have kids" says Tory MP', *HuffPost*, 8 Oct 2010, https://www.huffingtonpost.co.uk/2010/10/08/if-you-haven-t-got-the-money-you-shouldn-t-have-kids-says-tory-mp_n_7394858.html

76 Nigel Nelson, 'Boris Johnson "plans to resign next spring after complaining about £150k salary"', *Mirror*, 18 Oct 2020, https://www.mirror.co.uk/news/politics/boris-johnson-plans-resign-next-22863780

77 Mikey Smith, 'Boris Johnson dismissed £250,000 second job as "chicken feed" in unearthed clip', *Mirror*, 13 Nov 2021, https://www.mirror.co.uk/news/politics/boris-johnson-dismissed-250000-second-25450261

78 Surena Chande, 'What is Boris Johnson's net worth as Prime Minister resigns from Number 10', *Evening Standard*, 8 Jul 2022, https://www.standard.co.uk/news/politics/what-is-boris-johnson-net-worth-prime-minister-resigns-b1010964.html

79 Oliver Wright, Francis Elliott and Matt Chorley, 'Overburdened, underpaid and "misery on his face": Boris Johnson gets the blues', *The Times*, 19 Sep 2020, https://www.thetimes.co.uk/article/overburdened-underpaid-and-misery-on-his-face-boris-johnson-gets-the-blues-r9jl63m2q

80 Atul Singh, 'Do Rumors of Boris Johnson's Purported Twelfth Child Matter?', *Fair Observer*, 21 May 2022, https://www.fairobserver.com/politics/do-rumors-of-boris-johnsons-purported-twelfth-child-matter/

81 Gaby Hinsliff, 'Boris Johnson sacked by Tories over private life', *Guardian*, 14 Nov 2004, https://www.theguardian.com/politics/2004/nov/14/uk.conservatives

82 Peter Walker, 'Tory MP blames food poverty on lack of cooking skills', *Guardian*, 11 May 2022, https://www.theguardian.com/uk-news/2022/may/11/tory-mp-condemned-after-blaming-food-poverty-on-lack-of-cooking-skills

83 'Number of people receiving three days' worth of emergency food by Trussell Trust foodbanks in the United Kingdom from 2008/09 to 2021/22', Statista, https://www.statista.com/statistics/382695/uk-foodbank-users/

84 Kate Hardcastle, 'A visit to the "poshest shop in Britain" as Daylesford Organic celebrates two decades of premium retail', *Forbes*, 5 May 2022, https://www.forbes.com/sites/katehardcastle/2022/03/05/a-visit-to-the-poshest-shop-in-britain-as-daylesford-organic-celebrates-two-decades-of-premium-retail/?sh=701fa23b371c

85 David Wilcock and Simon Walters, 'Downing Street insists "the PM pays his own bills" as it is revealed Boris Johnson and Carrie Symonds have dined in style during lockdown on £12,500 of gourmet takeaways smuggled in from Britain's poshest farm shop owned by Tory donor', *Daily Mail*, 5 Mar 2021, https://www.dailymail.co.uk/news/article-9330277/No10-insists-PM-pays-bills-amid-row-12-500-gourmet-takeaways.html

86 Jen Mills, 'Butler smuggled £27,000 of organic food into Downing Street for Boris', *Metro*, 22 May 2021, https://metro.co.uk/2021/05/22/butler-smuggled-27000-of-organic-food-into-downing-street-for-boris-14628328/

87 'Boris Johnson, Registered interests', UK Parliament, MPs and Lords, https://members.parliament.uk/member/1423/registeredinterests

88 David Wilcock and Simon Walters, 'Downing Street insists "the PM pays his own bills" as it is revealed Boris Johnson and Carrie Symonds have dined in style during lockdown on

£12,500 of gourmet takeaways smuggled in from Britain's poshest farm shop owned by Tory donor', *Daily Mail*, 5 Mar 2021, https://www.dailymail.co.uk/news/article-9330277/No10-insists-PM-pays-bills-amid-row-12-500-gourmet-takeaways.html

89 Jen Mills, 'Butler smuggled £27,000 of organic food into Downing Street for Boris', *Metro*, 22 May 2021, https://metro.co.uk/2021/05/22/butler-smuggled-27000-of-organic-food-into-downing-street-for-boris-14628328/

90 Kate Ng and Joe Sommerlad, 'Boris Johnson flat decoration: What were the controversial refurbishments carried out at Downing Street?', *Independent*, 9 Dec 2021, https://www.independent.co.uk/news/uk/politics/boris-johnson-flat-decoration-refurb-b1972813.html

91 Kate Plummer, '13 of the best reactions to Boris Johnson and Carrie Symond's "John Lewis Nightmare"', indy100, https://www.indy100.com/politics/john-lewis-boris-johnson-flat-b1838119

92 Archie Bland, 'Rishi Sunak's adviser Richard Sharp to be next BBC chair', *Guardian*, 6 Jan 2021, https://www.theguardian.com/media/2021/jan/06/former-goldman-sachs-banker-richard-sharp-to-be-next-bbc-chairman

93 Josiah Mortimer, 'BBC chairman donated tens of thousands of pounds to right-wing group funding criticism of BBC', *Byline Times*, 24 Feb 2023, https://bylinetimes.com/2023/02/24/bbc-chairman-donated-tens-of-thousands-of-pounds-to-right-wing-group-funding-criticism-of-bbc/

94 Steerpike, 'Fresh questions for Boris over financial advice', *Spectator*, 28 Jan 2023, https://www.spectator.co.uk/article/fresh-questions-for-boris-over-financial-advice/

95 Best for Britain [@BestForBritain], Twitter, 7 Feb 2023, https://twitter.com/BestForBritain/status/1622903559044866048

96 Harry Yorke, Gabriel Pogrund, 'Boris Johnson was told: stop seeking Richard Sharp's advice on "financial matters"', *Sunday Times*, 28 Jan 2023, https://www.thetimes.co.uk/article/boris-johnson-was-told-stop-seeking-richard-sharps-advice-on-financial-matters-n2jgkjk7x

97 Mark Sweney, 'Panel approving Richard Sharp as BBC chair included Tory party donor', *Guardian*, 24 Jan 2023, https://www.theguardian.com/media/2023/jan/24/panel-approving-richard-sharp-as-bbc-chair-included-tory-party-donor

98 'Ministerial Code', GOV.UK, 22 Dec 2022, https://www.gov.uk/government/publications/ministerial-code/ministerial-code

99 Ffion Haf, 'BBC chairman Richard Sharp's position is in increased peril after MPs said he made "significant errors of judgment" by acting as a go-between for a loan for Boris Johnson', *Daily Mail*, 12 Feb 2022, https://www.dailymail.co.uk/news/article-11741059/BBC-chairmans-position-increased-peril-MPs-said-significant-errors-judgment.html

100 Daniel Thomas, 'BBC review finds outgoing chair Richard Sharp breached code of practice', *Financial Times*, 11 May 2023, https://www.ft.com/content/f8d2e932-62a4-4f49-9af6-b37717998d46

101 Jim Waterson, 'Richard Sharp resigns as BBC chair after failing to declare link to Boris Johnson loan', *Guardian*, 28 Apr 2023, https://www.theguardian.com/media/2023/apr/28/richard-sharp-resigns-as-bbc-chair-after-months-of-mounting-pressure

102 Gabriel Pogrund and Harry Yorke, 'The BBC chairman, the prime minister and the £800,000 loan guarantee', *Sunday Times*, 21 Jan 2023, https://www.thetimes.co.uk/article/the-bbc-chairman-the-prime-minister-and-the-800-000-loan-guarantee-f7nt5kfml

103 Simon Walters, 'Carrie on plotting: Boris Johnson's fiancée Carrie Symonds tried to damage career of top woman civil servant who refused to sign off No 10 flat refurb and made crude sexual insult about another woman tipped to become his Cabinet Secretary', *Daily Mail*, 26 Feb 2021, https://www.dailymail.co.uk/news/article-9305603/Boris-Johnsons-fianc-e-Carrie-Symonds-tried-damage-careers-women-civil-servants.html

104 Oliver Wainwright, '"Trump-like madness!" – our critic's verdict on Boris Johnson's £200,000 No 11 refurb', *Guardian*, 8 Jul 2022, https://www.theguardian.com/artanddesign/2022/jul/08/the-johnsons-downing-street-refurb-a-lurid-hellscape-lined-with-gilded-tat

105 Simon Walters, 'Number 10 makeover scandal: New leaked memo shows Conservative Party chief knew £58,000 donation was earmarked for Boris Johnson's Downing Street flat', *Daily Mail*, 20 Apr 2021, https://www.dailymail.co.uk/news/article-9492829/Leaked-memo-shows-Tory-chief-knew-58-000-donation-Boris-Johnsons-Downing-Street-flat.html

106 Peter Walker and Aubrey Allegretti, '"Mad and totally unethical": Dominic Cummings hits out at Boris Johnson', *Guardian*, 23 Apr 2021, https://www.theguardian.com/politics/2021/apr/23/dominic-cummings-launches-attack-on-boris-johnson

107 Hansard UK Parliament, 28 Apr 2021, https://hansard.parliament.uk/Commons/2021-04-28/debates/1E773197-C43C-40B4-9A52-BBF454C196AA/Engagements

108 Xander Richards, 'Boris Johnson told to explain Lord Brownlow messages about No 11 flat refurb', *The National*, 6 Jan 2022, https://www.thenational.scot/news/19830141.boris-johnson-told-explain-lord-brownlow-messages-no-11-flat-refurb/

109 Mikey Smith, 'Inside Boris Johnson's lavish No10 refurb as estimate shows £7k rug and £3k paint', *Mirror*, 8 Jul 2022, https://www.mirror.co.uk/news/politics/inside-boris-johnsons-lavish-no10-27429850

110 Simon Walters, 'Number 10 makeover scandal: New leaked memo shows Conservative Party chief knew £58,000 donation was earmarked for Boris Johnson's Downing Street flat', *Daily Mail*, 20 Apr 2021, https://www.dailymail.co.uk/news/article-9492829/Leaked-memo-shows-Tory-chief-knew-58-000-donation-Boris-Johnsons-Downing-Street-flat.html

111 George Grylls, 'Boris Johnson's flat donor Lord Brownlow made pitch for £115m exhibition', *The Times*, 1 Jun 2022, https://www.thetimes.co.uk/article/boris-johnsons-flat-donor-lord-brownlow-made-pitch-for-115m-exhibition-rgft6crpk

112 George Grylls, 'Boris Johnson's flat donor Lord Brownlow made pitch for £115m exhibition', *The Times*, 1 Jun 2022, https://www.thetimes.co.uk/article/boris-johnsons-flat-donor-lord-brownlow-made-pitch-for-115m-exhibition-rgft6crpk

113 Xander Richards, 'Boris Johnson told to explain Lord Brownlow messages about No 11 flat refurb', *The National*, 6 Jan 2022, https://www.thenational.scot/news/19830141.boris-johnson-told-explain-lord-brownlow-messages-no-11-flat-refurb/

114 Derek Healey, 'Unboxed: What is the "festival of Brexit" and why are people angry about it?', *The Courier*, 19 Jun 2022, https://www.thecourier.co.uk/fp/politics/scottish-politics/3111167/festival-of-brexit/

115 Julian Knight, 'We must find out where the government's £120m Unboxed festival went so wrong', *PoliticsHome*, 15 Oct 2022, https://www.politicshome.com/thehouse/article/unboxed-festival-of-brexit-nao-investigation-julian-knight

116 Ben Quinn, 'Downing Street refurb: the money trail, inquiries and questions still to answer', *Guardian*, 9 Dec 2021, https://www.theguardian.com/politics/2021/dec/09/downing-street-refurb-the-money-trail-inquiries-and-questions-still-to-answer

117 Sophie Wingate, 'Boris Johnson's flat revamp cost £200,000, leaked invoice suggests', *Independent*, 8 Jul 2022, https://www.independent.co.uk/news/uk/boris-johnson-carrie-johnson-downing-street-the-independent-lord-b2118741.html

118 Steerpike, 'Eight awkward David Cameron quotes on lobbying', *Spectator*, 12 Apr 2021, https://www.spectator.co.uk/article/eight-awkward-david-cameron-quotes-on-lobbying/

119 Conal Urquart, 'David Cameron's "chillaxing" hobbies revealed in new biography', *Guardian*, 29 May 2012, https://www.theguardian.com/politics/2012/may/19/david-cameron-chillaxing-hobbies-biography

120 Conal Urquart, 'David Cameron's "chillaxing" hobbies revealed in new biography', *Guardian*, 29 May 2012, https://www.theguardian.com/politics/2012/may/19/david-cameron-chillaxing-hobbies-biography

121 Rajeev Syal, 'Lex Greensill had no contract for No 10 job, MPs are told', *Guardian*, 26 Apr 2021, https://www.theguardian.com/politics/2021/apr/26/lex-greensill-had-no-contract-for-no-10-job-mps-are-told

122 Rob Powell, 'Greensill: What is the lobbying scandal and why is David Cameron involved?', Sky News, 12 Apr 2021, https://news.sky.com/story/greensill-what-is-the-lobbying-scandal-and-why-is-david-cameron-involved-12272518

123 Rajeev Syal, 'Lex Greensill had no contract for No 10 job, MPs are told', *Guardian*, 26 Apr 2021, https://www.theguardian.com/politics/2021/apr/26/lex-greensill-had-no-contract-for-no-10-job-mps-are-told

124 Steven Swinford, 'David Cameron "told friends he would make $60m from Greensill deal"', *The Times*, 29 Mar 2021, https://www.thetimes.co.uk/article/david-cameron-greensill-deal-claims-lobbying-tfd6j7ln3

125 Rajeev Syal, 'Lex Greensill had no contract for No 10 job, MPs are told', *Guardian*, 26 Apr 2021, https://www.theguardian.com/politics/2021/apr/26/lex-greensill-had-no-contract-for-no-10-job-mps-are-told
126 Steerpike, 'Eight awkward David Cameron quotes on lobbying', *Spectator*, 12 Apr 2021, https://www.spectator.co.uk/article/eight-awkward-david-cameron-quotes-on-lobbying/
127 Steven Swinford, 'David Cameron "told friends he would make $60m from Greensill deal"', *The Times*, 29 Mar 2021, https://www.thetimes.co.uk/article/david-cameron-greensill-deal-claims-lobbying-tfd6j7ln3
128 Steerpike, 'Eight awkward David Cameron quotes on lobbying', *Spectator*, 12 Apr 2021, https://www.spectator.co.uk/article/eight-awkward-david-cameron-quotes-on-lobbying/
129 Denis Campbell, 'Greensill lobbying: how did David Cameron target the NHS?', *Guardian*, 18 Apr 2021, https://www.theguardian.com/business/2021/apr/18/greensill-lobbying-how-did-david-cameron-target-the-nhs
130 Louise Moon, 'David Cameron lobbied ex-colleagues for Greensill access to Covid loan scheme', *Telegraph*, 18 Mar 2021, https://www.telegraph.co.uk/business/2021/03/18/david-cameron-lobbied-former-colleagues-greensill-access-covid/
131 'Matt Hancock "had private drink" with David Cameron and Lex Greensill', BBC News, 11 Apr 2021, https://www.bbc.com/news/uk-56706619
132 Chris Jewers, 'David Cameron's financier friend Lex Greensill said "he spoke for the PM" as he sold civil servants loans – years before employing ex-Prime Minister as lobbyist', *Daily Mail*, 4 Apr 2021, https://www.dailymail.co.uk/news/article-9434067/David-Camerons-friend-Lex-Greensill-said-spoke-PM-sold-civil-servants-loans.html
133 Oliver Wright, 'Bill Crothers: Ex-civil servant's Greensill role not vetted', *The Times*, 31 Mar 2021, https://www.thetimes.co.uk/article/bill-crothers-ex-civil-servants-greensill-role-not-vetted-sclcl0gp8
134 Kalyeena Makortoff, Ben Butler and Joseph Smith, 'Greensill scandal: ex-civil servant had $8m stake in lender', *Guardian*, 13 Apr 2021, https://www.theguardian.com/politics/2021/apr/13/greensill-scandal-ex-civil-servant-faces-questions-over-whitehall-meetings
135 Rob Powell, 'Greensill: What is the lobbying scandal and why is David Cameron involved?', Sky News, 12 Apr 2021, https://news.sky.com/story/greensill-what-is-the-lobbying-scandal-and-why-is-david-cameron-involved-12272518
136 Aubrey Allegretti, 'David Cameron said to have made about $10m from Greensill Capital', *Guardian*, 9 Aug 2021, https://www.theguardian.com/politics/2021/aug/09/david-cameron-said-made-about-10m-greensill-capital-bbc
137 Rajeev Syal, '"No evidence" conflicts of interest were considered in Greensill contracts – NAO', *Guardian*, 29 Oct 2021, https://www.theguardian.com/business/2021/oct/29/no-evidence-conflicts-of-interest-were-considered-in-greensill-contracts-nao
138 'Ex-PM David Cameron cleared by lobbying watchdog', BBC News, 26 Mar 2021, https://www.bbc.co.uk/news/uk-politics-56541377
139 'Greensill had extraordinarily privileged access to government, says inquiry', BBC News, 22 Jul 2021, https://www.bbc.co.uk/news/uk-politics-57927390
140 'David Cameron lacked judgement over Greensill, MPs' report says', BBC News, 20 Jul 2021, https://www.bbc.co.uk/news/business-57889549
141 Steerpike, 'Eight awkward David Cameron quotes on lobbying', *Spectator*, 12 Apr 2021, https://www.spectator.co.uk/article/eight-awkward-david-cameron-quotes-on-lobbying/
142 'Opposition day: Lobbying of Government Committee', Votes in Parliament, 14 Apr 2021, https://votes.parliament.uk/Votes/Commons/Division/992
143 'Labour maintains strong lead over Conservatives', Survation, Mar 2022, https://www.survation.com/labour-maintains-strong-lead-over-conservatives/
144 '2019 electoral fraud data', The Electoral Commission, 31 Mar 2021, https://www.electoralcommission.org.uk/who-we-are-and-what-we-do/our-views-and-research/our-research/electoral-fraud-data/2019-electoral-fraud-data
145 '2022 Electoral Fraud Data', The Electoral Commission, https://www.electoralcommission.org.uk/who-we-are-and-what-we-do/our-views-and-research/our-research/electoral-fraud-data/2022-electoral-fraud-data
146 Ollie Corfe, 'Election ID laws to come into play despite just two voter fraud convictions in five years', *Express*, 21 Dec 2022, https://www.express.co.uk/news/uk/1709865/voter-id-laws-electoral-fraud-cases-uk-spt

147 Josiah Mortimer, 'Voter ID: it's far worse than any US state', *Byline Times*, 7 Nov 2022, https://bylinetimes.com/2022/11/07/voter-id-its-far-worse-than-any-us-state/
148 'Voter ID: an expensive distraction', Electoral Reform Society, https://www.electoral-reform.org.uk/campaigns/voter-id/
149 Rob Merrick, 'Matt Hancock admits only 6 voter fraud cases at last election, as protests grow over "photo ID" crackdown', *Independent*, 11 May 2021, https://www.independent.co.uk/news/uk/politics/matt-hancock-voter-fraud-photo-id-b1845363.html
150 Adam Bienkov, 'Jacob Rees-Mogg says Voter ID was attempt to "gerrymander" elections for the Conservatives', *Byline Times*, 15 May 2023, https://bylinetimes.com/2023/05/15/jacob-rees-mogg-says-voter-id-was-attempt-to-gerrymander-elections-for-the-conservatives/
151 'Generational Gerrymandering? New voter ID requirements will disenfranchise young people', Good Law Project, 21 Nov 2022, https://goodlawproject.org/generational-gerrymandering-new-voter-id-requirements-will-disenfranchise-young-people/
152 Peter Walker, 'Only 10,000 people in Great Britain have applied for government-issued voter ID', *Guardian*, 31 Jan 2023, https://www.theguardian.com/politics/2023/jan/31/only-10000-people-in-uk-have-applied-for-government-issued-voter-id
153 Rob Merrick, 'Matt Hancock admits only 6 voter fraud cases at last election, as protests grow over "photo ID" crackdown', *Independent*, 11 May 2021, https://www.independent.co.uk/news/uk/politics/matt-hancock-voter-fraud-photo-id-b1845363.html
154 Josiah Mortimer, 'Voter ID: it's far worse than any US state', *Byline Times*, 7 Nov 2022, https://bylinetimes.com/2022/11/07/voter-id-its-far-worse-than-any-us-state/
155 Adam Sundle, 'Global Ranking of Electoral Systems', 2022, https://citizen-network.org/library/global-ranking-of-electoral-systems.html
156 Freedom House, 'Countries and Territories', https://freedomhouse.org/countries/freedom-world/scores
157 'Voter ID: an expensive distraction', Electoral Reform Society, https://www.electoral-reform.org.uk/campaigns/voter-id/
158 Jon Stone, 'Electoral Commission "concerned" after Tories vote to place it under government control', *Independent*, 28 Apr 2022, https://www.independent.co.uk/news/uk/politics/electoral-commission-elections-bill-independence-b2067888.html
159 Best for Britain [@BestForBritain], Twitter, 1 Dec 2022, https://twitter.com/BestForBritain/status/1598378799997063177
160 Peter Walker, 'Tory plan to scrap election watchdog "undermines democracy"', *Guardian*, 31 Aug 2020, https://www.theguardian.com/politics/2020/aug/31/tory-plans-to-scrap-election-watchdog-undermines-democracy
161 'What are the Kill the Bill protests?', *The Big Issue*, 28 Feb 2022, https://www.bigissue.com/news/activism/what-are-the-kill-the-bill-protests-police-crime-sentencing-courts-bill/
162 Adam Bychawski, 'MPs vote through National Security Bill in "disaster for free press"', openDemocracy, 16 Nov 2022, https://www.opendemocracy.net/en/national-security-bill-amendment-public-interest-defence/
163 Sacha Deshmukh, 'UK: Dark day for civil liberties as "deeply authoritarian" Policing Bill passed by Lords', Amnesty International, 27 Apr 2022, https://www.amnesty.org.uk/press-releases/uk-dark-day-civil-liberties-deeply-authoritarian-policing-bill-passed-lords
164 Matt Honeycombe-Foster, '5 times Tory prime ministers talked up quitting the ECHR – and then didn't', *Politico*, 9 Mar 2023, https://www.politico.eu/article/tories-prime-minister-quit-echr-david-cameron-theresa-may-boris-johnson-liz-truss-rishi-sunak/
165 'National Address', International Churchill Society, 21 Mar 1943, https://winstonchurchill.org/resources/speeches/1941-1945-war-leader/national-address/
166 PoliticsJoe [@PoliticsJOE_UK], Twitter, 22 Nov 2022, https://twitter.com/PoliticsJOE_UK/status/1595095459567001601
167 'Predictive text? Why *Superforecasting* is top of Dominic Cummings' reading list', *Guardian*, 1 Jul 2020, https://www.theguardian.com/politics/2020/jul/01/predictive-text-why-superforecasting-is-top-of-dominic-cummings-reading-list
168 Otto English [@Otto_English], Twitter, 23 Apr 2021, https://twitter.com/otto_english/status/1385659107101876224

NOTES TO PP. 36–37

169 Graeme Paton, 'Michael Gove: schools failing to promote the classics', *Telegraph*, 1 Apr 2011, https://www.telegraph.co.uk/education/educationnews/8419770/Michael-Gove-schools-failing-to-promote-the-classics.html
170 Matthew Holehouse, 'Gove: Classics lessons to help state pupils compete for university places', *Telegraph*, 3 Feb 2014, https://www.telegraph.co.uk/education/education news/10614868/Gove-Classics-lessons-to-help-state-pupils-compete-for-university-places.html
171 'School buildings scheme scrapped', BBC News, 5 Jul 2010, https://www.bbc.co.uk/news/10514113
172 Lizzy Buchan, 'Education spending slashed by £7bn since 2011 with children "paying price for austerity", says Labour', *Independent*, 14 Jan 2019, https://www.independent.co.uk/news/uk/politics/labour-angela-rayner-funding-cuts-department-for-education-damian-hinds-a8726151.html
173 'Michael Gove heckled at head teachers' conference in Birmingham', BBC News, 18 May 2013, https://www.bbc.co.uk/news/education-22558756
174 Toby Helm, 'Cummings and Johnson face backlash over sacking of advisers', *Guardian*, 15 Feb 2020, https://www.theguardian.com/politics/2020/feb/15/boris-johnson-dominic-cummings-backlash-sacking-sonia-khan
175 Patrick Wintour, 'Dominic Cummings, master of the dark arts handed keys to No 10', *Guardian*, 26 Jul 2019, https://www.theguardian.com/politics/2019/jul/26/dominic-cummings-a-career-psychopath-in-downing-street
176 Rowena Mason, 'PM backs Michael Gove but suggests former aide was a "career psychopath"', *Guardian*, 18 Jun 2014, https://www.theguardian.com/politics/2014/jun/18/david-cameron-dominic-cummings-career-psychopath
177 Henry Mance, 'Combative Brexiter who took control of Vote Leave operation', *Financial Times*, 14 Jun 2016, https://www.ft.com/content/cceb7038-30cc-11e6-bda0-04585c31b153#axzz4H22r0hWH
178 Ben Chu, 'The real "Brexit dividend"? Minus £800m a week – and counting', *Independent*, 23 Jun 2021, https://www.independent.co.uk/news/uk/politics/brexit-vote-cost-trade-eu-b1843018.html
179 Andrew Woodcock, 'Brexit might have been a mistake, says Vote Leave supremo Dominic Cummings', *Independent*, 21 Jul 2021, https://www.independent.co.uk/news/uk/politics/dominic-cummings-brexit-bus-johnson-b1887457.html
180 Luke McGee, 'Fear sets in that Boris Johnson's Brexit government is ill equipped to handle a pandemic', CNN, 11 Oct 2020, https://edition.cnn.com/2020/10/10/uk/brexit-britain-pandemic-intl-gbr/index.html
181 'Dominic Cummings wanted to be "largely redundant" by the end of 2020', *Shropshire Star*, 13 Nov 2020, https://www.shropshirestar.com/news/uk-news/2020/11/13/dominic-cummings-wanted-to-be-largely-redundant-by-the-end-of-2020/
182 Rajeev Syal, 'Dominic Cummings calls for "weirdos and misfits" for No 10 jobs', *Guardian*, 2 Jan 2020, https://www.theguardian.com/politics/2020/jan/02/dominic-cummings-calls-for-weirdos-and-misfits-for-no-10-jobs
183 Andrew Woodcock, 'Dominic Cummings says he left Durham self-isolation to drive to Barnard Castle to "test his eyesight"', *Independent*, 25 May 2020, https://www.independent.co.uk/news/uk/politics/dominic-cummings-statement-barnard-castle-durham-eyesight-press-briefing-speech-a9531766.html
184 'My dog Dilyn can't control his romantic urges, says Boris Johnson', BBC News, 27 Jul 2021, https://www.bbc.co.uk/news/uk-politics-57987491
185 'UK PM's former adviser confirms Johnson said "let the bodies pile high"', *Reuters*, 26 May 2021, https://www.reuters.com/world/uk/uk-pms-former-adviser-confirms-johnson-said-let-bodies-pile-high-2021-05-26/
186 'Dominic Cummings says resignation linked to "illegal" moves by Carrie Symonds to "appoint friends to jobs"', Sky News, 26 May 2021, https://news.sky.com/story/cummings-says-resignation-linked-to-illegal-moves-by-carrie-symonds-to-appoint-friends-to-jobs-12317616
187 Ian Dunt, 'The architect of Britain's political culture war is gone. The culture war will go on', *Washington Post*, 17 Nov 2020, https://www.washingtonpost.com/outlook/2020/11/17/dominic-cummings-boris-johnson-politics/

188 'Dominic Cummings: the seven most explosive claims', BBC News, 26 May 2021, https://www.bbc.co.uk/news/uk-politics-57254915
189 Alix Culbertson, 'Dominic Cummings claims Boris Johnson was writing Shakespeare book instead of dealing with COVID', Sky News, 12 Nov 2021, https://news.sky.com/story/dominic-cummings-claims-boris-johnson-was-writing-shakespeare-book-instead-of-dealing-with-covid-12467178
190 Heather Stewart and Peter Walker, *Guardian*, 26 May 2021, 'Cummings lambasts Johnson in damning account of Covid crisis', https://www.theguardian.com/politics/2021/may/26/boris-johnson-is-unfit-to-be-prime-minister-says-dominic-cummings
191 'Coronavirus (COVID-19) Deaths', Our World In Data, https://ourworldindata.org/covid-deaths
192 'Dominic Cummings: thousands died needlessly after Covid mistakes', BBC News, 26 May 2021, https://www.bbc.co.uk/news/uk-politics-57253578
193 Peter Walker, 'Matt Hancock apologises after photos show him kissing aide', *Guardian*, 25 Jun 2021, https://www.theguardian.com/politics/2021/jun/25/matt-hancock-gina-coladangelo-grant-shapps-health-job
194 Gabriel Pogrund, 'Matt Hancock gave key Covid role to lobbyist pal', *Sunday Times*, 22 Nov 2020, https://www.thetimes.co.uk/article/matt-hancock-gave-key-covid-role-to-lobbyist-pal-tppg75t5c
195 Steve Bird, 'Gina Coladangelo: the millionaire lobbyist quietly appointed to top government roles', *Telegraph*, 15 Jul 2021, https://www.telegraph.co.uk/politics/2021/06/25/gina-coladangelo-met-matt-hancock-decades-quietly-appointed/
196 Mario Ledwith and Nick Enoch, 'Brother of millionaire lobbyist who enjoyed passionate clinch with married Matt Hancock is executive of healthcare company awarded series of NHS contracts', *Daily Mail*, 25 Jun 2021, https://www.dailymail.co.uk/news/article-9726425/Gina-Coladangelos-brother-healthcare-executive-company-got-NHS-contracts.html
197 Nicholas Cecil, 'Matt Hancock under fire over alleged affair with close aide Gina Coladangelo', *Evening Standard*, 25 Jun 2021, https://www.standard.co.uk/news/uk/matt-hancock-alleged-affair-close-aide-gina-coladangelo-b942615.html
198 Heather Stewart, 'Boris Johnson tries to claim credit for Matt Hancock departure', *Guardian*, 28 Jun 2021, https://www.theguardian.com/politics/2021/jun/28/boris-johnson-tries-to-claim-credit-for-matt-hancock-departure
199 Toby Helm, Michael Savage and Peter Walker, 'Matt Hancock resigns as health secretary after day of humiliation', *Guardian*, 26 Jun 2021, https://www.theguardian.com/politics/2021/jun/26/matt-hancock-resigns-after-questions-over-relationship-with-aide
200 'Letters: Will the police break up Armistice Day ceremonies on Wednesday?', *Telegraph*, 9 Nov 2020, https://www.telegraph.co.uk/opinion/2020/11/09/letterswill-police-break-armistice-day-ceremonies-wednesday/
201 Rajeev Syal and Rowena Mason, 'Who are the Conservatives' most controversial new MPs?', *Guardian*, 16 Dec 2019, https://www.theguardian.com/politics/2019/dec/16/who-are-the-conservatives-most-controversial-new-mps
202 'Number of people receiving three days' worth of emergency food by Trussell Trust foodbanks in the United Kingdom from 2008/09 to 2021/22', Statista, https://www.statista.com/statistics/382695/uk-foodbank-users/
203 'Conservative MP quits government job over free school meals', BBC News, 22 Oct 2020, https://www.bbc.co.uk/news/uk-politics-54642788
204 'Conservative MP quits government job over free school meals', BBC News, 22 Oct 2020, https://www.bbc.co.uk/news/uk-politics-54642788
205 'Letters: Will the police break up Armistice Day ceremonies on Wednesday?', *Telegraph*, 9 Nov 2020, https://www.telegraph.co.uk/opinion/2020/11/09/letterswill-police-break-armistice-day-ceremonies-wednesday/
206 'Education group membership', National Trust, https://www.nationaltrust.org.uk/membership/education-group-membership
207 'Letters: Will the police break up Armistice Day ceremonies on Wednesday?', *Telegraph*, 9 Nov 2020, https://www.telegraph.co.uk/opinion/2020/11/09/letterswill-police-break-armistice-day-ceremonies-wednesday/

208 P. Jackson and A. Shekhovtsov, *The Post-War Anglo-American Far Right: A Special Relationship of Hate*, 2014, Palgrave Pivot, ISBN-13 978-1137396198, https://books.google.co.uk/books?id=VbLSBAAAQBAJ, https://www.amazon.co.uk/Post-War-Anglo-American-Far-Right/dp/1137396199/

209 Arj Singh, 'Taking the knee: Tory MP Lee Anderson admits he is "annoyed" about boycotting Euros final over the gesture', *iNews*, 9 Jul 2021, https://inews.co.uk/news/politics/taking-the-knee-tory-mp-lee-anderson-boycott-euros-final-england-gesture-1095251

210 Xander Elliards, 'Lee Anderson linked to "far-right" man with white supremacist tattoo', *The National*, 9 Feb 2023, https://www.thenational.scot/news/23311580.lee-anderson-linked-far-right-man-white-supremacist-tattoo/

211 Mikey Smith and Katherine Denkinson, 'Deputy Tory chairman Lee Anderson faces fresh questions "over link to white supremacists"', *Mirror*, 11 Feb 2023/updated 12 Feb 2023, https://www.mirror.co.uk/news/politics/deputy-tory-chairman-lee-anderson-29194474

212 Gary Langer, '63% support Black Lives Matter as recognition of discrimination jumps: POLL', *ABC News*, 21 Jul 2020, https://abcnews.go.com/Politics/63-support-black-lives-matter-recognition-discrimination-jumps/story?id=71779435

213 Mikey Smith, 'Tory MP compares England players taking the knee to Nazi salutes', *Mirror*, 7 Jun 2021, https://www.mirror.co.uk/news/politics/tory-mp-compares-england-players-24268237

214 Sarah Fitton, 'Scott Benton: former Calderdale councillor now Blackpool MP suspended from Tory party after reportedly filmed offering lobbying services in sting operation', *Halifax Courier*, 5 Apr 2023, https://www.halifaxcourier.co.uk/news/politics/scott-benton-former-calderdale-councillor-now-blackpool-mp-suspended-from-tory-party-after-reportedly-filmed-offering-lobbying-services-in-sting-operation-4094448

215 James Graves, 'Blackpool MP and Calderdale councillor Scott Benton facing separate investigations relating to his conduct and finances', *Halifax Courier*, 2 Nov 2020, https://www.halifaxcourier.co.uk/news/politics/blackpool-mp-and-calderdale-councillor-scott-benton-facing-separate-investigations-relating-to-his-conduct-and-finances-3022033

216 John Greenwood, 'Calderdale councillor and Blackpool South MP breached Parliamentary rules', *Halifax Courier*, 12 Jan 2021, https://www.halifaxcourier.co.uk/news/politics/calderdale-councillor-and-blackpool-south-mp-breached-parliamentary-rules-3092855

217 Rowena Mason and Peter Walker, 'Nine MPs accepted free Euro 2020 tickets from gambling companies', *Guardian*, 15 Jul 2021, https://www.theguardian.com/politics/2021/jul/15/nine-mps-free-euro-2020-tickets-gambling-companies

218 George Greenwood, 'Scandal MP lobbied against gambling watchdog candidates', *The Times*, 7 Apr 2023, https://www.thetimes.co.uk/article/7f9915b0-d570-11ed-a308-364551a39b53

219 Billy Kenber and Arthi Nachiappan, 'Exposed: how Tory MP offered to lobby for gambling investors', *The Times*, 6 Apr 2023, https://www.thetimes.co.uk/article/tory-mp-scott-benton-lobbying-investigation-ckhzrfqg0

220 Robert Wright, 'Scott Benton loses Tory whip after video of lobbying meeting published', *Financial Times*, 6 Apr 2023, https://www.ft.com/content/7c3e54e4-0b3f-42c8-967f-3eb3f72e1acb

221 'Scott Benton suspended as Tory MP after lobbying sting', BBC News, 5 Apr 2023, https://www.bbc.co.uk/news/uk-politics-65193097

222 Rajeev Syal, '"Merry" Michael Gove seen dancing "alone" in Aberdeen nightclub', *Guardian*, 29 Aug 2021, https://www.theguardian.com/politics/2021/aug/29/merry-michael-gove-seen-dancing-alone-in-aberdeen-nightclub

223 Adam Bienkov and Henry Dyer, 'Boris Johnson plans to resign after the next election to "make money and have fun", says Dominic Cummings', *Business Insider*, 16 Jun 2021, https://www.businessinsider.com/boris-johnson-resign-after-election-to-make-money-cummings-2021-6

224 'Our Plan | Conservative Manifesto 2019', Conservatives, https://www.conservatives.com/our-plan

225 Jonny Bairstow, 'Boris Johnson flies to green G7 summit in private jet', *Energy Live News*, 10 Jun 2021, https://www.energylivenews.com/2021/06/10/boris-johnson-flies-to-green-g7-summit-in-private-jet/
226 Dan Sabbagh, 'Boris Johnson repaint may ruin plane for military use, says ex-pilot', *Guardian*, 19 Jun 2020, https://www.theguardian.com/politics/2020/jun/19/boris-johnson-planes-paint-job-may-render-it-useless-for-military-purposes-says-ex-pilot
227 Dan Sabbagh, 'Boris Johnson repaint may ruin plane for military use, says ex-pilot', *Guardian*, 19 Jun 2020, https://www.theguardian.com/politics/2020/jun/19/boris-johnson-planes-paint-job-may-render-it-useless-for-military-purposes-says-ex-pilot
228 Steven Brown, 'RAF defend Boris's £900,000 plane after critics claim Union Jack is UPSIDE DOWN', *Express*, 26 Jun 2020, https://www.express.co.uk/news/uk/1301529/RAF-union-jack-boris-johnson-plane-union-jack-upside-down-Royal-Air-Force-news
229 Jack Newman, 'How green are you really Boris? PM used JCB tycoon's £47million private jet and helicopter and pumped out 21 tonnes of CO2 during local election campaign it emerges . . . as he prepares to host COP26 climate summit', *Daily Mail*, 24 Oct 2021, https://www.dailymail.co.uk/news/article-10124465/Boris-Johnson-pumped-21-tonnes-CO2-using-JCB-tycoons-private-jet-local-elections.html
230 Mikey Smith, 'Boris Johnson's luxury private plane habit laid bare as he spends £216k on flights', *Mirror*, 30 Oct 2021, https://www.mirror.co.uk/news/politics/boris-johnsons-luxury-private-plane-25337866
231 Rowena Mason, 'Boris Johnson took official jet home from weekend with family in Cornwall', *Guardian*, 3 Jul 2022, https://www.theguardian.com/politics/2022/jul/03/boris-johnson-took-official-jet-home-from-weekend-with-family-in-cornwall
232 Chris Matthews, 'Boris Johnson "planned £150,000 treehouse for son Wilf at Chequers but was forced to scrap idea after police raised security fears"', *Daily Mail*, 25 Jun 2022, https://www.dailymail.co.uk/news/article-10951425/Boris-Johnson-planned-150-000-treehouse-son-Wilf-Chequers-forced-scrap-idea.html
233 Richard Partington, 'UK exports to EU fell by £20bn last year, new ONS data shows', *Guardian*, 11 Feb 2022, https://www.theguardian.com/politics/2022/feb/11/uk-exports-to-eu-fell-by-20bn-last-year-new-ons-data-shows
234 Phillip Adnett, 'Over 40% of British products have disappeared from EU shelves since Brexit', Institute of Export and International Trade, 29 Nov 2022, https://www.export.org.uk/news/624530/Over-40-of-British-products-have-disappeared-from-EU-shelves-since-Brexit.htm
235 'UK agreed "reasonable" compromise on fish – PM Johnson', *Reuters*, 24 Dec 2020, https://www.reuters.com/world/uk/uk-agreed-reasonable-compromise-fish-pm-johnson-2020-12-24/
236 'The Observer view on the grim effects of Brexit being impossible to hide', *Observer*, 14 Mar 2021, https://www.theguardian.com/commentisfree/2021/mar/14/the-observer-view-on-the-grim-effects-of-brexit-being-impossible-to-hide
237 William Schomberg, 'UK's Johnson says lots of Brexit teething problems, employers fear worse to come', *Reuters*, 28 Jan 2021, https://www.reuters.com/article/us-britain-eu-johnson-idUSKBN29X2E0
238 George Parker, 'UK trade deal with Japan stalls over blue cheese demands', *Financial Times*, 10 Aug 2020, https://www.ft.com/content/dbfff350-f404-4c10-96fc-64da55a8fb09
239 Michelle Manetti, 'Japanese Restaurateur Pays $118K For Endangered Fish', *The Food Press*, 5 Jan 2016, http://foodpress.net/tsukiji-fish-market-auction/
240 Lisa O'Carroll, 'Data shows collapse of UK food and drink exports post-Brexit', *Guardian*, 22 Mar 2021, https://www.theguardian.com/business/2021/mar/22/data-shows-collapse-of-uk-food-and-drink-exports-post-brexit
241 Joanna Partridge, 'UK forced to delay checks on imports from EU by six months', *Guardian*, 11 Mar 2021, https://www.theguardian.com/politics/2021/mar/11/uk-forced-to-delay-import-checks-on-eu-goods-by-six-months-2022-border-post-not-ready
242 'United Kingdom – Country Commercial Guide', *International Trade Administration*, 11 Sep 2022, https://www.trade.gov/country-commercial-guides/united-kingdom-agricultural-sectors

243 Peter Morris, 'Brexit to blame for empty trucks and shelves', *Guardian*, 13 Oct 2021, https://www.theguardian.com/business/2021/oct/13/brexit-to-blame-for-empty-trucks-and-shelves
244 Alex Whiteman, 'More than 25% of trucks leaving the UK for EU are empty as exports dive', *The Loadstar*, 10 Mar 2021, https://theloadstar.com/more-than-25-of-trucks-leaving-the-uk-for-eu-are-empty-as-exports-dive/
245 William James, 'BP says nearly a third of its UK fuel stations running on empty', *Reuters*, 26 Sep 2021, https://www.reuters.com/world/uk/behave-normally-uk-transport-minister-tells-britons-queuing-fuel-2021-09-26/
246 'Fuel issues persist in south but "over" elsewhere', BBC News, 3 Oct 2021, https://www.bbc.com/news/business-58781445
247 'Latest petrol and diesel fuel prices', Heycar, 18 Jan 2023, https://heycar.co.uk/blog/latest-fuel-prices
248 Larry Elliott, 'Slowdown in UK recovery may be more than a supply chain issue', *Guardian*, 26 Aug 2021, https://www.theguardian.com/business/2021/aug/26/slowdown-in-uk-recovery-may-be-more-than-a-supply-chain-issue
249 Caroline Davies, 'McDonald's runs out of milkshakes amid "supply chain issues"', *Guardian*, 24 Aug 2021, https://www.theguardian.com/business/2021/aug/24/mcdonalds-runs-out-of-milkshakes-due-to-supply-chain-issues
250 'Consumers experiencing a shortage of food items in Great Britain between September 22 and October 17 2021, by type and region', Statista, https://www.statista.com/statistics/1268805/food-shortage-region-great-britain
251 Sarah Butler, 'Supermarkets using cardboard cutouts to hide gaps left by supply issues', *Guardian*, 22 Oct 2021, https://www.theguardian.com/business/2021/oct/22/supermarkets-using-cardboard-cutouts-to-hide-gaps-left-by-supply-issues
252 'Inflation: food price rises are terrifying, warns industry', BBC News, 19 Oct 2021, https://www.bbc.co.uk/news/business-58962049
253 Sarah Butler, 'Cost of British food basics increases by up to 80% in a year', *Guardian*, 18 Apr 2023, https://www.theguardian.com/business/2023/apr/18/cost-of-british-food-basics-increases-by-up-to-80-in-a-year
254 Elly Blake, 'One in four Londoners unable to buy essential food in past fortnight, study says', *Evening Standard*, 25 Oct 2021, https://www.standard.co.uk/news/london/one-four-londoners-essential-food-ons-food-shortages-fuel-b962312.html
255 Peter Davidson, '"Get in the real world" Scots Tory MP scolded over views on Brexit food shortages', *Daily Record*, 6 Sep 2021, https://www.dailyrecord.co.uk/news/politics/get-real-world-scots-tory-24919301
256 Tom Rees, 'Supermarket crisis is a good thing, says Tory MP', *Telegraph*, 3 Oct 2021, https://www.telegraph.co.uk/business/2021/10/03/supermarket-shortages-good-thing-says-tory-mp/
257 Zoe Wood, 'Not enough turkeys for Christmas due to Brexit, poultry producers warn', *Guardian*, 19 Aug 2021, https://www.theguardian.com/environment/2021/aug/19/chicken-producers-brexit-staff-supply-shortages-uk-immigration-jobs-eu
258 '"Don't let Brexit obliterate us": pig farmers protest at Tory conference amid cull warning', LBC, 4 Oct 2021, https://www.lbc.co.uk/news/dont-let-brexit-obliterate-us-pig-farmers-protest-at-tory-conference-amid-cull-w/
259 Chris Burn, 'Mass culling of 35,000 pigs and tonnes of crops being left to rot "caused by Brexit", committee finds', *Yorkshire Post*, 6 Apr 2022, https://www.yorkshirepost.co.uk/country-and-farming/mass-culling-of-35000-pigs-and-tonnes-of-crops-being-left-to-rot-caused-by-brexit-committee-finds-3642244
260 'Number of people receiving three days' worth of emergency food by Trussell Trust foodbanks in the United Kingdom from 2008/09 to 2021/22', Statista, https://www.statista.com/statistics/382695/uk-foodbank-users/
261 'UK vows to match EU funds, farm subsidies after Brexit', *Daily Star*, 13 Aug 2016, https://www.thedailystar.net/world/uk-vows-match-eu-funds-farm-subsidies-after-brexit-1269250
262 'What support would farmers get after Brexit?', Farming UK, 14 Jun 2016, https://www.farminguk.com/news/what-support-would-farmers-get-after-brexit-_42108.html

263 Tom Levitt and Andrew Wasley, '"No running water": foreign workers criticise UK farm labour scheme', *Guardian*, 12 Jan 2022, https://www.theguardian.com/global-development/2022/jan/12/no-running-water-foreign-workers-criticise-uk-farm-labour-scheme
264 Helena Horton, 'Revealed: farmers received less than 0.5% of post-Brexit money last year', *Guardian*, 12 Feb 2023, https://www.theguardian.com/environment/2023/feb/12/farmers-post-brexit-payments
265 'Investigation into the management of backlogs in driving licence applications', National Audit Office, 4 Nov 2022, https://www.nao.org.uk/reports/investigation-into-the-management-of-backlogs-in-driving-licence-applications
266 'Unemployment rate in the United Kingdom (UK) from 1999 to 2021', Statista, https://www.statista.com/statistics/263709/unemployment-rate-in-the-united-kingdom/
267 Sasha Mistlin, 'Minister urges firms to invest in UK-based workers in HGV driver shortage', *Guardian*, 28 Aug 2021, https://www.theguardian.com/business/2021/aug/28/minister-urges-firms-to-invest-in-uk-based-workers-in-hgv-driver-shortage
268 Zoe Wood, 'Not enough turkeys for Christmas due to Brexit, poultry producers warn', *Guardian*, 19 Aug 2021, https://www.theguardian.com/environment/2021/aug/19/chicken-producers-brexit-staff-supply-shortages-uk-immigration-jobs-eu
269 Alexander McNamara, 'Coronavirus: Mandatory face masks "could save up to 50,000 lives"', *BBC Science Focus*, 16 Jun 2020, https://www.sciencefocus.com/news/coronavirus-mandatory-face-masks-could-save-up-to-50000-lives/
270 Lynne Peeples, 'Face masks: what the data say', *Nature*, 6 Oct 2020, https://www.nature.com/articles/d41586-020-02801-8
271 John Kampfner, 'English exceptionalism doesn't apply to Covid', *The Times*, 22 Oct 2021, https://www.thetimes.co.uk/article/english-exceptionalism-doesnt-apply-to-covid-xddhhtjwg
272 James Morris, 'Rees-Mogg: Tories don't wear masks in Parliament because we are friends', LBC, 21 Oct 2021, https://www.lbc.co.uk/news/jacob-rees-mogg-masks-parliament/
273 Chris Smyth, 'Jacob Rees-Mogg tells opposition MPs: Work harder and you won't need a mask', *The Times*, 16 Sep 2021, https://www.thetimes.co.uk/article/jacob-rees-mogg-tells-labour-mps-work-harder-and-you-wont-need-a-mask-8p8hvkgbh
274 Stephen Bates, 'Lord Rees-Mogg obituary', *Guardian*, 29 Dec 2012, https://www.theguardian.com/media/2012/dec/29/william-rees-mogg-obituary
275 'Coronavirus (COVID-19) in the UK', GOV.UK, https://coronavirus.data.gov.uk/details/vaccinations
276 'Deaths in the United Kingdom', GOV.UK, https://coronavirus.data.gov.uk/details/deaths
277 Jamie Grierson, 'Tory minister says face masks should not become a "sign of virtue"', *Guardian*, 22 Oct 2021, https://www.theguardian.com/politics/2021/oct/22/tory-minister-says-face-masks-should-not-become-a-sign-of-virtue
278 Connor Boyd, 'The great political divide . . . on face masks! Tory benches opt against own guidance on wearing coverings in packed Commons debate over Afghanistan – but opposition masks up', *Daily Mail*, 18 Aug 2021, https://www.dailymail.co.uk/news/article-9905359/The-great-political-divide-face-masks-Tory-benches-opt-against-guidance-Commons.html
279 Will Dahlgreen, 'Memories of Iraq: did we ever support the war?', YouGov, 3 Jun 2015, https://yougov.co.uk/topics/politics/articles-reports/2015/06/03/remembering-iraq
280 Eugene Kiely and Robert Farley, 'Timeline of U.S. Withdrawal from Afghanistan', FactCheck.org. 17 Aug 2021, https://www.factcheck.org/2021/08/timeline-of-u-s-withdrawal-from-afghanistan/
281 'Afghanistan', Hansard, 8 Jul 2021, https://hansard.parliament.uk/commons/2021-07-08/debates/CBB76087-2079-42F0-A58C-2DFEBED899F1/Afghanistan
282 'Missing in action: UK leadership and the withdrawal from Afghanistan', Parliament Publications, 24 May 2022, https://publications.parliament.uk/pa/cm5803/cmselect/cmfaff/169/report.html
283 'Missing in action: UK leadership and the withdrawal from Afghanistan', Parliament Publications, 24 May 2022, https://publications.parliament.uk/pa/cm5803/cmselect/cmfaff/169/report.html

284 'Missing in action: UK leadership and the withdrawal from Afghanistan', Parliament Publications, 24 May 2022, https://publications.parliament.uk/pa/cm5803/cmselect/cmfaff/169/report.html

285 Eugene Kiely and Robert Farley, 'Timeline of U.S. Withdrawal from Afghanistan', FactCheck.org, 17 Aug 2021, https://www.factcheck.org/2021/08/timeline-of-u-s-withdrawal-from-afghanistan/

286 Kate Devlin, 'Raab's "refusal to speak to time-waster staff led to Afghanistan evacuation delays"', Independent, 19 Nov 2022, https://www.independent.co.uk/news/uk/politics/dominic-raab-staff-afghanistan-evacuation-b2228586.html

287 Jasmine Cameron-Chileshe, 'UK withdrawal from Afghanistan was a "disaster" and "betrayal"', Financial Times, 24 May 2022, https://www.ft.com/content/a0b34ccc-845c-4f94-8093-caf40a710000

288 Kate Townshend, '"The sea was closed": Even Dominic Raab knows it's a ridiculous excuse, so why let him get away with it?', Independent, 25 Aug 2021, https://www.independent.co.uk/voices/dominic-raab-taliban-kabul-politicians-b1908571.html

289 'Missing in action: UK leadership and the withdrawal from Afghanistan', Parliament Publications, 24 May 2022, https://publications.parliament.uk/pa/cm5803/cmselect/cmfaff/169/report.html

290 Tom Peck, 'Dominic Raab really does think his own personal failures on Afghanistan are "silly season stuff"', Independent, 31 Aug 2021, https://www.independent.co.uk/voices/dominic-raab-kabul-taliban-holiday-b1911777.html

291 Rt. Hon Ben Wallace MP [@BWallaceMP], Twitter, 25 Aug 2021, https://twitter.com/BWallaceMP/status/1430327318434754568

292 Jasmine Cameron-Chileshe, 'UK withdrawal from Afghanistan was a "disaster" and "betrayal"', Financial Times, 24 May 2022, https://www.ft.com/content/a0b34ccc-845c-4f94-8093-caf40a710000

293 'Missing in action: UK leadership and the withdrawal from Afghanistan', Parliament Publications, 24 May 2022, https://publications.parliament.uk/pa/cm5803/cmselect/cmfaff/169/report.html

294 Madeleine Brand and Sanden Totten, 'How to spot a psychopath', KPCC, 18 May 2011, https://www.kpcc.org/2011-05-18/how-spot-psychopath

295 'Dominic Raab faces further pressure over Afghanistan delays as it emerges phone call delegated to junior minister never took place', Sky News, 20 Aug 2021, https://news.sky.com/story/dominic-raab-faces-further-pressure-over-afghanistan-delays-as-it-emerges-phone-call-delegated-to-junior-minister-never-took-place-12385654

296 'Tom Tugendhat – 2021 Speech on Afghanistan', UK Pol, 20 Aug 2021, https://www.ukpol.co.uk/tom-tugendhat-2021-speech-on-afghanistan/

297 'Operation Warm Welcome under way to support Afghan arrivals in the UK', GOV.UK, 1 Sep 2021, https://www.gov.uk/government/news/operation-warm-welcome-underway-to-support-afghan-arrivals-in-the-uk

298 Holly Bancroft and Andrew Woodcock, 'Just four Afghan refugees brought to the UK since fall of Kabul', Independent, 1 Dec 2022, https://www.independent.co.uk/news/uk/home-news/afghan-refugees-acrs-arap-home-office-b2237159.html

299 Sean Coughlan, 'Gavin Williamson: how has he survived?', BBC News, 13 Jan 2021, https://www.bbc.co.uk/news/education-55640335

300 Will Hazell, 'A-levels and GCSEs U-turn: Gavin Williamson claims he only discovered unfairness in Ofqual algorithm "over the weekend"', iNews, 17 Aug 2020, https://inews.co.uk/news/education/a-levels-gcses-u-turn-gavin-williamson-says-he-only-ofqual-algorithm-weekend-581910

301 Sean O'Grady, 'He may have failed to make the grade, but Boris Johnson cannot get rid of Gavin Williamson', Independent, 4 Aug 2021, https://www.independent.co.uk/independentpremium/politics-explained/gavin-williamson-schools-latin-boris-johnson-b1896083.html

302 Gavin Coughlan, 'Gavin Williamson on coping with "lonely" leadership', BBC News, 12 Mar 2021, https://www.bbc.co.uk/news/education-56375664

303 'Reshuffle: Boris Johnson fires Gavin Williamson as he rings cabinet changes', BBC News, 15 Sep 2021, https://www.bbc.co.uk/news/uk-politics-58571935

304 'College lecturer photographs MP Elizabeth Truss for 209 Women initiative', West Suffolk College, 14 Dec 2018, https://www.wsc.ac.uk/about-the-college/news/4819-college-lecturer-photographs-liz-truss-for-209-women-initiative
305 Alex Finnis, 'Liz Truss cheese speech: How Tory leadership favourite's viral comments on UK imports spawned countless memes', *iNews*, 5 Sep 2022, https://inews.co.uk/news/politics/conservatives/liz-truss-cheese-speech-tory-leadership-contestant-uk-imports-memes-1753951
306 Matt Chorley, '"New-fangled" desserts like Angel Delight are to blame for the decline of the English apple, claims Environment Secretary', *Daily Mail*, 24 Sep 2014, https://www.dailymail.co.uk/news/article-2768071/New-fangled-desserts-like-Angel-Delight-blame-decline-English-apple-claims-Environment-Secretary.html
307 'About Angel Delight', https://www.angeldelightdesserts.co.uk/
308 Andrew Anthony, '"She often speaks without thinking": Nadine Dorries, our new minister for culture wars', *Guardian*, 31 Oct 2021, https://www.theguardian.com/politics/2021/oct/31/she-often-speaks-without-thinking-nadine-dorries-our-new-minister-for-culture-wars
309 Peter Walker, 'BBC staffed by people "whose mum and dad worked there", says Nadine Dorries', *Guardian*, 4 Oct 2021, https://www.theguardian.com/politics/2021/oct/04/bbc-staffed-by-people-whose-mum-and-dad-worked-there-says-nadine-dorries
310 Ellie Buchdahl, 'MP Nadine Dorries paid her daughters up to £80k from the public purse to work in her office . . . and gave one a £15k pay rise', *Daily Mail*, 14 Sep 2013, https://www.dailymail.co.uk/news/article-2420625/MP-Nadine-Dorries-pays-daughters-75k-public-purse-work-office.html
311 John Nicholson MP [@MrJohnNicolson], Twitter, 5 Nov 2021, https://twitter.com/MrJohn Nicolson/status/1456656898338525189
312 Ben Glaze, 'Tory MP Nadine Dorries threatens to "nail Sunday Mirror reporter's testicles to the floor using own front teeth"', *Mirror*, 24 Nov 2013, https://www.mirror.co.uk/news/uk-news/tory-mp-nadine-dorries-threatens-2845154
313 Maya Oppenheim, 'Tory MP who called James O'Brien a "public school posh boy f**kwit" sends daughter to same school as presenter', *Independent*, 30 Mar 2017, https://www.independent.co.uk/news/uk/politics/james-o-brien-nadine-dorries-tory-mp-posh-boy-daughter-goes-to-same-public-school-lbc-presenter-a7658236.html
314 Kate Nicholson, 'Nadine Dorries doesn't know how Channel 4 is funded and no one can believe it', *HuffPost*, 24 Oct 2021, https://www.huffingtonpost.co.uk/entry/nadine-dorries-channel-4-funding-twitter_uk_619e6964e4b0ae9a42a9919e
315 Greg Evans, 'Awkward clip of Boris Johnson jogging just 10 metres from his car resurfaces', *Indy100*, 27 Jun 2022, https://www.indy100.com/politics/boris-johnson-jogging-running-car
316 'World-leading Environment Act becomes law', GOV.UK, 10 Nov 2021, https://www.gov.uk/government/news/world-leading-environment-act-becomes-law
317 'Labour governments' achievements', Shrewsbury Labour, https://www.shrewsburylabour.org.uk/labours-top-50-achievements/
318 'Tory MPs defend votes after uproar over sewage proposals', BBC News, 25 Oct 2021, https://www.bbc.co.uk/news/uk-politics-59040175
319 'Official figures reveal not one river or lake in England is in good health', Wildlife and Countryside Link, 17 Sep 2020, https://www.wcl.org.uk/not-one-river-in-england-in-good-health.asp
320 Tom Bawden, 'UK needs 30 new reservoirs to protect water supply from drought after failing to build one in 31 years', *iNews*, 13 Aug 2022, https://inews.co.uk/news/environment/uk-needs-30-new-reservoirs-protect-water-supply-drought-31-years-1793414
321 Helena Horton, 'Water companies in England "will take 2,000 years to replace pipe network"', *Guardian*, 23 Aug 2022, https://www.theguardian.com/environment/2022/aug/23/water-companies-in-england-expecting-sewers-to-last-2000-years
322 Rachel Salvidge, 'Water firms in England and Wales lost 1tn litres via leaky pipes in 2021', *Guardian*, 19 Aug 2021, https://www.theguardian.com/environment/2022/aug/19/water-firms-england-wales-litres-leaky-pipes-ofwat
323 Colin Fernandez, 'Fury as water companies make £2.8BILLION in profits amid scandal of dumping raw sewage in rivers', *Daily Mail*, 11 Feb 2022, https://www.dailymail.co.uk/news/

article-10503873/Fury-water-companies-make-2-8BILLION-profits-amid-scandal-dumping-raw-sewage-rivers.html
324 'Tory MPs vote for 15 more years of sewage dumping', Liberal Democrats, 26 Jan 2023, https://www.libdems.org.uk/news/adlib-articles/conservative-mps-vote-for-15-more-years-of-sewage-dumping
325 Soraya Ebrahimi, 'UK households to see largest water bill rise in 20 years', *The National*, 9 Feb 2023, https://www.thenationalnews.com/world/uk-news/2023/02/02/uk-households-to-see-largest-water-bill-rise-in-20-years/
326 'Govt rail subsidy of £4.8 billion is double mid-1980s level', RMT, 13 Oct 2016, https://www.rmt.org.uk/news/govt-rail-subsidy-of-48-billion-is-double-mid-1980s-level/
327 Laurie McFarlane, 'Our railways have failed – what next?', New Economics Foundation, 10 Jan 2017, https://neweconomics.org/2017/01/railways-failed-next
328 'UK commuters spend up to 5 times as much of their salary on rail fares as other Europeans, finds TUC', TUC, 2 Jan 2018, https://www.tuc.org.uk/news/national/uk-commuters-spend-5-times-much-their-salary-rail-fares-other-europeans-finds-tuc
329 Chris Lo, 'UK rail: measuring passenger satisfaction', Railway Technology, 10 Mar 2013, https://www.railway-technology.com/features/featureuk-rail-passenger-satisfaction-british-public/
330 'RMT policy briefing on profiteering on Great British railways', RMT, 17 June 2021, https://www.rmt.org.uk/news/publications/rmt-policy-briefing-on-profiteering-on-great-british-railways/
331 Michiel Willems, 'Revealed: Brits are paying the highest electricity bills in the entire world', *CityA.M.*, 14 Jan 2023, https://www.cityam.com/revealed-brits-are-paying-the-highest-electricity-bills-in-the-entire-world/
332 Rachel Millard, 'Hinkley Point nuclear plant faces risk of 11-year delay', *Telegraph*, 29 Dec 2022, https://www.telegraph.co.uk/business/2022/11/29/hinkley-point-nuclear-plant-faces-risk-11-year-delay/
333 Mathew Lawrence, 'The energy sector isn't "broken", it's cooking on gas – if you're a profit-hungry shareholder', *Guardian*, 17 Feb 2023, https://www.theguardian.com/commentisfree/2023/feb/17/energy-sector-gas-shareholder-profits
334 Sean Farrell, 'Royal Mail sale underpriced by £1bn, says scathing select committee report', *Guardian*, 11 Jul 2014, https://www.theguardian.com/uk-news/2014/jul/11/royal-mail-sale-lost-1bn-says-select-committee
335 'Royal Mail struggles to reduce customer complaints post-privatisation', Consultancy.uk, 23 Aug 2018, https://www.consultancy.uk/news/18390/royal-mail-struggles-to-reduce-customer-complaints-post-privatisation
336 Clive Lewis, 'Three years on from its sale, the privatisation of Royal Mail is a story of our times', *HuffPost*, 15 Oct 2017, https://www.huffingtonpost.co.uk/clive-lewis/royal-mail-sale_b_12500394.html
337 Jim Waterson, 'Tory MPs receive £15.2m from second jobs since 2019 election', *Guardian*, 8 Jan 2023, https://www.theguardian.com/politics/2023/jan/08/tory-mps-receive-152m-second-jobs-since-2019-election
338 Arj Singh, 'Ports firm advised by Chris Grayling "wins £35m" Brexit cash as others get "next to nothing"', *HuffPost*, 17 Dec 2020, https://www.huffingtonpost.co.uk/entry/brexit-ports-grayling-labour-reeves_uk_5fdb2f28c5b6094c0fef9680
339 '"Plebgate" row: Timeline', BBC News, 27 Nov 2014, https://www.bbc.co.uk/news/uk-24548645
340 Rowena Mason, 'At least a quarter of Tory MPs have second jobs, earning over £4m a year', *Guardian*, 9 Nov 2021, https://www.theguardian.com/politics/2021/nov/09/at-least-a-quarter-of-tory-mps-have-second-jobs-earning-5m-a-year
341 Rowena Mason, 'At least a quarter of Tory MPs have second jobs, earning over £4m a year', *Guardian*, 9 Nov 2021, https://www.theguardian.com/politics/2021/nov/09/at-least-a-quarter-of-tory-mps-have-second-jobs-earning-5m-a-year
342 Stefan Boscia, 'Jacob Rees-Mogg may have broken parliamentary rules by not declaring £6m in loans', *CityA.M.*, 14 Nov 2021, https://www.cityam.com/jacob-rees-mogg-may-have-broken-parliamentary-rules-by-not-declaring-6m-in-loans/

343 Sophie Huskisson, 'Hypocrite Tory Lee Anderson to rake in £100k from TV show after MP second jobs rant', *Mirror*, 22 Mar 2023, https://www.mirror.co.uk/news/politics/hypocrite-tory-lee-anderson-rake-29526814
344 Ethan Shone, 'Exclusive poll: 68% of people think MPs shouldn't be able to have second jobs outside Parliament', NationalWorld, 8 Nov 2021, https://www.nationalworld.com/news/politics/exclusive-poll-68-of-people-think-mps-shouldnt-be-able-to-have-second-jobs-outside-parliament-3447415
345 Shirley Tart, 'Owen Paterson back and fighting for Brexit', *Shropshire Star*, 3 Sep 2018, https://www.shropshirestar.com/news/politics/2018/09/03/owen-paterson-back-and-fighting-for-brexit/
346 Damian Carrington, 'Owen Paterson: true blue countryman putting wind up green campaigners', *Guardian*, 11 Oct 2012, https://www.theguardian.com/politics/2012/oct/11/owen-paterson-environment-guardian-profile
347 Mehdi Hasan, 'Why is climate change denier Owen Paterson still in his job?', *HuffPost*, 2 Nov 2014, https://www.huffingtonpost.co.uk/mehdi-hasan/uk-floods-owen-paterson_b_4767153.html
348 Richard Vaughan, 'Owen Paterson: former cabinet minister faces 30-day suspension for "egregious" breach of lobbying rules', *iNews*, 26 Oct 2021, https://inews.co.uk/news/politics/tory-mp-owen-paterson-hits-back-faces-30-day-suspension-flouting-lobbying-rules-1268153
349 'Mr Owen Paterson', Parliament.uk, 26 Oct 2021, https://publications.parliament.uk/pa/cm5802/cmselect/cmstandards/797/79703.htm
350 Rupert Neate, Juliette Garside, Felicity Lawrence and Rob Evans, 'Healthcare firm advised by Owen Paterson won £133m coronavirus testing contract unopposed', *Guardian*, 11 May 2020, https://www.theguardian.com/world/2020/may/11/healthcare-firm-advised-by-owen-paterson-won-133m-coronavirus-testing-contract-unopposed
351 Mikey Smith, 'Tories say they "can't locate" vital papers on firm that got £600m Covid contracts', *Mirror*, 17 Nov 2021, https://www.mirror.co.uk/news/politics/tories-say-cant-locate-vital-25481797
352 Sophie Morris, 'Owen Paterson: Minister confirms government "unable to locate" minutes of call between ex-Tory MP, Randox and officials', Sky News, 17 Nov 2021, https://news.sky.com/story/owen-paterson-minister-confirms-government-unable-to-locate-minutes-of-meeting-between-ex-tory-mp-randox-and-officials-12470899
353 Geraldine Scott, 'Messages show how disgraced MP Owen Paterson lobbied health secretary Matt Hancock for Randox', *Independent*, 4 Feb 2022, https://www.independent.co.uk/news/uk/politics/owen-paterson-matt-hancock-randox-commons-government-b2007986.html
354 Juliette Garside and Joseph Smith, 'Tory-linked firm involved in testing failure given new £347m Covid contract', *Guardian*, 4 Nov 2020, https://www.theguardian.com/world/2020/nov/04/tory-linked-firm-involved-in-testing-failure-awarded-new-347m-covid-contract
355 Rob Evans, David Pegg and Felicity Lawrence, 'UK health department played "fast and loose" when awarding Covid contracts to Randox', *Guardian*, 27 Jul 2022, https://www.theguardian.com/politics/2022/jul/27/uk-health-department-played-fast-and-loose-when-awarding-covid-contracts-to-randox
356 Rob Evans, David Pegg and Felicity Lawrence, 'UK health department played "fast and loose" when awarding Covid contracts to Randox', *Guardian*, 27 Jul 2022, https://www.theguardian.com/politics/2022/jul/27/uk-health-department-played-fast-and-loose-when-awarding-covid-contracts-to-randox
357 Rob Evans, David Pegg and Felicity Lawrence, 'Matt Hancock's stay at mansion of Randox founder revealed by FoI request', *Guardian*, 24 Apr 2022, https://www.theguardian.com/world/2022/apr/24/matt-hancocks-stay-at-mansion-of-randox-founder-revealed-by-foi-request
358 'Owen Paterson faces 30-day Commons suspension for rule breach after watchdog report', BBC News, 26 Oct 2021, https://www.bbc.co.uk/news/uk-politics-59049243
359 'Committee on Standards – Amendment (a)', Votes in Parliament, 3 Nov 2021, https://votes.parliament.uk/Votes/Commons/Division/1124#notrecorded

360 Mark Harper [@Mark_J_Harper], Twitter, 4 Nov 2021, https://twitter.com/bbclaurak/status/1456232047832403968
361 Christopher Hope, '"Cruel world of politics": inside story of the Tory U-turn that meant Owen Paterson's career was over', *Telegraph*, 4 Nov 2021, https://www.telegraph.co.uk/politics/2021/11/04/cruel-world-politics-u-turn-sunk-owen-patersons-political-career/
362 'PM U-turns on controversial review of Owen Paterson's lobbying suspension', *Shropshire Star*, 4 Nov 2021, https://www.shropshirestar.com/news/uk-news/2021/11/04/pm-backtracks-on-controversial-review-of-owen-patersons-lobbying-suspension/
363 'Tories lose North Shropshire seat they held for 115 years', BBC News, 17 Dec 2021, https://www.bbc.co.uk/news/uk-england-shropshire-59693102
364 Toby Helm, Jon Ungoed-Thomas, Michael Savage and Tom Wall, 'Return of the sleazy party: the Conservatives and the Owen Paterson affair', *Guardian*, 7 Nov 2021, https://www.theguardian.com/politics/2021/nov/07/return-of-the-sleazy-party-the-conservatives-and-the-owen-paterson-affair
365 Toby Helm, Jon Ungoed-Thomas, Michael Savage and Tom Wall, 'Return of the sleazy party: the Conservatives and the Owen Paterson affair', *Guardian*, 7 Nov 2021, https://www.theguardian.com/politics/2021/nov/07/return-of-the-sleazy-party-the-conservatives-and-the-owen-paterson-affair
366 Susannah Butter, 'Sleazopedia: the anatomy of the Tories' week from hell', *Evening Standard*, 11 Nov 2021, https://www.standard.co.uk/news/politics/sleaze-tories-boris-johnson-owen-paterson-geoffrey-cox-b965629.html
367 Mark Travers, 'Narcissists prefer the romantic company of other narcissists, according to new research', *Forbes*, 17 Dec 2020, https://www.forbes.com/sites/traversmark/2020/12/17/narcissists-prefer-the-romantic-company-of-other-narcissists-according-to-new-research/?sh=3fe4601f6be1
368 Pippa Crerar, 'Boris Johnson "broke Covid lockdown rules" with Downing Street parties at Xmas', *Mirror*, 30 Nov 2021, https://www.mirror.co.uk/news/politics/boris-johnson-broke-covid-lockdown-25585238
369 'Seven Downing Street parties and government explanations that just do not stack up – as the warren of rooms at the storm's centre are revealed', *Daily Mail*, 10 Dec 2021, https://www.dailymail.co.uk/news/article-10298281/Seven-Downing-Street-parties-government-explanations-just-not-stack-up.html
370 Nicholas Cecil, 'Minister fails to follow No10 line on Boris Johnson party', *Evening Standard*, 2 Dec 2021, https://www.standard.co.uk/news/politics/minister-george-freeman-no10-boris-johnson-party-tier-3-b969609.html
371 Pippa Crerar, 'Boris Johnson "broke Covid lockdown rules" with Downing Street parties at Xmas', *Mirror*, 30 Nov 2021, https://www.mirror.co.uk/news/politics/boris-johnson-broke-covid-lockdown-25585238
372 'Seven Downing Street parties and government explanations that just do not stack up – as the warren of rooms at the storm's centre are revealed', *Daily Mail*, 10 Dec 2021, https://www.dailymail.co.uk/news/article-10298281/Seven-Downing-Street-parties-government-explanations-just-not-stack-up.html
373 Anna Isaac, 'Operation Save Big Dog: Boris Johnson draws up plan for officials to quit over partygate so he can keep job', *Independent*, 14 Jan 2022, https://www.independent.co.uk/news/uk/politics/boris-johnson-downing-street-partygate-b1993433.html
374 'Do police normally investigate things that happened a year ago?', FullFact, 8 Dec 2021, https://fullfact.org/law/dominic-raab-police-investigate-downing-street-party/
375 Pippa Crerar [@PippaCrerar], Twitter, 20 Dec 2021, https://twitter.com/PippaCrerar/status/1472907231460999168
376 Aubrey Allegretti, 'First pictures released of Boris Johnson's new £2.6m briefing room', *Guardian*, 15 Mar 2021, https://www.theguardian.com/politics/2021/mar/15/no-10-offers-first-sight-of-26m-white-house-style-briefing-room
377 Lucy Campbell, 'Boris Johnson used £2.6m Downing Street briefing room to watch new Bond film', *Guardian*, 22 Oct 2021, https://www.theguardian.com/politics/2021/oct/22/boris-johnson-used-26m-downing-street-briefing-room-to-watch-new-bond-film
378 Peter Walker, Aubrey Allegretti and Jamie Grierson, 'PM accused of lying after No 10 officials caught joking about Christmas party', *Guardian*, 7 Dec 2021, https://www.

theguardian.com/politics/2021/dec/07/leaked-video-shows-no-10-officials-joking-about-holding-christmas-party
379 Peter Walker, 'Johnson "apologises unreservedly" over No 10 Christmas party video', *Guardian*, 8 Dec 2021, https://www.theguardian.com/politics/2021/dec/08/boris-johnson-apologises-unreservedly-over-no-10-christmas-party-video

2022: 'It's Bollocks, Utter Bollocks'

1. Rob Merrick, 'Liz Truss "insisted" on £1,400 taxpayer-funded lunch at private club owned by Tory donor', *Independent*, 2 Jan 2022, https://www.independent.co.uk/news/uk/politics/liz-truss-tory-donor-leadership-b1985560.html
2. Emily Ferguson, 'Liz Truss channels Margaret Thatcher with tank photo op as poll finds Foreign Secretary most popular minister', *iNews*, 30 Nov 2021, https://inews.co.uk/news/politics/liz-truss-margaret-thatcher-tank-photo-foreign-secretary-most-popular-minister-1327348
3. Liz Truss [@trussliz], Twitter, 15 Dec 2021, https://twitter.com/trussliz/status/1471045885446533129
4. Instagram [elizabeth.truss.mp], https://www.instagram.com/elizabeth.truss.mp/
5. Giulia Crouch, 'Prime Minister Liz Truss – everything you need to know about the new PM', *Evening Standard*, 5 Sep 2022, https://www.standard.co.uk/insider/liz-truss-who-is-she-foreign-secretary-conservative-leadership-b1013289.html
6. Glen Owen, 'Foreign Secretary Liz Truss hires an "Instagram guru" to project her image on social media – and combat the slick online efforts of rival Rishi Sunak', *Daily Mail*, 23 Oct 2021, https://www.dailymail.co.uk/news/article-10124181/Foreign-Secretary-Liz-Truss-hires-Instagram-guru-project-image-social-media.html
7. Matt Bodell, 'Health Secretary accused of "desperately looking for ways not to negotiate with nurses"', NursingNotes, 19 Jan 2023, https://nursingnotes.co.uk/news/politics/health-secretary-accused-of-desperately-looking-for-ways-not-to-negotiate-with-nurses/
8. Andrew Woodcock, 'More than 22,000 EU nationals have left NHS since Brexit referendum, figures show', *Independent*, 10 Dec 2019, https://www.independent.co.uk/news/uk/politics/brexit-eu-citizens-nhs-crisis-migration-boris-johnson-hospital-health-a9239791.html
9. 'How the new nursing bursary works', Nurses.co.uk, 22 Oct 2020, https://www.nurses.co.uk/blog/how-the-new-nursing-bursary-works
10. 'Large drop in the number of new nurses coming from the EU to work in the UK', The Health Foundation, https://www.health.org.uk/chart/chart-large-drop-in-the-number-of-new-nurses-coming-from-the-eu-to-work-in-the-uk
11. Jessica Morris, 'How much is Covid-19 to blame for growing NHS waiting times?', Nuffield Trust, 5 Sep 2022, https://www.nuffieldtrust.org.uk/resource/how-much-is-covid-19-to-blame-for-growing-nhs-waiting-times
12. Luke Haynes, 'Hancock denies PPE shortages caused any of 1,500 NHS staff deaths from COVID-19', GP Online, 10 June 2021, https://www.gponline.com/hancock-denies-ppe-shortages-caused-1500-nhs-staff-deaths-covid-19/article/1718813
13. 'Mayor declares "major incident" following rapid spread of Covid-19', London.gov, 8 Jan 2021, https://www.london.gov.uk/press-releases/mayoral/hospitals-at-risk-of-being-overwhelmed-in-capital
14. 'Covid: Lincolnshire hospitals declare "critical incident" over staff shortages', BBC News, 3 Jan 2022, https://www.bbc.co.uk/news/uk-england-lincolnshire-59858887
15. 'Omicron variant of the SARS-CoV-2: a quest to define the consequences of its high mutational load', National Library of Medicine, 18 Dec 2021, https://www.ncbi.nlm.nih.gov/pmc/articles/PMC8683309/
16. 'Omicron is "killing people" and should not be called "mild", WHO warns', *Euronews*, 7 Jan 2022, https://www.euronews.com/2022/01/07/omicron-is-killing-people-and-should-not-be-called-mild-who-warns
17. 'Covid news: Omicron detected in US; UK reports 48,374 new cases and 171 deaths – as it happened', *Guardian*, 2 Dec 2021, https://www.theguardian.com/world/live/2021/dec/01/covid-news-live-who-advises-vulnerable-against-travel-over-omicron-greece-to-fine-those-over-60-who-refuse-vaccine

18 'Travel to England from another country during coronavirus (COVID-19)', GOV.UK, 22 Jun 2021, https://www.gov.uk/guidance/travel-to-england-from-another-country-during-coronavirus-covid-19
19 Andrew Gregory, 'Covid self-isolation cut to seven days with negative test in England', *Guardian*, 22 Dec 2021, https://www.theguardian.com/world/2021/dec/22/covid-self-isolation-cut-to-seven-days-for-jabbed-people-in-england
20 Peter Walker, Andrew Gregory and Linda Geddes, 'No new Covid restrictions before Christmas, Boris Johnson confirms', *Guardian*, 22 Dec 2021, https://www.theguardian.com/politics/2021/dec/21/no-new-covid-measures-before-christmas-boris-johnson-confirms
21 'Deaths within 28 days of positive test by date of death', GOV.UK, https://coronavirus.data.gov.uk/details/deaths
22 'As-it-happened: PM warns of challenging weeks, as cases top 200k', BBC News, 4 Jan 2022, https://www.bbc.co.uk/news/live/uk-59865257
23 Becky Morton, 'Covid: UK records more than 150,000 deaths', BBC News, 8 Jan 2022, https://www.bbc.co.uk/news/uk-59923936
24 Phillip Inman, 'UK inflation rises to highest level in almost 30 years at 5.4%', *Guardian*, 19 Jan 2022, https://www.theguardian.com/business/2022/jan/19/uk-inflation-hits-near-three-decade-high-rising-to-54
25 Jillian Ambrose, 'Millions face second record energy price hike this year, analysts warn', *Guardian*, 17 Jan 2022, https://www.theguardian.com/money/2022/jan/17/millions-face-second-record-energy-price-hike-this-year-analysts-warn
26 'Global Energy Crisis', IEA, https://www.iea.org/topics/global-energy-crisis
27 Jack Peat, 'Brutal Brexit assessment from US embassy has played out precisely as predicted', *London Economic*, 5 Feb 2022, https://www.thelondoneconomic.com/politics/brutal-brexit-assessment-from-us-embassy-has-played-out-precisely-as-predicted-310787/
28 Asher McShane, 'Dover lorry queues "sparked by Brexit checks" so long they can be seen from space', LBC, 22 Jan 2022, https://www.lbc.co.uk/news/uk/dover-lorry-queues-sparked-by-brexit-delays-so-long-they-can-be-seen-from-space/
29 'Lack of trust in politics threatens democracy: New report and poll', Carnegie UK, 20 Jan 2022, https://www.carnegieuktrust.org.uk/news-stories/lack-of-trust-in-politics-threatens-democracy-new-report-and-poll/
30 'Gender identity, England and Wales: Census 2021', ONS, 2021, https://www.ons.gov.uk/peoplepopulationandcommunity/culturalidentity/genderidentity/bulletins/genderidentityenglandandwales/census2021
31 'Transgender people over four times more likely than cisgender people to be victims of violent crime', Williams Institute, UCLA, 23 Mar 2021, https://williamsinstitute.law.ucla.edu/press/ncvs-trans-press-release/
32 'Met to contact two people over party for Shaun Bailey at Conservative HQ', *Guardian*, 16 Dec 2021, https://www.theguardian.com/politics/2021/dec/16/met-to-contact-two-people-over-party-for-shaun-bailey-at-conservative-hq
33 Paul Brand, 'Email proves Downing Street staff held drinks party at height of lockdown', ITV News, 10 Jan 2022, https://www.itv.com/news/2022-01-10/email-proves-downing-street-staff-held-drinks-party-at-height-of-lockdown
34 Pippa Crerar, 'Boris Johnson's "wine time Fridays" – No10 staff held drinks EVERY week during pandemic', *Mirror*, 14 Jan 2022, https://www.mirror.co.uk/news/politics/boris-johnsons-wine-time-fridays-25951853
35 Paul Brand, 'ITV News podcast reveals Boris Johnson joked about "the most unsocially distanced party in the UK"', ITV News, 12 Jan 2023, https://www.itv.com/news/2023-01-10/exclusive-boris-johnson-joked-about-most-unsocially-distanced-party-in-the-uk
36 Dan Bloom, 'Inside Downing Street party with "suitcase of wine", DJ and broken kid's swing', *Mirror*, 14 Jan 2022, https://www.mirror.co.uk/news/politics/inside-downing-street-party-suitcase-25945525
37 Adam Forrest, 'Boris Johnson staff "had sex at No 10 lockdown party"', *Independent*, 12 Jan 2023, https://www.independent.co.uk/news/uk/politics/boris-johnson-sex-partygate-covid-b2260903.html
38 Heather Stewart, Rowena Mason, Jessica Murray and Steven Morris, 'No 10 apologises to Queen over parties on eve of Prince Philip funeral', *Guardian*, 14 Jan 2022, https://www.

theguardian.com/politics/2022/jan/14/no-10-apologises-palace-parties-eve-prince-philip-funeral-queen-covid
39 Aletha Adu, 'Dame Priti and Sir Jacob: the allies and aides in Johnson's honours list', *Guardian*, 9 Jun 2023, https://www.theguardian.com/politics/2023/jun/09/dame-priti-and-sir-party-marty-the-aides-and-allies-in-boris-johnsons-honours-list
40 Andrew Sparrow, 'Report of Boris Johnson pouring drinks "implies he started lockdown party"', *Guardian*, 17 Apr 2022, https://www.theguardian.com/politics/2022/apr/17/report-of-boris-johnson-pouring-drinks-implies-he-started-lockdown-party-says-labour-partygate
41 'Michael Fabricant rushes to defend Boris Johnson; says it's not like there were pole dancers at the "parties"', *The National*, 12 Apr 2022, https://www.thenational.scot/news/20063457.michael-fabricant-rushes-defend-boris-johnson-says-not-like-pole-dancers-parties/
42 Sophie Barnett, 'Sexist of the Year award handed out at lockdown-breaking Downing Street Christmas party', LBC, 2 May 2022, https://www.lbc.co.uk/news/sexist-award-downing-street-christmas-party/
43 Lara Keay, 'Sue Gray report key findings: Karaoke machine, drunkenness and panic button triggered', Sky News, 26 May 2022, https://news.sky.com/story/sue-gray-report-all-the-key-criticisms-of-the-government-12621059
44 Camilla Cavendish, 'Partygate lays bare the casual carelessness of Boris Johnson's ancien régime', *Financial Times*, 15 Apr 2022, https://www.ft.com/content/fcafe048-ca40-496f-bc2a-40789ea6f3c8
45 'Partygate: Boris Johnson "told barefaced lie", says Labour, as Covid victim group urges Tory MPs to remove PM – as it happened', *Guardian*, 19 May 2022, https://www.theguardian.com/politics/live/2022/may/19/boris-johnson-news-uk-politics-live-cost-of-living-latest
46 Rosaleen Fenton, 'Boris Johnson's worst quotes – from slamming single mums to Partygate apology', *Mirror*, 6 Sep 2022, https://www.mirror.co.uk/news/politics/boris-johnsons-worst-quotes-slamming-27893087
47 Paul Brand [@PaulBrandITV], Twitter, 22 Mar 2023, https://twitter.com/PaulBrandITV/status/1638500578278924289
48 Michael Howie, 'Simon Case: Cabinet Secretary "recuses himself" from Partygate inquiry after new allegations', *Evening Standard*, 17 Dec 2021, https://www.standard.co.uk/news/uk/simon-case-boris-johnson-parties-downing-street-oliver-dowden-cabinet-office-b972676.html
49 Paul Brand, 'ITV News podcast reveals Boris Johnson joked about "the most unsocially distanced party in the UK"', ITV News, 12 Jan 2023, https://www.itv.com/news/2023-01-10/exclusive-boris-johnson-joked-about-most-unsocially-distanced-party-in-the-uk
50 Sophie Morris, 'Downing Street parties: Rees-Mogg refuses to apologise for calling partygate scandal "fluff" as first fines issued by Metropolitan Police', Sky News, 4 Apr 2022, https://news.sky.com/story/downing-street-parties-rees-mogg-refuses-to-apologise-for-calling-partygate-scandal-fluff-as-first-fines-issued-by-metropolitan-police-12582088
51 'In the name of God go, David Davis tells Boris Johnson', BBC News, 19 Jan 2022, https://www.bbc.co.uk/news/uk-politics-60056482
52 'Looks like checkmate for Boris Johnson, says senior Tory Steve Baker', BBC News, 20 Jan 2022, https://www.bbc.co.uk/news/uk-politics-60071311
53 'In the name of God go, David Davis tells Boris Johnson', BBC News, 19 Jan 2022, https://www.bbc.co.uk/news/uk-politics-60056482
54 Peter Walker and Jessica Elgot, 'Tory defector says whips told him to back PM or lose school funds', *Guardian*, 20 Jan 2022, https://www.theguardian.com/politics/2022/jan/20/ministers-attempting-blackmail-colleagues-who-might-oppose-pm-alleges-tory-mp-william-wragg-boris-johnson
55 'Boris Johnson: I've seen no evidence of plotters being blackmailed', BBC News, 21 Jan 2022, https://www.bbc.co.uk/news/uk-politics-60068612
56 Clea Skopeliti, 'About a dozen Tory MPs said to have accused party whips of blackmail', *Guardian*, 22 Jan 2022, https://www.theguardian.com/politics/2022/jan/22/about-a-dozen-tory-mps-said-to-have-accused-party-whips-of-blackmail

57 Graeme Demianyk, 'Ghana slaps down Boris Johnson's "Operation Red Meat" in humiliation for UK', *HuffPost*, 18 Jan 2022, https://www.huffingtonpost.co.uk/entry/ghana-operation-red-dead-meat-boris-johnson_uk_61e6f512e4b05645a6ed0b63

58 Graeme Demianyk, 'Ghana slaps down Boris Johnson's "Operation Red Meat" in humiliation For UK', *HuffPost*, 18 Jan 2022, https://www.huffingtonpost.co.uk/entry/ghana-operation-red-dead-meat-boris-johnson_uk_61e6f512e4b05645a6ed0b63

59 Jack Peat, 'Leaked: Chief whip's nicknames for Tory backbenchers', *London Economic*, 24 Jan 2022, https://www.thelondoneconomic.com/politics/leaked-chief-whips-nick names-for-tory-backbenchers-309242/

60 Press Association, 'Chief whip comes forward as person behind "Muslimness" sacking claim', *Observer*, 22 Jan 2022, https://www.theguardian.com/politics/2022/jan/22/tory-mp-says-muslimness-given-as-reason-for-losing-job

61 Gabriel Pogrund [@Gabriel_Pogrund], Twitter, 22 Jan 2022, https://twitter.com/Gabriel_Pogrund/status/1485017363661602821

62 Gavin Cordon, 'PM met with Tory MP to discuss "extremely serious" Muslim sacking claims', *Evening Standard*, 23 Jan 2022, https://www.standard.co.uk/news/uk/mark-spencer-nusrat-ghani-downing-street-muslim-b978240.html

63 Peter Walker, 'Johnson orders inquiry into Nusrat Ghani "Muslimness" sacking claims', *Guardian*, 24 Jan 2022, https://www.theguardian.com/politics/2022/jan/24/boris-johnson-calls-for-inquiry-into-nusrat-ghani-muslimness-sacking-claims

64 David Wilcock and Bhvishya Patel, 'Boris Johnson told to call in human rights commissioners to investigate "Muslimness" row after MP Nusrat Ghani said she was sacked because of her religion', *Daily Mail*, 23 Jan 2022, https://www.dailymail.co.uk/news/article-10432927/Tory-MP-Michael-Fabricant-says-claim-minister-sacked-Muslim-faith-stinks.html

65 Niamh McIntyre, Pamela Duncan and Josh Halliday, 'Levelling-up: some wealthy areas of England to see 10 times more funding than poorest', *Guardian*, 2 Feb 2022, https://www.theguardian.com/inequality/2022/feb/02/levelling-up-funding-inequality-exposed-by-guardian-research

66 Toby Helm, 'Boris Johnson's "bus back better" plan in tatters as Treasury cuts funding by half', *Guardian*, 23 Jan 2022, https://www.theguardian.com/politics/2022/jan/23/boris-johnsons-bus-back-better-red-wall-levelling-up-treasury-cuts-funding

67 Elizabeth Piper and Kate Holton, 'Fuelling Scots anger, UK confident on solving post-Brexit "teething" woes', *Reuters*, 14 Jan 2021, https://www.reuters.com/world/europe/fuelling-scots-anger-uk-confident-solving-post-brexit-teething-woes-2021-01-14/

68 Graeme Demianyk, 'Jacob Rees-Mogg says it could take 50 years to reap the benefits of Brexit', *HuffPost*, 23 Jul 2018, https://www.huffingtonpost.co.uk/entry/jacob-rees-mogg-economy-brexit_uk_5b54e3b5e4b0de86f48e3566

69 Jon Stone, 'Jacob Rees-Mogg issues plea to readers of The Sun to flag possible Brexit benefits to him', *Independent*, 10 Feb 2022, https://www.independent.co.uk/news/uk/politics/jacob-reesmogg-brexit-benefits-the-sun-b2012162.html

70 Kate Plummer, 'Jacob Rees-Mogg names scrapping "funny numbers" as another Brexit benefit', *Indy100*, 24 Jun 2022, https://www.indy100.com/politics/jacob-rees-mogg-brexit-benefits

71 Phillip Inman, 'Brexit damaging trade with EU, says public accounts committee', *Guardian*, 9 Feb 2022, https://www.theguardian.com/politics/2022/feb/09/brexit-damaging-trade-with-eu-says-public-accounts-committee

72 Kate Plummer, 'Brexit: Disbelief after minister claims traffic jams in Dover are because of EU', *Indy100*, 10 Feb 2022, https://www.indy100.com/politics/brexit-natalie-elphicke-dover-eu

73 Stefan Boscia, 'Rees-Mogg backs post-Brexit push for UK to adopt other countries' regulations', *CityA.M.*, 14 Feb 2022, https://www.cityam.com/rees-mogg-backs-post-brexit-push-for-uk-to-adopt-other-countries-regulations/

74 Rob Merrick, 'Cabinet split over plans to force UK firms to put goods through costly post-Brexit tests', *Independent*, 22 Feb 2022, https://www.independent.co.uk/news/uk/politics/brexit-red-tape-jacob-rees-mogg-b2020748.html

75 Peter Foster [@pmdfoster], Twitter, 22 Feb 2022, https://twitter.com/pmdfoster/status/1496135118272008194

76 Tevye Markson, 'Rees-Mogg pledges to cut 65,000 civil service jobs to get headcount "under control"', *Civil Service World*, 21 Feb 2022, https://www.civilserviceworld.com/professions/article/reesmogg-sets-out-plans-to-shrink-civil-service-and-get-it-under-control

77 'Civil Service Numbers', Dec 2022, https://www.civilservant.org.uk/information-numbers.html

78 Mia Hunt, 'Number of UK civil servants working on Brexit trebles in two years', Global Government Forum, 20 Jan 2020, https://www.globalgovernmentforum.com/number-of-uk-civil-servants-working-on-brexit-trebles-in-two-years/

79 Nick Eardley, 'Ministers set to drop UK ban on foie gras and fur imports', BBC News, 19 Feb 2022, https://www.bbc.co.uk/news/uk-politics-60439796

80 Heather Stewart and Jessica Elgot, 'Rishi Sunak: the polished "tech bro" with low-tax dreams', *Guardian*, 21 Jan 2022, https://www.theguardian.com/politics/2022/jan/21/rishi-sunak-the-polished-tech-bro-with-low-tax-dreams

81 Rachael Burford, 'Tory treasury minister Lord Agnew resigns over how government handled fraudulent Covid business loan', *Evening Standard*, 24 Jan 2022, https://www.standard.co.uk/news/politics/lord-agnew-resigns-minister-covid-business-loans-fraudulent-house-of-lords-b978486.html

82 Sophie Morris, 'Treasury minister Lord Agnew resigns over government's "lamentable" record on tackling COVID business loan fraud', Sky News, 24 Jan 2022, https://news.sky.com/story/treasury-minister-lord-agnew-resigns-over-governments-lamentable-record-on-tackling-covid-business-loan-fraud-12524460

83 Stefan Boscia, 'Ex-minister: Billions lost in Covid fraud "one of biggest cock-ups" in recent history', *CityA.M.*, 15 Mar 2022, https://www.cityam.com/ex-minister-billions-lost-in-covid-fraud-one-of-biggest-cock-ups-in-recent-history/

84 'Tackling fraud and corruption against government', National Audit Office, 30 Mar 2023, https://www.nao.org.uk/wp-content/uploads/2023/03/tackling-fraud-and-corruption-against-government-summary.pdf

85 Jemma Forte [@jemmaforte], Twitter, 11 Apr 2023, https://mobile.twitter.com/jemmaforte/status/1645682438830452736

86 Daniel Martin and Stephen Wynn-Davies, 'Rishi Sunak's relationship with Boris Johnson "completely disintegrated" and he "considered resigning" over National Insurance hike, one MP claims', *Daily Mail*, 19 Mar 2022, https://www.dailymail.co.uk/news/article-10629537/Rishi-Sunak-considered-resigning-row-National-Insurance-one-MP-claims.html

87 Jim Waterson, 'Children's TV makers say British shows could die as ministers scrap £44m fund', *Guardian*, 24 Jan 2022, https://www.theguardian.com/tv-and-radio/2022/jan/24/british-kids-tv-shows-under-threat-ministers-end-funding

88 Jessica Elgot, 'Lying to parliament a resigning matter, says Raab, amid claims PM misled MPs', *Guardian*, 18 Jan 2022, https://www.theguardian.com/politics/2022/jan/18/raab-admits-lying-to-parliament-a-resigning-matter-amid-claims-pm-misled-mps-boris-johnson

89 Andrew Sparrow, 'Downing Street parties: No 10 denies talking to Met police about Gray report and what could be published – as it happened', *Guardian*, 28 Jan 2022, https://www.theguardian.com/politics/live/2022/jan/28/boris-johnson-gray-report-partygate-downing-street-parties-met-police-covid-coronavirus-live-news

90 Danielle Sheridan, 'Sue Gray "partygate" report will not be published in full, Cabinet ministers suggest', *Telegraph*, 24 Jan 2022, https://www.telegraph.co.uk/politics/2022/01/24/sue-gray-partygate-report-will-not-published-full-cabinet-ministers/

91 'Downing Street parties: Calls grow for Sue Gray report to be published', BBC News, 28 Jan 2022, https://www.bbc.co.uk/news/uk-politics-60166997

92 Dale Millar, 'Downing Street parties: Boris Johnson says at PMQs he will publish full Sue Gray report', *The Scotsman*, 26 Jan 2022, https://www.scotsman.com/news/politics/pmqs-johnson-says-he-will-publish-full-sue-gray-report-3542466

93 George Parker [@GeorgeWParker], Twitter, https://twitter.com/GeorgeWParker/status/1488212798693851147

NOTES TO PP. 103-6

94 Aubrey Allegretti, 'Tory MPs are frogs in boiling water amid Johnson's "partygate" defence', *Guardian*, 31 Jan 2022, https://www.theguardian.com/politics/2022/jan/31/tory-mps-are-frogs-in-boiling-water-amid-johnsons-partygate-defence
95 Lizzy Buchan, 'Sue Gray report delayed or watered down as Met Police want key details removed', *Mirror*, 28 Jan 2022, https://www.mirror.co.uk/news/politics/breaking-police-ask-sue-gray-26072289
96 '"A man without shame": Boris Johnson attacked after Sue Gray report condemns "failure of leadership"', ITV News, 31 Jan 2022, https://www.itv.com/news/2022-01-31/sue-gray-report-condemns-serious-failure-in-number-10-to-observe-rules
97 'Keir Starmer led the CPS when it did not charge Jimmy Savile, but he wasn't the reviewing lawyer', Full Fact, 26 Jun 2020, https://fullfact.org/online/keir-starmer-prosecute-jimmy-savile/
98 'No evidence for Boris Johnson's claim about Keir Starmer and Jimmy Savile', BBC Reality Check, 3 Feb 2022, https://www.bbc.co.uk/news/60213975
99 Sophie Morris, 'Boris Johnson: PM "won't apologise" for Savile remark to Starmer as Commons speaker warns MPs "words have consequences"', Sky News, 8 Feb 2022, https://news.sky.com/story/boris-johnson-pm-wont-apologise-for-savile-remark-to-starmer-as-commons-speaker-warns-mps-words-have-consequences-12535971
100 Matthew Weaver, 'Starmer blames PM's Savile slur for inciting mob that accosted him', *Guardian*, 10 Feb 2022, https://www.theguardian.com/uk-news/2022/feb/10/keir-starmer-blames-pm-boris-johnson-savile-slur-inciting-mob
101 Andrew Woodcock, 'Boris Johnson backs down on Jimmy Savile smear and admits Keir Starmer had "nothing to do" with case', *Independent*, 3 Feb 2022, https://www.independent.co.uk/news/uk/politics/boris-johnson-savile-smear-starmer-b2006872.html
102 'Boris Johnson's policy chief Munira Mirza resigns over PM's Savile remarks', BBC News, 3 Feb 2022, https://www.bbc.co.uk/news/uk-politics-60250036
103 Justin Parkinson, 'Munira Mirza: The student radical who became "Boris's brain"', BBC News, 4 Feb 2022, https://www.bbc.co.uk/news/uk-politics-60257702
104 'Birthday celebration for PM sparks new party row', BBC News, 25 Jan 2022, https://www.bbc.co.uk/news/uk-60121572
105 Jon Stone, 'Furious Tory MPs put Boris Johnson on notice over No 10 lockdown party revelations', *Independent*, 15 Jan 2022, https://www.independent.co.uk/news/uk/politics/boris-johnson-andrew-bridgen-lockdown-parties-no10-b1993908.html
106 'Sutton Coldfield Tory MP withdraws support for Boris Johnson', BBC News, 1 Feb 2022, https://www.bbc.co.uk/news/uk-england-birmingham-60205883
107 'COVID-19: Boris Johnson has "lost moral authority to lead" and he should "do the honourable thing" and resign, says Andrew Bridgen', Sky News, 15 Jan 2022, https://news.sky.com/story/covid-19-boris-johnson-has-lost-moral-authority-to-lead-and-he-should-do-the-honourable-thing-and-resign-says-andrew-bridgen-12516445
108 'Veterans in politics by CampaignForce', 18 Nov 2020, https://veteransinpolitics.buzzsprout.com/1394725/6308446-stuart-anderson-mp
109 'Sutton Coldfield Tory MP withdraws support for Boris Johnson', BBC News, 1 Feb 2022, https://www.bbc.co.uk/news/uk-england-birmingham-60205883
110 Channel 4 News [@Channel4News], Twitter, 26 Jan 2022, https://twitter.com/channel4news/status/1486446088777314310
111 Steerpike, 'Jacob Rees-Mogg offers up another laughable defence of Boris', *Spectator*, 26 Jan 20220, https://www.spectator.co.uk/article/another-rees-mogg-newsnight-outing/
112 Aubrey Allegretti, Rowena Mason and Peter Walker, 'Boris Johnson attended leaving do during strict January lockdown', *Guardian*, 1 Feb 2022, https://www.theguardian.com/politics/2022/feb/01/boris-johnson-attended-leaving-do-during-strict-january-lockdown
113 Miranda Bryant, 'Full list of Tory MPs who have urged Boris Johnson to stand down', *Guardian*, 5 Feb 2022, https://www.theguardian.com/politics/2022/feb/05/full-list-of-tory-mps-who-have-urged-boris-johnson-to-stand-down
114 Charles Harrison, 'Boris Johnson's new staffer drops major clue Prime Minister might be gone within 6 months', *Express*, 6 Feb 2022, https://www.express.co.uk/news/politics/1561763/Boris-Johnson-gone-six-months-new-director-of-communications

115 Kevin Schofield, 'Boris Johnson's new spin doctor once accused him of "digging his political grave"', *HuffPost*, 6 Feb 2022, https://www.huffingtonpost.co.uk/entry/guto-harri-boris-johnson_uk_61ff6fa1e4b05004242e4d3b

116 Simon Walters, 'Boris Johnson threatens to prosecute his former spin doctor amid spat over his "sexual incontinence" following a cancelled TV interview', *Daily Mail*, 15 Sep 2018, https://www.dailymail.co.uk/news/article-6170129/Boris-Johnson-threatens-prosecute-former-spin-doctor-following-cancelled-TV-interview.html

117 'Boris Johnson apologizes for attending illegal party during lockdown—but says it "did not occur to me" that it broke COVID rules', CBS News, 19 Apr 2022, https://www.cbsnews.com/news/boris-johnson-partygate-apology-covid-lockdown/

118 Rowena Mason, 'Keep your friends close: why Boris Johnson hired Guto Harri', *Guardian*, 6 Feb 2022, https://www.theguardian.com/politics/2022/feb/06/keep-your-friends-close-why-boris-johnson-hired-guto-harri

119 Katie Strick, 'Guto Harri: Does Boris Johnson's new communications chief risk becoming the new Scaramucci?', *Evening Standard*, 10 Feb 2022, https://www.standard.co.uk/insider/guto-harri-no10-downing-street-comms-chief-boris-johnson-b981335.html

120 Jacob Bentley-York, 'YOU CAN CALL ME AL What is Boris Johnson's full name?', *Sun*, 5 Jul 2021, https://www.thesun.co.uk/news/15496495/boris-johnsons-full-name/

121 Jennifer Savin, 'Sidenote: did we all know that Boris Johnson is not the PM's actual name?', *Cosmopolitan*, 7 Jul 2022, https://www.cosmopolitan.com/uk/reports/a38745090/boris-johnson-name/

122 Jonathan Este, 'Scruffy Boris Johnson's "man of the people" look is part of a long British tradition', *The Conversation*, 5 Oct 2021, https://theconversation.com/scruffy-boris-johnsons-man-of-the-people-look-is-part-of-a-long-british-tradition-168773

123 Ian Jack, 'Rees-Mogg's roots tell a true Conservative tale – just not the one he wants us to hear', *Guardian*, 22 Jan 2022, https://www.theguardian.com/commentisfree/2022/jan/22/jacob-rees-mogg-roots-conservative-mp

124 Christopher Hope, 'Still toiling at 80: Nanny Rees-Mogg going strong after 57 years in service', *Telegraph*, 18 Nov 2022, https://www.telegraph.co.uk/news/2022/11/18/still-toiling-80-nanny-rees-mogg-going-strong-57-years-service/

125 Anabelle Dickson, 'Steve Barclay: The backroom fixer sent to save Boris Johnson', *Politico*, 7 Feb 2022, https://www.politico.eu/article/steve-barclay-boris-johnson-partygate-downing-street-conservative-party/

126 Michael Howie, 'Steve Barclay: Questions over how Boris Johnson's new chief of staff will tackle three jobs at once', *Evening Standard*, 6 Feb 2022, https://www.standard.co.uk/news/politics/steve-barclay-chief-of-staff-three-jobs-boris-johnson-downing-street-b980974.html

127 Greg Heffer, 'Boris Johnson's new triple-jobbing top aide Steve Barclay swerves the House of Commons', Sky News, 7 Feb 2022, https://news.sky.com/story/boris-johnsons-new-triple-jobbing-top-aide-steve-barclay-swerves-the-house-of-commons-12535724

128 Simon Calder, 'Liz Truss flew by private jet to Australia at cost of £500,000 to taxpayers', *Independent*, 28 Jan 2022, https://www.independent.co.uk/travel/news-and-advice/liz-truss-australia-private-jet-flight-cost-b2002588.html

129 Daniel Hurst, 'Former Australian PM Paul Keating criticises Liz Truss over "demented" China comments', *Guardian*, 24 Jan 2022, https://www.theguardian.com/australia-news/2022/jan/24/former-australian-pm-paul-keating-criticises-liz-truss-over-demented-china-comments

130 Tim Witherow, 'Liz Truss's Australia trade deal is not good for the UK and we have been "on the back foot repeatedly", former minister says', *Daily Mail*, 15 Nov 2022, https://www.dailymail.co.uk/news/article-11428133/Liz-Trusss-Australia-trade-deal-not-good-UK-former-minister-says.html

131 Latika Bourke, '"One sided": Sunak says Australia's free trade deal was bad for British farmers', *Sydney Morning Herald*, 2 Aug 2022, https://www.smh.com.au/world/europe/one-sided-sunak-says-australia-s-free-trade-deal-was-bad-for-british-farmers-20220802-p5b6fu.html

132 Graham Lanktree, 'UK's Liz Truss was warned of blow to food sector under Australia and New Zealand trade deals', *Politico*, 12 Jul 2022, https://www.politico.eu/article/liz-truss-uk-food-sector-australia-new-zealand-trade-deal/
133 Thomas Harding, 'Alok Sharma: Cop26 "just words on a page" unless promises delivered', *National News*, 24 Jan 2022, https://www.thenationalnews.com/world/uk-news/2022/01/24/alok-sharma-cop26-just-words-on-a-page-unless-promises-delivered/
134 Simon Calder, 'Liz Truss flew by private jet to Australia at cost of £500,000 to taxpayers', *Independent*, 28 Jan 2022, https://www.independent.co.uk/travel/news-and-advice/liz-truss-australia-private-jet-flight-cost-b2002588.html
135 'Better to get fossil fuels "from our own green and pleasant land" says Jacob Rees-Mogg after Welsh coal mine expansion', *Nation Cymru*, 27 Jan 2022, https://nation.cymru/news/better-to-get-fossil-fuels-from-our-own-green-and-pleasant-land-says-jacob-rees-mogg-after-welsh-coal-mine-expansion/
136 Michael Settle, 'Brexit is costing Britain £800m a week or £80bn since EU referendum, says Bank of England policymaker', *Herald Scotland*, 14 Feb 2022, https://www.heraldscotland.com/news/17434006.brexit-costing-britain-800m-week-80bn-since-eu-referendum-says-bank-england-policymaker/
137 Kevin McGwin, 'Greenland and the UK are heading towards a free trade deal', *Polar Journal*, 4 Feb 2022, https://polarjournal.ch/en/2022/02/04/greenland-the-uk-are-heading-towards-a-free-trade-deal/
138 Steve Anglesey, 'Brex Factor: Fined pundit Grimes is fine by Sky News', *New European*, 11 Apr 2019, https://www.theneweuropean.co.uk/brexit-news-brex-factor-darren-grimes-sky-news-44818/
139 Joe Duggan, 'Nadine Dorries in awkward BBC interview refuses to say if she has spoken to Boris Johnson in the last 24 hours', *iNews*, 5 Feb 2022, https://inews.co.uk/news/politics/nadine-dorries-awkward-bbc-interview-refuses-say-spoken-boris-johnson-1445382
140 John O'Neill, 'Nadine Dorries leads calls for Cameron's resignation', *Spectator*, 29 May 2016, https://www.spectator.co.uk/article/nadine-dorries-leads-calls-for-cameron-s-resignation/
141 James Morris, 'Nadine Dorries calls for Theresa May to resign as "she has let me down" on Brexit', *Evening Standard*, 26 Sep 2018, https://www.standard.co.uk/news/politics/nadine-dorries-calls-for-theresa-may-to-resign-as-she-has-let-me-down-on-brexit-a3946801.html
142 Joe Duggan, 'Nadine Dorries in awkward BBC interview refuses to say if she has spoken to Boris Johnson in the last 24 hours', *iNews*, 5 Feb 2022, https://inews.co.uk/news/politics/nadine-dorries-awkward-bbc-interview-refuses-say-spoken-boris-johnson-1445382
143 Gary Gibbon, 'Boris Johnson throws Tory MPs into panic', Channel 4 News, 22 Feb 2016, https://www.channel4.com/news/by/gary-gibbon/blogs/boris-johnson-throws-tory-mps-panic
144 'The United Kingdom's exit from, and new partnership with, the European Union', Department for Exiting the European Union, GOV.UK, 15 May 2017, https://www.gov.uk/government/publications/the-united-kingdoms-exit-from-and-new-partnership-with-the-european-union-white-paper/the-united-kingdoms-exit-from-and-new-partnership-with-the-european-union--2#preface-by-the-secretary-of-state
145 Pippa Crerar, 'UK ministers 'trying to avoid scrutiny' by releasing 150 documents in 48 hours', *Guardian*, 2 Apr 2023, https://www.theguardian.com/politics/2023/apr/02/uk-ministers-trying-avoid-scrutiny-releasing-150-documents-48-hours
146 Jon Ungoed-Thomas, 'Give me back my £200,000, major donor tells Tories', *Observer*, 5 Feb 2022, https://www.theguardian.com/politics/2022/feb/05/give-me-back-my-200000-major-donor-tells-tories
147 Adam Bienkov [@AdamBienkov], Twitter, 25 Feb 2022, https://twitter.com/AdamBienkov/status/1497139951552671744
148 Jon Stone, 'All the times the UK has changed prime minister during a war', *Independent*, 13 Apr 2022, https://www.independent.co.uk/news/uk/politics/change-prime-minister-during-war-partygate-boris-johnson-b2057168.html

149 Claudia Rowan, 'Andrew Bridgen withdraws no confidence letter as Boris Johnson's "partygate" troubles ease', *Telegraph*, 16 Mar 2022, https://www.telegraph.co.uk/politics/2022/03/16/andrew-bridgen-withdraws-no-confidence-letter-boris-johnson/

150 Patrick Wintour, 'Liz Truss arrives in Moscow with "toughest sanctions" plan delayed', *Guardian*, 10 Feb 2022, https://www.theguardian.com/politics/2022/feb/09/liz-truss-moscow-toughest-russia-sanctions-plan-doubt

151 Layla Moran [@LaylaMoran], Twitter, 22 Feb 2022, https://twitter.com/LaylaMoran/status/1496106541241573377

152 Ben Chapman, 'UK sanctions will have little impact on Putin despite Boris Johnson's claims, say experts', *Independent*, 25 Feb 2022, https://www.independent.co.uk/news/business/russia-uk-sanctions-putin-impact-b2022683.html

153 Patrick Wintour, 'No 10 pressured me to drop anti-money laundering measures, says ex-minister', *Guardian*, 15 Feb 2022, https://www.theguardian.com/politics/2022/feb/15/no-10-pressure-money-laundering-measures-lord-faulks

154 Rupert Neate and Jessica Elgot, 'UK accused of being "toothless" in sanctions enforcement', *Guardian*, 24 Feb 2022, https://www.theguardian.com/politics/2022/feb/24/uk-sanctions-enforcement-toothless-russia-deterrent

155 Rupert Neate and Jessica Elgot, 'UK accused of being "toothless" in sanctions enforcement', *Guardian*, 24 Feb 2022, https://www.theguardian.com/politics/2022/feb/24/uk-sanctions-enforcement-toothless-russia-deterrent

156 'Why have there been delays to UK Russia sanctions?', BBC News, 15 Mar 2022, https://www.bbc.co.uk/news/60524666

157 Rupert Neate and Aubrey Allegretti, 'Russian oligarchs on UK sanctions list were granted "golden visas"', *Guardian*, 30 Mar 2022, https://www.theguardian.com/uk-news/2022/mar/30/russian-oligarchs-on-uk-sanctions-list-were-granted-golden-visas

158 Rowena Mason, 'Questions raised over time-lag on UK moves to sanction oligarchs', *Guardian*, 1 Mar 2022, https://www.theguardian.com/world/2022/mar/01/questions-raised-over-time-lag-on-uk-moves-to-sanction-oligarchs

159 Rowena Mason, Aubrey Allegretti and Jasper Jolly, 'Oligarchs under EU and US sanctions linked to £200m in UK property', *Guardian*, 2 Mar 2022, https://www.theguardian.com/world/2022/mar/02/oligarchs-under-eu-and-us-sanctions-linked-to-pounds-200m-uk-property-ukraine-invasion

160 Rowena Mason, 'Foreign owners of UK properties to be identified in new register', *Guardian*, 28 Feb 2022, https://www.theguardian.com/business/2022/feb/28/foreign-owners-of-uk-properties-to-be-identified-in-new-register

161 Adam Forrest, 'Boris Johnson says Putin has "singled out" UK for "leading" on global sanctions', *Independent*, 9 Mar 2022, https://www.independent.co.uk/news/uk/politics/russia-sanctions-global-putin-boris-johnson-b2031992.html

162 Rupert Neate and Aubrey Allegretti, 'Russian oligarchs on UK sanctions list were granted "golden visas"', *Guardian*, 30 Mar 2022, https://www.theguardian.com/uk-news/2022/mar/30/russian-oligarchs-on-uk-sanctions-list-were-granted-golden-visas

163 Thomas Kingsley, 'US government fears dirty money in "Londongrad" would kneecap sanctions on Russia', *Independent*, 28 Jan 2022, https://www.independent.co.uk/news/uk/home-news/russia-ukraine-us-government-sanctions-b2002591.html

164 Kate Elliott, 'The 6 Russian oligarchs who donated £2m to Tory party since Boris became PM', *Express*, 3 Mar 2022, https://www.express.co.uk/news/uk/1574370/Russian-oligarchs-linked-conservative-party-tory-donor-evg

165 Martin Williams, 'Tories have taken £62,000 from Russia-linked donors since war began', *openDemocracy*, 9 Jun 2022, https://www.opendemocracy.net/en/dark-money-investigations/conservative-party-russia-donors-ukraine-invasion/

166 Jon Stone, 'Corruption experts warn Boris Johnson's government is worst since WWII', *Independent*, 29 Jan 2022, https://www.independent.co.uk/news/uk/politics/boris-johnson-corruption-b2002869.html

167 'Chancellor calls on firms to stop investing in Russia', HM Treasury, 13 Mar 2022, https://www.gov.uk/government/news/chancellor-calls-on-firms-to-stop-investing-in-russia

168 Rupert Neate, 'Sunak under pressure over wife's Russia-related "blood money" dividends', *Guardian*, 28 Mar 2022, https://www.theguardian.com/politics/2022/mar/28/sunak-under-pressure-over-wifes-russia-related-blood-money-dividends

169 Alan McGuinness, 'Rishi Sunak challenged over wife's links to company Infosys that has presence in Russia', Sky News, 25 Mar 2022, https://news.sky.com/story/rishi-sunak-challenged-over-wifes-links-to-company-infosys-that-has-presence-in-russia-12574093

170 Daniel Boffey and Andrew Roth, 'Infosys still operating from Russia eight months after saying it was pulling out', *Guardian*, 4 Nov 2022, https://www.theguardian.com/world/2022/nov/04/infosys-still-operating-russia-rishi-sunak-akshata-murty

171 Michael O'Dwyer and Kate Beloley, 'MPs criticise UK government for weak enforcement of sanctions regime', *Financial Times*, 12 Dec 2022, https://www.ft.com/content/2d9b41a9-c125-43fd-9037-1d471dcc0304

172 Angus Cochrane, 'Liz Truss mocked for geography gaffe as British diplomacy dubbed "worthless"', *Yahoo! News*, 2 Feb 2022, https://uk.news.yahoo.com/liz-truss-mocked-geography-gaffe-154259362.html

173 Michael Savage, '"Instagram diplomacy": concerns grow over Liz Truss's publicly funded five photos a day', *Observer*, 12 Feb 2022, https://www.theguardian.com/politics/2022/feb/12/liz-truss-instagram-diplomacy-five-photos-a-day-foreign-secretary-flickr

174 Kate Plummer, 'All the times Liz Truss has been accused of dressing like Margaret Thatcher', *Indy100*, 27 Jul 2022, https://www.indy100.com/politics/liz-truss-margaret-thatcher-comparisons-2657745286

175 Michael Savage, '"Instagram diplomacy": concerns grow over Liz Truss's publicly funded five photos a day', *Observer*, 12 Feb 2022, https://www.theguardian.com/politics/2022/feb/12/liz-truss-instagram-diplomacy-five-photos-a-day-foreign-secretary-flickr

176 Jedidajah Otte, 'Liz Truss tests positive for Covid after speaking in packed Commons', *Guardian*, 31 Jan 2022, https://www.theguardian.com/politics/2022/jan/31/liz-truss-tests-positive-for-covid-after-speaking-in-packed-commons

177 'COVID-19: UK reports another 534 coronavirus-related deaths, as latest figures include "backlog"', Sky News, 2 Feb 2022, https://news.sky.com/story/covid-19-uk-reports-another-534-coronavirus-related-deaths-highest-daily-figure-since-february-last-year-12531239

178 'Everything you need to know about face coverings in schools and colleges – who must wear them, why they're important and when will they stop having to wear them', GOV.UK, 7 Jan 2022, https://educationhub.blog.gov.uk/2022/01/07/everything-you-need-to-know-about-face-coverings-in-schools-and-colleges-who-must-wear-them-why-theyre-important-and-when-will-they-stop-having-to-wear-them/

179 Sally Weale, 'Pupils in England reluctant to return to school after lockdown, says report', *Guardian*, 7 Feb 2022, https://www.theguardian.com/education/2022/feb/07/pupils-in-england-reluctant-to-return-to-school-after-lockdown-says-report

180 Julie Henry and James Tapper, 'Schools in England reinstate mask wearing rules as Covid cases soar', *Guardian*, 29 Jan 2022, https://www.theguardian.com/world/2022/jan/29/schools-in-england-reinstate-mask-wearing-rules-as-covid-and-absenteeism-soar

181 Jane Croft, 'UK acted unlawfully in appointing Dido Harding to key Covid role, judges rule', *Financial Times*, 15 Feb 2022, https://www.ft.com/content/f13c3d34-ae79-4615-a748-a08ef00bcaba

182 'Endorsements in the 2019 United Kingdom general election', Wikipedia, https://en.wikipedia.org/wiki/Endorsements_in_the_2019_United_Kingdom_general_election

183 Elaine McCallig, 'Resurfaced clip of Boris Johnson on his "strategy" to confuse the media goes viral', *Indy100*, 30 Jan 2022, https://www.indy100.com/politics/boris-johnson-strategy-confuse-media

184 Lisa O'Carroll, 'Northern Ireland first minister resigns over Brexit checks on goods', *Guardian*, 3 Feb 2022, https://www.theguardian.com/uk-news/2022/feb/03/northern-ireland-first-minister-poised-to-quit-over-brexit-reports-say

185 Rory Carroll, 'Police arrest three men over shooting of off-duty detective in Omagh', *Guardian*, 24 Feb 2023, https://www.theguardian.com/uk-news/2023/feb/23/police-name-off-duty-detective-injured-in-omagh-shooting-john-caldwell

186 'Britain raises domestic threat level for Northern Ireland to "severe"', NBC News, 28 Mar 2023, https://www.nbcnews.com/news/world/britain-raises-domestic-threat-level-northern-ireland-severe-rcna76960
187 Jeremy Warner, 'Project Fear was right all along', Telegraph, 15 Oct 2022, https://www.telegraph.co.uk/business/2022/10/15/project-fear-right-along/
188 Peter Walker, 'Gavin Williamson awarded knighthood by Boris Johnson', Guardian, 3 Mar 2022, https://www.theguardian.com/politics/2022/mar/03/gavin-williamson-awarded-knighthood-by-boris-johnson
189 'Home Office claim to have launched first Ukrainian visa scheme lacks context', Full Fact, 10 Mar 2022, https://fullfact.org/immigration/ukraine-family-visa-scheme/
190 Muvija M and William James, 'UK refuses to drop visa requirement for Ukraine refugees', Reuters, 7 Mar 2022, https://www.reuters.com/world/europe/britain-may-ease-immigration-rules-ukrainian-refugees-sun-2022-03-07/
191 Jon Ungoed-Thomas, 'UK urged to suspend "golden visas" after fast tracking of Russian millionaires', Guardian, 30 Jan 2022, https://www.theguardian.com/world/2022/jan/30/calls-for-uk-to-suspend-golden-visas-after-fast-tracking-of-russian-millionaires
192 'Visit the UK as a Standard Visitor', GOV.UK, https://www.gov.uk/standard-visitor/apply-standard-visitor-visa
193 Andrew Woodcock, 'Priti Patel accused of misleading MPs over help for Ukrainian refugees at Calais', Independent, 8 Mar 2022, https://www.independent.co.uk/news/uk/politics/priti-patel-ukraine-refugees-calais-b2030979.html
194 Andy Lines and Antony Thrower, '"Insulting" Calais sign for Ukraine refugees after Patel blunder over UK visa centre', Mirror, 8 Mar 2022, https://www.mirror.co.uk/news/uk-news/insulting-calais-sign-still-awaiting-26411526
195 Lizzie Dearden, 'Transport operators face £2,000 fines for bringing Ukrainians without visas to UK', Independent, 7 Mar 2022, https://www.independent.co.uk/news/uk/home-news/ukrainian-refugees-france-uk-fines-b2030429.html
196 'Ukraine: Refugees to UK turned back at Calais over paperwork', BBC News, 8 Mar 2022, https://www.bbc.co.uk/news/uk-60659786
197 Rajeev Syal and Peter Walker, 'Priti Patel under fire over chaotic Ukrainian refugee policy', Guardian, 7 Mar 2022, https://www.theguardian.com/world/2022/mar/07/uk-minister-denies-plans-for-humanitarian-route-for-ukrainian-refugees
198 Sue Austin, 'Shrewsbury MP Daniel Kawczynski defends taxpayer-funded Polish lessons', Shropshire Star, 4 Jan 2022, https://www.shropshirestar.com/news/politics/2022/01/04/shrewsbury-mp-daniel-kawczynski-defends-claiming-expenses-for-polish-lessons/
199 Jon Stone, 'Tory MP says it would be "immoral" for Britain to take more Ukrainian refugees', Independent, 10 Mar 2022, https://www.independent.co.uk/news/uk/politics/ukraine-refugees-tory-mp-daniel-kawczynski-b2032409.html
200 Dominic Robertson, 'Daniel Kawczynski: Shrewsbury MP accused of 'immoral and offensive bile' over Ukrainian refugees', Shropshire Star, 10 Mar 2022, https://www.shropshirestar.com/news/politics/ukraine-war/2022/03/10/daniel-kawczynski--shrewsbury-mp-accused-of-immoral-and-offensive-bile-over-ukrainian-refugees/
201 David Tooley, 'Shrewsbury MP Daniel Kawczynski deletes Twitter after row over Ukrainian refugee post', Shropshire Star, 14 Mar 2022, https://www.shropshirestar.com/news/politics/2022/03/14/shrewsbury-mp-daniel-kawczynski-deletes-twitter-after-row-over-ukrainian-refugee-post/
202 Lizzie Dearden, 'Britain fails to set up refugee route as thousands flee Ukraine after Russian invasion', Independent, 24 Feb 2022, https://www.independent.co.uk/news/uk/home-news/ukraine-war-refugees-uk-visas-b2022567.html
203 Tevye Markson, 'Home Office helpline "was not ready" to help Ukrainian refugees come to the UK after visas extended', Civil Service World, 2 Mar 2022, https://www.civilserviceworld.com/news/article/home-office-helpline-not-ready-ukraine-family-members-visa-scheme-refugees-come-to-uk
204 Diane Taylor, 'Ukrainians denied entry to UK despite being eligible for visa', Guardian, 28 Feb 2022, https://www.theguardian.com/world/2022/feb/28/ukrainians-denied-entry-to-uk-despite-being-eligible-for-visa

205 Lizzie Dearden, 'Britain fails to set up refugee route as thousands flee Ukraine after Russian invasion', *Independent*, 24 Feb 2022, https://www.independent.co.uk/news/uk/home-news/ukraine-war-refugees-uk-visas-b2022567.html
206 Sky News [@SkyNews], Twitter, 26 Feb 2022, https://twitter.com/SkyNews/status/1497688938881945601
207 Colin Yeo [@ColinYeo1], Twitter, 25 Feb 2022, https://twitter.com/ColinYeo1/status/1497322354044817409
208 Anthea Simmons, 'The tweet heartless Kevin Foster didn't want you to see', *West Country Voices*, 26 Feb 2022, https://westcountryvoices.co.uk/the-tweet-heartless-kevin-foster-didnt-want-you-to-see/
209 Kevin Foster [@kevin_j_foster], Twitter, 27 Apr 2022, https://twitter.com/kevin_j_foster/status/1519320965452288013
210 Andrew Woodcock, 'Government buildings fly Ukrainian flag in mark of solidarity', *Independent*, 25 Feb 2022, https://www.independent.co.uk/news/uk/politics/ukraine-russia-flag-mi6-downing-b2023415.html
211 Matthew Smith, 'Support for taking in Ukraine refugees rises to 76%', YouGov, 2 Mar 2022, https://yougov.co.uk/topics/politics/articles-reports/2022/03/02/support-taking-ukraine-refugees-rises-76
212 Alix Culbertson, 'Ukraine war: More than 130,000 Britons register interest in housing Ukrainian refugees', Sky News, 16 Mar 2022, https://news.sky.com/story/ukraine-war-more-than-100-000-britons-register-interest-to-house-ukrainian-refugees-12566826
213 May Bulman, 'Britons hoping to host Ukrainian refugees will need to know their names first', *Independent*, 14 Mar 2022, https://www.independent.co.uk/news/uk/home-news/ukraine-refugees-sponsorship-name-uk-b2035310.html
214 Mark Townsend, 'Homes For Ukraine whistleblower says UK refugee scheme is "designed to fail"', *Guardian*, 23 Apr 2022, https://www.theguardian.com/world/2022/apr/23/homes-for-ukraine-whistleblower-says-uk-refugee-scheme-is-designed-to-fail
215 Charles Hymas, 'We've been giving Ukrainian refugees wrong guidance, admits Home Office', *Telegraph*, 5 Apr 2022, https://www.telegraph.co.uk/news/2022/04/05/home-office-admits-giving-wrong-call-centre-guidance-ukrainian/
216 'Prime Minister pledges UK's unwavering support to Ukraine on visit to Kyiv: 9 April 2022', GOV.UK, 9 Apr 2022, https://www.gov.uk/government/news/prime-minister-pledges-uks-unwavering-support-to-ukraine-on-visit-to-kyiv-9-april-2022
217 'How many Ukrainian refugees are there and where have they gone?', BBC News, 4 Jul 2022, https://www.bbc.co.uk/news/world-60555472
218 Martin Evans and Ben Riley-Smith, 'Downing Street is the most fined address in the country for Covid breaches', *Telegraph*, 12 May 2022, https://www.telegraph.co.uk/politics/2022/05/12/fresh-partygate-fines-met-police-downing-street-parties/
219 Nina Lloyd, 'Bereaved Covid families boo ministers at Boris Johnson's dinner as Partygate fines issued', *Independent*, 29 Mar 2022, https://www.independent.co.uk/news/uk/politics/boris-johnson-party-downing-street-boo-b2046847.html
220 Michael Fabricant [@Mike_Fabricant], Twitter, 30 Mar 2022, https://twitter.com/Mike_Fabricant/status/1509088870952054785
221 Connor Ibbetson and Isabelle Kirk, 'Snap poll: following lockdown fines, most say Boris Johnson should resign', YouGov, 12 Apr 2022, https://yougov.co.uk/topics/politics/articles-reports/2022/04/12/lockdown-fine-public-think-johnson-sunak-resign
222 Ashley Cowburn, Chiara Giordano and Joe Sommerlad, 'How many Tory MPs are calling for Boris Johnson to quit and who are they?', *Independent*, 6 Jun 2022, https://www.independent.co.uk/news/uk/politics/tory-mps-confidence-vote-johnson-b2102714.html
223 Andrew Sparrow, 'Chris Patten says Johnson is "moral vacuum"', *Guardian*, 4 Feb 2022, https://www.theguardian.com/politics/live/2022/feb/04/uk-politics-live-boris-johnson-tories-fresh-ultimatum-no-10-staffer-quits-downing-street-parties-latest-updates
224 Anushka Asthana [@AnushkaAsthana], Twitter, 31 Jan 2022, https://twitter.com/AnushkaAsthana/status/1488233820855881729

225 Toby Helm, 'Tories despair after Gray delay prolongs their leadership crisis', *Observer*, 30 Jan 2022, https://www.theguardian.com/politics/2022/jan/30/tories-despair-after-gray-delay-prolongs-their-leadership-crisis
226 Phillip Thompson, 'Alex Chalk says "an election is coming" as he faces Cheltenham residents at impromptu meeting', *Gloucestershire Live*, 10 Sep 2019, https://www.gloucestershirelive.co.uk/news/cheltenham-news/alex-chalk-says-an-election-3305913
227 Amelia Jenne, 'P&O Ferries: Political unity after company sacks 800', Channel 4 News, 18 Mar 2022, https://www.channel4.com/news/po-ferries-political-unity-after-company-sacks-800
228 Josh Martin, 'Outrage and no ferries after mass P&O sackings', BBC News, 18 Mar 2022, https://www.bbc.co.uk/news/business-60779001
229 Helen Coffey, Simon Calder, Lucy Thackray and Jane Dalton, 'P&O Ferries news: Firm denies insensitive behaviour, "aims to have services up and running in a day or two"', *Independent*, 24 Mar 2022, https://www.independent.co.uk/travel/news-and-advice/p-o-ferries-cruises-dover-calais-latest-suspended-b2038703.html
230 Heather Stewart, Gwyn Topham and Matthew Weaver, 'P&O Ferries told it could face unlimited fine if sackings unlawful', *Guardian*, 18 Mar 2022, https://www.theguardian.com/business/2022/mar/18/po-ferries-could-face-an-unlimited-fine-if-sackings-unlawful
231 Gwyn Topham, 'P&O Ferries has "got away with it", say unions as Shapps backtracks on action', *Guardian*, 31 Mar 2022, https://www.theguardian.com/business/2022/mar/31/p-and-o-ferries-unions-shapps-backtracks-action-sacking
232 Gwyn Topham, 'P&O Ferries has "got away with it", say unions as Shapps backtracks on action', *Guardian*, 31 Mar 2022, https://www.theguardian.com/business/2022/mar/31/p-and-o-ferries-unions-shapps-backtracks-action-sacking
233 Nadine Dorries [@NadineDorries], Twitter, 9 Mar 2022, https://twitter.com/NadineDorries/status/1501507023321681922
234 Geraldine Scott, 'Social media executives could face jail if they do not comply with new rules', *Independent*, 5 Feb 2022, https://www.independent.co.uk/news/uk/nadine-dorries-bill-mark-zuckerberg-government-children-b2008410.html
235 Annabelle Dickson, 'Nadine Dorries, Britain's Big Tech slayer', *Politico*, 14 Mar 2022, https://www.politico.eu/article/nadine-dorries-digital-minister-big-tech/
236 Harry Fletcher, 'Did Nadine Dorries actually say "we've had the internet for 10 years"?', *Indy100*, 7 Feb 2022, https://www.indy100.com/politics/nadine-dorries-internet-sky-interview
237 Oliver Browning, 'Culture Secretary Nadine Dorries tells MPs she's "amazed to learn" young people use YouTube', *Independent*, 17 Jan 2022, https://www.independent.co.uk/tv/news/culture-secretary-nadine-dorries-tells-mps-she-s-amazed-to-learn-young-people-use-youtube-b2190311.html
238 'Nadine Dorries raps and mic drops in TikTok video on online safety – video', *Guardian*, 27 May 2022, https://www.theguardian.com/politics/video/2022/may/27/nadine-dorries-raps-and-mic-drops-in-tiktok-video-on-online-safety-video
239 Jim Waterson, 'Nadine Dorries claims dyslexia made her say "downstream" films', *Guardian*, 23 Apr 2022, https://www.theguardian.com/politics/2022/apr/23/nadine-dorries-claims-dyslexia-made-her-say-downstream-films
240 Nadine Dorries [@NadineDorries], Twitter, 4 Apr 2022, https://twitter.com/NadineDorries/status/1511076442980896769
241 Edward Helmore, 'Netflix shares fall more than 35% after streamer loses over 200,000 subscribers', *Guardian*, 20 Apr 2022, https://www.theguardian.com/media/2022/apr/20/netflix-shares-fall-losing-subscribers
242 'Oral Answers to Questions', Hansard, 3 Dec 2018, https://hansard.parliament.uk/Commons/2018-12-03/debates/F47C685B-9683-4EA7-B21C-3625B7930C37/OralAnswersToQuestions#contribution-A1A6749C-85AA-482D-AA8B-C2ADFAA8AB71
243 Gabriel Pogrund, 'Tory MP David Warburton in hospital after sex and cocaine claims', *Sunday Times*, 3 Apr 2022, https://www.thetimes.co.uk/article/tory-mp-david-warburton-suspended-after-sex-and-drugs-allegations-h3t8ghj0q
244 Steve Bird and Edward Malnick, 'Tory MP David Warburton has whip withdrawn during investigation into drug and sex allegations', *Telegraph*, 2 Apr 2022, https://www.telegraph.

co.uk/politics/2022/04/02/tory-mp-david-warburton-has-whip-withdrawn-amid-investigation/
245 Gabriel Pogrund, 'Tory MP David Warburton in hospital after sex and cocaine claims', *Sunday Times*, 3 Apr 2022, https://www.thetimes.co.uk/article/tory-mp-david-warburton-suspended-after-sex-and-drugs-allegations-h3t8ghj0q
246 Adam Forrest, 'Tory MP broke rules over £150,000 loan from Russian businessman, watchdog finds', *Independent*, 21 Nov 2022, https://www.independent.co.uk/independentpremium/uk-news/conservative-mp-russia-david-warburton-b2230785.html
247 Greg Heffer, 'Tory MP David Warburton won't face any sanction despite being found to have breached Commons' rules over £150,000 loan from a Russian-born businessman he provided a character reference for', *Daily Mail*, 21 Nov 2022, https://www.dailymail.co.uk/news/article-11453393/Tory-MP-David-Warburton-wont-face-sanction-despite-breaching-rules-150k-loan.html
248 Mark Tovey, 'Tory whips "were warned two weeks ago" that MP David Warburton faced sexual assault and cocaine allegations but did not suspend him until it came out in the press', *Daily Mail*, 4 Apr 2022, https://www.dailymail.co.uk/news/article-10682613/Tory-whips-warned-two-weeks-ago-MP-David-Warburtons-drug-sex-scandal.html
249 Adam Forrest, 'Tory MP broke rules over £150,000 loan from Russian businessman, watchdog finds', *Independent*, 21 Nov 2022, https://www.independent.co.uk/independentpremium/uk-news/conservative-mp-russia-david-warburton-b2230785.html
250 Chiara Giordano, 'David Warburton: Tory MP admitted to psychiatric hospital after sexual harassment and drug allegations', *Independent*, 3 Apr 2022, https://www.independent.co.uk/news/uk/politics/david-warburton-tory-mp-hospital-b2050008.html
251 Denis Campbell, 'Swamped NHS mental health services turning away children, say GPs', *Guardian*, 3 Apr 2022, https://www.theguardian.com/society/2022/apr/03/swamped-nhs-mental-health-services-turning-away-children-say-doctors
252 'Voting Record—David Warburton MP, Somerton and Frome', The Public Whip, https://www.publicwhip.org.uk/mp.php?id=uk.org.publicwhip/member/42703&showall=yes
253 Gabriel Pogrund and Hannah Al-Othman, 'First it was sex and drugs. Now David Warburton faces financial claims', *Sunday Times*, 11 Feb 2023, https://www.thetimes.co.uk/article/david-warburton-first-it-was-sex-and-drugs-now-mp-faces-financial-allegations-9x2nb6k52
254 Tylar Green and Jacob Richmond, 'NASA Says 2022 Fifth Warmest Year on Record, Warming Trend Continues', NASA, 12 Jan 2023, https://www.nasa.gov/press-release/nasa-says-2022-fifth-warmest-year-on-record-warming-trend-continues
255 Sophie Morris, 'Energy security strategy: Boris Johnson pledges to "do more" on cost of living crisis as he defends energy strategy', Sky News, 7 Apr 2022, https://news.sky.com/story/energy-security-strategy-boris-johnson-pledges-to-do-more-to-ease-cost-of-living-crisis-as-energy-security-strategy-criticised-12584281
256 Sam Blewett, 'Rees-Mogg downplays fracking risk and eyes "every last drop" of North Sea oil', *Evening Standard*, 4 Apr 2022, https://www.standard.co.uk/news/uk/jacob-reesmogg-cabinet-north-sea-grant-shapps-prime-minister-b992366.html
257 Rowena Mason, Rob Davies and Helena Horton, 'Boris Johnson blows cold on onshore wind faced with 100-plus rebel MPs', *Guardian*, 5 Apr 2022, https://www.theguardian.com/environment/2022/apr/05/boris-johnson-blows-cold-on-onshore-wind-faced-with-100-plus-rebel-mps
258 'What the manifestos say on energy and climate change', *Carbon Brief*, 22 Nov 2019, https://www.carbonbrief.org/election-2019-what-the-manifestos-say-on-energy-and-climate-change/
259 'Conservative Party Manifesto 2019', Conservatives, https://www.conservatives.com/our-plan/conservative-party-manifesto-2019
260 Helen-Ann Smith, 'National Insurance rise: How will it work and what will it mean for you?', Sky News, 6 Apr 2022, https://news.sky.com/story/national-insurance-rise-how-will-it-work-and-what-will-it-mean-for-you-12583071

261 Kate Morgan, 'Pension triple lock: what is it and why is it changing?', *Unbiased*, 14 Feb 2022, https://www.unbiased.co.uk/news/pensions/pension-triple-lock-what-is-it-and-why-is-it-changing
262 Gordon Rayner, 'No-one will have to sell their house to pay for social care under Tories, says Boris Johnson', *Telegraph*, 20 Nov 2019, https://www.telegraph.co.uk/politics/2019/11/20/no-one-will-have-sell-house-pay-social-care-tories-says-boris/
263 Jasmine Cameron-Chileshe and Laura Hughes, 'Boris Johnson appears to acknowledge social care plans undermine manifesto', *Financial Times*, 23 Nov 2021, https://www.ft.com/content/3917a988-275a-4156-a0f9-a64242afefb0
264 Jon Stone, 'Northern Powerhouse Rail isn't being cut back – it's being cancelled', *Independent*, 15 Nov 2021, https://www.independent.co.uk/news/uk/politics/northern-powerhouse-rail-hs2-integrated-rail-plan-b1958009.html
265 Andrew Woodcock, 'Tory pledge to build 40 new hospitals under fire as minister admits funding in place for just six', *Independent*, 29 Sep 2019, https://www.independent.co.uk/news/uk/politics/nhs-new-hospital-funding-boris-johnson-matt-hancock-health-secretary-a9125101.html
266 William Worley, 'Breaking: UK cuts aid budget to 0.5% of GNI', *DevEx*, 25 Nov 2020, https://www.devex.com/news/breaking-uk-cuts-aid-budget-to-0-5-of-gni-98640
267 Aubrey Allegretti and Libby Brooks, 'LGBTQ+ conference cancelled over conversion practices furore', *Guardian*, 5 Apr 2022, https://www.theguardian.com/society/2022/apr/05/lgbt-government-adviser-quits-over-conversion-practices-uturn
268 Heather Stewart, Harriet Sherwood, 'Boris Johnson backtracks over LGBT conversion practices ban after backlash', *Guardian*, 31 Mar 2022, https://www.theguardian.com/world/2022/mar/31/boris-johnson-ditches-plans-for-ban-on-lgbt-conversion-practices
269 'Jamie Wallis MP says he wants to begin gender transition process "as quickly as possible" as he describes rape and blackmail ordeal', Sky News, 24 Apr 2022, https://news.sky.com/story/jamie-wallis-mp-says-he-wants-to-begin-gender-transition-process-as-quickly-as-possible-as-he-describes-rape-and-blackmail-ordeal-12596079
270 Glen Owen, 'I'm a naked Tory MP stuck in a brothel . . . get me out of here! Politician calls senior colleague for help after waking up unable to find his clothes at 4am', *Daily Mail*, 1 Apr 2023, https://www.dailymail.co.uk/news/article-11928613/Tory-MP-wakes-naked-brothel-unable-clothes-calls-senior-colleague-help.html
271 Peter Walker, 'Tory MP blames food poverty on lack of cooking skills', *Guardian*, 11 May 2022, https://www.theguardian.com/uk-news/2022/may/11/tory-mp-condemned-after-blaming-food-poverty-on-lack-of-cooking-skills
272 Andy Gregory and Matt Mathers, 'History of controversial comments by deputy Tory chairman who backs death penalty', *Independent*, 9 Feb 2023, https://www.independent.co.uk/news/uk/politics/lee-anderson-food-banks-nurses-claims-b2
273 Dave Burke, 'Tory MP says economy will only have a "big problem" when Wetherspoons is empty', *Mirror*, 2 Oct 2022, https://www.mirror.co.uk/news/politics/tory-mp-says-economy-only-28136853
274 Peter Walker, 'Tory MP blames food poverty on lack of cooking skills', *Guardian*, 11 May 2022, https://www.theguardian.com/uk-news/2022/may/11/tory-mp-condemned-after-blaming-food-poverty-on-lack-of-cooking-skills
275 Asher McShane, '"Worst queues I've ever seen": Lorry drivers face 12-hour waits and "30 mile jam" at Dover', LBC, 7 Apr 2022, https://www.lbc.co.uk/news/worst-queues-ever-lorry-drivers-12-hour-waits-23-mile-jam-dover-p-and-o/
276 Sharon Marris, 'Energy bills expected to hit £4,200 in January, according to dire new forecast', Sky News, 9 Aug 2022, https://news.sky.com/story/energy-bills-forecast-to-rise-even-higher-than-previously-thought-12668906
277 'France has capped energy price rises at 4% – could UK do the same?', Sky News, 30 Aug 2022, https://news.sky.com/story/france-has-capped-energy-price-rises-at-4-could-uk-do-the-same-12675068
278 Paul Waugh, 'Rishi Sunak's £200 "energy rebate" is really a "loan-not-loan" that fools no one', *iNews*, 8 Apr 2022, https://inews.co.uk/opinion/rishi-sunak-energy-rebate-loan-not-loan-fools-1565690

279 Tim Hanlon, 'Question Time: Howls of laughter as energy minister says £200 bills "discount" not a loan', *Mirror*, 8 Apr 2022, https://www.mirror.co.uk/news/politics/question-time-howls-laughter-energy-26663601
280 Rob Merrick, 'Cabinet minister admits £200 help with fuel bills is "a loan" despite Rishi Sunak's denials', *Independent*, 2 Apr 2022, https://www.independent.co.uk/news/uk/politics/fuel-bills-200-loan-sunak-lewis-b2049507.html
281 James Tapsfield and David Pilditch, 'Revealed: Millionaire Rishi Sunak borrowed £12,000 Kia Rio from Sainsbury's worker before putting in £30.01 of petrol for photo-op (but he says he actually drives a VW Golf)', *Daily Mail*, 25 Mar 2022, https://www.dailymail.co.uk/news/article-10648305/Rishi-borrowed-12-000-Kia-Rio-Sainsburys-worker-photo-op.html
282 Harshith KN, 'UK PM Rishi Sunak's car collection: From VW Golf to Jaguar XJ', *Times of India*, 26 Oct 2022, https://timesofindia.indiatimes.com/auto/cars/uk-pm-rishi-sunaks-car-collection-from-vw-golf-to-jaguar-xj/articleshow/95095538.cms
283 Ralph Blackburn, 'Watch: Rishi Sunak's bizarre contactless card fail at New Cross Sainsbury's petrol station', *London World*, 24 Mar 2022, https://www.londonworld.com/news/politics/watch-rishi-sunaks-bizarre-contactless-card-fail-at-new-cross-sainsburys-petrol-station-3625509
284 Rowena Mason, 'Rishi Sunak and wife donate over £100,000 to Winchester college', *Guardian*, 5 Apr 2022, https://www.theguardian.com/politics/2022/apr/05/rishi-sunak-and-wife-donate-over-100000-to-winchester-college
285 Gordon Rayner, 'Santa Monica beckons for Rishi Sunak as his political stock continues to plummet', *Telegraph*, 10 Apr 2022, https://www.telegraph.co.uk/politics/2022/04/10/santa-monica-beckons-rishi-sunak-political-stock-continues-plummet/
286 Jane McLeod, 'Rishi Sunak tax rise: 15 times the Tory Chancellor has hiked taxes', *The National*, 6 Apr 2022, https://www.thenational.scot/news/20048696.rishi-sunak-tax-rise-15-times-tory-chancellor-hiked-taxes/
287 Jack Barnett, 'UK households to be saddled with heaviest tax burden since 1940s', *CityA.M.*, 23 Mar 2022, https://www.cityam.com/uk-households-to-be-saddled-with-heaviest-tax-burden-since-1940s/
288 Andrew Sparrow, 'Spring statement 2022: living standards "set for historic fall", says OBR after Sunak mini budget – as it happened', *Guardian*, 23 Mar 2022, https://www.theguardian.com/politics/live/2022/mar/23/spring-statement-2022-rishi-sunak-poorest-families-likely-to-be-worst-hit-by-impact-of-ukraine-war-live-updates
289 Professor Ronen Palan, 'What is a non-dom? An expert answers questions about the tax status claimed by Rishi Sunak's wife and other wealthy people', City, University of London, 8 Apr 2022, https://www.city.ac.uk/news-and-events/news/2022/04/what-is-a-non-dom-an-expert-answers-questions-about-the-tax-status-claimed-by-rishi-sunaks-wife-and-other-wealthy-people
290 'Why Rishi Sunak's wife's tax status isn't a direct consequence of her citizenship', Full Fact, 8 Apr 2022, https://fullfact.org/economy/rishi-sunak-akshata-murty-non-dom-tax/
291 Peter Walker, Kalyeena Makortoff, Graeme Wearden, Jessica Elgot and Rupert Neate, 'Akshata Murty may have avoided up to £20m in tax with non-dom status', *Guardian*, 7 Apr 2022, https://www.theguardian.com/politics/2022/apr/07/rishi-sunaks-wife-says-its-not-relevant-to-say-where-she-pays-tax-overseas
292 'Chancellor Rishi Sunak held US green card until last year', BBC News, 8 Apr 2022, https://www.bbc.co.uk/news/uk-politics-61044847
293 Anna Isaac, 'Revealed: Rishi Sunak "listed in tax haven as trust beneficiary" while chancellor', *Independent*, 8 Apr 2022, https://www.independent.co.uk/news/uk/politics/rishi-sunak-akshata-murty-tax-haven-b2054179.html
294 Nick Sommerlad and Will Maule, 'Firm owned by family of Rishi Sunak's wife allegedly won £50m in taxpayer-funded deals', *WalesOnline*, 8 Apr 2022, https://www.walesonline.co.uk/news/uk-news/firm-owned-family-rishi-sunaks-23630660
295 'Full text: Theresa May's conference speech', *Spectator*, 5 Oct 2016, https://www.spectator.co.uk/article/full-text-theresa-may-s-conference-speech/

296 Anna Isaac, Ashley Cowburn, 'Cabinet ministers refuse to publicly declare offshore interests and non-dom status', *Independent*, 15 Apr 2022, https://www.independent.co.uk/news/uk/politics/cabinet-ministers-offshore-interest-tax-b2058176.html
297 'Full text of David Cameron's speech', *Guardian*, 8 Oct 2009, https://www.theguardian.com/politics/2009/oct/08/david-cameron-speech-in-full
298 Joe Roberts, 'Rishi Sunak "orders" inquiry into who leaked his wife's tax status', *Metro*, 10 Apr 2022, https://metro.co.uk/2022/04/10/rishi-sunak-orders-inquiry-into-who-leaked-his-wifes-tax-status-16439170/
299 Adam Payne, 'Ethics adviser clears Rishi Sunak over tax affairs and green card', *PoliticsHome*, 27 Apr 2022, https://www.politicshome.com/news/article/rishi-sunak-cleared-over-us-green-card-by-independent-adviser
300 Andrew Woodcock, 'Boris Johnson promises to "set the record straight" on Partygate fine in parliament next week', *Independent*, 14 Apr 2022, https://www.independent.co.uk/news/uk/politics/boris-johnson-party-fine-covid-b2057933.html
301 Tim McNulty, '"Stayed three minutes and left" Tory grandee Gale walks out of Boris charm offensive chat', *Express*, 20 Apr 2022, https://www.express.co.uk/news/politics/1598388/Boris-Johnson-news-Sky-News-partygate-latest-Conservative-Party-news-Parliament-live-vn
302 Jim Waterson, 'Tories face heavy local election losses over Partygate, PM told', *Guardian*, 23 Apr 2022, https://www.theguardian.com/politics/2022/apr/23/tories-face-heavy-local-election-losses-over-partygate-pm-told
303 Aubrey Allegretti, 'Justice minister resigns over No 10 Partygate revelations', *Guardian*, 23 Apr 2022, https://www.theguardian.com/politics/2022/apr/13/justice-minister-david-wolfson-resigns-partygate-boris-johnson
304 Robert Peston, 'Boris Johnson no longer "worthy", says senior Tory MP Mark Harper calling for resignation', ITV News, 19 Apr 2022, https://www.itv.com/news/2022-04-19/tory-mp-mark-harper-calls-for-pm-to-resign-as-he-is-no-longer-worthy-of-office
305 Kevin Schofield, '"We are better than this": David Davis Condemns PM's Rwanda asylum plan', *HuffPost*, 19 Apr 2022, https://www.huffingtonpost.co.uk/entry/david-davis-boris-johnson-rwanda-asylum_uk_625e4f71e4b052d2bd656c0d
306 'Migration and Brexit', *Migration Observatory*, https://migrationobservatory.ox.ac.uk/projects/migration-and-brexit/
307 'Which Scottish island will Priti Patel want to put asylum seekers on?', *The National*, 1 Oct 2020, https://www.thenational.scot/news/18763966.scottish-island-will-priti-patel-want-put-asylum-seekers/
308 Vincent Wood, 'Priti Patel "explored shipping asylum seekers to South Atlantic volcanic island to be processed"', *Independent*, 30 Sep 2020, https://www.independent.co.uk/news/uk/politics/priti-patel-asylum-ascension-island-atlantic-immigration-process-centre-b703625.html
309 Jonathon Read, 'Priti Patel "considered wave machines" to stop migrants crossing English Channel', *New European*, 1 Oct 2020, https://www.theneweuropean.co.uk/brexit-news-westminster-news-priti-patel-migrants-english-channel-plans-268062/
310 Archie Bland, 'Forty-three times the Conservatives tried (and failed) to tackle Channel crossings', *Guardian*, 7 Mar 2023, https://www.theguardian.com/uk-news/2023/mar/07/conservatives-channel-crossings-small-boats-tories-rwanda-deportation
311 Harriet Grant, 'Legal challenge seeks to end UK's jailing of asylum seekers who steer boats', *Guardian*, 12 Dec 2021, https://www.theguardian.com/politics/2021/dec/12/legal-challenge-seeks-to-end-uks-jailing-of-asylum-seekers-who-steer-boats
312 Richard Ford, 'Sending in the navy to tackle migrants is a "potty" idea, Ministry of Defence source says', *The Times*, 7 Aug 2020, https://www.thetimes.co.uk/article/sending-in-the-navy-to-tackle-migrants-is-a-potty-idea-ministry-of-defence-source-says-0svwpfz2r
313 'Timeline: Policy and legislative changes affecting migration to the UK', GOV.UK, https://assets.publishing.service.gov.uk/government/uploads/system/uploads/attachment_data/file/1010857/user-guide-policy-changes-jun21.ods

314 Archie Bland, 'Forty-three times the Conservatives tried (and failed) to tackle Channel crossings', *Guardian*, 7 Mar 2023, https://www.theguardian.com/uk-news/2023/mar/07/conservatives-channel-crossings-small-boats-tories-rwanda-deportation

315 Rajeev Syal and Nadeem Badshah, 'UK to send asylum seekers to Rwanda for processing', *Guardian*, 13 Apr 2022, https://www.theguardian.com/uk-news/2022/apr/13/priti-patel-finalises-plan-to-send-asylum-seekers-to-rwanda

316 'How many people do we grant asylum or protection to?', GOV.UK, 23 Sep 2022, https://www.gov.uk/government/statistics/immigration-statistics-year-ending-june-2022/how-many-people-do-we-grant-asylum-or-protection-to

317 'World Migration Report 2020', IOM UN Migration, 2022, https://worldmigrationreport.iom.int/wmr-2020-interactive/

318 'Poorest countries in the world 2023, ranked', Atlas and Boots, 30 Nov 2022, https://www.atlasandboots.com/travel-blog/poorest-countries-in-the-world-ranked/

319 Sami Quadri, 'Rwanda says it can only bring in 200 migrants from UK under controversial deportation scheme', *Evening Standard*, 23 Jul 2022, https://www.standard.co.uk/news/uk/rwanda-asylum-deal-uk-asylum-seekers-yolande-makolo-b1014266.html

320 Holly Christodoulou, 'The towns where homeowners pay a £600,000 premium to live in a picturesque village', *Sun*, 24 Oct 2016, https://www.thesun.co.uk/living/2036200/the-towns-where-homeowners-pay-a-600000-premium-to-live-in-a-picturesque-village/

321 Amelia Gentleman and Aubrey Allegretti, 'UN refugee agency condemns Boris Johnson's Rwanda asylum plan', *Guardian*, 15 Apr 2022, https://www.theguardian.com/uk-news/2022/apr/15/un-refugee-agency-condemns-johnsons-rwanda-asylum-plan

322 Joseph Lee and Doug Faulkner, 'Rwanda asylum flight cancelled after legal action', BBC News, 15 Jun 2022, https://www.bbc.co.uk/news/uk-61806383

323 Adam Forrest, 'Liz Truss "prepared to withdraw" UK from European Convention on Human Rights', *Independent*, 13 Jul 2022, https://www.independent.co.uk/news/uk/politics/liz-truss-uk-human-rights-convention-b2122084.html

324 Matt Dathan, 'Britain pays Rwanda extra £20m despite no migrant deportations', *The Times*, 18 Oct 2022, https://www.thetimes.co.uk/article/britain-pays-rwanda-extra-20m-despite-no-migrant-deportations-8nxmwfwt7

325 Alex Russell, 'Rwanda's Paul Kagame—is he just another dictator?', *Financial Times*, 6 Apr 2021, https://www.ft.com/content/678b2d31-cbe2-447a-8774-639087dfb863

326 Molly Blackall, 'Money paid by UK to Rwanda for migrant deportations is not being scrutinised, says country's opposition leader', *iNews*, 30 Oct 2022, https://inews.co.uk/news/money-uk-rwanda-migrant-deportations-not-monitored-opposition-leader-1939416

327 'Tackling fraud and corruption against government', National Audit Office, 30 Mar 2023, https://www.nao.org.uk/wp-content/uploads/2023/03/tackling-fraud-and-corruption-against-government-summary.pdf

328 Toby Helm, 'Rishi Sunak's hopes of becoming prime minister are over, say top Tories', *Observer*, 9 Apr 2022, https://www.theguardian.com/politics/2022/apr/09/rishi-sunaks-hopes-of-becoming-prime-minister-are-over-say-top-tories

329 Faye Brown, 'Imran Ahmad Khan: Former Tory MP who groped boy, 15, released from prison after serving half his sentence', Sky News, 21 Feb 2023, https://news.sky.com/story/imran-ahmad-khan-former-tory-mp-who-groped-boy-15-released-from-prison-after-serving-half-his-sentence-12816508

330 Rachel Russell, 'Crispin Blunt reiterates defence of ex-Tory MP Imran Ahmad Khan as he claims sex offender "did not get fair trial"', Sky News, 22 May 2022, https://news.sky.com/story/crispin-blunt-reiterates-defence-of-ex-tory-mp-imran-ahmad-khan-as-he-claims-sex-offender-did-not-get-fair-trial-12618859

331 Jessica Elgot, 'Crispin Blunt quits as LGBTQ+ group chair after Imran Ahmad Khan comments', *Guardian*, 12 Apr 2022, https://www.theguardian.com/politics/2022/apr/12/crispin-blunt-urged-to-apologise-for-comments-on-imran-ahmad-khan-case

332 Ben Quinn and Helena Horton, 'Neil Parish: Tory MP at centre of Commons pornography scandal', *Guardian*, 29 Apr 2022, https://www.theguardian.com/politics/2022/apr/29/neil-parish-tory-mp-scandal-profile

333 'Neil Parish MP: I'm resigning after porn moment of madness', BBC News, 30 Apr 2022, https://www.bbc.co.uk/news/uk-politics-61284686

334 Adam Forrest, 'Partygate: Boris Johnson joked No 10 party was "most unsocially distanced in UK"', *Independent*, 11 Jan 2023, https://www.independent.co.uk/news/uk/politics/boris-johnson-partygate-unsocially-distanced-b2259942.html
335 Chris Hughes and Tom Pettifor, 'Met Police "stitch up" claim as Sajid Javid's brother oversees Partygate complaint', *Mirror*, 31 Jan 2022, https://www.mirror.co.uk/news/politics/met-police-stitch-up-claim-26102172
336 Henry Zeffman, Oliver Wright, Steven Swinford and Chris Smyth, 'Boris Johnson: Tory MPs told to block inquiry into Downing Street parties', *The Times*, 20 Apr 2022, https://www.thetimes.co.uk/article/boris-johnson-tory-mps-told-to-block-inquiry-downing-street-lockdown-parties-hlfjqph2f
337 Jessica Elgot and Heather Stewart, 'Partygate: No 10 denies Boris Johnson asked Sue Gray to ditch report', *Guardian*, 24 May 2022, https://www.theguardian.com/politics/2022/may/24/partygate-boris-johnson-meeting-sue-gray-lockdown-parties-downing-street
338 Peter Walker, 'Sue Gray report: full breakdown of findings about No 10 parties', *Guardian*, 25 May 2022, https://www.theguardian.com/politics/2022/may/25/sue-gray-report-full-breakdown-findings-no-10-parties
339 'Sue Gray partygate report: "Humbled" Boris Johnson "surprised and disappointed" at revelations', Sky News, 25 May 2022, https://news.sky.com/story/boris-johnson-says-he-was-surprised-and-disappointed-at-partygate-revelations-in-sue-gray-report-12621061
340 'Sue Gray: Failure of leadership over Downing Street lockdown parties', BBC News, 31 Jan 2022, https://www.bbc.co.uk/news/uk-politics-60203287
341 Peter Walker, 'Boris Johnson to face no-confidence vote today as scores of Tory MPs call on him to go', *Guardian*, 6 Jun 2022, https://www.theguardian.com/politics/2022/jun/06/boris-johnson-face-confidence-vote-scores-tory-mps-call-on-him-to-go
342 Aubrey Allegretti and Peter Walker, 'Jeremy Hunt urges Tory MPs to vote no confidence in Boris Johnson', *Guardian*, 6 Jun 2022, https://www.theguardian.com/politics/2022/jun/06/boris-johnson-jeremy-hunt-tory-mps-vote-no-confidence
343 Rowena Mason, 'Boris Johnson wins no-confidence vote despite unexpectedly large rebellion', *Guardian*, 6 Jun 2022, https://www.theguardian.com/politics/2022/jun/06/boris-johnson-wins-no-confidence-vote-despite-unexpectedly-large-rebellion
344 Kate Nicholson, 'Neil Parish's wife chases him with scissors saying "snip-snap" after tractor porn scandal', *HuffPost*, 7 Apr 2022, https://www.huffingtonpost.co.uk/entry/tractor-porn-neil-parish-wife-scissors-boris-johnson_uk_62c2c4abe4b0f6125729ad21
345 Peter Walker, 'Tories lose two key byelections on same night in Wakefield and Tiverton and Honiton', *Guardian*, 24 Jun 2022, https://www.theguardian.com/politics/2022/jun/24/tories-lose-byelections-wakefield-tiverton-honiton-labour-lib-dems
346 Sinead Butler, 'Tory by-election candidate hid in dance studio to avoid reporters following humiliating defeat', *Indy100*, 24 Jun 2022, https://www.indy100.com/politics/tory-lost-by-election-hid-dance-studio
347 Andrew Sparrow, 'Backlash from Tory MPs as Boris Johnson misses Tory "red wall" conference to make surprise visit to Kyiv – as it happened', *Guardian*, 17 Jun 2022, https://www.theguardian.com/politics/live/2022/jun/17/boris-johnson-lord-geidt-uk-politics-live-latest
348 Peter Walker, 'Oliver Dowden resigns as Conservative party chair after byelection losses', *Guardian*, 24 Jun 2022, https://www.theguardian.com/politics/2022/jun/24/oliver-dowden-resigns-as-conservative-party-chair-in-wake-of-byelection-losses
349 Emma Soteriou, ' "We've done incredibly well": Priti says govt will "crack on" despite by-election wipeout', LBC, 24 Jun 2022, https://www.lbc.co.uk/news/boris-johnson-by-election-results-wakefield-tiverton-honiton/
350 Sophia Sleigh, 'Priti Patel says there will not be any more resignations after by-election wipe out', *HuffPost*, 24 Jun 2022, https://www.huffingtonpost.co.uk/entry/priti-patel-says-there-will-not-be-any-more-resignations-after-by-election-wipe-out_uk_62b564e8e4b0cf43c862a99b

351 Lewis Adams, 'Priti Patel and other north Essex MPs react to by-election', *Essex County Gazette*, 24 Jun 2022, https://www.gazette-news.co.uk/news/20234013.priti-patel-north-essex-mps-react-by-election/

352 Kirsten Robertson, 'Boris Johnson says he will "listen to voters" following humiliating by-election defeats', *Metro*, 24 Jun 2022, https://metro.co.uk/2022/06/24/boris-johnson-has-said-he-will-listen-to-voters-but-keep-going-16883470/

353 Matthew Smith, 'Most Conservative party members want Boris Johnson to resign', YouGov, 7 Jul 2022, https://yougov.co.uk/topics/politics/articles-reports/2022/07/07/most-conservative-party-members-want-boris-johnson

354 Flavia Krause-Jackson, 'A defiant Boris Johnson says he'll stay UK leader into 2030s', *Bloomberg*, 25 Jun 2022, https://www.bloomberg.com/news/articles/2022-06-25/a-defiant-boris-johnson-says-he-s-staying-uk-leader-into-2030s

355 Rajeev Syal and Rowena Mason, 'Michael Howard calls on Boris Johnson to resign after byelection defeats', *Guardian*, 24 Jun 2022, https://www.theguardian.com/politics/2022/jun/24/boris-johnson-insists-he-will-keep-going-despite-byelection-defeats

356 George Parker, 'Boris Johnson's ethics adviser quits after "exceptionally busy" year', *Financial Times*, 15 Jun 2022, https://www.ft.com/content/6c72c771-7bb0-4ab6-9b2b-ea2dce43f224

357 Jamie Grierson, '"You can't pretend it doesn't matter": Johnson urged not to scrap Lord Geidt's role', *Guardian*, 17 Jun 2022, https://www.theguardian.com/politics/2022/jun/17/boris-johnson-urged-not-to-scrap-ethics-adviser-role-lord-geidt

358 Rob Hull, 'Revealed: 337k drivers with medical conditions awaiting DVLA to process licence applications as backlog grows by TWO THIRDS in a year', *This Is Money*, 18 May 2022, https://www.thisismoney.co.uk/money/cars/article-10825511/Driving-licence-backlog-medical-conditions-swells.html

359 Ben Chapman, 'UK farmers face "existential crisis" as Ukraine invasion hits grain, energy and fertiliser supplies', *Independent*, 8 Mar 2022, https://www.independent.co.uk/news/business/farming-ukraine-russia-food-prices-b2030784.html

360 Andrew Sparrow, 'Government wins vote on second reading of Northern Ireland protocol bill – as it happened', *Guardian*, 27 Jun 2022, https://www.theguardian.com/politics/live/2022/jun/27/boris-johnson-tories-g7-government-latest-updates

361 Andrew Sparrow, 'Government wins vote on second reading of Northern Ireland protocol bill – as it happened', *Guardian*, 27 Jun 2022, https://www.theguardian.com/politics/live/2022/jun/27/boris-johnson-tories-g7-government-latest-updates?page=with:block-62b95b5a8f0814a0d5d43e2a#block-62b95b5a8f0814a0d5d43e2a#block-62b95b5a8f0814a0d5d43e2a

362 Jessica Elgot, 'Boris Johnson could face new confidence vote within days', *Guardian*, 6 Jul 2022, https://www.theguardian.com/politics/2022/jul/06/boris-johnson-could-face-new-confidence-vote-within-days-1922-committee

363 Torchuil Crichton, 'Boris Johnson will be judged at the "bollocks box" says Tory Minister in TV slip up', *Daily Record*, 17 Jun 2022, https://www.dailyrecord.co.uk/news/politics/boris-johnson-judged-bollocks-box-27259101

364 Aidan Radnedge, 'Boris accused of announcing Ukraine calls "whenever No 10 hits new crisis"', *Metro*, 20 Jun 2022, https://metro.co.uk/2022/06/20/boris-accused-of-announcing-ukraine-calls-when-no-10-hits-new-crisis-16854993/

365 Helen Coffey, '"Major queues" return to Dover ferry port as P&O warns of two-hour wait', *Independent*, 27 Jul 2022, https://www.independent.co.uk/travel/news-and-advice/dover-port-ferries-delays-queues-b2132099.html

366 Gwyn Topham, 'Rail strikes: passengers face disruption as Britain's biggest walkout in decades begins', *Guardian*, 21 Jun 2022, https://www.theguardian.com/uk-news/2022/jun/21/passengers-face-disruption-as-britains-biggest-rail-strike-for-decades-begins

367 Adam Forrest, 'Brexit "completely" to blame for airport chaos, says Ryanair boss – predicting summer-long disruption', *Independent*, 21 Jun 2022, https://www.independent.co.uk/news/uk/politics/brexit-airport-flights-disruption-ryanair-b2105790.html

368 Mark Jenkinson [@markjenkinsonmp], Twitter, 21 Jun 2022, https://twitter.com/markjenkinsonmp/status/1539136883678412800

369 Mario Cacciottolo, 'The Streisand Effect: When censorship backfires', BBC News, 15 Jun 2022, https://www.bbc.co.uk/news/uk-18458567

370 Peter Stubley, 'Boris Johnson "wrote letter backing Jennifer Arcuri for £100k job at government-funded firm"', *Independent*, 6 Oct 2019, https://www.independent.co.uk/news/uk/politics/boris-johnson-jennifer-arcuri-leaked-emails-job-reference-company-a9144696.html

371 Jim Waterson, Rowena Mason and Aubrey Allegretti, 'No 10 confirms it asked the Times to drop Carrie Johnson story', *Guardian*, 20 Jun 2022, https://www.theguardian.com/uk-news/2022/jun/20/no-10-confirms-asked-the-times-drop-carrie-johnson-story

372 Tom Gordon, 'PM facing fresh ethics controversy on eve of crunch byelections', *Yahoo! Finance*, 22 Jun 2022, https://uk.finance.yahoo.com/news/pm-facing-fresh-ethics-controversy-040300103.html

373 Bill Bostock, 'Everything you need to know about Boris Johnson's fiancée Carrie Symonds, who just gave birth to a baby boy', *Business Insider*, 29 Apr 2022, https://www.businessinsider.com/who-is-carrie-symonds-boris-johnson-partner-2019-7

374 Helen Davidson, 'Boris Johnson having sex in the office: a case of misconduct in public office?', *Yorkshire Bylines*, 30 Jun 2022, https://yorkshirebylines.co.uk/news/home-affairs/boris-johnson-having-sex-in-the-office-a-case-of-misconduct-in-public-office/

375 James Tapsfield, 'It's not Princess Nut Nuts, it's Princess Nut Nut: Cummings allies' nasty nickname for Carrie Symonds "has been used for MONTHS"', *Mail Online*, 15 Nov 2022, https://www.dailymail.co.uk/news/article-8950507/Cruel-Princess-Nut-Nut-nickname-Carrie-used-months.html

376 Shaun Connolly, 'Conservative Whip refers himself to police over behaviour claims', *Independent*, 5 Nov 2017, https://www.independent.co.uk/news/uk/politics/conservative-party-whip-chris-pincher-alex-story-olympic-rower-bathrobe-pound-shop-harvey-weinstein-a8039216.html

377 Laura Hughes, 'Tory Whip Chris Pincher refers himself to the police after claim of unwanted pass at former Olympic rower', *Telegraph*, 5 Nov 2017, https://www.telegraph.co.uk/news/2017/11/05/tory-whip-chris-pincherrefers-police-claim-unwanted-pass-former/

378 Shaun Connolly, 'Conservative Whip refers himself to police over behaviour claims', *Independent*, 5 Nov 2017, https://www.independent.co.uk/news/uk/politics/conservative-party-whip-chris-pincher-alex-story-olympic-rower-bathrobe-pound-shop-harvey-weinstein-a8039216.html

379 Jon Craig, 'Chris Pincher: Disgraced MP "incredibly drunk" on the night he is alleged to have groped two men', Sky News, 3 Jul 2022, https://news.sky.com/story/chris-pincher-disgraced-mp-incredibly-drunk-on-the-night-he-is-alleged-to-have-groped-two-men-12644720

380 John Walsh, 'Behind closed doors: the secrets of London's gentlemen's clubs revealed', *The Times*, 17 Jul 2022, https://www.thetimes.co.uk/article/behind-closed-doors-the-secrets-of-londons-gentlemens-clubs-revealed-8sbdg6gzr

381 Rowena Mason, 'Chris Pincher: a timeline of allegations and investigations', *Guardian*, 4 Jul 2022, https://www.theguardian.com/politics/2022/jul/04/chris-pincher-a-timeline-of-allegations-and-investigations

382 Dominic McGrath, 'Neil Parish complains of "double standards" in Pincher controversy', *Independent*, 1 Jul 2022, https://www.independent.co.uk/news/uk/neil-parish-chris-pincher-conservatives-parliament-tiverton-b2113896.html

383 Sophie Morris, 'Boris Johnson makes second surprise visit to Kyiv after pulling out of major red wall summit at the last minute', Sky News, 18 Jul 2022, https://news.sky.com/story/boris-johnson-makes-second-surprise-visit-to-kyiv-12635686

384 Rowena Mason, 'Chris Pincher: a timeline of allegations and investigations', *Guardian*, 4 Jul 2022, https://www.theguardian.com/politics/2022/jul/04/chris-pincher-a-timeline-of-allegations-and-investigations

385 Camilla Turner et al., 'Chris Pincher suspended from Conservative Party after groping allegations', *Telegraph*, 1 Jul 2022, https://www.telegraph.co.uk/politics/2022/07/01/chris-pincher-suspended-conservative-party-groping-allegations/

386 Esther Webber, 'Revealed: The "minders" tasked with keeping Britain's drunk or misbehaving MPs in line', *Politico*, 2 Jul 2022, https://www.politico.eu/article/minder-task-britain-drunk-misbehaving-mp/

387 Zac Sherratt, 'Worthing MP Peter Bottomley message to Chris Pincher', *Argus*, 4 Jul 2022, https://www.theargus.co.uk/news/20254656.worthing-mp-peter-bottomley-message-chris-pincher/

388 GB News [@GBNEWS], Twitter, 4 Jul 2022, https://twitter.com/GBNEWS/status/1543971850753130496

389 Adam Forrest, 'Tory men do not have particular problem with sexual harassment, says cabinet minister', *Independent*, 3 Jul 2022, https://www.independent.co.uk/news/uk/politics/chris-pincher-tory-mps-sexual-harassment-b2114691.html

390 'Charlie Elphicke: Ex-MP jailed for sex assaults on women', BBC News, 15 Sep 2020, https://www.bbc.co.uk/news/uk-england-kent-54161766

391 Brendan Carlin and Kieran Corcoran, 'Pictured: Brazilian rent boy, 19, whose sex and drugs claims forced Tory MP to resign as Minister's aide', *Mail on Sunday*, 30 Mar 2014, https://www.dailymail.co.uk/news/article-2592478/Tory-MP-Mark-Menzies-quits-drug-rent-boy-claims.html

392 Heather Stewart and Haroon Siddique, 'Tory minister faces inquiry after getting female assistant to buy sex toys', *Guardian*, 29 Oct 2017, https://www.theguardian.com/politics/2017/oct/29/minister-mark-garnier-conservative-admits-asking-assistant-to-buy-sex-toys

393 Steve Robson and Gavin Cordon, 'Westminster "sexual harassment" scandal breaks: Tory MP Stephen Crabb admits sexting 19-year-old while another called his secretary "sugar t*ts" and made her buy sex toys', *Mirror*, 29 Oct 2017, https://www.mirror.co.uk/news/politics/tory-mp-stephen-crabb-sorry-11428747

394 Paul Bentley, Eleanor Harding and Martin Robinson, 'Tory MP Brooks Newmark sent explicit texts to single mother telling her "I am desperate for sex with you" during alleged two year affair', *Daily Mail*, 12 Oct 2014, https://www.dailymail.co.uk/news/article-2790302/wife-moves-family-home-tory-mp-shamed-texting-explicit-pictures-vows-fight-demons-residential-psychiatric-facility.html

395 Nina Massey, 'Brooks Newmark: I am a complete fool for sending X-rated picture', *Mirror*, 28 Sep 2014, https://www.mirror.co.uk/news/uk-news/brooks-newmark-am-complete-fool-4337653

396 Alan Selby and Nicola Small, 'Andrew Griffiths' lewd and depraved text message demands to two barmaids revealed', *Mirror*, 15 Jul 2018, https://www.mirror.co.uk/news/politics/tory-mp-andrew-griffiths-lewd-12919733

397 Jessica Elgot, 'Damian Green: I wasn't inappropriate to Kate Maltby', *Guardian*, 20 Feb 2018, https://www.theguardian.com/politics/2018/feb/20/damian-green-i-wasnt-inappropriate-to-kate-maltby

398 Gordon Rayner, 'Westminster sexual harassment scandal: 36 Tory MPs accused in "dirty dossier" as PM vows to sack ministers involved', *Telegraph*, 30 Oct 2017, https://www.telegraph.co.uk/news/2017/10/29/theresa-may-will-sack-cabinet-ministers-found-sex-pests-13-mps/

399 Rachel Roberts, 'Tory MP says female journalists are fuelling Westminster sex scandal and behaving like "wilting flowers"', *Independent*, 11 Nov 2017, https://www.independent.co.uk/news/uk/politics/sir-roger-gale-tory-mp-female-journalists-wilting-flowers-sex-scandal-westminster-a8050206.html

400 Fiona Simpson, 'MP sex pest scandal: 36 Tories named over sexual misconduct allegations in Tory spreadsheet of shame', *Evening Standard*, 30 Oct 2017, https://www.standard.co.uk/news/politics/leaked-spreadsheet-reveals-sexual-harassment-claims-against-36-mps-a3670961.html

401 Rachael Bunyan, 'Boris Johnson is facing allegations that he groped women and misused public funds. Here's what to know', *Time*, 2 Oct 2019, https://time.com/5689788/boris-johnson-charlotte-edwardes-jennifer-arcuri/

402 Jack Peat, 'BBC journalist says "dogs on the street in Westminster" knew what Pincher was like', *London Economic*, 5 Jul 2022, https://www.thelondoneconomic.com/politics/bbc-journalist-says-dogs-on-the-street-in-westminster-knew-what-pincher-was-like-328438/

403 Andrew Sparrow, 'Johnson has call with Ukrainian president as No 10 faces renewed claims it lied over Chris Pincher scandal', *Guardian*, 5 Jul 2022, https://www.theguardian.

com/politics/live/2022/jul/05/boris-johnson-accused-not-telling-truth-chris-pincher-politics-live?page=with:block-62c419ed8f0824967a54c3f7#block-62c419ed8f0824967a54c3f7

404 Sophie Morris, 'Boris Johnson apologises for appointing Chris Pincher as deputy chief whip and said "it was the wrong thing to do"', Sky News, 5 Jul 2022, https://news.sky.com/story/boris-johnson-apologises-for-appointing-chris-pincher-as-deputy-chief-whip-and-said-it-was-the-wrong-thing-to-do-12646408

405 Sajid Javid [@sajidjavid], Twitter, 5 Jul 2022, https://twitter.com/sajidjavid/status/1544366218789937152

406 Jim Waterson, 'Daily Mail out to stop "traitor" Sunak as Tory rivals vie for press backing', *Guardian*, 13 Jul 2022, https://www.theguardian.com/politics/2022/jul/13/daily-mail-out-to-stop-rishi-sunak-as-tory-rivals-vie-for-press-backing

407 First Edition [@FirstEdition], Twitter, 5 Jul 2022, https://twitter.com/FirstEdition/status/1544388951435247625

408 Alex Chalk [@AlexChalkChelt], Twitter, 5 Jul 2022, https://twitter.com/AlexChalkChelt/status/1544437737771655169

409 Haggis UK [@Haggis_UK], Twitter, 7 Jul 2022, https://twitter.com/Haggis_UK/status/1545126381733937155

410 Holly Patrick, 'Jacob Rees-Mogg says Boris Johnson could last as prime minister for over 20 years', *Independent*, 6 Jul 2022, https://www.independent.co.uk/tv/news/boris-johnson-pm-jacob-rees-b2116886.html

411 Hollie Bone, 'Bungling Nadine Dorries congratulates Nadhim Zahawi for wrong job in epic Twitter fail', *Mirror*, 6 Jul 2022, https://www.mirror.co.uk/news/politics/bungling-nadine-dorries-congratulates-nadhim-27408342

412 Heather Stewart, 'Priti Patel urges PM to go', *Guardian*, 6 Jul 2022, https://www.theguardian.com/politics/live/2022/jul/06/boris-johnson-rishi-sunak-sajid-javid-resignations-uk-politics-live-latest?filterKeyEvents=false&page=with:block-62c5e00a8f08ae7c89443ce7#block-62c5e00a8f08ae7c89443ce7

413 Adam Forrest, 'Boris Johnson: Six more ministers quit at once as PM clings onto power', *Independent*, 6 Jul 2022, https://www.independent.co.uk/news/uk/politics/boris-johnson-tory-ministers-resign-latest-b2117093.html

414 Chris Mason [@ChrisMasonBBC], Twitter, 6 Jul 2022, https://twitter.com/ChrisMasonBBC/status/1544778322973949953

415 Ashley Cowburn and Matt Mathers, '"Do the right thing and go": Nadhim Zahawi tells Boris Johnson to resign two days after appointed chancellor', *Independent*, 7 Jul 2022, https://www.independent.co.uk/news/uk/politics/nadhim-zahawi-boris-johnson-resign-twitter-b2117741.html

416 Michael Savage and Jon Ungoed-Thomas, 'Revealed: officials raised "flag" over Nadhim Zahawi's tax affairs before he was appointed chancellor', *Observer*, 9 Jul 2022, https://www.theguardian.com/uk-news/2022/jul/09/revealed-officials-raised-flag-over-nadim-zahawis-tax-affairs-before-he-was-appointed-chancellor

417 Samantha Booth, 'Education secretary Michelle Donelan resigns after less than two days', *Schools Week*, 7 Jul 2022, https://schoolsweek.co.uk/education-secretary-michelle-donelan-resigns-after-less-than-two-days/

418 Kevin Schofield, 'Five ministers quit government at once as Boris Johnson's premiership nears the end', *HuffPost*, 7 Jul 2022, https://www.huffingtonpost.co.uk/entry/five-ministers-resign-at-same-time_uk_62c58ff2e4b02e0ac90e3d5e

419 Liam James, 'Boris Johnson's flagship levelling up department left with only one paid minister after Gove sacked', *Independent*, 6 Jul 2022, https://www.independent.co.uk/news/uk/politics/boris-johnson-levelling-up-gove-b2117535.html

420 'Live news updates from July 6: More than 40 members of UK government quit, Boris Johnson sacks Michael Gove', *Financial Times*, 6 Jul 2022, https://www.ft.com/content/54d14d6b-4cb3-4972-b22d-397b8ea3fdd5#post-0038b1e3-8cfc-43dd-b6af-35734533cb02

421 Rory Stewart [@RoryStewartUK], Twitter, 6 Jul 2022, https://twitter.com/RoryStewartUK/status/1544594449149427715

422 Sebastian Payne [@SebastianEPayne], Twitter, 8 Jul 2022, https://twitter.com/SebastianEPayne/status/1545446272240422917

423 Allegra Stratton, 'Tory bill attempts to water down minimum wage', *Guardian*, 13 May 2009, https://www.theguardian.com/politics/2009/may/13/minimum-wage-tory-bill
424 'Low Pay Commission summary of findings 2022', GOV.UK, 17 Nov 2022, https://www.gov.uk/government/publications/minimum-wage-rates-for-2023/low-pay-commission-summary-of-findings-2022
425 Tim Shipman, 'The rebels' smartphone spreadsheet that means Liz Truss is still in deep trouble', *The Times*, 8 Oct 2022, https://www.thetimes.co.uk/article/the-rebels-smartphone-spreadsheet-that-means-liz-truss-is-still-in-deep-trouble-0shzg86hq
426 'Labour leader says new Northern Ireland Secretary asked if passport for Derry was needed', ITV News, 13 Jul 2022, https://www.itv.com/news/utv/2022-07-13/labour-leader-says-new-ni-secretary-asked-if-passport-for-derry-was-needed
427 Jane Dalton, 'MP who gave Boris Johnson protesters the middle finger promoted to education minister', *Independent*, 8 Jul 2022, https://www.independent.co.uk/news/uk/politics/andrea-jenkyns-finger-education-minister-b2119196.html
428 Camilla Turner, 'Boris Johnson suffers most ministerial resignations in modern history', *Telegraph*, 6 Jul 2022, https://www.telegraph.co.uk/politics/2022/07/06/boris-johnson-suffers-ministerial-resignations-24-hours-since/
429 Jack Guy, Luke McGee and Ivana Kottasová, 'UK Prime Minister Boris Johnson resigns after mutiny in his party', CNN, 7 Jul 2022, https://www.cnn.com/2022/07/07/europe/boris-johnson-resignation-intl/index.html
430 Noa Hoffman [@hoffman_noa], Twitter, 7 Jul 2022, https://twitter.com/hoffman_noa/status/1545009832205467651
431 Sophie Morris, 'UK heatwave: Boris Johnson told to "turn up for work" as he is set to miss third COBRA meeting', Sky News, 18 Jul 2022, https://news.sky.com/story/uk-heatwave-boris-johnson-told-to-turn-up-for-work-as-he-is-set-to-miss-third-cobra-meeting-12654184
432 Liam O'Dell, 'Boris Johnson skips heatwave Cobra meeting for "Chequers party" and people are rightly furious', *Indy100*, 16 Jul 2022, https://www.indy100.com/politics/boris-johnson-party-chequers-cobra
433 Sophie Morris, 'Boris Johnson compares his premiership to a Typhoon flight as he prepares to hand over the controls', *Sky News*, 18 Jul 2022, https://news.sky.com/story/boris-johnson-compares-his-premiership-to-a-typhoon-flight-as-he-prepares-to-hand-over-the-controls-12654261
434 Adam Forrest, 'Brexit: Boris Johnson suggests Keir Starmer and "deep state" plotting to take UK back into EU', *Independent*, 18 Jul 2022, https://www.independent.co.uk/news/uk/politics/brexit-boris-johnson-eu-deep-state-labour-b2125940.html
435 Asher McShane, 'Tobias Ellwood MP stripped of Tory party whip after abstaining in confidence vote', LBC, 19 Jul 2022, https://www.lbc.co.uk/news/tobias-ellwood-mp-stripped-tory-party-whip-abstaining-confidence-vote/
436 Andy Gregory, 'Knives out as Tory leadership teams "create dirty dossiers on rivals"', *Independent*, 10 Jul 2022, https://www.independent.co.uk/news/uk/politics/tory-leadership-race-dirty-dossiers-b2119655.html
437 Matthew Smith, 'Ben Wallace clear favourite for next Conservative leader among party members', YouGov, 7 Jul 2022, https://yougov.co.uk/topics/politics/articles-reports/2022/07/07/ben-wallace-clear-favourite-next-conservative-lead
438 Peter Walker, 'Ben Wallace rules himself out of Tory leadership race', *Guardian*, 9 Jul 2022, https://www.theguardian.com/politics/2022/jul/09/ben-wallace-rules-himself-out-tory-leadership-race
439 'Next Tory Leader. Which MP is backing whom – the updated list. Truss on 149, Sunak on 132. The Foreign Secretary's lead amongst MPs grows', *Conservative Home*, 25 Aug 2022, https://conservativehome.com/2022/08/25/next-tory-leader-whos-backing-whom-our-working-list/
440 Kay Balls, 'Truss pitches herself as continuity Boris', *Spectator*, 14 Jul 2022, https://www.spectator.co.uk/article/truss-pitches-herself-as-continuity-boris/
441 Alexandra Rogers, 'Liz Truss allies reject she is Boris Johnson "continuity" candidate', *HuffPost*, 13 Jul 2022, https://www.huffingtonpost.co.uk/entry/liz-truss-allies-reject-she-is-boris-johnson-continuity-candidate_uk_62cecf9ee4b0c0bdba653461

442 Chris York, 'Jeremy Hunt makes "terrible mistake" about his own wife during debut in China', *HuffPost*, 30 Jul 2018, https://www.huffingtonpost.co.uk/entry/jeremy-hunt-wife-gaffe_uk_5b5ec339e4b0fd5c73d0d152
443 Kate Gill, 'Jeremy Hunt names Esther McVey as his deputy prime minister after launching leadership bid', *Independent*, 10 Jul 2022, https://www.independent.co.uk/tv/news/jeremy-hunt-esther-mcvey-prime-minister-b2119839.html
444 Sebastian Payne, 'Boris Johnson allies accuse Rishi Sunak of treachery', *Financial Times*, 9 Jul 2022, https://www.ft.com/content/ea706ae0-284c-43f3-adb8-55c3ad8bc250
445 Jennifer Scott, 'Boris Johnson and Rishi Sunak reject calls to resign over lockdown fines', BBC News, 13 Apr 2022, https://www.bbc.co.uk/news/uk-politics-61083402
446 'UK's Sunak to run for PM as "serious candidate" with integrity – Times', *Reuters*, 8 Jul 2022, https://www.reuters.com/world/uk/uks-sunak-run-pm-serious-candidate-with-integrity-times-2022-07-08/
447 Oliver Wright and George Grylls, 'My weakness is aiming for perfection, Rishi Sunak says', *The Times*, 16 Jul 2022, https://www.thetimes.co.uk/article/my-weakness-is-aiming-for-perfection-rishi-sunak-says-27jpbt0tw
448 Elly Blake, 'Rishi Sunak mocked by eagle-eyed viewers over spelling mistake on Tory leadership campaign banner', *Evening Standard*, 15 Jul 2022, https://www.standard.co.uk/news/politics/rishi-sunak-spelling-mistake-campaign-tory-leadereship-contest-latest-b1012663.html
449 Alona Ferber, 'Don't make the Tory leadership contest about the trans culture war', *New Statesman*, 12 Jul 2022, https://www.newstatesman.com/quickfire/2022/07/trans-culture-war-tory-leadership-women
450 Tim Shipman [@ShippersUnbound], Twitter, 11 Jul 2022, https://twitter.com/ShippersUnbound/status/1546444860944785409
451 Adam Bienkov [@AdamBienkov], Twitter, 10 Jul 2022, https://twitter.com/AdamBienkov/status/1546070277771198470
452 Hugh Carr, 'British PM candidate shares bizarre proposal to form alliance with "Viking parliaments", including Ireland', JOE, 10 Jul 2022, https://www.joe.ie/news/tugendhat-ireland-751514
453 Katherine McPhillips, 'Britain First urges supporters to back "anti-woke" candidate Kemi Badenoch', *Express*, 19 Jul 2022, https://www.express.co.uk/news/politics/1642512/britain-first-back-kemi-badenoch-ont
454 Helena Horton, 'Kemi Badenoch moves away from net zero by 2050, in double climate U-turn', *Guardian*, 19 Jul 2022, https://www.theguardian.com/environment/2022/jul/19/kemi-badenoch-moves-away-from-net-zero-by-2050-in-double-climate-u-turn
455 Robert Peston [@peston], Twitter, 23 Jul 2022, https://twitter.com/Peston/status/1547123276266217474
456 Laura Webster, 'Jacob Rees-Mogg as prime minister? Right-wing MP considering leadership bid, reports say', *The National*, 11 Jul 2022, https://www.thenational.scot/news/20270526.jacob-rees-mogg-prime-minister-right-wing-mp-considering-leadership-bid-reports-say/
457 Lara Keay, 'Who is Penny Mordaunt, the ex-magician's assistant looking to conjure up victory in PM race?', *Sky News*, 24 Oct 2022, https://news.sky.com/story/penny-mordaunt-has-been-the-dark-horse-in-the-tory-leadership-race-can-she-make-it-all-the-way-12651726
458 Mark Nichol, 'Senior officers question Penny Mordaunt's claims about Royal Navy credentials', *Daily Mail*, 15 Jul 2022, https://www.dailymail.co.uk/news/article-11015669/Senior-officers-questioned-Penny-Mordaunts-Navy-claims.html
459 Tom Tugendhat, https://www.tomtugendhat.org/aboutom
460 Dan Sabbagh, 'Penny Mordaunt: what her 85 days as defence secretary tell us about her', *Guardian*, 19 Jul 2022, https://www.theguardian.com/politics/2022/jul/19/penny-mordaunt-what-her-85-days-as-defence-secretary-tell-us-about-her
461 Mark Nichol, 'Senior officers question Penny Mordaunt's claims about Royal Navy credentials', *Daily Mail*, 15 Jul 2022, https://www.dailymail.co.uk/news/article-11015669/Senior-officers-questioned-Penny-Mordaunts-Navy-claims.html

462 Harry Cole, 'Penny as our new Defence Chief? She'll drink to that! Minister delights top brass as she sports badge showing she passed Navy rum-drinking test', *Daily Mail*, 4 May 2019, https://www.dailymail.co.uk/news/article-6992951/Penny-new-Defence-Chief-Shell-drink-that.html

463 'Penny Mordaunt: Who is the Navy reservist running for PM?', *Forces.net*, 21 Oct 2022, https://www.forces.net/politics/penny-mordaunt-who-navy-reservist-and-former-defence-secretary-running-pm

464 Joey Nolfi, 'Daniel Craig and James Bond now hold the same rank in the British Royal Navy', *EW*, 24 Sep 2021, https://ew.com/movies/james-bond-daniel-craig-is-now-an-honorary-commander-british-navy/

465 Sophie Barnett, 'Champion sprinter demands pic axed from Tory hopeful Penny Mordaunt's campaign video', LBC, 20 Oct 2022, https://www.lbc.co.uk/news/sprinter-demands-pic-axed-from-penny-mordaunts-campaign-video/

466 Rebecca Perring, 'Bungling Tory MP vows to "level" Stoke and spells his OWN name wrong in leadership gaffe', *Express*, 15 Jul 2022, https://www.express.co.uk/news/politics/1641159/Tory-mp-leader-race-penny-mordaunt-Jack-Brereton

467 Russell Jones [@RussInCheshire], Twitter, 8 Jul 2022, https://twitter.com/russincheshire/status/1545435669639700481

468 Helena Horton, 'Anti-green MP Steve Baker considering running for PM', *Guardian*, 7 Jul 2022, https://www.theguardian.com/politics/2022/jul/07/anti-green-mp-steve-baker-considering-running-for-pm-if-boris-johnson-goes

469 Jon Stone, 'Tory leadership candidate says she will "eliminate" right to protection from torture and inhuman treatment', *Independent*, 14 Jul 2022, https://www.independent.co.uk/independentpremium/uk-news/tory-leadership-candidate-suella-braverman-torture-human-rights-b2124323.html

470 'We couldn't find any results for "Rehman Chishti"', YouGov, https://yougov.co.uk/ratings/politics/fame/politicians-political-figures/all(popup:search/Rehman%20Chishti)

471 'Neil Hamilton', YouGov, https://yougov.co.uk/topics/politics/explore/public_figure/Neil_Hamilton

472 Rehman Chishti [@Rehman_Chishti], Twitter, 10 Jul 2022, https://twitter.com/Rehman_Chishti/status/1546240922043695107

473 Sophie Wingate, 'Rehman Chishti's unlikely Tory leadership bid ends with zero backers', *Independent*, 12 Jul 2022, https://www.independent.co.uk/news/uk/foreign-office-mps-grant-shapps-government-boris-johnson-b2121593.html

474 Jessica Elgot, 'Nadine Dorries's "disturbing" tweets on Sunak condemned by Tory MPs', *Guardian*, 31 Jul 2022, https://www.theguardian.com/politics/2022/jul/31/nadine-dorries-disturbing-tweets-on-rishi-sunak-condemned-by-tory-mps

475 Aubrey Allegretti, '"FFS Nadine! Muted": fears Truss-Sunak race is plunging into horrific nastiness', *Guardian*, 25 Jul 2022, https://www.theguardian.com/politics/2022/jul/25/ffs-nadine-muted-fears-truss-sunak-race-is-plunging-into-horrific-nastiness

476 Liam O'Dell, 'Tory leadership poll finds 6 per cent of people know "a great deal" about fake MP "Stewart Lewis"', *Indy100*, 14 Jul 2022, https://www.indy100.com/politics/stewart-lewis-tory-leadership-poll

477 Andy Gregory, 'Tom Tugendhat clear winner of first Tory leadership debate, snap poll finds' *Independent*, 16 Jul 2022, https://www.independent.co.uk/news/uk/politics/tory-leadership-debate-poll-tugendhat-winner-b2124458.html

478 Peter Walker and Nadeem Badshah, 'TV debate between Truss and Sunak cancelled after presenter faints', *Guardian*, 26 Jul 2022, https://www.theguardian.com/politics/2022/jul/26/tv-debate-between-truss-and-sunak-cancelled-after-presenter-faints

479 Seán Clarke and Anna Leach, 'How Truss beat Sunak: round by round Tory leadership results', *Guardian*, 5 Sep 2022, https://www.theguardian.com/politics/ng-interactive/2022/sep/05/tory-leadership-election-full-results-liz-truss-rishi-sunak

480 Sophie Thompson, 'Liz Truss just got lost trying to leave her own leadership launch', *Indy100*, 14 Jul 2022, https://www.indy100.com/politics/liz-truss-leadership-launch-lost

481 Arj Singh, Chloe Chaplain, 'Tory leadership race: Liz Truss completes U-turn by pledging billions of pounds-worth of energy bill help', *iNews*, 26 Aug 2022, https://inews.co.uk/news/politics/tory-leadership-race-liz-truss-completes-u-turn-by-pledging-billions-of-pounds-worth-of-energy-bill-help-1819000

482 Dave Burke and Dan Bloom, 'All Liz Truss and Rishi Sunak's worst gaffes, U-turns and awkward moments so far', *Mirror*, 16 Aug 2022, https://www.mirror.co.uk/news/politics/liz-truss-rishi-sunaks-worst-27640981

483 Jessica Elgot and Heather Stewart, 'Liz Truss U-turns on plan to cut public sector pay outside London', *Guardian*, 2 Aug 2022, https://www.theguardian.com/politics/2022/aug/02/liz-truss-u-turns-plan-cut-public-sector-pay-outside-london-tory-leadership

484 Dave Burke, 'All Liz Truss and Rishi Sunak's worst gaffes, U-turns and awkward moments so far', *Mirror*, 16 Aug 2022, https://www.mirror.co.uk/news/politics/liz-truss-rishi-sunaks-worst-27640981

485 Rowena Mason, 'Liz Truss accused of offensive remarks about Jewish people and civil service', *Guardian*, 12 Aug 2022, https://www.theguardian.com/politics/2022/aug/12/liz-truss-protect-british-jews-antisemitism-woke-culture

486 Dan Bloom, 'Liz Truss makes amusing first gaffe two minutes after getting onto Tory leadership ballot', *Mirror*, 20 Jul 2022, https://www.mirror.co.uk/news/uk-news/liz-truss-makes-amusing-first-27533842

487 Kiran Stacey and Jessica Elgot, 'Rishi Sunak saved £300,000 in tax thanks to cut he voted for in 2016', *Guardian*, 23 Mar 2023, https://www.theguardian.com/politics/2023/mar/23/rishi-sunak-saved-tax-capital-gains-cut-voted-for-in-2016

488 Matthew Dresch and Aaron Morris, '"Out of touch" Rishi Sunak blasted over "no working class friends" in unearthed BBC clip', *Chronicle Live*, 11 Jul 2022, https://www.chroniclelive.co.uk/news/north-east-news/rishi-sunak-working-class-friends-24461141

489 Robert Booth, 'What Rishi Sunak's Tunbridge Wells boast may mean for levelling up', *Guardian*, 26 Oct 2022, https://www.theguardian.com/politics/2022/oct/26/rishi-sunak-garden-party-levelling-up-agenda-tunbridge-wells-funding-tory-heartlands

490 Rajeev Syal, 'Rishi Sunak admits taking money from deprived areas', *Guardian*, 5 Aug 2022, https://www.theguardian.com/politics/2022/aug/05/video-emerges-of-rishi-sunak-admitting-to-taking-money-from-deprived-areas

491 Kate Plummer, '14 of Rishi Sunak's biggest gaffes and most awkward moments', *Indy100*, 25 Oct 2022, https://www.indy100.com/politics/rishi-sunak-pm-gaffes-memes

492 Daniel Martin, 'Liz Truss elected Tory leader by narrowest margin since members got the vote', *Telegraph*, 5 Sep 2022, https://www.telegraph.co.uk/politics/2022/09/05/liz-truss-elected-tory-leader-narrowest-margin-record/

493 Mark Townsend, 'Boris Johnson's busy post-resignation schedule . . . of luxury holidays', *Guardian*, 23 Oct 2022, https://www.theguardian.com/politics/2022/oct/23/boris-johnson-busy-post-resignation-schedule-of-luxury-holidays

494 'Contributions for Boris Johnson', Hansard, https://hansard.parliament.uk/search/MemberContributions?endDate=2022-11-15&memberId=1423&outputType=List&partial=False&searchTerm=uxbridge&startDate=2015-05-07&type=Spoken

495 Samuel Osborne, 'Boris Johnson's reference to Roman dictator Cincinnatus hints at his return', *Sky News*, 6 Sep 2022, https://news.sky.com/story/boris-johnsons-reference-to-roman-dictator-cincinnatus-hints-at-his-return-12691090

496 'Cincinnatus', Digital Encyclopaedia of George Washington, https://www.mountvernon.org/library/digitalhistory/digital-encyclopedia/article/cincinnatus/

497 Mark Townsend, 'Boris Johnson's busy post-resignation schedule . . . of luxury holidays', *Guardian*, 23 Oct 2022, https://www.theguardian.com/politics/2022/oct/23/boris-johnson-busy-post-resignation-schedule-of-luxury-holidays

498 Josh Salisbury, 'Boris Johnson tops public poll of worst post-war Prime Ministers with half saying he did bad job', *Evening Standard*, 31 Aug 2022, https://www.standard.co.uk/news/uk/boris-johnson-worst-prime-minister-ipsos-poll-b1022192.html

499 Archie Mitchell, 'The 12 words that sparked Boris Johnson's downfall', *Independent*, 14 June 2023, https://www.independent.co.uk/news/uk/politics/boris-johnson-partygate-misled-parliament-b2357197.html

500 'Tory aides invited to "Jingle and Mingle" Covid party', BBC News, 20 Jun 2023, https://www.bbc.co.uk/news/uk-politics-65952298

501 Alice Lilly, 'Privileges Committee investigation into Boris Johnson', Institute for Government, 15 Jun 2023, https://www.instituteforgovernment.org.uk/explainer/privileges-committee-investigation-boris-johnson

502 Joshua Nevett and Paul Seddon, 'Boris Johnson's taxpayer-funded legal bill rises to £245,000', BBC News, 10 May 2023, https://www.bbc.co.uk/news/uk-politics-65401587
503 'The Current Legal Aid Financial Eligibility Rules – Summary', Ministry of Justice, 2013, https://consult.justice.gov.uk/digital-communications/legal-aid-eligibility-and-universal-credit/supporting_documents/annexcsummaryofcurrentlegalaidfinancialeligibilityrules.pdf
504 Ethan Stone, 'Boris Johnson has received earnings, donations, gifts and hospitality worth £6 million since leaving No 10', *National World*, 27 Jan 2023, https://www.nationalworld.com/news/politics/boris-johnson-received-earnings-donations-gifts-and-hospitality-worth-ps6-million-since-leaving-no-10-4004634
505 'Ministers: Legal Costs', Questions for the Cabinet Office, 15 June 2023, https://questions-statements.parliament.uk/written-questions/detail/2023-06-15/189774
506 Alice Lilly, 'Privileges Committee investigation into Boris Johnson', Institute for Government, 15 Jun 2023, https://www.instituteforgovernment.org.uk/explainer/privileges-committee-investigation-boris-johnson
507 Seán Clarke, 'How did your MP vote on the Boris Johnson privileges committee report?', *Guardian*, 19 Jun 2023, https://www.theguardian.com/politics/ng-interactive/2023/jun/19/how-did-your-mp-vote-on-the-boris-johnson-privileges-committee-report
508 Kevin Schofield, 'Tory MP gets rinsed after explaining why he's snubbing the Boris Johnson vote', *HuffPost*, 19 Jun 2023, https://www.huffingtonpost.co.uk/entry/tory-mp-rinsed-after-explaining-why-hes-snubbing-johnson-vote_uk_64905a57e4b06725aee8073f
509 Jacqueline Howard, 'How Boris Johnson became the first prime minister to deliberately mislead the UK parliament', *ABC*, 15 June 2023, https://www.abc.net.au/news/2023-06-16/boris-johnson-first-pm-to-deliberately-mislead-parliament/102486004
510 Jon Stone, 'Which Tories voted to punish Boris Johnson – and which didn't', *Independent*, 20 Jun 2023, https://www.independent.co.uk/news/uk/politics/boris-johnson-vote-rishi-sunak-punishment-b2360409.html
511 Anthony Robinson, 'Johnson's "disciplined and deluded collection of stooges" is turning on him', *Yorkshire Bylines*, 18 Nov 2021, https://yorkshirebylines.co.uk/politics/johnsons-disciplined-deluded-collection-of-stooges-turning-on-him/

Part 2: How to Lose a Country in Ten Days
2022: 'It Would Almost Be Endearing if it Wasn't so Completely and Utterly Fucking Mad'

1. 'UK think tanks and campaigns rated for funding transparency', Who Funds You, https://www.opendemocracy.net/en/who-funds-you/
2. Nafeez Ahmed, 'How US climate deniers are working with far-right racists to hijack Brexit for Big Oil', *Le Monde Diplomatique*, 20 Jun 2019, https://mondediplo.com/outsidein/brexit-climate-deniers
3. Tobias Hübinette, 'Race and Sweden's Fascist Turn', *Boston Review*, 19 Oct 2022, https://www.bostonreview.net/articles/race-and-swedens-fascist-turn/
4. Nicole Winfield, 'How a party of neo-fascist roots won big in Italy', *Associated Press*, 26 Sep 2022, https://apnews.com/article/elections-rome-italy-6aa9fcb003071c307190a4053f199d98
5. Carole Cadwalladr, 'Shahmir Sanni: "Nobody was called to account. But I lost almost everything"', *Observer*, 21 Jul 2018, https://www.theguardian.com/politics/2018/jul/21/shahmir-sanni-nobody-was-called-to-account-but-i-lost-almost-everything
6. Carole Cadwalladr, 'Brexit, the ministers, the professor and the spy: how Russia pulls strings in UK', *Observer*, 4 Nov 2017, https://www.theguardian.com/politics/2017/nov/04/brexit-ministers-spy-russia-uk-brexit

7   Tom Bawden, 'The address where Eurosceptics and climate change sceptics rub shoulders', *Independent*, 10 Feb 2016, https://www.independent.co.uk/news/uk/politics/eu-referendum-eurosceptics-climate-change-sceptics-55-tufton-street-westminster-a6866021.html
8   James Dale Davidson and Lord William Rees-Mogg, *The Sovereign Individual*, Simon & Schuster, 1999, https://www.simonandschuster.com/books/The-Sovereign-Individual/James-Dale-Davidson/9780684832722
9   Andy Beckett, 'How to explain Jacob Rees-Mogg? Start with his father's books', *Guardian*, 9 Nov 2018, https://www.theguardian.com/books/2018/nov/09/mystic-mogg-jacob-rees-mogg-willam-predicts-brexit-plans
10 Sam Bright, 'Liz Truss: the Tufton Street candidate', *Byline Times*, 18 Jan 2022, https://bylinetimes.com/2022/01/18/liz-truss-the-tufton-street-candidate/
11 Mat Hope, 'Brexit & climate science denial, the Tufton Street network', *Byline Times*, 10 Jun 2019, https://bylinetimes.com/2019/06/10/brexit-and-climate-science-denial-johnson-gove-and-raab-all-part-of-the-tufton-street-network/
12 'Centre for Policy Studies', Desmog, https://www.desmog.com/centre-policy-studies/
13 'BBC finally insists opaquely funded think tanks declare their interests', *Byline Times*, 30 Aug 2019, https://bylinetimes.com/2019/08/30/bbc-finally-insists-opaquely-funded-think-tanks-declare-their-interests/
14 Adam Curtis, 'The Curse of TINA', BBC News, 13 Sep 2011, https://www.bbc.co.uk/blogs/adamcurtis/entries/fdb484c8-99a1-32a3-83be-20108374b985
15 Tom Bawden, 'The address where Eurosceptics and climate change sceptics rub shoulders', *Independent*, 10 Feb 2016, https://www.independent.co.uk/news/uk/politics/eu-referendum-eurosceptics-climate-change-sceptics-55-tufton-street-westminster-a6866021.html
16 Matthew Lesh [@matthewlesh], Twitter, 23 Sep 2022, https://twitter.com/matthewlesh/status/1573219352622637056
17 'Awkward silence from Tories after Liz Truss claims Boris Johnson is "admired from Kyiv to Carlisle"', YouTube, 5 Sep 2022, https://www.youtube.com/watch?v=v7kOQoPz2Lk
18 'Factbox: Key quotes from Liz Truss's victory speech after winning UK leadership contest', *Reuters*, 5 Sep 2022, https://www.reuters.com/world/uk/key-quotes-liz-trusss-victory-speech-after-winning-uk-leadership-contest-2022-09-05/
19 'How the new nursing bursary works', Nurses.co.uk, 22 Oct 2020, https://www.nurses.co.uk/blog/how-the-new-nursing-bursary-works
20 Michael Savage, 'Stressed NHS staff in England quit at record 400 a week, fuelling fears over care quality', *Guardian*, 26 Feb 2022, https://www.theguardian.com/society/2022/feb/26/stressed-nhs-staff-quit-at-record-rate-of-400-a-week-fuelling-fears-over-care-quality
21 'Number of COVID-19 patients in hospital', Our World In Data, https://ourworldindata.org/grapher/current-covid-patients-hospital?country=GBR
22 Daniel Keane, 'Number of London nurses leaving NHS rises by 24% in a year', *Evening Standard*, 30 Sep 2022, https://www.standard.co.uk/news/london/number-of-london-nurses-leaving-nhs-rises-year-b1029266.html
23 Daniel Keane, 'Therese Coffey: Government "has already acted" to help nurses with cost of living', *Evening Standard*, 16 Oct 2022, https://www.standard.co.uk/news/health/therese-coffey-nurses-dont-need-pay-rise-government-helped-cost-living-b1032055.html
24 'What's the typical starting wage for a nurse in the UK in 2022?', Nurses.co.uk 1 Mar 2022, https://www.nurses.co.uk/blog/what-s-the-typical-starting-wage-for-a-nurse-in-the-uk-in-2022/
25 'Graduate Area Manager Programme', Aldi, https://www.aldirecruitment.co.uk/area-manager-programme/graduate-area-manager-programme
26 John Ely, 'Therese Coffey says nurses can LEAVE if they're unhappy about their pay as Health Secretary claims No10 has "already" helped with cost of living crisis', *Daily Mail*, 16 Oct 2022, https://www.dailymail.co.uk/health/article-11315195/Nurses-LEAVE-theyre-unhappy-pay-Health-Secretary-says.html
27 Ione Wells, 'New cabinet: Who is in Liz Truss's top team?', BBC News, 7 Sep 2022, https://www.bbc.co.uk/news/uk-politics-62796077

28. Christopher McKeon and Dan Bloom, 'Jacob Rees-Mogg's Tory donor pal handed LIFE-long Lords seat for just 26 days in government', *Mirror*, 31 Oct 2022, https://www.mirror.co.uk/news/politics/jacob-rees-moggs-tory-donor-28373131
29. 'Universal Credit calculator 2023: How much can I claim and how do I apply?', *Sun*, 3 Apr 2022, https://www.thesun.co.uk/money/10163368/universal-credit-calculator-how-much/
30. Rowena Mason, 'Jacob Rees-Mogg's business partner given senior ministerial role', *Guardian*, 2 Oct 2022, https://www.theguardian.com/politics/2022/oct/02/jacob-rees-mogg-business-partner-dominic-johnson-given-senior-minister-role
31. Susie Watkins, 'Tittle tattle – the Prime Minister always tells the truth – Midsomer Norton's Jacob Rees Mogg MP defends the PM', *Midsomer Norton*, 5 Jul 2022, https://midsomernorton.nub.news/news/local-news/tittle-tattle-the-prime-minister-always-tell-the-truth-midsomer-nortons-jacob-rees-mogg-mp-defends-the-pm-140491
32. 'Kwasi Kwarteng', UK Parliament, https://members.parliament.uk/member/4134/career
33. Peter Walker, 'Kwasi Kwarteng was logical choice as chancellor but hubris was his downfall', *Guardian*, 14 Oct 2022, https://www.theguardian.com/politics/2022/oct/14/kwasi-kwarteng-logical-choice-chancellor-hubris-downfall
34. Dylan Butts, 'New UK PM, finance minister have previously supported crypto, blockchain', *Forkast*, 7 Sep 2022, https://forkast.news/headlines/uk-pm-finance-minister-blockchain-crypto/
35. Will Taylor, 'The Queen gives rare glimpse of Balmoral drawing room complete with roaring fire before appointing Liz Truss as PM', LBC, 6 Sep 2022, https://www.lbc.co.uk/news/liz-truss-prime-minister-official/
36. Alain Tolhurst, 'Parliament may sit for extra days after Queen's death paused proceedings', *Civil Service World*, 15 Sept 2022, https://www.civilserviceworld.com/news/article/parliament-may-sit-for-extra-days-after-queens-death-paused-proceedings
37. Alistair Smout et al., 'PM Truss to accompany King Charles on tour of Britain to lead mourning', *Reuters*, 10 Sep 2022, https://www.reuters.com/world/uk/pm-truss-accompany-king-charles-tour-britain-lead-mourning-2022-09-10/
38. Jessica Elgot, 'Liz Truss will not accompany King Charles on UK tour, says No 10', *Guardian*, 11 Sep 2022, https://www.theguardian.com/uk-news/2022/sep/11/liz-truss-not-accompanying-king-charles-on-uk-tour-says-no-10
39. Dan Bloom, 'Liz Truss says her tax cuts are "fair" in front of big graph showing they help the rich', *Mirror*, 4 Sep 2022, https://www.mirror.co.uk/news/politics/liz-truss-says-tax-cuts-27903759
40. Esther Webber, 'UK's Liz Truss admits US trade deal out of reach', *Politico*, 20 Sep 2022, https://www.politico.eu/article/liz-truss-admits-us-trade-deal-out-of-reach/
41. 'UK-US trade deal', Trade Justice Movement, https://www.tjm.org.uk/trade-deals/a-uk-us-trade-deal
42. 'UK Perspectives 2016: Trade with the EU and beyond', ONS, 25 May 2016, https://www.ons.gov.uk/businessindustryandtrade/internationaltrade/articles/ukperspectives2016tradewiththeeuandbeyond/2016-05-25
43. Jack Peat, 'US considers suspending "special relationship" label after Liz Truss visit', *London Economic*, 23 Sep 2022, https://www.thelondoneconomic.com/politics/us-considers-suspending-special-relationship-label-after-liz-truss-visit-335751/
44. Dan Bloom, 'Top Tory Simon Clarke moans the Conservatives haven't had a "clear run" all decade', *Mirror*, 22 Sep 2022, https://www.mirror.co.uk/news/politics/top-tory-simon-clarke-moans-28053140
45. 'Simon Clarke', TheyWorkForYou, https://www.theyworkforyou.com/mp/25657/simon_clarke/middlesbrough_south_and_east_cleveland/votes
46. Michiel Williams, 'Senior Tory shrugs off partygate: Boris Johnson was given "a fine for eating a slice of cake between meetings"', *CityA.M.*, 23 May 2022, https://www.cityam.com/senior-tory-shrugs-off-partygate-boris-johnson-was-given-a-fine-for-eating-a-slice-of-cake-between-meetings/
47. Faisal Islam, 'Treasury refuses to publish UK economic forecast', BBC News, 20 Sep 2022, https://www.bbc.co.uk/news/business-62970803

48. Peter Walker, 'Tom Scholar, permanent secretary to the Treasury, sacked by Liz Truss', *Guardian*, 8 Sep 2022, https://www.theguardian.com/uk-news/2022/sep/08/tom-scholar-permanent-secretary-to-the-treasury-sacked-by-liz-truss
49. Toby Helm, Michael Savage and Kalyeena Makortoff, 'Ten days that shook the British political world: the inside story of Tory collapse', *Guardian*, 2 Oct 2022, https://www.theguardian.com/politics/2022/oct/02/ten-days-that-shook-the-british-political-world-the-inside-story-of-tory-collapse
50. Jennifer Scott, 'Who is Kwasi Kwarteng? The new chancellor who has been unafraid of upsetting his party', Sky News, 7 Sep 2022, https://news.sky.com/story/who-is-kwasi-kwarteng-the-new-chancellor-who-has-been-unafraid-of-upsetting-his-party-12690759
51. 'The Growth Plan 2022 speech', GOV.UK, 23 Sep 2022, https://www.gov.uk/government/speeches/the-growth-plan-2022-speech
52. 'Public sector net debt expressed as a percentage of gross domestic product in the United Kingdom from 1920/21 to 2021/22', Statista, 24 Aug 2022, https://www.statista.com/statistics/282841/debt-as-gdp-uk/
53. Rory Stewart, '"Being an MP was bad for my brain, body and soul": Rory Stewart on politics, privilege and podcast stardom', *Guardian*, 29 Aug 2022, https://www.theguardian.com/lifeandstyle/2022/aug/29/rory-stewart-politics-privilege-podcast-stardom
54. Aubrey Allegretti, 'Affordable housing provision in wider building projects could be ditched', *Guardian*, 21 Sep 2022, https://www.theguardian.com/politics/2022/sep/21/provision-of-affordable-housing-in-wider-building-project-could-be-ditched
55. Rob Merrick, 'Freeports of no economic benefit says Treasury watchdog, in damning verdict', *Independent*, 27 Oct 2021, https://www.independent.co.uk/news/uk/politics/freeports-office-budget-responsibility-sunak-b1946497.html
56. Richard Partington and Aubrey Allegretti, 'Kwasi Kwarteng's mini-budget: key points at a glance', *Guardian*, 23 Sep 2022, https://www.theguardian.com/uk-news/2022/sep/23/kwasi-kwarteng-mini-budget-key-points-at-a-glance
57. Craig Stirling, 'Fifty years of tax cuts for rich didn't trickle down, study says', *Bloomberg*, 16 Dec 2020, https://www.bloomberg.com/news/articles/2020-12-16/fifty-years-of-tax-cuts-for-rich-didn-t-trickle-down-study-says
58. Tim Shipman, Oliver Shah and Gabriel Pogrund, 'Kwasi Kwarteng's "budget day" cocktail party with financiers who may have profited from crash', *Sunday Times*, 1 Oct 2022, https://www.thetimes.co.uk/article/kwasi-kwartengs-budget-day-cocktail-party-with-financiers-who-may-have-profited-from-crash-kwdbs72g0
59. Tim Shipman, Harry Yorke and Caroline Wheeler, '"Biscotti mini-budget" exposes gulf between Liz Truss and Keir Starmer – and more tax cuts are on the cards', *The Times*, 24 Sep 2022, https://www.thetimes.co.uk/article/biscotti-mini-budget-exposes-gulf-between-liz-truss-and-keir-starmer-and-more-tax-cuts-are-on-the-cards-j2mj5zncs
60. Matt Mathers, 'Conservative Party receives £3.6m from hedge fund tycoons and finance firms', *Independent*, 29 Oct 2022, https://www.independent.co.uk/news/uk/politics/tory-party-donations-hedge-funds-b2197963.html
61. 'What is the International Space Station?', NASA, 30 Oct 2020, https://www.nasa.gov/audience/forstudents/5-8/features/nasa-knows/what-is-the-iss-58.html
62. Sagarika Jaisinghani, 'UK markets have lost $500 Billion since Liz Truss took over', *Bloomberg*, 27 Sep 2022, https://www.bloomberg.com/news/articles/2022-09-27/uk-markets-have-lost-500-billion-since-truss-took-over
63. Sam Bright [@WritesBright], Twitter, https://twitter.com/WritesBright/status/1574790996969267200
64. Freya Thomson, 'British pound sterling drops to record low', *Open Access Government*, 29 Sep 2022, https://www.openaccessgovernment.org/british-pound-sterling-drops-to-record-low/144564/
65. Bill McLoughlin, 'Treasury minister tweets "great to see sterling strengthening" moments before colossal slump', *Evening Standard*, 23 Sep 2022, https://www.standard.co.uk/news/politics/budget-politics-sterling-slump-chris-philp-b1027751.html
66. 'British pound breaks $2 barrier', *Al Jazeera*, 18 Apr 2007, https://www.aljazeera.com/news/2007/4/18/british-pound-breaks-2-barrier

67 Graeme Demianyk, 'Treasury Minister dunked on for premature celebration of rising pound', *HuffPost*, 23 Sep 2022, https://www.huffingtonpost.co.uk/entry/chris-philp-pound-twitter_uk_632dd5e2e4b00e36d1af0e92
68 Tommy Stubbington, Josephine Cumbo and Chris Flood, 'How Kwasi Kwarteng's mini-Budget broke the UK bond market', *Financial Times*, 28 Sep 2022, https://www.ft.com/content/4e6b89a3-a63e-49df-8a04-0488b69e84f5
69 Jon Stone, 'How Kwasi Kwarteng's budget damaged the economy and what will happen now', *Independent*, 30 Sep 2022, https://www.independent.co.uk/news/uk/politics/kwasi-kwarteng-pound-mini-budget-b2182460.html
70 Larry Elliott, 'IMF criticises Kwarteng again over tax cuts and energy package', *Guardian*, 11 Oct 2022, https://www.theguardian.com/business/2022/oct/11/imf-criticises-kwasi-kwarteng-tax-cuts-energy-inflation
71 Harvey Jones, 'Bank of England steps in to stop £1.5 trillion pensions meltdown – 20m pensioners at risk', *Express*, 29 Sep 2022, https://www.express.co.uk/finance/personalfinance/1675372/Bank-of-England-pensions-defined-benefit-schemes-financial-crisis-Kwasi-Kwarteng
72 Patrick Tooher, 'Former Chancellor Kwasi Kwarteng's Budget fire sale has cost pensions £75bn, according to a report by a US investment bank', *Financial Mail on Sunday*, 5 Nov 2022, https://www.msn.com/en-gb/money/other/former-chancellor-kwasi-kwarteng-s-budget-fire-sale-has-cost-pensions-75bn-according-to-a-report-by-a-us-investment-bank/ar-AA13MvzO?ocid=msedgntp&cvid=73a8ec1a41fd4a5d9e1af2ba18360e46
73 Jonathan Portes, '"Factual errors" and "slipshod research" – the Britannia Unchained Tories must try harder', *New Statesman*, 13 Sept 2012, https://www.newstatesman.com/business/economics/2012/09/factual-errors-and-slipshod-research-britannia-unchained-tories-must-try-hard
74 Ben Riley-Smith, Nick Gutteridge and Tony Diver, 'How Truss and Kwarteng were warned of danger before the pound nosedived', *Telegraph*, 28 Sep 2022, https://www.telegraph.co.uk/politics/2022/09/28/how-truss-kwarteng-warned-danger-pound-nosedived/
75 Rowena Mason and Phillip Inman, 'Kwasi Kwarteng refuses to let OBR release forecasts with mini-budget', *Guardian*, 20 Sep 2022, https://www.theguardian.com/politics/2022/sep/20/kwasi-kwarteng-urged-to-allow-release-of-obr-forecasts-with-mini-budget
76 Dan Ladden-Hall, 'New British PM Liz Truss' first month in power is officially a record-breaking sh*tshow', *Yahoo! Money*, Oct 2022, https://money.yahoo.com/truss-first-month-power-officially-155735611.html
77 Tim Shipman, Harry Yorke and Caroline Wheeler, '"Biscotti mini-budget" exposes gulf between Liz Truss and Keir Starmer – and more tax cuts are on the cards', *The Times*, 24 Sep 2022, https://www.thetimes.co.uk/article/biscotti-mini-budget-exposes-gulf-between-liz-truss-and-keir-starmer-and-more-tax-cuts-are-on-the-cards-j2mj5zncs
78 Jim Pickard [@PickardJE], Twitter, 23 Sep 2022, https://twitter.com/PickardJE/status/1573376413368975361
79 Michael Savage, '"It's extraordinary": Liz Truss's low-tax gamble has yet to convince Tory MPs', *Guardian*, 24 Sep 2022, https://www.theguardian.com/politics/2022/sep/24/its-extraordinary-liz-trusss-low-tax-gamble-has-yet-to-convince-tory-mps
80 Tom Sanders, 'Senior Tory claims MPs are already writing letters of no confidence in Liz Truss', *Metro*, 26 Sep 2022, https://metro.co.uk/2022/09/26/senior-tory-claims-mps-are-already-plotting-to-get-rid-of-liz-truss-17450187/
81 Dan Bloom, 'Where is Liz Truss? PM "missing" as UK descends into chaos after disastrous mini-budget', *Mirror*, 28 Sep 2022, https://www.mirror.co.uk/news/politics/liz-truss-pm-missing-uk-28105984
82 Rowena Mason and Jessica Elgot, 'Truss and Kwarteng had row over sterling crisis response, say Whitehall sources', *Guardian*, 27 Sep 2022, https://www.theguardian.com/politics/2022/sep/27/no-10-denies-row-between-truss-and-kwarteng-over-sterling-crisis-response
83 Liz Truss [@lizztruss], Twitter, 26 Sep 2022, https://twitter.com/trussliz/status/1574476937015304192

84 Rowena Mason, 'Liz Truss faces questions over Foreign Office spending', *Guardian*, 23 Sep 2022, https://www.theguardian.com/politics/2022/sep/23/liz-truss-questions-foreign-office-spending-hair-norwich-city
85 'Liz Truss "painted over" Boris Johnson's £840-a-roll No 10 gold wallpaper, says Jeremy Hunt', *Telegraph*, 24 Nov 2022, https://www.telegraph.co.uk/politics/2022/11/24/liz-truss-painted-boris-johnsons-840-a-roll-no-10-gold-wallpaper/
86 Ala Evans, 'Liz Truss spent £500,000 of taxpayers' money on a private flight to Australia', *JOE*, 27 Jan 2022, https://www.joe.co.uk/news/liz-truss-spent-500000-of-taxpayers-money-on-a-private-flight-to-australia-313876
87 Aubrey Allegretti, 'Liz Truss travel bill in last months as foreign secretary hit nearly £2m', *Guardian*, 9 Oct 2022, https://www.theguardian.com/politics/2022/oct/09/liz-truss-foreign-secretary-overseas-trips-cost
88 Rowena Mason, 'Liz Truss faces questions over Foreign Office spending', *Guardian*, 23 Sep 2022, https://www.theguardian.com/politics/2022/sep/23/liz-truss-questions-foreign-office-spending-hair-norwich-city
89 Gabriel Pogrund, 'Liz Truss chief of staff Mark Fullbrook is paid through his lobbying company', *The Times*, 24 Sep 2022, https://www.thetimes.co.uk/article/top-liz-truss-aide-mark-fullbrook-paid-through-his-private-company-b90hdkj5z
90 Gabriel Pogrund [@Gabriel_Pogrund], Twitter, 24 Sep 2022, https://twitter.com/Gabriel_Pogrund/status/1573738991685353473
91 Joshua Nevett, 'Chancellor Kwasi Kwarteng to set out debt plan earlier than planned', BBC News, 4 Oct 2022, https://www.bbc.co.uk/news/uk-politics-63123880
92 Rebecca Cook, 'GMB's Susanna Reid grills Tory MP on tax cuts for the wealthy in heated exchange', *Mirror*, 26 Sep 2022, https://www.mirror.co.uk/tv/tv-news/gmbs-susanna-reid-grills-tory-28080524
93 Peter Walker and Patrick Butler, 'Ministers consider plan to ease £20-a-week universal credit cut', *Guardian*, 23 Sept 2021, https://www.theguardian.com/society/2021/sep/23/ministers-consider-plan-to-ease-20-a-week-universal-credit-cut
94 Esther Addley, 'Nothing to see here: Truss allies' curious excuses for financial meltdown', *Guardian*, 29 Sep 2022, https://www.theguardian.com/politics/2022/sep/29/truss-allies-excuses-financial-meltdown-economy-pound
95 LBC [@lbc], Twitter, 27 Sep 2022, https://twitter.com/LBC/status/1574793344810713092
96 Oliver Gill, 'Remainers are to blame for the run on the pound, claims hedge fund tycoon Crispin Odey', *Telegraph*, 27 Sept 2022, https://www.telegraph.co.uk/business/2022/09/27/remainers-blame-run-pound-claims-hedge-fund-tycoon-crispin-odey/
97 Kalyeena Makortoff, 'Tory donor says bets against UK government bonds "gifts that keep giving"', *Guardian*, 27 Sept 2022, https://www.theguardian.com/business/2022/sep/27/tory-donor-says-bets-against-uk-government-bonds-gifts-that-keep-giving
98 Graeme Demianyk, 'Tory peer Lord Frost doesn't think "anything has gone wrong", as pound touches record low', *HuffPost*, 26 Sep 2022, https://www.huffingtonpost.co.uk/entry/lord-frost-pound-mini-budget_uk_63320402e4b00f7fcb5571d6
99 Dominic McGrath, 'Fears of Labour Government caused market turmoil, claims Tory peer Daniel Hannan', *Evening Standard*, 28 Sep 2022, https://www.standard.co.uk/news/politics/daniel-hannan-comment-conservative-home-labour-keir-starmer-government-b1028697.html
100 Phillip Inman, 'More than 40% of mortgages withdrawn as market reels after mini-budget', *Guardian*, 29 Sep 2022, https://www.theguardian.com/business/2022/sep/29/mortgages-withdrawn-housing-market-mini-budget-lenders-economic-uncertainty
101 Padraig Prendergast, 'Just what is a AAA rating and why did the UK lose it?', BBC News, 28 Jun 2016, https://www.bbc.co.uk/news/newsbeat-36652494
102 Wayne Cole, 'Moody's warns UK unfunded tax cuts are "credit negative"', *Reuters*, 28 Sep 2022, https://www.reuters.com/world/uk/moodys-warns-uk-unfunded-tax-cuts-are-credit-negative-2022-09-28/
103 Steve Goldstein, 'New Truss government is like a doomsday cult, UBS economist says', *MarketWatch*, 26 Sep 2022, https://www.marketwatch.com/story/new-truss-government-is-like-a-doomsday-cult-ubs-economist-says-11664201615

104 Lizzie Dearden, 'Home secretary tells police she "expects" them to cut murders by 20% – but does not say how', *Independent*, 24 Sep 2022, https://www.independent.co.uk/news/uk/politics/suella-braverman-police-crime-targets-b2174238.html
105 Mark Townsend, 'Revealed: Suella Braverman sets Home Office "No boats crossing the Channel" target', *Guardian*, 10 Sep 2022, https://www.theguardian.com/politics/2022/sep/10/revealed-suella-braverman-sets-home-office-no-boats-crossing-the-channel-target
106 Rachael Molitor, 'Love Island: the psychological challenges contestants – and viewers – could face after the show is over', *The Conversation*, 2 Aug 2022, https://theconversation.com/love-island-the-psychological-challenges-contestants-and-viewers-could-face-after-the-show-is-over-187948
107 Peter Walker, 'Coffey urges staff to be positive, be precise, and not use Oxford commas', *Guardian*, 15 Sep 2022, https://www.theguardian.com/politics/2022/sep/15/coffey-urges-staff-to-be-positive-be-precise-and-not-use-oxford-commas
108 Nick Triggle, 'GP waiting time target "scrapped"', BBC News, 21 June 2010, https://www.bbc.co.uk/news/10364566
109 'Guide to NHS waiting times in England', NHS, 2 Dec 2019, https://www.nhs.uk/nhs-services/hospitals/guide-to-nhs-waiting-times-in-england/
110 Andrew Woodcock, 'More than 22,000 EU nationals have left NHS since Brexit referendum, figures', *Independent*, 10 Dec 2019, https://www.independent.co.uk/news/uk/politics/brexit-eu-citizens-nhs-crisis-migration-boris-johnson-hospital-health-a9239791.html
111 John Burn-Murdoch, 'Britons now have the worst access to healthcare in Europe, and it shows', *Financial Times*, 4 Nov 2022, https://www.ft.com/content/de8fc348-0025-4821-9ec5-d50b4bbacc8d
112 'Number of patients waiting more than 18 weeks for NHS treatment at highest in over a decade', Royal College of Surgeons of England, 12 Sep 2019, https://www.rcseng.ac.uk/news-and-events/media-centre/press-releases/nhs-performance-data-rtt-july-2019/
113 'NHS backlog data analysis', BMA, Oct 2022, https://www.bma.org.uk/advice-and-support/nhs-delivery-and-workforce/pressures/nhs-backlog-data-analysis
114 Jessica Elgot, 'PR agencies bidding for UK Covid inquiry risk "farcical conflict of interest"', *Guardian*, 20 Sep 2022, https://www.theguardian.com/society/2022/sep/20/pr-agencies-bidding-uk-covid-inquiry-potential-conflict-interest
115 Jessica Elgot, 'Bereaved families to ask Covid contract PR firms not to bid for inquiry work', *Guardian*, 14 Oct 2022, https://www.theguardian.com/uk-news/2022/oct/14/covid-inquiry-pr-firms-families-urge-tender-process-withdrawal
116 Denis Campbell, 'Thérèse Coffey scraps promised paper on health inequality', *Guardian*, 29 Sep 2022, https://www.theguardian.com/politics/2022/sep/29/therese-coffey-scraps-promised-paper-on-health-inequality
117 Andrew Gregory, 'Growing gap in healthy life expectancy between poorest and richest in England', *Guardian*, 25 Apr 2022, https://www.theguardian.com/society/2022/apr/25/growing-gap-in-healthy-life-expectancy-between-poorest-and-richest-in-england
118 Denis Campbell, 'Thérèse Coffey scraps promised paper on health inequality', *Guardian*, 29 Sep 2022, https://www.theguardian.com/politics/2022/sep/29/therese-coffey-scraps-promised-paper-on-health-inequality
119 Adam Forrest, 'Brexit "opportunities" role ditched with no replacement for Jacob Rees-Mogg', *Independent*, 7 Sep 2022, https://www.independent.co.uk/independentpremium/uk-news/brexit-opportunities-jacob-rees-mogg-b2162781.html
120 Helena Horton, 'Rees-Mogg: "Britain must get every cubic inch of gas out of North Sea"', *Guardian*, 23 Sep 2022, https://www.theguardian.com/politics/2022/sep/23/rees-mogg-tells-staff-britain-must-get-every-cubic-inch-gas-out-of-north-sea
121 Jacob Paul, 'Rees-Mogg officially lifts UK fracking ban as he savages Putin's "weaponisation of energy"', *Express*, 22 Sep 2022, https://www.express.co.uk/news/science/1672698/jacob-rees-mogg-fracking-earthquakes-energy-crisis-bills-gas
122 Helena Horton, 'Fracking caused daily earthquakes at UK's only active site', *Guardian*, 19 Oct 2022, https://www.theguardian.com/environment/2022/oct/19/fracking-caused-daily-earthquakes-at-uks-only-active-site

123 Adam Bienkov [@AdamBienkov], Twitter, https://twitter.com/AdamBienkov/status/1572910961941684225
124 Nafeez Ahmed, 'Fracking minister funded by fossil fuel investor', *Byline Times*, 22 Sep 2022, https://bylinetimes.com/2022/09/22/fracking-minister-funded-by-fossil-fuel-investor/
125 Jon Ungoed-Thomas, 'Jacob Rees-Mogg's imperial measurements consultation "biased" after no option given to say no', *Guardian*, 18 Sep 2022, https://www.theguardian.com/politics/2022/sep/18/metric-system-imperial-measures-consultation-brexit
126 Steven Swinford, 'Pay pain for workers as public sector squeezed', *The Times*, 26 Sep 2022, https://www.thetimes.co.uk/article/pay-pain-for-workers-as-public-sector-squeezed-spcfnhkf0
127 Sam Coates [@SamCoatesSky], Twitter, 29 Sep 2022, https://twitter.com/SamCoatesSky/status/1575553979286958080
128 Millie Cookie, 'Big beast Tory MPs poised to boycott own conference as Sunak tells Truss to "own moment"', *Express*, 28 Sep 2022, https://www.express.co.uk/news/politics/1675352/rishi-sunak-liz-truss-conservative-party-conference-chancellor-torkshire
129 Peter Walker and Pippa Crerar, 'Truss says she has "right plan" on economy and will not change course', *Guardian*, 29 Sep 2022, https://www.theguardian.com/politics/2022/sep/29/truss-says-she-has-right-plan-on-economy-mini-budget
130 '"Repeatedly misleading": Fact-checkers call out Liz Truss's claim no one will pay more than £2,500 on energy', *Sky News*, 29 Sep 2022, https://news.sky.com/story/repeatedly-misleading-fact-checkers-call-out-liz-trusss-claim-no-one-will-pay-more-than-2-500-on-energy-12707677
131 Peter Walker and Pippa Crerar, 'Truss says she has "right plan" on economy and will not change course', *Guardian*, 29 Sep 2022, https://www.theguardian.com/politics/2022/sep/29/truss-says-she-has-right-plan-on-economy-mini-budget
132 Valentina Romei, 'UK remains only G7 economy to languish below pre-pandemic levels', *Financial Times*, 30 Sep 2022, https://www.ft.com/content/4edae69b-c82d-49fb-ae5a-03d14ca8caa6
133 Alastair Lockhart, 'Tory party would win just THREE seats under Liz Truss if an election was held today, as Starmer's Labour storms ahead with 33-point lead, new poll shows', *Daily Mail*, 29 Sep 2022, https://www.dailymail.co.uk/news/article-11264115/Tories-win-just-THREE-seats-Liz-Truss-election-held-today-Labour-storm-ahead.html
134 Xander Elliards, 'Tory MPs round on Liz Truss and Kwasi Kwarteng as UK enters economic crisis', *The National*, 28 Sep 2022, https://www.thenational.scot/news/22800913.tory-mps-round-liz-truss-kwasi-kwarteng-uk-enters-economic-crisis/
135 George Parker et al., 'Tory MPs question Kwasi Kwarteng's future as market turmoil continues', *Financial Times*, 28 Sep 2022, https://www.ft.com/content/a46e53bb-e23d-4450-a70e-05f71d2e57ef
136 Nick Gutteridge, '1922 Committee rules: How Tory MPs could oust Liz Truss', *Telegraph*, 13 Oct 2022, https://www.telegraph.co.uk/politics/2022/10/13/tory-mps-plotting-coronation-new-leader-replace-liz-truss/
137 Rowena Mason and Aubrey Allegretti, 'Tory MPs furious with Liz Truss and Kwasi Kwarteng as pound crashes', *Guardian*, 26 Sep 2022, https://www.theguardian.com/politics/2022/sep/26/kwasi-kwarteng-refuses-to-comment-as-pound-hits-all-time-low-against-dollar
138 'Liz Truss commits to "absolutely" no cuts to public spending at PMQs – video', *Guardian*, 12 Oct 2022, https://www.theguardian.com/politics/video/2022/oct/12/liz-truss-commits-to-absolutely-no-cuts-to-public-spending-at-pmqs-video
139 Sam Coates, 'Cabinet to be asked to find "efficiency savings" in Whitehall despite Truss promising no cuts', *Sky News*, 28 Sep 2022, https://news.sky.com/story/cabinet-to-be-asked-to-find-efficiency-savings-in-whitehall-despite-truss-promising-no-cuts-12707062
140 Sam Coates [@SamCoatesSky], Twitter, 28 Sep 2022, https://twitter.com/samcoatessky/status/1575157707421601799
141 Vicky Shaw, 'The Treasury deletes tweet after Martin Lewis hit out at "irresponsible" first-time buyer messaging', *WalesOnline*, 3 Oct 2022, https://www.walesonline.co.uk/news/cost-of-living/martin-lewis-hits-out-irresponsible-25163097

142 Gavin Cordon, 'Liz Truss and Kwasi Kwarteng double down on mini-budget as Chancellor visits Darlington', *Chronicle Live*, 29 Sep 2022, https://www.chroniclelive.co.uk/news/north-east-news/kwasi-kwarteng-darlington-liz-truss-25141641
143 Holly Patrick, 'Liz Truss "prepared to be unpopular" with plans to "grow British economy"', *Independent*, 28 Sep 2022, https://www.independent.co.uk/tv/news/liz-truss-british-economy-plans-b2171353.html
144 Greg Evans, 'Liz Truss left speechless after being asked: "How many people voted for your plan?"', *Indy100*, 2 Oct 2022, https://www.indy100.com/politics/liz-truss-kuennsberg-voted-plan
145 Adam Forrest, 'Kwasi Kwarteng admits losing sleep over market chaos he failed to anticipate', *Independent*, 2 Oct 2022, https://www.independent.co.uk/news/uk/politics/kwasi-kwarteng-economy-pound-markets-b2190852.html
146 Paul Seddon, 'I told Liz Truss she was going too fast, says Kwasi Kwarteng', BBC News, 11 Nov 2022, https://www.bbc.co.uk/news/uk-politics-63592909
147 Adam Forrest, 'Kwasi Kwarteng admits losing sleep over market chaos he failed to anticipate', *Independent*, 2 Oct 2022, https://www.independent.co.uk/news/uk/politics/kwasi-kwarteng-economy-pound-markets-b2190852.html
148 Zoe Gardner [@ZoeJardiniere], Twitter, 29 Sep 2022, https://twitter.com/ZoeJardiniere/status/1575360674124947456
149 Steven Swinford, 'Simon Clarke interview: "Truss is enjoying her chance to pull Britain out of its fool's paradise"', *The Times*, 20 Sep 2022, https://www.thetimes.co.uk/article/simon-clarke-interview-truss-is-enjoying-her-chance-to-pull-britain-out-of-its-fools-paradise-rndrm9kn6
150 Tamara Cohen, 'Liz Truss's U-turn on 45p tax rate for highest earners will embolden her many critics in the Tory party', Sky News, 3 Oct 2022, https://news.sky.com/story/liz-trusss-u-turn-on-45p-tax-rate-for-highest-earners-will-embolden-her-many-critics-in-the-tory-party-12711039
151 Douglas Ross [@Douglas4Moray], Twitter, 23 Sep 2022, https://twitter.com/douglas4moray/status/1573317413772427265
152 Number of people receiving three days' worth of emergency food by Trussell Trust foodbanks in the United Kingdom from 2008/09 to 2021/22, Statista, https://www.statista.com/statistics/382695/uk-foodbank-users/
153 Gareth Davies, 'Jake Berry: I regret telling people worried about bills to get better jobs', *Telegraph*, 6 Oct 2022, https://www.telegraph.co.uk/politics/2022/10/06/jake-berry-regret-telling-people-worried-bills-get-better-jobs/
154 Jon Stone, 'Tory minister on £115k salary says workers must accept "pay restraint" to control inflation', *Independent*, 27 Jul 2022, https://www.independent.co.uk/news/uk/politics/tory-minister-pay-restraint-salary-rmt-rail-strike-b2132276.html
155 Sky News [@SkyNews], Twitter, 4 Oct 2022, https://twitter.com/SkyNews/status/1577226553154576385
156 Kitty Donaldson, 'Truss says it was Kwarteng who decided to cut UK's top tax rate', *Bloomberg*, 2 Oct 2022, https://www.bloomberg.com/news/articles/2022-10-02/truss-says-her-government-mishandled-announcement-on-uk-tax-cuts
157 Pippa Crerar [@PippaCrerar], Twitter, 3 Oct 2022 https://twitter.com/pippacrerar/status/1576819652902400000
158 George Parker [@GeorgeWParker], Twitter, 3 Oct 2022, https://twitter.com/GeorgeWParker/status/1576823678331138050
159 Harrison Jones, 'Young Tory told to get out of Birmingham after calling it a dump', *Metro*, 2 Oct 2022, https://metro.co.uk/2022/10/02/young-conservative-told-to-leave-birmingham-after-branding-it-a-dump-17489103/
160 Snigdha[@snigskitchen], Twitter, 1 Oct 2022, https://twitter.com/snigskitchen/status/1576185285129314304
161 Zoe Beaty, 'Why did Liz Truss wear the same outfit as a fictional fascist?', *Guardian*, 5 Oct 2022, https://www.theguardian.com/politics/shortcuts/2022/oct/05/dictator-chic-why-did-liz-truss-wear-the-same-outfit-as-a-fictional-fascist
162 'Party Chairman Jake Berry at #CPC22 | We're Getting Britain Moving', YouTube, 5 Oct 2022, https://www.youtube.com/watch?v=3d7fRwxIbT4

163 'Full text: Liz Truss's Tory conference speech', *Spectator*, 5 Oct 2022, https://www.spectator.co.uk/article/full-text-liz-truss-s-tory-conference-speech/
164 Rowena Mason, 'Liz Truss promises "growth, growth and growth" in protest-hit speech', *Guardian*, 5 Oct 2022, https://www.theguardian.com/politics/2022/oct/05/liz-truss-says-she-wants-growth-growth-and-growth-in-protest-hit-speech-tory-conference
165 Maria Elena Vizgaino, 'UK's credit outlook cut to negative by Fitch on fiscal risk', *Bloomberg*, 5 Oct 2022, https://www.bloomberg.com/news/articles/2022-10-05/uk-s-credit-outlook-cut-to-negative-by-fitch-on-fiscal-risk
166 'Full text: Liz Truss's Tory conference speech', *Spectator*, 5 Oct 2022, https://www.spectator.co.uk/article/full-text-liz-truss-s-tory-conference-speech/
167 'The Moggcast', *Apple Podcasts*, https://podcasts.apple.com/gb/podcast/the-moggcast/id1335312124
168 'Full text: Liz Truss's Tory conference speech', *Spectator*, 5 Oct 2022, https://www.spectator.co.uk/article/full-text-liz-truss-s-tory-conference-speech/
169 Nadine Dorries [@NadineDorries], Twitter, 6 Sep 2022, https://twitter.com/NadineDorries/status/1567077192798015489
170 Liam James, 'Former minister calls Truss's plans "cruel" and warns over "lurch to the right"', *Independent*, 5 Oct 2022, https://www.independent.co.uk/news/uk/politics/nadine-dorries-liz-truss-b2196547.html
171 Sami Quadri, 'Nadine Dorries suggests Liz Truss should call election as she doesn't have mandate', *Evening Standard*, 3 Oct 2022, https://www.standard.co.uk/news/politics/nadine-dorries-liz-truss-general-election-conservative-party-labour-no-mandate-b1029834.html
172 Peter Davidson, 'Liz Truss blames Chancellor Kwasi Kwarteng for decision to slash income tax for rich', *Daily Record*, 2 Oct 2022, https://www.dailyrecord.co.uk/news/politics/liz-truss-blames-chancellor-kwasi-28134259
173 Ashley Cowburn, 'Michael Gove attacks Liz Truss's tax cuts for richest Brits as "display of wrong values"', *Mirror*, 2 Oct 2022, https://www.mirror.co.uk/news/politics/michael-gove-attacks-liz-trusss-28133755
174 Matt Dathan [@matt_dathan], Twitter, 4 Oct 2022, https://twitter.com/matt_dathan/status/1577269259696209921
175 Martina Bet, 'Badenoch urges colleagues: We need to have dissent in a grown-up fashion', *Evening Standard*, 3 Oct 2022, https://www.standard.co.uk/news/politics/kemi-badenoch-birmingham-prime-minister-michael-gove-government-b1029920.html
176 Archie Bland, '"Arghhhhhhhhh": the 10 angriest Tories at Conservative conference', *Guardian*, 5 Oct 2022, https://www.theguardian.com/politics/2022/oct/05/arghhhhhhhhh-the-10-angriest-tories-at-conservative-conference
177 Julian Smith [@JulianSmithUK], Twitter, 27 Sep 2022, https://mobile.twitter.com/JulianSmithUK/status/1574888103298441223
178 Michael Savage, 'Liz Truss approval ratings reach new lows after Tory conference', *Guardian*, 8 Oct 2022, https://www.theguardian.com/politics/2022/oct/08/liz-truss-approval-ratings-reach-new-lows-after-tory-conference
179 'Cabinet minister Liz Truss "overheard saying Sajid Javid or Jeremy Hunt will replace Theresa May and everyone hates Michael Gove"', *Independent*, 4 Dec 2018, https://www.independent.co.uk/news/uk/politics/liz-truss-theresa-may-sajid-javid-jeremy-hunt-michael-gove-cabinet-brexit-conservatives-brexit-a8666971.html
180 The News Agents [@TheNewsAgents], Twitter, 4 Oct 2022, https://twitter.com/TheNewsAgents/status/1577341771004231687
181 'Cocaine found in toilets at the Conservative Party conference during raucous parties', *Daily Record*, 9 Oct 2022, https://www.dailyrecord.co.uk/news/scottish-news/cocaine-found-toilets-conservative-party-28189687
182 Stefan Boscia, 'Minister says Rees-Mogg wants to ditch "all business regulations" for SMEs', *CityA.M.*, 2 Oct 2022, https://www.cityam.com/minister-says-rees-mogg-wants-to-ditch-all-business-regulations-for-smes/
183 David Lynch, 'UK's first prototype fusion energy plant to be built by 2040 – Rees-Mogg', *Evening Standard*, 3 Oct 2022, https://www.standard.co.uk/tech/science/jacob-reesmogg-conservative-party-birmingham-david-lynch-oxfordshire-b1029912.html

184 Rob Edwards, 'Brexit threat to nuclear safety laws', *The Ferret*, 13 Nov 2022, https://theferret.scot/brexit-threat-nuclear-safety-laws/
185 Peter Walker and Helena Horton, 'Rees-Mogg seeking to evade scrutiny of new fracking projects, email shows', *Guardian*, 4 Oct 2022, https://www.theguardian.com/politics/2022/oct/04/jacob-rees-mogg-fracking-email-hse
186 Peter Foster, Jim Pickard and George Parker, 'Liz Truss quashes Jacob Rees-Mogg's "half-baked" labour market reforms', *Financial Times*, 3 Oct 2022, https://www.ft.com/content/799ed62c-86bc-469d-a442-d1553c6e47ec
187 'Jacob Rees-Mogg says he doesn't mind being called "Tory scum" – video', *Guardian*, 3 Oct 2022, https://www.theguardian.com/politics/video/2022/oct/03/jacob-rees-mogg-does-not-mind-being-called-tory-scum-video
188 Dan Bloom, 'Universal Credit claimants who already have a job "should be working", top Tory moans', *Mirror*, 5 Oct 2022, https://www.mirror.co.uk/news/politics/universal-credit-claimants-who-already-28157717
189 Anoosh Chakelian, 'Britain braces itself for the devastation of austerity 2.0', *New Statesman*, 6 Oct 2022, https://www.newstatesman.com/society/2022/10/uk-austerity-measures-meaning-devastation
190 Lizzie Dearden, 'Suella Braverman says it is her "dream" and "obsession" to see a flight take asylum seekers to Rwanda', *Independent*, 5 Oct 2022, https://www.independent.co.uk/news/uk/politics/suella-braverman-rwanda-dream-obsession-b2195296.html
191 'Do any European countries send asylum seekers to Rwanda?', Full Fact, 30 Mar 2023, https://fullfact.org/news/sir-jake-berry-asylum-seekers-rwanda/
192 'UNHCR: UK's migration partnership with Rwanda is unlawful and incompatible with the Refugee Convention', Electronic Immigration Network, 10 Jun 2022, https://www.ein.org.uk/news/unhcr-uks-migration-partnership-rwanda-unlawful-and-incompatible-refugee-convention
193 Kevin Schofield, 'Suella Braverman insists Rwanda is safe despite deaths of 12 refugees', *HuffPost*, 2 Apr 2023, https://www.huffingtonpost.co.uk/entry/suella-braverman-insists-rwanda-is-safe-country-despite-12-protester-deaths_uk_642947dce4b00c95175297f7
194 Lizzie Dearden, 'Revealed: Suella Braverman's trips to Rwanda to teach government lawyers', *Independent*, 27 Nov 2022, https://www.independent.co.uk/news/uk/politics/suella-braverman-rwanda-law-migrants-b2233102.html
195 Barney Davis, 'Suella Braverman accused of faking contribution to law textbook when "all she was asked to do was photocopy"', *Evening Standard*, 4 Oct 2022, https://www.standard.co.uk/news/politics/suella-braverman-accused-faking-contribution-law-textbook-b1030013.html
196 Sam Freedman[@Samfr], Twitter, 3 Oct 2022, https://twitter.com/samfr/status/1576918288025767936
197 Peter Walker[@peterwalker99], Twitter, 3 Oct 2022, https://twitter.com/peterwalker99/status/1576976672930136064
198 Adam Forrest, 'Tory members "subjected to disgusting homophobic abuse" at LGBT event', *Independent*, 6 Oct 2022, https://www.independent.co.uk/news/uk/politics/tories-conference-lgbt-homophobia-abuse-b2196724.html
199 Michael Savage and Miranda Bryant, 'Conor Burns sacked after being seen "touching young man's thigh", witness says', *Observer*, 8 Oct 2022, https://www.theguardian.com/politics/2022/oct/08/conor-burns-sacked-after-being-seen-touching-young-mans-thigh-witness-says
200 Sophie Zeldin-O'Neill, 'Tory whip restored to Conor Burns after being cleared of misconduct', *Guardian*, 3 Dec 2022, https://www.theguardian.com/politics/2022/dec/03/tory-whip-restored-conor-burns-conservative-party
201 LGBT+ Conservatives [@LGBTCons], Twitter, 7 Oct 2022, https://twitter.com/LGBTCons/status/1578413980342632452
202 Andrew Goldman, 'Bournemouth West MP Conor Burns sacked as trade minister', *Daily Echo*, 8 Oct 2022, https://www.bournemouthecho.co.uk/news/23031761.bournemouth-west-mp-conor-burns-whip-suspended/
203 'Tobias Ellwood suspended as Tory MP after missing confidence vote', BBC News, 19 Jul 2022, https://www.bbc.co.uk/news/uk-politics-62221445

204 Caroline Wheeler, Tim Shipman, Harry Yorke and Gabriel Pogrund, 'Conor Burns, minister sacked for misconduct claims, is on track for knighthood from Boris Johnson', *The Times*, 8 Oct 2022, https://www.thetimes.co.uk/article/conor-burns-minister-sacked-for-misconduct-claims-is-on-track-for-knighthood-from-boris-johnson-5v2tpdszh

205 Melanie Brown MBE [@OfficialMelB], Twitter, 7 Oct, https://twitter.com/OfficialMelB/status/1578487276707143682

206 Miranda Bryant, 'Mel B challenges sacked Tory minister over "what you said to me in lift"', *Guardian*, 8 Oct 2022, https://www.theguardian.com/politics/2022/oct/08/mel-b-tweets-sacked-tory-minister-conor-burns-about-lift-incident

207 'Voting Intention: Con 22%, Lab 52% (6-7 Oct 2022)', YouGov, 8 Oct 2022, https://yougov.co.uk/topics/politics/articles-reports/2022/10/08/voting-intention-con-22-lab-52-6-7-oct-2022

208 David Wilcock, 'UK-India free trade deal "on the verge of collapse" after "disrespectful" Home Secretary Suella Braverman sparks outrage in Delhi with attack on Indian migrants saying they are worst offenders for overstaying their visas', *Daily Mail*, 12 Oct 2022, https://www.dailymail.co.uk/news/article-11307029/UK-India-free-trade-deal-verge-collapse-Suella-Braverman-blasts-Indian-migrants.html

209 Lizzie Dearden, 'Suella Braverman scraps year-long recruitment process for modern slavery watchdog', *Independent*, 9 Jan 2023, https://www.independent.co.uk/news/uk/home-news/modern-slavery-watchdog-braverman-migrants-b2258937.html

210 Lizzie Dearden, 'Suella Braverman's modern slavery "abuse" claims questioned by former watchdog', *Independent*, 5 Oct 2022, https://www.independent.co.uk/news/uk/politics/suella-braverman-modern-slavery-abuse-b2195548.html

211 Rajeev Syal, 'Liz Truss plans more immigration in effort to fill vacancies and drive growth', *Guardian*, 25 Sep 2022, https://www.theguardian.com/uk-news/2022/sep/25/liz-truss-plans-more-immigration-in-effort-to-fill-vacancies-and-drive-growth

212 Rajeev Syal, 'Suella Braverman revives Tory pledge to cut net migration to "tens of thousands"', *Guardian*, 4 Oct 2022, https://www.theguardian.com/politics/2022/oct/04/suella-braverman-revives-tory-pledge-to-cut-net-migration-to-tens-of-thousands

213 Rajeev Syal, 'No 10 rejects reports that Braverman could make cannabis class A', *Guardian*, 10 Oct 2022, https://www.theguardian.com/society/2022/oct/10/no-10-rejects-reports-suella-braverman-could-make-cannabis-class-a

214 Rachel Wearmouth [@REWearmouth], Twitter, 12 Oct 2022, https://twitter.com/rewearmouth/status/1580276459154784256

215 Aubrey Allegretti and Peter Walker, 'No 10 dismisses rumours of Liz Truss U-turn on tax cuts', *Guardian*, 13 Oct 2022, https://www.theguardian.com/politics/2022/oct/13/removing-truss-would-be-disastrously-bad-idea-says-cabinet-ally

216 Adam Forrest, 'Liz Truss loyalist tells Tory critics to "shut up" as pressure on PM builds', *Independent*, 13 Oct 2022, https://www.independent.co.uk/news/uk/politics/liz-truss-christopher-chope-shut-up-b2202028.html

217 Alexander Brown [@AlexofBrown], Twitter, 13 Oct 2022, https://twitter.com/AlexofBrown/status/1580496835105665025

218 Bron Maher, 'Daily Star lettuce world exclusive first interview: We're "not anti-Tory, we're anti-idiot"', *Press Gazette*, 20 Oct 2022, https://pressgazette.co.uk/news/daily-star-lettuce/

219 Neil Shaw, 'Rishi Sunak will run to be the next Prime Minister, allies say', *WalesOnline*, 20 Oct 2022, https://www.walesonline.co.uk/news/uk-news/rishi-sunak-run-next-prime-25314933

220 Louise Ashworth, 'Quantifying Britain's moron risk premium', *Financial Times*, 19 Oct 2022, https://www-ft-com.ezp.lib.cam.ac.uk/content/08908266-cc47-4cda-b8d4-97a8ac433a6d

221 Andrew Woodcock, 'Liz Truss's Tories slump below 20% in bombshell poll', *Independent*, 14 Oct 2022, https://www.independent.co.uk/news/uk/politics/liz-truss-poll-labour-conservatives-b2202716.html

222 BBC Radio 4 Today [@BBCr4today], Twitter, 13 Oct 2022, https://twitter.com/BBCr4today/status/1580468411175665664

223 Andrew Marr [@AndrewMarr9], Twitter, 13 Oct 2022, https://twitter.com/andrewmarr9/status/1580526813738336256

224 '"Back again? Dear, oh dear": King Charles holds audience with Liz Truss – video', *Guardian*, 13 Oct 2022, https://www.theguardian.com/politics/video/2022/oct/13/back-again-dear-oh-dear-king-charles-holds-audience-with-liz-truss-video

225 Kalyeena Makortoff, 'Mini-budget an "international embarrassment" says NatWest boss', *Guardian*, 6 Dec 2022, https://www.theguardian.com/business/2022/dec/06/mini-budget-an-international-embarrassment-says-natwest-boss

226 Sophie Morris and Faye Brown, 'Chancellor Kwasi Kwarteng insists he is "not going anywhere" – and hints at mini-budget U-turn', Sky News, 14 Oct 2022, https://news.sky.com/story/chancellor-kwasi-kwarteng-insists-he-is-not-going-anywhere-and-hints-at-mini-budget-u-turn-12719504

227 Politics Joe [@PoliticsJOE_UK], Twitter, 14 Oct 2022, https://twitter.com/politicsjoe_uk/status/1580855684412846080

228 Joe Easton, '"Uninvestable" UK Market Lost £300 Billion in Truss's First Month', *Bloomberg*, 6 Oct 2022, https://www.bloomberg.com/news/articles/2022-10-06/-uninvestable-uk-market-lost-300-billion-in-truss-first-month

229 Peter Walker, Jessica Elgot and Aubrey Allegretti, 'Liz Truss to raise corporation tax in another humiliating U-turn', *Guardian*, 14 Oct 2022 https://www.theguardian.com/politics/2022/oct/14/liz-truss-to-raise-corporation-tax-in-another-humiliating-u-turn'

230 'Pound pares losses as Jeremy Hunt appointed chancellor after Kwarteng sacking', *Yahoo! News*, 14 Oct 2022, https://uk.news.yahoo.com/kwarteng-pound-markets-price-mini-budget-u-turns-092647154.html

231 Peter Walker and Aubrey Allegretti, 'Liz Truss adviser suspended after Sajid Javid was insulted', *Guardian*, 19 Oct 2022, https://www.theguardian.com/politics/2022/oct/19/liz-truss-adviser-jason-stein-suspended-sajid-javid

232 Jon Stone, 'Liz Truss aides "pretended her relatives had died" to get her out of going on TV', *Independent*, 20 Oct 2022, https://www.independent.co.uk/news/uk/politics/liz-truss-question-time-relatives-die-tv-b2206063.html

233 Ian Jones, 'Jeremy Hunt is fourth Chancellor in just over three months', *Independent*, 14 Oct 2022, https://www.independent.co.uk/news/uk/jeremy-hunt-kwasi-kwarteng-nadhim-zahawi-chancellor-sajid-javid-b2202897.html

234 The News Agents [@TheNewsAgents], Twitter, 1 Nov 2022, https://twitter.com/TheNewsAgents/status/1587551747915980802

235 'Secretary of State for Work and Pensions', Wikipedia, https://en.wikipedia.org/wiki/Secretary_of_State_for_Work_and_Pensions

236 'Secretary of State for Education', Wikipedia, https://en.wikipedia.org/wiki/Secretary_of_State_for_Education

237 'Parliamentary Under-Secretary of State for Housing', Wikipedia, https://en.wikipedia.org/wiki/Parliamentary_Under-Secretary_of_State_for_Housing

238 'Minister of State for Energy and Climate', Wikipedia, https://en.wikipedia.org/wiki/Minister_of_State_for_Energy_and_Climate

239 Andrew Sparrow, 'Was that it? Eight-minute Liz Truss press conference will not steady ship', *Guardian*, 14 Oct 2022, https://www.theguardian.com/politics/2022/oct/14/liz-truss-press-conference-verdict-corporation-tax-kwasi-kwarteng

240 Kate Devlin, 'Tory donors turn on Liz Truss even as Jeremy Hunt rips up disastrous mini-Budget', *Independent*, 15 Oct 2022, https://www.independent.co.uk/news/uk/politics/liz-truss-jeremy-hunt-donors-b2203571.html

241 Sophia Sleigh, 'Liz Truss is "not under a desk" hiding, Penny Mordaunt tells Commons', *HuffPost*, 17 Oct 2022, https://www.huffingtonpost.co.uk/entry/liz-truss-is-not-under-a-desk-hiding-penny-mordaunt-tells-commons_uk_634d700ae4b04cf8f37b1a34

242 Sam Lister [@sam_lister_], Twitter, 17 Oct 2022, https://twitter.com/sam_lister_/status/1582033441746321408

243 Hugo Gye, Chloe Chaplain, 'Up to 100 Tories have written to Graham Brady demanding vote of no-confidence in Liz Truss, MPs believe', *iNews*, 16 Oct 2022, https://inews.co.uk/news/politics/up-to-100-tories-have-written-to-graham-brady-demanding-no-confidence-in-liz-truss-mps-believe-1915033

244 'Suella Braverman blames "Guardian-reading, tofu-eating wokerati" for disruptive protests – video', *Guardian*, 18 Oct 2022, https://www.theguardian.com/politics/video/2022/oct/18/suella-braverman-blames-guardian-reading-tofu-eating-wokerati-for-disruptive-protests-video

245 Aubrey Allegretti, 'Suella Braverman resignation letter: what she said and totally meant', *Guardian*, 19 Oct 2022, https://www.theguardian.com/politics/2022/oct/19/suella-braverman-resignation-letter-what-she-said-and-totally-meant

246 Tim Shipman [@ShippersUnbound], Twitter, 25 Oct 2022, https://twitter.com/ShippersUnbound/status/1584939423703396352

247 Steven Swinford, 'Suella Braverman broke security rules on emails six times', *The Times*, 1 Nov 2022, https://www.thetimes.co.uk/article/suella-braverman-email-leak-urged-explain-lv0rftgqm

248 Oliver Wright, 'Tory waverers press-ganged to back Cameron on gay marriage vote', *Independent*, 3 Feb 2013, https://www.independent.co.uk/news/uk/politics/tory-waverers-press-ganged-to-back-cameron-on-gay-marriage-vote-8478712.html

249 'Spalding and the Deepings MP John Hayes writes on sex and identity', *Spalding Today*, 29 Oct 2018, https://www.spaldingtoday.co.uk/news/hayes-in-the-house-sex-and-identity-9047705/

250 'John Hayes MP pursues Cardinal's call for abortion law reform', *Conservative Home*, 23 Jun 2006, https://conservativehome.blogs.com/torydiary/2006/06/john_hayes_mp_p.html

251 Benjamin Kentish, 'Tory MP asks government to consider bringing back death penalty', *Independent*, 3 Nov 2018, https://www.independent.co.uk/news/uk/politics/tory-mp-bring-back-death-penalty-john-hayes-lincolnshire-capital-punishment-a8615731.html

252 David Barrett, 'Worst March snow for 30 years brings chaos', *Telegraph*, 23 Mar 2013, https://www.telegraph.co.uk/news/weather/9950516/Worst-March-snow-for-30-years-brings-chaos.html

253 Joshua Nevett, 'Why high UK energy bills were decades in the making', BBC News, 7 Nov 2022, https://www.bbc.co.uk/news/uk-politics-63477214

254 'Analysis: Why UK energy bills are soaring to record highs – and how to cut them', *Carbon Brief*, 12 Aug 2022, https://www.carbonbrief.org/analysis-why-uk-energy-bills-are-soaring-to-record-highs-and-how-to-cut-them/

255 Adam Bienkov [@AdamBienkov], Twitter, 30 Oct 2022, https://twitter.com/AdamBienkov/status/1586647873210535936

256 Tim Shipman and Caroline Wheeler, 'Is the tide going out on Boris Johnson's comeback?', *The Times*, 22 Oct 2022, https://www.thetimes.co.uk/article/is-the-tide-going-out-on-boris-johnsons-comeback-x5xb6vj8b

257 Pippa Crerar, Peter Walker and Aubrey Allegretti, 'Suella Braverman forced to resign as UK home secretary', *Guardian*, 19 Oct 2022, https://www.theguardian.com/politics/2022/oct/19/suella-braverman-departs-as-uk-home-secretary-liz-truss

258 John Burn-Murdoch, 'The Tories have become unmoored from the British people', *Financial Times*, 30 Sep 2022, https://www.ft.com/content/d5f1d564-8c08-4711-b11d-9c6c7759f2b8

259 Jamie Grierson, 'What will new UK home secretary Grant Shapps bring to the role?', *Guardian*, 19 Oct 2022, https://www.theguardian.com/politics/2022/oct/19/what-will-new-uk-home-secretary-grant-shapps-bring-to-the-role

260 Joel Day, 'Inside Grant Shapps' "fabled spreadsheet" used to bring down Tory prime ministers', *Express*, 19 Oct 2022, https://www.express.co.uk/news/politics/1684382/grant-shapps-spreadsheet-liz-truss-rory-stewart-rest-is-politics-spt

261 Jamie Phillips, 'Health Secretary Therese Coffey admits to illegally sharing antibiotics with friends and family as she faces backlash over plan for pharmacies to offer the medicines without prescriptions', *Daily Mail*, 16 Oct 2022, https://www.dailymail.co.uk/news/article-11320893/Health-Secretary-Therese-Coffey-admits-illegally-sharing-antibiotics-friends-family.html

262 Ben Quinn, 'Thérèse Coffey had to leave Oxford University – but made it to deputy PM', *Guardian*, 7 Sep 2022, https://www.theguardian.com/politics/2022/sep/07/therese-coffey-had-to-leave-oxford-university-but-made-it-to-deputy-pm

263 Ruth Hayhurst, 'Fracking moratorium – the unanswered questions', Drill or Drop, 4 Nov 2019, https://drillordrop.com/2019/11/04/fracking-moratorium-the-unanswered-questions/
264 'Conservative Party Manifesto', Conservatives, https://www.conservatives.com/our-plan/conservative-party-manifesto-2019
265 Fiona Harvey, 'Fracking won't work in UK says founder of fracking company Cuadrilla', *Guardian*, 21 Sep 2022, https://www.theguardian.com/environment/2022/sep/21/fracking-wont-work-uk-founder-chris-cornelius-cuadrilla
266 Helena Horton, 'Fracking caused daily earthquakes at UK's only active site', *Guardian*, 19 Oct 2022, https://www.theguardian.com/environment/2022/oct/19/fracking-caused-daily-earthquakes-at-uks-only-active-site
267 'Labour motion to force vote on a bill to ban fracking rejected by MPs', ITV News, 19 Oct 2022, https://www.itv.com/news/2022-10-19/fracking-vote-described-as-confidence-vote-in-government-by-tory-whips
268 Sam Blewett, 'Tories make Labour fracking motion "confidence vote" in Liz Truss's government', *Independent*, 19 Oct 2022, https://www.independent.co.uk/climate-change/news/liz-truss-mps-tories-labour-lancashire-b2205920.html
269 Nicholas Cecil, 'Liz Truss threatened with Tory revolt in showdown "confidence vote" on fracking', *Evening Standard*, 19 Oct 2022, https://www.standard.co.uk/news/politics/liz-truss-prime-minister-fracking-confidence-vote-b1033761.html
270 Aubrey Allegretti [@breeallegretti], Twitter, 19 Oct 2022, https://twitter.com/breeallegretti/status/1582792387952508928
271 Sam Blewett, 'Liz Truss meets 1922 Committee chairman after acknowledging "difficult day"', *Independent*, 20 Oct 2022, https://www.independent.co.uk/news/uk/liz-truss-graham-brady-prime-minister-suella-braverman-annemarie-trevelyan-b2206800.html
272 Adam Bienkov [@AdamBienkov], Twitter, 29 Oct 2022, https://twitter.com/AdamBienkov/status/1582802654786297856
273 Cat Smith [@CatSmithMP], Twitter, 19 Oct 2022, https://twitter.com/CatSmithMP/status/1582820285723869184
274 Peter Walker, Aubrey Allegretti and Pippa Crerar, 'Crunch Commons vote on fracking descends into farce', *Guardian*, 19 Oct 2022, https://www.theguardian.com/politics/2022/oct/19/crunch-commons-vote-on-fracking-descends-into-farce
275 'Chief whip remains in post after reportedly resigning earlier', ITV News, 19 Oct 2022, https://www.itv.com/news/2022-10-19/conservative-chief-whip-resigns-in-further-blow-to-pm-liz-truss
276 'The Conservative Party', Gresham College, 26 Sep 2017, https://www.gresham.ac.uk/watch-now/conservative-party
277 Peter Walker, Aubrey Allegretti and Pippa Crerar, 'Crunch Commons vote on fracking descends into farce', *Guardian*, 19 Oct 2022, https://www.theguardian.com/politics/2022/oct/19/crunch-commons-vote-on-fracking-descends-into-farce
278 Kate Plummer, 'These are the 40 Tory MPs that didn't vote on fracking – including Liz Truss', *Indy100*, 20 Oct 2022, https://www.indy100.com/politics/fracking-vote-mps-liz-truss
279 The Telegraph [@Telegraph], Twitter, 19 Oct 2022, https://twitter.com/Telegraph/status/1582816759316635648
280 Camilla Turner, 'Just nine per cent have a favourable view of Liz Truss', *Telegraph*, 13 Oct 2022, https://www.telegraph.co.uk/politics/2022/10/13/just-nine-per-cent-have-favourable-view-liz-truss/
281 Mark Sweney, 'Prices of staples such as pasta and tea soar in UK, hitting poorest hard', *Guardian*, 25 Oct 2022, https://www.theguardian.com/business/2022/oct/25/prices-staples-surge-cost-of-living-crisis-inflation-ons
282 Chas Geiger, 'Liz Truss wanted government turned up to 11, says former aide', BBC News, 3 Dec 2022, https://www.bbc.co.uk/news/uk-politics-63834307
283 'Liz Truss: I'm a fighter, not a quitter', BBC News, 19 Oct 2022, https://www.bbc.co.uk/news/av/uk-politics-63313539
284 Laura O'Callaghan, 'Liz Truss says she was relieved when resigning as UK's prime minister', *The National*, 23 Oct 2022, https://www.thenationalnews.com/world/uk-news/2022/10/23/liz-truss-says-she-was-relieved-when-resigning-as-uks-prime-minister/

285 Seren Morris, 'Did Liz Truss serve long enough as PM to receive the £115k a year payout for the rest of her life?', *Evening Standard*, 21 Oct 2022, https://www.standard.co.uk/news/politics/liz-truss-prime-minister-115k-pdca-allowance-b1034215.html
286 Sophie Wingate, 'Boris Johnson's flat revamp cost £200,000, leaked invoice suggests', *Independent*, 8 Jul 2022, https://www.independent.co.uk/news/uk/boris-johnson-carrie-johnson-downing-street-the-independent-lord-b2118741.html
287 Aletha Adu, 'Liz Truss Jenga-style podium cost taxpayers £4,175', *Guardian*, 18 Jan 2023, https://www.theguardian.com/politics/2023/jan/18/liz-truss-jenga-style-podium-cost-taxpayers-4175
288 Greg Evans, 'Liz Truss's time as prime minister in numbers', *Indy100*, 20 Oct 2022, https://www.indy100.com/politics/liz-truss-pm-in-numbers
289 Oliver Browning, '1922 Committee chair Graham Brady confirms rules of Tory leadership contest', *Independent*, 20 Oct 2022, https://www.independent.co.uk/tv/news/liz-truss-resigned-tory-leadership-b2207228.html
290 John Johnston, 'Tory Party sets out new rules for running week-long leadership contest', *PoliticsHome*, 20 Oct 2022, https://www.politicshome.com/news/article/tory-party-set-out-new-rules-for-running-week-long-leadership-contest
291 Will Hayward, 'Boris Johnson the favourite among Tory members to take over as leader from Liz Truss', *WalesOnline*, 18 Oct 2022, https://www.walesonline.co.uk/news/politics/boris-johnson-favourite-among-tory-25291273
292 Tim Shipman and Caroline Wheeler, 'Is the tide going out on Boris Johnson's comeback?', *The Times*, 22 Oct 2022, https://www.thetimes.co.uk/article/is-the-tide-going-out-on-boris-johnsons-comeback-x5xb6vj8b
293 George Parker et al., 'Investors and MPs take fright at prospect of Boris Johnson's return', *Financial Times*, 22 Oct 2022, https://www.ft.com/content/e8d941eb-c435-4897-b957-dbc87ece56ac
294 'United Kingdom: Sovereign credit ratings', *The Global Economy*, https://www.theglobaleconomy.com/United-Kingdom/credit_rating/
295 'Boris Johnson jets back to UK as Tories split on his expected leadership bid', *Bloomberg*, 22 Oct 2022, https://www.bloomberg.com/news/articles/2022-10-22/boris-johnson-jets-back-to-uk-as-tories-split-on-his-expected-leadership-bid
296 'No one thought mini-budget was a "bad idea", senior minister admits', *The Comet*, 18 Oct 2022, https://www.thecomet.net/news/national/23057239.no-one-thought-mini-budget-bad-idea-senior-minister-admits/
297 Sam Blewett, 'Rishi Sunak "first contender to pass threshold of 100 Tory MPs"', *Independent*, 22 Oct 2022, https://www.independent.co.uk/news/uk/boris-johnson-penny-mordaunt-tobias-ellwood-mps-liz-truss-b2208258.html
298 'Sunak leads among Tory MPs but Johnson camp claims growing support', BBC News, 22 Oct 2022, https://www.bbc.co.uk/news/live/uk-politics-63338261
299 Chris Mason, 'Penny Mordaunt speech: Fowl play or light-hearted fun?', BBC News, 1 Dec 2014, https://www.bbc.co.uk/news/uk-politics-30280120
300 Nadine Dorries, 'Nadine Dorries: Boris Johnson is a proven winner. He alone has an electoral mandate', *Daily Mail*, 22 Oct 2022, https://www.dailymail.co.uk/debate/article-11344347/NADINE-DORRIES-Boris-Johnson-proven-winner-electoral-mandate.html
301 Nadine Dorries [@NadineDorries], Twitter, 23 Oct 2022, https://twitter.com/NadineDorries/status/1584093885487542272
302 Theo Usherwood [@theousherwood], Twitter, 24 Oct 2022, https://twitter.com/theousherwood/status/1584430262540062720
303 'Endorsements in the October 2022 Conservative Party leadership election', Wikipedia, https://en.wikipedia.org/wiki/Endorsements_in_the_October_2022_Conservative_Party_leadership_election
304 Toby Helm, 'Boris Johnson "quit PM race over risk to £10m earnings", sources say', *Guardian*, 6 Nov 2022, https://www.theguardian.com/politics/2022/nov/06/boris-johnson-quit-pm-race-over-risk-to-10m-earnings-sources-say
305 GB News [@GBNEWS], Twitter, 24 Oct 2022, https://twitter.com/GBNEWS/status/1584496850106601472
306 Kevin Schofield [@KevinASchofield], Twitter, 23 Oct 2022, https://twitter.com/KevinASchofield/status/1584278017966149632

307 Adam Solomons, 'Boris Johnson's withdrawal statement in full as he quits race for No 10', LBC, 23 Oct 2022, https://www.lbc.co.uk/news/boris-johnsons-withdrawal-statement-in-full-as-he-quits-race-for-no-10/
308 Clea Skopeliti, '"Best of a bad bunch": voters share their views on Rishi Sunak', *Guardian*, 25 Oct 2022, https://www.theguardian.com/politics/2022/oct/25/best-of-a-bad-bunch-voters-share-their-views-on-rishi-sunak

Part 3: Crazy Rich Asian
2022: 'Screams from a Madhouse'

1. Liam O'Dell, '8 times Rishi Sunak's government definitely led with "integrity, professionalism and accountability"', *Indy100*, 9 Nov 2022, https://www.indy100.com/politics/rishi-sunak-government-integrity-professionalism
2. James FitzGerald, 'Sunak warns of economic challenge as he prepares to become PM', BBC News, 23 Oct 2022, https://www.bbc.co.uk/news/live/uk-politics-63327087
3. Emily Cleary, '"The Rishbot": Rishi Sunak's awkward pause at end of first speech as incoming PM goes viral', *Yahoo! News*, 25 Oct 2022, https://uk.news.yahoo.com/rishi-sunaks-awkward-pause-end-first-speech-viral-081828504.html
4. Peter Evans, 'New chancellor Rishi Sunak cashed in on fund that helped break banks', *Sunday Times*, 16 Feb 2020, https://www.thetimes.co.uk/article/new-chancellor-rishi-sunak-cashed-in-on-fund-that-helped-break-banks-rb7zgfqkz
5. Joshua Nevett, 'Rishi Sunak calls for stability and unity as he wins contest to be PM', BBC News, 25 Oct 2022, https://www.bbc.co.uk/news/uk-politics-63375281
6. Cnaan Liphshiz/JTA, 'Dominic Raab, whose father was a Jewish refugee, is Britain's acting PM', *Jerusalem Post*, 8 Apr 2020, https://www.jpost.com/diaspora/dominic-raab-whose-father-was-a-jewish-refugee-is-britains-acting-pm-623994
7. 'Sadiq Khan', *The Muslim 500*, https://themuslim500.com/profiles/sadiq-khan/
8. Parveen Akhtar, 'It matters that Rishi Sunak has become the UK's first prime minister of Indian descent', *The Conversation*, 24 Oct 2022, https://theconversation.com/it-matters-that-rishi-sunak-has-become-the-uks-first-prime-minister-of-indian-descent-193154
9. 'Women are more likely to experience persistent poverty', National Education Union, 17 Jan 2019, https://neu.org.uk/advice/women-and-poverty
10. Miranda Bryant, 'Women £570 a year worse off after 12 years of Conservatives, says Labour', *Guardian*, 19 Nov 2022, https://www.theguardian.com/politics/2022/nov/19/women-570-year-worse-off-12-years-conservatives-labour
11. Andrew Sparrow, 'More than half of UK's black children live in poverty, analysis shows', *Guardian*, 2 Jan 2022, https://www.theguardian.com/world/2022/jan/02/more-than-half-of-uks-black-children-live-in-poverty-analysis-shows
12. Arj Singh, Jane Merrick, Richard Vaughan and Hugo Gye, '"Everything has to wait": Inside paralysed Whitehall as Rishi Sunak faces the UK's permacrisis', *iNews*, 5 Nov 2022, https://inews.co.uk/news/politics/everything-has-to-wait-inside-paralysed-whitehall-as-rishi-sunak-faces-uks-permacrisis-1954552
13. Michiel Willems, 'Revealed: Brits are paying the highest electricity bills in the entire world', *CityA.M.*, 14 Jan 2023, https://www.cityam.com/revealed-brits-are-paying-the-highest-electricity-bills-in-the-entire-world/
14. Neil Turnbull, 'Permacrisis: what it means and why it's word of the year for 2022', *The Conversation*, 11 Nov 2022, https://theconversation.com/permacrisis-what-it-means-and-why-its-word-of-the-year-for-2022-194306
15. 'Word of the year', Wikipedia, https://en.wikipedia.org/wiki/Word_of_the_year
16. Jess Bacon, 'I'm a Celebrity releases voting figures for finale', *Digital Spy*, 29 Nov 2022, https://www.digitalspy.com/tv/reality-tv/a42092628/im-a-celebrity-finale-voting-figures/

17 Karla Adam, 'Richer than the royals: Win puts Rishi Sunak's wealth in the spotlight', *Washington Post*, 24 Oct 2022, https://www.washingtonpost.com/world/2022/10/24/rishi-sunak-net-worth/
18 Press Association, 'Honest mistake: Jeremy Hunt sorry for failure to declare luxury flats purchase', *Guardian*, 13 Apr 2018, https://www.theguardian.com/politics/2018/apr/13/jeremy-hunt-sorry-for-luxury-flat-purchase-errors
19 Rowena Mason and Helena Horton, 'Rishi Sunak U-turns on decision not to attend Cop27 climate summit', *Guardian*, 2 Nov 2022, https://www.theguardian.com/environment/2022/nov/02/rishi-sunak-u-turns-decision-not-to-attend-cop27-climate-summit
20 Pippa Crerar and Jessica Elgot, 'Rishi Sunak to ditch key Tory leadership campaign pledges', *Guardian*, 2 Nov 2022, https://www.theguardian.com/politics/2022/nov/02/rishi-sunak-to-ditch-key-tory-leadership-campaign-pledges
21 'Rishi Sunak: "I pledge to serve you with integrity and humility"', *Daily Mail*, 24 Oct 2022, https://www.dailymail.co.uk/video/news/video-2801651/Video-Rishi-Sunak-pledge-serve-integrity-humility.html
22 'Rishi Sunak sported £3,500 bespoke suit as he prepared for crunch leadership vote', *Daily Mail*, 21 Jul 2022, https://www.dailymail.co.uk/news/article-11033847/Rishi-Sunak-sported-3-500-bespoke-suit-prepared-crunch-leadership-vote.html
23 '1975: Tories choose first woman leader', BBC News, 11 Feb 1975, http://news.bbc.co.uk/onthisday/hi/dates/stories/february/11/newsid_2539000/2539451.stm
24 Rob Merrick, 'Housebuilding figures under Conservatives lowest since the Second World War', *Independent*, 1 Jan 2019, https://www.independent.co.uk/news/uk/politics/england-house-building-record-second-world-war-conservative-government-home-a8706776.html
25 'How much has homelessness increased in the UK', Greater Change, 8 Jun 2022, https://www.greaterchange.co.uk/post/how-much-has-homelessness-increased-in-the-uk
26 Adam Forrest, 'Jacob Rees-Mogg admitted profiting from sale of abortion pills', *Independent*, 29 Nov 2022, https://www.independent.co.uk/news/uk/politics/rees-mogg-abortion-pills-profit-b2235424.html
27 Helena Horton, 'Anti-green MP Steve Baker considering running for PM', *Guardian*, 7 Jul 2022, https://www.theguardian.com/politics/2022/jul/07/anti-green-mp-steve-baker-considering-running-for-pm-if-boris-johnson-goes
28 Andy McSmith, 'Michael Gove: The modest moderniser', *Independent*, 27 Sep 2008, https://www.independent.co.uk/news/people/profiles/michael-gove-the-modest-moderniser-944074.html
29 Maurice Cowling, 'The Present Position', in Maurice Cowling (ed.), *Conservative Essays*, Cassell, 1978
30 Tim Bale, 'The Tory "war on woke" has a manifesto – and its targets are crushingly familiar', *Guardian*, 25 May 2021, https://www.theguardian.com/commentisfree/2021/may/25/tory-war-on-woke-manifesto-common-sense-group
31 David Pegg, Felicity Lawrence and Rob Evans, 'Tory Brexit faction censured for using public funds for campaigning', *Guardian*, 14 Sep 2018, https://www.theguardian.com/politics/2018/sep/14/tory-brexit-faction-erg-censured-for-using-public-funds-for-campaigning
32 'Meet our team and supporters', Blue Collar Conservatism, https://www.bluecollarconservatism.co.uk/team
33 Emily Maskell, '"Deep concern" as anti-trans MP Kemi Badenoch re-appointed Equalities Minister', *Attitude*, 26 Oct 2022, https://www.attitude.co.uk/news/uk/kemi-badenoch-mp-appointed-equalities-minister-416513/
34 Jon Stone, 'Equalities minister Kemi Badenoch attacks LGBT magazine in parliament', *Independent*, 26 Oct 2022, https://www.independent.co.uk/news/uk/politics/kemi-badenoch-lgbt-trans-rights-b2210909.html
35 Patrick Kelleher, 'Kemi Badenoch as equalities minister leaves LGBTQ+ activists "deeply fearful" for the future', *PinkNews*, 26 Oct 2022, https://www.thepinknews.com/2022/10/26/kemi-badenoch-women-equalities-lgbtq
36 Sophie Perry, 'Kemi Badenoch appoints anti-trans JK Rowling fan and ex-GB News host to advise on gender policy', *PinkNews*, 13 Jan 2022, https://www.thepinknews.com/2023/01/13/mercy-muroki-kemi-badenoch-gender-policy-fellow-trans/

37 Aletha Adu and Aubrey Allegretti, 'Tory MP under fire for transphobic comments about Eddie Izzard', *Guardian*, 26 Oct 2022, https://www.theguardian.com/culture/2022/oct/26/tory-mp-under-fire-for-transphobic-comments-about-eddie-izzard

38 Lizzy Buchan, 'Tories should fight next election on "culture wars and trans debate", says Lee Anderson', *Mirror*, 14 Feb 2023, https://www.mirror.co.uk/news/politics/tories-should-fight-next-election-29211636

39 Freddie Whittaker, 'Gillian Keegan becomes fifth education secretary in four months', *Schools Week*, 25 Oct 2022, https://schoolsweek.co.uk/gillian-keegan-becomes-fifth-education-secretary-in-four-months/

40 Paul Withers and David Maddox, '"Deeply unhappy" Tory MPs drafting letters of no confidence after Sunak's Cabinet purge', *Express*, 31 Oct 2022, https://www.express.co.uk/news/politics/1689774/rishi-sunak-no-confidence-letters-tory-mps-cabinet-reshuffle-suella-braverman

41 Henry McDonald, 'Former Tory donor's housing project "unlawfully approved to avoid £40m hit"', *Guardian*, 27 May 2020, https://www.theguardian.com/politics/2020/may/27/richard-desmond-housing-project-unlawfully-approved-robert-jenrick-isle-dogs-london-avoid-40m-hit

42 Heather Stewart, Dan Sabbagh and Peter Walker, 'Gavin Williamson: "I was tried by kangaroo court – then sacked"', *Guardian*, 1 May 2019, https://www.theguardian.com/politics/2019/may/01/gavin-williamson-sacked-as-defence-secretary-over-huawei-leak

43 Pippa Crerar, Peter Walker and Aubrey Allegretti, 'Suella Braverman forced to resign as UK home secretary', *Guardian*, 19 Oct 2022, https://www.theguardian.com/politics/2022/oct/19/suella-braverman-departs-as-uk-home-secretary-liz-truss

44 Piers Morgan Uncensored [@PiersUncensored], Twitter, 26 Oct 2022, https://twitter.com/PiersUncensored/status/1585361104062058508

45 Yvette Cooper [@YvetteCooperMP], Twitter, 26 Oct 2022, https://twitter.com/YvetteCooperMP/status/1585375081123172352

46 Jonathan Reilly and Kate Ferguson, 'Home Secretary Suella Braverman was probed over allegations she leaked sensitive details on Northern Ireland Protocol', *Sun*, 29 Oct 2022, https://www.thesun.co.uk/news/politics/20264308/home-secretary-suella-probed-leaked-protocol/

47 Matt Dathan, 'MI5 security lessons for "Leaky Sue"', *The Times*, 27 Oct 2022, https://www.thetimes.co.uk/article/mi5-security-lessons-for-leaky-sue-wtws56pxd

48 David Barrett, 'Exclusive: Suella was embroiled in probe over leak that raised "concerns" at MI5', *Mail Plus*, 26 Oct 2022, https://www.mailplus.co.uk/edition/news/politics/232140

49 Adam Bienkov [@AdamBienkov], Twitter, 16 Oct 2022, https://twitter.com/AdamBienkov/status/1585233808710053889

50 Chris Bryant [@RhonddaBryant], Twitter, 27 Oct 2022, https://twitter.com/RhonddaBryant/status/1585707873912643584

51 'British Nationality and Status of Aliens Act 1914', https://www.legislation.gov.uk/ukpga/1914/17/pdfs/ukpga_19140017_en.pdf

52 Jeanne Batalova, 'Top Statistics on Global Migration and Migrants', Migration Policy Institute, 21 Jul 2022, https://www.migrationpolicy.org/article/top-statistics-global-migration-migrants

53 Niall McCarthy, 'The Biggest Empires in Human History', Statista, 25 May 2020, https://www.statista.com/chart/20342/peak-land-area-of-the-largest-empires/

54 Ritchie Ovendale, 'Great Britain and the Anglo-American invasion of Jordan and Lebanon in 1958', *International History Review*, 1 Dec 2010, https://www.tandfonline.com/doi/abs/10.1080/07075332.1994.9640677

55 Thom Brooks, 'Increase in small boat crossings caused by no returns agreement after Brexit', *North East Bylines*, 15 Feb 2023, https://northeastbylines.co.uk/increase-in-small-boat-crossings-caused-by-no-returns-agreement-after-brexit/

56 Thom Brooks, 'Increase in small boat crossings caused by no returns agreement after Brexit', *North East Bylines*, 15 Feb 2023, https://northeastbylines.co.uk/increase-in-small-boat-crossings-caused-by-no-returns-agreement-after-brexit/

57 Callum May, Judith Burns and Kate Whannel, 'Suella Braverman: We have failed to control our borders', BBC News, 23 Nov 2022, https://www.bbc.co.uk/news/uk-politics-63730054
58 Tom Sasse, Rhys Clyne and Sachin Savur, 'Asylum backlog', Institute for Government, 24 Feb 2023, https://www.instituteforgovernment.org.uk/article/explainer/asylum-backlog
59 Daniel Waldron, 'UK immigration budget slashed by £40 million', Work Permit, 8 Aug 2021, https://workpermit.com/news/uk-immigration-budget-slashed-ps40-million-20211008
60 Tom Sasse, Rhys Clyne and Sachin Savur, 'Asylum backlog', Institute for Government, 24 Feb 2023, https://www.instituteforgovernment.org.uk/article/explainer/asylum-backlog
61 Diane Taylor, 'Sunak used incorrect asylum backlog figures, statistics watchdog says', *Guardian*, 25 Mar 2023, https://www.theguardian.com/uk-news/2023/mar/25/sunak-used-incorrect-asylum-backlog-figures-statistics-watchdog-says
62 Tom Sasse, Rhys Clyne and Sachin Savur, 'Asylum backlog', Institute for Government, 24 Feb 2023, https://www.instituteforgovernment.org.uk/article/explainer/asylum-backlog
63 'Refugees by Country 2022', World Population Review, 2022, https://worldpopulationreview.com/country-rankings/refugees-by-country
64 Laura Parnaby, 'Lineker claim on UK taking "far fewer refugees" than Europe supported by data', *Independent*, 8 Mar 2023, https://www.independent.co.uk/news/uk/europe-robert-jenrick-austria-twitter-parliament-b2296719.html
65 'How does the UK compare with other countries?', SWVG, https://swvg-refugees.org.uk/about-asylum/asylum-facts/uk-compare-countries/
66 Tom Sasse, Rhys Clyne and Sachin Savur, 'Asylum backlog', Institute for Government, 24 Feb 2023, https://www.instituteforgovernment.org.uk/article/explainer/asylum-backlog
67 'Long-term international migration, provisional: year ending December 2020', ONS, 25 Nov 2021, https://www.ons.gov.uk/peoplepopulationandcommunity/populationandmigration/internationalmigration/bulletins/longterminternationalmigrationprovisional/yearendingdecember2020
68 Mark Townsend, 'Home Office admits no evidence to support key claim on small boat crossings', *Guardian*, 8 Apr 2023, https://www.theguardian.com/uk-news/2023/apr/08/home-office-admits-no-evidence-to-support-key-claim-on-small-boat-crossings
69 'Timeline: Policy and legislative changes affecting migration to the UK', GOV.UK, https://assets.publishing.service.gov.uk/government/uploads/system/uploads/attachment_data/file/1010857/user-guide-policy-changes-jun21.ods
70 Mohammed Amin, 'For years, I urged minorities to join the Tories. But now there's Suella Braverman, I say – get out!', *Guardian*, 17 Apr 2023, https://www.theguardian.com/commentisfree/2023/apr/17/minorities-join-tories-suella-braverman-boris-johnson
71 Aletha Adu, Jessica Elgot and Kiran Stacey, 'Senior Conservatives hit out at Suella Braverman's "racist rhetoric"', *Guardian*, 13 Apr 2023, https://www.theguardian.com/world/2023/apr/13/senior-conservatives-hit-out-at-suella-bravermans-racist-rhetoric
72 Melissa Bell and Saskya Vandoorne, 'Migrants risk death at sea to reach Britain as prices spike on traditional routes', CNN, 6 Dec 2018, https://edition.cnn.com/2018/12/06/europe/migrants-channel-dinghies-gbr-intl/index.html
73 Matt Dathan, Chris Smyth and Oliver Wright, 'Rishi Sunak battles to save immigration bill from Tory rebellion', *The Times*, 24 Mar 2023, https://www.thetimes.co.uk/article/illegal-migration-bill-rishi-sunak-tory-rebellion-9nh3tmdzc
74 '£7 million daily cost of hotel accommodation includes cost of housing Afghan refugees', Full Fact, 6 Feb 2023, https://fullfact.org/immigration/hotel-accommodation-asylum-seeker-cost/
75 Christian Dustmann and Tommaso Frattini, 'The Fiscal Effects of Immigration to the UK', University College London, https://www.ucl.ac.uk/economics/about-department/fiscal-effects-immigration-uk
76 'The Fiscal Impact of Immigration on the UK', Oxford Economics, June 2018, https://www.oxfordeconomics.com/resource/the-fiscal-impact-of-immigration-on-the-uk/

77 'Public sector expenditure on education in the United Kingdom in 2021/22, by sub-function', Statista, 2021/22, https://www.statista.com/statistics/298910/united-kingdom-uk-public-sector-expenditure-education/
78 Thom Brooks, 'Priti Patel's immigration reform is a confusing mess that will leave us worse off', *Independent*, 29 May 2021, https://www.independent.co.uk/voices/priti-patel-immigration-reform-b1855684.html
79 Diane Taylor, 'Manston health concerns raised with Home Office weeks before outbreak', *Guardian*, 6 Feb 2023, https://www.theguardian.com/uk-news/2023/feb/06/manston-health-concerns-home-diptheria-outbreak
80 Diane Taylor, 'Manston health concerns raised with Home Office weeks before outbreak', *Guardian*, 6 Feb 2023, https://www.theguardian.com/uk-news/2023/feb/06/manston-health-concerns-home-diptheria-outbreak
81 Harry Yorke and Tim Shipman, 'Suella Braverman "ignored advice" that detaining asylum seekers was breaking the law', *Sunday Times*, 29 Oct 2022, https://www.thetimes.co.uk/article/suella-braverman-ignored-advice-and-illegally-detained-asylum-seekers-ttbrtrfxp
82 Matt Dathan, 'Manston migrants centre emptied after outbreaks of infections', *The Times*, 22 Nov 2022, https://www.thetimes.co.uk/article/manston-migrants-centre-emptied-after-outbreaks-of-infections-h5cfn65lh
83 Lizzie Dearden, 'Afghan family detained in tent for a month amid "chaotic" Home Office response to Channel boats', *Independent*, 26 Oct 2022, https://www.independent.co.uk/news/uk/home-news/channel-boats-afghan-refugees-tent-b2210891.html
84 Holly Bancroft, 'Suella Braverman arrives at Manston migrant centre by Chinook helicopter', *Independent*, 3 Nov 2022, https://www.independent.co.uk/news/uk/home-news/suella-braverman-dover-manston-immigration-chinook-b2217000.html
85 Matthew Weaver, 'Petrol bombs thrown at immigration centre in Dover', *Guardian*, 30 Oct 2022, https://www.theguardian.com/uk-news/2022/oct/30/dover-petrol-bomb-immigration-centre-border-force
86 Rajeev Syal, ' "Come to Germany and learn": Albanian PM criticises UK's immigration stance', *Guardian*, 4 Nov 2022, https://www.theguardian.com/uk-news/2022/nov/03/belize-paraguay-and-peru-deny-reports-of-asylum-deal-talks-with-uk
87 Connie Dimsdale, ' "Manston feels like prison": Young girl pleads for help in letter thrown over fence at immigration centre', *iNews*, 2 Nov 2022, https://inews.co.uk/news/manston-feels-like-prison-young-girl-pleads-for-help-in-letter-thrown-over-fence-at-immigration-centre-1950155
88 Scott Benton [ScottBentonMP], Twitter, 3 Nov 2022, https://twitter.com/ScottBentonMP/status/1588209008799776768
89 Rachel Hall, 'Hundreds moved from Kent immigration centre amid overcrowding', *Guardian*, 2 Nov 2022, https://www.theguardian.com/uk-news/2022/nov/02/hundreds-moved-manston-migrant-centre-kent-overcrowding
90 'Dover migrant centre attack driven by right-wing ideology – police', BBC News, 5 Nov 2022, https://www.bbc.co.uk/news/uk-england-63526659
91 Jon Stone, 'Tory MP names hotel where asylum seekers will stay 48 hours after firebomb attack', *Independent*, 1 Nov 2022, https://www.independent.co.uk/news/uk/politics/jonathan-gullis-tory-mp-hotel-asylum-seekers-b2215096.html
92 Adam Bienkov [@AdamBienkov], Twitter, 7 Nov 2022, https://twitter.com/AdamBienkov/status/1589643413963489280
93 Adam Bienkov [@AdamBienkov], Twitter, 7 Nov 2022, https://twitter.com/AdamBienkov/status/1589659446124240897
94 Kate Plummer, 'Suella Braverman sounds lost speaking about the UK's asylum system', *Indy100*, 23 Nov 2022, https://www.indy100.com/politics/suella-braverman-tim-loughton-asylum
95 'Asylum: Afghanistan', *TheyWorkForYou*, 3 Apr 2023, https://www.theyworkforyou.com/wrans/?id=2023-03-15.166166.h&s=robert+jenrick#g166166.r0
96 'Asylum in the UK', UNHCR, https://www.unhcr.org/uk/asylum-in-the-uk.html
97 'The 1951 Refugee Convention', UNHCR, https://www.unhcr.org/uk/1951-refugee-convention.html

98 Adam Forrest, 'UN condemns "legal errors" in asylum report backed by Suella Braverman', *Independent*, 5 Dec 2022, https://www.independent.co.uk/independentpremium/uk-news/suella-braverman-asylum-ban-un-b2240019.html
99 'About Suella', https://www.suellabraverman.co.uk/about-suella
100 Becky Morton, 'UK is compassionate, says PM after Suella Braverman invasion row', BBC News, 1 Nov 2022, https://www.bbc.co.uk/news/uk-politics-63475511
101 Peter Walker and Jessica Murray, 'Priti Patel looked at idea of sending asylum seekers to South Atlantic', *Guardian*, 30 Sep 2020, https://www.theguardian.com/politics/2020/sep/30/priti-patel-looked-at-idea-of-sending-asylum-seekers-to-south-atlantic
102 Harry Yorke, 'Suella Braverman is fuelling Farage politics, says former adviser', *Sunday Times*, 17 Dec 2022, https://www.thetimes.co.uk/article/suella-braverman-is-fuelling-farage-politics-says-nimco-ali-g3blc6lqq
103 '£7 million daily cost of hotel accommodation includes cost of housing Afghan refugees', Full Fact, 8 Feb 2023, https://fullfact.org/immigration/hotel-accommodation-asylum-seeker-cost/
104 Harry Horton [@harry_horton], Twitter, 9 Feb 2023, https://twitter.com/harry_horton/status/1623738699321118725
105 Gregory Davis, 'Exposed: Tory County Councillor was key member of fascist group', Hope Not Hate, 15 Nov 2022, https://hopenothate.org.uk/2022/11/15/exposed-tory-county-councillor-was-key-member-of-fascist-group/
106 Rachel Sylvester, 'Andrew Mitchell: We used to be a foreign aid superpower, but our reputation has declined', *The Times*, 26 Nov 2022, https://www.thetimes.co.uk/article/andrew-mitchell-tory-interview-britain-uk-aid-budget-8lzbftgmk
107 Adam Forrest, 'NHS forced to spend £180m a year on "pointless" visa charges', *Independent*, 26 Nov 2022, https://www.independent.co.uk/news/uk/politics/nhs-visas-immigration-home-office-b2233508.html
108 Andrew Woodcock, 'More than 22,000 EU nationals have left NHS since Brexit referendum, figures show', *Independent*, 10 Dec 2019, https://www.independent.co.uk/news/uk/politics/brexit-eu-citizens-nhs-crisis-migration-boris-johnson-hospital-health-a9239791.html
109 Denis Campbell, 'Brexit has worsened shortage of NHS doctors, analysis shows', *Guardian*, 27 Nov 2022, https://www.theguardian.com/society/2022/nov/27/brexit-worsened-shortage-nhs-doctors-eu
110 Chris Smyth, 'Stop training so many doctors, universities told', *The Times*, 25 Jan 2023, https://www.thetimes.co.uk/article/stop-training-so-many-doctors-universities-told-xd3p3p37q
111 Anna Fazackerley, 'Government refuses to fund UK students at new medical school despite "chronic" doctor shortage', *Guardian*, 14 Jan 2023, https://www.theguardian.com/education/2023/jan/14/ministers-refuse-fund-medical-school-uk-doctor-shortage
112 'Number of job vacancies in the United Kingdom from June 2001 to February 2023', Statista, 2023, https://www.statista.com/statistics/283771/monthly-job-vacancies-in-the-united-kingdom-uk/
113 'UK productivity among the lowest of the G7, finds ONS', HR Magazine, 24 Jan 2022, https://www.hrmagazine.co.uk/content/news/uk-productivity-among-the-lowest-of-the-g7-finds-ons/
114 Peter Walker, 'UK will not ease immigration barriers to plug skills shortages, says minister', *Guardian*, 21 Nov 2022, https://www.theguardian.com/world/2022/nov/21/uk-will-not-ease-immigration-barriers-to-plug-skills-shortages-insists-minister
115 Hamish Morrison, 'Rishi Sunak "Keep Brexit Safe" video mocked as "vapid" and "embarrassing"', *The National*, 8 Aug 2022, https://www.thenational.scot/news/20608495.rishi-sunak-keep-brexit-safe-video-mocked-vapid-embarrassing/
116 Tom Parfitt, '"I will make Brexit work" FTSE falls by just 0.7% as Osborne says UK is open for business', *Express*, 27 June 2016, https://www.express.co.uk/news/politics/683640/Brexit-George-Osborne-EU-referendum-finance
117 'In hindsight, do you think Britain was right or wrong to vote to leave the European Union?', Statista, Mar 2023, https://www.statista.com/statistics/987347/brexit-opinion-poll/

118 Kate Devlin, 'Brexit poll: Two-thirds of Britons now support future referendum on rejoining the EU', *Independent*, 1 Jan 2023, https://www.independent.co.uk/news/uk/politics/brexit-poll-referendum-rejoin-eu-b2250813.html
119 Caroline Wheeler, Harry Yorke and Tim Shipman, 'Britain mulls Swiss-style ties with Brussels', *Sunday Times*, 20 Nov 2022, https://www.thetimes.co.uk/article/britain-mulls-swiss-style-ties-with-brussels-nr0f7fw2k
120 Theo Usherwood [@theousherwood], Twitter, 21 Nov 2022, https://twitter.com/theousherwood/status/1594596168348073984
121 Jasmine Cameron-Chileshe and Daniel Thomas, 'Rishi Sunak rules out Swiss-style trade deal with EU', *Financial Times*, 21 Nov 2022, https://www.ft.com/content/5bc9fd89-dd20-4848-b1ba-8abe646c643c
122 Toby Helm, Robin McKie, James Tapper and Phillip Inman, "What have we done?': six years on, UK counts the cost of Brexit', *Guardian*, 25 Jun 2022, https://www.theguardian.com/politics/2022/jun/25/what-have-we-done-six-years-on-uk-counts-the-cost-of-brexit
123 David Conn, Russell Scott and David Pegg, 'Firm with mystery investors wins £200m of PPE contracts via "high-priority lane"', *Guardian*, 21 Dec 2020, https://www.theguardian.com/world/2020/dec/21/firm-with-mystery-investors-wins-200m-of-ppe-contracts-via-high-priority-lane
124 Chris Smyth, 'Ministers write off £10bn on lost, unusable or overpriced PPE', *The Times*, 2 Feb 2022, https://www.thetimes.co.uk/article/ministers-write-off-9-billion-on-lost-unusable-or-overpriced-ppe-262kpdr8v
125 Haroon Siddique, 'Use of "VIP lane" to award Covid PPE contracts unlawful, high court rules', *Guardian*, 12 Jan 2022, https://www.theguardian.com/politics/2022/jan/12/use-of-vip-lane-to-award-covid-ppe-contracts-unlawful-high-court-rules
126 'Half of VIP lane companies supplied PPE worth £1 billion that was not fit for purpose', Spotlight On Corruption, 11 Feb 2022, https://www.spotlightcorruption.org/half-of-vip-lane-companies-supplied-ppe-worth-1-billion-that-was-not-fit-for-purpose/
127 'Profits jumped 500% at Uniserve after firm landed "VIP" contracts', Good Law Project, 4 Oct 2021, https://goodlawproject.org/update/uniserve-profits-500-vip-contracts/
128 Sam Bright, 'Firm owned by Conservative donor nets additional £81.8 million government PPE deals', *Byline Times*, 28 Sep 2020, https://bylinetimes.com/2020/09/18/firm-meller-designs-conservative-donor-nets-millions-government-ppe-deals/
129 Sebastien Ash and Daniel Kraemer, 'Coronavirus: Conservative councillor PPE contracts questioned', BBC News, 10 Jul 2020, https://www.bbc.co.uk/news/uk-politics-53361167
130 Sam Bright, 'Firm that gave £400,000 to Conservatives wins £93.8 million government PPE deal', *Byline Times*, 16 Sep 2020, https://bylinetimes.com/2020/09/16/company-conservative-donations-government-ppe-procurement-deal/
131 'Investigation into government procurement during the COVID-19 pandemic', National Audit Office, 26 Nov 2020, https://www.nao.org.uk/press-releases/government-procurement-during-the-covid-19-pandemic/
132 'Coronavirus: Protective Clothing', Hansard and TheyWorkForYou, 25 Nov 2021, https://www.theyworkforyou.com/wrans/?id=2021-11-22.79399.h&p=25429
133 Adam Bychawski, '"VIP" lane led to "systemic bias" in UK government COVID contracts', *openDemocracy*, 22 Apr 2021, https://www.opendemocracy.net/en/opendemocracyuk/vip-lane-led-to-systemic-bias-in-uk-government-covid-contracts/
134 'Covid-19: One in five government contracts had signs of possible corruption, report finds', *BMJ*, 23 Apr 2021, https://www.bmj.com/content/373/bmj.n1072
135 Daniel Sanderson, 'Michelle Mone's office guilty of "Wiki Washing" her online biography', *Herald*, 20 Aug 2015, https://www.heraldscotland.com/news/13614216.michelle-mones-office-guilty-wiki-washing-online-biography/
136 Douglas Dickie, 'Did Michelle Mone create "Erin Brockovich bra" worn by Julia Roberts in hit movie?', *Scottish Daily Express*, 6 Dec 2022, https://www.scottishdailyexpress.co.uk/news/weird-news/michelle-mone-create-erin-brockovich-28669181

137 Daniel Sanderson, 'Michelle Mone's office guilty of "Wiki Washing" her online biography', *Herald*, 20 Aug 2015, https://www.heraldscotland.com/news/13614216.michelle-mones-office-guilty-wiki-washing-online-biography/
138 Michael Glackin, 'Lingerie boss drops her support for Labour', *Sunday Times*, 25 Apr 2009, https://www.thetimes.co.uk/article/lingerie-boss-drops-her-support-for-labour-sb37305smpz
139 Daniel Sanderson, 'Millionaire businessman calls on UK government to explain Mone appointment', *Herald*, 15 Aug 2015, https://www.heraldscotland.com/news/13599093.millionaire-businessman-calls-uk-government-explain-mone-appointment/
140 Tom Gordon, 'Major Tory donor latest to question Mone's government appointment', *Herald*, 23 Aug 2015, https://www.heraldscotland.com/news/13620827.major-tory-donor-latest-question-mones-government-appointment/
141 Euan McColm, 'Scots Tory cringe over Michelle Mone', *Scotsman*, 16 Aug 2015, https://www.scotsman.com/news/opinion/columnists/euan-mccolm-scots-tory-cringe-over-michelle-mone-2466967
142 Daniel Sanderson, 'Millionaire businessman calls on UK government to explain Mone appointment', *Herald*, 15 Aug 2015, https://www.heraldscotland.com/news/13599093.millionaire-businessman-calls-uk-government-explain-mone-appointment/
143 'Rod defends Pen over lingerie-gate', *Evening Standard*, 28 Mar 2004, https://www.standard.co.uk/hp/front/rod-defends-pen-over-lingeriegate-7235277.html
144 David Conn and Paul Lewis, 'Michelle Mone referred company for PPE contracts five days before it was incorporated', *Guardian*, 7 Jan 2022, https://www.theguardian.com/politics/2022/jan/07/michelle-mone-referred-company-for-ppe-contracts-five-days-before-it-was-incorporated
145 Sam Bright, 'Government awards £122 million PPE contract to one-month-old firm', *Byline Times*, 14 Sep 2020, https://bylinetimes.com/2020/09/14/government-awards-122-million-ppe-contract-to-one-month-old-firm/
146 Inderdeep Bains, '"Aggressive" Michelle Mone was "threatening" over Covid tests: In his explosive Pandemic Diaries, Matt Hancock accuses the Tory peer of throwing around "wild accusations" to try to help firm win Covid contract', *Daily Mail*, 4 Dec 2022, https://www.dailymail.co.uk/news/article-11500789/Matt-Hancock-accuses-Michelle-Mone-wild-accusations-try-help-firm-win-Covid-contract.html
147 David Conn, 'Government paid firm linked to Tory peer £122m for PPE bought for £46m', *Guardian*, 27 Mar 2022, https://www.theguardian.com/politics/2022/mar/27/government-paid-firm-linked-to-tory-peer-122m-for-ppe-bought-for-46m
148 Dominic Yeatman, 'Michelle Mone accused of trying to "bully" ministers over £200,000,000 PPE contract', *Metro*, 5 Dec 2022, https://metro.co.uk/2022/12/05/mone-accused-of-trying-to-bully-ministers-over-200m-ppe-contract-17876901/
149 Anna Gross and Kadhim Shubber, 'PPE Medpro gave "invalid" accreditation for gowns, UK government claims', *Financial Times*, 4 Jan 2023, https://www.ft.com/content/7a2093f8-55f8-400f-9176-2225b9193e05
150 David Conn, 'Gove under pressure to explain role in PPE deals for Mone-linked firm', *Guardian*, 24 Nov 2022, https://www.theguardian.com/uk-news/2022/nov/24/michael-gove-under-pressure-explain-role-ppe-deals-michelle-mone
151 David Conn, 'Revealed: Tory peer Michelle Mone secretly received £29m from "VIP lane" PPE firm', *Guardian*, 23 Nov 2022, https://www.theguardian.com/uk-news/2022/nov/23/revealed-tory-peer-michelle-mone-secretly-received-29m-from-vip-lane-ppe-firm
152 Andrew Ellson, 'Company linked to Michelle Mone bought private jet after PPE windfall', *The Times*, 9 Dec 2022, https://www.thetimes.co.uk/article/company-linked-to-michelle-mone-bought-private-jet-after-ppe-windfall-02j75t97m
153 David Conn, 'Michelle Mone's PPE denials v what we know', *Guardian*, 23 Nov 2022, https://www.theguardian.com/uk-news/2022/nov/23/michelle-mones-ppe-denials-v-what-we-know
154 Gabriel Pogrund and Jack Clover, 'The PPE Rich List: Covid firms unmasked', *Sunday Times*, 11 Dec 2022, https://www.thetimes.co.uk/article/the-ppe-rich-list-covid-firms-unmasked-6270fk8xw

155 Rory Woods, 'UK government spent billions on substandard PPE, as private sector made a killing', *WSWS*, 18 Feb 2022, https://www.wsws.org/en/articles/2022/02/19/nofi-f19.html

156 'Tory donor's company awarded £4.5 million government contract to take care of mountain of unusable PPE waste', Good Law Project, 12 Dec 2022, https://goodlawproject.org/revealed-tory-donors-company-awarded-4-5-million-government-contract-to-take-care-of-mountain-of-unusable-ppe-waste/

157 David Conn, 'Michelle Mone's PPE denials v what we know', *Guardian*, 23 Nov 2022, https://www.theguardian.com/uk-news/2022/nov/23/michelle-mones-ppe-denials-v-what-we-know

158 David Conn, 'PPE Medpro: UK government alleges firm supplied defective gowns to NHS', *Guardian*, 5 Jan 2023, https://www.theguardian.com/uk-news/2023/jan/04/ppe-medpro-uk-government-alleges-firm-supplied-defective-gowns-nhs

159 '£11m spent so far in Medpro PPE legal case', *Three.FM*, 7 Jan 2023, https://www.three.fm/news/isle-of-man-news/11m-spent-so-far-in-medpro-ppe-legal-case/

160 David Conn, Paul Lewis, Vikram Dodd and Kevin Rawlinson, 'Michelle Mone's home raided as PPE firm linked to Tory peer investigated', *Guardian*, 29 Apr 2022, https://www.theguardian.com/uk-news/2022/apr/29/nca-launches-investigation-ppe-firm-linked-to-michelle-mone

161 David Conn, 'HMRC names three schemes linked to Mone's husband as tax avoidance', *Guardian*, 20 Jan 2023, https://www.theguardian.com/politics/2023/jan/20/hmrc-names-three-schemes-linked-to-michelle-mone-husband-as-tax-avoidance

162 Jessica Elgot, Aubrey Allegretti and Rowena Mason, 'Sunak vows to bring "integrity" to No 10 but gambles by restoring Braverman', *Guardian*, 25 Oct 2022, https://www.theguardian.com/politics/2022/oct/25/sunak-vows-to-bring-integrity-to-no-10-but-gambles-by-restoring-braverman

163 Sophie Morris, 'Baroness Michelle Mone takes a leave of absence from House of Lords amid PPE contracts controversy', Sky News, 7 Dec 2022, https://news.sky.com/story/baroness-michelle-mone-takes-a-leave-of-absence-from-house-of-lords-amid-ppe-contracts-controversy-12762711

164 Rowena Mason, 'Nadine Dorries apologises to MPs over I'm a Celebrity appearance fee', *Guardian*, 11 Nov 2013, https://www.theguardian.com/politics/2013/nov/11/nadine-dorries-im-a-celebrity-apology

165 Isobel Lewis, 'I'm a Celeb: Matt Hancock finally discusses dyslexia after saying he would raise awareness in jungle', *Independent*, 21 Nov 2022, https://www.independent.co.uk/arts-entertainment/tv/news/im-a-celebrity-matt-hancock-dyslexia-b2229414.html

166 David Hughes [@DavidHughesPA], Twitter, 1 Nov 2022, https://twitter.com/DavidHughesPA/status/1587403568692207617

167 'Care home discharges during Covid ruled "unlawful"', Disability Rights UK, 4 May 2022, https://www.disabilityrightsuk.org/news/2022/may/care-home-discharges-during-covid-ruled-%E2%80%98unlawful%E2%80%99

168 Tom Ambrose, 'Matt Hancock donates just 3% of I'm a Celebrity fee', *Guardian*, 27 Jan 2023, https://www.theguardian.com/politics/2023/jan/27/matt-hancock-donates-three-per-cent-of-im-a-celebrity-fee

169 Ava Santina [@AvaSantina], Twitter, 9 Nov 2022, https://twitter.com/AvaSantina/status/1590259110108631042

170 'Matt Hancock: Covid campaigners fly banner over I'm A Celebrity jungle', BBC News, 15 Nov 2022, https://www.bbc.co.uk/news/entertainment-arts-63634006

171 'I'm a Celebrity: "Matt Hancock should let someone else be our MP"', BBC News, 28 Nov 2022, https://www.bbc.co.uk/news/uk-england-suffolk-63781019

172 Lauren Williams, 'I'm A Celebrity backlash: Matt Hancock jungle stint prompts over 2,000 Ofcom complaints', *Express*, 16 Nov 2022, https://www.express.co.uk/showbiz/tv-radio/1697488/Im-A-Celebrity-Ofcom-complaints-2000-Matt-Hancock

173 Jessica Elgot, Nadia Khomami and Henry Dyer, 'Matt Hancock loses Tory whip after agreeing to appear on I'm a Celebrity', *Guardian*, 1 Nov 2022, https://www.theguardian.com/politics/2022/nov/01/matt-hancock-loses-tory-whip-after-agreeing-to-appear-on-im-a-celebrity

174 Peter Walker, 'Row grows over Matt Hancock's announcement he is quitting as MP', *Guardian*, 7 Dec 2022, https://www.theguardian.com/politics/2022/dec/07/matt-hancock-will-not-stand-conservatives-next-election

175 Anna Isaac, 'Worst fall in UK living standards since records began, says OBR', *Guardian*, 17 Nov 2022, https://www.theguardian.com/business/2022/nov/17/obr-confirms-uk-enters-year-long-recession-with-half-a-million-job-losses-likely

176 'UK citizens pay the highest electricity bills in the world', *Oil Price*, 16 Nov 2022, https://oilprice.com/Energy/Energy-General/UK-Citizens-Pay-The-Highest-Electricity-Bills-In-The-World.html

177 Geoff Tily, '17-year wage squeeze the worst in two hundred years', TUC, 11 May 2018, https://www.tuc.org.uk/blogs/17-year-wage-squeeze-worst-two-hundred-years

178 Pedro Goncalves, 'Migration data shows Johnson's Brexit will not result in a high wage economy', *Yahoo! News*, 17 Feb 2022, https://uk.news.yahoo.com/migration-data-shows-johnsons-brexit-will-drive-high-wage-economy-a-false-claim-000147191.html

179 Laurie MacFarlane, 'Boris Johnson's vision for a high-wage economy is built on shaky foundations', *openDemocracy*, 7 Oct 2021, https://www.opendemocracy.net/en/oureconomy/boris-johnsons-vision-for-a-high-wage-economy-is-built-on-shaky-foundations/

180 LaToya Harding, 'Brexit deal will see a £470 real terms cut in worker pay every year', *Yahoo! News*, 22 Jun 2022, https://uk.news.yahoo.com/brexit-legacy-uk-will-be-poorer-in-decade-ahead-study-says-230105346.html

181 Rowena Mason, 'Tory chairman's "NHS strikes help Putin" claim dismissed as "ludicrous"', *Guardian*, 4 Dec 2022, https://www.theguardian.com/uk-news/2022/dec/04/striking-uk-workers-playing-into-putins-hands-says-zahawi

182 Gwyn Topham, 'Rail strikes cost UK £1bn and settling would have been cheaper, minister admits', *Guardian*, 18 Jan 2023, https://www.theguardian.com/uk-news/2023/jan/18/rail-strikes-cost-uk-1bn-and-settling-would-have-been-cheaper-minister-admits

183 'Do you support or oppose the train drivers and rail transport workers strikes taking place this week?', YouGov, 6 Oct 2022, https://yougov.co.uk/topics/economy/survey-results/daily/2022/10/06/338b8/1

184 'Support for nurses' strikes lower than last month's but blame placed mainly with the government', Ipsos, 18 Jan 2023, https://www.ipsos.com/en-uk/support-nurses-strikes-lower-last-months-blame-placed-mainly-government

185 Delphine Strauss, Sarah Neville and Bethan Staton, 'Nurses' rejection of pay offer leaves UK government strategy in disarray', *Financial Times*, 14 Apr 2023, https://www.ft.com/content/9c8e065d-65e4-4eb3-8b88-b9efa2be8fc0

186 'Health Secretary is putting lives at risk by refusing to hold urgent talks', *Mirror*, 7 Apr 2023, https://www.mirror.co.uk/news/politics/health-secretary-putting-lives-risk-29658768

187 Matt Bodell, 'Health Secretary accused of "desperately looking for ways not to negotiate with nurses"', NursingNotes, 19 Jan 2023, https://nursingnotes.co.uk/news/politics/health-secretary-accused-of-desperately-looking-for-ways-not-to-negotiate-with-nurses/

188 Mikey Smith, 'Health Secretary Steve Barclay faces questions over meetings with nightclub owners', *Mirror*, 8 Apr 2023, https://www.mirror.co.uk/news/politics/health-secretary-steve-barclay-faces-29663525

189 Sky News [@SkyNews], Twitter, 12 Apr 2023, https://twitter.com/SkyNews/status/1646042272553746432

190 'Annual salary of Members of Parliament (MPs) in the United Kingdom from 2010/11 to 2023/24', Statista, Feb 2023, https://www.statista.com/statistics/388885/mp-salary-uk/

191 Denis Campbell, 'Non-NHS healthcare providers given £96bn in a decade, says Labour', *Guardian*, 3 May 2021, https://www.theguardian.com/society/2021/may/03/non-nhs-healthcare-providers-given-96bn-in-a-decade-says-labour

192 Larry Elliott, 'Tory austerity "has cost UK half a trillion pounds of public spending since 2010"', *Guardian*, 3 Mar 2023, https://www.theguardian.com/business/2023/mar/03/tory-austerity-has-cost-uk-half-a-trillion-pounds-of-public-spending-since-2010

193 Timeline of prehistory, Wikipedia, https://en.wikipedia.org/wiki/Pig

194 Ned Simons, 'Andrew Bridgen summoned by Tory whips after calling for David Cameron to go', *HuffPost*, 10 Jun 2013, https://www.huffingtonpost.co.uk/2013/06/10/andrew-bridgen-cameron-whips_n_3414009.html

195 Dan Martin, 'In full: Andrew Bridgen's stinging no-confidence letter blasts Theresa May's Brexit plan', *Leicestershire Live*, 11 Jul 2018, https://www.leicestermercury.co.uk/news/local-news/full-andrew-bridgens-stinging-no-1770043
196 Christopher Hope, 'Brexiteer becomes fifth Tory MP this week to submit Boris Johnson no confidence letter', *Telegraph*, 13 Jan 2022, https://www.telegraph.co.uk/politics/2022/01/13/brexiteer-becomes-fifth-tory-mp-week-submit-boris-johnson-no/
197 Dominic Penna, 'Jamie Wallis becomes third Tory MP to urge Liz Truss to quit', *Telegraph*, 16 Oct 2022, https://www.telegraph.co.uk/politics/2022/10/16/liz-truss-jeremy-hunt-new-chancellor-income-tax/
198 'AB Produce near Measham risks losing licence over "urine" smell', BBC News, 14 Aug 2014, https://www.bbc.co.uk/news/uk-england-leicestershire-28785285
199 Gabriel Pogrund and Matt Chorley, '"Dishonest" MP Bridgen "lied" about conduct in family dispute', *The Times*, 17 Apr 2022, https://www.thetimes.co.uk/article/12ba7432-bdb8-11ec-84c4-70cc6ae427fb
200 Gabriel Pogrund and Matt Chorley, '"Dishonest" MP Bridgen "lied" about conduct in family dispute', *The Times*, 17 Apr 2022, https://www.thetimes.co.uk/article/12ba7432-bdb8-11ec-84c4-70cc6ae427fb
201 Gabriel Pogrund and Matt Chorley, '"Dishonest" MP Bridgen "lied" about conduct in family dispute', *The Times*, 17 Apr 2022, https://www.thetimes.co.uk/article/12ba7432-bdb8-11ec-84c4-70cc6ae427fb
202 Jenna Corderoy, 'Tory MP facing suspension after openDemocracy reveals lobbying scandal', openDemocracy, 3 Nov 2022, https://www.opendemocracy.net/en/conservative-mp-andrew-bridgen-suspension-lobbying/
203 Rachael Burford, 'Andrew Bridgen: Tory MP facing five-day Commons suspension over "significant" rule breaches this week', *Evening Standard*, 9 Jan 2023, https://www.standard.co.uk/news/politics/tory-mp-andrew-bridgen-commons-suspension-lobbying-rule-b1051630.html
204 Jenna Corderoy, 'Tory MP facing suspension after openDemocracy reveals lobbying scandal', openDemocracy, 3 Nov 2022, https://www.opendemocracy.net/en/conservative-mp-andrew-bridgen-suspension-lobbying/
205 Rachael Burford, 'Andrew Bridgen: Tory MP facing five-day Commons suspension over "significant" rule breaches this week', *Evening Standard*, 9 Jan 2023, https://www.standard.co.uk/news/politics/tory-mp-andrew-bridgen-commons-suspension-lobbying-rule-b1051630.html
206 Paul Seddon and Rachel Schraer, 'Andrew Bridgen suspended as Tory MP over Covid vaccine comments', BBC News, 1 Jan 2023, https://www.bbc.co.uk/news/uk-politics-64236687
207 Rowena Mason, 'The tarantula stays: Tory chief whip won't remove pet spider from office', *Guardian*, 23 Nov 2016, https://www.theguardian.com/politics/2016/nov/23/the-tarantula-stays-tory-chief-whip-wont-remove-pet-spider-from-office-gavin-williamson
208 Jacob Jarvis, 'Gavin Williamson "swears on his children's lives" he was not behind Huawei leak', *Evening Standard*, 1 May 2019, https://www.standard.co.uk/news/politics/gavin-williamson-swears-on-his-children-s-lives-he-was-not-behind-huawei-leak-a4131901.html
209 Aubrey Allegretti, Dan Sabbagh and Pippa Crerar, 'Senior MoD figures thought Gavin Williamson caused national security leak', *Guardian*, 10 Nov 2022, https://www.theguardian.com/politics/2022/nov/10/senior-mod-figures-thought-gavin-williamson-caused-national-security-leak
210 Camilla Turner, 'Gavin Williamson and Ofqual divided over A-level exam grades', *Daily Telegraph*, 17 Aug 2020, https://www.telegraph.co.uk/news/2020/08/16/top-figures-ofqual-want-government-u-turn-award-students-predicted/
211 Adam Bienkov [@AdamBienkov], Twitter, 9 Nov 2022, https://twitter.com/AdamBienkov/status/1590267517582254080
212 Aletha Adu and Rowena Mason, 'Sunak under pressure over Williamson's "vile messages" to Wendy Morton', *Guardian*, 4 Nov 2022, https://www.theguardian.com/politics/2022/nov/04/rishi-sunak-under-pressure-over-gavin-williamson-vile-messages-to-wendy-morton

213 Gabriel Pogrund, 'No 10 refuses to endorse Gavin Williamson as threatening texts revealed', *Sunday Times*, 5 Nov 2022, https://www.thetimes.co.uk/article/no-10-refuses-to-endorse-gavin-williamson-as-threatening-texts-revealed-xnqj03kkm
214 Jessica Elgot, 'Rishi Sunak under pressure over Gavin Williamson texts', *Guardian*, 6 Nov 2022, https://www.theguardian.com/politics/2022/nov/06/oliver-dowden-defends-gavin-williamson-texts-as-heat-of-the-moment
215 Pippa Crerar, 'Senior civil servant claims Gavin Williamson told them to "slit your throat"', *Guardian*, 7 Nov 2022, https://www.theguardian.com/politics/2022/nov/07/senior-civil-servant-claims-gavin-williamson-told-them-slit-your-throat
216 Channel 4 News [@Channel4News], Twitter, 8 Nov 2022, https://twitter.com/Channel4News/status/1590043429656223744
217 Pippa Crerar and Rowena Mason, 'Gavin Williamson quits cabinet after claims of "unethical and immoral" behaviour', *Guardian*, 8 Nov 2022, https://www.theguardian.com/politics/2022/nov/08/pressure-grows-on-unethical-and-immoral-gavin-williamson
218 Sophie Morris, 'Prime Minister's Questions: Rishi Sunak says it is "absolutely right" Gavin Williamson resigned – and admits "regret" over appointment', Sky News, 9 Nov 2022, https://news.sky.com/story/prime-ministers-questions-rishi-sunak-says-it-is-absolutely-right-gavin-williamson-resigned-and-admits-regret-over-appointment-12742539
219 Pippa Crerar, 'Senior civil servant claims Gavin Williamson told them to "slit your throat"', *Guardian*, 7 Nov 2022, https://www.theguardian.com/politics/2022/nov/07/senior-civil-servant-claims-gavin-williamson-told-them-slit-your-throat
220 Jack Maidment [@jrmaidment], Twitter, 3 Nov 2022, https://twitter.com/jrmaidment/status/1588115651054505984
221 Sophie Morris, 'Prime Minister's Questions: Rishi Sunak says it is "absolutely right" Gavin Williamson resigned – and admits "regret" over appointment', Sky News, 9 Nov 2022, https://news.sky.com/story/prime-ministers-questions-rishi-sunak-says-it-is-absolutely-right-gavin-williamson-resigned-and-admits-regret-over-appointment-12742539
222 Iain Watson, 'Gavin Williamson: More MPs planned to complain before resignation', BBC News, 10 Nov 2022, https://www.bbc.co.uk/news/uk-politics-63578525
223 Jasper King, 'Dominic Raab "hurled three tomatoes across a room at staff in fit of rage"', *Metro*, 12 Nov 2022, https://metro.co.uk/2022/11/12/dominic-raab-hurls-three-tomatoes-at-staff-in-fit-of-rage-17746668/
224 Gina Miller, 'I was bullied and demeaned by Dominic Raab', *Independent*, 2 Feb 2023, https://www.independent.co.uk/voices/dominic-raab-bullying-allegations-gina-miller-b2274570.html
225 Kate Devlin, 'Dominic Raab faces claims he "bullied and demeaned" leading anti-Brexit campaigner', *Independent*, 3 Feb 2023, https://www.independent.co.uk/news/uk/politics/gina-miller-dominic-raab-bullied-b2274685.html
226 Jon Stone and William Mata, 'Dominic Raab: Timeline of bullying claims against deputy prime minister', *Independent*, 20 Apr 2023, https://www.independent.co.uk/news/uk/politics/dominic-raab-bullying-complaints-timeline-b2275186.html
227 Jon Stone and William Mata, 'Dominic Raab: Timeline of bullying claims against deputy prime minister', *Independent*, 20 Apr 2023, https://www.independent.co.uk/news/uk/politics/dominic-raab-bullying-complaints-timeline-b2275186.html
228 Kate Devlin, '"Plausible" for Raab to be characterised as someone who could bully, former top civil servant warns', *Independent*, 14 Nov 2022, https://www.independent.co.uk/news/uk/politics/dominic-raab-bully-simon-mcdonald-b2224725.html
229 Rajeev Syal, 'Priti Patel reaches £340,000 settlement with ex-Home Office chief Philip Rutnam', *Guardian*, 4 Mar 2021, https://www.theguardian.com/politics/2021/mar/04/priti-patel-reaches-six-figure-settlement-with-ex-home-office-chief-philip-rutnam
230 Pippa Crerar and Aubrey Allegretti, 'Top Whitehall official had to apologise over alleged bad behaviour by Raab', *Guardian*, 21 Nov 2022, https://www.theguardian.com/politics/2022/nov/21/top-whitehall-official-had-to-apologise-over-alleged-bad-behaviour-by-dominic-raab

231 Ben Riley-Smith, 'Boris Johnson warned Dominic Raab about his conduct and gave evidence to bullying investigation', *Telegraph*, 8 Mar 2023, https://www.telegraph.co.uk/politics/2023/03/08/boris-johnson-warned-dominic-raab-conduct-gave-evidence-bullying/
232 Jess Bowie and Beckie Smith, 'EXCL: Raab telling MoJ staff he has zero tolerance for bullying "felt like gaslighting"', *Civil Service World*, 15 Nov 2022, https://www.civilserviceworld.com/professions/article/dominic-raab-moj-staff-bullying-zero-tolerance-felt-like-gaslighting-belittling-intimidating
233 Jon Stone and William Mata, 'Dominic Raab: Timeline of bullying claims against deputy prime minister', *Independent*, 20 Apr 2023, https://www.independent.co.uk/news/uk/politics/dominic-raab-bullying-complaints-timeline-b2275186.html
234 Michael Savage and Toby Helm, 'Dominic Raab: more civil servants in bullying complaint than previously thought', *Observer*, 5 Feb 2023, https://www.theguardian.com/politics/2023/feb/05/dominic-raab-more-civil-servants-in-bullying-complaint-than-previously-thought
235 Jon Stone and William Mata, 'Dominic Raab: Timeline of bullying claims against deputy prime minister', *Independent*, 20 Apr 2023, https://www.independent.co.uk/news/uk/politics/dominic-raab-bullying-complaints-timeline-b2275186.html
236 Pippa Crerar [@PippaCrerar], Twitter, 16 Nov 2022, https://twitter.com/PippaCrerar/status/1592856932016324608
237 Pippa Crerar [@PippaCrerar], Twitter, 15 Nov 2022, https://twitter.com/PippaCrerar/status/1592612651267678208
238 Liam O'Dell, '8 times Rishi Sunak's government definitely led with "integrity, professionalism and accountability"', *Indy100*, 9 Nov 2022, https://www.indy100.com/politics/rishi-sunak-government-integrity-professionalism
239 Jon Stone and William Mata, 'Dominic Raab: Timeline of bullying claims against deputy prime minister', *Independent*, 20 Apr 2023, https://www.independent.co.uk/news/uk/politics/dominic-raab-bullying-complaints-timeline-b2275186.html
240 Pippa Crerar, 'Sunak urges officials with concerns about Raab to come forward', *Guardian*, 15 Nov 2022, https://www.theguardian.com/politics/2022/nov/15/sunak-urges-officials-with-concerns-about-raab-to-come-forward
241 Michael Savage and Toby Helm, 'Dominic Raab: more civil servants in bullying complaint than previously thought', *Observer*, 5 Feb 2023, https://www.theguardian.com/politics/2023/feb/05/dominic-raab-more-civil-servants-in-bullying-complaint-than-previously-thought
242 Jessica Elgot, 'Candidates snub Sunak's ethics adviser role left vacant for five months', *Guardian*, 28 Nov 2022, https://www.theguardian.com/politics/2022/nov/28/candidates-snub-sunak-ethics-adviser-role-left-vacant-for-five-months
243 Peter Walker and Henry Dyer, 'Sir Laurie Magnus named Rishi Sunak's new ethics adviser', *Guardian*, 22 Dec 2022, https://www.theguardian.com/politics/2022/dec/22/sir-laurie-magnus-named-rishi-sunak-independent-adviser-ministers-interests
244 Aletha Adu, 'Braverman says she "never ignored legal advice" about housing asylum seekers', *Guardian*, 31 Oct 2022, https://www.theguardian.com/uk-news/2022/oct/31/suella-braverman-says-never-ignored-legal-advice-housing-asylum-seekers
245 Jon Stone and William Mata, 'Dominic Raab: Timeline of bullying claims against deputy prime minister', *Independent*, 20 Apr 2023, https://www.independent.co.uk/news/uk/politics/dominic-raab-bullying-complaints-timeline-b2275186.html
246 Pippa Crerar, Aubrey Allegretti and Kiran Stacey, 'Dominic Raab quits as report criticises his "unreasonably aggressive conduct"', *Guardian*, 21 Apr 2023, https://www.theguardian.com/politics/2023/apr/21/dominic-raab-resigns-as-deputy-pm-after-bullying-allegations
247 Aubrey Allegretti and Pippa Crerar, 'Raab fights for political future as PM ponders "stinging" bullying report', *Guardian*, 20 Apr 2023, https://www.theguardian.com/politics/2023/apr/20/dominic-raab-fights-for-political-future-as-pm-ponders-stinging-bullying-report
248 David Burke, 'Dithering Rishi Sunak slammed over Dominic Raab "farce" as deputy PM faces D-Day', *Mirror*, 21 Apr 2023, https://www.mirror.co.uk/news/politics/dithering-rishi-sunak-slammed-over-29769909
249 Ben Riley-Smith, 'Bullying report sets "dangerous precedent", warns Dominic Raab as he resigns', *Telegraph*, 21 Apr 2023, https://www.telegraph.co.uk/politics/2023/04/21/dominic-raab-resigns-justice-minister-dangerous-precedent/

250 'No evidence for Rishi Sunak's claim about "record" number of new homes built', Full Fact, 2 Nov 2022, https://fullfact.org/economy/rishi-sunak-house-building-pmq/
251 Emily Twinch, 'Tory infighting as Villiers tables bid to scrap housing targets', *Housing Today*, 21 Nov 2022, https://www.housingtoday.co.uk/news/tory-infighting-as-villiers-tables-bid-to-scrap-housing-targets/5120564.article
252 Oliver Wright, 'UK housing crisis: planning targets scrapped in "win for nimbys"', *The Times*, 7 Apr 2023, https://www.thetimes.co.uk/article/uk-housing-supply-crisis-home-building-england-2023-v0wjkwl0j
253 Isabel Hardman, 'What is the Tory party's legacy after so many years in power? Pretty thin gruel', *Observer*, 27 Nov 2022, https://www.theguardian.com/commentisfree/2022/nov/27/what-is-the-tory-party-legacy-after-so-many-years-in-power-pretty-thin-gruel
254 Jessica Elgot, 'Bright Blue founder to quit, condemning Tory party "betrayal" of millennials', *Guardian*, 22 Nov 2022, https://www.theguardian.com/uk-news/2022/nov/22/bright-blue-founder-to-quit-over-tory-partys-betrayal-of-millennials
255 'Engagements', Hansard, 30 Nov 2022, https://hansard.parliament.uk/commons/2022-11-30/debates/1BFA1A26-3814-40E6-B310-418F6C03ED30/Engagements
256 'UK government debt and deficit: December 2018', ONS, 17 Apr 2019, https://www.ons.gov.uk/economy/governmentpublicsectorandtaxes/publicspending/bulletins/ukgovernmentdebtanddeficitforeurostatmaast/december2018
257 'UK government debt and deficit: September 2022', ONS, 31 Jan 2023, https://www.ons.gov.uk/economy/governmentpublicsectorandtaxes/publicspending/bulletins/ukgovernmentdebtanddeficitforeurostatmaast/september2022
258 'United Kingdom Inflation Rates: 1989 to 2023', *Rate Inflation*, Mar 2023, https://www.rateinflation.com/inflation-rate/uk-historical-inflation-rate/
259 Richard Partington, 'Number of days lost to strikes is highest since the Thatcher era', *Guardian*, 14 Feb 2023, https://www.theguardian.com/uk-news/2023/feb/14/nearly-million-days-lost-strikes-december-uk-pay-growth
260 'Long-term international migration, provisional: year ending June 2022', ONS, 24 Nov 2022, https://www.ons.gov.uk/peoplepopulationandcommunity/populationandmigration/internationalmigration/bulletins/longterminternationalmigrationprovisional/yearendingjune2022
261 Faye Brown, 'Lee Anderson: New Tory deputy chairman says he would support return of death penalty', Sky News, 9 Feb 2023, https://news.sky.com/story/lee-anderson-new-tory-deputy-chairman-says-he-would-support-return-of-death-penalty-12806408
262 Peter Walker, 'Rishi Sunak rebukes Tory vice-chair for backing death penalty', *Guardian*, 9 Feb 2023, https://www.theguardian.com/politics/2023/feb/09/lee-anderson-tory-vice-chair-backed-death-penalty-and-naval-standoff-in-channel
263 Ellie Harrison, "How ashamed are they?' Carol Vorderman calls out Conservative MPs who hide role on social media', *Independent*, 4 Apr 2023, https://www.independent.co.uk/arts-entertainment/tv/news/carol-vorderman-conservative-tories-b2313721.html
264 Brendan McFadden, 'Conservative MP Lee Anderson likens government to the "band on the Titanic"', *iNews*, 29 Jan 2023, https://inews.co.uk/news/conservative-mp-lee-anderson-likens-government-to-the-band-on-the-titanic-2115473

2023: 'A Whiny, Unpleasant, Bitchy Row'

1 'The EEC and Britain's late entry', The National Archives, https://www.nationalarchives.gov.uk/cabinetpapers/themes/eec-britains-late-entry.htm
2 Joe Evans, 'Brexit deal done: the key dates in the UK exit from the EU', *The Week*, 24 Dec 2020, https://www.theweek.co.uk/100284/brexit-timeline-key-dates-in-the-uk-s-break-up-with-the-eu
3 Ben Walker, 'Rishi Sunak at day 100: the least popular prime minister in recent history', *New Statesman*, 2 Feb 2023, https://sotn.newstatesman.com/2023/02/rishi-sunak-day-100-least-popular-prime-minister
4 Phillip Inman, 'Decision on bringing forward UK pension age rise to 68 delayed until after election', *Guardian*, 30 Mar 2023, https://www.theguardian.com/money/2023/mar/30/decision-on-bringing-forward-uk-pension-age-rise-to-68-delayed-until-after-election

5   Lucy Garcia, 'NHS: Sajid Javid calls for people to PAY for GP visits and A&E trips', *The National*, 21 Jan 2023, https://www.thenational.scot/news/23267086.nhs-sajid-javid-calls-people-pay-gp-visits-e-trips/
6   Billy Kenber, 'Nadhim Zahawi "may have avoided millions in tax with trust"', *The Times*, 16 Jul 2022, https://www.thetimes.co.uk/article/nadhim-zahawi-may-have-avoided-millions-in-tax-with-trust-0n8mt7kj7
7   Jon Ungoed-Thomas, 'Zahawi urged to explain source of £26m mystery loans', *Guardian*, 17 Jul 2022, https://www.theguardian.com/uk-news/2022/jul/17/zahawi-urged-to-explain-source-of-26m-mystery-loans
8   Josh Halliday and Heather Stewart, 'How we got here: events leading up to Nadhim Zahawi's sacking for breaching ministerial code', *Guardian*, 29 Jan 2023, https://www.theguardian.com/uk-news/2023/jan/29/seven-occasions-when-nadhim-zahawi-broke-the-ministerial-code
9   Simon Walters, 'Nadhim Zahawi: New chancellor's finances secretly investigated by National Crime Agency', *Independent*, 6 Jul 2022, https://www.independent.co.uk/news/uk/politics/chancellor-nadhim-zahawi-nca-investigation-b2117197.html
10 Josh Halliday and Heather Stewart, 'How we got here: events leading up to Nadhim Zahawi's sacking for breaching ministerial code', *Guardian*, 29 Jan 2023, https://www.theguardian.com/uk-news/2023/jan/29/seven-occasions-when-nadhim-zahawi-broke-the-ministerial-code
11 Michael Savage and Jon Ungoed-Thomas, 'Revealed: officials raised "flag" over Nadhim Zahawi's tax affairs before he was appointed chancellor', *Guardian*, 9 Jul 2022, https://www.theguardian.com/uk-news/2022/jul/09/revealed-officials-raised-flag-over-nadim-zahawis-tax-affairs-before-he-was-appointed-chancellor
12 Jim Pickard, 'Pressure builds on Nadhim Zahawi to explain his finances', *Financial Times*, 10 Jul 2022, https://www.ft.com/content/a57b6f7d-003f-4651-a6b8-3e880293efc1
13 Dan Neidle, 'Worse than careless? The Zahawi cover-up', Tax Policy Associates, 24 Jan 2023, https://www.taxpolicy.org.uk/2023/01/24/coverup/
14 Billy Kenber, George Greenwood and Mario Ledwith, 'Nadhim Zahawi "may have avoided millions in tax with trust"', *The Times*, 16 Jul 2022, https://www.thetimes.co.uk/article/nadhim-zahawi-may-have-avoided-millions-in-tax-with-trust-0n8mt7kj7
15 Richard Hattersley, 'Chancellor legal letters reject tax "smears"', *Accounting Web*, 27 Jul 2022, https://www.accountingweb.co.uk/tax/personal-tax/chancellor-legal-letters-reject-tax-smears
16 Billy Kenber, George Greenwood and Mario Ledwith, 'Nadhim Zahawi "may have avoided millions in tax with trust"', *The Times*, 16 Jul 2022, https://www.thetimes.co.uk/article/nadhim-zahawi-may-have-avoided-millions-in-tax-with-trust-0n8mt7kj7
17 Heather Stewart, 'Labour challenges Nadhim Zahawi over tax and £26m business loan', *Guardian*, 18 Jul 2022, https://www.theguardian.com/uk-news/2022/jul/18/labour-challenges-nadhim-zahawi-over-tax-and-26m-business-loan
18 Francesca Gillet, 'Nadhim Zahawi: Tax error was careless and not deliberate', BBC News, 21 Jan 2023, https://www.bbc.co.uk/news/uk-politics-64360260
19 Kalyeena Makortoff and Peter Walker, 'HMRC boss tells MPs "innocent errors" are not penalised, amid Zahawi tax row', *Guardian*, 26 Jan 2023, https://www.theguardian.com/politics/2023/jan/26/hmrc-boss-tells-mps-innocent-errors-dont-attract-penalties-after-nadhim-zahawi-tax-row
20 Toby Helm, Michael Savage, Jon Ungoed-Thomas and Phillip Inman, 'Sleaze, scandal and the ghost of Boris Johnson – can "hopelessly weak" Sunak handle the job?', *Guardian*, 29 Jan 2023, https://www.theguardian.com/politics/2023/jan/29/is-the-prime-ministers-job-just-too-big-for-rishi-sunak
21 'Zahawi sacking letters in full', BBC News, 29 Jan 2023, https://www.bbc.co.uk/news/uk-politics-64444315
22 Peter Walker, 'Rishi Sunak vows to "restore integrity" after sacking Nadhim Zahawi', *Guardian*, 30 Jan 2023, https://www.theguardian.com/uk-news/2023/jan/30/nadhim-zahawi-pushback-helen-whately
23 Aubrey Allegretti, 'Watchdog looks into £220,000 public funding for Johnson Partygate defence', *Guardian*, 1 Feb 2023, https://www.theguardian.com/politics/2023/feb/01/watchdog-examines-220000-public-funding-for-boris-johnson-partygate-defence

24 Dominic McGrath and Alex Green, 'Dorries "broke rules" on post-ministerial jobs with TalkTV role', *Belfast Telegraph*, 27 Jan 2023, https://www.belfasttelegraph.co.uk/entertainment/news/dorries-broke-rules-on-post-ministerial-jobs-with-talktv-role/136411248.html

25 Scott Bryan [@scottygb], Twitter, 25 Oct 2022, https://twitter.com/scottygb/status/1584853529864175616

26 Ed Power, 'Friday Night with Nadine Dorries, review: Carefully rationed Boris Johnson pre-record lacks bite', *Telegraph*, 4 Feb 2023, https://www.telegraph.co.uk/tv/0/friday-night-nadine-dorries-review-carefully-rationed-boris/

27 John Stevens, 'Nadine Dorries told to return £84k MP salary as she hasn't spoken in Commons for 8 months', *Mirror*, 28 Feb 2023, https://www.mirror.co.uk/news/politics/nadine-dorries-told-return-84k-29338148

28 Aletha Adu, 'Boris Johnson: anyone who thinks I covered up parties is out of their mind', *Guardian*, 1 Feb 2023, https://www.theguardian.com/politics/2023/feb/01/boris-johnson-anyone-who-thinks-i-covered-up-parties-is-out-of-their-mind

29 Alix Culbertson, 'Boris Johnson "joked he was at most unsocially distanced party in UK" during No 10 lockdown party', Sky News, 11 Jan 2023, https://news.sky.com/story/boris-johnson-joked-he-was-at-most-unsocially-distanced-party-in-uk-during-no-10-lockdown-party-12784217

30 Ione Wells [@ionewells], Twitter, 10 Jan 2023, https://twitter.com/ionewells/status/1612777957113892864

31 Sherelle Jacobs, 'Britain is going to rejoin the EU far sooner than anyone now imagines', *Telegraph*, 16 Jan 2023, https://www.telegraph.co.uk/news/2023/01/16/britain-going-rejoin-eu-farsooner-anyone-now-imagines/

32 Toby Helm, 'Revealed: secret cross-party summit held to confront failings of Brexit', *Guardian*, 11 Feb 2022, https://www.theguardian.com/politics/2023/feb/11/revealed-secret-cross-party-summit-held-to-confront-failings-of-brexit

33 Angela Symons, 'Food shortages: The perfect storm that led to UK supermarkets rationing fruit and vegetables', *Euronews*, 23 Feb 2022, https://www.euronews.com/green/2023/02/22/food-shortages-why-are-uk-supermarkets-rationing-fruit-and-vegetables

34 David Lynch, '"Let them eat turnips": Tory minister wades in on how to ease supermarket shortages', *Independent*, 23 Feb 2023, https://www.independent.co.uk/news/uk/politics/therese-coffey-turnips-tomato-shortages-b2288274.html

35 James Tapper, 'Thérèse Coffey's "eat turnips" message leaves bitter taste after UK's biggest grower gives up', *Guardian*, 18 Mar 2023, https://www.theguardian.com/food/2023/mar/18/therese-coffeys-eat-turnips-message-leaves-bitter-taste-after-uks-biggest-grower-gives-up

36 Matthew Field, 'Electric car battery maker Britishvolt enters administration with the loss of hundreds of jobs', *Telegraph*, 17 Jan 2023, https://www.telegraph.co.uk/business/2023/01/17/electric-car-battery-maker-britishvolt-collapses/

37 'What is corporation tax and who pays it?', BBC News, 15 Mar 2023, https://www.bbc.co.uk/news/business-63255747

38 Peter Campbell, 'China's BYD blames Brexit as it rules out UK for Europe car plant', *Financial Times*, 12 Mar 2023, https://www.ft.com/content/a38acb75-23ab-4eae-b5c3-d4e880748986

39 Larry Elliott, 'Britain the only G7 economy forecast to shrink in 2023', *Guardian*, 21 Jan 2023, https://www.theguardian.com/business/2023/jan/31/britain-only-g7-economy-expected-shrink-2023-imf

40 Tom Rees, 'Paris overtakes London as Europe's largest stock market', *Telegraph*, 14 Nov 2022, https://www.telegraph.co.uk/business/2022/11/14/paris-overtakes-london-europes-largest-stock-market/

41 Xander Elliards, 'WVS: What we learned from a huge international poll on Brexit and EU', *The National*, 30 Mar 2023, https://www.thenational.scot/news/23421343.wvs-learned-huge-international-poll-brexit-eu/

42 'The EU transition period ended on Dec 31st 2020. Since then, do you think Brexit has gone well or badly?', YouGov, 24 Nov 2022, https://yougov.co.uk/topics/politics/survey-results/daily/2022/11/24/40567/1

43 Ellen Manning, 'This is how many British people think the Earth is flat', *Yahoo! News*, 9 May 2019, https://uk.style.yahoo.com/three-in-100-britons-think-the-earth-is-flat-143259242.html
44 Xander Elliards, 'WVS: What we learned from a huge international poll on Brexit and EU', *The National*, 30 Mar 2023, https://www.thenational.scot/news/23421343.wvs-learned-huge-international-poll-brexit-eu/
45 Adam Forrest, 'Tories braced for mass exodus of MPs as December deadline looms', *Independent*, 23 Nov 2022, https://www.independent.co.uk/independentpremium/uk-news/tory-mps-quit-general-election-b2232390.html
46 'National campaign to recruit 20,000 police officers launches today', GOV.UK, 5 Sep 2019, https://www.gov.uk/government/news/national-campaign-to-recruit-20000-police-officers-launches-today
47 'Reality Check: Are there 20,000 fewer police?', BBC News, 2 May 2017, https://www.bbc.co.uk/news/uk-politics-39779288
48 'Annual growth of gross domestic product in the United Kingdom from 1949 to 2022', Statista, 31 Mar 2023, https://www.statista.com/statistics/281734/gdp-growth-in-the-united-kingdom-uk
49 Camilla Turner, 'Liz Truss: I was brought down by the left-wing economic establishment', *Telegraph*, 4 Feb 2023, https://www.telegraph.co.uk/politics/2023/02/04/liz-truss-tory-conservative-party-sunak-economy/
50 Jessica Elgot, 'Liz Truss admits cutting 45p tax rate was "perhaps a bridge too far"', *Guardian*, 6 Feb 2023, https://www.theguardian.com/politics/2023/feb/06/liz-truss-admits-cutting-45p-tax-rate-was-perhaps-a-bridge-too-far
51 Politics Joe [@PoliticsJOE_UK], Twitter, 5 Feb 2023, https://twitter.com/PoliticsJOE_UK/status/1622642727341916169
52 Paul Routledge and Simon Hoggart, 'Major hits out at Cabinet', *Guardian*, 25 Jul 1993, https://www.theguardian.com/politics/1993/jul/25/politicalnews.uk
53 Paul Dallison, 'Nigel Farage duped into sending pro-IRA message', *Politico*, 12 Oct 2021, https://www.politico.eu/article/nigel-farage-pro-ira-message-birthday-cameo-video/
54 Sophie Thompson, 'Nigel Farage gets tricked into promoting Led By Donkeys', *Indy100*, 6 Apr 2023, https://www.indy100.com/politics/nigel-farage-led-by-donkeys
55 Peter Raven, 'One in five who voted for Brexit now think it was the wrong decision', YouGov, 17 Nov 2022, https://yougov.co.uk/topics/politics/articles-reports/2022/11/17/one-five-who-voted-brexit-now-think-it-was-wrong-d
56 'Britain was wrong to leave the EU', UnHerd, Dec 2022, https://britain.unherd.com/britain-was-wrong-to-leave-the-eu/
57 Adam Forrest, 'Brexit is doomed, says Boris Johnson's favourite paper', *Independent*, 17 Jan 2023, https://www.independent.co.uk/news/uk/politics/brexit-doomed-boris-johnson-economy-b2263675.html
58 Michelle Fox, 'Former Brexit secretary: Prime minister's deal takes away all economic benefits of EU divorce', CNBC, 16 Nov 2018, https://www.cnbc.com/2018/11/16/david-davis-pm-mays-deal-takes-away-all-economic-benefits-of-brexit.html
59 Adam Forrest, 'Brexit is doomed, says Boris Johnson's favourite paper', *Independent*, 17 Jan 2023, https://www.independent.co.uk/news/uk/politics/brexit-doomed-boris-johnson-economy-b2263675.html
60 Julia Kollewe, 'Brexit is a "complete disaster" and "total lies", says former Tory donor', *Guardian*, 31 Jan 2023, https://www.theguardian.com/business/2023/jan/31/brexit-lies-tory-billionaire-guy-hands-uk-eu-economy
61 'Since January 2022 Brexit has cost us', Cost of Brexit, 20 Apr 2023, http://costofbrexit.com/
62 Dominic Casciani, 'Chronic backlog of serious-crime cases hits courts', BBC News, 9 Feb 2023, https://www.bbc.co.uk/news/uk-64586483
63 'New research reveals: Labour is better at handling the economy than the Conservatives', *London Economic*, 18 Oct 2021, https://www.thelondoneconomic.com/business-economics/new-research-reveals-labour-is-better-at-handling-the-economy-than-the-conservatives-295748/
64 Rachel Russell, 'Sunday Times Rich List 2022: Sunaks join wealthy elite as UK billionaires swell to record level', Sky News, 19 Aug 2022, https://news.sky.com/story/sunday-times-rich-list-2022-uk-has-a-record-number-of-billionaires-12617181

65 Farrukh [@implausibleblog], Twitter, 2 Feb 2023, https://twitter.com/implausibleblog/status/1621162191792803840

Part 4: P.S. They Hate You
'Putting the Gini Back in the Bottle'

1. 'The story of social housing', Shelter, https://england.shelter.org.uk/support_us/campaigns/story_of_social_housing
2. Dennis Kavanagh and Peter Morris, *Consensus Politics from Attlee to Major*, Blackwell, 1994, pp. 4–6
3. Chris McCall, 'UK benefits system "least generous" in northern Europe claims SNP', *Daily Record*, 4 Aug 2021, https://www.dailyrecord.co.uk/news/politics/uk-benefits-system-least-generous-24689158
4. 'Gross Domestic Product: Year on Year growth: CVM SA %', ONS, 22 Dec 2022, https://www.ons.gov.uk/economy/grossdomesticproductgdp/timeseries/ihyp/pn2
5. 'Gini coefficient of the United Kingdom from 1977 to 2021', Statista, 2023, https://www.statista.com/statistics/872472/gini-index-of-the-united-kingdom/
6. 'The Scale of Economic Inequality in the UK', The Equality Trust, https://www.equalitytrust.org.uk/scale-economic-inequality-uk
7. Clifford Singer, '8 reasons to share the wealth', New Economics Foundation, 15 Dec 2022, https://neweconomics.org/2022/12/8-reasons-to-share-the-wealth
8. 'John Kenneth Galbraith Quotes', BrainyQuote, https://www.brainyquote.com/quotes/john_kenneth_galbraith_107301
9. 'How much did people earn in the 1960s?', RetroWow, https://www.retrowow.co.uk/social_history/60s/earnings_1960s.php
10. Patrick Collinson, 'Oh for the 1960s! People earned less but could afford more', *Guardian*, 10 Dec 2016, https://www.theguardian.com/money/blog/2016/dec/10/sixties-pay-people-earned-less-but-could-afford-more
11. Clifford Singer, '8 reasons to share the wealth', New Economics Foundation, 15 Dec 2022, https://neweconomics.org/2022/12/8-reasons-to-share-the-wealth
12. Rupert Neate, '70% of central London properties sold this year bought with cash – Savills', *Guardian*, 5 Jul 2023, https://www.theguardian.com/uk-news/2023/jul/05/70-of-central-london-properties-sold-this-year-bought-with-cash-savills
13. Patrick Collinson, 'Oh for the 1960s! People earned less but could afford more', *Guardian*, 10 Dec 2016, https://www.theguardian.com/money/blog/2016/dec/10/sixties-pay-people-earned-less-but-could-afford-more
14. Edaein O'Connell, 'The average solo first-time buyer now needs a £74,000 deposit to get on the ladder', *Metro*, 11 Jun 2022, https://metro.co.uk/2022/06/11/the-average-solo-first-time-buyer-now-needs-a-74000-deposit-16809472/
    Erin Yudray, 'Average Household Savings & Wealth UK 2023', Nimblefins, 18 Jan 2023, https://www.nimblefins.co.uk/savings-accounts/average-household-savings-uk
15. Patrick Collinson, 'One in three UK retirees will have to rely solely on state pension', *Guardian*, 21 Oct 2017, https://www.theguardian.com/money/2017/oct/21/uk-retirees-state-pension-financial-future
16. Laurence Cadieux, '7 Terrible Products That Never Should Have Existed', Devolutions, 9 Jun 2022, https://blog.devolutions.net/2022/06/7-terrible-products-that-never-should-have-existed/
17. Kavita Puri, '£3 in my pocket: the pioneering migrants who came to 1950s Britain from India', History Extra, 5 Mar 2014, https://www.historyextra.com/period/20th-century/3-in-my-pocket-the-pioneering-migrants-who-came-to-1950s-britain-from-india/
18. Tendayi Bloom and Katie Tonkiss, 'History offers Britain an important lesson on shutting down immigration', *The Conversation*, 26 Sep 2016, https://theconversation.com/history-offers-britain-an-important-lesson-on-shutting-down-immigration-65840

19. Alan Manning, 'The top rate of income tax', LSE, 22 Apr 2015, https://blogs.lse.ac.uk/politicsandpolicy/the-top-rate-of-income-tax-2/
20. 'United Kingdom Personal Income Tax Rate', Trading Economics, 2022–2023, https://tradingeconomics.com/united-kingdom/personal-income-tax-rate
21. 'Finance Act 1980', Legislation.gov, part III, chapter I, para 19, https://www.legislation.gov.uk/ukpga/1980/48/enacted
22. 'Finance Act 2021', Legislation.gov, https://www.legislation.gov.uk/ukpga/2021/26/enacted
23. Clifford Singer, '8 reasons to share the wealth', New Economics Foundation, 15 Dec 2022, https://neweconomics.org/2022/12/8-reasons-to-share-the-wealth
24. Joseph E Stiglitz, 'Opinion: The world will plunge into chaos if we don't tax windfall profits', CNN, 19 Jan 2023, https://edition.cnn.com/2023/01/19/opinions/windfall-profits-tax-stiglitz/index.html
25. Robert Booth, Holly Watt and David Pegg, 'David Cameron admits he profited from father's Panama offshore trust', Guardian, 7 Apr 2016, https://www.theguardian.com/news/2016/apr/07/david-cameron-admits-he-profited-fathers-offshore-fund-panama-papers
26. Anna Isaac, 'Revealed: Rishi Sunak "listed in tax haven as trust beneficiary" while chancellor', Independent, 8 Apr 2022, https://www.independent.co.uk/news/uk/politics/rishi-sunak-akshata-murty-tax-haven-b2054179.html
27. Cynthia Kroet, 'Theresa May's husband works for investment fund with stake in tax dodging companies: report', Politico, 13 Jul 2016, https://www.politico.eu/article/theresa-mays-husband-works-for-investment-fund-with-stake-in-tax-dodging-companies-report/
28. Anna Fleck, 'The UK's rich are getting richer', Statista/Sunday Times, 23 May 2022, https://www.statista.com/chart/27505/uks-richest-are-getting-richer/
29. Patrick Butler, 'UK benefits fall short of minimum living cost by £140 a month, charities say', Guardian, 26 Feb 2023, https://www.theguardian.com/society/2023/feb/26/uk-benefits-fall-short-of-minimum-living-cost-by-140-a-month-charities-say
30. George Easton, '"This country doesn't invest in its own future": Torsten Bell on why the UK is being hit hardest', New Statesman, 4 Jan 2023, https://www.newstatesman.com/encounter/2023/01/britain-invest-own-future-torsten-bell-uk-fell-rivals
31. 'Biggest economies in 2021 by gross domestic product', World Data, https://www.worlddata.info/largest-economies.php
32. 'A Theory of Justice', John Rawls, Wikipedia, https://en.wikipedia.org/wiki/A_Theory_of_Justice
33. Ros Atkins [@BBCRosAtkins], Twitter, 20 Mar 2023, https://twitter.com/BBCRosAtkins/status/1637884030795259926
34. Ros Atkins [@BBCRosAtkins], Twitter, 20 Mar 2023, https://twitter.com/BBCRosAtkins/status/1637884035300032513
35. Ros Atkins [@BBCRosAtkins], Twitter, 20 Mar 2023, https://twitter.com/BBCRosAtkins/status/1637884037422370816
36. Dave Burke, 'Rishi Sunak splashes huge sum ramping up power to private pool as leisure centres close', Mirror, 12 Mar 2023, https://www.mirror.co.uk/news/politics/rishi-sunak-splashes-huge-sum-29436243
37. Duncan Lamont, 'What 175 years of data tell us about house price affordability in the UK', Schroders, 20 Feb 2023, https://www.schroders.com/en-gb/uk/individual/insights/what-174-years-of-data-tell-us-about-house-price-affordability-in-the-uk/
38. 'Direct taxes: rates and allowances 2022/23', House of Commons Library, 7 Nov 2022, https://commonslibrary.parliament.uk/research-briefings/cbp-9489/
39. 'Capital Gains Tax rates and allowances', HMRC, 4 Jun 2018, https://www.gov.uk/guidance/capital-gains-tax-rates-and-allowances
40. Mathieu Gallard[@mathieugallard], Twitter, https://twitter.com/mathieugallard/status/1610950639147798528
41. Ross Clark, 'Are a growing number of Brits choosing not to work?', Spectator, 14 Dec 2021, https://www.spectator.co.uk/article/are-a-growing-number-of-brits-choosing-not-to-work/
42. John Moylan, 'Union membership has halved since 1980', BBC News, 7 Sep 2012, https://www.bbc.co.uk/news/business-19521535

43 'Trade Union Membership, UK 1995–2019: Statistical Bulletin', Department for Business, Energy and Industrial Strategy, 27 May 2020, https://assets.publishing.service.gov.uk/government/uploads/system/uploads/attachment_data/file/887740/Trade-union-membership-2019-statistical-bulletin.pdf
44 'More than 70% of England's water industry owned by foreign companies', GMB, 27 Sep 2018, https://www.gmb.org.uk/news/more-70-englands-water-industry-owned-foreign-companies
45 Matt Brooks, 'Who owns Great Britain's electricity supply? Market share of energy companies British Gas, EDF and E.On explained', NationalWorld, 10 May 2021, https://www.nationalworld.com/lifestyle/money/who-owns-great-britains-electricity-supply-market-share-of-energy-companies-british-gas-edf-and-eon-explained-3231013
46 Philip Aldrick, 'UK slips behind India to become world's sixth biggest economy', *Bloomberg*, 2 Sep 2022, https://www.bloomberg.com/news/articles/2022-09-02/uk-slips-behind-india-to-become-world-s-sixth-biggest-economy
47 Simon Duffy, 'Welfare Myth Five – The UK is Rich', *HuffPost*, 12 Jan 2016/updated 29 Nov 2017, https://www.huffingtonpost.co.uk/dr-simon-duffy/welfare-myth-five-the-uk-_b_13296512.html

A Note on the Author

Russell Jones is the man behind the *Sunday Times* bestselling *The Decade in Tory*. He publishes #TheWeekInTory, a regular breakdown of the government's regular breakdowns on social media, writing as @RussInCheshire. *Four Chancellors and a Funeral* is his second book.

Index

A B Produce, 287–8
Advisory Committee on Business Appointments, 26
Afghanistan, 56–61, 64, 77, 84, 142, 258, 293
Afolami, Bim, 160
Agnew, Lord, 101–2
agriculture, 52–3, 309
Ahmed, Lord, 202
Albania, 266, 328
Aldi, 190
Ali, Nimco, 269
Amersi, Mohamed, 113
Amess, David, 171
Amnesty International, 34
Anderson, Iain, 253
Anderson, Lee, 19, 42–3, 65, 73, 135–6, 253, 297–9
Anderson, Stuart, 105
antibiotics, 231
Anti-Growth Coalition, 215
antisemitism, 42, 173
Arcuri, Jennifer, 154
artificial intelligence, 250
Ashcroft, Lord, 154
Association of School and College Leaders, 253
Attenborough, Sir David, 65–6
austerity, 3–4, 71, 85, 100, 174, 204–5, 243–4, 259, 286, 309, 318, 332
Australian trade deal, 109–10
authoritarianism, 34–5, 241

Badenoch, Kemi, 16, 168, 171, 216, 250, 252–3

Bailey, Shaun, 91–2
Baker, Steve, 12–13, 94, 128, 140, 161, 170, 249
Balshore Investments, 301–3
Bamford, Lord, 19, 22–3, 47
Bank of England, 199, 211
bankers' bonuses, 196
Barclay, Steve, 102–3, 106–9, 286, 298, 306
Barnier, Michel, 335
Barrowman, Douglas, 279–80
BBC, 20–3, 67, 120, 186, 188, 216, 256, 312, 318
BBC Reality Check, 104
Bell, Aaron, 76, 104
Benton, Scott, 43–4, 266–7
Berry, Jake, 174, 213–14, 218, 256, 292
Bethell, Lord, 40, 74
Biden, Joe, 57
billionaires, 3, 19, 27–8, 117, 133, 186–7, 255, 319, 329
Black Lives Matter, 15–16, 42–3
Blaine, David, 228
Blair, Tony, 243, 249
Blenkinsop, Tom, 155
Blunt, Crispin, 145–6
Blyth, Sam, 20–1
Bone, Peter, 163
Bottomley, Peter, 157
Bowie, Andrew, 52
Boy George, 283
Bradley, Ben, 15
Brady, Graham, 94, 141, 148, 228

Braverman, Suella, 170–1, 191, 204–5, 216, 218–19, 221–3, 250
 forced resignation, 228–30
 and Sunak premiership, 255–8, 260–2, 265–71, 295, 301
Brereton, Jack, 169–70
Brexit, 4–5, 7–12, 26, 29–30, 34–7, 46, 48–54, 62, 71, 73, 78, 84, 94, 97, 114, 129, 134, 136, 141, 151, 153, 158, 164, 167, 170, 180, 235, 243, 292, 294, 297, 323–4, 333–7
 anniversaries, 300, 315–16, 319
 and Covid vaccines, 7–9
 cross-party summit, 307–8
 economic impacts, 87–9, 98–9, 110–12, 276, 306–12, 315–19
 and falling living standards, 285–6, 335
 and immigration, 258–60, 264
 and Irish border, 120–1, 151, 256, 274
 and Johnson premiership, 48–9, 52–3, 89, 97, 112, 120–1, 180, 258, 274–6, 285–6, 306, 316, 319

and NHS, 36-7, 86,
    272, 316-17
  opinion polling, 274,
    310, 316, 333
  and sovereignty,
    111-12, 121, 187,
    336
  and Sunak
    premiership,
    252-3, 272-6
  tariffs, 10-11
  and Truss
    premiership,
    192-5, 198,
    203-5, 207, 209,
    216-17
  Unboxed festival,
    24-5
  and US trade deal,
    193-4
Bridgen, Andrew, 50, 105,
  114, 203, 287-9
Bright Blue, 297
Britain First, 168
Britannia Unchained, 199
British Election Study,
  230
British Leyland, 328
British Medical
  Association, 55
British Medical Journal,
  8, 277
British Poultry Council,
  52
British Retail
  Consortium, 53
Britishvolt, 308
Brothers of Italy, 186
Brown, Melanie, 221
Brownlow, Lord, 23-4,
  48
Bruce, Fiona, 137
Bryant, Chris, 176-7,
  256
Buffett, Warren, 247
Burns, Conor, 102,
  155-6, 220-1
BYD, 309

Cabinet Office, 21-2, 28,
  103, 107, 177, 292-4,
  302
cabotage, 50, 53-4
Calderdale Council,
  43-4
Cameron, David, 4, 16,
  29, 34, 36, 111, 231,
  243, 287, 311

  and Baroness Mone,
    278, 280
  lobbying scandal,
    25-9, 77, 157
  pig-fucking, 3
  tax affairs, 329
cannabis, 223
capital punishment, 229,
  298
CapX news website, 187
Case, Simon, 94,
  229-30
Cates, Miriam, 220
Cayman Islands, 139, 175,
  242
Centre for Policy Studies,
  185, 188
Centre for the Study of
  Corruption, 116
Centre for Welfare
  Reform, 32
Centrica, 71
Chalk, Alex, 128, 160
Channel 4, 8, 67, 112,
  131, 284, 312
Charity Commission, 17
Charles III, King, 136,
  193, 224, 244
cheese exports, 49
Chequers, 48
child poverty, 42, 242
China, 114, 122
Chishti, Rehman,
  170-1
Churchill, Winston, 35,
  114, 152. 178, 275
Cincinnatus, Lucius
  Quinctius, 176
City of London,
  309, 316
civil service numbers, 99
Clandestine Channel
  Threat Commander,
  265
Clarke, Simon, 194, 213,
  236, 298
Clarke-Smith, Brendan,
  41-3, 179
Clean Air Act, 328
Clegg, Nick, 26
Cleverley, James, 157,
  163, 191, 224, 253
climate change, 3, 46,
  110, 133, 168, 217,
  249-50, 257, 264,
  317
coal-mining, 110
cocaine, 131-2, 217, 221

Coffey, Thérèse, 158-60,
  190-1, 205-6, 231,
  233, 308
Cohen, Benjamin,
  253
Coladangelo, Gina, 40
Colston, Edward, 15
Commission on Race and
  Ethnic Disparities,
  16-17
Common Sense Group,
  41-3
Confederation of British
  Industry (CBI), 273
Conservative Friends of
  Russia, 186
Conservative Home, 63,
  292
Conservative Muslim
  Forum, 261
Conservative Party
  factions, 249-51
Conservative Way
  Forward, 170
conversion therapy, 134,
  252
COP26 climate summit,
  47, 69, 110
COP27 climate summit,
  244
Corbyn, Jeremy, 253
Cornwall
  Spaceport, 306
cost-of-living crisis, 87-8,
  100, 164, 173, 196,
  224
Council of Europe, 35
council tax, 247
Covid-19, 6-14, 28,
  37-8, 51, 68, 71,
  118-19, 195, 265,
  282-3, 285, 318, 325,
  334
  death rates, 7, 9, 12,
    38, 55, 87, 118
  hospitalisations, 190,
    205
  impact on NHS,
    86-7, 205-6
  inquiry, 38-40, 206
  and Johnson
    premiership, 8,
    12-13, 38, 46, 76,
    86-7, 118, 180
  loan fraud, 101-2,
    145
  and mask-wearing,
    54-6, 118

INDEX

Omicron variant, 86–7
PPE contracts, 101, 113, 276–81, 283
Randox contract, 73–4
and schools, 63
vaccines, 6–9, 13–14, 46, 55, 289
see also Partygate
Covid Memorial Wall, 127
Covid Recovery Group (CRG), 12–13
Cowling, Maurice, 250
Cox, Geoffrey, 72
Crabb, Stephen, 159
Craig, Daniel, 169
crime figures, 204–5
critical race theory, 220
Crothers, Bill, 28
cryptocurrencies, 192, 199
Cuadrilla, 232
Cultural Marxism, 42
Culture Select Committee, 67
culture wars, 14, 30, 89–90, 167–8, 250, 252–3, 298, 312, 323
Cummings, Dominic, 23, 35–40, 77–8, 81, 146, 150, 154
Czech Republic, 333

Daily Express, 315
Daily Mail, 78, 144, 154, 209, 256, 265, 274, 315
Daily Mirror, 79
Daily Star, 223
Daily Telegraph, 18, 40, 67, 95, 127, 181, 187, 218, 238, 274, 290, 305, 307, 313, 315
Dartford Tunnel, 98
Davies, Andrew R. T., 150
Davies, Howard, 225
Davies, Hunter, 107
Davis, David, 94, 97, 112, 141, 151, 310, 316
Daylesford, 19
Debenhams, 10
Dechan, Steve, 277
Defence Committee, 164
Disraeli, Benjamin, 242

Doctor Who, 250
Donelan, Michelle, 162, 253
Dorrell, Stephen, 286
Dorries, Nadine, 7–8, 64–8, 78, 102, 105, 110–11, 130–1, 134, 161, 163, 171, 181, 216, 282
and Johnson leadership bid, 236–8
TalkTV show, 305–6
Dowden, Oliver, 91, 150, 162, 291
Downing Street, press briefing room, 82
Downing Street Trust, 23–4
Doyle, Jack, 93, 104
DPD, 10
Duncan Smith, Iain, 78
Durham Law School, 264
DVLA, 54
dyslexia, 131, 282–4

Economist, 223
Eddy, Richard, 15
Edmonds, Noel, 119
education, 36, 63, 95, 102, 220, 253, 290, 309, 316
Edwardes, Charlotte, 159
election fraud, 30–3
Electoral Commission, 23, 25, 33
Elizabeth II, Queen, 5, 76, 85, 92, 136, 192, 201
her funeral, 175, 291
Elliott, Matthew, 186
Ellwood, Tobias, 104, 164–5
Elphicke, Charlie, 158
Elphicke, Natalie, 98–9
energy bills, 87–8, 136–7, 151, 193, 195, 209, 243, 276, 284
energy industry, 70–1, 187, 309
England football team, 42
Environment Act, 68–9
Environment, Food and Rural Affairs Committee, 53
Equatorial Guinea, 336

European Convention on Human Rights (ECHR), 34–5, 144
European Medicines Agency, 7–8
European Research Group (ERG), 12, 128, 255, 274–5
Eustice, George, 109
exports, 4, 9–12, 30, 48–50, 121, 151, 274, 309
Exxon, 186

Fabricant, Michael, 93, 97, 127, 154, 157, 160, 179, 238
Fair Vote UK, 33
far right, 42–3, 186, 188, 250, 311, 315
Farage, Nigel, 11, 263, 307, 315
farming subsidies, 53
Farthing, Pen, 60
Faulks, Lord, 115
Financial Conduct Authority, 132–3, 252, 284
Financial Times, 103, 144, 302
fisheries, 11–12, 71, 274
Floyd, George, 15
Food and Drink Federation, 52
food shortages, 51–2, 292, 308, 317
foodbanks, 3, 19, 23, 41, 53, 135–6, 138, 213
football, 3, 42–4, 71, 312
Fortnum & Mason, 10, 201
Foster, Kevin, 125
Fox, Liam, 97
fracking, 133–4, 203, 207, 217, 232–3
Francois, Mark, 165
free school meals, 42, 317
free speech, 67, 220
Freeman, George, 79–80
freeports, 130, 298
Frost, Lord David, 97, 204
Full Fact, 8, 81, 104, 209
Fullbrook, Mark, 202

G7 summit, 46–7
Galbraith, J. K., 326
Gale, Roger, 76, 159

INDEX

gambling, 44
Garnier, Mark, 158
Gates, Bill, 14
GB News, 66, 73, 146, 187, 252, 275
GDP, 4, 7, 195, 210, 271, 276, 325, 331
Geidt, Lord, 23–4, 140, 145, 150, 295
gerrymandering, 31
Ghana, 95–7, 141–2
Ghani, Nusrat, 96–7
Gini coefficient, 325, 330
Globus (Shetland) Ltd, 277
Goldman Sachs, 242
Good Friday Agreement, 120–1
Gove, Michael, 36, 45, 75, 112, 161–2, 181, 188, 216, 250, 279, 307
Grainger, Daniel, 214
Grantham Institute, 189
Gray, Sue, 94, 103, 147
Grayling, Chris, 72
Green, Damian, 159
Greenland trade deal, 110
Greensill, Lex, 26–8
Greensill Capital, 26–9, 74, 77
Griffiths, Andrew, 159
Guardian, 66, 209, 228, 232, 275, 312
Gullis, Jonathan, 14, 54–5, 165, 267

Hague, William, 186, 236, 242
Hamilton, Alexander, 198
Hamilton, Neil, 171
Hancock, Matt, 7–9, 28, 32, 38–41, 74, 118, 243, 279, 282–4
Hands, Greg, 137, 171
Hands, Guy, 316
Hannan, Dan, 204
Harding, Dido, 119, 151
Harman, Harriet, 177
Harper, Mark, 76, 141
Harri, Guto, 106, 109, 157
Hart, Simon, 173
Hayes, Sir John, 17, 229
Healey, Denis, 39
Health Service Journal, 8
Heaton-Harris, Chris, 236
hedge funds, 197–8, 242
Henry, Darren, 17

HGV drivers, 51, 53–4
Hoare, Simon, 124, 171
homophobia, 65, 220–1
Horne, Alex, 296
housing, 246–8, 296–7, 309, 317, 324, 326–7, 329, 332–3, 336
Howard, Michael, 150, 307
human rights, 34–5, 42, 144, 187, 195, 267, 278, 312
Hunt, Jeremy, 18
  chancellorship, 226, 228, 231, 313–14
  leadership bid, 148–9, 166, 171–2
Hunt, Tom, 17
Hurford, Helen, 149
Hutchison Ports Europe, 72

I'm a Celebrity, 111, 282–4
immigration, 90, 95–7, 112, 116, 141–5, 151–2, 191, 222–3, 242, 249, 257–73, 285, 328–9
  Dover attack, 266–7
  Ghana scheme, 95–7, 141–2
  and hotel accommodation, 263–4, 269
  Manston detention centre, 264–6, 269, 295
  Rwanda scheme, 141, 143–5, 218–19, 271
  and small boats, 96, 142, 152, 258, 260–2, 270, 311–12
imperial measurements, 207–8
Independent, 302
Index on Censorship, 34
inequality, 3, 17, 197, 246, 248, 257, 325, 327, 329, 332
inflation, 52, 87–8, 139, 151, 190–1, 211, 213, 234, 285, 297–8, 312, 318, 326

Information Commissioner's Office, 222
Infosys, 116, 139
Institute for Fiscal Studies, 172
Institute for Government, 108
Institute for Policy Research (IPR), 20
Institute of Economic Affairs, 185, 188–9
Intelligence and Security Committee, 186
International Monetary Fund (IMF), 199, 225, 309
Iraq War, 56, 258
Islamophobia, 97
Izzard, Eddie, 253

Javid, Sajid, 79, 147, 160, 172, 226, 301
Jenkinson, Mark, 153
Jenkyns, Andrea, 163, 219–20
Jenrick, Robert, 255, 268, 273
John Lewis, 10, 20
Johnson, Boris, 5–9, 28, 30, 33–4, 37–8, 41, 43, 180–2
  and Afghanistan, 57–8, 60–1, 77
  and Andrew Bridgen, 287–9
  and Brexit, 48–9, 52–3, 89, 97, 112, 120–1, 180, 258, 274–6, 285–6, 306, 316, 319
  and Carriegate, 154–5
  and Chequers treehouse, 48
  and Chris Pincher, 155–7
  and conversion therapy, 134
  and Covid, 8, 12–13, 38, 46, 76, 86–7, 118, 180
  and Dominic Raab, 293–4
  downfall, 104–8, 111–13, 119–20, 127–8, 135–6,

428

INDEX

148–51, 160–2, 175–82
and environment, 47, 68–9, 133
financial pressures, 18–25, 77
and Gavin Williamson, 63–4
groping accusation, 159
and honours, 92, 122, 179, 221, 289
and Islamophobia, 97
and leadership contest, 166–7, 170–1, 175–6
narcissism, 78, 88, 119, 180–2
and 1922 Committee, 140–1
office blowjobs, 155–7
and Operation Red Meat, 95–7, 127
and Operation Save Big Dog, 80, 127
and Owen Paterson, 75–8
and P&O Ferries, 129
and Partygate, 79–83, 91–5, 102–6, 118, 127, 140–1, 147–8, 176–9, 195, 216, 305
and Priti Patel, 150, 293
and private jet, 46–7
privileges inquiry, 176–80, 182
and racism, 15–16, 18
renewed leadership bid, 235–8
and Starmer smear, 104
and Sunak premiership, 244, 273–6, 300, 304–6
and Truss premiership, 189, 201–2, 210, 216, 228, 235
and Tufton Street, 186, 188

and Ukraine, 114–16, 125–6, 152, 156, 160–5
Johnson (Symonds), Carrie, 19–20, 22, 37, 81, 105, 127, 154–5, 157
Johnson, Dominic, 190–1
Jordan, 258
Joukovski, Roman, 132

Kagame, Paul, 144
Kawczynski, Daniel, 124, 165
Keegan, Gillian, 56, 253
Khan, Imran Ahmad, 145, 158
Kilgour, Robert, 278
King, Martin Luther, 218
Koch brothers, 186, 250
Kolvin, Philip, 219
kompromat, 165
Kuenssberg, Laura, 193, 212
Kwarteng, Kwasi, 53–4, 129, 192, 194–201, 203–4, 208–13, 216, 225–7, 236, 314

Lammy, David, 104
Lamont, Norman, 307
Lawson, Nigel, 100–1
Leadsom, Andrea, 75
Lebanon, 258
Led By Donkeys, 315
legal aid, 177
Leigh, Sir Edward, 267
Levelling Up, 97, 162, 174, 249
Lewis, Brandon, 137
Lewis, Stewart, 172
LGBTQ+, 134, 145–6, 220, 252–3
Liberty, 31
Libya, 219
Lineker, Gary, 66, 312
living standards, falling, 139, 284–5, 335
lobbying, 25–9, 40, 44, 74, 77, 157, 202, 279, 288–9
Loder, Chris, 52
Logistics UK, 53
London Olympics, 317
London School of Economics, 189, 196–7

London Stock Exchange, 310
Lopez, Julia, 277
Loughton, Tim, 268
Love Island, 205
Lytle, Lulu, 20, 24, 82, 93

McCririck, John, 146
McDonald's, 51
MacNamara, Helen, 22
McVey, Esther, 166
Magna Carta, 89
Magnus, Laurie, 295
Major, John, 29, 315
Mallett, Ben, 92
Malthouse, Kit, 253
Mangnall, Anthony, 96
Manston detention centre, 264–6, 269, 295
Marks & Spencer, 10, 277
Martin, Trayvon, 15
May, Theresa, 4–5, 30, 34, 72, 97, 111, 115, 134, 148–9, 173, 215, 251, 274, 287, 290, 330
media, Conservative-supporting, 119–20
Meller, David, 177
mental health, 133, 205, 291
Menzies, Mark, 158
Mercer, Johnny, 250
Mercer, Robert, 186
Mere Plantations, 288
Merriman, Huw, 285
Metropolitan Police, 18, 103, 127, 147
MHRA, 7–8
MI5, 256
Microsoft, 130
Miliband, Ed, 336
Miller, Gina, 292
Milton, Anne, 291
minimum wage, 163, 244
ministerial code, 21, 102, 150, 256, 293, 302, 304
ministerial resignations, 227
Mirza, Munira, 16, 104
Mitchell, Andrew, 72, 105, 271–2
modern slavery, 222, 267
Mone, Baroness Michelle, 277–81
Moody's, 204, 236

429

INDEX

Moran, Layla, 252
Mordaunt, Penny, 113, 168–9, 171, 216, 228, 237–8, 290
Morecambe, Eric, 215
Morton, Wendy, 290
MPs' second jobs, 71–3
Muroki, Mercy, 252–3
Murray, Al, 15
Murty, Akshata, 116–17, 138–9

Nalobin, Sergey, 186
Napoleon Bonaparte, 284
National Association of Head Teachers, 36
National Audit Office, 102, 305
National Crime Agency, 162, 281, 302
national debt, 3, 195, 297–8, 332
National Insurance, 102, 134, 196
National Leathersellers' College, 73
National Security Bill, 34
National Security Council, 122, 290
National Trust, 42–3, 312
National Union of Journalists, 34
Nationality and Borders Act, 258
Neidle, Dan, 303
neoconservatives, 250
Netflix, 131
New British Union, 272
New IRA, 121
New York City Council, 32
Newmark, Brooks, 159
Newsnight, 185
NewsWatch, 20
NHS, 3, 9, 41, 71, 84–7, 151, 190–1, 195, 205–6, 255, 272–4, 276, 316–18, 329, 332
  and Brexit, 36–7, 86, 272, 316–17
  and Greensill scandal, 27–8
  and PPE contracts, 280–1
  strikes, 285–6

1922 Committee, 94, 140–1, 148, 210, 223, 228, 235
Norman, Jesse, 28
North Korea, 249
North Shropshire by-election, 76
Northern Ireland Assembly, 30
Northern Ireland border, 120–1, 151, 256, 274
Northern Powerhouse Rail, 134
Norwich City FC, 202
Nowzad, 60
NSPCC, 130
Nureyev, Rudolf, 23

Obama, Barack, 170
obesity, 206, 231
O'Brien, James, 67
Odey, Crispin, 198, 203, 207
Office for Budget Responsibility (OBR), 139, 173, 195–6, 200
Office of the Prime Minister, 148
O'Leary, Michael, 153
Olulode, Kunle, 17
Online Safety Bill, 130
Operation Brock, 136
Operation Red Meat, 95–7, 127
Operation Rolling Thunder, 195
Operation Save Big Dog, 80, 127
Organisation for Economic Co-operation and Development (OECD), 331
Osborne, George, 26, 86, 100, 274, 308
overseas aid (international development), 129, 134, 271–2
Oxford comma, 205

P&O, 128–30, 136, 256
Pannick, Lord, 177
Papua New Guinea, 142
Parish, Neil, 146, 149, 156

Partygate, 41, 79–84, 90–5, 102–6, 114, 118, 127, 140–1, 147–8, 160, 176–9, 195, 216, 282, 305
passports, 257
Patel, Priti, 6, 9, 34, 122–3, 125, 134, 141–2, 144, 161, 191, 199, 204, 249, 260–1, 269
  bullying allegations, 150, 293, 310
Paterson, Owen, 73–8, 80, 105, 157, 188
Patten, Chris, 128
Peacock, Johnnie, 169
Penrose, John, 151
pension funds, collapse of, 199
pensions, 134, 327–8
Percy, Andrew, 229–30
'permacrisis' (the word), 243
Peston, Robert, 194
Philip, Prince, 92
Philp, Chris, 192, 194, 197–9, 209–11, 217
Pincher, Chris, 155–60
Pink Floyd, 245
PinkNews, 252
Pirsig, Robert M., 323–4
Pistorius, Oscar, 169
Police, Crime, Sentencing and Courts Bill, 33
police officers, 311, 317
political interviews, 39
poll tax, 247
Posner, Bob, 33
post-war settlement, 246, 248, 335
potholes, 317
Poulter, Dan, 231
Powell, Enoch, 238
PPE Medpro, 278–81
press freedom, 34
Previn, André, 215
private jets, 47, 109, 202, 280
privatisation, 69–72, 336
Privileges Committee inquiry, 176–80, 182
protests, 33–5
Public Accounts Committee, 28, 98
public ownership, 328, 334
public sector pay, 173

INDEX

public spending, 211, 249, 286–7
public transport, 97, 318
Purchasing Power Parity, 336
Putin, Vladimir, 114–17, 123, 125, 207, 285

Question Time, 137, 185
Quin, Jeremy, 292

Raab, Dominic, 12, 35, 108, 152, 165, 188, 199, 202, 266
  and Afghanistan, 58–61, 64, 71, 84
  bullying allegations, 292–6, 301, 308, 310
  and Partygate, 80–1, 94, 102–3
racism, 15–18, 42–3, 45, 65, 253, 261–2, 269, 271
railcards, 31–2
railways, 70, 110, 285
Randox, 73–4, 77
raw sewage, 69
Rawls, John, 330–1
Red Wall, 99, 149, 250–1, 297
Redwood, John, 216
Rees-Mogg, Jacob, 7–8, 12–13, 31–2, 55, 65, 72–3, 78, 94, 97, 105, 110, 161, 179, 181, 187, 267, 307
  and abortion, 249
  and environment, 133–4, 217, 232
  family background, 107–8
  and leadership contests, 165, 169, 236
  minister for Brexit opportunities, 98–9, 207
  and Truss premiership, 191–2, 194, 207–8, 216–17, 232–4
Rees-Mogg, William, 107–8, 187
Reynolds, Martin, 92
Richardson, Angela, 75–6, 105, 171

Rifkind, Malcolm, 186
Roberts, Julia, 277
Robinson, Nick, 160
Ronson, Jon, 60
Ross, Douglas, 114, 213
Royal African Company, 15
Royal Ascot, 44
Royal Mail, 71
Royal Navy, 142, 169, 238, 264
Runnymede Trust, 17
Russian oligarchs, 33, 115–16, 123, 207
Rwanda, 141, 143–5, 218–19, 271
Ryder, Sir Ernest, 177

same-sex marriage, 229, 252
Saudi Arabia, 124
Savile, Jimmy, 104
Saxby, Selaine, 308
Scargill, Arthur, 334
Science Focus, 54
Scottish Conservatives, 105
Scully, Paul, 152
Sewell, Tony, 16, 18, 253
Shakespeare, William, 6, 38
Shapps, Grant, 41, 129, 152–3, 165, 167, 172, 217, 230–1, 306
Sharma, Alok, 110, 236
Sharp, Richard, 20–3, 188
Sheffield Hallam University, 317
Shelley, Mary, 251
Shipman, Harold, 283
Shorthouse, Ryan, 297
Single Market, 30, 274
Skidmore, Chris, 233
small-state libertarianism, 100–1
Smith, Chloe, 203
Smith, Greg, 203
social care, 134, 312
Soros, George, 66
Spectator, 21, 105, 313–14
Spencer, Mark, 96–7
Spotlight on Corruption, 115
stamp duty, 196, 204
Standards Committee, 75–6, 289

Starmer, Keir, 104, 204, 298
Stein, Jason, 226
sterling crash, 198–9, 203, 226
Stewart, Rod, 278
Stewart, Rory, 162
Stiglitz, Joseph, 329
Stone, Kathryn, 288–9
Story, Alex, 155
Stratton, Allegra, 82
Streisand, Barbra, 153–4
strikes, 284–5
Stuart, Graham, 233
Sugar, Alan, 109
Sun, The, 98
Sunak, Rishi, 20, 28, 34, 85, 100–2, 109, 127, 180, 231
  and Andrew Bridgen, 289
  and Baroness Mone, 281
  and Brexit, 273–6
  and Covid fraud, 102, 145
  and Dominic Raab, 294–6
  and energy bills, 137–8
  and Gavin Williamson, 290–2
  and immigration, 269–70
  lack of mandate, 243–4, 300
  leadership bids, 102, 109, 113, 137–8, 140, 145, 148, 160, 166–7, 171, 174–5, 236–7
  and Nadhim Zahawi, 302, 304
  PPE degree, 242
  premiership, 192, 241–5, 251–4, 273–6, 292, 296–301, 309
  his swimming pool, 332
  tax affairs, 138–40, 145, 157, 167, 174, 329
  and Ukraine war, 116–17

431

INDEX

Sunday Times, 107, 290, 327
Swayne, Desmond, 14, 54–5
Sweden Democrats, 186
swimming pools, 332–3

tax, 62, 100–1, 130, 134, 139, 155, 165, 308, 329–33
  Andrew Bridgen and, 288
  Baroness Mone and, 278, 281
  and leadership contest, 172, 174
  Nadhim Zahawi and, 301–4
  non-dom status, 138–40, 168, 332
  and Sunak premiership, 243, 246–8, 254–5, 275, 284, 298
  Sunak's affairs, 138–40, 145, 157, 167, 174, 329
  tax-and-spend, 251
  and Truss premiership, 193, 195–8, 202–3, 208, 213, 226, 254, 275, 300, 313
tax credits, 218, 325
TaxPayers' Alliance, 20, 185
Thatcher, Margaret, 29, 39, 69, 75, 85, 109, 117–18, 168, 225, 246, 325–6
Thiel, Peter, 250
TikTok, 130
Times, The, 44, 154–5, 200, 263
Times Educational Supplement, 220
Tiverton and Honiton by-election, 149
Today programme, 79, 208
Tory donors, 7, 19–21, 23, 84, 113, 116, 192, 198, 207, 255, 277–8, 281, 316
trade unions, 334, 336

trans people, 90, 134–5, 167, 229, 252–3, 312
Transparency International, 116, 277
Treasury Committee, 29
Trevelyan, Anne-Marie, 236
trickle-down economics, 196–7
Trump, Donald, 57–9, 186, 250, 311
Truss, Liz, 34, 49, 64, 72, 84–5, 97, 99–100, 128, 187, 308
  apologia, 313–15
  Australian trade deal, 109–10
  confidence vote and resignation, 232–5
  leadership bid, 148, 163, 165–6, 171–5
  premiership, 189–217, 223–5, 286, 294
  and public money, 201–2
  radio interviews, 208–9
  and Rwanda scheme, 144–5
  and Sunak premiership, 237, 241, 243–5, 273–5
  and Ukraine, 115, 117–18
Trussell Trust, 135
TS Lombard, 224
Tufton Street, 185–9, 201
Tugendhat, Tom, 61, 96, 167–9, 171–2
turnips, 308

UBS Global Wealth Management, 204
UK credit rating, 204, 215, 236
UKIP, 4, 98, 249, 315, 324
Ukraine, 52, 84, 88, 113–18, 122–6, 152, 156, 160–1, 165, 285, 318–19
  refugee crisis, 122–6, 151

  and sanctions, 114–17, 139
UN High Commissioner for Refugees (UNHCR), 61, 124, 144, 268
UN Refugee Agency, 219
Unboxed festival, 24–5
Union of Jewish Students, 173
Uniserve, 276–7
Universal Credit, 192, 203
University of Worcester, 272
US and 'special relationship', 194, 201

Vara, Shailesh, 163
Vietnam War, 195
Virgin Health, 286
virtue signalling, 42, 126
Vote Leave, 36
voter ID, 30–2, 35

Wakefield by-election, 149
Wakeford, Christian, 94–5
Walker, Charles, 234
Wallace, Ben, 60, 165, 236, 250
Wallis, Jamie, 134
Walpole, Robert, 161
Warburton, David, 131–3, 135–6, 159
Warsi, Baroness Sayeeda, 104, 262
water industry, 69–70, 335
Weatherhead, Andy, 271
Wheeler, Marina, 154
Which? magazine, 70
Whittaker, Craig, 128, 233
Whittington, John, 44
Who Funds You, 186
Williams-Walker, Shelley, 92
Williamson, Gavin, 62–4, 96, 122, 157, 213, 255
  bullying allegations, 289–92, 301, 310
Wimbledon, 44

INDEX

Winchester College, 138, 174, 241
wind power, 133–4, 229, 250, 275
Winter of Discontent, 204, 236
Wintour, Patrick, 36
'wokeness', 64–6, 250, 273
Wolfson, Lord, 141
Woolley, Lord, 17

World Food Programme, 61
World Health Organization (WHO), 86–7
Wragg, William, 95, 128

xenophobia, 3, 11, 243, 271, 308

YouGov, 301, 303

Young Conservative Network, 214
YouTube, 130

Zahawi, Nadim, 13, 161–2, 168, 171–2, 238, 285, 301–4
Zelenskiy, Volodomyr, 160
Zimmerman, George, 15

Unbound is the world's first crowdfunding publisher, established in 2011.

We believe that wonderful things can happen when you clear a path for people who share a passion. That's why we've built a platform that brings together readers and authors to crowdfund books they believe in – and give fresh ideas that don't fit the traditional mould the chance they deserve.

This book is in your hands because readers made it possible. Everyone who pledged their support is listed below. Join them by visiting unbound.com and supporting a book today.

Joe #FBRTL
Zahra Abdeali
Maarten Abele
Matthew Abercrombie
Conan Ablewhite
Alison Adams
Lesley Adams
Mark Adams
James Afford
Kerry Agnew
Konstantinos Agrafiotis
Zoe Alderman
Fiona Alexander
Syeda Ali
Julie Allan

Richard Allard
Jenni Allen
Richard Allen
Stephanie Allison
Nicola Alloway
Peter Allum
Michael Anders
Adelaine Anderson
Alison Anderson
Carolyn B Anderson
Keith Anderson
Susan Anderson
Tracey Andre
Luke Andrews
Stewart Andrews
Igor Andronov
Marie Angell

Kirk Annett
Tanya AnsteyMudd
Ana Araujo
Niina Arjanne
Anne B Armstrong
David Armstrong
Heather Arnold
Malc Arnold
David Ashcroft
Tim Ashcroft
Chris Ashdown
Nicola Ashdown
Hilary Ashton
Nick Ashton
Simon Ashworth
Penny Asquith-Evans

SUPPORTERS

Helen Astley	Andrew Barnard	Grahame Bell
Richard Atkin	Heidi Barnard	Richard Bellinger
Denise Atkins	Tom Barnard	Chafika
Lorraine Atkins	Chris Barnes	Benkherroubi
Lisa Aubrey-Cosslett	Mary Barney	Carey Benn
Ed Austin	Andrew Barrett	Sarah Benn
Luke Austin	Lizzie Barrett	David Bennett
Marc Austin	Mike Barron	Margaret Bennett
Derek Avery	Claire Barrow	Maria Bennett
Sally Backhouse	Gordon Barrs	Phillip
Trevor Baden	Wolf C. Bartholomae	Bennett-Richards
Alison Bailey	Felix Bartle	Shaun Bent
Becky Bailey	James Bartoli	Mark Bentley
Janice Bailey	Yves Bastide	Kasia Bera
Peter Baird	Andrew Batchelor	Liam Bergin
Richard Bairwell	Hannah Lauren	Lorna Bernard
Andrea Baker	Batchelor	Eyvind Bernhardsen
Caroline Baker	Kaye Batchelor	Christopher Berry
Jeremy Baker	Lynne Batik	Colin Berry
Rebecca Baker	Caroline Baxter	Ruth Berry
Susan Baker	Tracy Bayly	BIL
Suzan Baker	Dave Beal	Rebekah Billingsley
Bernie Baldwin	Michael Beaufoy	Simon Binks
Ian Ball	Bob Beaupre	Chris Binner
Robin Ball	Samantha Beavis	Alan Birse
Sara Ball	Jennifer Becker	David Bishop
Stephen Ball	Chris Beddoes	Sara Bishop
Haydon Bambury	Dave Beech	Andrew Blackburn
Vanessa Bamford	Simon Beeforth	Simon Blackham
John Banks	Simon Beevers	Colin Blackman
Kitty Banks	Alex Bell	Simon Blackwell
Paul Barlow	Catherine Bell	Hamish Blair
Moo Barman	David Bell	Christine Blake

Rognvald Blance
Russell Blandamer
Amy Louise Blaney
Lynne Blaylock
Graham Blenkin
Anthony Blews
Paul Blinkhorn
Colin Bloor
Patrick Bolger
Keith Bollands
Catherine Bolt
Mark Boltman
Hannah Bolton
Chris Bond
Tracey Booth
Nic Boothby
Wendy&David
   Boother
Kate Born
David Boughton
Matt Boulton
Joanna Susan Bowe
Mike Bowker
David Bowler
Emma Bowles
Danny Boyd
Graham Brack
Carolina Bracken
Elizabeth Bradley
John Bradley
Neil Bradley
Sarah Bradley
Simon Bradley

Paula Bradshaw
Maryam Brady
Douglas Brain
Matt Brain
Caroline Braithwaite
Sarah Brammall
Jo Brass
Paul Bray
Emma Breen
Isabelle Brennan
Katrine Bretner
Henk-Martijn
   Breunese
Richard Bridge
Simon Brilliant
Margaret Brinkley
Rachel Brock
Michael Brockbanks
The Brollinsons
Alan Brook
Jim Brookbank
Amy Brooke
Adrian Brooks
Brad Brooks
Liam Broom
Rachel Brougham
Bill Brown
Caroline Brown
Graham Leslie
   Brown
Heather Brown
Ian Brown
Ishbel Brown

Julia Brown
Robert Brown
Sara Brown
Brian Browne
Barbara Browning
Lesley Bruce
Thomas Bruce
Vanessa Bryan
Danny Buchanan
Keith Buckby
Andrew Buckley
Claire Budd
Yvonne Budden
Lia Buddle
Jane Budge
Charles Budworth
Alison Bunce
John Burdall
Andrea Burden
Kevin Burgess
Matt Burgess
Kate Burnell
Tim Burnett
David Burns
Christine Burns
   MBE
Deirdre Burrell
Andrea Burton
The Burton-Clabers
Morris Butler
Adam Butterworth
Olivia Butterworth
Stephen Buxton

SUPPORTERS

Kit & Shellie Byatt
Tom Cadmore
Jane Cahill
Maria-Elena Calderon
Jane Caldwell
Ruth Calladine
Phil Callaghan
Sarah Callanan
Lewis Cameron
Tony Cameron
Kirsty Campbell
Lore Campbell
Steven Cannavan
John Cantelo
Lara Cappuccini
Janet Carberry
David Carlill
Guy Carmichael
Oliver Carpenter
Chris 'the cake runner' Carr
Micah Carr-Hill
Jon Carricker
Claire Carroll
Jonny Carroll
Anne-Marie Carslaw
Alex Carter
Damon Carter
Mandy Carter
Richard Carter-Ferris
Isabel Cartmail

Mike Cartmel
Sandy Cartmell
Lizzie Carver
Hannah Casey
Keith Cass
Beth Caswell
Andrew Cattanach
William Cave
Lucy Cavell
Andrea Caven
Jim Cessford
Marie Chadwick
Chalet One Saint Foy Tarentaise
Jack Challen
Debbie Challis
jenni chambers
Shelley Chambers
Sally Champion
Colin Chapman
Jonathan Chapman
Richard Chapman
Andy Charlton
Kate Charlton
Chris Chatterton
Maria Chauhan
Chesh
James Chiles
Robert Chilton
Michael Chilvers
Sadia Chishti
Annie Cholewa
Jamie Christie

Kostis Christodoulou
Edward Churchill
Ian Chuter
Debby Claber
Peter Clapham
Guy Clapperton
Doug Clark
Phil Clark
Simon Clark
Ian Clarke
Belle Claudi
Chris Clegg
Richmond Clements
Joe Clifford
Soo Coates
Philippa Cochrane
Andrew Cogan
Genevieve Cogman
Elliot Cohen
Chris Coldwell
Ben Cole
Michael Cole
Lucy Rose Coleman
Ady Coles
Rachel Coleshill
Joanna Colin
Ian Collier
Peter Collier
Alan Collins
Katie Collins
Marguerite Collins
Geoff Collyer

SUPPORTERS

Daniel Connelly
Martin Connolly
John Connor
Rachel Constable
Helen Convery
Denny Conway
George A. J. Cook
Stephen Cook
John Cooksley
Adam Cooper
Alison Cooper
Fiona Cooper
Jane Cooper
John Cooper
Vicky Cooper
Mike Coote
Gary Copland
Kate Corden
Suzanne Cordier
Nic Corke
Mike & Rosie Corlett
Nick Corlett
David Corne
Will Cornelius
Ian Cornick
John Corvesor
Tony Cottam
Jacqui Cottrell
Richard Courtney
Ken Cousen
Christine Coutts
Katharine Cowley
Rob Cowlin

Jean Cox
Andrew Coyle
Nick Craggs
Fiona Craig
Malcolm Craik
Neil Crane
John Crawford
Jon Crawford
Adam Crawte
David Creasey-Benjamin
Robert Crerar
Ewald Cress
Paul Crompton
Tamsin Cromwell
Martin Crookall
Nyssa Crorie
Stella Croskery
Adrian Cross
Jason Crosswaite
James Crowe
Geoff Crump
Andrew Crysell
Steven Culliford
Graham Cumming
Brian Cunningham
Ian Cunningham
Sam Curran
Neil Curry
Jon Curwen
Renata Czinkotai
Phillip Dack
John Dady

Kae Dale
Eleanor Dalglish
John Dallimore
Tony Daly
Jeri Dansky
Kieron Darcy
Tanya Das
Jon Dasilva
Judgement Dave
Chris Davenport
Gary and Lesley Davey
Claire Louise Davidson
Elizabeth Davidson
Andrew Davies
Barry Davies
Nigel Davies
Philippa Davies
Sian Davies
Sophie Davies
M.R. Davies, Esq.
E R Andrew Davis
Nigel Davis
Tisha Davis
Jon Davison
Peter Davison
Darren Dawson
Pat Dawson
Martin Dean
Richard Deans
Christine Dee
Andy Deegan

Simon Dell
Heather Delonnette
Tracy Demianczuk
Nick Dempsey
Sian Denereaz
Andrew Denman
Calum Dennehy
Jim Dennett
Jo and Ian Dennis
Mark Dennison
Colin Dente
Peter Denyer
Will Derrick
Frederic Dervin
Gerry
   Devine-McGovern
Katie Dexter
Candy Diamond
Stephen Dick
Rob Dickens
Ian Diddams
Lisa Diver
Stuart Dix
DJG
Adrian Doggett
Craig Doherty
David Donnelly
Doodan
Barry Dooley
Marc Doran
Marvin Dorfler
Andy Doswell
Mark Douglas

Emma Doward
James Dowling
Stephen Down
Karen Doyle
Neil Doyle
Paul Drage
Gaynor Drake
Kinza Drewett
Charlotte Drury
Emma Dry
Miranda Dubner
Charlie Duboc
Richard Ducker
Michael Duffy
Shane Duggan
Heidi & Sam Dulai
Tracy Dunbar
Cara Duncan
Anne Duncanson
Pam Dunn
Jane Dunsmore
Peter Durbin
Howard Durdle
Elan Durham
Rodney Dykeman
Dave Eagle
Robert Eardley
Kara Earl
Richard Earney
Reuben Easom
Lynne Maria East
John Ebdon
Janet Edington

Annette Edmondson
Andrew Edmonstone
Dan Edwards
Mark Edwards
Paul Edwards
Rachel and Sean
   Edwards
Dave Edwards
   @RealDaveEdwards
Birgit Einhoff
Sarah Ellingworth
Chris Elliott
Graham Elliott
Carla Ellis
Graham Ellis
Helen Ellis
Linda Ellis
Mark Ellis
Viv Ellis
John Ellison
Todd Ellner
Lesley Elrick
Brad Emerson
Tricia
   Emlyn-Williams
Andrew Engel
Russell England
Michael Englefield
Peter English
Olivier Epaulard
Arlene Esdaile
Rose Esposito
Victoria Esposito

SUPPORTERS

Liz Etheridge
David Evans
Gareth Evans
Jake Evans
Mike Evans
James Eyre
Stephen Eyre
Clint Fabergé
Andrea Fairhurst
Paul Fairie
Andrew Falvey
Colin Farquhar
Mrs M Farquhar
Louise Farquharson
Maureen Farr
Julie Farrar
Matt Farrington
Desmond Farthing
Simon Fathers
David Faulkes
Craig Faulkner
Judy Faulkner
Ron Faulkner
Felicity Feek
Ciarán Fegan
Tony Fenn
Mark Ferguson
Alex Ferrie
Chris Fett-Worsfold
Imogen Fett-Worsfold
Jakob Fey
Patric ffrench Devitt
Sally Field
Paula Finn
Gretchen Fisher
James Fisher
Nick Fisher
Lisa Fitt
Nick Fitzsimons
Tom Flannery
Alastair Fleck
Ralph Fleming
Janet Folland
Stuart Forbes
Simon Ford
Derek Fordham
Karl Fordham
Stephen Foreshew-Cain
Chris Forrest
Peter Forrest
G Foskett
Brian Foster
Louise Foster
Rob Foster
Elisha Foust
Nicola Fowler
Steve Fowler
Caroline Fox
Michael Fox
Joanne Foxton
Stephanie Frackowiak
Kelvin France
Pauline France
Nathan Franks
Oliver Franks
Lyndsey Fraser
Stuart Fraser
Peta Free
Rob Freeland
Emma Freeman
Jake Freeman
Julian Freeman
Harry French
david frew
Peter Friel
Vicki Frost
David J Fry
Mike Fryer
Steve Fuller
Callum Furner
Mike Furness
Myles Furr
Naoise Gaffney
Nick Gage
Caroline Gale
Alison Galletly
Marjorie Galloway
Lukas Gamble
Mark Gamble
Paul Gardiner
Karen Gardner
Iain Garioch
Alison Garner
Richard Garner
Helen Louise Gateley
Stuart Gaunt

SUPPORTERS

Luke Gawin
Abigail Gawith
James Gawman
Marcus Gearini
Amanda George
Dani Georgieva
Caroline Gerrard
Terry Gibson
Tom Gidden
Jane Gidman
Julie Giles
Ben Gill
Christine Gill
Dave Gill
Matthew Gill
Roy Gillett
Jane Gilliland
Bill Gillingham
Martin Gilmore
Tony Gilmore
Caroline Gisbourne
Matt Gittins
Jennie Gladwin
Andrew Gledhill
David & Nyk
  Glennie
Ryan Gliddon
Vicki Gloak
Alex Glonek
Sue Glover
Tony Glover
Paul Godden
Deirdre Godfray

Roger Godfrey
Duane Godwin
Chris Goff
Simon Goff
Sophie Goldspink
Mercedes Gonzalez
Laurence Good
Adam Gooding
Susan Goose Cross
Annette Goosey
Nicola
  Gordon-Thaxter
Frank Gorman
Will Gormley
Evelyn Gothard
Fred Gough
Richard Gough
Ros Gough
Jane Gould
Fiona Govan
Ian Govier
Claire Gowson
Tom Grace
Peter Gracey
Paul Graham
Yoan Graignic
James Grant
Russell Grant
Liz Gratton
Paul Grave
Carolyn Gray
Peter Greatbanks
Yuko Greatrex

David Greaves
Anne Green
Clare Green
Deb Green
Jen Green
Ste Greenall
Wayne Greenfield
Robert Greenhalgh
Dave Greenham
Tony Greenham
Julie Greenslade
Andrew Gregg
Louise Gregory
Michael Gregory
Phil Gregson
Griff Griffith
William Griffiths
James Grizzell-Jones
Julie Groom
Christine Grove
Kenny Grue
Laura Guerrero
Bedwyr Gullidge
Sanjay Gupta
Andy Guttridge
Jonathan Guy
Geoff Haederle
Sharman Hague
Philip Haigh
Ruba Halabi
Paul Hale
Alan Duncan Hall
Irene Hall

SUPPORTERS

Jenny Hall
Greg Hallam
Neil Hallam
Dr Robert Hallett
Steve Halley
Dave Hallwood
Gareth Haman
David Hammond
Tim Handley
Suzie Hanna
Phil Hanson
Donna Hardcastle
Julie Hardiment
Gary Hardy
Lakshmi Hariprasad
Roy Harmsworth
Jo Harnett
Mel Harper
Miranda Harper
Alex Harrington
Jacqueline Harrington
Leonard Harris
Lynne Harris
Nigel Harris
Paul Harris
Steve Harris
Chris Harrison
Peter Harrison
Tim J Harrison
Matthew Hart
Rita Hart
Chris Hartness
Dave Harvey
Graham Harvey
Jon Harvey
Mark Harwood
Yusaf Hassan
Joanne Haswell
D C Hatch
Chris Hawes
Kathleen Hawkin
Ed Hawkins
Judith Hawkins
David Hawksworth
Martin Hay
Peter Haydon
Bernadette Hayes
Chris Hayes
Sharon Hayes
Spencer Hayes
John S Haynes
Lord High Master of the Universe: Chris Haynes
Damien Healey
Barbara Healy
Joyce Heard
Cis Heaviside
Andrew Hedges
Stuart Hemming
Jane Hemstritch
Matt Hemsworth
John Henderson
Jude Henderson
Bill Hendry
Gary Hendry
Adam Henley
Elizabeth Henwood
Sarah Herring
Lee Herron
Alison Hesketh
Tim Hewitt
Kat Heywood
Mark Hiatt
Calvin Vincey Hibbard
Nick Hickman
Stephen Hickman
Gary Hicks
Virtual Colin Hicks
Chris Higgins
Steve Higgins
Terry Higgins
Stephen Higginson
Barrie Higham
Paul Higham
David Hilary
Nigel Hiley
Matthew Hill
Sam Hill
Suzanne Hillman
Christopher Hilton
Graham Hind
Jennifer Hirst
Michael Hirst
Tony Hirst
John Hobson
Steven Hodges

Frances Hodgson
Kathryn Hodgson
Diane Holden
Dave Hollands
Paul Hollingsworth
Ian Holloway
Jack Holloway
Edward Holmes
Joe Holsman
Mike & Janet Holt
Katherine Honan
Euan Hope
James Hope
Simon Horbury
Stephanie Horner
Rich Horsfall
Matt Horsnell
Barry Horton
Angela Hosie
Matthew Hothersall
Gary Houghton
Sean Houlihane
Jules Hoult
Paul Hoult
Rich House
Daniel Howarth
Karen Howat
Steven Howell
David Howker
Tony Howse
Karen Hoyles
Karen Hubbard
Louis James Hudson
Andrew Hughes
Ben Hughes
Gareth Hughes
Gareth N Hughes
Pete Hughes
Sheila Hughes
Warren Hughes
Chris Hulbert
Kathrin Hulse
Jay Humphrey
Michael Humphrey
Suzanne Humphries
Ian Hunneybell
Allan Hunt
Finlay Hunt
Gordon Hunt
Michael Hunt
Paul Hunt-Terry
Scott Hunter
Martin Huntford
Jan Hurst
Martin Hussey
Steven Hutchinson
Dan J. Hutson
Desmond Hutton
Mark Hymers
Hilda Ibrahim
Steve Ingamells
Christine Ingram
Maggie Innes
John Ireland
Jonathan Ison
Graham Ives
Andy Ivory
Adam Jackson
Andrew Robert
    Jackson
Carole Jackson
Dr Ian Jackson
Judith Jackson
Ross Jackson
Pascal Jacquemain
    (@jacquep.bsky.
    social)
Lisa Jain
Nick James
Mark Jamieson
Miss Jane Jane
David Janning
Simon Jarvis
Leah Jeffery
Steve Jeffery
Alexandra Jeffries
Betty Jenkins
Rigby Jerram
Tom Jin
Joanna
Andrea Johnson
Claire Johnson
Darren C S L
    Johnson
Liam Johnson
Neil Johnson
Rob Johnson
Doug Johnston
Riona Johnston

SUPPORTERS

Alexander Jones
Alison Jones
Alistair Jones
Heather Jones
Jim Jones
John Jones
Kerry Jones
Lee Jones
Matthew Jones
Mike Jones
Tony Jones
Michael Jordan
Ronan Jouffe
Indra Joyce
Jane Joyce
Kevin Joynes
JPL
Jason Judge
Nick Kaijaks
Ranjit Kaur
Lesley Kazan-Pinfield
Mike Keal
Andy Keany
Helen Keay
Paula Keay
Chris Keen
David Keighley
Morag Keith
Margaret Kelly
Andrew Kemp
Hilary Kemp
Simon Kempton

Ian Kenny
Stephen Kent
Neil Kerr
Alexandra Kershaw
Helen Kershaw
Rob Kevan
Mike Khan
Fozia Khanam
Ifat Khawaja
Dan Kieran
David Kiernan
Nicola Kilduff
Martin King
S Kinnear
Ian Kirby
J Kirby
Blake Kirk
Richard Kirk
Jackie Kirkham
Tony Kitson
Michael Kitt
Peel Kittens
Lisa Kitto
Ashley Knight
Ian Knight
Lindi Knight
Matt Knight
Terry Knipe
Gill Knowles
Mirella Koleva
Daniel Kraemer
Sunil Kumar
Kenneth Kwek

Nick Lacey
Anthony Lacny
Robert Laedlein
Iain Laird
Anu Laitakari
Sally Lake
Ben Lambert
James Lambert
Sarah Lambeth
Steve Lambley
David Langlands
Gavin Large
Mike Latham
Ben Lathbury
Leigh Lawrence
Lyn Lawrence
Nathan Lawrence
Sharon Laws
Adam Le Boutillier
Dean Lea
Dame Andrea Leadsom
Jo Leatham
Gordon Lee
Kevin Lee
Mark Lee
Michael Lee
Stevie Lee
Emma Leech
Malcolm Lees
@1kiwiboy
The Leftlungs
Richard Legge

SUPPORTERS

Mary Leigh
Kate Leimer
Moonika Leisson
David Leonard
Helen Lester
Fraser Levey
Shena Lewington
Gillian Lewis
Paul Lewis
Philip Lewis
Lawrence Lilley
Andrew Lillywhite
Steven Linnington
Jenny Livy
Linda Lloyd
Elizabeth Locke
George Lockley
Rachael Loftus
Gareth Logue
Matt Longshaw
Dermot Loughnane
Antony Loveless
Stephen Lovering
Craig Lowe
Peter Lowe
Sebastian Lucas
Clare Luery
Maureen Luff
Min Luk
Shen Luk
Andy Lulham
Mark Lumby
Elizabeth Lupton

Sally Luxmoore
Chris Lydon
Andrew Lyman
Jonathan and Clare Lynas
Fiona Lynch
Carie Lyndene
Christopher Lyndon
Neal Lyon
Gerard Lyons
Richard "#IndyRef2" Lyons
L M
Peter M.f.K.
Cathal Mac Elhatton
Liz Macaulay
Cass Macdonald
Sharon Macdonald
Pauline MacDougall
Liz Mace
Robert Macfarlane
Lorna MacGillivray (@Elemjay1 on Twitter)
Steve Mack
John Mackenzie
Roderick Mackenzie
Denise Mackie
Richard Mackie
Mhairi Maclennan
Sharon Macpherson
Joe MacVeigh
Karen Maddock

Zahir Mahmood
Graeme M Mair
David Male
Marcin Malinow
Dana Mallon
Tim Mallon
Jessica Maloney
Wendy Maloney
Dale Maltby
Claire Mankowitz
Helen and Libby Manktelow
Katrin Mansfeld
Deborah Manzoori
Anita Maria from Cheshire
Hayleigh Marks Talabis
Markus
Andrew Marmot
Kevin Marnell
John Marr
Andrew Marren
Richard Marsh
Leigh Marsh Horgan
Jim Marshall
Joseph Marshall
Peter Marshall
Anthony Martin
Jacqueline Mason
Rick Mason
Gordon Massey
Frederic Massoubre

SUPPORTERS

Dan Masters
Emily Mates
Ian Mathewson
David Matkins
Matlock the Hare
Benjamin C. S. Matthews
Catherine Matthews
Eileen Ann Matthews
Jessica Matthews
Matthew Maude
Indigo Maughn
Stuart Maw
David Maxwell-Lyte
Paul May
Tina May
Dawood Mayet
Mark Mazzara
Allan McAllister
LaToyah McAllister-Jones
Jacqueline McCallum
Judith McCarron
Stephen McClay
Duncan David McColl
Bill McConnell
Graham McConnell
Pam McCormac
Dave McCraw
John McCubbin
Fiona McDaid
Ian McDougall
Lauchlan McEwan
Jessica McEwan Chambers
Michael McFarlane
Boaty McGammonface
Adam McGee
Conor McGeown
Liz McGhee
Mandy Mcgill
Caomhan McGlinchey
Anna McGrail
Sean McGrath
Mitch McGregor
Nicole McGuire
Amelia Rose McGurk
Kathleen McGurl
Bernie McIlvenny
Bryan McIlvenny
Gavin McKeown
Andrew McKeown-Henshall
Paul McKernan
Jim McKie
William McKinnon
Andrew McLachlan
Chris McLoughlin
Kerry McMahon
Stephen McMahon
Susan McMillan
Graham McNeill
Hugo McNestry
Bruce McPherson
Jenny McQuillan
Ruth McQuinn
New Elites' Andrew & Fiona McRait
Lorna McWilliam
Elizabeth Meenagh
Victor Meldrew
Ellen Mellor
Helen Mellor
John Mellors
Kay Melmoth
Angela Melton
Simon Melton
Neil Melville-Kenney
Edward Mercer
Leah Meredith
Luke Meredith
Alastair Merrill
Rachel Metcalf
Ciaron Metcalfe-Lynch
Marc Meyer
Sam Michel
Elaine Micklewright
Ali Middle
Kathryn Middleton
Cecile Midrouillet
Birgit Mikus

SUPPORTERS

Philippa Milbourne
Eleanor Miller
Ian Miller
John Miller
Judy Miller
Ryan Miller
Tony Miller
Gareth Mills
Alex Milne
Barry Mitchell
Peter Mitchell
John Mitchinson
Jane Moaveni
Carolyn Moir
Phillipa Moir
Catherine Molloy
Paul Monks
Martin Moon
Annabelle Mooney
Brigid Moore
C Moore
Chris Moore
Simon Moore
Harriett Moore-Boyd
Mike Moran
Laura Morgan
Richard Morgan
Dorita Morito
Rob Morley
Tony Morley
Karen Morrell
Olivia Morris
Sam Morrison

Dylan Mortimer Hughes
David Moss
Kathryn Moss
Hilary Moules
Paul Mountain
Stuart Mozley
Tim Mullen
Graeme 'Mulv' Mulvey
Lauren Mulville
Craig Munn
Robert Munro
Sarah Murdoch
Cat Murphy
Colin Murphy
James Murphy
Siobhan Murphy
Evtimia Murray
Stig Myken
Malcolm Myles-Hook
Andy N @fintanbear
Francesca Nandy
Sue Nash
Carlo Navato
Vivek Nayak
John Neary
Antony Neill
Roderick Neilson
Antony Nelson
Kirsty Nelson
Ritchie Nelson

Sabina Netherclift
Lisa Newby
Gary Nicol
Niels Aagaard Nielsen
Salil Nizar
Linda Norman
Daniel Northover
Chris Novakovic
Julia Nowak
Clare Nunan
Abigail Nunes-Richards
Ugochi Nwulu
Andrew O'Brien
Kevin O'Neill
Paul O'Neill
Sean O'Neill
Ann O'Shaughnessy
Denise Ogden
Susan Olney
Tomasz Ondrusz
Christina ONeill
Tony Orchard
Nir Oren-Woods
Neil Orford
Jane Ormrod
Lewis Orrow
Simona Orru
Karen Osborne
Tim Owen
Robin Owen-Morley
Rob P

SUPPORTERS

Grant Palmer
Tara Palmer
Colin Pari
Cathy Parker
Stephen Parker
Steve Parker
Jeni Parsons
Mathew Partington
Jane Paterson
Uto Patrick
Cath Payne
Harry Payne
Julie Payne
Sam Payne
Russell Peaker
Debbie Pearce
Joanne Pearce
Rob Pearson
Juliet Pedrazas
Christopher Pell
Joanna Pellereau
Rich Pemberton
Ronnie Pemberton
Louise Pengelly
Chris Pennell
Mike Pennell
Chris Penney
Kathryn Percival
Monika Peretz
Celia Perez Mourin
Graham Perkins
Michele Perry
Sue Perry

Pete
Alex Peters
Mark Phillips
Nancy Phillips
Sean Phillips
Douglas Philp
Emma Pickard
Daniel Piddock
Clay Pilfold
Mike Pilkington
Seb Pillon
Colin Pink
Terry Piper
Ben Platt
Philip Platt
Tom Pleasant
Adam
   Poland-Goodyer
Justin Pollard
Amy Pomeroy
Steve Pont
Will Poole
Richard Porges
Lee Porte
Simon Porter
Jack Pottage
Alistair Potter
Libby Potter
Jeff Povey
Colin Powers
Leigh Poynter
Jane Pratt
Leo Preece

Rebecca Prentice
Linda Price
Sarah Price
Belinda Priestley
Sam Proctor
Simon Proctor
Lorelai Prosser
David Proudlove
Tim Pugh
Becky Pulley
Joris Quaatbloet
Becki Quigley
Samantha Quill
Mike Quin
Becky Quinn
Dan Rackham
Richard Rackham
Adam Radcliffe
Chris Radcliffe
Catherine Radley
Kieran Rae
Louise Elizabeth
   Raines
Marvin Rajaram
Sarah Ramage
Miguel Ramírez
   Moreno
Robyn Ramsay
Julie Ramsdale
Rowan Ramsey
Natalie Randall
Stephen Rapley
Edward Ratnam

SUPPORTERS

Heather Rawlin
Maggie Rawlings
Rauf Rawson
Wendy Rayner
Paul Rayski
Colette Reap
Simon Reap
Darryl Reidy
Joe Reilly
Julian Rendall
Scott Renton
Alistair Renwick
Liverpool Resurgent
Josh Reynolds
Julien Reynolds
Tina Reynolds
Ian Rhodes
John-Paul Rhodes
Sarah Rhodes
Rhys & Becky
Liz Rice
Chris Richards
Ian Richards
Lindsay Richards
Melanie Richards
Mark
   Richards-
    Littlefield
David Richardson
Heather Richardson
Rich Rickett
Simon Riden
Petra Rigby

Christopher Riley
William Neil Riley
Tracy Rimmer
Huw Ringer
Jonathan Risby
Paul Robbins
Robbo
Adam Roberts
Deb Roberts
Gwen Roberts
Hazel Roberts
Jean Roberts
Martin Roberts
Simon Roberts
Douglas Robertson
Duncan Robertson
Sue Robertson
Adam Robinson
Phil Robinson
Shaun Robinson
Simon Robinson
John Roden
Roland Rodgers
Rebecca Roe
Jeremy Roebuck
Jane Rogers
Kevin Rogers
Kinga Rona
Helen Rose
Malcolm Rose
Sonja Ross
Adam Ross Patterson
Claire Rouse

Anna Route
Nicholas Rowles
Dave Rowlings
Zoë Roylance
Andy Royle
Janine Rudge
Sally Ruffer
Simon Ruffle
Nicole Rugman
Lisa Rull
Jon Rumfitt
Nicholas Rusbatch
Greg Russell
Amanda Rutter
Miriama Ruzbacka
Bruce Ryan
Paul Ryan
Sarah-Jane Ryan
Paul Sabourin
Luke Saker
Jayne Samuel-Walker
Louise Sarjeant
Dave Sarre
Jo Sastrr
Karen Satterley
Tracy Saunders
Shreya Sawhney
David Saxon
Darrell and Helen
   Saxton
Gabriella
   Schleinkofer
Thierry Schmidlin

Julia Schnabel
Caroline Schofield
Christopher Schofield
Peter Schofield
Devin Scobie
Alasdair Scott
Gemma Scott
Ian Scott
Jane Scott
Michelle Scully
Phil Scully
Hazel Seal
Henry Seal
Matthew Searle
Andrea See
Antony Seedhouse
Marie Segar
Gill Selby
Trudy Sellers
Karen Selley
Karen Semple
Nigel Sergeant
Roland Serjeant
Mark Seton
Daniel Sewell
Bryan Sexton
Janet Shackleton
Gillian Shankland
Patrick Shannon
Rebecca Shannon
James Sharp
Elizabeth Sharp née Nixon
Ritchie Sharpe
Brigid Shaw
Darren Shaw
Graham Shaw
Sue Shaw
Siobhan K M Shea
Rob Shelton & Mark Grubb
David Shepherd
Robin Sheppard
Su Sheppard
Sue Sheridan
Steven Shiel
Ian Shipley
John Shirley
Paul Shodimu
Andy Shuker
Jon Shute
Tanya Siann
Laura Sibra
Ronnie Sievewright
Rachel Sim
Andy Sime
Jeremy Simmonds
Dr B Simon
Simon
Caroline Simpson
Heva Simpson
Julian Simpson
Alan Sims
Joan Sinclair
Martin Sinclair
Katie Singer
Guru Singh
Robert Singleton
Deborah Sippitt
Paul Skinner
Maggie Slaughter
Ruth Slavin
Andy Slee
Anthony Sloane
Peter Smales
Adrian Smith
Andrea Smith
David Smith
Emma F V Smith
Eoin Smith
Gavin Smith
Gwyn Smith
Jane Smith
John Smith
Kevin Smith
Lauren Smith
Leigh Smith
Martyn Smith
Ron Smith
Stuart Smith
Mark Smitham
Jamie Snashall
Des Snowdon
Kirsty Softley
Amar Solanki
Ian Sorensen
Nadine Southern

Carrie Spacey
Elizabeth Spall
Simon Spall
Chris Spear
Ruth Speare
Colin Speers
Jane Spensley
James Spibey
David Spinolli Tyler
SpooksDavey
Dave Spring
Siobhan Spurle
Simon Stacey
Susan Stainer
Cathy Stalker
Lyndsay Stallard
Ann Stapleton
Andrew Stark
Emily Starling
Marios Stavridis
Jane Steed
Ben Stephen
Jessica Stephens
Jessica Stephens QC
Robin Stephenson
Andy Steven
Melville Stevens
Gary Stewart
John Stewart
Amanda Stiltz
Catriona Stirling
Frank Stirling
Tina Stojko

David Stokes
Jitka Stollova
Lauren Stoner
Chris Storer
Bekah Stott
Marin Stoychev
Charles Strange
Jim Strange
Mathilda Streets
Nick Stringer
Cathy Stubbs
Sophia Stutter
Mike Sum
Amanda Summers
Geraldine Sutcliffe
James Sutherland
Kenneth Sutherland
Pauline Swales
Anthony Swan
Chris Swan
Mary Swan
Luke Sweeney
Christina Swindells-Nader
Helen Szewczyk
Tim T.
Mads Taanquist
Nila Tailor
Anne Tait
Marzieh Talebi
Robert Tallis
James Tams
Maria Tate

Oliver Tate
Brian Taylor
David Taylor
Helen Taylor
Jo Taylor
Kev Taylor
Leanne Taylor
Steve Taylor
Wayne Taylor
Emma Taylor Northey
Anton Teasdale
Alistair Tease
Lorraine Templeton
Judith Thomas
Nigel Thomas
Sam Thomas
Stella-Maria Thomas
Stephen Thomas
Su Thomas
Amanda Thompson
Andy Thompson
Ann Thompson
Bob Thompson
Ian A Thompson
Katherine Thompson
Lisa Thompson
Lynn Thompson
Richard Thompson
Sarah Thompson Turvey
Dr John S Thomson
Ann Thornton

SUPPORTERS

Charlie Thwaites
Theresa Tilley
Therese Timlin
Alec Tinker
Alex Tischer
Mike Tobyn
Giles Todd
Selim Toker
Michael Toland
Stu Tomlinson
Jo and John Toon
Jedihomer Townend
Ian Travis
Scott Treacy
Gareth Tregidon
Dave Triffitt
Luke Trimmings
Mark Trotter
Harold Truett
Jill Trumper
Pem Tshering
Kerry Tucker
Richard Tuckett
Aphra Tulip-Briggs
John Turley
Andrew Turner
Richard Turner
Ben Twemlow
Chris Tye
Mike Tynan
Maureen Unsworth
David Urquhart
Andrew van Doorn
Anton van Heesewijk
Christine van Sluiters
Caroline Vanzie
Ralph Varcoe
Dominic Varley
Paul Vaughan
Rococo Velázquez
Mark Vent
Paul Verbinnen
P Vermoter
John Vesey
Sue Vickers-Thompson
Kerri Victoria
Peter Vize
Marcel Volker
Andy Wace
Fazrie Wahid
Laura Wailes
Simon Wailling
John Wainwright
Nicola Wake
Jamie Wakefield
Martin and Lin Wakeford
Elly Wakeling
Dave Wakely
Amy Waldie
Laura Wales
Bridget Walker
Nick and Kate Walker
Simon Walker
Zoe Walker
Barry Walsh
Denise Walsh
Amanda Walters
Geoffrey Walton
Kellie Walton
Carole-Ann Warburton
David Ward
Luke Ward
Rob Ward
Charlie Wardrop
Heather Wareing
Martin Waters
Adam Watkins
Ivor Watkins
Kim Watkiss
Carl Watson
Christine Watson
Karen Watson
Michelle Watson
Paul Watson
Wattovich
Gwyneth Watts
Revd Matthew Watts
Artur Wawrowski
David Way
Tim Way
Lin Webb
Amy Webber
Ben Webster
Chris Weight

Margaret Weir
Jen Welch
Nigel Welham
John Wells
Anthea West
Paul Westhead
Neil Westlake-Guy
Mike Wheeler
Liz Whelen
Richard Whitaker
Matt White
Nigel White
Paul White
Steven White
Adam White-Bower
Kirsten Whitehead
Mark Whittingham
Adrian Widdowson
Eve Wigham
Patricia Wightman
Ben Wilczynski
Ian Wilkins
Dave Wilkinson
Rachel Wilkinson
Samantha Wilkinson
Susan Wilkinson
Suzanne Wilkinson
Christopher Williams
David Williams
Donna Williams
Gareth Williams
Jacquie Williams
Judi Williams
Julia Michelle Williams
Sharon Williams
Tim Williams
Giles Williams (Your Helmsman)
Dan Williamson
Brian Willis
Mark Willis
Natasha Willmott
Maurice Wilsdon
David Wilson
Drew Wilson
Kerry Wilson
Kevin Wilson
Nigel Wilson
Jez Wingham
Michael Winiberg
Roger Winter
Chris Winters
Annette With
Theresa Witziers
Jazz Wood
Matt J. Wood
Melanie Wood
Mark Woodfield
Colin Woodfinden
Alexander Woodgate
Darren Woodiwiss
Ian Woods
Annette Woollam
Noel Woollard
Jem Woolley
Mick Woolley
Lisa Worledge
Lea Worrall
Louise Worsfold
Chris Wray
Amanda Wright
Graham A. N. Wright
Hannah Wright
Jo Wright
Neil Wright
Solveig Wright
Ian Wrigley
Helen Wroe
Curly Wyer
Mike Yorwerth
Clarissa Young
Dave Young
Jenn Young
Mark Young
Erica Youngman
Frances Yule
Andrey Zaytsev
Maik Zumstrull